When Democracy Breaks

Studies in Democratic Erosion and Collapse, from Ancient Athens to the Present Day

Edited by
ARCHON FUNG, DAVID MOSS, AND
ODD ARNE WESTAD

OXFORD
UNIVERSITY PRESS

Oxford University Press is a department of the University of Oxford. It furthers
the University's objective of excellence in research, scholarship, and education
by publishing worldwide. Oxford is a registered trade mark of Oxford University
Press in the UK and certain other countries.

Published in the United States of America by Oxford University Press
198 Madison Avenue, New York, NY 10016, United States of America.

© Oxford University Press 2024

Some rights reserved. No part of this publication may be reproduced, stored in
a retrieval system, or transmitted, in any form or by any means, for commercial purposes,
without the prior permission in writing of Oxford University Press, or as expressly
permitted by law, by licence or under terms agreed with the appropriate
reprographics rights organization.

This is an open access publication, available online and distributed under the terms of a
Creative Commons Attribution – Non Commercial – No Derivatives 4.0
International licence (CC BY-NC-ND 4.0), a copy of which is available at
http://creativecommons.org/licenses/by-nc-nd/4.0/.

You must not circulate this work in any other form
and you must impose this same condition on any acquirer.

Library of Congress Cataloging-in-Publication Data
Names: Fung, Archon, 1968– editor. | Moss, David A., 1964– editor. | Westad, Odd Arne, 1960– editor.
Title: When democracy breaks : studies in democratic erosion and collapse,
from ancient Athens to the present day / Archon Fung, David Moss,
Odd Arne Westad.
Description: New York, NY : Oxford University Press, [2024] | Includes index.
Identifiers: LCCN 2023052080 (print) | LCCN 2023052081 (ebook) |
ISBN 9780197760789 (hardback) | ISBN 9780197760796 (paperback) |
ISBN 9780197760819 (epub)
Subjects: LCSH: Democracy—History—Cross-cultural studies. |
Social conflict—Political aspects—Cross-cultural studies. | World politics. |
Democratization—History—Cross-cultural studies.
Classification: LCC JC421 .W52 2024 (print) | LCC JC421 (ebook) |
DDC 320.9—dc23/eng/20231226
LC record available at https://lccn.loc.gov/2023052080
LC ebook record available at https://lccn.loc.gov/2023052081
DOI: 10.1093/oso/9780197760789.001.0001

Contents

List of Contributors	vii

1. Introduction: When Democracy Breaks   1
   David Moss, Archon Fung, and Odd Arne Westad

2. Democratic Collapse and Recovery in Ancient Athens (413–403)   25
   Federica Carugati and Josiah Ober

3. The U.S. Secession Crisis as a Breakdown of Democracy   43
   Dean Grodzins and David Moss

4. The Breakdown in Democracy in 1930s Japan   108
   Louise Young

5. Weimar Germany and the Fragility of Democracy   142
   Eric D. Weitz

6. The Failures of Czech Democracy, 1918–1948   161
   John Connelly

7. September 11, 1973: Breakdown of Democracy in Chile   189
   Marian Schlotterbeck

8. The Indian Emergency (1975–1977) in Historical Perspective   221
   Sugata Bose and Ayesha Jalal

9. Democratic Breakdown in Argentina, 1976   237
   Scott Mainwaring

10. Why Russia's Democracy Broke   277
    Chris Miller

11. A Different "Turkish Model": Exemplifying De-democratization in the AKP Era   299
    Lisel Hintz

12. Venezuela's Autocratization, 1999–2021: Variations in Temporalities, Party Systems, and Institutional Controls   327
    Javier Corrales

Index	351

List of Contributors

Editors

Archon Fung. Winthrop Laflin McCormack Professor of Citizenship and Democracy at the Harvard University Kennedy School of Government.

David Moss. Paul Whiton Cherington Professor at Harvard Business School and founder of the Tobin Project.

Odd Arne Westad. Elihu Professor of History and Global Affairs at Yale University.

Contributors

Sugata Bose. Gardiner Professor of Oceanic History and Affairs at Harvard University.

Federica Carugati. Lecturer in history and political economy at King's College London.

John Connelly. Sidney Hellman Ehrman Professor of European History at the University of California, Berkeley.

Javier Corrales. Dwight W. Morrow 1895 Professor of Political Science at Amherst College.

Dean Grodzins. Independent scholar and former senior researcher at the Harvard Business School.

Lisel Hintz. Assistant professor of European and Eurasian studies at Johns Hopkins University.

Ayesha Jalal. Mary Richardson Professor of History, Arts and Sciences at Tufts University.

Scott Mainwaring. Eugene and Helen Conley Professor of Political Science at the University of Notre Dame.

Chris Miller. Associate professor of international history at Tufts University.

Josiah Ober. Markos & Eleni Kounalakis Chair in Honor of Constantine Mitsotakis and professor of political science and classics at Stanford University.

Marian Schlotterbeck. Associate professor of history at the University of California, Davis.

Eric D. Weitz. Professor of history at the City University of New York. Professor Weitz passed away July 1, 2022

Louise Young. Professor of history at the University of Wisconsin, Madison.

1

Introduction

When Democracy Breaks

David Moss, Archon Fung, and Odd Arne Westad

Democracy is often described in two opposite ways, as either wonderfully resilient or dangerously fragile. Curiously, both characterizations can be correct, depending on the context. In a relatively small number of countries, democracy has survived numerous shocks across many generations, while in others it has faltered or collapsed, whether after just a short time or after a long period of apparent strength. Some broken democracies have reconstituted themselves as democracies once again, while others have notably failed to do so.[1]

Democratization around the world has sometimes occurred in waves—such as the so-called third wave of democratization in Latin America and Asia over the 1970s and 1980s. Other periods have exhibited the opposite: in the 1920s and 1930s, several democracies in Europe and Asia fell to fascism. More recently, many indicators suggest that liberal democracy suffered significant retrenchment during the early twenty-first century.[2] This "democratic backsliding," which was especially visible in Latin America, Asia, and Eastern Europe, has dispelled the illusion that democratic institutions, once established, can be taken for granted and that the passage of time brings the inexorable expansion and deepening of democratic practices. Indeed, this reversal has sparked growing interest in the sources of democratic weakness and, in particular, what differentiates democracies that break from those that endure during periods of stress.

---

[1] Among the cases treated in this volume, Ancient Athens and India after the 1975 emergency are the clearest cases of broken democracies reconstituting themselves. Weimar Germany and Japan are clear cases where democracy was not reinstated until an outside power installed a new structure after defeating the countries in war. Czechoslovakia in 1948, Chile in 1973, and Argentina in 1976 all endured long periods of authoritarian government, but when democracy did eventually reemerge it was largely driven by forces from within those countries. The cases from the very recent past—Russia, Turkey, and Venezuela—are still unfolding. The United States after the Civil War is a difficult case. If one focuses on the Southern states, the conclusion might be that democratic procedures were installed from outside by a conquering army. If one thinks of the breakage in terms of the United States as a whole, then it arguably becomes an instance of a (proto-)democracy reconstituting itself.

[2] V-Dem Institute, "Autocratization Turns Viral: Democracy Report 2021," March 2021, https://www.v-dem.net/static/website/files/dr/dr_2021.pdf.

David Moss, Archon Fung, and Odd Arne Westad, *Introduction* In: *When Democracy Breaks*. Edited by: Archon Fung, David Moss, and Odd Arne Westad, Oxford University Press. © Oxford University Press 2024. DOI: 10.1093/oso/9780197760789.003.0001

2 WHEN DEMOCRACY BREAKS

This book aims to deepen our understanding of these differences—of what separates democratic resilience from democratic fragility—by focusing on the latter. Specifically, we explore eleven episodes of democratic breakdown from ancient to modern times. Although no single factor emerges as decisive, linking together all of the episodes of breakdown, a small number of factors do seem to stand out across the various cases. The notion of democratic culture, while admittedly difficult to define and even more difficult to measure, could play a role in all of them.

The necessary conditions for a well-functioning democracy have long been a subject of intense examination and experimentation, dating back at least to the Ancient Greeks. Notably, the power of democratic culture has figured prominently along the way. In his mid-nineteenth-century *History of Greece*, George Grote observed that Cleisthenes, one of the fathers of Athenian democracy, had instilled a robust democratic "sentiment" within the citizens of Athens that helped ensure strength and resilience over time:

> It was necessary to create in the multitude, and through them to force upon the leading ambitious men, that rare and difficult sentiment which we may term a constitutional morality—a paramount reverence for the forms of the constitution, enforcing obedience to the authorities acting under and within those forms, yet combined with the habit of open speech, of action subject only to definite legal control, and unrestrained censure of those very authorities as to all their public acts—combined, too, with a perfect confidence in the bosom of every citizen, amidst the bitterness of party contest, that the forms of the constitution will be not less sacred in the eyes of his opponents than in his own.[3]

Over two millennia after Cleisthenes, Americans working to build a republic picked up on a similar theme. James Madison, a Virginia slaveholder and perhaps the principal author of the U.S. Constitution, highlighted the pivotal role of "national sentiment" in America's emerging (white male) democracy. When pressed by his friend—and fellow slaveholder—Thomas Jefferson following the Convention of 1787 about the absence of a bill of rights in the new Constitution, Madison responded that he did not view "the omission a material defect." Among other things, "experience proves the inefficacy of a bill of rights on those occasions when its controul is most needed." He pointed out, in particular, that "[r]epeated violations of these parchment barriers have been committed by overbearing majorities in every State."[4] Of what use, then, was a bill of rights,

---

[3] George Grote, *A History of Greece: From the Earliest Period to the Close of the Generation Contemporary with Alexander the Great* (New York: Wm. L Allison & Son, 1882), 2:86.

[4] See especially National Archives, James Madison to Thomas Jefferson, October 17, 1788, https://founders.archives.gov/documents/Madison/01-11-02-0218; National Archives, Jefferson to Madison, December 20, 1787, https://founders.archives.gov/documents/Madison/01-10-02-0210.

INTRODUCTION   3

and why did Madison ultimately support adding one to the Constitution? His answer: "The political truths declared in that solemn manner acquire by degrees the character of fundamental maxims of free Government, and as they become *incorporated with the national sentiment*, counteract the impulses of interest and passion." In short, a bill of rights is nothing but a set of "parchment barriers" against the will of "overbearing majorities" until, crucially, "they become incorporated with the national sentiment."[5]

Strikingly, Grote suggested that the sentiment of "constitutional morality" Cleisthenes had aimed to establish in Athens could also "be found in the aristocracy of England (since about 1688) as well as in the democracy of the American United States: and because we are familiar with it, we are apt to suppose it a natural sentiment; though there seem to be few sentiments more difficult to establish and diffuse among a community, judging by the experience of history."[6]

In the chapters that follow, we will see again and again that the written rules of democracy are insufficient to protect against tyranny. They are mere "parchment barriers" unless embedded within a strong culture of democracy—a strong democratic sentiment—that embraces and gives life not only to the written rules themselves but to the essential democratic values that underlie them.[7] We will see, in graphic detail, just how far society can descend, into chaos or even madness, when this sentiment supporting a common commitment to democratic process and values breaks down.[8]

* * *

There is of course no universally accepted definition of democracy. For our purposes, we will rely on a highly capacious definition: that democracy requires

---

[5]   Madison to Jefferson, October 17, 1788, emphasis added.

[6]   Grote, *History of Greece*, 2:86–87.

[7]   But who must embrace this commitment to sustain democracy? Cleisthenes and Madison both worried that democratic sentiments would not be strongly held among citizens themselves, perhaps at least in part out of a concern that citizens would prove vulnerable to the appeals of demagogues. Prominent recent scholarship, by contrast, has suggested that weak commitment to democracy among political elites may be of central importance. See, e.g., Steven Levitsky and Daniel Ziblatt, *How Democracies Die* (New York: Broadway Books, 2018); Juan J. Linz and Alfred Stepan, eds., *The Breakdown of Democratic Regimes* (Baltimore: Johns Hopkins University Press, 1978). The case studies in this volume offer multiple perspectives on the relative roles of mass and elite commitment to democracy.

[8]   While direct evidence of "democratic sentiment" is difficult to obtain, several patterns are plausibly connected to a deep cultural commitment to democracy, including electoral participation; respect for civic institutions, laws, processes, and norms; expressions of faith in democracy and democratic process; willingness to compromise; respect for minority rights; honoring of fair electoral outcomes; and peaceful transitions of power.

4 WHEN DEMOCRACY BREAKS

both majoritarianism, on the one hand, and meaningful rights to express dissent, to oppose and contest, on the other.[9]

In modern representative democracies, the right to vote is expected to be nearly universal among adult citizens, whereas in earlier times—and until relatively recently in many societies—the franchise was typically limited to a favored group, such as white males in the pre–Civil War United States (or, in the early American republic, propertied white males). Basic political rights, including voting rights, were far too narrowly distributed in Ancient Athens and antebellum America for their political systems to qualify as democracies by modern standards. We have nevertheless chosen to examine both Athens and antebellum America as part of this volume not only because they were recognized as democracies in their own time but also because they represent early exercises in combining majoritarianism with a right to dissent—exercises that broke down in spectacular fashion but that were also ultimately restored in both settings. As such, these early *quasi-democracies* are useful to us in studying the breakdown of *modern* democracies, even though they were a far cry from democracy as we understand it today.[10]

---

[9] Our expectation is that the word in this definition that is most fraught, at least in academic circles, is "majoritarianism." We use the term broadly to mean a shared *belief* that in democratic decision-making the will of the majority should, all else equal, win out. We do not mean to follow the narrower usage of some political scientists who treat majoritarianism as one extreme on a spectrum of democratic forms. In this narrower usage, majoritarianism is contrasted with democratic regimes that limit majority rule or impose heightened requirements upon it, including supermajority requirements for certain types of decisions. See, e.g., Arend Lijphart, *Democracies: Patterns of Majoritarian and Consensus Government in Twenty-One Countries* (New Haven: Yale University Press, 1984). Our sense, meanwhile, is that all democracies, across any relevant spectrum, demonstrate some significant commitment to majoritarianism, broadly defined. If there is not a widely shared belief that a majority vote, whether by citizens themselves or their elected representatives, typically carries special weight or legitimacy in the selection of candidates or the enactment of policies, then the regime is not meaningfully democratic. The second half of our definition—regarding rights to express dissent, to oppose and contest—often stands in dynamic tension with the majoritarian requirement, and ensuring these rights has long been seen as a legitimate justification for certain limits on pure majority rule. See, e.g., James Madison, *Vices of the Political System of the United States* (1787), esp. §11; Jon Elster, "On Majoritarianism and Rights," *East European Constitutional Review* 1, no. 3 (Fall 1992): 19–24. To the extent that limits on (or departures from) majority rule are seen as necessary to sustain meaningful rights to dissent, to oppose, and to contest, those limits should not be thought of as antidemocratic under our definition. Indeed, this is the essence of *liberal* democracy. Notably, in his introduction to a foundational collection of case studies on democratic failure, co-edited with Alfred Stepan and published in 1978, Juan Linz offered a widely cited and far more precise definition of democracy, which he himself acknowledged was highly restrictive (and which we concluded may be too restrictive for this volume): "Our criteria for a democracy may be summarized as follows: legal freedom to formulate and advocate political alternatives with the concomitant rights to free association, free speech, and other basic freedoms of person; free and nonviolent competition among leaders with periodic validation of their claim to rule; inclusion of all effective political offices in the democratic process; and provision for the participation of all members of the political community, whatever their political preferences. Practically, this means the freedom to create political parties and to conduct free and honest elections at regular intervals without excluding any effective political office from direct or indirect electoral accountability. Today 'democracy' implies at least universal male suffrage, but perhaps in the past it would extend to the regimes with property, taxation, occupational, or literacy requirements of an earlier period, which limited suffrage to certain social groups" (Linz and Stepan, *The Breakdown of Democratic Regimes*, 5).

[10] These qualifiers on the scope of democracy in Ancient Athens and the antebellum American South are not meant to suggest an absence of significant limitations on participation in the more

INTRODUCTION 5

Scholars of democratic failure often classify two types of breakdown based on the speed of decline. Democracies may appear to break down either quickly or slowly—to be the victims of either shock or slide. Democracy in Weimar Germany, for example, is often said to have come to a sudden stop when Adolf Hitler, whose National Socialist (Nazi) Party had won a plurality in the November 1932 parliamentary elections and who himself had been appointed chancellor in late January, seized emergency powers soon after the mysterious Reichstag fire of February 27, 1933. One additional election allowing opposition parties was held in Germany in early March, but it was the last one, and conducted in the shadow of Nazi terror. Opposition to the Nazi Party was completely banned in all subsequent elections under the Nazi regime. In the chapters that follow, we'll see many other sudden shocks to democracy, including in Ancient Athens (411 BCE), the United States (1860–1861), Czechoslovakia (1948), Chile (1973), India (1975–1977), and Argentina (1976).

Not all democratic breakdowns proceed this way, however. The democratic crisis in modern-day Venezuela, for example, occurred more gradually, beginning mostly after Hugo Chávez was elected president in 1998. From that point forward, multiparty elections were still held, but other core democratic institutions, including those safeguarding dissent, regularly came under attack, and opposition parties were increasingly constrained and sidelined. Sometimes referred to as "illiberal" democracy or democracy with other adjectives such as "controlled," "restrictive," or "electoral," the model of democratic breakdown that Venezuela has experienced retains an ostensible commitment to majoritarianism and multiparty elections, but with ever fewer political protections for minority and opposition groups, until democracy as we know it disappears.[11] Democratic breakdowns in interwar Japan as well as modern-day Russia and Turkey (highlighted in Chapters 4, 10, and 11) showed similar characteristics.

Although in principle it should be easy to distinguish a democracy that collapses suddenly from one that slides into oblivion as key protections are gradually dismantled, in practice there is almost always a long period of democratic erosion preceding any breakdown. Democracies that ultimately collapse typically face multiple but differing forms of erosion over preceding years and even decades. All of the democracies covered in this volume experienced the rise of antidemocratic political actors prior to breakdown; all experienced significant degrees of political violence; and all experienced intense political polarization. Most faced losses of legitimacy as a result of economic, security, or other crises,

modern cases we consider. As the cases will show, even where formally given suffrage, religious and ethnic minorities (including ethnic Germans in Czechoslovakia, Muslims in India, and Kurds in Turkey) frequently had their ability to fully participate in democratic governance circumscribed.

[11] David Collier and Steve Levitsky, "Democracy with Adjectives: Conceptual Innovation in Comparative Research," *World Politics* 49, no. 3 (1997): 430–451.

6   WHEN DEMOCRACY BREAKS

widely perceived as failures of democratic governance, and some, but not all, failed to receive support from other democracies at crucial moments. Beyond problems of democratic erosion, moreover, many of the democracies examined in this volume were compromised, often from the start, by weaknesses of institutional design or failures of political inclusion.

Germany. Frequently presented as the classic case of abrupt democratic collapse, Weimar Germany had in fact suffered democratic weakness and erosion from the very beginning. As Eric Weitz shows in his masterful chapter, conservative groups that were actively hostile to democracy remained deeply entrenched in the German power structure, even after the Revolution of 1918/19. Social Democrats tolerated them in the pursuit of stability, but the presence of antidemocratic elements throughout the ministries, and especially their dominance within the military and other security services, ultimately proved catastrophic. Although the new republic experienced a surge in democratic spirit and an extraordinary cultural renaissance, the conservatives' violent assault on the far left—up to and including high-level political assassinations—destabilized Weimar politics and profoundly undercut democratic legitimacy. When the Great Depression struck and the German economy collapsed, the republic's already weakened legitimacy collapsed with it. "In some ways," Weitz writes, "the Republic was already overthrown in 1930." From 1930 to 1932, Germany experienced a presidential dictatorship after President Paul von Hindenburg invoked emergency powers under Article 48 of the Weimar Constitution. When traditional conservatives around Hindenburg joined in support of the newly ascendant radical right (the Nazi Party) and the appointment of Hitler as chancellor in January 1933, this effectively marked the death of Weimar, even before the Reichstag fire and all that followed.

Nor was Weimar exceptional in this respect. In case after case, the seemingly sudden collapse of a democracy—typically the result of a coup or declaration of emergency powers—was itself made possible by deeper vulnerabilities, including institutional weaknesses and flagging democratic commitment from many political actors that long preceded the moment of reckoning.

Athens. The breakdown of Athenian democracy in 411 BCE—and its restoration in 403 BCE—provides a particularly telling example. As Federica Carugati and Josiah Ober argue in their marvelously original chapter on the Athenian saga, the abrupt conversion from democracy to oligarchy in 411 BCE, in which the democracy "in effect, voted itself out of existence," was the result of three intersecting factors: (1) a devastating military defeat in Sicily in 413 BCE, which put the regime under tremendous economic and political pressure; (2) the existence of an antidemocratic elite that feared popular expropriation of their wealth to fund continued war against Sparta, and that was willing to utilize political violence to prevent the demos from taking such action; and (3) a democratic order that, by putting virtually no checks or constraints on the demos, invited erratic and inconsistent decision-making, particularly in times of stress, further undercutting democratic legitimacy. Although this combination of factors was enough to convince (or perhaps frighten) the demos into empowering an oligarchy at an extreme moment of crisis following the defeat in Sicily, it was apparently not enough to destroy the deep underlying commitment to democracy—Grote's "constitutional morality"—that had grown strong outside of certain elites and that would ultimately drive the return to democracy, briefly in 410 BCE, and then on an ongoing basis (for the next eighty years) beginning in 403 BCE. Notably, as Carugati and Ober point out, the new democracy launched in 403 corrected the key design flaws of the prior democratic regime, imposing a range of checks and constraints on the demos that helped ensure more consistent policymaking and, ultimately, greater legitimacy even in times of crisis.

United States. In their chapter on the breakdown of American democracy in 1860–1861, Dean Grodzins and David Moss also find that extended decay preceded a sudden democratic break. Specifically, they reassess the question of why so many Southern states rejected the outcome of the 1860 presidential election, deciding to secede from the Union rather than recognize Abraham Lincoln's electoral victory. Moving beyond the standard explanations for this remarkably risky choice, Grodzins and Moss suggest that at least part of the answer is that Southern secession grew out of a long process of democratic erosion and distorted decision-making over the previous thirty or more years. As fears of slave insurrections began to grow among white Southerners, especially following publication of David Walker's abolitionist *Appeal* in 1829 and Turner's Rebellion in 1831, many Southern states began enacting statutes aggressively limiting speech that was critical of slavery. In time, even a book suggesting that the institution of slavery was undercutting Southern economic performance was banned as seditious. Most strikingly, the Republican Party itself, when it emerged in the mid-1850s, was effectively prohibited across much of the South for the same reason, because of the critique of slavery that the party invoked. Meanwhile, political violence against those with unpopular views, particularly about slavery, was becoming increasingly common in the South, from North Carolina to Texas. With virtually all dissent against slavery and its consequences silenced, many Southern political leaders apparently began to believe their own propaganda about both the moral and economic superiority of the Southern social system, rooted in slavery. Indeed, this belief became so all-consuming that it ultimately superseded their commitment to electoral institutions. So when the Republican Lincoln won a plurality of the popular vote and a clear majority of the electoral college in November 1860, it didn't seem like such a large leap for many of these Southern leaders simply to reject the outcome of the election and to call for secession, strangely confident that they would prevail against a larger and far more

8 WHEN DEMOCRACY BREAKS

industrialized North on the basis of the South's slave-centered social system and its principal economic product, cotton.

Czechoslovakia. Nearly a century later, the Communist coup in Czechoslovakia in 1948 constituted another abrupt democratic breakdown. Once again this sudden development was deeply rooted in an already troubled democratic system. "Democracy did not simply collapse," writes John Connelly in his riveting chapter on the subject: "it had been eroded in a process extending backward, to before the war." Connelly argues that already by the dawn of the first Czechoslovak Republic in 1918, the nation was well positioned for success as a liberal democracy, with relatively high incomes, high education levels, low inequality, and a well-developed civil society. The democracy that took shape, however, was contorted by the desire of Czechs to dominate the political system in a multiethnic state. This was accomplished through the formation of a united front of Czech parties and select Slovak allies, which left Germans, Hungarians, Communists, and many Slovaks with virtually no influence at all. When Czechoslovak democracy was reconstituted after World War II, it retained a strong nationalist (and even stronger anti-German) bent, but now Communists were part of the National Front government rather than outside of it. The trauma of Munich in 1938 and the war itself had turned allegiances eastward, away from the liberal democratic West, which had abandoned Czechoslovakia, and toward the Soviet Union, which had liberated it. Despite having received only 10% of the vote in elections of the 1930s, the Communists met no resistance from their National Front partners when they sought control of key ministries immediately after the war, including the Interior Ministry, which gave them authority over the police. With Communists taking the lead, and again with no resistance from their political partners, the National Front government quickly undertook the mass expulsion of Germans and Hungarians starting in 1945–1946, trampling over individual rights, rule of law, and basic human decency in the process. In some ways, it was a warm-up to the coup in 1948, when Communists seized full control of the government—and the country—without firing a shot. Czechoslovakia's democracy died in 1948, but the truth is that it had been far from healthy before the war and was essentially on life support afterward.

Chile. The long-term roots of democratic breakdown were also visible in Chile, where democracy was extinguished in 1973. At the time, Chile's democracy was the oldest in Latin America, having been continuously in place since the 1930s. Yet, as Marian Schlotterbeck explains in her notable chapter on the subject, its longevity masked deep-seated weaknesses. Political tensions exploded in the late 1940s, following an experiment in coalition politics involving the left and center-left known as the Popular Front. Turning on his former Popular Front partners, President Gabriel González Videla of the middle-class Radical Party sent in the military to shut down strikes by copper and coal miners,

INTRODUCTION 9

forcibly deported thousands of Communist workers to internment camps, and outlawed the Communist Party. Although multiparty elections continued (with Communists excluded until 1958), Schlotterbeck suggests that political stability rested on an implicit—and highly tenuous—bargain protecting elite interests, rather than on democratic legitimacy per se. "Chile's democracy endured," she writes, "as long as social relations in the countryside, particularly on the large landed estates (*haciendas*), remained unchanged." Passage of the Agrarian Reform Law of 1967 and the election of Salvador Allende, a Socialist, to the presidency in 1970 effectively shattered the bargain. The political right organized a far-reaching campaign to delegitimize Allende, especially in the eyes of the middle classes, while the Nixon administration in the United States was secretly mobilizing American resources to achieve the same ultimate objective, the removal of Allende, even if it meant destabilizing Chile and destroying Chilean democracy in the process. When Christian Democrats, who had long occupied the center of Chilean politics, "[threw] their support behind the antidemocratic right to destabilize the Allende government and call[ed] for military intervention," the game was nearly up. If the center and right had had enough votes to impeach Allende, they would have; failing that, they turned to the military, which was itself now highly politicized and fully aligned with the right, for an extraconstitutional solution. As is well known, the coup, led by Augusto Pinochet, came on September 11, 1973, setting up Pinochet as the nation's military dictator for the next seventeen years.

Argentina. Chile's neighbor, Argentina, saw its democracy collapse three years later, and for similar reasons. Unlike Chile, Argentina had not experienced a long-lived democracy, having suffered democratic breakdowns in 1930, 1951/55, 1962, and 1966. Scott Mainwaring writes in his deeply insightful chapter on the Argentine coup of 1976 that the country was "one of the world champions of democratic breakdowns in the twentieth century." In explaining why democracy failed yet again in Argentina in 1976, just three years after it had been reestablished, Mainwaring emphasizes three principal causes: (1) the existence of violent extremist actors on the right and left, both with "complete disdain for democracy," which sought to destroy each other through "bombings, kidnappings, politically motivated assassinations, factory seizures," and countless other violent acts; (2) the democratic regime's inability to effectively manage either these pervasive public security threats or the severe economic challenges then plaguing the nation, which together "generated a widespread sense of chaos"; and (3) indifference and even outright hostility to democracy among top political leaders in the government, including Juan Perón, whose active collaboration with extremist, antidemocratic forces "helped forge the cauldron in which democracy died." When Perón himself died on July 1, 1974, he was succeeded as president by his third wife, Isabel Martínez de Perón, whom he had handpicked as vice president. Describing her as "ill-prepared to become president," Mainwaring observes that Isabel Perón's term "marked a sharp but erratic turn toward the authoritarian far right." The nation was soon plunged into an orgy of political violence, including that sponsored by the government itself. Mainwaring concludes that any real semblance of democracy was gone by the second half of 1975, even before the military finally seized power from Isabel Perón in a widely anticipated coup on March 24, 1976.

India. In India, meanwhile, President Fakhruddin Ali Ahmed, at the request of Prime Minister Indira Gandhi, had declared a state of internal emergency under Article 352 of the Constitution on June 25, 1975, effectively suspending the nation's democracy. The emergency, lasting nearly two years, provided cover for countless abuses, including the imprisonment of more than 100,000 political opponents, dissenters, and activists. In their chapter on the emergency, Sugata Bose and Ayesha Jalal consider the immediate reasons why Article 352 was invoked (deteriorating political support, a growing economic crisis, mounting unrest and dissent, and a serious legal challenge to Gandhi herself). But they devote greater attention to exploring why Article 352 was added to the Indian Constitution in the first place. There was certainly sharp criticism of the provision (originally numbered Article 275) when the Constitution was being drafted in the late 1940s. Hari Vishnu Kamath, for example, declared in August 1949 that he had "ransacked most of the constitutions of democratic countries of the world" and that the only comparable provision he could find in any of them was Article 48 of the Weimar Constitution—the very provision Hitler had used to secure emergency powers in 1933. The chair of the drafting committee of the Indian Constitution, Dr. B. R. Ambedkar, acknowledged that the emergency powers provision could conceivably be abused but expressed hope that it would "never be called into operation and . . . would remain a dead letter." While Bose and Jalal are careful not to reach beyond the documentary evidence in interpreting why Ambedkar supported a provision he hoped would never be used, they suggest that part of the reason may be that he worried about the Indian people's readiness for democracy. Remarkably, after first citing Ambedkar quoting Grote on the importance of "constitutional morality" and democratic "sentiment," they next quote him announcing, "Constitutional morality . . . is not a natural sentiment. It has to be cultivated. We must realize that our people have yet to learn it." And just in case there was any doubt, they also quote Ambedkar saying, "Democracy in India is only a top-dressing on an Indian soil, which is essentially undemocratic." The irony, then, may be that Gandhi was able to suspend democracy in 1975 not because the Indian people lacked the proper democratic sentiment, but because their political leaders in 1949 thought they did. In any case, when Gandhi finally called elections in early 1977, apparently willing to end the emergency because she was certain she would win the vote, she and her party were instead decisively

INTRODUCTION 11

rejected at the polls. "The resort to overt authoritarianism," Bose and Jalal write, "had been emphatically repudiated by India's electorate." Perhaps democratic sentiment in India was more than just topsoil after all.

If sudden democratic breakdowns, from Athens to India, are typically rooted in deficiencies that date back much further, it is also true that not all democratic breakdowns even appear to occur suddenly. In this volume, we examine four cases—interwar Japan and modern-day Russia, Turkey, and Venezuela—where democratic shortfalls cumulate gradually to breakdown rather than manifesting as a sudden shock.

Japan. The story of interwar Japan is different from the other three. In fact, it is different from all of the other cases covered in this volume. As Louise Young argues in her remarkable chapter on the rise and fall of Japan's Taishō democracy, the nation's democratic breakdown "did not occur suddenly or through institutional rupture." It was the product of "an authoritarian slide," but unlike other cases of slide, in Japan there was no strongman at the center who won election and then gradually dismantled the guardrails of democracy. Instead, the Japanese military, often provoked or goaded by isolated cliques of junior officers, gradually expanded its power over virtually every aspect of the state and society until, in the end, democracy was replaced by dictatorship—and mostly with broad support from the Japanese people. To the extent there was a turning point, it was the Manchurian Incident of 1931–1933, which began when "conspirators" within the Japanese army framed Chinese troops for an attack on a Japanese railway that they themselves had staged. This became "the pretext for Japanese forces on the spot to launch an invasion of Manchuria, acting without authorization from the high command." Particularly against the backdrop of the Great Depression, when public faith in the democratic government's capacity to address the nation's massive economic challenges was collapsing, the invasion—wildly successful in both military and economic terms—proved enormously popular with the Japanese public. Within Japan, meanwhile, "groups of junior military officers joined hands with civilian organizations to enact a rapid-fire series of violent conspiracies aimed at reclaiming command over the state." These actions included attempted coups as well as assassinations of major business and political figures. Although members of the military leadership had mostly not been involved, they quickly exploited these situations, "work[ing] hard to gather the levers of power in their hands." This involved the exclusion of political parties from forming cabinets in 1932 (and the elimination of independent political parties in 1940); far-reaching censorship and brutal punishment of dissent that ultimately gave rise to "a de facto police state"; steadily increasing military control of the bureaucracy; and full economic mobilization for war that concentrated economic power in the military's hands. Young maintains that "Japan was a military dictatorship for all practical purposes" by the time of the attack on Pearl Harbor in 1941. This was

12   WHEN DEMOCRACY BREAKS

accomplished, she explains, not by the abrupt overthrow of existing institutions, as in Germany and Italy, but by the gradual "repurposing of existing institutions" and the "voluntary, if reluctant, relinquishing of influence" by political leaders, who too often made "Faustian bargains" with the military simply to gain short-term advantage over political rivals, but ultimately at the expense of the democracy as a whole.

Russia. Although Russia's democratic breakdown at the start of the twenty-first century, like Japan's in the interwar period, is best characterized as a slide into authoritarianism, there was (unlike in Japan) a strongman at the center of the process in Russia. In his revealing chapter on the subject, Chris Miller suggests that Vladimir Putin leveraged his close relationship with the nation's security services to destroy the oligarchs' hold on Russian politics. By eliminating his political competition, Putin rebuilt the one-party state around himself. Miller emphasizes that prior to Putin's becoming president in 2000, Russia's political system was only marginally democratic, but at least its elections were competitive, mainly as a result of competition between the oligarchs. All of this began to change once Putin took charge. All media came under state control, meaningful political opposition became pointless or even suicidal, and election outcomes became entirely predictable. Notably, Putin's antidemocratic moves generated little opposition. Partly this was because there was only minimal public support for democracy to begin with, given both the relentless anti-Western propaganda under the Soviets and the country's poor economic performance when democracy was tried in the 1990s. Among those who did support democracy, moreover, there was widespread fear of a Weimar-style putsch from extremist elements, and Putin's assertion of strength in the center proved reassuring in this context. The result, however, was that Russian democracy was destroyed not by a shock, as befell Weimar Germany, but by an insidious slide into authoritarianism. As Miller observes, "rather than being overturned in a coup or a rebellion, Russian democracy was degraded steadily over time."

Turkey. Democratic breakdown in Turkey has also revolved around a strongman, Recep Tayyip Erdoğan, who, after first taking power in 2003, steadily dismantled checks on his authority and degraded (even destroyed) the capacity for meaningful political opposition or resistance. As Lisel Hintz demonstrates in her highly evocative chapter, Erdoğan's first step was to neutralize the principal institutional threats to his power, including the military and the judiciary, under the guise of strong democratic reforms needed for EU accession. Historically, these institutions—especially the military—had fiercely defended the Republican Nationalist identity (secular, modern, and Western-oriented, derived from the nation's "founding father," Mustafa Kemal Atatürk) against Ottoman Islamist parties and other threats. Indeed, Erdoğan himself, as a member of one such party (the RP), had spent time in jail in 1999

INTRODUCTION   13

for referencing a poem that was said to incite religious hatred. In founding a new party, the AKP, in 2001, Erdoğan denied it was Islamist (instead preferring the label "conservative democrat"), which helped provide room for his highly effective—and ostensibly pro-democracy and pro-EU—maneuvers against the military, the judiciary, and other bastions of Republican Nationalist identity. From there, Hintz maintains, Erdoğan and the AKP were able to create "space for marginalizing opposition actors with a reduced fear of recrimination through institutional checks." While the AKP pursued many avenues for silencing opposition and dominating the political space, from control of the media to large-scale political patronage, Hintz focuses particularly on Erdoğan's strategy of "rhetorical vilification," which he has deployed against opponents. By regularly belittling, defaming, and demonizing opponents through derogatory language (calling them everything from "hooligans" and "looters" to "provocateurs" and "terrorists"), and by focusing attention on isolated or manufactured incidents of violence associated with them, Erdoğan and the AKP have largely succeeded in delegitimizing many of their opponents. This in turn has provoked a firestorm of nationalist anger and violence, which has been used to justify such steps as incarceration of opponents and, in the case of many Kurdish mayors, removal from democratically elected office. "The AKP's vilifying rhetoric," Hintz writes, "has gained tremendous momentum, targeting many different forms of opposition and cementing antagonistic us-versus-them relations along multiple identity lines." Ultimately, in deploying these methods, Erdoğan has managed to suppress political competition and free expression, forcefully assert an Ottoman Islamist identity for Turkey (despite earlier denials), and, in Hintz's words, "secure his place as the most powerful individual in Turkey since Atatürk—indeed, openly challenging the founder's legacy by putting in place a 'New Turkey' undergirded by a fundamentally different understanding of what it means to be Turkish."

Venezuela. A third example of a country sliding into authoritarianism through the emergence and machinations of a democratically elected strongman is modern-day Venezuela. As Javier Corrales argues in his chapter, however, Venezuela fell further than almost any other country on record: "No other cases in Latin America except Nicaragua, and few cases of democratic backsliding worldwide, end up undergoing this degree of autocratic intensification. Few cases of democratic backsliding worldwide started from such a high level of democracy and ended so low." Although backsliding had already started before Chávez, most of it took place afterward. Indeed, Corrales maintains that Venezuela's especially long descent from democracy occurred mainly in two stages. Under Chávez, who served as president from 1999 to 2013, democracy deteriorated steadily but only reached a status of "semi-authoritarianism," according to Corrales, before 2010. Month after month and year after year, Chávez chipped away at core democratic institutions—dramatically expanding the

14 WHEN DEMOCRACY BREAKS

powers of the president, significantly restricting who could compete in elections, ensuring partisan control over election administration and the courts, limiting what topics the press could cover, and so forth. Although Chávez initially attacked institutions of liberal democracy while seeming, at the same time, to *expand* the scope of participatory democracy, before long Venezuela was seeing democratic backsliding on all fronts. The process reached a new level after 2010, especially once Chávez died and was succeeded by Nicolás Maduro in 2013. In what Corrales describes as a second wave of autocratization, Maduro carried the country into "full-fledged authoritarianism," comparable to Cuba. Notably, whereas Chávez took most of his steps away from democracy when he was politically strongest (and his opposition was fragmented and weak), Maduro pursued even more far-reaching authoritarian measures, from militarizing the cabinet to suspending elections, when he faced a series of potentially regime-crushing crises and the opposition was relatively unified and posed the largest threat. Against this backdrop, Maduro was able to draw on a remarkably deep reservoir of autocratic options inherited from Chávez to suppress the opposition and maintain his grip on power.

* * *

The eleven cases of democratic breakdown explored in this volume are far from exhaustive. A great many democracies, mostly nascent ones, have failed over time—too many to document in detail in a single volume. Still, the eleven case studies presented here cover a great deal of ground, reflecting many of the core themes flagged in the academic literature on the subject, while also suggesting new insights into democratic fragility that could help deepen understanding going forward.

The existing scholarly literature highlights a number of factors commonly associated with democratic breakdown. Poor macroeconomic performance is one such a factor, potentially raising doubts about governmental effectiveness and undercutting democratic legitimacy. Scholars have also found, at various times, that high levels of economic inequality are associated with democratic breakdown; that highly polarized democracies are more vulnerable to collapse than less polarized ones; that racial or ethnic divisions provide opportunities for political leaders to foment polarization; that presidential as opposed to parliamentary democracies show a somewhat higher risk of failure; and that new democratic states (perhaps not surprisingly) break down more frequently than old ones.[12]

---

[12] On macroeconomic performance and democratic breakdown, see Mark Gasiorowski, "Economic Crisis and Political Regime Change: An Event History Analysis," *American Political Science Review* 89, no. 4 (Dec. 1995): 882–897; Stephan Haggard and Robert Kaufman, *The Political Economy of Democratic Transitions* (Princeton: Princeton University Press, 1997); Christian

INTRODUCTION   15

The degree of academic consensus surrounding these factors varies greatly. Researchers have shown a reasonably high degree of consensus about the adverse effects of poor macroeconomic performance (such as negative GDP growth), though even here the most recent research has suggested that negative economic shocks were more of a factor in twentieth-century democratic breakdowns (which tended to be more sudden, Weimar-style) than in twenty-first-century breakdowns (which have tended to be more gradual, as in Chávez's Venezuela). In fact, Matthew Singer has argued that favorable economic performance can bolster the antidemocratic activity of an elected strongman like Chávez. It may be that good economic performance generates "output legitimacy" that supports existing regimes, whether democratic or authoritarian (e.g., China in recent decades). Notably, Adam Przeworski and his coauthors have shown that the *level* of per capita income also matters—that it is negatively correlated with democratic breakdown (i.e., lower-income democracies are more likely to break

---

Stogbauer, "The Radicalization of the German Electorate: Swinging to the Right and to the Left in the Twilight of the Weimar Republic," *European Review of Economic History* 5 (Aug. 2001): 251–280; Jørgen Møller, Alexander Schmotz, and Svend-Erik Skaaning, "Economic Crisis and Democratic Breakdown in the Interwar Years: A Reassessment," *Historical Social Research* 40, no. 2 (2015): 301–318. On inequality and democratic breakdown, see Ross E. Burkhart, "Comparative Democracy and Income Distribution: Shape and Direction of the Causal Arrow," *Journal of Politics* 59, no. 1 (Feb. 1997): 148–164; Adam Przeworski, Michael E. Alvarez, José Antonio Cheibub, and Fernando Limongi, *Democracy and Development: Political Institutions and Material Well-Being in the World, 1950–1990* (Cambridge: Cambridge University Press, 2000), esp. 117–122; Daron Acemoglu and James A. Robinson, *Economic Origin of Dictatorship and Democracy* (Cambridge: Cambridge University Press, 2006); Stephan Haggard and Robert R. Kaufman, "Inequality and Regime Change: Democratic Transitions and the Stability of Democratic Rule," *American Political Science Review* 106, no. 3 (Aug. 2012): 495–516; Luca Tomini, *When Democracies Collapse: Assessing Transitions to Non-Democratic Regimes in the Contemporary World* (New York: Routledge, 2018), 14. On polarization and democratic breakdown, see Giovanni Sartori, *Parties and Party Systems: A Framework for Analysis* (Cambridge: Cambridge University Press, 1976); Juan J. Linz, *The Breakdown of Democratic Regimes: Crisis, Breakdown, and Reequilibration* (Baltimore: John Hopkins University Press, 1978); Alan Siaroff, "The Fate of Centrifugal Democracies: Lessons from Consociational Theory and System Performance," *Comparative Politics* 32, no. 3 (Apr. 2000): 317–332; Jennifer McCoy, Tahmina Rahman, and Murat Somer, "Polarization and the Global Crisis of Democracy: Common Patterns, Dynamics, and Pernicious Consequences for Democratic Polities," *American Behavioral Scientist* 62, no. 1 (Jan 2018): 16–42; Dan Slater and Aries A. Arugay, "Polarizing Figures: Executive Power and Institutional Conflict in Asian Democracies," *American Behavioral Scientist* 62, no. 1 (2018): 92–106. On presidential regimes and democratic breakdown, see Linz, *Breakdown of Democratic Regimes*; Juan J. Linz, "The Perils of Presidentialism," *Journal of Democracy* 1, no. 1 (Winter 1990): 51–69; Scott Mainwaring, "Presidentialism, Multipartism, and Democracy: The Difficult Combination," *Comparative Political Studies* 26, no. 2 (July 1993): 198–228; Abraham Diskin, Hanna Diskin, and Reuven Y. Hazan, "Why Democracies Collapse: The Reasons for Democratic Failure and Success," *International Political Science Review* 26, no. 3 (July 2005): 291–309. On new democracies and breakdown, see Jack A. Goldstone, Robert H. Bates, David L. Epstein, Ted Robert Gurr, Michael B. Lustik, Monty G. Marshall, Jay Ulfelder, and Mark Woodward, "A Global Model for Forecasting Political Instability," *American Journal of Political Science* 54, no. 1 (Jan. 2010): 190–208; Milan W. Svolik, "Which Democracies Will Last? Coups, Incumbent Takeovers, and the Dynamic of Democratic Consolidation," *British Journal of Political Science* 45, no. 4 (Oct. 2015): 715–738; Tomini, *When Democracies Collapse*, 15.

16 WHEN DEMOCRACY BREAKS

down) and that no democracy with a real per capita income above Argentina's in 1975 has ever broken down.[13]

Although high levels of political polarization are also widely seen as connected with democratic breakdown, the types of polarization that scholars highlight vary considerably. Some focus mainly on the positioning of parties within a multiparty system, whereas others have stressed polarization among elites, irrespective of the number of parties, or so-called affective polarization—the antipathy that political partisans feel toward those who support their opponents. Still others, more recently, have shown how democratically elected strongmen have actively provoked us-versus-them polarization to isolate their opponents and strengthen their own positions.[14]

While the evidence showing that presidential democracies break down more frequently than parliamentary democracies appears strong, Mainwaring has suggested that perhaps the most vulnerable presidential democracies historically were multiparty presidential systems. Mainwaring and Shugart, moreover, pointed out in 1997 that parliamentary democracies had tended to be more stable than presidential democracies, at least in part because the former frequently had a heritage of British colonial rule, which had itself been identified as a factor correlated with the successful adoption of democracy at least in some regions.[15]

In exploring these various correlations, it is essential not to lose sight of what is arguably the most important question that stands behind them: *Why, in certain democratic countries, does dissatisfaction with the status quo lead to breakdown of democracy itself, rather than simply provoke punishment of incumbents and potentially a change of government through standard electoral means?* Why, for example, did the Great Depression seem to precipitate the rise of Hitler and the collapse of democracy in Germany, while merely leading to a shift in power from Republicans to Democrats, via the ballot box, in the United States?

---

[13] Larry Diamond, "The Impact of the Economic Crisis: Why Democracies Survive," *Journal of Democracy* 22, no. 1 (Jan. 2011): 17–30; Matthew Singer, "Delegating Away Democracy: How Good Representation and Policy Successes Can Undermine Democratic Legitimacy," *Comparative Political Studies* 51, no. 13 (Nov. 2018): 1754–1788; Przeworski et al., *Democracy and Development*, esp. 98.

[14] Sartori, *Parties and Party Systems*; Linz, *Breakdown of Democratic Regimes*; Nancy Bermeo, *Ordinary People in Extraordinary Times: The Citizenry and the Breakdown of Democracy* (New Haven: Yale University Press, 2003); McCoy, Rahman, and Somer, "Polarization and the Global Crisis of Democracy"; Marc Hetherington and Thomas J. Rudolph, *Why Washington Won't Work: Polarization, Political Trust, and the Governing Crisis* (Chicago: University of Chicago Press, 2015); Jennifer McCoy and Murat Somer, "Toward a Theory of Pernicious Polarization and How It Harms Democracies: Comparative Evidence and Possible Remedies," *Annals of the American Academy of Political and Social Science* 681, no. 1 (Jan. 2019): 234–271.

[15] Mainwaring, "Presidentialism, Multipartism, and Democracy"; Diskin, Diskin, and Hazan, "Why Democracies Collapse"; Scott Mainwaring and Matthew S. Shugart. "Juan Linz, Presidentialism, and Democracy: A Critical Appraisal," *Comparative Politics* 29, no. 4 (July 1997): 449–471.

INTRODUCTION   17

Notably, if we try to address this last question drawing only on the variables most frequently highlighted in the academic literature on democratic breakdown, we don't necessarily gain a great deal of clarity. On the one hand, by the start of the Great Depression, Germany almost certainly faced higher levels of political polarization compared to the United States, and Germany's democracy was clearly younger than America's.[16] Greater polarization and a newer democracy both would suggest that Germany faced a *higher* likelihood of democratic breakdown. On the other hand, inequality was lower in Germany than in the United States, and Germany had (arguably) a parliamentary system, whereas the United States had a presidential system.[17] These differences, according to much of the literature, would suggest Germany faced a *lower* likelihood of breakdown. Additionally, while income per capita was higher in the United States than in Germany at the time, both countries' per capita incomes were below the Przeworski cutoff, suggesting that both democracies were vulnerable to failure.[18] So, focusing on these variables alone, some considerable uncertainty would remain why, as the Great Depression drove up unemployment and drove down incomes in both countries, democracy would collapse in one while surviving in the other.

Against the backdrop of this question, one of the main themes to emerge from the case studies in this volume—that democratic breakdown is very frequently preceded by years or even decades of democratic erosion—takes on particular significance. As we will see, it is possible that these periods of erosion represent not only warning signs of breakdowns to come, but also critical first phases of the breakdowns themselves. Many examples of democratic erosion—such as using violence to achieve political ends, suppressing political speech, and jailing political opponents—involve active assaults on democratic values, processes, or institutions, potentially weakening the political system and its legitimacy and increasing the likelihood of a full breakdown later on. At the same time, even if it

[16] On political polarization in Weimar, see, e.g., Benjamin Carter Hett, *The Death of Democracy: Hitler's Rise to Power and the Downfall of the Weimar Republic* (New York: Henry Holt, 2018). Hett writes, "Divisions, increasingly bitter, increasingly irreconcilable, in matters of politics, religion, social class, occupation, and region, were the hallmark of the Weimar Republic" (66).

[17] On inequality in Germany and the United States during this period, see Tony Atkinson, Joe Hasell, Salvatore Morelli, and Max Roser, *The Chartbook of Economic Inequality*, 2017, https://www. chartbookofeconomicinequality.com/inequality-by-country/; the full data set is available as an Excel file at http://chartbookofeconomicinequality.com/wp-content/uploads/DataForDownload/ AllData_ChartbookOfEconomicInequality.xlsx.

[18] For GDP per capita estimates for Germany and the United States during the relevant period, see Maddison Project Database 2020, https://www.rug.nl/ggdc/historicaldevelopment/maddison/relea ses/maddison-project-database-2020. The Maddison Project presents real per capita GDP figures in 2011$. Corrected for inflation using the CPI, the Przeworski cutoff would be about $12,700 in 2011$, which is higher than the per capita GDP of either Germany ($5,359) or the United States ($8,381) in 1932 (in 2011$). Prior to the depression, Germany had peaked at $6,519 in 1928, and the United States had peaked at $11,954 in 1929 (both in 2011$).

18   WHEN DEMOCRACY BREAKS

is not clear whether particular instances of democratic erosion contribute to subsequent breakdowns, they may reflect a less visible—though no less important—deterioration in the underlying commitment to democracy, which could be the most dangerous development of all.

One of the most powerful lines of defense within a democracy—arguably *the* most powerful line of defense—derives from the refusal of regular citizens and political leaders alike to sacrifice democratic institutions or values, even for the chance to get their way on pivotal issues of public policy, legal arrangements, or government personnel. Among scholars who subscribe to this view, some argue that democracy primarily requires commitment to democratic processes and norms among political leaders.[19] Others argue that democratic commitments must be more broadly shared, among citizens and leaders alike. Supporting this latter view, Rousseau wrote more than two centuries ago, "As soon as any man says of the affairs of the State *What does it matter to me?* the State may be given up for lost."[20]

But however one comes out on this question, it is essential that such commitment not be restricted to one party or one portion of the political spectrum. As Grote observed, ostensibly channeling Cleisthenes, "It was necessary to create . . . a perfect confidence in the bosom of every citizen . . . that the forms of the constitution will be not less sacred in the eyes of his opponents than in his own."[21] In other words, although participants in a democracy can safely disagree about nearly everything, they must share a deep and overriding—even sacred—commitment to democratic process and the outcomes it yields. By extension, the success and survival of democracy depend fundamentally on the willingness of citizens and their political leaders to *lose*, whether elections or other political battles, even to those with whom they most vehemently disagree, because of their abiding faith in the legitimacy of the democratic process and their abiding belief that their opponents are equally willing to lose when the votes turn against them, for the same reasons.

In a very real sense, democratic erosion—in nearly all of its forms—reflects a creeping rejection of such a willingness to lose or compromise, and thus a creeping rejection of democracy itself. The resort to political violence, for example, is implicitly an acknowledgment that the same objectives might not be achieved peacefully, through electoral or other democratic means. It is also an acknowledgment that the objectives at issue supersede the democratic principles

---

[19] For a sampling of leading democracy scholars who focus on the role of political elites, rather than the citizenry more generally, in upholding democratic norms, see especially Linz and Stepan, *The Breakdown of Democratic Regimes;* Bermeo, *Ordinary People in Extraordinary Times;* and Levitsky and Ziblatt, *How Democracies Die.*

[20] Jean-Jacques Rousseau, *The Social Contract* (1762), Book III, Chapter 15.

[21] Grote, *History of Greece,* 2:86.

INTRODUCTION 19

being trampled, at least in the eyes of those willing to commit the violence—as well as those not directly involved but willing to look the other way. Similarly, the rise of explicitly antidemocratic political actors almost definitionally indicates a decline in democratic commitment, among both the actors and their most ardent followers, at a minimum, and perhaps among many of their less ardent followers as well.

One additional factor that deserves special consideration, political polarization, represents a special case of democratic erosion. Unlike political violence or the rise of antidemocratic actors, which are worrisome even in small amounts, some degree of political polarization is normal in a democracy. In fact, in many contexts, intense partisanship is associated with productive—even highly productive—democratic governance, surfacing new ideas and policy approaches in much the same way that intense competition in the economic marketplace can generate vital innovation in commercial products and processes.[22] Intense political polarization can of course also prove highly destructive—in the lead-up to the American Civil War, for example. So we're left with the question of what leads political conflict and polarization to be either productive or destructive. High polarization can strain the commitment to democracy because losing in the face of moderate disagreement is less painful than losing in the face of vehement disputes, when the stakes seem existential.[23] Political polarization can prove especially dangerous when it infects core institutions, such as the military, leading these institutions to be clearly identified with one political side or another. This was plainly the case in Chile in 1973, for instance, when the military became strongly aligned with political opponents of the president. Another possibility is that even intense partisan conflict can prove productive when set against the backdrop of a strong culture of democracy—a deep commitment to democratic process, institutions, and values—but can quickly turn destructive when that commitment fades, as it apparently did in the pre–Civil War American South.[24]

---

[22] David Moss, *Democracy: A Case Study* (Cambridge, MA: Harvard University Press, 2017), esp. 6–8.

[23] Archon Fung, "Afterword: Does Deliberative Democracy Have a Role in Our Time of Political Crisis?," *Journal of Deliberative Democracy* 16, no. 1 (2020): 75.

[24] See, e.g., Moss, *Democracy*, 682, characterizing a strong culture of democracy as "a sort of societal glue, binding people together even in the face of intense political disagreement." Institutions that enable productive negotiation between strongly opposed factions can also preserve democratic sentiments, though scholars disagree about what institutional structures most facilitate such productive negotiation. In his book *Breaking the Two-Party Doom Loop* (New York: Oxford University Press, 2020), for example, Lee Drutman argues that multiparty democracies are more likely to be stable in the face of strong disagreements than the fully sorted two-party system in the United States in the early twenty-first century. Yet Scott Mainwaring, in "Presidentialism, Multipartism, and Democracy: The Difficult Combination," *Comparative Political Studies* 26, no. 2 (1993): 198–228, argues that the combination of presidentialism and multiparty systems can be especially conducive to democratic breakdown. Giovanni Sartori, *Parties and Party Systems: A Framework for Analysis* (New York: Cambridge University Press, 1976), meanwhile, argues that the number of parties in a

20 WHEN DEMOCRACY BREAKS

Either way, this idea that political conflict and polarization can be associated with a well-functioning democracy, or with a democracy on the verge of collapse, depending on the precise circumstances, points to a larger challenge both for this volume and for our collective understanding of democratic fragility and resilience. While we can say with a high degree of confidence that democratic erosion often precedes democratic breakdown, we cannot say with an equally high degree of confidence that erosion doesn't also precede democratic survival. In fact, some degree of democratic erosion, in this or that part of the political system, is likely present at nearly all times in all democracies. To what extent, then, is democratic erosion a meaningful warning sign or simply an inevitable fact of democratic life?

And this brings us back to the question of why the Great Depression seemed to provoke or accelerate democratic collapse in Germany, while provoking or accelerating only an electoral realignment in the United States. What role, if any, did democratic erosion play in all of this? Certainly, we saw significant signs of democratic erosion in Weimar Germany, even well before the depression took hold. This included not only intense political polarization but also significant political violence and the rise of explicitly antidemocratic political actors. It seems reasonable to infer that these developments may have contributed to—or at least signaled—the full breakdown to come. Yet the analysis cannot end there, because even a cursory look at the United States would reveal significant signs of democratic weakness or erosion prior to the Great Depression, including everything from modest electoral corruption to brutal political violence directed against Black Americans, particularly in the American South. Since American democracy survived, how can we be sure that democratic erosion or weakness is in fact a precursor to democratic collapse? This volume focuses on the path from erosion to breakdown, but it is important to recognize that other trajectories are possible as well.

Ideally, to better understand these varying trajectories, we would like to have quantitative measures that allow us to compare democratic strength or weakness across countries and across time. Various efforts along these lines have emerged over past decades (and, in some cases, over just the past few years), offering quantitative measures of everything from freedom of the press to electoral integrity. V-Dem's composite liberal-democracy index allows us to compare the overall quality of liberal democracy, according to V-Dem's measure, across countries and time. Looking specifically at Germany and the United States from 1900 to the early 1930s, we see that the United States consistently scored well above Germany until 1918 (with the United States averaging 0.386 vs. Germany

---

multiparty system is an important factor in determining whether parties will have incentives to negotiate responsibly.

0.216, on a scale of 0 to 1), and that Germany then rose rapidly with the birth of the Weimar Republic, actually overtaking the United States by 1920, according to the index (Germany 0.495 vs. U.S. 0.385 in that year). Over the next decade, the United States gradually rose while Germany gradually declined, such that by 1930 the United States had again taken the lead by a small margin (U.S. 0.485 vs. Germany 0.430).[25] The index suggests that while both democracies were very far from perfect (i.e., well below a perfect score of 1), the Weimar Constitution was quite advanced for the time (delivering a score above that of the United States for most of the 1920s); it also suggests that Germany experienced at least some degree of democratic erosion over the 1920s, while the United States saw the quality of its liberal democracy modestly improve, on net.

Although in some ways the V-Dem data are broadly consistent with what one might have expected (namely, that both democracies were imperfect and that Germany's democracy deteriorated prior to its collapse), the differences in the two countries' liberal-democracy scores over the 1920s and early 1930s hardly seem large enough to explain the radically different political outcomes these two countries experienced. By 1932, immediately before its descent into fascism, Germany's score was still significantly higher than America's had been in 1920 or even 1925. Looking beyond the Weimar period itself, one can see from the longer path of Germany's V-Dem scores—as well as from literally any relevant textbook—that its democracy was still very young by the early 1930s, and this may be part of why the Weimar Republic proved so vulnerable to an economic shock like the Great Depression. As we have seen, the academic literature suggests that newer democracies are more likely to fail than older ones. This seems obvious enough—but why, exactly? And why would the liberal-democracy scores themselves not reflect this deeper weakness?

Weimar's "model" constitution ensured that, at least on paper, its democracy rivaled or exceeded the best democracies in the world at the time, which helps to explain why Weimar Germany initially emerged as a bastion of personal freedom and also, perhaps, why its liberal-democracy score was higher than America's through most of the 1920s.[26] Still, Madison's observation that constitutional provisions are little more than "parchment barriers" unless "incorporated with

---

[25] Michael Coppedge et al., "V-Dem Dataset v10," Varieties of Democracy (V-Dem) Project, 2020, https://papers.ssrn.com/sol3/papers.cfm?abstract_id=3557877. See also Michael Coppedge et al., "V-Dem Codebook v10" Varieties of Democracy (V-Dem) Project, https://papers.ssrn.com/sol3/papers.cfm?abstract_id=3557877. Notably, Germany's score rose sharply to 0.472 in 1931, but only for a single year, and returned to 0.430 in 1932 (before collapsing to 0.089 in 1933, when Hitler took power, and 0.021 the following year).

[26] Herbert J. Spiro, *Government by Constitution: The Political Systems of Democracy* (New York: Random House, 1959). According to Spiro, "[a]t the time of its adoption, the Weimar Constitution was widely hailed as the very model of modern constitutionalism" (421). In this volume, Eric Weitz writes, "Globally, the Weimar Constitution was probably *the* most democratic constitution of its time."

22   WHEN DEMOCRACY BREAKS

the national sentiment" seems especially pertinent here. How strong was democratic sentiment in Weimar Germany, and how did it compare with sentiment in the United States? Unfortunately, in the absence of relevant public opinion surveys from the time, reliable quantitative data on the nature of democratic sentiment from bygone eras—about how wide or deep commitment to democracy ran in Weimar Germany or interwar America, for example—are simply not available.

In this context, historical case studies can prove especially valuable. The newness of democracy in Germany after World War I might vaguely suggest weaker democratic commitment relative to the United States, but careful historical examination can provide us with more precise clues, even when quantitative survey data from the period are lacking. Weitz's chapter on Weimar Germany provides an excellent illustration. As he argues, politics in Weimar Germany were shaped by two powerful traditions: a "150-year-long humanistic and democratic tradition," on the one hand, and a "highly authoritarian" tradition, bringing together elements of both conservative traditionalism and "right-wing populism," on the other. Descendants of the authoritarian tradition, Weitz maintains, proved "not just anti-Socialist but fundamentally antidemocratic as well." All of this indicates that democratic sentiment ran deep in certain quarters, contributing to "the vast expansion of democracy, social reform, and cultural efflorescence in the Weimar years," but also that it was far from universally held in Germany and even actively resisted, including from bastions of authoritarianism within the state itself.

In the pages that follow, in one chapter after another, portraits emerge of weak or weakening democracies. Individuals and groups with the strongest democratic leanings struggle against antidemocratic forces but ultimately succumb, sometimes in the face of extreme violence or superior force but in many cases without a shot being fired. One apparent lesson is that although circumstances vary greatly from one country to the next, the destruction of democracies typically comes with years of warning, as in the case of Weimar, but that these warnings often go unheeded or at least largely unheeded in many quarters, as citizens and their political leaders seem to grow increasingly inured to each successive insult to democratic values or institutions. One might conclude that democratic commitment softens or wavers long before democracy itself collapses.

We say "apparent lesson" because this volume aims to generate insights about democratic fragility on the basis of individual case studies, rather than to test existing hypotheses using quantitative methods. We know that while the list of polities where democracy has failed is long, the variation across them—including variation in institutional context—is so large that it often confounds meaningful statistical analysis. We also know that some of the variables of greatest interest, such as democratic commitment, are among the most difficult to capture in consistent ways. And, of course, we have focused in this volume on cases of democratic breakdown, without developing comparable cases on polities where democracy survived, uninterrupted.

Our expectation is that in countries where democracy fails, prior democratic erosion is likely to have been more pronounced—and the level and breadth of democratic commitment lower, among both the general public and political leaders—than in countries where democracy survives, despite equivalent shocks. Of course, this remains only a hypothesis, for all of the reasons highlighted in the previous paragraph. Although our focus on individual case studies is not conducive to rigorous hypothesis testing, it does provide visibility into the antecedents of democratic breakdown that may not be available any other way.

The last time a collection of this kind was put together was more than forty years ago, in 1978, when Juan Linz and Alfred Stepan (and their many co-authors) published *The Breakdown of Democratic Regimes*. A monumental contribution, this work has helped to shape understanding of democratic fragility in the decades since and has offered a foundation on which many other scholars have built. In the meantime, the field has progressed quite considerably, even as a dangerous new wave of democratic backsliding and breakdown has become reality, particularly in the twenty-first century. In fact, the amount of new, book-length work published on democratic failure over just the past few years is striking.[27] Much of this work, including Steven Levitsky and Daniel Ziblatt's widely acclaimed *How Democracies Die*, provides vital insight into the latest mode of autocratic assault on democracy. As Levitsky and Ziblatt explain:

> This is how elected autocrats subvert democracy—packing and "weaponizing" the courts and other neutral agencies, buying off the media and the private sector (or bullying them into silence), and rewriting the rules of politics to tilt the playing field against opponents. The tragic paradox of the electoral route to authoritarianism is that democracy's assassins use the very institutions of democracy—gradually, subtly, and even legally—to kill it.[28]

---

[27] See, e.g., Bermeo, *Ordinary People in Extraordinary Times*; Larry Diamond, Marc F. Plattner, and Christopher Walker, *Authoritarianism Goes Global: The Challenge to Democracy* (Baltimore: Johns Hopkins University Press, 2016); Jan-Werner Müller, *What Is Populism?* (Philadelphia: University of Pennsylvania Press, 2016); Timothy Snyder, *On Tyranny: Twenty Lessons from the Twentieth Century* (New York: Tim Duggan Books, 2017); Barry Eichengreen, *The Populist Temptation: Economic Grievance and Political Reaction in the Modern Era* (New York: Oxford University Press, 2018); William A. Galston, *Anti-Pluralism: The Populist Threat to Liberal Democracy* (New Haven: Yale University Press, 2018); Tom Ginsburg and Aziz Z. Huq, *How to Save a Constitutional Democracy* (Chicago: University of Chicago Press, 2018); Hett, *The Death of Democracy*; Levitsky and Ziblatt, *How Democracies Die*; Yascha Mounk, *The People vs. Democracy: Why Our Freedom Is in Danger and How to Save It* (Cambridge, MA: Harvard University Press, 2018); Frances McCall Rosenbluth and Ian Shapiro, *Responsible Parties: Saving Democracy from Itself* (New Haven: Yale University Press, 2018); Tomini, *When Democracies Collapse*; Sheri Berman, *Democracy and Dictatorship in Europe: From the Ancien Régime to the Present Day* (New York: Oxford University Press, 2019).

[28] Levitsky and Ziblatt, *How Democracies Die*, 8.

24 WHEN DEMOCRACY BREAKS

Levitsky and Ziblatt, among many others, have done a superb job documenting and analyzing this "electoral route to authoritarianism" (or "illiberal democracy"), which has been so characteristic of democratic breakdown in the twenty-first century up until this point.[29] All of the contributors to this volume—and perhaps especially the authors covering the most contemporary cases on Russia, Turkey, and Venezuela—have benefited a great deal from this growing body of work, and there are many points of agreement.

At the same time, the main goal of this volume is to widen the aperture, to explore democratic failure across a broad range of cases, recent and long past, with the aim of exposing not only notable commonalities but notable differences as well. When it comes to differences, some relate to the fact-patterns of the cases themselves (abrupt vs. gradual seizure of power, for example), while others relate to diverging interpretations among contributing authors and editors. As a case in point, some contributors to this volume, following Juan Linz, see strong democratic commitment as being especially vital among political elites, even as others believe political leaders can be counted upon to adhere to essential norms only if democratic commitments remain strongly held throughout the citizenry at large.

We see this diversity, of both cases and viewpoint, as a core strength of the volume. Especially at a time when democracy appears to be under very significant stress around the world, having as broad a perspective as possible on the history of democratic breakdown seems particularly valuable. The next threat that emerges could look a great deal like what we have seen most recently in Turkey or Venezuela, but it also could look closer to what unfolded in America in the lead-up to the Civil War or in India in 1975 or even in Germany in 1933. We need to continue thinking hard about why democratic crises of the twenty-first century seem so far to have taken a particular path, mostly following the "electoral route to authoritarianism" and "illiberal democracy," but without assuming that new threats, following very different patterns, cannot or will not emerge. History is by no means a perfect guide to what's possible, but it is one of the best guides we have—and this, to be sure, has been a principal motivation for the volume.

Above all, we believe that history, and especially the history of democratic breakdown, can provide new insight into the line separating democratic resilience from democratic fragility. We hope that the chapters that make up this volume contribute to that project and serve as an ongoing reminder not only of what can go wrong, but of what is at stake.

---

[29] On an early use of "illiberal democracy," see Fareed Zakaria, "The Rise of Illiberal Democracy," *Foreign Affairs* 76, no. 6 (Nov.–Dec. 1997): 22–43. See also Collier and Levitsky, "Democracy with Adjectives," 438–440.

2
Democratic Collapse and Recovery in Ancient Athens (413–403)

Federica Carugati and Josiah Ober

Introduction

Rich and consolidated democracies don't usually die—until they do.[1] This chapter explores the collapse and recovery of the world's first democracy: Ancient Athens. The Greek city-state of Athens was, by our definition (below), a democracy for at least 180 years (508–322 BCE). During that period, the Athenians pushed back foreign invasions, built and then lost an Aegean empire, suffered military catastrophes, experienced a period of democratic collapse, recovered to become a major center of Mediterranean trade and culture, and were finally forced to accept the hegemony of imperial Macedon. Athens provides a remarkable case study for analyzing the causes and consequences of democratic breakdown. First, the collapse defies broadly accepted social scientific findings, casting a shadow over what we think we know about the survival of today's rich and consolidated democracies. Second, unlike in many other experiments with democracy, past and present, democracy in Athens collapsed but then recovered. The restoration of democracy saw the resurrection of past institutions, as well as the creation of new ones.

The question of what conditions cause democracy to break is of obvious relevance today. This volume is but one of many contributions devoted to developing some answers. The evidence from the contemporary world suggests that

---

[1] On the conditions for democratic survival, see Adam Przeworski and Fernando Limongi, "Modernization: Theories and Facts," *World Politics* 49, no. 2 (1997): 155–183; Milan Svolik, "Authoritarian Reversals and Democratic Consolidation," *American Political Science Review* 102, no. 2 (2008): 153–168; Tom Ginsburg and Aziz Huq, *How to Save a Constitutional Democracy* (Chicago: University of Chicago Press, 2018), 55–56. For Christian Houle, homogeneity also contributes to survival: "Ethnic Inequality and the Dismantling of Democracy: A Global Analysis," *World Politics* 67, no. 3 (2015): 469–505. With a proviso: relevant cleavages in the literature cited are religion and ethnicity; see also James Fearon and David Laitin, "Ethnicity, Insurgency, and Civil War," *American Political Science Review* 97, no. 1 (2003): 75–90. These cleavages were not prevalent in Ancient Greece, but there were other relevant cleavages, e.g., socioeconomic status and regime preferences.

Federica Carugati and Josiah Ober, *Democratic Collapse and Recovery in Ancient Athens (413–403)*
In: *When Democracy Breaks*. Edited by: Archon Fung, David Moss, and Odd Arne Westad, Oxford University Press.
© Oxford University Press 2024. DOI: 10.1093/oso/9780197760789.003.0002

26 WHEN DEMOCRACY BREAKS

democratic breakdown occurs in the aftermath of military coups[2] or when leaders lose legitimacy or cannot solve political problems,[3] and it is more likely under presidentialism,[4] when inequality is high,[5] or when the country has past experiences with authoritarian institutions.[6] Breakdown also occurs through the erosion of checks on elected leaders.[7] Democratic stability rests instead on economic growth, strong states, and liberal institutions, such as a robust rule of law, free and fair elections, and individual rights.[8]

A limited literature exists which seeks to account for the collapse of democracy in Athens. The scholarly tradition has long interpreted the breakdown as a temporary suspension of normal democratic practice. Those who have delved into its causes have tended to rely on the account of the Athenian historian Thucydides. For Thucydides, democracy collapsed during the Peloponnesian War because it was an inferior system of governance, relying on the faulty opinions of laymen sitting on a hill at the top of the political hierarchy and fatally prone to squabbling. Its survival depended on rare personal characteristics and political talents uniquely well conjoined in its best-known general, Pericles. Thucydides's account leads to a simplistic counterfactual: had Pericles survived, Athens would have won the war, and the democracy would not have collapsed. This account obscures the deeper institutional questions that are central to our explanation of the democracy's breakdown, as well as its recovery and performance.[9]

Taking up this ancient polity as a comparative case study requires that we address two questions at the outset: What does it mean to speak of democracy in Ancient Athens? And then, what does it mean to suggest that Athens was a rich and consolidated democracy? Neither Przeworski's GDP threshold of $6,000, nor the mantra of recurring free and fair elections[10] applies to Athens.

---

[2] Guillermo O'Donnell, *Modernization and Bureaucratic Authoritarianism: Studies in South American Politics* (Berkeley: Institute of International Studies, University of California, 1973).

[3] Juan Linz and Alfred Stepan, eds., *The Breakdown of Democratic Regimes: Crisis, Breakdown, and Reequilibration* (Baltimore: Johns Hopkins University Press, 1978).

[4] Juan Linz, "The Perils of Presidentialism," *Journal of Democracy* 1, no. 1 (1990): 61–69.

[5] Charles Boix, *Democracy and Redistribution* (Cambridge: Cambridge University Press, 2003); Christian Houle, "Inequality and Democracy: Why Inequality Harms Consolidation but Does Not Affect Democratization," *World Politics* 61, no. 4 (2009): 589–622.

[6] Antonio Cheibub, *Presidentialism, Parliamentarianism, and Democracy* (New York: Cambridge University Press, 2007).

[7] Daniel Levitsky and Stephen Ziblatt, *How Democracies Die* (New York: Crown, 2018); Ginsburg and Huq, *How to Save a Constitutional Democracy*; Scott Mainwaring and Fernando Bizzarro, "The Fates of Third-Wave Democracies," *Journal of Democracy* 301, no. 1 (2019): 99–113.

[8] For a literature review, see Federica Carugati, "Democratic Stability: A Long View," *Annual Review of Political Science* 23, no. 4 (2020): 1–17.

[9] We do not address here the ultimate loss of Athenian independence after 322 BCE—which is a story about the emergence of imperial nation-states in Macedon and Rome, not about "how democracies die." Josiah Ober, *The Rise and Fall of Classical Greece* (Princeton: Princeton University Press, 2015), ch. 10.

[10] Przeworski and Limongi, "Modernization: Theories and Facts"; Jay Diamond, *The Spirit of Democracy: The Struggle to Build Free Societies throughout the World* (New York: Holt Paperbacks, 2008).

Preindustrial GDP growth cannot be meaningfully compared with that achieved by moderns.[11] The Athenians elected some officials, but most functions of government were carried out by citizens selected by lot. Athens also did not develop many of the liberal values that are normally associated, indeed often equated with contemporary democracy—among these, concepts of personal autonomy, inalienable rights, and distributive justice. So Athens was not a "liberal democracy." Athens was a slave society that failed to extend citizenship to women. Yet it seems absurd to deny the label of "democracy" to a demos that ruled itself for the best part of two centuries (roughly from 508 to 322 BCE) and whose rule coincided with a period of remarkably high economic performance. Athens's regime, then, was both "rich" and "consolidated." But was it a democracy? Our answer is that Athens was a "basic democracy": a system of collective self-rule by an extensive and socially diverse demos legitimately empowered to seek and capable of achieving the goals of security, prosperity, and nontyranny.[12]

Our account of democratic breakdown and recovery in Athens highlights a series of factors. Military defeats and the presence of an organized opposition played an important role in the democracy's collapse. However, we identify a deeper, root cause: a crisis of legitimacy precipitated by performance failures but ultimately traceable (then and now) to a fundamental defect of institutional design.

We do not take the restoration of democracy as a foregone conclusion. Instead, we delve into a decade of political turmoil during which democracy was put into question, collapsed, reemerged, and was tested, collapsed again, and was eventually restored in a revised form. This happened at the end of the fifth century BCE, about a hundred years after democracy was first established and at the end of a century that saw Athens rise from an unexceptional Greek city-state into an imperial capital and, in Pericles's words, "the school of Greece."[13] The pressure of the long, difficult Peloponnesian War (from 431 to 404 BCE) certainly played a role in straining Athens's institutions. A powerful and rich elite with strong sympathies for oligarchy and the cultural and social resources to organize for collective action also played a role.

---

[11] Ian Morris, *Why the West Rules—For Now: The Patterns of History, and What They Reveal about the Future* (London: Profile Books, 2010); Andreas Berg and Carl Lyttkens, "Measuring Institutional Quality in Ancient Athens," *Journal of Institutional Economics* 10, no. 2 (2014): 279–310; Ober, *The Rise and Fall of Classical Greece*.

[12] Josiah Ober, *Demopolic: Democracy Before Liberalism in Theory and Practice* (Cambridge: Cambridge University Press, 2017), chs. 1–2. We discuss the features of basic democracy, and address the distinction between basic and modern democracy, in the next section. The discussion suggests that Athens fares well according to measures of both electoral and liberal democracy in V-Dem, which include freedom of assembly and speech, rule of law, constraints on executive, and protection of personal liberties.

[13] Thucydides, 2.41.

28　WHEN DEMOCRACY BREAKS

But the Athenian democracy did not collapse solely because of external forces. In fact, the conditions for its progressive erosion are ultimately institutional and can be traced back to the democracy's very establishment. In particular, we highlight the lack of checks on the power of the demos as a critical factor of democratic breakdown. This design defect had its roots in the democracy's emergence from a past of tyranny and elite infighting. Against these forces, a powerful demos was a necessary counterweight.[14] But as time went by, as we will see, this design proved detrimental to the stability of democracy. We do not mean to suggest that political systems simply age badly, and that at some point collapse will ensue because circumstances have changed. Indeed, if institutional design were solely responsible for the collapse of democracy in Athens, it would be hard to explain why it took almost a century for democracy to break down.

In the end, what did democracy in was a crisis of legitimacy that was the result of a combination of the aforementioned factors: design defects, organized opposition, and military pressures. The crisis of legitimacy manifested as a breakdown in the belief that the democracy was a fair system of social cooperation—that the costs I incur for my cooperation as a member of the group are compensated by the benefits that participation bestows on me, both as an individual and as a part of a community whose flourishing I value, and the belief that my fellow citizens are similarly motivated. The crisis of legitimacy was a crisis of those beliefs. We use the word "legitimacy" to mean a form of Weberian descriptive legitimacy in which I commit to obey the rules even when I know that I can get away with violation.[15] The case of Athens suggests that democracy requires, at a minimum, this form of descriptive legitimacy. When legitimacy is lost, overcoming the crisis requires reconfiguring legitimacy at the institutional level, as well as at the level of political culture.

Our contribution combines history, normative political theory, and positive political science to shed light on the manifold causes of democratic breakdown. We emphasize institutions alongside political culture, and we seek to uncover proximate as well as ultimate causes. In diagnosing an ancient case study, we provide a prognosis for the future of our fragile modern democracies: it takes a lot to shake a rich, consolidated democracy, but in the end even these rare beasts can die when we, its citizens, lose faith in the value and efficacy of our mutual obligations.

[14] Sara Forsdyke, *Exile, Ostracism, and Democracy: The Politics of Expulsion in Ancient Greece* (Princeton: Princeton University Press, 2005).

[15] Max Weber, *The Theory of Social and Economic Organization*, ed. Talcott Parsons (New York: Free Press, 1964); Fabienne Peter, "Political Legitimacy," in *The Stanford Encyclopedia of Philosophy*, ed. Edward Zalta (2017), https://plato.stanford.edu/entries/legitimacy/.

Athens's Institutions, Culture, and History

Classical Athens is by far the best-documented and most thoroughly studied example of a premodern democracy in a complex state. Athens was governed by a large and economically (if not culturally, ethnically, or religiously) diverse citizenry through sophisticated legislative, judicial, and executive institutions. Many of the institutions of the mature classical democracy were established early on.[16]

The Council (Boule) was a deliberative body of five hundred members selected every year by lot among the citizen (free, adult, native male) population. The mandate lasted one year, and no member could iterate his participation more than once, and not in consecutive years. Given Athens's demographics, this meant that a very large number of Athenian citizens participated directly in governance. The Council set the agenda for each meeting of the citizen Assembly, either providing policy recommendations or mandating that an issue be openly debated on the floor of the Assembly. Assembly meetings, attended by six thousand to eight thousand citizens, typically featured multiple speeches on policy proposals, followed by a vote by show of hands. Councilors received pay for service, and from the early fourth century onward, so did assemblymen. During the democracy's first century, decisions of the Assembly were final and no appeal mechanisms existed. In the popular courts, large panels of lay citizen jurors, also selected by lot, resolved private and public disputes. Each year, six thousand men were sworn in as jurors. On each day that the courts were in session, panels of varying size (usually ranging between 201 and 501) were allotted to disputes through complex selection mechanisms. Jurors listened to speeches from the contending parties and then voted by secret ballot. They did not deliberate before the vote, and their decision was final. Finally, a number of magistrates, some selected by lot and some elected, were tasked with a variety of functions related to administration, the military, infrastructure, and finance. Law, understood as both written statutes and unwritten norms, played an important role in setting the rules of the game and controlling powerful actors.[17]

---

[16] The citizen population consisted of some 30,000 of a total population of perhaps 250,000 in the time of Aristotle, in the later fourth century BCE; citizens constituted perhaps up to 50,000 of a substantially larger total population in the imperial-democracy era of Pericles in the mid-fifth century BCE (about 350,000). Mogens Herman Hansen, *Three Studies in Athenian Demography* (Copenhagen: Munksgaard, 1988); Mogens Herman Hansen, *The Shotgun Method: The Demography of the Ancient Greek City-State Culture* (Columbia; University of Missouri Press, 2006). The development of Athens in the context of the world of the city-states is detailed in Ober, *The Rise and Fall of Classical Greece*, chs. 6–9. Federica Carugati, *Creating a Constitution: Law, Democracy, and Growth in Ancient Athens* (Princeton: Princeton University Press, 2019) is a detailed analysis of the crisis period of the late fifth and early fourth centuries.

[17] For a survey of democratic institutions, see Mogens Herman Hansen, *The Athenian Democracy in the Age of Demosthenes: Structure, Principles, and Ideology* (Norman: University of Oklahoma Press, 1999). As Sara Forsdyke argues, in the fifth century the Athenians made important strides toward establishing elements of what we may today call a rule of law: namely, legal supremacy and legal equality. Sara Forsdyke, "Ancient and Modern Conceptions of the Rule of Law," in *Ancient Greek*

30 WHEN DEMOCRACY BREAKS

These formal institutions were underpinned by a political culture predicated on rejection of autocratic (tyrannical, oligarchic) forms of government. Athens was a democracy, in the first instance, because its citizens refused to be subjects and were willing to put their bodies on the line in resisting threats of subjugation. Meanwhile, an emerging ideology of democratic citizenship emphasized political liberties—freedom of speech and assembly—and political equality, expressed in the equality of each citizen's vote and in lotteries for the selection of public officials. The political culture, furthermore, protected civic dignity: strong social norms, ultimately backed up by threats of legal sanction, pushed back against the tendency of wealthy and well-connected residents to engage in public behaviors likely to humiliate or infantilize their poorer fellow citizens. The freedom, equality, and dignity associated with the status of citizen were essential parts of the value package that compensated each citizen for the costs of participating in a relatively time-consuming regime of self-government and national defense.[18]

In comparison to a modern democracy, Athenian democracy may be described as "basic."[19] Most striking, Athenian democracy was not liberal, either in a classical liberal sense of being designed to defend the autonomy and natural rights of the individual against the intrusive potential of a strong central government, or in the contemporary liberal sense of promoting an egalitarian ideal of social justice and universal human rights. Freedom, equality, and dignity remained civic values, arising from and defended by the political participation of citizens. Athenian democracy did have certain redistributive effects: taxes on the rich enabled poorer citizens to be full participants in politics, and income inequality remained relatively low in comparison to other well-studied premodern societies.[20] Moreover, there were certain spillover effects such that noncitizens—slaves and resident foreigners—were to some degree protected by law and norms from certain forms of abuse. But those protections were not based on rights, and they depended for enforcement on the goodwill of the citizenry.[21]

History and Contemporary Social Science, ed. Mirko Canevaro, Andrew Erskine, Benjamin Gray, and Josiah Ober (Edinburgh: Edinburgh University Press, 2018), 186. On the rule of law in Athens in comparative perspective see also Paul Gowder, *The Rule of Law in the Real World* (New York: Cambridge University Press, 2016); Mirko Canevaro, "The Rule of Law as the Measure of Political Legitimacy in the Greek City States," *Hague Journal on the Rule of Law* 9, no. 1 (2017): 211–236; Carugati, "The Rule of Law through the Ages," in *The Routledge Handbook of the Rule of Law* (Routledge, forthcoming).

[18] Josiah Ober, *Demopolis: Democracy before Liberalism in Theory and Practice* (Cambridge: Cambridge University Press, 2017), ch. 2.

[19] Ober, *Demopolis*, ch. 1.

[20] Josiah Ober, "Inequality in Late-Classical Democratic Athens: Evidence and Models," in *Democracy and Open Economy World Order*, ed. George Bitros and Nicholas Kyriazis (New York: Springer, 2017), 125–146.

[21] Federica Carugati, "Tradeoffs of Inclusion: Development in Ancient Athens," *Comparative Political Studies* 53, no. 1 (2019): 144–170.

DEMOCRATIC COLLAPSE AND RECOVERY IN ATHENS   31

Among the striking features of Athenian democracy are its relative stability and prosperity. From its origin (usually dated to the aftermath of the "Athenian Revolution" of 508 BCE)[22] to its overthrow by the victorious Macedonian dynasts following the conquests of Alexander the Great (322 BCE), Athens was almost continuously ruled by a participatory (i.e., political participation-rights holding) citizenry that included virtually all free, native, adult males. This system sustained remarkably high levels of economic and social development.[23]

In the fifth century, Athens's stability and prosperity depended in large part on the empire, which the city-state came to control after the Persian Wars (490 and 480–479 BCE). The empire brought wealth, prestige, and stability to the polis. Imperial revenues, in the form of both rents and tribute from the allies, funded the polis's democratic institutions, its military might, and conspicuous public building programs. They also helped justify democratic institutions and culture before the eyes of rich Athenians who may have preferred a different type of government.

If the empire contributed to Athens's success, it was also responsible for triggering the conflict that would eventually bring the polis to its knees. According to Thucydides, "[t]he growth of the power of Athens, and the alarm which this inspired in Sparta, made war inevitable."[24] The first phase of the Peloponnesian War (the so-called Archidamian War, from 431 to 421 BCE) progressively eroded the conspicuous human and financial resources that Athens

[22] Josiah Ober, *The Athenian Revolution: Essays on Ancient Greek Democracy and Political Theory* (Princeton: Princeton University Press, 1996), ch. 4.

[23] Economic growth: aggregate consumption measured at 0.6–0.9% per annum—as compared to Holland's 0.5%; per capita consumption measured at 0.15% per annum—as compared to Holland's 0.2% and Rome's 0.1%. Ian Morris, "Economic Growth in Ancient Greece," *Journal of Institutional and Theoretical Economics* 160, no. 4 (2004): 709–742; Ian Morris, "The Eighth Century Revolution," Princeton/Stanford Record Papers in Classics, Paper no. 120507, 2005, https://papers.ssrn.com/sol3/papers.cfm?abstract_id=1426851Richard Saller "Framing the Debate over Growth in the Ancient Economy," in *The Ancient Economy*, ed. Ian Morris and J. G. Manning (Palo Alto: Stanford University Press, 2005); Josiah Ober, "Wealthy Hellas," *Transactions of the American Philological Association* 140, no. 2 (2010): 241–286; Ober, *The Rise and Fall of Classical Greece*, ch. 5. On healthy and urbanized populations, see Morris, "Economic Growth in Ancient Greece"; Anna Lagia, "Diet and the Polis: An Isotopic Study of Diet in Athens and Laurion during the Classical, Hellenistic, and Imperial Roman Periods," in *Archaeodiet in the Greek World: Dietary Reconstruction from Stable Isotope Analysis*, ed. Anastasia Papathanasiou, Michael P. Richards, and Sherry C. Fox (Princeton: American School of Classical Studies at Athens, 2015); Hansen, *The Shotgun Method*. On high real wages, see Walter Scheidel, "Real Wages in Early Economies: Evidence from Living Standards from 1800 BCE to 1300 CE," *Journal of the Social and Economic History of the Orient* 53 (2010): 425–462. Low inequality: wealth: 0.708 Gini; landholding: 0.44 Gini; income: 0.38 (the last measure includes slaves and resident foreigners): Geoffrey Kron, "The Distribution of Wealth in Athens in Comparative Perspective," *Zeitschrift für Papyrologie und Epigraphic* 179 (2011): 129–138; Geoffrey Kron, "Comparative Evidence and the Reconstruction of the Ancient Economy: Greco-Roman Housing and the Level and Distribution of Wealth and Income," in *Quantifying the Greco-Roman Economy and Beyond*, ed. François de Callataÿ (Beri: Edipuglia, 2014), 123–146; Julian Gallego, "El campesinado y la distribución de la tierra en la Atnas del siglo IV a.C.," *Gerion Revista de Historia Antigua* 34 (2016): 43–75; Ober, "Inequality in Late-Classical Democratic Athens."

[24] Robert Strassler, trans., *The Landmark Thucydides* (New York: Free Press, 1996), 1.23.6.

32   WHEN DEMOCRACY BREAKS

had accumulated in the fifth century.[25] In a bid to restore Athens's strength through conscripted manpower and booty, in 415 the Athenian Assembly enthusiastically voted to send a massive military expedition to Sicily with the aim of radically expanding the empire. The campaign (415–413 BCE) proved an utter disaster for Athens.[26]

The defeat in Sicily plunged the city into a severe financial crisis, triggering political instability. Between 411 and 403 BCE, a series of regimes replaced the democracy that had governed Athens for almost a century. The oligarchy of the Four Hundred was established in 411 BCE and ruled Athens for about four months. When the Four Hundred collapsed, another oligarchy—the regime of the Five Thousand—took power for another handful of months. Democracy was restored in 410/9 BCE and remained in place until the end of the Peloponnesian War in 404 BCE. After Athens's defeat, Spartan interference in the polis's domestic affairs led to the establishment of the oligarchy of the Thirty (404/3 BCE). Efforts to rid the city of the Thirty devolved into civil war. Democracy was eventually reestablished in 403 BCE.

First Collapse: 413–410 BCE. The Four Hundred and the Five Thousand

When news of the Sicilian disaster arrived at Athens in 413 BCE, the Athenians voted to appoint an advisory board of ten elders (*probouloi*) "to advise upon the state of affairs, as occasion should arise," and passed a series of emergency economic measures.[27] The duties of the board remained ill-specified, and the regular democratic organs of government—the citizen Assembly and the deliberative citizen Council—at first continued to operate as before. However, this was an unprecedented move to curtail the power of the demos. As the demos lost trust in the efficacy of the democratic system, the elite began to fear that the demos would expropriate their wealth to continue funding the Peloponnesian War against Sparta. For Thucydides, "the most powerful citizens suffered most severely from the war" because military expenditures fell largely on them.[28] After Sicily, the burden could only have kept increasing. By how much, no one knew, because in the absence of procedural checks on the Assembly, the demos could vote to extract from the elite as much as they wished. The state's

[25] Loren Samons, *Empire of the Owl: Athenian Imperial Finance* (Stuttgart: Steiner, 2000).

[26] Ten thousand Athenians may have died in Sicily (Hansen, *Three Studies in Athenian Demography*, 15–16). On Athenian finances in this period, see Alec Blamire, "Athenian Finance, 454–404 BC," *Journal of the American School of Classical Studies at Athens* 70, no. 1 (2001): 114–115; Samons, *Empire of the Owl*, ch. 6.

[27] Thucydides, 8.1.3.

[28] Thucydides, 8.48.1.

DEMOCRATIC COLLAPSE AND RECOVERY IN ATHENS   33

immediate problem was in fact raising funds to counter an expected attack from both Sparta and Syracuse, while rebuilding the navy and maintaining a fleet in the northern Aegean.

At this critical juncture, Alcibiades, a former Athenian general who had defected to Sparta in 415 BCE, boasted that he would be able to bring the Persian Empire and its vast financial resources over to the Athenian side, but only if Athens changed its government to oligarchy. This was a self-interested move, as Alcibiades hoped that the new government would reinstate him in power. Nonetheless, the proposal attracted the support of oligarchic sympathizers who began a campaign of systematic terrorism, assassinating prominent democratic politicians. The historian Thucydides reports that the terror campaign was effective in undermining trust among Athenian citizens and in leading the Athenians to overestimate the strength of the oligarchic faction.[29]

The advisory board of elders appointed after the defeat in Sicily was expanded in 411 BCE and authorized to make new constitutional proposals that would be brought before the citizen assembly. The board recommended the lifting of the *graphe paranomon* procedure, which allowed for the indictment of anyone making unconstitutional proposals in the Assembly. If we follow Thucydides (rather than Aristotle), the oligarchs successfully manipulated the discussion at the key meeting of the Assembly, which was held away from the city and whose participants overrepresented the Athenian upper classes. The Assembly granted what amounted to complete authority to a body of four hundred oligarchs. The Four Hundred were charged with creating a new, restricted body of five thousand citizens, but they kept postponing doing so. The Council was disempowered, as was the citizen Assembly itself. Democracy had, in effect, voted itself out of existence.

The Athenian citizens serving as rowers in the Aegean fleet, stationed on the island of Samos, rejected the new oligarchic government and set themselves up as a democratic government in exile, while continuing to act as a branch of the Athenian armed forces in operations against the Spartan fleet in the northern Aegean. The Four Hundred at Athens, under pressure to name the five thousand, sought a separate peace with Sparta. One of their leaders was assassinated, and the generals of the Four Hundred lost a key naval battle, which led to the revolt of the city-states on the highly strategic island of Euboea, off Athens's east coast. Soon after, the Four Hundred were deposed (later 411 BCE).

After the fall of the Four Hundred, the government was entrusted to the Five Thousand, whose membership was defined as those Athenians able to afford heavy infantry weapons and armor. Under this new oligarchy, praised by Thucydides as a mixture of high and low, Athens won a series of naval battles

---

[29] Thucydides, 8.65.2–66.5.

34 WHEN DEMOCRACY BREAKS

against the Spartans and Syracusans.[30] However, in the aftermath of those victories, the democracy was restored. The reasons for the demise of the Five Thousand are unclear. But it is possible that this compromise government lacked critical support. It also seems likely that, after the disastrous experience with the Four Hundred, the demand for democracy grew stronger once again. In a public ceremony, the Athenians swore an oath to kill anyone who sought to overthrow the democracy.[31]

Second Collapse: 404–403 BCE. The Thirty and Civil War

The democracy remained in place until Athens's defeat in the Peloponnesian War. In this period, through fiscal and legal reforms, the Athenians sought to restore internal order and assuage the tensions between masses and elites— tensions that were heightened by a dire financial and human crisis.[32]

When Athens surrendered to Sparta in the summer of 404 BCE, after twenty-seven years of war, the citizen population was very much reduced. It is likely that the number of free adult male natives was less than half of what it had been before the outbreak of the war.[33] Notably, the losses were heavily concentrated in the lower classes who had served in the navy. The surrender mandated the elimination of Athens's empire and the effective dismantling of its armed forces and city walls.[34] The democracy was also eliminated at the behest of the victorious Spartan general, Lysander, who called an assembly and surrounded the assembly place with Spartan soldiers. The upshot was the appointment of thirty Athenian aristocrats, all Spartan sympathizers.

The Thirty, led by Critias, uncle of Plato and sometime student of Socrates, had full executive authority and were charged with drafting new constitutional laws. It is difficult to decide what sort of positive plan the Thirty may have had. In any event, they never established a working constitutional government but rather ruled by executive decree and organized terror. They requested and received a Spartan garrison. To pay for the garrison, they executed and seized the property of wealthy resident foreigners and citizens. Many other Athenians were driven into exile. A split between Critias and more moderate members of the Thirty led to the judicial murder of the leaders of the moderates.

---

[30] Thucydides, 8.97.

[31] David Teegarden, *Death to Tyrants: Ancient Greek Democracy and the Struggle against Tyranny* (Princeton: Princeton University Press, 2014).

[32] Blamire, "Athenian Finance."

[33] Barry Strauss, *Athens after the Peloponnesian War: Class, Faction, and Policy, 403–386 BC* (Ithaca, NY: Cornell University Press, 1987); Hansen, *Three Studies in Athenian Demography*.

[34] Xenophon, *Hellenica*, 2.2.20.

DEMOCRATIC COLLAPSE AND RECOVERY IN ATHENS   35

In the winter of 404/3 BCE, a body of pro-democrats seized a strongpoint in the Athenian countryside and defeated the forces sent by the Thirty against them. The democrats soon moved to take control of Piraeus, Athens's port. The Thirty, meanwhile, grew increasingly violent: their recorded actions included the mass killing of the population of the Athenian town of Eleusis. The democrats eventually defeated the forces of the Thirty in a full-scale battle in which Critias was killed. The oligarchs then fell into disarray. The Thirty were replaced by a new government of "the Ten," which appealed to Sparta to put down the democrats. But the Spartans were divided in their counsels. Lysander, who might have crushed the democratic revolt had he been given a free hand, was under suspicion, and Sparta's king Pausanias preferred negotiating a peace between the warring Athenian factions.

Democracy was restored and a general amnesty passed that forbade prosecuting those Athenians who had collaborated with the oligarchic governments. Those oligarchs who were not willing to be reconciled were given control of Eleusis, which temporarily became a separate state. By September 403 the democrats were in control of the city and celebrated with a procession to the sacred Acropolis. New constitutional laws were enacted and new institutions and procedures created to check the power of the demos. Competing proposals to offer citizenship to noncitizens who had fought on the side of the democrats and to restrict the citizen body to property owners were defeated. In 401, after an armed conflict, the oligarchic state at Eleusis was forcibly reincorporated into the democratic state of Athens. The new democracy remained in place for the next eighty years.

Analysis

Why did the Athenian democracy collapse? And why did it recover? In this section, we discuss each process in turn.[35]

Democratic Breakdown

Democracy in Athens collapsed twice in the span of a few years. In each case, a military setback of unprecedented scale was a proximate cause. In the first instance, the catastrophe was the loss in 413 BCE of most of Athens's navy and a major expeditionary force after an aborted attempt to conquer Sicily. In the

---

[35] This section is based primarily on the detailed analysis offered in Carugati, *Creating a Constitution*.

36 WHEN DEMOCRACY BREAKS

second instance, democracy was overthrown after Athens surrendered in 404 BCE to Sparta at the end of the long Peloponnesian War.

Certainly, such major military defeats played a role in weakening the democracy. But Athens had survived previous military failures. The disaster would probably not have occasioned the failure of democracy, at least in the first case, had there not been an active opposition ready and able to exploit the situation. While the number of oligarchic sympathizers seems to have been fairly small, they were well organized and willing to use violence to achieve their ends.[36] In 411 BCE, the democrats were thrown on the defensive by terror attacks and proved unable to solve the collective action problem that the oligarchs purposefully exacerbated by assassinating democratic leaders. In 404 BCE, the Spartans were in a position of forcing a regime change on their defeated rival—the alternative was the extermination of the Athenian male population, an expedient urged by some of Sparta's allies. But once again, oligarchic elements at Athens were ready and willing to collaborate in the overthrow of the democratic government.

Terroristic violence helped the oligarchs accomplish their ends, both in destabilizing democracy and in consolidating oligarchy against internal opposition. But in both cases, oligarchy proved unstable and incapable of establishing secure new grounds for acquiescence to the new regime and general willingness to obey its rules. The failure of oligarchy was rooted in part in the oligarchs' abysmal performance while in power and in part in Athens's democratic culture.[37] By the late fifth century BCE, the political culture of democracy, which had long been defined in contradistinction to tyranny and oligarchy, was deeply ingrained. That culture did not immunize the Athenians against crises of confidence in their government institutions. But it made it difficult for any nondemocratic government to sustain itself in the absence of an existential external threat. The oligarchs had been successful in precipitating a legitimacy crisis, which contributed to persuading many in Athens to acquiesce to a new government. But the oligarchs were unable to produce the conditions in which oligarchy would be accepted as legitimate, such that obedience to the new regime would be general and sustained. By "legitimacy," it is worth stressing again, we mean a concept akin to Weber's descriptive legitimacy, which describes a situation where most people follow the rules most of the time. But justifying the failure of oligarchy is not tantamount to accounting for the success of democracy—particularly of the democracy that arose from the ashes of the Civil War, which differed substantially

---

[36] The overthrow of democracy, in both instances, occurred in the context of citizen assemblies. But the institutional façade hid a violent backdrop.

[37] The Four Hundred failed to secure a deal with Persia (Thucydides, 8.48) and then a peace with Sparta (Thucydides, 8.70–71). In addition, they suffered the revolt and loss of Euboea, Athens's strategic ally. [Aristotle,] *Athenaion Politeia* 33.1; Thucydides, 8.96–97. The Thirty failed to secure the support of Sparta, partly due to division within the Spartans themselves, and they were defeated in a series of military engagements with the democratic resistance (Xenophon, *Hellenica,* 2.4.28–30).

DEMOCRATIC COLLAPSE AND RECOVERY IN ATHENS   37

from the one that had collapsed in 411 BCE. We return to this point in the next subsection.

So far, we have identified military defeats and the presence of an organized opposition as proximate causes for the collapse of democracy in Athens. More specifically, we suggested that the breakdown was catalyzed by military defeats and brought to completion when the opposition to democracy was sufficiently organized and willing to use violence (i.e., ease of collective action within the group and ability to prevent collective action among the democrats, or the citizenry writ large). But clearly these reasons are insufficient. Athens experienced many dire military defeats in the course of its democratic history, but democracy did not always collapse. Equally, oligarchic sentiments and actors were quite widespread among the elite throughout the fifth and the fourth century BCE.[38] We need to dig deeper.

We argue that the collapse of democracy was due to a crisis of legitimacy, which in turn was rooted in an underlying institutional design defect. The Athenian democracy in the fifth century BCE lacked the capacity to credibly commit itself to a future course of action; that is, the Assembly was unable to convince relevant agents that it would keep promises made via legislation. This problem depended on three main factors. First, no other institution existed to check the legislative power of the Assembly.[39] Second, there were no systematic procedures to collect and archive Assembly decisions (laws and decrees).[40] Third, there was no clear rule of legal constraint, priority, or noncontradiction. As a result, decisions made by the Assembly today were valid tomorrow only insofar as the demos was willing to respect its previous pronouncements. Should a past decision appear inconvenient, it could be ignored or overridden by a simple majority vote.

To understand how this design defect affected the functioning of democracy, it is useful to go back to the very establishment of democracy in 508 BCE. Democracy was designed in response to certain demands for popular voice and to control infighting among the elite. The original structure—a popular Assembly, a participatory agenda-setting Council, and people's courts to hear appeals against the decisions of magistrates—initially worked very well. Even too well. In the span of only thirty years, Athens rose from a small, homogeneous

---

[38] Josiah Ober, *Political Dissent in Democratic Athens: Intellectual Critics of Popular Rule* (Princeton: Princeton University Press, 1998).

[39] Especially in cases of open *probouleumata* (where the Council makes no formal recommendation to the Assembly), and in cases where the *prytaneis* (the executive body of the Council, which rotated among the tribes such that each tribe would occupy the position for one-tenth of the year) are silenced by the crowd.

[40] In the fifth century, the Athenians sought to address the problem of credible commitment in certain specific domains, notably foreign policy, through entrenchment clauses. Melissa Schwartzberg, "Athenian Democracy and Legal Change," *American Political Science Review* 98, no. 2 (2004): 311–325; Melissa Schwartzberg, *Democracy and Legal Change* (Cambridge: Cambridge University Press, 2007).

38   WHEN DEMOCRACY BREAKS

community of civic equals to a large imperial power.[41] Initially, the empire provided opportunities for voice and enrichment to the upper and lower classes alike, smoothing social conflict and ushering in a period of remarkable growth. But as time went by, and as circumstances changed, this structure began to show some deficiencies. Take the famous Melian dialogue, where the Melians' arguments for fair treatment and autonomy are met with the Athenians' blunt realist logic: the assembly determined that Melos was advantageous to Athens as a subject, a liability if left independent, and that it would be treated accordingly without regard to background norms of interstate relations.[42] This logic of imperial acquisition, driven by the assumption that Athenian safety required constant expansion, also provided the justification for the decision to invade Sicily.[43]

A state of constant war put enormous pressure on the structure of democracy. In particular, the process of decision-making started to break down in the face of the scale, volume, and time-sensitivity of the decisions that had to be made. Long before Sicily, Thucydides reports how, in 427 BCE, the Athenian Assembly voted to dispatch a trireme (warship) to a victorious Athenian general, ordering him to punish a revolting ally—the city of Mytilene, on the island of Lesbos—by killing all adult males and selling women and children as slaves.[44] But the following day, the harshness of their pronouncement having come to seem excessive, the Athenians summoned a second assembly to reevaluate and eventually modify the decision. Thucydides recounts that the trireme carrying the second decision arrived in Mytilene just in the nick of time to avoid the massacre.

That the Athenians struggled with the lack of a system to constrain the scope of the demos's decisions and to bind the state's hands once a decision had been made emerges perhaps most evidently in the creation, sometimes between 427 and 415 BCE, of the *graphe paranomon*. The *graphe paranomon* enabled the revision of Assembly decisions by allowing any participant (*ho boulomenos*— lit. whoever wishes) in the course of any given assembly to indict a proposed measure as against the laws (*paranomon*) or inconvenient (*asymphoron*) in the sense of failing to foster the interests of the Athenian demos. But at least in the fifth century, the *graphe paranomon* remained a futile procedure.[45] The problem emerged clearly in the famous case of Arginusae, when the Assembly voted against existing laws to condemn their generals without trial for failing

---

[41] Of course, democracy was not solely responsible for Athens's success. In particular, democracy did not cause the empire, which was the result of a series of contingencies. But, as Ober has shown, democracy played a significant role in Athens's performance. Josiah Ober, *Democracy and Knowledge* (Princeton: Princeton University Press, 2008).

[42] Thucydides, 5.84–116.

[43] Thucydides, 6.18.2.

[44] Thucydides, 3.36–49.

[45] Adriaan Lani and Adrian Vermeule, "Precautionary Constitutionalism in Ancient Athens," *Cardozo Law Review* 34 (2013): 893.

to rescue the survivors of a naval battle. A proposed *graphe paranomon* to block that decision was withdrawn when its proposer was himself threatened with prosecution.[46]

In sum, there were cracks in the system long before Sicily. Athens's decisive defeat in Sicily was, to borrow a phrase from Timur Kuran, its "now out of never" moment.[47] Sicily was indubitably a shock like few others. But we cannot properly account for the timing of the subsequent democratic collapse if we neglect the difficulties that accompanied the fateful decision to launch the expedition in the first place—including a blunt violation, justified with an appeal to the will of the majority, of the procedural norm that votes be taken only on issues listed on a precirculated agenda.[48] By the same token, democracy collapsed after Sicily because specific conditions were met. Events like those surrounding the revolt of Mytilene must have alerted at least some Athenians to the risks inherent in unrestrained popular power. Already before Sicily, relentless war pressures had eroded human, material, and financial resources. In short, the collapse did not require all the unique circumstances attending the failure in Sicily. The collapse occurred because at this juncture the conditions for basic democracy—legitimacy, security, and welfare—were no longer in place. A question therefore emerged for the Athenian demos: Can we trust ourselves? And if we can't trust ourselves, whom should we trust? These questions created the opportunity for constitutional change—an opportunity that oligarchic sympathizers were ready and capable of exploiting.

Crisis and Recovery

Ten years after the disaster in Sicily, eight years after the democracy's collapse, a new constitutional structure emerged. It is perhaps not entirely surprising now, but certainly was not obvious at the time, that such a structure would be a democracy. By the time of the collapse of democracy in 411 BCE, Athens's democratic culture was well established. In addition, the oligarchs failed to consolidate their power by persuading others of the legitimacy of their rule. These reasons played a role in making democracy once again a viable constitutional option. But the democracy that emerged in 403 BCE was different from the one that collapsed in 411. In particular, the new democracy put a number of measures in place to fix the underlying design defect discussed in the previous section.

---

[46] Xenophon, *Hellenica*, 1.5.27–7.35.

[47] Timur Kuran, "Now out of Never: The Element of Surprise in the East European Revolutions of 1989," *World Politics* 44, no. 1 (1991): 7–48.

[48] Ober, *Political Dissent in Democratic Athens*, 104–113.

40 WHEN DEMOCRACY BREAKS

The reforms enhanced the credibility of the demos's commitments, contributing to resolve the legitimacy crisis that had brought down the fifth-century democracy. The Athenians imposed limits on the previously unrestrained decision-making power of the Assembly by introducing another legislative institution, the *nomothesia* (lit. lawmaking), and by specifying a series of procedures to be followed in the process of legislation. The *nomothesia* made it much harder to pass new laws by creating multiple veto points.[49] Moreover, a complex system of check and balances was created to coordinate the legislative process and define the relative spheres of influence of the two institutions. First, the Assembly maintained the power to pass decrees (*psephismata*), subject to the provision that decrees could not contradict existing laws (*nomoi*).[50] Second, laws were the domain of the *nomothetai* (lawmakers), but their power to pass legislation was in turn limited by the provision that the *nomothetai* could be convened only by the Assembly. Finally, both decrees of the Assembly and laws of the *nomothetai* had to conform to the body of existing laws, which were collected and republished between 410 and 399 BCE.[51]

The reforms themselves did not emerge out of nowhere. They were the product of a constitutional debate that began with the appointment of the board of elders in 413 BCE and continued throughout the crisis. The debate contributed to restoring the legitimacy of democracy by forging a consensus on basic principles of self-government. The consensus was minimalistic and, to borrow a term from

---

[49] According to Canevaro's recent reconstruction, the process involved four institutions—the Council, the Assembly, the law courts, and the *nomothetai* (lit. lawgivers)—and seven stages, including a preliminary vote in the Assembly to allow new proposals, a period for the publication of the new proposals in front of the statue of the Eponymous Heroes concomitant with readings in subsequent Assemblies, the summon of *nomothetai*, the repeal of existing laws that contradicted the new proposal, and an approval stage. Whether this final approval stage took place in the courts before judges selected by lot from the body of those who had sworn the jurors' oath, or in an Assembly labeled *nomothetai*, the many steps that preceded the final stage made it extremely hard for a proposer of new legislation to predict, ex-ante, how each different body would vote on a given proposal and act strategically to manipulate the proceedings. Mirko Canevaro, "Nomothesia in Classical Athens: What Sources Should We Believe?," *Classical Quarterly* 63, no. 1 (2013): 139–160. On *nomothetai* as judges, see Douglas MacDowell, "Lawmaking at Athens in the 4th Century BC," *Journal of Hellenic Studies* 95 (1975): 62–74; Mogens Herman Hansen, "Athenian Nomothesia," *Greek, Roman, and Byzantine Studies* 26 (1985): 363–365, 371; P. J. Rhodes, "Sessions of Nomothetai in Fourth-Century Athens," *Classical Quarterly* 53, no. 1 (2003): 124–129; Christos Kremmydas, *A Commentary on Demosthenes against Leptines* (Oxford: Oxford University Press, 2012), 16–31, 350–351. On *nomothetai* as a special session of the Assembly, see Marcel Piérart, "Qui étaient les nomothètes a l'époque de Démosthène?," in *La Codification des lois dan l'antiquité*, ed. Edmond Levy (Paris: De Boccard, 2000), 229–256.

[50] The Athenians may have been the first to establish a distinction between laws and decrees as two levels of man-made law. The locus classicus for the distinction between laws (general rules) and decrees (rules that apply to specific cases) is Aristotle, *Nicomachean Ethics*, 1137 b 13–32. The distinction was customary in fourth-century Athens: Douglas MacDowell, *The Law in Classical Athens* (Ithaca, NY: Cornell University Press, 1978), 43–46.

[51] The revision of the laws began in 410 and lasted until Athens's defeat in the Peloponnesian War in 404. It was then picked up again in 403 and ended in 399.

John Rawls, overlapping.[52] It was overlapping in the sense that the consensus united people holding different views of the good society under a common commitment to a *procedure* for making new rules, based on the core *value* of legality. It was minimalistic because, far from being predicated on a set of thick, normatively demanding principles, it expressed instead an obligation to respect the laws of the city, particularly when it came to protecting citizens' persons, property, and dignity.[53]

In sum, the restoration of democracy in Athens relied on processes aimed at reconfiguring legitimacy at the institutional level, as well as at the level of political culture. Athens did not experience other episodes of democratic breakdown until it was conquered by Macedon in 322 BCE, about eighty years after the restoration of democracy. During this period, Athens suffered many dire military defeats, including the defeat at the hands of Philip and Alexander at Chaeronea in 338 and the defeat in the Social War of 357–355. Similarly, opposition to democracy surely did not die out among the elite; in fact, the fourth century is, in many respects, the golden age of Athens's antidemocratic intellectual culture, when Plato, Aristotle, and the rhetorician Isocrates wrote deep and influential criticisms of Athens's democracy. Therefore, some of the triggers for the collapse of democracy in 411 BCE remained, but democracy did not collapse. At the same time, the reforms that addressed the design defect that, we suggested, was the ultimate cause of the collapse of democracy in the late fifth century remained in place until the final Macedonian conquest. The reforms presided over a long period of political stability and economic growth. Concomitant stability and growth, in turn, contributed to strengthening the legitimacy of the new democracy.

Conclusion

In this chapter, we explored the collapse and recovery of the world's first rich and consolidated democracy. We identified a series of proximate and ultimate causes for the collapse: military defeats, the presence of an organized opposition, and a crisis of legitimacy traceable to a fundamental defect of institutional design. We also suggested that democratic recovery depended on reengineering both institutions and culture.

In the fifth century, Athens developed a sophisticated democratic culture and institutions. The history of imperial Athens suggests that a "good enough"

---

[52] John Rawls, *A Theory of Justice* (Cambridge, MA; Belknap Press of Harvard University Press, 1999), 340; John Rawls, *Political Liberalism* (New York: Columbia University Press, 2005), 11–15, 133–172.

[53] Carugati, *Creating a Constitution.*

constitution, even one with a deep flaw, can drive growth and achieve high levels of legitimacy under good conditions, even in the face of internal opposition. But when subjected to sufficient stress (e.g., a long war), the flaw will become evident through performance failures. The resulting loss of legitimacy will open the way for opponents to overthrow democracy. If those opponents are incapable of establishing a reasonably high-performing, legitimate, alternative constitutional order, they will in turn open the way for democrats to overthrow the oligarchic order. The threat of a devolutionary cycle of constitutions in which the pattern of overthrow and replacement is indefinitely repeated on a short time horizon can be avoided by the recognition and rectification of the original constitutional flaw, in the context of a recommitment to some core values shared broadly among the population.

Our account brings the case of Ancient Athens to bear on the debate over the fate of contemporary rich and consolidated democracies and suggests that the time may have come for recommitting to shared values as well as fixing those institutions that are jeopardizing security, prosperity and nontyranny.

3

The U.S. Secession Crisis as a Breakdown of Democracy

Dean Grodzins and David Moss

This chapter examines the U.S. secession crisis of 1860–1861 as a case of democratic breakdown.[1] From December 1860 to early June 1861, eleven of the fifteen slaveholding states in the U.S. South declared secession from the Union. The trigger for the crisis was Abraham Lincoln's victory in the presidential election of November 1860. Many Southerners rejected the outcome of the election as intolerable. Together, the seceding states tried to form a new, proslavery nation, the Confederate States of America (CSA). They went to war with the United States to win their independence, only to be completely defeated within four years. The death toll from the war was approximately 750,000 (on both sides).[2] Importantly, the war also led to the emancipation of four million enslaved Americans.

The secession crisis involved both the mass rejection of a lawful electoral outcome and a large-scale turn to violence to resolve political differences. Notably, almost no one seriously disputed the procedural results of the election. Lincoln had won a plurality of the national popular vote and a majority of the Electoral College. Under the Constitution, he had won the election and was the president-elect. Indeed, until this point in U.S. history, no matter how bitterly contested a presidential election had been (and some had been very bitterly fought), the losers had always abided the outcome, believing that they could continue to defend their interests through the constitutional political process.

This time was different. Lincoln's Republican Party had pronounced slavery among the "relics of barbarism" and opposed the spread of slavery to federal territories in the American West.[3] Lincoln himself argued in his famous "House Divided" speech in 1858 that this restriction would place slavery on the path

---

[1] The authors are deeply grateful to Kimberly Hagan, research associate at Harvard Business School, for her outstanding feedback on multiple drafts and for reviewing and fact-checking the document with such care.

[2] J. David Hacker, "A Census-Based Count of the Civil War Dead," *Civil War History* 57, no. 4 (2011): 307–348.

[3] Quotation from the Republican Party Platform of 1856, https://www.presidency.ucsb.edu/documents/republican-party-platform-1856.

Dean Grodzins and David Moss, *The U.S. Secession Crisis as a Breakdown of Democracy* In: *When Democracy Breaks*. Edited by: Archon Fung, David Moss, and Odd Arne Westad, Oxford University Press. © Oxford University Press 2024. DOI: 10.1093/oso/9780197760789.003.0003

44　WHEN DEMOCRACY BREAKS

to "ultimate extinction."[4] Yet Republicans, including Lincoln, also repeatedly declared that they would not "interfere" with slavery in the states where it already existed, believing they lacked the constitutional right to do so.[5] Nonetheless, many Southern leaders insisted that the fifteen slaveholding states of the South must not "submit" to Republican "rule," but instead exercise a controversial constitutional right (one that even a significant number of Southerners denied existed) to secede from the Union.[6]

The secession crisis is not normally treated as a case of democratic breakdown. This may be because the Civil War itself (1861–1865) dramatically overshadowed the reality of democratic corrosion and collapse. Also, many modern observers understandably do not regard the antebellum South as having been any sort of democracy in the first place, given the existence of slavery and the exclusion of nearly all but white men from the franchise. In this chapter, we will suggest that although the antebellum South was not remotely a democracy by modern standards, it was widely regarded as a democratic republic at the time and can usefully be studied as a kind of quasi-democracy, in some ways analogous to Ancient Athens, which also enforced slavery and excluded the majority of adults from formal participation in political governance.

With this in mind, we will advance two core arguments regarding secession and the associated pattern of democratic breakdown: first, we will demonstrate that most Southern states suffered significant democratic erosion over the antebellum period, stemming in particular from their crackdown on any and all criticism of slavery; second, we will show that this democratic erosion, which involved far-reaching suppression of dissent, contributed directly to secession by limiting information flow and, in turn, limiting the ability of leading Southern political figures to see and understand the economic, political, and military realities that rendered secession far less likely to succeed than they seemed to believe.

Perhaps it should not be surprising that the perilous political act of secession, which was achieved through notably undemocratic means in the early seceding states and which, by design, broke the American republic in two, was itself born out of a critical erosion of democratic norms that gradually reshaped the South

---

[4] Abraham Lincoln, "A House Divided," speech, in *The Collected Works of Abraham Lincoln*, 9 vols., ed. Roy P. Basler (New Brunswick, NJ: Rutgers University Press, 1953), 2:461.

[5] Lincoln repeatedly denied that he wanted to interfere with slavery in the South, or that he believed he had the constitutional right to do so. See, for example, Lincoln, *Collected Works*, 3:16, 87, 300, 402, 404, 440; 4:263–264, 267. The Republican Party Platform of 1860 declared "inviolate" the "right of each state to order and control its own domestic institutions according to its own judgment exclusively." Republican Party Platform of 1860, Declaration 4, https://www.presidency.ucsb.edu/documents/republican-party-platform-1860.

[6] See, e.g., Eric H. Walther, *The Fire-Eaters* (Baton Rouge: Louisiana State University Press, 1992), 179; William W. Freehling and Craig M. Simpson, eds., *Secession Debated: Georgia's Showdown in 1860* (New York: Oxford University Press, 1992), 58.

THE U.S. SECESSION CRISIS   45

through the antebellum period. Yet the story of this erosion and its connection to secession has remained largely untold until now. It is to this story—and the broader story of secession and democratic breakdown—that we now turn.

Leading Explanations for Secession

Historians have written extensively on the secession crisis and the outbreak of the Civil War, and the leading explanations mostly fall into three broad categories. The first emphasizes growing economic and ideological divergence between the slaveholding South and the non-slaveholding North, which is thought to have made war between them almost inevitable. Although both North and South had commercial, market-dominated economies, and the two were interconnected, the differences between them were obvious, both to people at the time and since. The Southern economy, especially that of the Lower South, was based on the export of staple crops produced on slave plantations, while the Northern economy was based on free labor, with an agricultural sector grounded mostly in small farms, a strong merchant sector, and a growing industrial sector. The economic differences separating North and South inevitably led to sectional disputes, because leaders of each section tended to champion different federal economic policies regarding trade, banking, and internal improvements, among others, and had different visions of national expansion.[7] Historians have also recognized a growing ideological divide between the sections. They have focused on how Southern leaders after 1830 moved away from what had arguably been a shared belief among most white people across both sections that slavery was a "necessary evil," to the claim that it was a "positive good."[8] Northerners, meanwhile, generally rejected "proslavery" thought. Most Northern voters came to support the Republican Party, which emerged in 1854 and promoted "free labor" and a ban on slavery in the Western territories.[9]

---

[7] On this point, see Marc Egnal, *Clash of Extremes: The Economic Origins of the Civil War* (New York: Hill and Wang, 2009).

[8] Harold D. Tallant, *Evil Necessity: Slavery and Political Culture in Antebellum Kentucky* (Lexington: University Press of Kentucky, 2003), 4–7. A useful introduction remains Drew Gilpin Faust, ed., *The Ideology of Slavery: Proslavery Thought in the Antebellum South, 1830–1860* (Baton Rouge: Louisiana State University Press, 1981).

[9] See Eric Foner, *Free Soil, Free Labor, Free Men: The Ideology of the Republican Party before the Civil War*, 2nd ed. (1970; New York: Oxford University Press, 1995). More broadly, the Republicans advocated for the idea that freedom was national, and slavery merely a state institution. According to Republicans, slavery violated natural law, and therefore could exist only when explicitly sanctioned by "positive law." Republicans argued that the U.S. Constitution recognized slavery only in specific, defined instances, such as allowing slaves to be counted as three-fifths of a person for purposes of congressional representation and federal taxation, but that it otherwise did not sanction slavery. (The word "slavery" did not even appear in it.) The logic of the Republican position was that Congress had no authority to recognize the existence of slavery in the Western territories but did have the authority to ban it there. On the "Freedom National" idea, see James Oakes, *Freedom National: The Destruction*

46   WHEN DEMOCRACY BREAKS

Another category of historical explanation focuses on political developments in the 1850s, especially the breakdown of what historians call the Second Party System (of Whigs versus Democrats, in which each party enjoyed significant support in both North and South), the rise of the sectional Republican Party in the North, and the split of the Democratic Party between its Northern and Southern wings. Historians advancing this view tend to portray the outbreak of the Civil War as a contingent event, which could have been avoided had political leaders been more willing to compromise at critical junctures or to resist the temptation to exploit sectional differences for short-term political advantage.[10]

Finally, there are historians who focus less on the conflict between the sections and more on developments within the South itself. These scholars suggest that whether the war was inevitable or not, the cause of it must ultimately lie in the South because the South initiated the conflict. Scholars in this vein examine a wide range of tensions within the South (including political, cultural, economic, ideological, and racial), particularly those produced or intensified by slavery, to explain the growth of support for secession there, especially among leaders of the Lower South.[11]

While the historical scholarship on the coming of the Civil War is rich and varied, we believe we can contribute to it by calling attention to significant democratic erosion in the South prior to the war (specifically, the erosion of certain democratic freedoms for white Southerners) and how such erosion ultimately strengthened the drive for secession.[12]

---

of Slavery in the United States, 1861–1865 (New York: W. W. Norton, 2013), 2–4; a celebrated statement of the idea was Charles Sumner, *Freedom National; Slavery Sectional: Speech of Hon. Charles Sumner of Massachusetts* (Washington, DC: Buell & Blanchard, 1852), 6–14.

[10] Michael F. Holt, *The Political Crisis of the 1850s* (New York: Wylie, 1978); Daniel W. Crofts, *Reluctant Confederates: Upper South Unionists in the Secession Crisis* (Chapel Hill: University of North Carolina Press, 1989); Michael E. Woods, *Arguing until Doomsday: Stephen Douglas, Jefferson Davis, and the Struggle for American Democracy* (Chapel Hill: University of North Carolina Press, 2020); Michael F. Holt, *The Fate of Their Country: Politicians, Slavery Extension, and the Coming of the Civil War* (New York: Hill and Wang, 2004).

[11] William W. Freehling, *The Road to Disunion*, Vol. 1: *Secessionists at Bay, 1776–1854* (New York: Oxford University Press, 1990) and *The Road to Disunion*, Vol. 2: *Secessionists Triumphant, 1854–1861* (New York: Oxford University Press, 2007); Manisha Sinha, *The Counterrevolution of Slavery: Politics and Ideology in Antebellum South Carolina* (Chapel Hill: University of North Carolina Press, 2000); Keri Leigh Merritt, *Masterless Men: Poor Whites and Slavery in the Antebellum South* (New York: Cambridge University Press, 2017). See also William L. Barney's useful historiographical essay on the literature concerning how internal Southern tensions produced secession, in the introduction to the 2004 edition of Barney, *The Secessionist Impulse: Alabama and Mississippi in 1860* (1974; Tuscaloosa: University of Alabama Press, 2004), xv–xxiv.

[12] Some politically significant democratic erosion occurred in the North. Most notably, a small number of Northern antislavery activists, the most famous being John Brown, became advocates of violent revolution to end slavery. There were also examples of systematic anti-abolitionist violence in the North. Overall, however, we believe there was much less democratic erosion in the North than in the South. The suppression of the Republican Party and the rise of radical secessionism, for example, had far more mainstream political support in the South than antislavery violence or anti-abolitionist violence ever did in the North. For the case of a leading radical abolitionist whose support

Can the Antebellum South Be Studied as a Democracy?

We believe the antebellum South's democratic institutions merit careful study, even though the region was not nearly a democracy by modern standards. It is obviously painful to connect the word "democracy" in any way with a society that enforced chattel slavery and restricted suffrage to a privileged subset of the population. In 1860, 32% of the total population of the Southern states was enslaved. This enslaved population, entirely of African descent, comprised 94% of all people of African descent across the South and a majority of the population of two states, South Carolina and Mississippi.[13] Moreover, of the free population in the South in 1860, almost no person classified as Black, and almost no white women, could vote.[14] Yet slavery and major restrictions on suffrage in the antebellum South should not prevent scholars from studying its democratic institutions, just as the existence of slavery and restricted suffrage have not stopped scholars from studying the democratic institutions of Ancient Athens or, for that matter, the United States as a whole at the time of its founding, when slavery as well as race, sex, or property restrictions on suffrage could be found in every state.[15]

Notably, the United States—including the South—was commonly viewed as a democratic republic through the antebellum period. Some abolitionists denied that the South was a democracy, owing to slavery there, but these views were not widespread.[16] Most white Northerners did not see themselves as compromising democracy when they voted for slaveholding candidates for president, and eight

---

for antislavery violence was limited by commitment to democracy, see Dean Grodzins, "Wendell Phillips, the Rule of Law, and Antislavery Violence," in *Wendell Phillips, Social Justice, and the Power of the Past*, ed. A J Aiséirithe and Donald Yacovone (Baton Rouge: Louisiana State University Press, 2016), 89–110.

[13] Here and elsewhere, we use the term "Southern states" as Americans did in the 1850s, to refer to all fifteen slaveholding states, including the four Border South states of Delaware, Maryland, Kentucky, and Missouri, which would later side with the Union in the Civil War. For population data, see Roger L. Ransom, "Population of the Slave States, by State, Race, and Slave Status: 1860–1870," Table Eh1-7, in *Historical Statistics of the United States, Earliest Times to the Present: Millennial Edition*, ed. Susan B. Carter, Scott Sigmund Gartner, Michael R. Haines, Alan L. Olmstead, Richard Sutch, and Gavin White (New York: Cambridge University Press, 2006).

[14] Free Black men had the formal right to vote (in that there was no explicit racial exclusion) in Delaware until 1792, Kentucky until 1799, Maryland until 1801, Tennessee until 1834, and North Carolina until 1835; how often they were able to exercise this right is unclear. A small group of Black men retained the formal right to vote in Tennessee after 1834. Also, starting in 1838, white property-holding women (meaning single women, as wives' property at this time belonged to their husbands) could vote in school-related elections in Kentucky. See Alexander Keyssar, *The Right to Vote: The Contested History of Democracy in the United States*, revised ed. (2000; New York: Basic Books, 2009), 315–319, 365.

[15] Keyssar, *The Right to Vote*, 306–307. Note that in New Jersey, from 1776 to 1807, women and free Black people could vote if they met a property and residency requirement (43–44).

[16] See, e.g., Theodore Parker, *The Relation of Slavery to a Republican Form of Government: A Speech Delivered at the New England Anti-Slavery Convention* (Boston: William Kent, 1858).

of the first twelve U.S. presidents owned slaves while in office.[17] Meanwhile, the French scholar Alexis de Tocqueville—who traveled through the North and South in the early 1830s, wrote his seminal study *Democracy in America* based on his observations, and hated slavery—never seems to have questioned that he was in a democracy wherever he went, North or South.[18]

This nineteenth-century perspective on American democracy, held by so many white Americans and Europeans, frequently rested on deeply racist beliefs about the unsuitability of Black people for equal citizenship.[19] Still, there are reasons why the antebellum South was viewed as a democracy at the time and has often been treated by scholars as such—or at least as having some of the attributes of democracy—in the years since. By the 1840s, suffrage among white men was effectively universal in every Southern state except Virginia and North Carolina, which dropped their property-based suffrage restrictions in 1850 and 1854, respectively.[20] This translated into average suffrage rates of about 30% of all adults in the late antebellum South.[21] By contrast, in Britain in the 1840s, only about 7% of all adults were entitled to vote, and in Tocqueville's France (when he wrote *Democracy in America*), fewer than 2% of adults could vote.[22] Moreover, voters in the American South actively exercised their suffrage; in the presidential elections of 1852, 1856, and 1860, voter turnout in the region (among white male adults who were permitted to vote) was 59%, 69%, and 74%, respectively.[23]

---

[17] The following U.S. presidents were Southerners who owned slaves while president: George Washington (Virginia, 1789–1797); Thomas Jefferson (Virginia, 1801–1809); James Madison (Virginia, 1809–1817); James Monroe (Virginia, 1817–1825); Andrew Jackson (Tennessee, 1829–1837); John Tyler (Virginia, 1841–1845); James Polk (Tennessee, 1845–1849); Zachary Taylor (Louisiana, 1849–1850). Two other presidents, who did not own slaves while in office, had come from slaveholding families and themselves owned slaves at some point before becoming president: Martin Van Buren (New York, 1837–1841) and William Henry Harrison (Ohio, 1841). The only presidents before 1850 who had never owned slaves were John Adams (Massachusetts, 1797–1801) and his son John Quincy Adams (Massachusetts, 1825–1829). A useful compilation of information can be found at https://millercenter.org/us-presidents-and-slavery (accessed Nov. 28, 2023) and in Stephen A. Jones and Eric Freedman, *Presidents and Black America: A Documentary History* (Washington, DC: CQ Press, 2012).

[18] A standard scholarly edition in English is Alexis de Tocqueville, *Democracy in America*, ed. J. P. Mayer, trans. George Lawrence (Garden City, NY: Doubleday, 1969).

[19] Tocqueville unfortunately shared these attitudes (*Democracy in America*, 353–358).

[20] Keyssar, *Right to Vote*, 308–314. (South Carolina had a property requirement for voting, but the requirement could be waived with six months' residency in the state [314n1].)

[21] Ransom, "Population of the Slave States"; Michael R. Haines, "State Populations," Series Aa2244–6550, in Carter et al., *Historical Statistics of the United States.*

[22] Stefano Bartolini, "Franchise Expansion," in *International Encyclopedia of Elections*, ed. Richard Rose (Washington, DC: CQ Press, 2000), 119–120. It is worth noting that the rate of enfranchisement in France increased to 36% in 1848 with the adoption of universal male suffrage, but elections would not be "free and fair" until at least 1870. See Andrew McLaren Carstairs, *A Short History of Electoral Systems in Western Europe* (Boston: George Allen & Unwin, 1980), 176–177; Peter Campbell, *French Electoral Systems and Elections 1789-1957* (London: Faber and Faber Limited, 1958), 20, 64–66.

[23] Curtis Gans and Matthew Mulling, *Voter Turnout in the United States, 1788-2009* (Washington, DC: CQ Press, 2011), 168–169. These figures were calculated by totaling votes cast in fourteen of the fifteen slaveholding states and then dividing by the combined voter-eligible population for those

THE U.S. SECESSION CRISIS   49

Local, state, and national political offices in the South were filled by election, and elections to fill them took place frequently; in nine Southern states by the 1850s, even the judiciary was entirely elected.[24] Partisan electoral conflict in most Southern states was vigorous in the late antebellum period, between Democrats and Whigs, and after the Whig Party collapsed in the mid-1850s, between Democrats and the (short-lived) Know-Nothing or Constitutional Union Parties or between Democrats and "Oppositionists." Until 1860–1861, moreover, transfers of power after elections in the South typically took place peacefully.

According to one prominent list of criteria for what constitutes a democracy, proposed by Juan Linz in a landmark 1978 volume on the breakdown of democratic regimes, the political system of the antebellum South, *as experienced by white Southerners*, would largely seem to qualify. Linz's list includes "legal freedom to formulate and advocate political alternatives with the concomitant rights to free association, free speech, and other basic freedoms of person; free and nonviolent competition among leaders with periodic validation of their claim to rule; inclusion of all effective political offices in the democratic process; and provision for the participation of all members of the political community, whatever their political preferences." In turn, these criteria suggest "the freedom to create political parties and to conduct free and honest elections at regular intervals without excluding any effective political office from direct or indirect electoral accountability." Linz also observes that " 'democracy' implies at least universal male suffrage, but perhaps in the past it would extend to the regimes with property, taxation, occupational, or literacy requirements of an earlier period, which limited suffrage to certain social groups."[25]

Notably, while suggesting that sex-based exclusion from the franchise could fit within his definition of democracy, Linz does not comment on how or whether race-based exclusion from voting or citizenship would factor in. Clearly, neither of these exclusions would be remotely consistent with democracy as we understand it today. As we will show, however, even beyond the issue of legal exclusions based on race or sex, some of the core freedoms on Linz's list—including especially the rights to free speech and association and to create

---

states. (The fifteenth slaveholding state, South Carolina, did not hold popular elections for presidential electors.)

[24] Jed Handelsman Shugerman, *The People's Courts: Pursuing Judicial Independence in America* (Cambridge, MA: Harvard University Press, 2012), 276–277. The nine Southern states with fully elective judiciaries were Florida, Kentucky, Louisiana, Maryland, Mississippi, Missouri, Tennessee, Texas, and Virginia. Two more Southern states, Alabama and Arkansas, elected circuit judges. In Georgia, the judiciary was fully elective except for the state supreme court, which the legislature created in 1845 and changed to popular election in 1896 (61; https://www.gasupreme.us/court-information/history/).

[25] Juan J. Linz, "Introduction," in *The Breakdown of Democratic Regimes*, ed. Juan J. Linz and Alfred Stepan (Baltimore: Johns Hopkins University Press, 1978), 5.

50   WHEN DEMOCRACY BREAKS

political parties—existed for white males in the early antebellum South, but were significantly eroded by 1860.

Still, despite this clear and (we will suggest) highly consequential democratic erosion in the lead-up to secession, the only regions of the world in 1860 with more developed democratic institutions than the slaveholding states of the American South were arguably the non-slaveholding states of the American North and West. Although almost no women could vote in the Northern and Western states, and men not identified as white were mostly disenfranchised, these states had universal suffrage for white men, frequent elections, vigorous partisan conflict and public debate, and voter turnout that ranged from 66% in 1852 to 79% in 1860.[26]

Contrasting Southern with Northern and Western states does highlight features of several Southern state constitutions—beyond slavery itself—that made them seem less democratic, even by American standards of the time. Most notable was the peculiar constitutional system of South Carolina, the state in 1860 with the highest share of its population enslaved (57%), and a hotbed of secessionism (the first state to secede in the crisis of 1860–1861).[27] In South Carolina, although it had universal white male suffrage, property as well as population determined representation in the legislature; there were high wealth qualifications for holding office; and neither the governor nor presidential electors were chosen by popular vote.[28] The handful of other states with property-based representation and property qualifications for office were also located in the South.[29]

---

[26] In the sixteen non-slaveholding states in 1855, Black men were formally excluded from suffrage in all except Maine, New Hampshire, Vermont, Massachusetts, and Rhode Island, and were partially excluded in New York. Taxpaying women in Michigan could vote in school-related elections, starting in 1855. See Keyssar, *Right to Vote*, 69, 315–319, 365. For turnout, see Gans, *Voter Turnout*, 168–169. The turnout figures for Northern and Western (non-slaveholding) states were calculated by totaling votes cast in these states and then dividing by the states' combined voter-eligible population. The resulting turnout in these states for the presidential elections of 1852, 1856, and 1860 were 66.2%, 75.6%, and 79.1%, respectively. (California in 1856 was excluded from these calculations, because Gans lacked accurate information on turnout. Minnesota and Oregon are included only for the election of 1860, because they were not admitted as states until 1858 and 1859, respectively. There were eighteen non-slaveholding states by 1860, all in the North and West.)

[27] Ransom, "Population of the Slave States."

[28] See the South Carolina Constitution of 1790, which remained in effect, with amendments, until the Secession Convention in December 1860; see Benjamin Perley Poore, *The Federal and State Constitutions, Colonial Charters, and Other Organic Laws of the United States* (Washington, DC: Government Printing Office, 1877), 2:1628–1636. For property requirements for officeholding, see Art. I, Secs. 6, 8; Art. II, Sec. 2; for property representation, see the amendment of 1808; for indirect election of the governor, see Art. II, Sec. 1.

[29] South Carolina, North Carolina, Georgia, Florida, and Louisiana all had systems in which property (sometimes specifically in the form of slaves) helped determine representation in their legislatures. Virginia did this unofficially. Its constitutions of 1829 and 1850 did not formally count property toward legislative representation, but in practice, ownership of slaves influenced representation. The way Virginia legislative districts were drawn, voters from the eastern part of the state, which had more slaves, had more representatives in the legislature than voters from the western part of the state, which had fewer slaves. See Ralph A. Wooster, *The People in Power: Courthouse and Statehouse in the Lower South, 1850–1860* (Knoxville: University of Tennessee Press, 1969), 7–8,

THE U.S. SECESSION CRISIS   51

Yet these undemocratic features, which limited popular influence even among white males, did not characterize the political systems of most Southern states. Mississippi, for example, had none of them, despite being the only other majority-slave state in 1860, and the second state to declare secession; and all Southern states except South Carolina held popular elections for governor and presidential electors.[30] Many white Southerners, moreover, made clear that they did not regard the political system of South Carolina as a model. In 1861, during a referendum on secession in Texas, a group of Texas Unionists urged voters not to follow South Carolina in declaring secession, attacking the state as unworthy of emulation in part because its government was "less popular in its form than the government of any other State in the Union, that it is in fact the only State in the Union in which the politicians can act in conformity with law, without consulting the people."[31] Such criticism of South Carolina, from within the South, speaks to the degree of commitment to popular government in the region, even as it was grounded upon both a distressingly narrow definition of the electorate and—most tragically—the mass enslavement of human beings.

Slavery, Sedition, and the Erosion of Democratic Institutions in the Antebellum South

As we will show, the breakdown of democratic norms across much of the South, evidenced most strikingly by the rejection of Lincoln's election in 1860, was in part the product of years of democratic erosion, itself the consequence of an increasingly ardent and absolutist defense of slavery. Over the years, opposition to slavery had become tantamount to sedition in many slaveholding states, and in time, even an antislavery tract asserting that slavery undercut economic performance was widely seen as seditious and effectively banned in many locations.

Until around 1830, while slavery was a central feature of the Southern economic, social, and legal systems, and the number of slaveholding states steadily increased, criticism of slavery in the South was not uncommon. Thomas Jefferson embodied the contradictions of many Southern leaders in

10–15, 17–18; David Brown, *Southern Outcast: Hinton Rowan Helper and the Impending Crisis of the South* (Baton Rouge: Louisiana State University Press, 2006), 83–85, 83–84n29 (on North Carolina); Freehling, *Road to Disunion*, 1:511–515 (on Virginia).

[30] See the Mississippi Constitution of 1832, in Poore, *Federal and State Constitutions*, 2:1067–1078. See also "Presidential Elections: Methods of Choosing Electors" and "Gubernatorial Elections: Methods of Election" in *Guide to U.S. Elections* (Thousand Oaks, CA: CQ Press/Sage, 2010), 820–822, 1560.

[31] Martin D. Hart [and twenty-three other signers], "Address to the People of Texas!" [Texas. Convention. First Session, 1861], Broadside Collection, OD 1300, WF 173, Dolph Briscoe Center for American History, University of Texas, Austin.

52 WHEN DEMOCRACY BREAKS

this era regarding slavery. He wrote the Declaration of Independence, which asserted that "all men are created equal."[32] Yet he owned more than six hundred enslaved persons during his lifetime, while freeing only a small number of them (several now believed to have been his children with an enslaved woman, Sally Hemings, who was in the eyes of the law his property).[33] In his book *Notes on the State of Virginia* (1787), he claimed that slavery could not be abolished soon, not only because he thought it was economically necessary for the South, but because he thought Black people were likely "inferior to the whites in the endowments both of body and mind." He further insisted that, if slavery ended, there would be "provocations" and "convulsions" ending in the "extermination of the one or the other race."[34] Still, in the very same text, Jefferson also strongly criticized slavery, writing that the "whole commerce between master and slave is a perpetual exercise of the most boisterous passions, the most unremitting despotism on the one part, and degrading submissions on the other." He professed that slavery in America made him "tremble for my country when I reflect that God is just."[35]

Notably, Jefferson predicted that slavery would someday disappear and expressed support for policies that he saw as indirectly promoting that goal. In 1784, he drafted a proposal (not enacted) that would have banned slavery from all western territories after 1800. As president, he enthusiastically endorsed the 1807 law, which took effect in 1808, banning importation of slaves into the United States and forbidding Americans from participating in the international slave trade.[36] He also tentatively suggested gradual emancipation in his home state of Virginia (by freeing slaves born after a certain date), so long as all freed Black people could be "colonized" (deported) out of the state.[37]

Despite Jefferson's provisional suggestion of gradual emancipation for Virginia, the legislature never considered the issue before his death, in 1826.[38] Then, in 1831, the enslaved preacher Nat Turner led a slave uprising in Southampton, Virginia. The sixty to eighty rebels killed sixty white Virginians

[32] For the official National Archives transcription of the Declaration, see https://www.archives.gov/founding-docs/declaration-transcript.

[33] Lucia Stanton, *"Those Who Labor for My Happiness": Slavery at Thomas Jefferson's Monticello* (Charlottesville: University of Virginia Press, 2012), esp. 106, 179–180, 248–249; see also Annette Gordon-Reed, *Thomas Jefferson and Sally Hemings: An American Controversy* (Charlottesville: University of Virginia Press, 1997) (with author's 1999 preface), and https://www.monticello.org/site/research-and-collections/slaves-who-gained-freedom.

[34] Thomas Jefferson, *Notes on the State of Virginia* (London: John Stockdale, 1787), 229–240 (quotations 229, 239).

[35] Jefferson, *Notes on the State of Virginia*, 270, 272.

[36] Freehling, *Road to Disunion*, 1:136, 138.

[37] Freehling, *Road to Disunion*, 1:126–127, 130–131. See also Jefferson, *Notes on the State of Virginia*, 228–229.

[38] Eva Sheppard Wolf, *Race and Liberty in the New Nation* (Baton Rouge: Louisiana State University Press, 2006), 102–104.

before militiamen stopped them.[39] In the aftermath, as white authorities and vigilantes executed hundreds of Black people, many white Virginians began calling for an end to slavery out of fear of a future uprising. The legislature responded in 1831–1832 with its first public debate on emancipation. Various plans were proposed, including one by Jefferson's grandson, Thomas Jefferson Randolph. The latter would have freed enslaved people born after 1840—women when they turned eighteen (therefore, starting in 1858), and men when they turned twenty-one (in 1861). In the end, however, the legislature rejected emancipation as "inexpedient." Even assuming, as Randolph did, that many enslaved people would be sold out of state before they could be freed, emancipation would have greatly increased the free Black population in Virginia. Many white Virginians, like Jefferson, were unwilling to consider emancipation without a plan for the mass deportation of free Black people from the state; and though many supported the concept of mass deportation, no workable plan was ever developed.[40]

Before the Virginia debate, no Southern state legislature had debated an emancipation plan; afterward, none came as close to enacting one. A shift in Southern white opinion, from seeing slavery as a "necessary evil" to viewing it as a "positive good," became especially widespread in the 1830s, partly in response to the emergence of the abolitionist movement.[41]

Abolitionism drew on the tradition of antislavery agitation that had produced gradual emancipation in the North, the push to end the importation of enslaved people to the United States, and the effort to prevent the admission of Missouri as a slave state in 1820. Abolitionism was launched by a coalition of Black Northerners and an initially small number of white ones, many of the latter being Quakers, a religious denomination with a history of opposition to slavery.[42] Abolitionists denounced slaveholding as a crime and a sin, which had to be "immediately" renounced. They also rejected the idea that free Black people had to leave the country, arguing that they were entitled to full citizenship. After several years of movement-building, abolitionists established the American Anti-Slavery Society (AASS) in 1833. Headquartered in New York City, it had over 100,000 members in the free states by 1838.[43]

[39] On the Turner Rebellion, see Kenneth S. Greenberg, ed., *Nat Turner: A Slave Rebellion in History and Memory* (New York: Oxford University Press, 2003).

[40] See Erik S. Root, ed., *Sons of the Fathers: The Virginia Slavery Debates of 1831–1832* (Lanham, MD: Lexington Books, 2010); Wolf, *Race and Liberty*, 196–234; Freehling, *Road to Disunion*, 1:178–196.

[41] Tallant, *Evil Necessity*, 4–7.

[42] For a history of the movement, see Manisha Sinha, *The Slave's Cause: A History of Abolition* (New Haven: Yale University Press, 2016).

[43] Sinha, *The Slave's Cause*, 243, 252. In the 1850s, abolitionists suffered what they saw as major setbacks, including congressional enactment of the Fugitive Slave Law of 1850 and the Kansas-Nebraska Act (1854), as well as the *Dred Scott* decision of the U.S. Supreme Court (1857). In light of these setbacks, some Black abolitionists began to advocate for Black emigration to Canada, Liberia,

54   WHEN DEMOCRACY BREAKS

Despite this growth, abolitionists remained a relatively small, unpopular minority. Most white Northerners did not want slavery in their own states, but they also typically rejected abolitionists as dangerous radicals.[44] In the mid-1830s, the movement faced a violent backlash in the North. In the South, rejection of abolitionism went further. Southern states outlawed antislavery speech as "incendiary" or "seditious," claiming that it could incite enslaved people to revolt.

The earliest laws banning antislavery speech were in fact passed in the wake of a major uprising by enslaved people in the French Caribbean colony of Saint-Domingue, not far from American shores. A slave revolution began there in 1791 and culminated in 1804, when a former slave, Jean-Jacques Dessalines, proclaimed it the independent nation of Haiti.[45] Evidently in response to the Haitian declaration of independence, Georgia in 1804 outlawed speech "tending to incite" slave unrest, the guilty to be banished from the state. South Carolina, where many white refugees from the Haitian Revolution had fled, passed a law in 1805 outlawing "inflammatory discourse, tending to alienate the affection and seduce the fidelity of any slave or slaves"; those convicted were to receive a punishment, unspecified but short of the death penalty, to be determined by the trial court.[46]

In 1820, the governor of South Carolina asked the legislature to pass a second law, warning that the "expression of opinions and doctrines" sparked by the Missouri debate could both "threaten our security" and "diminish" the "value" of human property.[47] The legislature responded by outlawing the circulation of written or printed speech intended "to disturb the peace and security" of the state "in relation to the slaves of the people of this state." White people convicted of this crime faced a fine and imprisonment, while free Black people faced a fine

---

Haiti, or elsewhere. Most took pains to distinguish their support for emigration from proposals to "colonize" free Black people abroad. Martin Delany is probably the most notable Black abolitionist who became an advocate of emigration. See Robert S. Levine, ed., *Martin R. Delany: A Documentary Reader* (Chapel Hill: University of North Carolina Press, 2003).

[44] Many white Northerners sought to exclude Black people generally from their states, along with the institution of slavery. Several Northern states, including Ohio, enacted laws that strongly discouraged Black immigration (by requiring Black immigrants to post expensive bonds or face deportation out of the state, for example). On these so-called Black Laws and the opposition to them, focusing especially on the Ohio case, see Kate Masur, *Until Justice Be Done: America's First Civil Rights Movement, from the Revolution to Reconstruction* (New York: W. W. Norton, 2021), 1–41.

[45] For a useful introduction to this subject, see Jeremy D. Popkin, *A Concise History of the Haitian Revolution* (West Sussex: Wiley-Blackwell, 2012).

[46] Sinha, *The Slave's Cause*, 61, refers to white refugees from the Haitian Revolution in Charleston, South Carolina. "Charity," *Charleston (S.C.) Courier*, Feb. 22, 1805, 2, is a plea to the public to give money to aid impoverished white refugees from Haiti.

[47] "South Carolina," *National Gazette and Literary Register* (Philadelphia), Dec. 7, 1820, 2; Marina Wikramanayake, *A World in Shadow: The Free Black in Antebellum South Carolina* (Columbia: University of South Carolina Press, 1973), 163–164.

THE U.S. SECESSION CRISIS 55

for the first offense, and for the second, whipping and banishment from the state. (See appendix.)

A series of new incendiary speech laws were enacted starting in 1829, largely in reaction to a pamphlet by the Black abolitionist David Walker and mounting fears of slave rebellions. Walker, born free in lowland North Carolina, probably around 1796, had moved to Boston by 1825, where he opened a used-clothing shop and became a prominent figure in the Black community.[48] In 1829 and 1830, he self-published three editions of his pamphlet, *Appeal... to the Coloured Citizens of the World... but in particular... Those of the United States of America*. As the title indicates, he intended to address a primarily Black audience. He declared that freedom was their "natural right" and decried slavery as a "*curse to nations*" and "*hell upon earth.*" He rejected Jefferson's claim that Black people were "an *inferior* and *distinct race*" and urged his "*beloved Brethren and Fellow Citizens*" to "acquire learning" and oppose colonization. He denounced slaveholders who professed to be Christian or republican as hypocrites, prophesied that God would inevitably bring judgment upon them in the form of a slave revolution, and argued that the enslaved were justified in killing their enslavers.[49]

Walker mailed copies of his *Appeal* to the South and gave others to sailors, some of them Black, to distribute in Southern ports. Almost immediately, the pamphlets were discovered there and seized by authorities.[50] The *Appeal* so alarmed the governments of four states—Georgia, North Carolina, Mississippi, and Louisiana—that they enacted incendiary speech laws in 1829–1831.[51] Virginia almost enacted an incendiary speech law in response to Walker, and finally did so in 1832, after the Nat Turner Rebellion (and after voting down gradual emancipation). That same year, Alabama enacted an incendiary speech law, while the Territory of Florida, which already had a law on its books against incitement of slave unrest, enacted a new one.[52] (See appendix.)

---

[48] Peter Hinks, *To Awaken My Afflicted Brethren: David Walker and the Problem of Antebellum Slave Resistance* (University Park: Pennsylvania State University Press, 1997).

[49] David Walker, *Walker's Appeal, in Four Articles, Together with a Preamble, to the Coloured Citizens of the World, but in Particular, and Very Expressly, to Those of the United States of America*, revised ed. with an introduction by Sean Wilentz (New York: Hill and Wang, 1995), 3, 11, 19, 22, 31, 71. The title page of the first printing contains the date September 28, 1829; the title page of the third is marked "Third and Last Edition, with additional notes, corrections, &c."

[50] Hinks, *To Awaken My Afflicted Brethren*, 118–126, 134–138, 145–146, 149, 152; Amy Reynolds, "The Impact of Walker's *Appeal* on Northern and Southern Conceptions of Free Speech in the Nineteenth Century," *Communication Law and Policy* 9, no. 1 (2004): 83–84.

[51] Reynolds, "Impact of Walker's *Appeal*," 84, 86–87; Clement Eaton, *The Freedom-of-Thought Struggle in the Old South*, revised and enlarged ed., New York: Harper & Row, 1964), 121–125. Originally published as *Freedom of Thought in the Old South*, 1940.

[52] Reynolds, "Impact of Walker's *Appeal*," 94; Eaton, *Freedom-of-Thought Struggle*, 123; http://www.natturnerproject.org/laws-passed-march-15-1832, chapter 22, section 7.

56   WHEN DEMOCRACY BREAKS

The laws were harsh. The North Carolina statute, for example, made it a felony to publish or circulate any "written or printed pamphlet or paper . . . the evident tendency whereof would be to excite insurrection, conspiracy or resistance in the slaves or free negroes and persons of colour within the State, or which shall advise or persuade slaves or free persons of colour to insurrection, conspiracy or resistance." Anyone found guilty "shall for the first offence be imprisoned not less than one year and be put in the pillory and whipped, at the discretion of the court; and for the second offence shall suffer death without benefit of clergy." Moreover, anyone who "by words" tried to excite in slaves "a spirit of insurrection, conspiracy or rebellion" would also be guilty of a felony, and if convicted should "receive thirty-nine lashes upon his or her bare back and be imprisoned for a year; and for the second offence shall suffer death without benefit of clergy."[53] The Georgia and Alabama laws, and the new Florida law, were even more severe, holding that first offenders should be put to death.

The laws enacted after 1829 were more expansive than the Georgia and South Carolina laws of 1804–1805, which had focused on incitement of enslaved people; all the new laws (except that of Florida) also banned incitement of free Black people, who lived in every slaveholding state. These laws were usually enacted at the same time as other laws, or as part of longer statutes, restricting the activity of free Black people and tightening existing restrictions on enslaved people. Georgia and North Carolina enacted laws, for example, requiring that out-of-state Black sailors arriving in a local port be jailed if they disembarked.[54] Both states also enacted laws forbidding anyone from teaching slaves to read. In North Carolina, the penalty for white people who did so was a stiff fine or prison; for free Black people, a fine, imprisonment, or whipping; and for enslaved Black people, "thirty-nine lashes on his or her bare back."[55] Within a few years, every slaveholding state except Arkansas, Kentucky, Maryland, and Tennessee had enacted prohibitions against slave literacy.[56]

Besides trying to limit the impact of Walker's pamphlet, Southern officials also tried to silence its author. In 1829, both the governor of Georgia and the mayor of Savannah, where copies of the *Appeal* had been found, wrote to Mayor Harrison Gray Otis of Boston, demanding that Walker be jailed. Otis wrote back that although "all sensible people regretted what . . . [Walker] wrote and what he was doing," Walker had violated no federal or Massachusetts law and so could not

---

[53] *Acts Passed by the General Assembly of the State of North Carolina, at the Session of 1830–31* (Raleigh: Lawrence & Lemay, 1831), chapter 5 (pp. 10–11).

[54] Reynolds, "Impact of Walker's *Appeal*," 84, 86. South Carolina had already enacted a "Negro Seaman's Act" in response to the alleged plot, uncovered in 1822, for a slave revolt in Charleston led by the literate free Black carpenter Denmark Vesey; see Sinha, *The Slave's Cause*, 196–197.

[55] Eaton, *Freedom-of-Thought Struggle*, 122; *Acts Passed by the General Assembly of the State of North Carolina*, chapter 6.

[56] Reynolds, "Impact of Walker's *Appeal*," 91–92.

THE U.S. SECESSION CRISIS   57

be arrested. Instead, Otis warned ship captains in Boston to search their vessels and crew for seditious publications and to confiscate them before sailing south.[57] Southern leaders considered responses like that of Otis wholly inadequate. As Governor John Floyd of Virginia wrote in his diary in 1831, "[A] man in our States may plot treason in one state against another without fear of punishment, whilst the suffering state has no right to resist by provisions of the Federal Constitution. If this is not checked it must lead to a separation of these states. If the forms of law will not punish, the law of nature will not permit men to have their families butchered before their eyes by their slaves and not seek by force to punish those who plan and encourage them to perpetrate these deeds."[58]

What Floyd apparently meant by "the law of nature" stopping incendiaries was that people would take matters into their own hands and potentially kill them. Reportedly, white Georgians placed a $1,000 bounty on Walker's head.[59] He did die in 1830, but of natural causes.[60]

Southern restrictions against abolitionism were tightened in 1835 and 1836, in response to an ambitious AASS "postal campaign." Abolitionists aimed to convert white Southerners to their cause with a mass mailing of antislavery literature. At the height of the campaign, in the summer of 1835, perhaps as many as 175,000 abolitionist publications—including pamphlets, tracts, and newspapers—were mailed from the free to the slaveholding states in a single month.[61] Although many in the AASS expressed respect for the recently deceased Walker, the Society's mostly white leadership renounced violence and insisted that abolitionists achieve their ends only through "moral suasion." Unlike Walker, moreover, the AASS aimed to distribute its publications in the South only to white readers, and these publications were sent to some twenty thousand Southern white political, religious, and community leaders.[62]

Southern lawmakers denounced the postal campaign as an attempt "to interfere with the relations existing between master and slave . . . and to excite in our coloured population a spirit of insubordination, rebellion and insurrection."[63]

---

[57] Reynolds, "Impact of Walker's *Appeal*," 85.
[58] Reynolds, "Impact of Walker's *Appeal*," 93. Floyd was here writing not about Walker specifically, but about the abolitionist newspaper *The Liberator*, which reprinted sections of Walker's *Appeal*.
[59] Reynolds, "Impact of Walker's *Appeal*," 86.
[60] Reynolds, "Impact of Walker's *Appeal*," 88; Hinks, *To Awaken My Afflicted Brethren*, 269–270.
[61] Richard John, *Spreading the News: The American Postal System from Franklin to Morse* (Cambridge, MA: Harvard University Press, 1995), 261; but see also Susan Wyly-Jones, "The 1835 Anti-Abolition Meetings in the South: A New Look at the Controversy over the Abolition Postal Campaign," *Civil War History* 47, no. 4 (2001), 299–300, who indicates this figure may be an exaggeration.
[62] John, *Spreading the News*, 262. John explains that abolitionists compiled the list of names and addresses "from city directories, the proceedings of religious bodies, and other compendia of prominent men of affairs."
[63] From the preamble to "An Act to suppress the circulation of incendiary publications. . .," Mar. 23, 1836, in *Acts of the General Assembly of Virginia, Passed at the Session of 1835–36* (Richmond: Thomas Ritchie, 1836), 44–45.

58 WHEN DEMOCRACY BREAKS

In July 1835, a vigilante group in Charleston, South Carolina, calling themselves the "Lynch Men," with a former governor possibly among them, seized abolitionist publications from the city post office and burned them in a bonfire that was watched by an "enthusiastic crowd of 2,000."[64] Over the coming months, postmasters across the South purged abolitionist mail, either sending it back North or destroying it. By December, at least 150 public meetings had been held in the slaveholding states to condemn abolitionism. Many of these meetings appointed "vigilance committees" (groups of citizens tasked to maintain law and order in an emergency), which arrested, tried, and punished white travelers from the North and free Black people suspected of disseminating abolitionist ideas.[65]

A vigilance committee in Nashville, Tennessee, arrested Amos Dresser, a white traveling Bible salesman from Ohio with antislavery views, convicted him of being an abolitionist agent (which he denied), and after debating hanging him, had him publicly whipped and expelled from the state.[66] Weeks later, writing in a Nashville newspaper, one of the vigilance committee members urged "nonslaveholding brethren" from Ohio and other states to "energetically assist" in restraining "emissaries" like Dresser. He defended the makeshift trial as necessary because, after all, no law yet existed for which Dresser could be properly tried. The absence of any Tennessee law, he wrote, was a "defect" to be "remedied," and "remedied" it was: Tennessee passed its first seditious speech act in 1836.[67] (See appendix.)

Virginia, meanwhile, enacted a new, stronger incendiary speech law that same year. The law empowered "any free white person" to arrest any member of an antislavery organization "who shall come into this state, and . . . advocate or advise the abolition of slavery." Those found guilty would be fined $50 to $200 and imprisoned from six months to three years. If an enslaved person was found guilty of circulating incendiary publications, he or she was to be "punished by stripes, not exceeding thirty-nine," and "transported and sold beyond the limits of the United States"; if a white person, he or she was to be imprisoned for two to five years. The law also mandated censorship of the U.S. mail. It required that if a

---

[64] John, *Spreading the News*, 257–259 (quotation 258); Wyly-Jones, "1835 Anti-Abolition Meetings," 289–290.

[65] On the concept of a vigilance committee, see Dean Grodzins, "'Constitution or No Constitution, Law or No Law': The Boston Vigilance Committees, 1841–1861," in *Massachusetts and the Civil War: The Commonwealth and National Disunion*, ed. Matthew Mason, Katheryn P. Viens, and Conrad Edick Wright (Amherst: University of Massachusetts Press, 2015), 47–48.

[66] Wyly-Jones, "1835 Anti-Abolition Meetings," 291–292, 303; see also Amos Dresser, *The Narrative of Amos Dresser* (New York: American Anti-Slavery Society, 1836).

[67] W. H. Hunt, "Amos Dresser—The Cincinnati Gazette," *National Banner and Nashville Whig*, Aug. 24, 1835, 3. The identity of the vigilance committee member and newspaper writer is disclosed in an earlier editorial he authored, and again in a response editorial by an Ohio paper: W. H. Hunt, "ABOLITIONISTS BEWARE!," *National Banner and Nashville Whig*, Aug. 10, 1835, 3; C. Hammond, "'Amos Dresser's' Case," *Cincinnati Daily Gazette*, Aug. 20, 1835, 2.

THE U.S. SECESSION CRISIS 59

postmaster found incendiary publications in the mail, he must notify a local justice of the peace, who was ordered to have the material "burned in his presence."[68]

Most white Northerners apparently did not object to slaveholding states censoring abolitionist mail. In fact, allowing them to do so soon became de facto federal policy.[69] Nor did many object to Southern states suppressing abolitionism in the South. Most white Northerners themselves likely rejected abolitionism. In 1835 and 1836, anti-abolitionist public meetings took place throughout the North (including one in Boston, led by Mayor Otis). The meetings heard speeches and passed resolutions condemning abolitionists for imperiling the safety of white Southerners and the Union.[70] White mobs, reportedly led by "gentlemen of property and standing," attacked abolitionist meetings, lecturers, editors, and presses in dozens of Northern communities, among them New York, Philadelphia, and Boston, often also rampaging through Black neighborhoods. Few if any people were ever arrested for participating in these mobs, and the Northern press tended to blame the abolitionists for provoking the trouble.[71]

Yet there was one Southern demand that Northerners consistently declined to meet: namely, to outlaw abolitionist organizations and speech in the North. The legislature of South Carolina passed resolutions calling on Northern legislatures to "suppress all those associations within their respective limits, purporting to be Abolition Societies" and "make it highly penal" to print, publish, or circulate material that would have "an obvious tendency to excite the slaves of the Southern States to insurrection and revolt."[72] The legislatures of North Carolina, Virginia, Georgia, and Alabama passed similar resolutions, as did Southern anti-abolitionist meetings.[73] A meeting in Charleston, South Carolina, for example, resolved that Northern states should "adopt the necessary measures to punish any vile incendiaries within their limits, who, not daring to appear in person among us, where the gallows and the stake await them, discharge their missiles of mischief in the security of distance."[74] A meeting in Camden County,

---

[68] "An Act to suppress the circulation of incendiary publications."

[69] Michael Kent Curtis, Free Speech, "The People's Darling Privilege": Struggles for Freedom of Expression in American History (Durham, NC: Duke University Press, 2000), 174–175.

[70] For accounts of the Boston meeting, with examples of the resolutions and speeches there, see "Public Meeting in Boston," "Faneuil Hall Resolutions," Boston Recorder, Aug. 28, 1835, 139, 140; "Speech of Harrison Gray Otis. In Faneuil Hall, Boston—August 22," Niles' Weekly Register, Sept. 5, 1835, 10.

[71] Sinha, The Slave's Cause, 231–234; Curtis, Free Speech, 131–151.

[72] "Committee on Federal Relations. In Senate, Dec. 16, 1835," in Acts and Resolutions of the General Assembly of the State of South Carolina, Passed in December, 1835 (Columbia: S. Weir, 1836), [118].

[73] Acts Passed by the General Assembly of the State of North Carolina, at the Session of 1835 (Raleigh: Philo White, 1835), 120–121; Acts of the General Assembly of Virginia, 395–396; Russel B. Nye, Fettered Freedom: Civil Liberties and the Slavery Controversy, 1830–1860, revised ed. (1949; East Lansing: Michigan State University Press, 1963), 139.

[74] Curtis, Free Speech, 151; for the date, see 462nn83–84.

60   WHEN DEMOCRACY BREAKS

North Carolina, declared that Northern states were "duty bound" to ban "incendiary and seditious associations whose avowed object is to disturb our peace" and declared that all of the Northern anti-abolitionist meetings and mobs meant little unless reinforced by "legal enactments."[75] As a meeting in Virginia affirmed, "nothing less than absolute legal restrictions can retard or avert the awful consequences of a wild fanaticism."[76] In 1835, Maryland enacted a law that may have been intended as a model for Northern states to follow regarding abolitionist speech: those found guilty of sending publications to other states or territories that might create "discontent" or "insurrection" among Black people there would be sentenced to ten to twenty years in prison. (See appendix.)

In 1835 and 1836, officials in some Northern states considered responding to these Southern calls for action. Yet they struggled to determine how to outlaw abolitionism without undermining freedom of speech and the press in the North. Governor William Marcy of New York, for example, sent a message to his state legislature suggesting that Northern states might consider enacting "laws for the trial and punishment . . . of residents within their limits, guilty of acts therein, which are calculated and intended to excite insurrection and rebellion in a sister State."[77] The New York legislature assigned Marcy's suggestion to a committee, which produced a report condemning abolitionists but declining to recommend any laws to silence them. As the committee observed, "[I]t is a most delicate and difficult task of discrimination for legislators to determine at what point . . . rational and constitutional liberty [of the press] terminates, and venality and licentiousness begin. It is indeed more safe to tolerate the licentiousness of the press than to abridge its freedom; for a corrective of the evil will be generally found in the force of truth."[78] A committee of the Ohio legislature, also tasked with considering anti-abolitionist laws, rejected them even more emphatically. The states, it declared, "have no power to restrain the publication of private opinion on any subject whatever, and the principle, if admitted, involves much greater evils to the peace of the states, than the toleration of errors and the excitements they cause can ever produce."[79]

In the end, no Northern state outlawed abolitionism. Senator John C. Calhoun of South Carolina noted with disappointment in 1836, the "just hopes" of the South "have not been realized. The Legislatures of the South . . . have called upon the non-slaveholding States to repress the movements made within the jurisdiction of those States against their peace and security. Not a step has been taken; not a law has been passed."[80] The legislature of Kentucky approved a

---

[75] Wyly-Jones, "1835 Anti-Abolition Meetings," 304.
[76] Wyly-Jones, "1835 Anti-Abolition Meetings," 304–305.
[77] Curtis, *Free Speech*, 184–185.
[78] Curtis, *Free Speech*, 188.
[79] Curtis, *Free Speech*, 190.
[80] Curtis, *Free Speech*, 186–187.

THE U.S. SECESSION CRISIS   61

report complaining that "under the miserably perverted name of free discussion, these incendiaries will be permitted to scatter their fire-brands throughout the country, with no check but that which may be imposed by the feeble operation of public opinion."[81]

Attacks on abolitionists, meanwhile, whether by mobs in the North or both mobs and laws in the South, seem only to have won the abolitionists greater support among white Northerners, many of whom began to see slavery as a threat to their own freedoms. Although proslavery writings continued to circulate freely in the North, after 1837 the number of Northern anti-abolitionist mobs declined sharply.[82] In the South, by contrast, more states outlawed antislavery speech as incendiary, starting with Missouri in 1837, which prohibited "the publication, circulation or promulgation of the abolition doctrines." Specifically, the Missouri law banned anyone from offering "facts, arguments, reasoning, or opinions, tending directly to excite any slave or slaves, or other persons of color . . . to rebellion, sedition, mutiny, insurrection or murder." Those found guilty would be subjected to a fine and imprisonment.[83] By 1861, every slaveholding state except Delaware had enacted laws banning antislavery speech.[84] (See appendix.)

The Suppression of Hinton Helper's *Impending Crisis*

The incendiary speech laws exerted a chilling effect on public criticism of slavery in the South. In December 1831, a member of the North Carolina legislature proposed a resolution directing the state attorney general to prosecute a newspaper editor in Greensboro for having recently published "seditious and libellous" statements—meaning, a letter that had condemned slavery as a "moral and political evil."[85] The legislature rejected the resolution, but two weeks later

---

[81] *Acts Passed at the First Session of the Forty-Fourth General Assembly of the Commonwealth of Kentucky* (Frankfort: J. H. Holeman, 1836), 685.

[82] Curtis attributes this shift in part to the Northern public reaction against the murder of the abolitionist newspaper editor Elijah Lovejoy; in November 1837, Lovejoy was killed trying to defend his press from being destroyed by a mob in Alton, Illinois. See Curtis, *Free Speech*, 216–270.

[83] *Laws of the State of Missouri passed at the First Session of the Ninth General Assembly . . . [1836–1837]* (Jefferson: Calvin Gunn, 1837), 3.

[84] In addition, proslavery forces enacted an incendiary speech law in Kansas Territory in 1855, which banned (1) speech "calculated to produce a disorderly, dangerous or rebellious disaffection among the slaves in this territory, or to induce such slaves to escape from the service of their masters, or to resist their authority" and (2) speech by free people denying "the right of persons to hold slaves in this territory." Punishment for any person printing, writing, publishing, or circulating was for (1) imprisonment at hard labor for at least five years and for (2) imprisonment at hard labor for at least two years. See *The Statutes of the Territory of Kansas* (Shawnee M.L. School: John T. Brady, 1855), 717.

[85] *Journals of the Senate & House of Commons of the General Assembly of the State of North Carolina, at the Session of 1830–31* (Raleigh: Lawrence & Lemay, 1831), 240 (Dec. 25, 1830). The resolution condemned an antislavery letter to the editor of the *Greensborough Patriot* of Dec. 15,

62   WHEN DEMOCRACY BREAKS

it approved a seditious speech law.[86] As one North Carolina newspaper correspondent remarked, these events "put the whole Editorial corps on the *qui vive*
[alert] throughout the State."[87]

In time, as sedition laws spread across the South, even debate over the economic effects of slavery grew more constrained. Since at least the 1820s,
Southerners could be found who criticized the economic impact of slavery. Some
had argued, including in the 1832 debates in Virginia, that slavery had "with-
ering and blasting effects" on Southern economic development. By the 1840s,
writers in both South and North were commenting on how the population of
the North was growing faster than that of the South, as economic activity in
the North attracted more immigration from abroad. The 1850 census even revealed net outward migration from the slaveholding states of the Upper South
to the free states of the Midwest. By this point, several writers had published
statistical comparisons between the free states and slave states in an attempt to
show that slavery stymied economic advance.[88] This argument could potentially
have had appeal in the South, most notably to the almost three-quarters of white
Southerners who were neither slaveholders nor from a slaveholding family,
and perhaps especially to the third of them, according to one recent estimate,

---

1830, and previous issues; see "Communications . . . for the Greensborough Patriot," *Greensborough
Patriot*, Dec. 15, 1830, 1.

[86] *Journals of the Senate & House of Commons*, 281 (Jan. 7, 1831).
[87] The "Raleigh correspondent of the Fayetteville Observer," quoted in *The Globe* (Washington,
DC), Jan. 8, 1831, 6 (italics original).
[88] Laurence Shore, *Southern Capitalists: The Ideological Leadership of an Elite, 1832–1885*
(Chapel Hill: University of North Carolina Press, 1986), 4, 9, 199n25. In 1829, Henry Clay of
Kentucky said that his state's failure to pass an emancipation plan had left it "in the rear of our
neighbors who are exempt from slavery, in the state of agriculture, the progress of manufactures,
the advance of improvement, and the general prosperity of society." Henry Clay, "To Gentlemen
of the Colonization Society of Kentucky," in *The Papers of Henry Clay*, vol. 8: *Candidate,
Compromiser, Whig, March 5, 1829–December 31, 1836*, ed. Robert Seager II and Melba Porter Hay
(Lexington: University Press of Kentucky, 1984), 142. For additional statements by Southerners
in the 1820s regarding slavery's economic effects, see Shore, *Southern Capitalists*, 199nn25–26;
an example is James Raymond, *Prize Essay on the Comparative Economy of Free and Slave Labor
in Agriculture* (Frederick, MD: Frederick County Agricultural Society, 1827). On economic
themes in the 1832 Virginia debate, see Shore, *Southern Capitalists*, 22–23; Charles Faulkner, *The
Speech of Charles Jas. Faulkner, (of Berkeley) in the House of Delegates of Virginia on the Policy of
the State with Respect to Her Slave Population, Delivered January 20, 1832* (Richmond: Thomas
W. White, 1832), 20; Thomas Marshall, *The Speech of Thomas Marshall, in the House of Delegates
of Virginia, on the Abolition of Slavery, Delivered January 20, 1832* (Richmond: Thomas W. White,
1832), 6. On responses to the Census of 1850 and outmigration from the South to the Midwest, see
James McPherson, *Battle Cry of Freedom: The Civil War Era* (New York: Oxford University Press,
1988), 91; Kenneth J. Winkle, *The Politics of Community: Migration and Politics in Antebellum
Ohio* (New York: Cambridge University Press, 1988), 13–15. For examples of antislavery writers'
use of statistics in the 1840s, and proslavery writers' "counterattack" in the late 1840s and early
1850s, see Shore, *Southern Capitalists*, 21, 31, 38–40. A prominent example of the antislavery position is Theodore Parker, *A Letter to the People of the United States Touching the Matter of Slavery*
(Boston: J. Munroe, 1848), esp. 42–60.

THE U.S. SECESSION CRISIS   63

who were "truly, cyclically poor."[89] Yet by the late 1850s, the claim that slavery weakened the Southern economy had become particularly controversial—even dangerous.[90] Indeed, white Southerners who made an economic argument for an end to slavery faced censure and censorship. The most famous example was that of Hinton Helper.[91]

[89] Fewer than 400,000 Southern families owned enslaved people in 1860, and even ardent proslavery apologists claimed that these families comprised no more than 2,250,000 white people. The total white population of the South in 1860, meanwhile, was over 8 million. See Susan B. Carter, "Slaveholding families, by state: 1790–1860" (Table Bb167–195), and Haines, "State Populations" (Series Aa2244–6550), in Carter et al., *Historical Statistics of the United States*; J. D. B. De Bow, *The Interest in Slavery of the Southern Non-Slaveholder* (Charleston, SC: Evans & Cogswell, 1860), 3. For the estimate of poverty among non-slaveholding white Southerners, see Merritt, *Masterless Men*, 16, 341–348.

[90] In his history of Southern economic thought, Joseph Persky writes that a "paranoid political style" prevailed by the late 1850s: "As the South moved toward secession it pulled in on itself and became impervious to external criticism. Increasingly, anything that belittled the region was considered subversive and disruptive. Every colonial argument that disparaged the traditional agriculture of the region thus became suspect. . . . This mind-set demanded the complete vindication of southern institutions, especially of the slave plantation." Although proponents of the "New South" movement would later argue that slavery had weakened the Southern economy, such views were "considered virtually treasonous before the war." Joseph Persky, *The Burden of Dependency: Colonial Themes in Southern Economic Thought* (Baltimore: Johns Hopkins University Press, 1992), 93, 99–100. Notably, even *proslavery* economic commentators sometimes met with alarm and disapproval when they proposed economic reforms that seemingly "promulgated too fundamental a critique of Southern society." This was the case, for example, when a group of proslavery reformers began in 1856 to call for a reopening of the international slave trade, believing that such a measure would create conditions for white non-slaveholders to join the slaveholding class. For writing about "nonslaveholders' hardships," one newspaper editor was accused of stirring up "a violent animosity in the poorer class against the richer" and eliciting the "slumbering venom of the folded snake that is in the midst of us" (Shore, *Southern Capitalists*, 55, 66). The proslavery editor J. D. B. De Bow was called an abolitionist (a "charge" he dismissed as "ridiculous") after he included in his *Review* a piece by a Northern writer whose opinions he disagreed with but still found "in the main liberal to the South." A biographer of De Bow suggests that in the 1850s, "[e]ven if De Bow wanted to present a more unbiased critique of the South, the increasingly isolated worldview of conservative southerners made it more difficult for him to be as critical of the South as he had once been in the *Review*." John F. Kvach, *De Bow's Review: The Antebellum Vision of a New South* (Lexington: University Press of Kentucky, 2013), 79; *De Bow's Review* 16 (Mar. 1854): 263; *De Bow's Review* 15 (Aug. 1853): 129. De Bow's own worldview narrowed significantly over the 1850s. Despite his early aspirations to be an "impartial and neutral" editor, by 1857 he had become an "unapologetic fire-eater" and his *Review* an "outlet for fanatic secessionists." De Bow "banned unfriendly newspapers" from reporting on a commercial convention he led in 1857 and by 1861 believed that it was best to suppress information that might be damaging to the Southern cause. Ottis Clark Skipper, *J. D. B. De Bow: Magazinist of the Old South* (Athens: University of Georgia Press, 1958), 122–123; Kvach, *De Bow's Review*, 86–87, 91–92, 135. More broadly, Michael Kent Curtis writes that speech on slavery was constrained both by "formal legal reactions" and by "the broader social reaction to dissent," observing that when "the community sees dissent on a subject as not only wrong, but illegitimate, free discussion of that topic is likely to disappear." Arguments about slavery's economic effects can be understood as speech that, while not necessarily banned, was inevitably shaped by the chilling effect of seditious speech laws and the "broader social reaction to dissent" (Curtis, *Free Speech*, 142). In fact, even if economic criticisms of slavery were not censored per se, "empirical investigations of slavery's effects" became virtually impossible in the political climate of the late 1850s. Margo J. Anderson notes that in planning for the 1860 census, Congress never proposed any questions to probe the "economic efficiency of southern agriculture" because such a set of questions would have been "politically explosive." Margo J. Anderson, *The American Census: A Social History* (New Haven: Yale University Press, 1988), 56.

[91] A less famous example comes from Georgia in 1860, when a poor white man named Pool went before a vigilance committee for saying that he would join with abolitionists, if given the chance,

64   WHEN DEMOCRACY BREAKS

Helper identified himself proudly as a "Southron."[92] He was a white native of the North Carolina Piedmont, an area that relied somewhat less on slave labor than the rest of the state. In 1856, he moved to Baltimore, Maryland (a rare Southern community that had an active, if small and sometimes persecuted, Republican Party), and the following year he published *The Impending Crisis of the South: How to Meet It.*[93]

In his book, Helper argued that slavery had made the South economically "subservient" to the North and severely limited the economic opportunities of non-slaveholding white Southerners like himself.[94] He made his case principally with scores of statistical tables, compiled mostly from U.S. census reports, comparing the Northern and Southern economies. He presented the two regions as having engaged in an economic contest, which began with the creation of the federal government, in 1789, when the two sections had roughly equal total population and wealth. His tables suggested that by 1850, the North had sped past the South by every important economic and social measure: total population and population density (the South had few major cities); value of agricultural products; agricultural output per acre; value of farms and domestic animals; tonnage of exports and imports; manufacturing; miles of canals and railroads built; bank capital; number of public schools, teachers, and students; number of public libraries; number of newspapers and rates of circulation; and literacy rates. Though some modern scholars have pointed out errors in Helper's figures (or questioned whether slavery hampered economic growth), Helper saw his tables as irrefutable evidence of slavery's effects.[95] He stressed that while the South was

in part because he thought that in the absence of slavery "he could get more for his work." The vigilance committee ultimately let him go, observing that no one had heard his comments "except a few other simple people of his own class, whose sympathies would only be increased by a martyr in their own class, however their tongues might be stilled by the terror of the example" (Shore, *Southern Capitalists*, 69–70).

[92] Hinton Rowan Helper, *The Impending Crisis of the South: How to Meet It* (New York: Burdick Brothers, 1857), vi.
[93] See David Brown, *Southern Outcast: Hinton Rowan Helper and the Impending Crisis of the South* (Baton Rouge: Louisiana State University Press, 2006); on Helper's move to Baltimore and the Republican Party there, see 74–76.
[94] Helper, *Impending Crisis*, 22.
[95] Brown, *Southern Outcast*, 88, 88n41. Margo Anderson has observed that both proslavery and antislavery writers, including Helper, "misuse[d] the data" (*American Census*, 53, 55). Robert Fogel and Stanley Engerman argued that Helper erred specifically in his estimates of agricultural production, exports, and land values. While conceding that the North surpassed the South in per capita income in 1840 and 1860, they attributed this gap to the exceptional wealth of the Northeast rather than to Southern economic weakness. They pointed out that the South was hardly an economic backwater, as it exceeded most nations in the world in per capita income in 1860. See Robert Fogel and Stanley Engerman, *Time on the Cross: The Economics of American Negro Slavery* (Boston: Little, Brown, 1974), 163–169, 247–257. Yet Fogel and Engerman also hypothesized that slavery might have impeded industrialization even while increasing Southern per capita income. Other historians have argued that "the appearance of economic vitality in the antebellum South was misleading" and that "the economic foundations of the slave economy were not conducive to long-term growth." See Roger Ransom,

THE U.S. SECESSION CRISIS   65

once economically self-sufficient, Southerners were now "compelled to go to the North for almost every article of utility and adornment, from matches, shoepegs and paintings up to cotton-mills, steamships, and statuary . . . we are dependent on Northern capitalists for the means necessary to build our railroads, canals and other public improvements . . . and . . . nearly all the profits arising from the exchange of commodities, from insurance and shipping offices, and from the thousand and one industrial pursuits of the country, accrue to the North."[96] The obvious cause of Southern inferiority, Helper argued, was slavery.

Helper thought that non-slaveholding Southern whites would have turned against slavery already, had not "the oligarchy" (meaning slaveholders) kept them "humbled in the murky sloughs of poverty and ignorance" and instilled "into their untutored minds passions and prejudices expressly calculated to strengthen and protect the accursed institution of slavery."[97] He declared "an exterminating war" against "slavery on the whole, and against slaveholders as a body."[98] He called for the abolition of slavery, without compensation to the owners. "Chevaliers of the lash," he argued, did not deserve compensation. He contended that land values in the South were far below those of the North, which in his view meant that farms of Southern non-slaveholders were worth, collectively, billions of dollars less than what they would have been worth without slavery. Helper charged slaveholders with having "defrauded" non-slaveholders of the difference—and himself, personally, of nearly $20,000 on the sale of his family farm in North Carolina. He urged non-slaveholders to peaceful revolution: they should vote all slaveholders out of office, enact high taxes on slave property to force owners to emancipate, and use the money raised to colonize freed slaves to Africa. Yet he also warned slaveholders that if they resisted, they would face terrible consequences:

> [Y]ou shall oppress us no longer. . . . It is for you to decide whether we are to have justice peaceably or by violence, for whatever consequences may follow,

Conflict and Compromise: The Political Economy of Slavery, Emancipation, and the American Civil War (New York: Cambridge University Press, 1989), 53n24, summarizing Gavin Wright, *Old South, New South: Revolutions in the Southern Economy since the Civil War* (New York: Basic Books, 1986), chapter 2. See also Gavin Wright, *Slavery and Economic Development* (2006; Baton Rouge: Louisiana State University Press, 2013), 61–62, 66–67, 73–76; Marvin Fischbaum and Julius Rubin, "Slavery and the Economic Development of the American South," *Explorations in Entrepreneurial History* 6 (Fall 1968): 116–127. In his own review of the 1850 census and other sources, James McPherson found significant regional disparities in literacy, population growth, technological improvements, manufacturing capacity, and banking capital, among other measures. James McPherson, *Ordeal by Fire: The Civil War and Reconstruction* (New York: Alfred A. Knopf, 1982), 23–25; McPherson, *Battle Cry of Freedom*, 91, 92n26, 95.

[96] Helper, *Impending Crisis*, 21–22.
[97] Helper, *Impending Crisis*, 59.
[98] Helper, *Impending Crisis*, 120.

66 WHEN DEMOCRACY BREAKS

we are determined to have it one way or the other. Do you aspire to become the victims of white non-slaveholding vengeance by day, and of barbarous massacre by the negroes at night? . . . Out of our effects your [*sic*] have long since overpaid yourselves for your negroes; and now, Sirs, you *must* emancipate them—speedily emancipate them, or we will emancipate them for you![99]

The Impending Crisis sold a respectable thirteen thousand copies its first year. In 1859, however, the book became a massive best-seller when the Republican Party issued a shortened version as a campaign pamphlet, called *Compendium of the Impending Crisis of the South.*[100] At Republican urging, Helper deleted what he called "passages . . . regarded as unnecessarily harsh toward slaveholders" (in the passage quoted above, for example, he cut everything after "one way or the other").[101] Yet the book nonetheless became the subject of intense political controversy, and by May 1860 about 140,000 copies of both the original book and the *Compendium* had been sold.[102]

Almost all of its sales, however, were in the North.[103] In the South, the book was denounced (for example, in resolutions passed by the Florida legislature in December 1859) as "treasonable," and anyone caught distributing copies risked running afoul of the Southern incendiary speech laws.[104] In fact, in 1859–1860, Texas and Kentucky enacted their first incendiary speech laws, and South Carolina enacted a new incendiary speech law, possibly in part to block circulation of the *Compendium.* The South Carolina and Texas laws followed the example of the Virginia law of 1836 in mandating censorship of antislavery publications in the U.S. mail.[105] (See appendix.)

---

[99] Helper, *Impending Crisis*, 123–135, quotations 125, 128, 129 (emphasis in original). While Helper in the late 1850s favored the elimination of slavery, he also expressed deeply racist views at that time, and his racism appears to have become even more virulent after emancipation. See George Frederickson, "Introduction," to Helper, *Impending Crisis* (Cambridge, MA: Belknap Press of Harvard University Press, 1968), xli–lxi; Brown, *Southern Outcast*, 43–68, 107–115, 213–247.

[100] The *Compendium* was about half the number of pages of the original book, owing to a smaller typeface and deleted passages, but it was not strictly an abridgment. It included a new chapter, "Testimony of Living Witnesses," a compilation of antislavery statements by contemporaries; also, a later, enlarged edition of the *Compendium* added statements of support for Helper's book from the Upper South. See Brown, *Southern Outcast*, 130, 141–144, 148.

[101] Brown, *Southern Outcast*, 142–144, quotation 142; compare Helper, *Impending Crisis*, 128–129, with Hinton Rowan Helper, *Compendium of the Impending Crisis of the South* (New York: A. B. Burdick, 1860), 65.

[102] Brown, *Southern Outcast*, 182. For how *The Impending Crisis* became involved in the bitterly fought contest for Speaker of the House in 1859–1860, which gave the book enormous publicity, see 152–184.

[103] Copies of the book are known to have circulated in the Upper South. See Brown, *Southern Outcast*, 146–147.

[104] *The Acts and Resolutions adopted by the General Assembly of Florida, at an Adjourned Session* (Tallahassee: Dyke & Carlisle, 1859), 96–97.

[105] *Acts of the General Assembly of the State of South Carolina, Passed in December 1859* (Columbia: R. W. Gibbes, 1859), 768–769; H. P. N. Gammel, comp., *The Laws of Texas 1822–1897*, 10

THE U.S. SECESSION CRISIS 67

There were notable prosecutions or attempted prosecutions of white Southerners seeking to sell or circulate Helper's book. In western Virginia, a Republican named William Stevenson was indicted in county court for loaning a copy of the book to his neighbors. When he arrived at court to contest the charge, a hostile mob apparently showed up, only to find that a posse of his neighbors was accompanying him. In the resulting "confusion" and "excitement," the trial was "postponed," and Stevenson remained a free man.[106] In South Carolina, Harold Wyllys was less fortunate; for giving away a copy of Helper's book, he was sentenced to a year in jail.[107] Perhaps the best-documented *Impending Crisis* case, however, occurred in North Carolina and involved Rev. Daniel Worth.

Worth, like Helper, was from upcountry North Carolina. Born in 1795 to a white Quaker family, he moved to Indiana in 1822 and eventually became a minister with the abolitionist-leaning Wesleyan Methodists.[108] In November 1857, he returned to his native state as a missionary. He settled near where he had grown up and where many of his slaveholding relatives still lived. Over the next two years, besides preaching antislavery sermons, he sold fifty copies of *The Impending Crisis* and ordered more.[109] He thereby risked prosecution under the North Carolina incendiary publications law, enacted thirty years earlier in response to David Walker's *Appeal*, and reenacted in slightly modified form in 1854. He would not have been the first. In 1850, another Wesleyan preacher had been prosecuted and convicted for giving a white girl a pamphlet that claimed slaveholders violated the Ten Commandments. Faced with whipping and imprisonment, he had been allowed to leave the state.[110] For Worth, matters came to a head in late 1859, when he began to be attacked in the North Carolina press. "*Why is not this man arrested?*" editorialized one newspaper. "If the law will not take hold of him, let the strong arm of an outraged people be stretched forth to arrest him in his incendiary work." On December 22, 1859, Worth was taken into custody.[111]

Over the next four months, Worth was tried twice, in two separate counties, before two separate juries (although the same judge). The trials received national

vols. (Austin: Gammel Book Co., 1898), 4:1461–1462; Harvey Myers, comp., *A Digest of the General Laws of Kentucky* (Cincinnati: Robert Clarke, 1866), 381.

[106] Eaton, *Freedom-of-Thought Struggle*, 245; quotation from Thomas C. Miller and Hu Maxwell, *West Virginia and Its People* (New York: Lewis Historical Publishing Company, 1913), 2:600. Stevenson was later a governor of West Virginia.

[107] Merritt, *Masterless Men*, 274.

[108] Noble J. Tolbert, "Daniel Worth: Tar Heel Abolitionist," *North Carolina Historical Review* 39, no. 3 (1962): 284, 286; on the Wesleyan Methodists, see John R. McKivigan, *The War against Proslavery Religion: Abolitionism and the Northern Churches, 1830–1865* (Ithaca, NY: Cornell University Press, 1984), 84–85.

[109] Curtis, *Free Speech*, 289.

[110] Curtis, *Free Speech*, 262–263.

[111] Curtis, *Free Speech*, 290–291; quotation in Tolbert, "Daniel Worth," 291–292.

68 WHEN DEMOCRACY BREAKS

attention, and Northerners paid for his legal counsel. Worth's lawyers argued that the incendiary publications law was being too broadly applied; it was intended to suppress the free distribution of pamphlets and leaflets to Black people, not the sale of books to white people.[112] The prosecution argued that if jurors did not convict, the "darkness of midnight would be lighted up with our burning buildings to see the massacred bodies of our wives and children."[113] Jurors sided with the prosecution. Worth was convicted in both trials and sentenced, as the law required for first offenders, to a year in jail. The judge chose not to exercise the option of having him "put in the pillory and whipped," possibly because he feared that flogging a senior white clergyman might help Republicans win votes in the North. Instead, the judge allowed Worth to post bail and leave the state. Worth left in a closed carriage, presumably out of fear that he would be attacked by a mob.[114] Meanwhile, state and local authorities interviewed every person thought to have bought a copy of *The Impending Crisis* from him and searched their homes.[115] The North Carolina legislature also in 1861 amended the seditious publication law. Punishment for a first offense would no longer be a year in jail, but death.[116] (See appendix.)

The Suppression of the Republican Party

The Republican Party, which promoted Helper's book, had been organized in 1854 and 1855 around the central demand of stopping the spread of slavery into the Western territories and thereby preventing the addition of more slaveholding states to the Union. In 1856, the Republicans ran their first candidate for president, John C. Frémont of California, who only narrowly lost to the Democratic candidate, James Buchanan of Pennsylvania. Almost all of Frémont's support came from outside the South. According to official returns, he received just a handful of votes in two of the fourteen slaveholding states in which a popular election was held (Delaware and Maryland), and no votes at all in the others.[117] Four years later, when Lincoln won the national election, he did only slightly better in the South, winning a small number of votes in five slaveholding states (Delaware, Maryland, Virginia, Kentucky, and Missouri) and none in the others.[118]

[112] Tolbert, "Daniel Worth," 300. Worth's lawyers would make these arguments the basis of an appeal to the North Carolina Supreme Court, where they would lose (the appeal took place after Worth left the state) (302).
[113] Tolbert, "Daniel Worth," 299.
[114] Tolbert, "Daniel Worth," 301.
[115] Tolbert, "Daniel Worth," 294–295.
[116] Curtis, *Free Speech*, 295–296.
[117] *Guide to U.S. Elections*, 763.
[118] *Guide to U.S. Elections*, 764.

THE U.S. SECESSION CRISIS   69

Historians have rarely examined why, according to official returns, Republicans received literally zero votes in most of the South in the elections of 1856 and 1860. This is particularly remarkable given that the formal barriers limiting a party's ability to obtain votes in this era were exceedingly low. Since the 1890s, when states began to adopt the Australian ballot, new parties have had to gain access to an official, government-printed ballot in order to receive many votes. This process can sometimes be complex and expensive and must be completed weeks or months before election day. In the elections of 1856 and 1860, by contrast, there were no government-printed ballots. Each voter simply turned in a "ticket" with his preferred candidates' names on it, which at that point became a legal "ballot." Anyone could print a ticket at any time, up to and including election day, and political parties typically printed ballots listing their candidates' names and distributed them to sympathetic voters. A few states (all in the South) did not even require ballots, allowing votes to be cast by voice. New, small parties could and sometimes did appear just days before an election in some places, distributing tickets and winning a substantial number of votes.[119]

These low barriers to political entry did not help the Republican Party in the South because—strikingly—the party was actively suppressed across most Southern states. Thus, the presidential elections of 1856 and 1860 in these states were anything but "free and fair." The suppression of the Republican Party grew logically from the earlier suppression of abolitionism, even though the Republicans denied that they were abolitionists. Many Southern leaders dismissed Republicans' promises not to "interfere" with slavery in the South as a smoke screen, intended to disguise the Republicans' true intentions.

Tellingly, white Southerners frequently referred to members of the party as "Black Republicans." Northern and Southern Democrats alike used this nickname to reinforce their claim that Republicans favored "negro equality." Yet in the South especially, other connotations of the term "Black Republican" came to the fore. It was a play on the term "Red Republican," commonly used in English-speaking countries to describe the red-cap-wearing radicals of the French Revolution of 1789 and the most radical European revolutionaries of 1848.[120] As John Townsend of South Carolina asked, "What difference would it make to us, whether our lives and fortunes were controlled by Red Republican France,

---

[119] See David Moss, Marc Campasano, and Dean Grodzins, "An Australian Ballot for California?," Harvard Business School Case 716-054, Feb. 2016; revised July 2017; Alicia Yin Cheng, *This Is What Democracy Looked Like: A Visual History of the Printed Ballot* (Hudson, NY: Princeton Architectural Press, 2020). The Southern states of Virginia, Kentucky, and Missouri also allowed *viva voce* voting in the 1856 and 1860 elections; see Paul Bourke and Donald DeBats, *Washington County: Politics and Community in Antebellum America* (Baltimore: Johns Hopkins University Press, 1995), 9.

[120] For the association of the terms "Black Republican" and "Red Republican," see Don H. Doyle, *The Cause of All Nations: An International History of the American Civil War* (New York: Basic Books, 2015), 91, 100; see also Merritt, *Masterless Men*, 268–269.

70   WHEN DEMOCRACY BREAKS

or Black Republican Massachusetts?"[121] He and other Southern political leaders considered the "Black Republicans" just like the Red, believing that both wanted to overthrow the existing social order and constitutional system and were willing to use violence to do it. "Those French desperadoes who design the destruction of life and property are called Red Republicans," noted another writer. "Why should not the reckless advocates of abolition . . . be called the Black Republicans?"[122]

Many white Southerners believed that the rise of the "Black Republicans" in the North was linked to a rise in slave unrest that they perceived in the South. During and immediately following the presidential election of 1856, white officials and vigilante groups charged enslaved people with plotting to massacre white people in Texas, Tennessee, Kentucky, Louisiana, Arkansas, Missouri, Mississippi, Alabama, Florida, Maryland, and Virginia. Vigilance committees killed many of the accused. A few of the plots were allegedly instigated by white men, usually natives of the North who had moved to the South and were thought to harbor antislavery beliefs. The accused individuals were subjected to arrest, expulsion from the South, whipping, and even lynching in some cases.[123]

When Republicans could not be credibly accused of directly instigating slave unrest, they were still often blamed for provoking it. A former Tennessee congressman explained how he thought such provocation had played out in his state. Just weeks after the 1856 election, white leaders in Tennessee claimed to have uncovered a murderous slave plot in the state. The Republican candidate, Frémont, seemed to have had no support in Tennessee (officially, he got zero votes), but Democratic and Know-Nothing stump speakers had crossed the state denouncing Republican ties to abolitionism. The speakers had drawn enthusiastic crowds wherever they went—and this, the former congressman thought, was the problem. As he explained in a letter to a newspaper, while the white listeners in every crowd had indignantly rejected the Republicans, "a long line of sable visages upon the outskirts . . . were turned eagerly toward the speaker. . . . They managed to comprehend one idea, and that was . . . that the institution of slavery would be much less secure if Frémont was elected." These enslaved people, the former congressman alleged, went home and talked about this "one idea . . . until at length they came to entertain the belief that the inhabitants of the North were so thoroughly enlisted in their cause that they would assist them in their work of slaughter."[124]

---

[121] [John Townsend], *The South Alone Should Govern the South, and African Slavery Should Be Controlled by Those Only, Who Are Friendly to It* (Charleston, SC: Evans & Cogswell, 1860), 10.

[122] Quoted in Merritt, *Masterless Men*, 269.

[123] Harvey Wish, "The Slave Insurrection Panic of 1856," *Journal of Southern History* 5, no. 2 (1939): 206–222. See also, e.g., "Slave Insurrections," *The Liberator* (Boston), Dec. 12, 1856.

[124] "Rumored Insubordination in the South," *Daily National Intelligencer*, Dec. 22, 1856, 3. The writer was Lucien Chase. For other contemporary observers making the same point, see Wish, "Slave Insurrection Panic," 207.

THE U.S. SECESSION CRISIS   71

Many white Southerners, in short, viewed the Republican Party as an existential threat. They were alarmed and outraged that some white Southerners, at least, found the Republican message or candidates appealing, and they feared that a Republican presence of any kind could incite enslaved people to resist or even rebel. For these reasons, they sought to eradicate the Republican Party from the South entirely. The following three vignettes—from Virginia, North Carolina, and Texas—suggest some of the ways that this was accomplished.

Virginia, 1856

The Republican national convention in Philadelphia in June 1856, which nominated Frémont, welcomed delegations from the slaveholding states of Delaware, Kentucky, Maryland, and Virginia. By party rules that year, Virginia, the most populous state in the South, was entitled to a delegation of forty-five members. Only three showed up, however.[125] One of them was John C. Underwood, a native New Yorker who had married into a prominent Virginia family. Since the 1840s, he and his wife had maintained an eight-hundred-acre farm in the northern part of the state, without use of enslaved labor.[126] Underwood spoke to the convention, asking why Virginia was not represented "here to-day as in 1776," when Virginians had been at the forefront of the American Revolution. He blamed the "blighting curse" of slavery, which had "crushed humanity" in his state. The "fate of Virginia," he declared, "should be a warning" to the nation.[127]

While Underwood was still in the North, news reports of his speech reached his white neighbors. They immediately held a public "indignation meeting," which one Virginia newspaper praised as "large and respectable." The meeting passed resolutions denouncing the "principles" of the Republican platform as "unjust and incendiary in their tendency," calling Underwood's claim to represent them "a libel upon our institutions and an insult to us as citizens." The meeting also appointed "a committee . . . to wait upon Mr. Underwood, and inform him . . . that they deem it just and advisable that he should leave the State as speedily as he can find it in his power so to do."[128] Both Underwood's brother and his wife wrote to him, urging him not to come home because "the excitement is so great against him that he will be mobbed." Underwood called for his wife and

---

[125] Richard G. Lowe, "The Republican Party in Antebellum Virginia, 1856–1860," *Virginia Magazine of History and Biography* 81, no. 3 (1973): 262.

[126] Lowe, "Republican Party," 261–262; Eaton, *Freedom-of-Thought Struggle*, 265.

[127] *Proceedings of the First Three Republican National Conventions of 1856, 1860, and 1864, Including Proceedings of the Antecedent National Convention Held at Pittsburgh, in February 1856, as Reported by Horace Greeley* (Minneapolis: C. W. Johnson, [1893]), 80.

[128] "Indignation Meeting," *Richmond Whig*, July 1, 1856, 2.

72   WHEN DEMOCRACY BREAKS

son to join him in temporary exile, and they stayed for the next several months in New York City.[129]

In August, five hundred Frémont supporters in Wheeling, in northwestern Virginia, attempted to hold a mass meeting. Hecklers interrupted the pro-Frémont speeches, and when the lead speaker, a local physician, tried to leave the hall, a mob attacked him. Anticipating that this might happen, he was carrying a knife. He tried to defend himself, but this only inflamed his attackers further. He probably would have been lynched had not the sheriff seized him and jailed him, apparently for his own protection; no member of the mob, however, was arrested.[130] Over the next few weeks, threats against "Frémont men" continued. A prominent citizen of Wheeling received an anonymous letter, telling him to stay away from any "black republican" meetings, or "[n]o one knows what will happen."[131] Nonetheless, other Frémont meetings were held in northwest Virginia. In September, a Republican convention defiantly gathered in Wheeling and nominated a ticket of presidential electors.[132]

During the fall campaign, Virginia Republicans faced continual harassment. One observer noted that many who liked Frémont did not "dare" vote for him, because anyone who tried would "hear himself held up as a black hearted villain and his cause as one of treason." Threats of physical violence against Frémont supporters were so common that Republicans grimly joked about having to write their wills before going to the polls. In November, on election day, some Republican voters were assaulted, and one, a native of Connecticut living in Norfolk, was run out of town by a mob. In the end, according to a Wheeling newspaper, Republicans received just 291 votes in the entire state.[133] Official returns, however, showed Frémont receiving zero votes in Virginia. (Official returns also indicated that Frémont received zero votes in two other states represented at the 1856 Republican convention, Kentucky and Missouri.)[134]

Benjamin Hedrick (North Carolina, 1856)

In September 1856, a New York newspaper backing Frémont claimed that Republicans had enough support in the South to field full slates of Frémont

[129] Lowe, "Republican Party," 263–264; quotation from "A Black Republican in Virginia," *Daily Advocate* (Baton Rouge), July 11, 1856, 2.

[130] "Republicanism in Virginia—What Freedom Means at the South," *New York Daily Times*, Aug. 26, 1856, 2; Lowe, "Republican Party," 264.

[131] "A Fremont Man in Virginia," *New York Herald*, Sept. 28, 1856, 2.

[132] Lowe, "Republican Party," 265.

[133] Lowe, "Republican Party," 265, 267.

[134] *Guide to U.S. Elections*, 763. The other slaveholding state represented at the 1856 Republican convention was Maryland; according to official returns, Frémont received 285 votes there.

THE U.S. SECESSION CRISIS   73

electors in Virginia, Kentucky, Maryland, Texas, and North Carolina. The *North Carolina Standard*, the most influential Democratic paper in the state, responded in an editorial that the claim was a "vile slander on the Southern people." If there were any Frémont supporters in North Carolina, the editorial added, they should "be silenced or required to leave," because "[t]he expression of black Republican opinions in our midst, is incompatible with our honor and safety as a people."[135]

The *Standard* apparently had someone specific in mind: twenty-nine-year-old Benjamin Sherwood Hedrick. Like Hinton Helper and Daniel Worth, he was a white native of the Piedmont region of North Carolina. Hedrick had graduated from the University of North Carolina, Chapel Hill, pursued graduate studies at Harvard University (on Sundays, going to Boston to hear antislavery preaching), and returned to Chapel Hill to take a position as professor of agricultural chemistry.[136] In August, when state elections had taken place, a student asked him whom he would vote for in the presidential race, and he responded that he wanted to vote for Frémont. Soon, rumors swirled around campus that he was an abolitionist, and students burned him in effigy. Then came the editorial response to the New York newspaper in the *North Carolina Standard*, which subsequently published an anonymous letter expressing alarm that "a professor at our State University is an open and avowed supporter of Fremont, and declares his willingness—nay, his desire—to support the black Republican ticket."[137] The letter-writer insisted that this situation "*ought and must be looked to. We must have certain security . . . that at State Universities at least we will have no canker worm preying at the very vitals of Southern institutions.*"[138]

Hedrick wrote to the *Standard* to defend himself. In a letter that the newspaper published on October 4, he explained that he would vote for Frémont because "I like the man" and because Republicans were right to oppose the extension of slavery. He argued that his position was not at all anti-Southern, pointing out that the "great Southern statesmen of the Revolution," such as Jefferson, had decried the evils of slavery. Hedrick also argued that slavery had limited the economic opportunities of white North Carolinians. He denied that he had ever tried to influence the political beliefs of his students and mocked the notion that he was somehow responsible for exposing them to antislavery ideas. To stop the students from encountering criticism of slavery, he pointed out, Jefferson's writings would have to be purged from the university library.[139]

---

[135] J. G. de Roulhac Hamilton, "Benjamin Sherwood Hedrick," *James Sprunt Historical Publications*, 10 (1910):8, https://books.google.com/books?id=dA3g05Q_m9UC&printsec=frontcover&source=gbs_ge_summary_r&cad=0#v=onepage&q&f=false.

[136] For a biography, see Michael Thomas Smith, *A Traitor and a Scoundrel: Benjamin Hedrick and the Cost of Dissent* (Newark: University of Delaware, 2003).

[137] Hamilton, "Benjamin Sherwood Hedrick," 10. Note that the quoted passage uses "Fremont" rather than "Frémont."

[138] Hamilton, "Benjamin Sherwood Hedrick," 10 (emphasis in original).

[139] Hamilton, "Benjamin Sherwood Hedrick," 12–15.

74 WHEN DEMOCRACY BREAKS

On October 6, an "indignation meeting" in Murfreesboro denounced Hedrick's views as "subversive of and inimical to the true interests of our rights as a people."[140] Every significant newspaper in the state attacked him (except one, edited by his uncle, who made no public comment but rebuked him privately for stirring up trouble).[141] The public clamor for Hedrick's dismissal from the university grew intense. On October 18, the Executive Committee of the university trustees voted to fire him, even though some of the members doubted that they had the legal authority to do so. As one trustee explained in a letter to the university president, "The 'outside pressure' was too great."[142]

Months earlier, Hedrick had agreed to attend an educational conference in Salisbury, his hometown. Now, despite having been fired, he decided to go. The first day of the conference passed uneventfully, but when he left it for the evening, he was met by a mob. It carried an effigy of him, on which was hung a sign: "Hedrick, leave or tar and feathers." The mob burned the effigy in his presence, then followed him to the friend's house where he was staying, heckling him all the way. He left Salisbury before sunrise.[143] Days later, he and his wife left the state altogether. He would spend the remainder of his career in New York and Washington, DC.[144] The *Standard*, which had launched the campaign against him, expressed satisfaction with the outcome: "Our object was to rid the University and the State of an avowed Fremont man; and we have succeeded.... [N]o man who is avowedly for John C. Fremont for President, ought to be allowed to breathe the air or to tread the soil of North Carolina."[145] According to official returns, Frémont received zero votes in North Carolina in the November 1856 election.

The "Texas Troubles" (1860)

In 1853, David Hoover, a white native of Indiana, moved to northern Texas, in the Dallas region. Within a few years, he owned eight hundred acres of land, with fifty under cultivation. Some people noticed that he neither owned enslaved people nor "hired" (rented) any to work for him, but rather employed only free white workers. Suspicious, they questioned him about his views on slavery. By

---

[140] Hamilton, "Benjamin Sherwood Hedrick," 21–22.

[141] Monty Woodall Cox, "Freedom during the Fremont Campaign: The Fate of One North Carolina Republican in 1856," *North Carolina Historical Review* 45, no. 4 (1968): 378–379; Smith, *A Traitor and a Scoundrel*, 83.

[142] Hamilton, "Benjamin Sherwood Hedrick," 32–33, quotation on 33.

[143] Hamilton, "Benjamin Sherwood Hedrick," 36–37; Smith, *A Traitor and a Scoundrel*, 84–85.

[144] See Smith, *A Traitor and a Scoundrel*.

[145] Hamilton, "Benjamin Sherwood Hedrick," 39. Again, the quoted passage uses "Fremont" rather than "Frémont."

THE U.S. SECESSION CRISIS   75

his own account, he told them that he "thought [slavery] was wrong," that he opposed "the further extension of slavery," but that he "was equally opposed to meddling with it in the States where it already existed by law." Hoover later recalled that he used only "cautious and temperate . . . language" when talking about slavery and had been "careful never to speak against slavery in the presence of negroes." It began to be "whispered around the neighborhood" that he was a "Black Republican."[146]

The rumors were apparently correct about his party preference. Hoover later reported that in the 1856 presidential election, he and another local man had voted for Frémont (although according to official returns, Frémont received zero votes in Texas).[147] "The fat was then in the fire," he recalled. "Whispers gave way to audible curses, and I was openly denounced as a 'd——d Abolitionist.'" Hoover's nephew overheard a group of men plotting to tie him to a "black jack" tree, strip him, and flog him with a rawhide whip.[148]

Hoover must have known this was not idle talk. In September 1856, in southeast Texas, vigilantes had announced that they had stopped an alleged slave insurrection organized by Mexicans. In response, the vigilantes executed five Black people, two by whipping them to death, and ordered all Mexicans to leave the county in five days or be killed. News of the alleged plot had caused alarm, and vigilance committees were formed across the state. In October 1856, one of them had seized a white migrant from Ohio for allegedly plotting a slave revolt and given him a hundred lashes.[149]

Hoover nonetheless stood his ground, possibly because he had allies among his fellow Northern Methodists. In 1844, the Methodist Episcopal Church (MEC)—the principal white Methodist denomination—had divided over whether to enforce an old denominational rule that clergy should not own slaves.[150] Proslavery members had broken away to form their own denomination, the MEC, South, called the "Southern Methodists." Those who chose not to break away came to be called "Northern Methodists." Most of them, like Hoover, rejected abolitionism.

---

[146] "An Indianan Driven Out of Texas," *Worthington White River Gazette*, Nov. 8, 1860, 4. This reprints a long extract of a letter by Hoover, which appeared originally in the *Lafayette Courier*. The article gives his name only as "D. O. Hoover"; but see also Charles Elliott, *South-Western Methodism: A History of the M.E. Church in the South-West, from 1844 to 1864* (Cincinnati: Poe & Hitchcock, 1868), 211, where his name is given as "David A. Hoover." That his fellow Northern Methodists would know his given name seems likely, so we use the name "David."

[147] "An Indianan Driven Out of Texas"; *Guide to U.S. Elections*, 763.

[148] "An Indianan Driven Out of Texas."

[149] Donald E. Reynolds, *Texas Terror: The Slave Insurrection Panic of 1860 and the Secession of the Lower South* (Baton Rouge: Louisiana State University Press, 2007), 13–14; Wish, "Slave Insurrection Panic," 208.

[150] The most important Black Methodist denominations in this era were the African Methodist Episcopal Church (AME), to which Walker had apparently belonged, and the African Methodist Episcopal Zion Church, which had been founded in 1821. Walker's involvement with Black Methodism is a theme in Hinks, *To Awaken My Afflicted Brethren*.

76   WHEN DEMOCRACY BREAKS

The Northern Methodists retained many Southern members, including four thousand slaveholders. (White Methodists with abolitionist views, such as Daniel Worth, tended to belong to the Wesleyan Methodists, while Black Methodists—among them, David Walker—usually belonged to an African Methodist denomination.)[151] Northern Methodists, despite mostly opposing abolitionism, were widely distrusted among white Texans as "unsound" on slavery.

Enough Northern Methodists had settled in northern Texas by the mid-1850s that the MEC sent missionaries to the region. The most senior of them was Rev. Anthony Bewley, a Tennessee native who had spent much of his career in Missouri. Sometime after the 1856 election, Bewley began holding religious meetings at Hoover's house. This development led Hoover's neighbors to escalate their threats. They told Hoover that they would "attend to" him and any Northern Methodist who preached at his house. As Hoover later explained, everyone "understood" what the threat meant: they would be tied to a tree and whipped and would have to leave Texas or be hanged "without judge or jury."[152]

Meanwhile, in March 1859, Bewley himself met with the threat of violence when he attended a Northern Methodist conference in Timber Creek, about forty miles from Dallas. The gathering alarmed some local leaders, who considered the participants to be "spies and forerunners of the invading army of abolitionism." These anxious leaders also held a public meeting that appointed a committee to "wait upon" the conference. On Sunday, March 12, the committee, accompanied by two hundred armed, mounted vigilantes, interrupted the delegates' worship services. The committee spokesman, a prominent local lawyer, strode to the front of the congregation and warned those present—Bewley among them—to end the meeting and stop their work in Texas. The conference quickly adjourned, and efforts to organize Northern Methodists in Texas collapsed. Bewley left the state in late 1859.[153]

Fear of antislavery infiltration into Texas did not subside, however, and strategies for how best to combat it became a topic of discussion in the state legislature. In December 1859 and January 1860, the Texas House of Representatives debated whether to ban persons from settling in Texas "who belong to any religious sect or association, political party or organization" that aimed "to abolish the institution of slavery as it now exists in this State." The Texas House also considered whether to require every potential settler to swear under oath "that he does not belong to such sect or party, or organization, and that he is not opposed to slavery."[154]

---

[151] McKivigan, *War against Proslavery Religion*, 84–87.

[152] "An Indianan Driven Out of Texas"; Reynolds, *Texas Terror*, 148–149.

[153] Reynolds, *Texas Terror*, 15–17, 149.

[154] *Texas House Journal, Eighth Legislature, Regular Session*, 249–250; see also *Texas State Gazette Appendix, Containing Debates in the House of Representatives of the Eighth Legislature, of the State of*

THE U.S. SECESSION CRISIS 77

A sponsor of these proposals argued that they had become necessary because "emissaries of a certain religious sect ... infested, some months ago, the northern section of this State, and ... in their boldness, sentiments were uttered upon the highways inimical to the institution of slavery."[155] Some legislators objected that the proposed ban was a religious test ("Are you going to establish an Inquisition here in Texas?" one asked), but most representatives from north Texas, including a leader of the attack on the Timber Creek conference, rejected the proposed laws on proslavery grounds.[156] Enacting such measures would only "give the abolitionists reasons to suppose there is a sympathy for them in this State." Even worse, the proposed legislation implied that the region was "unsound" on slavery. North Texans, one representative proudly pointed out, "have never yet allowed the utterance of sentiments antagonistic to the interests of the South to go unpunished."[157] Despite these objections, the proposals won a close preliminary vote in the Texas House, though they did not ultimately become law.[158]

In February 1860, the legislature did add a provision to the Texas penal code on the crime of "[e]xciting insurrection or insubordination." In many features, it followed the example of other Southern "incendiary speech" laws. Like them, it banned writing or printing, or circulating written or printed work, that was "calculated to produce in slaves a spirit of insubordination with the intent to advise or incite negroes in this State, to rebel or to make insurrection." The penalty was prison for up to seven years. The provision also banned, under penalty of two to four years in prison, anyone from making a public statement "that masters have not right of property in their slaves." To this, however, the law added a new element: it mandated a prison term of two to five years for any "free person" who "privately or otherwise than publicly" tried to "bring the institution of slavery (African) into dispute in the mind of any free inhabitant of this State, or of any resident for the time being therein." In other words, a white person who criticized slavery in private conversation with other white people, as David Hoover seemed to have done, would now be guilty of a serious crime. The law also mandated that the mail be censored, perhaps aiming to stop circulation of *The Impending Crisis*. Specifically, it required that U.S. postmasters in Texas intercept incendiary

---

Texas, vol. 4 (Austin: State Gazette Office, 1860), 68–70. These were proposed amendments to a "preemption" or "donation" bill, which would grant state-owned land to settlers.

[155] *Texas State Gazette Appendix*, 82; see also 66.

[156] Quotation in *Texas State Gazette Appendix*, 69; see also 75. On the involvement of Representative Robert H. Taylor of Fannin, Texas, in the Timber Creek incident, see 82. Taylor spoke at the "indignation" meeting the day prior to the attack; we have not yet determined whether he participated in the attack, but many of those who spoke in the meeting also participated in the attack; see Reynolds, *Texas Terror*, 15–17.

[157] *Texas State Gazette Appendix*, 75; see also 66.

[158] *Texas House Journal, Eighth Legislature, Regular Session*, 250. The version of the preemption law as finally enacted did not have these provisions; see Gammel, *The Laws of Texas*, 4:1384.

publications and turn them over to a local justice of the peace, who would be obliged to burn them.[159] (See appendix.)

Hoover now had not only public opinion against him, but arguably the law as well, and with the 1860 presidential election looming, anti-Northern sentiment and fears of slave unrest could be expected to run high. Then, on July 8, 1860, a fire burned much of Dallas to the ground. Over the coming days, other fires broke out in nearby north Texas communities. Phosphorous matches probably caused the blazes. Widely used at the time, these matches were known to combust in their boxes in hot weather, and the region was experiencing a heat wave. Yet prominent north Texans made an alarming announcement: the fires, they claimed, had been set by enslaved people, who had been incited to arson by a secret network of white Northern abolitionists operating throughout the state. The resulting panic produced what became known as the "Texas Troubles" (or sometimes the "Texas Terror"). Rumors flew that one town after another had been reduced to ashes. For nearly three months, vigilance committees arrested enslaved people and whipped them until they confessed that white Northerners had supplied them with matches, guns, and poison. The vigilantes acted on the principle that, as one explained to a newspaper, "it is better for us to hang ninety-nine innocent (suspicious) men than to let one guilty one pass, for the guilty one endangers the peace of society."[160] There were eyewitness and press reports of at least thirty people, Black and white, being lynched; perhaps as many as a hundred were killed altogether, and many settlers from the North were forced to leave the state.[161]

David Hoover was one of those who left, having realized sometime in August that he was in imminent danger of having his life "sacrificed at the hands of a brutal mob."[162] He fled on horseback, leaving behind his family, "some of whom were sick." Two months later, after a journey of over a thousand miles, he arrived in Illinois, penniless and ill. Yet he was more fortunate than his former minister Bewley. In Hoover's words, Bewley had been "sacrificed to the Moloch of slavery."[163]

---

[159] Gammel, *Laws of Texas*, 4:1461–1462 (see 1457 for the Act that included this law, and 1464 reflecting the Act's passage). See also "An Act, Supplementary to [and] amendatory of an act, entitled an act to adopt and establish a Penal Code for the State of Texas," Title 19, Chapter 1, Article 653. The authors would like to thank the Texas State Library and Archives Commission for supplying us with a copy of the manuscript of this Act, which lists its title and date of passage.

[160] [John Townsend], *The Doom of Slavery in the Union: Its Safety Out of It* (Charleston, SC: Evans & Cogswell, 1860), 34–37, quotation on 36.

[161] See "Texas Troubles," https://tshaonline.org/handbook/online/articles/vetbr; Reynolds, *Texas Terror*.

[162] "An Indianan Driven Out of Texas."

[163] "Returning," *Centerville Indiana True Republic*, Oct. 18, 1860, 2; "An Indianan Driven Out of Texas." Moloch is a pagan god condemned in the Bible, associated with child sacrifice. See Lev. 18:21, 20:2–5.

THE U.S. SECESSION CRISIS   79

Bewley had returned to Texas in the spring of 1860, planning to move to the southern part of the state and evangelize among the large community of German immigrants there, who were thought to be indifferent if not hostile to slavery.[164] He had stopped in north Texas, however, probably to spend time with old parishioners such as Hoover.[165] He was there when the Dallas fire occurred. Bewley had been the most prominent Northern Methodist missionary in Texas, and rumors began to circulate that he had been the ringleader of the alleged abolitionist conspiracy. Realizing that his life was in danger, he left Texas on July 17 in a wagon, accompanied by his wife and a young son. Vigilance committees offered a $1,000 bounty to anyone who captured him and brought him back for punishment. On September 3, a posse caught him in southwest Missouri. He was taken first to Arkansas, where he wrote a farewell letter to his family in which he protested his innocence and promised to meet them in heaven. Taken to Fort Worth late on September 13, he was immediately hanged. The next morning, his body was cut down and buried in a shallow grave. About three weeks later, his body was exhumed, his bones stripped, and his skeleton placed on display atop a Dallas warehouse. Boys would play with it, setting "the bones in a variety of attitudes by bending the joints of the arms and legs, and . . . mocked [the skeleton] by crying, 'old Bewley,' 'old abolitionist,' etc."[166]

Meanwhile, newspapers across the South spread reports of the "Abolition Plot in Texas." During the fall presidential election campaign, some white Southerners, mostly self-identified "Union men," questioned whether such a vast conspiracy could have existed and whether Bewley had really been guilty.[167] Others, especially those who declared the South would have to secede if Lincoln were elected, pointed to Texas as an example of what would happen throughout the slaveholding states "if the Black Republicans were in power."[168] After Lincoln's victory, secessionists again referenced Texas to help make their case. One prominent Georgia secessionist explained in a speech that, in his view, although most

---

[164] Most German immigrants in Texas did not own slaves and were "indifferent to the institution." See Walter L. Buenger, *Secession and the Union in Texas* (Austin: University of Texas Press, 1984), 83–84. The most prominent German critic of slavery in Texas was Adolph Douai, editor of the *San Antonio Zeitung*, who in Germany had participated in the 1848 revolutions and in Texas worked with the New York journalist and landscape architect Frederick Law Olmsted on a failed attempt to establish a free state in western Texas. Douai found himself isolated, impoverished, and sometimes physically threatened for his views; he had left the state in 1856. See Laura Wood Roper, "Frederick Law Olmsted and the Western Texas Free-Soil Movement," *American Historical Review* 56, no. 1 (1950): 58–64; see also Justine Davis Randers-Pehrson, *Adolph Douai, 1819–1888: The Turbulent Life of a German Forty-Eighter in the Homeland and in the United States*, New German-American Studies, vol. 22 (New York: Peter Lang, 2000).

[165] Reynolds, *Texas Terror*, 149.

[166] Reynolds, *Texas Terror*, 150–152, 163. Reynolds discusses a letter that was meant to implicate Bewley in the abolitionist plot, which he convincingly argues was a forgery (155–167).

[167] Reynolds, *Texas Terror*, 99–100, 155, 160–161.

[168] Reynolds, *Texas Terror*, 179.

80   WHEN DEMOCRACY BREAKS

slaves were loyal, a few might become "the incendiary or the poisoner" when "instigated by the unscrupulous emissaries of Northern Abolitionists. . . . What has given impulse to these fears, and aid and comfort to those outbreaks now, but the success of the Black Republicans—the election of Abraham Lincoln!"[169] Notably, Lincoln officially received zero votes in Texas.

From Erosion of Democracy to Secession

Constraints on free expression, public debate, and political organization during the years leading up to the Civil War inevitably distorted political decision-making in the South, including during the pivotal years of 1860 and 1861. The tendency of Southern leaders to deny or even criminalize facts that challenged their worldview may have left them less capable of reaching accurate conclusions about their economic and political strength. At the same time, by treating any challenge to slavery as an existential threat, they cultivated a political siege mentality that seemed to justify extraordinary and blatantly undemocratic measures in response to a perceived emergency.

An Exaggerated Sense of Southern Economic Power

Southern leaders had suppressed the views of those like Hinton Helper who identified weaknesses of the Southern economy and claimed that slavery was the cause. Publications that celebrated the Southern economy, meanwhile, whether written by Southerners themselves or by proslavery writers from outside the South, were welcomed. Apparently as a result, many Southern leaders developed an exaggerated sense of the economic power of the slaveholding states, relative both to the North and to Great Britain, the nation that purchased most Southern-grown cotton. Indeed, this exaggerated sense of economic power seems to have contributed to many Southern leaders' confidence in pursuing secession in 1860–1861.[170]

---

[169] Reynolds, *Texas Terror*, 183.

[170] "In early 1860, the predominant tone among proslavery voices was present prosperity and potential for future prosperity." See Shore, *Southern Capitalists*, 70–71 (listing several representative texts). One of the most important journals in the Lower South, *De Bow's Review*, included a number of prominent secessionist leaders among its readership, and by the late 1850s "obscured inherent weaknesses in the region's industrial and transportation sectors" rather than reporting "candidly [on] the South's shortcomings" (Shore, *Southern Capitalists*, 56; Kvach, *De Bow's Review*, 91–92, 132–134). (De Bow's biographer writes, "Caught up in the excitement of the growing secessionist movement, and feeling the pressure to justify southern independence, De Bow pandered to readers by overlooking or avoiding significant shortfalls in the South's industrial sector" [Kvach, *De Bow's Review*, 91].) Once the war was underway, De Bow believed that writing critically about the Confederate economy or military effort could hurt Southern morale, and his boosterism "distorted

THE U.S. SECESSION CRISIS   81

Key Southern leaders insisted, for example, that the North was economically dependent on the South—not, as Helper had indicated, the other way around—as was Britain, so that if the South declared its independence, the North would have no choice but to acquiesce without a fight and Britain to ally with the South. In a famous speech delivered to the U.S. Senate in 1858, the slaveholding senator James Henry Hammond of South Carolina had asserted that if any nation attempted to make war on the South, the South could "[w]ithout firing a gun . . . bring the whole world to our feet." The South, he argued, could easily go three years "without planting a seed of cotton," but if it did so, "England would topple headlong and carry the whole civilized world with her, save the South. No, you dare not make war on cotton. No power on earth dares to make war upon it. Cotton *is* king."[171] He added, addressing Northerners directly, that Southerners "have sustained you in great measure. You are our factors [cotton brokers]. You fetch and carry for us. . . . Suppose we were to discharge you; suppose we were to take our business out of your hands;—we should consign you to anarchy and poverty."[172]

Secessionists advanced similar points in 1860 and 1861.[173] Especially notable are the arguments of South Carolina slaveholder John Townsend, the most popular pro-secession pamphleteer, whose works together sold 165,000 copies in 1860–1861. Townsend insisted on Southern economic superiority in his pamphlet, *The South Alone Should Govern the South, and African Slavery Should Be Controlled by Those Only, Who Are Friendly to It*.[174] He argued that whatever apparent prosperity the North had, it was only owing to "*plunder of the South*" through federal tariffs and taxes.[175] Most Northerners, in his view, misunderstood the true source of their wealth: "They see this copious stream of treasure flowing in upon them, year by year; they see it lavishly expended among them, and every branch of their industry abundantly remunerated; and

---

information for unwitting readers" already "isolated by war" (135, 137, 142). After emancipation and the end of the war, De Bow conceded for the first time that he believed slavery "impeded industrialization," that "his editorial vision had been clouded by Southern nationalism," and that the South was not prepared for war (Skipper, *J. D. B. De Bow*, 216; Kvach, *De Bow's Review*, 133). Persky observes that, in the late 1850s, "the self-deprecatory quality of much Southern thought receded" and was replaced by "a new perception of economic buoyancy," "increasing optimism," and "exaggerated notions of Southern power." This overconfidence in Southern economic strength was, in his words, "an important social psychological event" and a "critical proposition" in the campaign for Southern independence (*Burden of Dependency*, 87–96).

[171] James Henry Hammond, *Selections from the Letters and Speeches of the Hon. James Henry Hammond, of South Carolina* (New York: John F. Trow, 1866), 316–317, emphasis in original.

[172] Hammond, *Selections from the Letters and Speeches of the Hon. James Henry Hammond*, 321.

[173] Hammond himself was hesitant to endorse secession in South Carolina, fearing that the state would act alone. See Freehling, *Road to Disunion*, 2:404–405, 415–418.

[174] Freehling, *Road to Disunion*, 2:391, 394; Merritt, *Masterless Men*, 298.

[175] [Townsend], *The South Alone*, 16, emphasis in original.

82   WHEN DEMOCRACY BREAKS

they innocently suppose that it springs up out of the soil, as it were, of their own section; and that they are indebted to no other people, but *themselves*, for their prosperity."[176] Northerners would discover the truth, Townsend believed, when the South became an independent nation, and "shall bank up this stream, and *turn back upon herself*, the fertilizing current, leaving parched and dry the hitherto luxuriant fields of Northern labor." Townsend predicted that with Southern independence, a "scramble for *profits*" would ensue between New England and the other Northern states. The intense competition, he thought, would lead the North to split into separate, small confederacies, presumably all vying for Southern favor.[177]

Townsend also dismissed the concern that Britain would pose a problem for an independent South, despite Britain having a reputation for "deadly hostility to *slavery* everywhere." Britain had emancipated the enslaved people in its Caribbean colonies in 1835 and had a large, well-established antislavery movement, which had helped inspire, and was closely allied with, the American abolitionist movement. Nevertheless, Townsend quoted from conservative, proslavery British writers to argue, first, that Britons now thought their emancipation policy had been "a great *political blunder*" and, second, that Britons recognized the "*Cotton States*" exerted an "immense influence" on their economy. Southerners, Townsend concluded, "may confidently expect no hostile intermeddling with our Institution from any of the great powers of christendom; but on the contrary, if they did not extend to it an active support and protection, seeing that their own prosperity so much depends upon it, that they would at least regard it with the kindness of friendly neighbors."[178]

Southern opponents of secession operated at a disadvantage in trying to refute these arguments because the fundamental assumption behind them, about the strength of the slave economy, could not always be openly disputed. Among those who tried nonetheless was Sam Houston, who had been a president of the independent Republic of Texas before it became a state, in 1845, and who was serving as governor of Texas during the crisis of 1860–1861. Although a slaveholder and proslavery, he strongly opposed disunion. He argued, first, that "peaceful secession" was a delusion, and that any move for Southern independence would inevitably lead to a catastrophic civil war that "will fill our fair land with untold suffering, misfortune and disaster."[179] He also ridiculed those who "gravely talk

---

[176] [Townsend], *The South Alone*, 17, emphasis in original.
[177] [Townsend], *The South Alone*, 17, emphasis in original.
[178] [Townsend], *The South Alone*, 19–20, 57, 55, 58, emphases original. On the British antislavery movement, see Adam Hochschild, *Bury the Chains: Prophets and Rebels in the Fight to Free an Empire's Slaves* (New York: Houghton Mifflin, 2005). On connections between British and American abolitionists, see Sinha, *The Slave's Cause*, 97–105.
[179] Sam Houston, *The Writings of Sam Houston, 1813–1863*, ed. Amelia W. Williams and Eugene C. Barker, 8 vols. (Austin: University of Texas Press, 1938–1943), 8:148, 298–299. On Houston's life,

THE U.S. SECESSION CRISIS   83

of holding treaties with Great Britain and other foreign powers."[180] Here, he may have been drawing at least in part on his own experience negotiating with Britain as president of Texas.[181] Whether he was or not, he could hardly believe what his fellow Southerners were suggesting: "Treaties with Great Britain! Alliance with foreign powers! Have these men forgotten history? Look at Spanish America! Look at every petty State, which by alliance with Great Britain is subject to continual aggression! . . . Is it reasonable to suppose that England, after starting this Abolition movement and fostering it, will form an alliance with the South to sustain slavery? No; but the stipulation to their recognition will be, *the abolition of slavery!*"[182] Houston's warnings, however, went unheeded, in Texas and in much of the South.

The experience of the South in the Civil War revealed how wrongheaded many of the leading secessionists' expectations had been. The North did not hesitate to go to war to suppress what it viewed as a "rebellion," and Southerners soon learned the limits of what came to be called "King Cotton Diplomacy."[183] In 1861, the South embargoed cotton exports with the goal of forcing Britain to intervene diplomatically or even militarily on its behalf. Faith in this strategy of economic coercion was so widespread that the Confederate government did not even have to enforce it; cotton exports were stopped instead, and very effectively, by the united action of state legislatures and vigilance committees, coupled with the almost unanimous support of the Southern press.[184] Yet Confederate leaders discovered that the South needed Britain more than Britain needed the South. Unable to buy cotton from America, British textile manufacturers soon switched suppliers, importing cotton from Egypt and India instead.[185] Moreover, British public opinion, outside of certain circles, was far more hostile to slavery than secessionists had led themselves to believe. Once Lincoln signed the Emancipation Proclamation, in 1863, and the war became clearly one of slavery versus antislavery, it became almost impossible politically for the

see Randolph B. Campbell, *Sam Houston and the American Southwest*, 3rd ed., Library of American Biography (New York: Pearson Longman, 2007).

[180] Houston, *Writings*, 8:148.

[181] As president of Texas, Houston had championed annexation to the United States. Many U.S. political leaders were reluctant to act, however, so he had sought to alarm them with the possibility that Texas might ally with antislavery Britain. As he explained years later in a speech, "I admit that I have recommended that treaties of reciprocity be made with England, squinting even to the future extinction of slavery in Texas. When at the same time my only object was to turn public opinion in the United States in favor of annexation" (Houston, *Writings*, 6:12).

[182] Houston, *Writings*, 8:148–149.

[183] A classic account is Frank Lawrence Owsley, *King Cotton Diplomacy: Foreign Relations of the Confederate States of America*, 2nd ed. (1931; Chicago: University of Chicago Press, 1959).

[184] Owsley, *King Cotton Diplomacy*, 23–42; see also Charles M. Hubbard, *The Burden of Confederate Diplomacy* (Knoxville: University of Tennessee Press, 1998), 26.

[185] Beckert, *Empire of Cotton*, 242–273.

84   WHEN DEMOCRACY BREAKS

British government to intervene on behalf of the South.[186] By 1865, as Southern defeat seemed increasingly inevitable, the Confederate government finally did as Houston predicted it would have to do and offered emancipation in exchange for diplomatic recognition. The offer, however, came far too late and was refused.[187]

Finally, despite all the bold claims of Northern economic weakness and Southern economic strength, the Union economy grew during the war. The Confederate economy, by contrast, suffered severely, plagued by chronic shortages and hyperinflation.[188]

Exaggerated Fears of "Black Republican" Rule?

After Lincoln's election victory, on November 6, 1860, secessionists insisted that a Republican administration posed such a threat to the South that slaveholding states must leave the Union before Lincoln took office as president, on March 4, 1861. This view prevailed in the seven states of the Lower South—South Carolina, Mississippi, Florida, Alabama, Georgia, Louisiana, and Texas—all of which declared secession between December and February. The Confederate States of America was established in February 1861, and over subsequent months four more states joined the Confederacy: Virginia, Arkansas, North Carolina, and Tennessee.[189]

To be sure, Lincoln's victory reinforced what many Southerners had long feared: that their political power was waning. Northern lawmakers had held a majority in the House of Representatives since the start of the republic, and that dominance had only increased as Northern population growth outstripped that of the South.[190] In the U.S. Senate, free and slaveholding states had been equally represented at the start of 1850, but the balance shifted to the free states that year with the admission of California to the Union. Over the ensuing decade, the free-state advantage in the Senate increased to three (with the admission of Minnesota and Oregon), while an intense Southern push to make Kansas a slaveholding state failed. If the Republicans' program to halt the expansion of

---

[186] See Doyle, *Cause of All Nations*, 240–256.

[187] Doyle, *Cause of All Nations*, 275–279.

[188] On deliberate hyperinflation as a Southern financial policy, see Michael Brem Bonner, *Confederate Political Economy: Creating and Managing a Southern Corporatist Nation* (Baton Rouge: Louisiana State University Press, 2016), 190–191. Bonner compares Confederate monetary policy to that of Weimar Germany (232n15).

[189] According to the Confederate government, Missouri and Kentucky also joined the Confederacy. They were represented in the Confederate Congress, and there are thirteen stars on the Confederate battle flag. Yet because Confederates in these states never achieved political control, historians generally do not consider Missouri and Kentucky to have been Confederate states.

[190] John P. McIver, "Apportionment of the House of Representatives: 1787–2000," Table Eb1-56, in Carter et al., *Historical Statistics of the United States*.

THE U.S. SECESSION CRISIS   85

slavery were enacted and enforced, there would be no additional slaveholding states, and the free-state majority in the Senate would only continue to grow. Finally, Southerners had dominated the Executive Branch until 1850, with eight of the first twelve presidents being Southern slaveholders (and the four non-slaveholding presidents all having slaveholding vice presidents), but Lincoln's election in 1860 (following those of Franklin Pierce in 1852 and James Buchanan in 1856, both non-slaveholders from Northern states) seemed to confirm that Northerners now controlled the presidency as well.[191]

Nonetheless, the secession movement struck at least some Southern leaders as politically unnecessary. Houston, for example, urged Southerners to continue advancing their interests through the existing political process, like countless Americans before them whose candidate or party had not prevailed in an election. Southerners were certainly not without conventional political resources after Lincoln's victory. Although Lincoln had won a majority of the popular vote in the North, he had won only a plurality of the national vote—just 39.8%, the lowest of any presidential candidate before (or since) to win an Electoral College majority.[192] The public could therefore plausibly be rallied against the Republican agenda. As Alexander Stephens of Georgia pointed out, in opposing the secession of his state, "Mr. Lincoln has been elected . . . by a minority of the people of the United States. . . . [A] majority of the constitutional conservative voters of the country were against him. . . . Therefore let us not be hasty and rash in our action."[193]

Houston agreed that there was no need for a Southern "revolution," observing further that the "checks and guarantees" of the Constitution—meaning, both

[191] See n.17 above. The four slaveholding vice presidents of non-slaveholding presidents before 1850 were Thomas Jefferson (Virginia, 1797–1801); John C. Calhoun (South Carolina, 1825–1829); Richard M. Johnson (Kentucky, 1837–1841); and John Tyler (Virginia, 1841). Note that Presidents Pierce and Buchanan had slaveholding vice presidents as well: respectively, William R. King (Alabama, 1853) and John C. Breckinridge (Kentucky, 1857–1861). The only other non-slaveholding president before 1860, Millard Fillmore, was himself a vice president who attained office on the death of a president (Zachary Taylor) and so had no vice president. Lincoln was therefore the first non-slaveholding president with a non-slaveholding vice president, Hannibal Hamlin (Maine). On the Southern domination of the federal government in the antebellum period, beyond the presidency and vice presidency, see Leonard L. Richards, *The Slave Power: The Free North and Southern Domination, 1780–1860* (Baton Rouge: Louisiana State University Press, 2000), 9; Matthew Karp, *This Vast Southern Empire: Slaveholders at the Helm of American Foreign Policy* (Cambridge, MA: Harvard University Press, 2016), 4, 226–227.

[192] *Guide to U.S. Elections*, 764, says 39.9%, but the correct figure (based on the underlying vote counts) is 39.8%. The only winning presidential candidate to get a lower popular vote percentage was John Quincy Adams in 1824, with 30.9%, and his was a special case. Adams had placed behind Andrew Jackson in both the popular and Electoral vote, but as no candidate had won an Electoral College majority, the presidential election was thrown to the U.S. House of Representatives, following the procedure of the Twelfth Amendment, which chose Adams.

[193] Freehling and Simpson, *Secession Debated*, 54–55. Later, after Georgia declared secession despite Stephens's objections, he would decide to support the Confederacy and agree to become the Confederate vice president.

86   WHEN DEMOCRACY BREAKS

Congress and the Supreme Court—were "in our favor."[194] Although Republicans had won the presidency in November 1860, they had not secured majorities in the House and Senate for the 37th Congress, originally scheduled to convene in December 1861.[195] The precise balance of power that would have existed in the absence of secession cannot be known because some congressional elections in the South were not scheduled to take place until late 1861 and thus were preempted by secession. Immediately after Lincoln's victory, however, during the first weeks of the Southern secession debate, advocates on both sides noted that Republicans would not fully control the upcoming Congress.[196] The Unionist Houston made this point; so did the secessionist Howell Cobb of Georgia, who reluctantly conceded that there would be a "majority in the two Houses of Congress" against Lincoln (although he insisted it would be "an uncertain and at best trembling" one).[197] Alexander Stephens, himself a longtime congressman and careful political observer, calculated that a majority of thirty would be against Lincoln in the House and a majority of four against him in the Senate. "The President of the United States is no emperor, no dictator," Stephens pointed out. "He can do nothing unless he is backed by power in Congress." With Congress against him, Stephens concluded, Lincoln would be "powerless."[198] As for the Supreme Court, seven of the nine justices sitting on the Court in 1860–1861 had endorsed the *Dred Scott* ruling of 1857, which found the Republican program of banning slavery in the territories to be unconstitutional.[199] Any of Lincoln's antislavery acts might therefore be subjected to successful legal challenge.

Southerners might also have taken comfort from Republicans' repeated statements, including from Lincoln himself, that although they opposed the spread of slavery, they would not "interfere" with it in the states where it already existed. In Lincoln's First Inaugural Address, in March 1861, he took care

[194] Houston, *Writings*, 8:194–195.

[195] Although the 37th Congress was originally scheduled to convene in December 1861, it in fact convened beginning on July 4, 1861. See https://history.house.gov/Institution/Session-Dates/30-39/ and https://www.senate.gov/artandhistory/history/resources/pdf/ExtraSessions.pdf.

[196] Contemporary analysis accords with this view. Most of the Northern states had held their congressional elections before secession, and the seats Republicans had secured so far (108 in the House and 31 in the Senate) were fewer than half of the full 238 and 68 seats in those chambers. Once the secessionists vacated their seats, the House and Senate shrank to 183 and 50 seats, respectively, affording Republicans a majority in the "Civil War" Congress. Kenneth C. Martis, *The Historical Atlas of Political Parties in the United States Congress, 1789–1989* (New York: Macmillan, 1989), 35–36.

[197] Martis, *The Historical Atlas of Political Parties*, 8:194; Howell Cobb, "Letter . . . to the People of Georgia" (1860), in *Southern Pamphlets on Secession, November 1860–April 1861*, ed. Jon L. Wakelyn (Chapel Hill: University of North Carolina Press, 1996), 97.

[198] Freehling and Simpson, *Secession Debated*, 56–57.

[199] Not only were all seven of the justices who made the *Dred Scott* ruling still on the Court in 1860–1861, but one of the dissenters from that case had been replaced by a justice understood to have Southern sympathies. Only one justice from this period, John McClean, was known to be sympathetic to the Republicans. See *Dred Scott v. Sandford* 60 U.S. 393 (1857), https://www.supremecourt.gov/about/members.aspx.

THE U.S. SECESSION CRISIS   87

once again to reassure Southerners: "I have no purpose, directly or indirectly to interfere with the institution of slavery in the States where it exists." He even announced that he had "no objection" to a proposed constitutional amendment that would have barred any subsequent amendment authorizing Congress "to abolish or interfere" with slavery "within any State."[200]

By this point, however, the Southern drive to defend not only slavery but a particular vision of slavery had gone so far, requiring severe erosion of basic democratic protections and even the suppression of the Republican Party itself as seditious, that it seemed virtually impossible that enough Southern leaders and voters would tolerate a "Black Republican" president, no matter what assurances were provided. Under these circumstances, the logic of secession appeared all but inevitable, particularly across the Lower South.

The Undemocratic Secession Process

Yet even against this backdrop, secessionists apparently felt the need to cut corners. Not only did secession in many ways represent a culmination of years of democratic erosion in the South—and also a literal manifestation of democratic breakdown, involving as it did the rejection of a lawful electoral outcome—but it also exemplified a profound corruption of democratic norms and process in the very way it was achieved.

Nominally, at least, secession was cast as a democratic project. In ten of the eleven seceded states, "supralegislative" conventions had been called, understood to represent the people acting in their "sovereign capacity."[201] Delegates to these conventions, chosen by special election, proceeded to debate and vote on whether to pass an "ordinance" of secession. Five states added popular referenda to the process: three referenda on whether to hold the convention at all, and three on whether to ratify secession.[202] By all appearances, states that declared

---

[200] Lincoln, "First Inaugural Address—Final Text," in *Collected Works*, 4:263, 270. The text of the proposed amendment can be found at https://www.usconstitution.net/constamfail.html.

[201] We borrow the term "supralegislative" to describe these conventions from Drew Gilpin Faust, *The Creation of Confederate Nationalism: Ideology and Identity in the Civil War South* (Baton Rouge: Louisiana State University Press, 1988), 34. For convention elections in ten of the eleven seceded states, see Ralph A. Wooster, *The Secession Conventions of the South* (Princeton: Princeton University Press, 1962), 14, 26, 51, 68, 82, 103, 141, 156, 179, 192. In Texas, the convention elections were not called by the legislature, but by a group of secessionists in the "Austin Call," as we discuss below.

[202] In February 1861, referenda on whether to call a secession convention were held in Arkansas, North Carolina, and Tennessee; a convention was approved in Arkansas and rejected in the latter two states (Wooster, *Secession Conventions*, 156–157, 179–180, 192–193). Once the Civil War began, the North Carolina legislature called a convention in spite of the earlier referendum result, and delegates, chosen by popular vote, approved secession (195, 203). The Tennessee legislature ultimately approved an ordinance of secession without holding a convention and submitted the secession ordinance for

88 WHEN DEMOCRACY BREAKS

secession acted with overwhelming popular approval. The convention votes for
the various state secession ordinances were lopsided, and in the three ratification
referenda, in Texas, Virginia, and Tennessee, voters approved secession by large
majorities.[203]

These procedures drew on various democratic precedents. Over the years,
some Southern states had called special conventions to determine and declare
the position of their "sovereign peoples" on notable issues of state-federal relations.[204] More generally, seceding states self-consciously followed the process
used to ratify the U.S. Constitution. In both 1787–1788 and 1860–1861, a series
of popularly elected state conventions did the work. The latter conventions, of
course, had a very different purpose: "deratification."[205] Of the eleven effective
"ordinances" of secession, seven were explicitly framed in terms of repealing ratification of the Constitution.[206] After deratifying the U.S. Constitution, the secession conventions proceeded to ratify the Constitution of the Confederacy.[207]
Finally, the secession conventions followed the example of prior state constitutional conventions.[208] Several of them, in fact, debated and proposed
amendments to their state constitutions.[209] Southerners could draw on abun-
dant experience here. Between 1790 and 1851, the Southern states held at least
twenty-two state constitutional conventions.[210] At least nine of these, including

popular approval (182). In all, ordinances of secession were submitted for approval by referendum in
Texas (in February), Virginia (in May), and Tennessee (in June) (132–133, 149, 188).

[203] For the convention vote results, see Wooster, *Secession Conventions*, 22, 37, 59, 74, 91, 111, 130,
149, 165, 182, 202–203. Missouri, which although claimed by the Confederacy was never really part
of it, held a convention that rejected secession 89–1 (232).

[204] One such convention produced the influential "Georgia Platform," endorsing the compromise
of 1850. See *Journal of the State Convention, Held in Milledgeville in December 1850* (Milledgeville,
GA: R. M. Orme, 1850).

[205] A comparison between the secession movement and the ratification of the Constitution, with
the argument that the two processes were analogous, appears in Mark Neely Jr., *Lincoln and the
Triumph of the Nation: Constitutional Conflict in the American Civil War* (Chapel Hill: University of
North Carolina Press, 2011), 241–248.

[206] The other four secession ordinances declared the state had withdrawn from the Union or that
its ratification of the Constitution was annulled. Note that the Confederate government recognized
thirteen secession ordinances; those of Kentucky and Missouri, however, were made by minority
governments that never controlled their states. The eleven effective secession ordinances are collected in Albert Bushnell Hart and Edward Channing, eds., *American History Leaflets, Colonial and
Constitutional, No. 12: Ordinances of Secession and Other Documents, 1860–1861* (New York: A.
Lovell, 1893).

[207] William C. Davis, *Look Away! A History of the Confederate States of America* (New York: Free
Press, 2002), 107–111.

[208] The Texas secessionist Oran Milo Roberts drew the analogy between the secession conventions
and state constitutional conventions in his *Speech . . . upon the "Impending Crisis"* ([Austin]: n.p.,
1860), 3, which became an immense best-seller (see Freehling, *Road to Disunion*, 2:451).

[209] Faust, *Creation of Confederate Nationalism*, 34, notes this, as does Neely, *Lincoln and the
Triumph of the Nation*, 263–264.

[210] Conventions that produced new or completely revised state constitutions were held in the following places and years: Alabama, 1819; Arkansas, 1836; Delaware, 1792, 1831; Florida, 1838 (for the
territory of Florida); Georgia, 1798; Kentucky, 1799, 1850; Louisiana, 1812, 1845, 1852; Maryland,

THE U.S. SECESSION CRISIS 89

the Texas constitutional convention of 1845 and the Virginia conventions of 1830 and 1850, had submitted their work to the voters for ratification, just as the 1861 conventions of Texas and Virginia submitted their ordinances of secession for popular approval.[211]

The secession process was therefore, in form, democratic. Voters participated either in the election of delegates to the secession conventions or in secession referenda, or both. Yet the process was in fact no more "free and fair" than the presidential elections of 1856 and 1860 had been in most Southern states. Based on various "ballot tests" of the time, one historian estimates that in the weeks following Lincoln's victory, most white Southerners, possibly over 70%, opposed immediate secession. Some considered secession to be treason, or at least reckless and foolish. But even many of those who were open to the possibility of secession thought it could be justified only in response to some "overt act" by the new Republican administration, or only after the complete breakdown of negotiations with the North, or only if all Southern states could agree to secede at the same time.[212] At first, those demanding immediate secession seem to

1851; Mississippi, 1817, 1832; Missouri, 1820; South Carolina, 1790; Tennessee, 1796, 1834; Texas, 1836 (for the independent Republic of Texas), 1845; Virginia, 1830, 1850. See Poore, *Federal and State Constitutions*, 1:32, 101, 278n, 289n, 317, 388n, 657, 668, 700, 711n, 725n, 837n; 2:1054n, 1067n, 1104n, 1628, 1667n, 1677n, 1754n, 1767n, 1912n, 1919n.

[211] The Texas Constitution of 1845 provides for its popular ratification in Art. XIII, Sec. 5; the Virginia Constitution of 1830 does so in its Preamble, and of 1850 does so under the heading Schedule, Sections 2 and 3. The others were the Florida Constitution of 1838 (Art. XVII, Sec. 5); the Louisiana Constitutions of 1845 (Title X, Arts. 150–152) and 1852 (Title XI, Arts. 150–152); the Mississippi Constitutions of 1817 and 1832 (see Poore, *Federal and State Constitutions*, 2:1054n, 1067n); the Tennessee Constitution of 1834 (see Poore, *Federal and State Constitutions*, 2:1677n, 1689–1690). For popular ratification of the Ordinances, see "1861, Feb. 1, Texas' Ordinance of Secession, Sec. 2" (Hart and Channing, *No. 12: Ordinances*, 15); "1861, April 17, Virginia's Ordinance of Secession," penultimate paragraph (18).

[212] The 70% estimate and the reference to "ballot tests" come from Freehling, *Road to Disunion*, 2:345. Freehling does not identify these tests, but we would include the November 1860 presidential election and state votes concerning secession conventions in February 1861. The presidential election is not an exact test, because there was only a general, not strict, correlation between support for certain candidates and support for secession or Unionism. Although all four candidates declared themselves Unionists, the Southern Democrat, John C. Breckinridge of Kentucky, was a champion of "Southern Rights" and had the conspicuous support of leading advocates of secession, such as John Townsend (although he also had the support of some committed Unionists). In the South, the contest was primarily between Breckinridge and the Constitutional Unionist candidate, John Bell of Tennessee, a champion of sectional compromise favored by most Southern opponents of secession. Besides Breckinridge and Bell, Southerners could vote for the Northern Democrat Stephen A. Douglas of Illinois, who competed in every Southern state and declared during the campaign that secession would be treason, and Lincoln, who competed in parts of five Upper South states. Bell and Douglas, generally seen as the principal anti-secessionist options, together received 53% of the total Southern vote, carried majorities in seven of the fifteen slaveholding states (Georgia, Kentucky, Louisiana, Maryland, Missouri, Tennessee, and Virginia), and fell just shy of half the vote in two others (Arkansas and North Carolina). Adding Lincoln's constrained Southern vote share of 2% (entirely from the Upper South) brings the overall vote in the South for candidates who opposed secession (Bell, Douglas, and Lincoln) to 55%. In the eight Upper South states, where almost two-thirds of white Southerners lived, Bell, Douglas, and Lincoln together received just over 60% of the vote.

90   WHEN DEMOCRACY BREAKS

have had majority support of the public and political leaders in only three Lower South states—South Carolina, Mississippi, and Florida—and even in these, there appears to have been significant resistance.[213] Nonetheless, the "immediatist" minority was able to seize control of the process in all seven Lower South states, which all declared secession in the winter of 1860–1861. Although the secessionist movement initially stalled in the eight Upper South states, the secession of the Lower South (and the Confederate firing on Fort Sumter on April 12) set the terms of political debate there, and four Upper South states eventually seceded in the spring of 1861.[214]

On the 1860 contest between Breckinridge, Bell, and Douglas, especially in the South, see Michael F. Holt, *The Election of 1860: "A Campaign Fraught with Consequences"* (Lawrence: University Press of Kansas, 2017), 141–152; for Douglas's declaration that secession would be treason, see 151; for population data, see Ransom, "Population of the Slave States"; for the election results, see *Guide to U.S. Elections*, 764. In February 1861, more direct electoral tests of secession occurred in the Upper South, where voters in five states cast ballots related to secession conventions. Three states held referenda on whether to hold secession conventions, along with elections for delegates to the conventions if they were held. In Tennessee (February 9), the convention was voted down 69,675–57,798, and anti-secessionist candidates won by a total of 91,803–24,749; in North Carolina (February 28), the convention was defeated 47,323–46,672, while anti-secessionist candidates won 78 of the 120 delegates and carried 52 of 82 counties. In Arkansas (February 18), voters approved the convention, but anti-secessionists won the delegate elections with 23,626 total votes to the secessionists' 17,927. In two other states, Virginia and Missouri, the state legislatures passed bills calling for a convention, and voters then elected the convention delegates; in Virginia (February 4), anti-secessionists captured between 106 and 120 of 152 seats, and in Missouri (February 18), delegates opposed to secession won by a total vote of 110,000 to 30,000. See Wooster, *Secession Conventions*, 179–180, 192–193, 156–157, 141–142, 225–226. In January, meanwhile, in Georgia, the most populous state in the Lower South, opponents of secession apparently won more votes than secessionists in delegate elections to the secession convention (see the main text).

[213] Freehling, *Road to Disunion*, 2:345; Stephanie McCurry, *Confederate Reckoning: Power and Politics in the Civil War South* (Cambridge, MA: Harvard University Press, 2010), 53–54.

[214] Four of the fifteen slaveholding states—Delaware, Maryland, Kentucky, and Missouri—sided with the Union in the Civil War. In addition, northwestern Virginia refused to join the rest of Virginia in declaring secession in 1861, and it ultimately entered the Union as the State of West Virginia in 1863. The usual factors historians highlight to explain the loyalty of these northernmost slaveholding states, called the Border South, are that they had close social and economic ties to the North; their economies and societies were less tied to slavery than elsewhere in the South; there was a regional political tradition of favoring sectional compromise; and they did not want to become Civil War battlegrounds. See William C. Harris, *Lincoln and the Border States: Preserving the Union* (Lawrence: University Press of Kansas, 2011), 2. We would add that while the Border South saw significant democratic erosion before the Civil War, this erosion appears to have been less severe than in the rest of the South. Three of the four border states that existed in 1860 had enacted one or more incendiary speech laws by this time: Missouri (1837, 1845, and 1855), Maryland (1842), and Kentucky (1860). Yet unlike in much of the rest of the South, the legal suppression of antislavery speech was not as strongly reinforced by extralegal terror. Across most of the South, the chronic threat of lethal violence against anyone even rumored to harbor abolitionist or "Black Republican" sympathies "encouraged silence, caution, and fear about broaching anything but unqualified praise of slavery." David Grimsted, *American Mobbing, 1828–1861* (New York: Oxford University Press, 1998), 123. By contrast, in the border region, although it had its own history of mobbing, criticism of slavery was to an extent tolerated. Many Kentuckians, for example, followed Henry Clay's lead in conceding that slavery was a "necessary evil," years after proslavery ("positive good") ideology became ascendant in other slaveholding states, especially across the Lower South (see Tallant, *Evil Necessity*, 1–7). Perhaps partly as a result, two notable white critics of slavery were able to have long careers in Kentucky: the newspaper editor and politician Cassius Marcellus Clay, who like Hinton Helper denounced slavery

THE U.S. SECESSION CRISIS   91

Secessionists triumphed in 1860–1861 in no small part because, just as they rejected the political legitimacy of the "Black Republicans," so they rejected that of their Southern opponents. They saw anti-secessionists as "submissionists," whose cowardly willingness to submit to Republican rule posed a dire threat to slavery. As a result, secessionists felt justified in subverting and manipulating the democratic process to override their critics. The secessionist John Townsend, in another of his best-selling pamphlets, *The Doom of Slavery in the Union: Its Safety Out of It*, forcefully expressed the secessionists' attitude:

> In this great turning point in the destiny of the South no man can remain neutral. . . . He who is not for her, in this hour of her extremity, is, without being conscious of it perhaps, against her, to the last end of her existence. Knowing, as he ought to know, the extreme dangers which are about to fall upon his country, THE 'UNIONIST' OF THE SOUTH IN 1860, IS THE 'SUBMISSIONIST,' NOW, AND WILL

as an economic disaster for white people (leading Helper to dedicate the *Compendium* to him) and who helped to organize the Kentucky Republican Party, and the abolitionist clergyman John G. Fee, who tried in the 1850s to establish a racially integrated school and college in Berea (which would eventually open as Berea College). Life for neither man was easy—both faced not only opposition but hostility and violent threats—but in the Lower South, they almost certainly would have been driven out sooner (as Fee ultimately was) or even killed. Clay's and Fee's careers are described in Freehling, *Road to Disunion*, 1:462–474; 2:222–245; see also Tallant, *Evil Necessity*, 116–128, 165–219; Grimsted, *American Mobbing*, 128–134. For Helper's dedication of his *Compendium* to Clay, see Helper, *Compendium of the Impending Crisis*, ii. Also, efforts to suppress the Republican Party along the border, unlike in the rest of the South, did not fully succeed: Republicans found a toehold there, and Lincoln won votes (not many, but also not zero) in all four border states that existed in 1860. Almost three-quarters of the popular votes that Lincoln received in Virginia (the only other slaveholding state where he received popular votes) were cast in the northwestern part of the state that would become West Virginia. On breakdowns of the 1860 vote in Virginia by county, see "The 1860 Presidential Vote in Virginia," accessed Nov. 28, 2023, https://archive.wvculture.org/hiStory/statehood/1860presidentialvote.html. To be sure, there was significant support for secession along the border—an estimated ninety thousand Confederate soldiers came from there, and Kentucky and Missouri even had minority secessionist governments, recognized by the CSA—yet support for the Union and "neutrality" was also strong, and secessionists never gained political control. For the estimate of Confederate soldiers enlisting from the Border South, see William W. Freehling, *The South vs. The South: How Anti-Confederate Southerners Shaped the Course of the Civil War* (New York: Oxford University Press, 2001), 61. There appears to be a correlation, therefore, between less severe democratic erosion on the one hand, and less expansive support for secession on the other, both of which were evident in the Border South as compared to the rest of the South. It is also true, however, that a lower share of the population was enslaved in the Border South as compared to the rest of the South (approximately 13% versus 40%), and this could potentially help to explain *both* lower degrees of democratic erosion *and* lower support for secession there. On shares of population enslaved, see Haines, "State Populations"; Susan B. Carter, "Black Population, by State and Slave/Free Status: 1790–1860," Series Bb1-98, in Carter et al., *Historical Statistics of the United States*; James Morton Callahan, *Semi-Centennial History of West Virginia* ([Charleston, W.V.]: Semi-Centennial Commission of West Virginia, 1913), 56. Complicating the analysis still further is the fact that the federal government intervened forcefully to ensure the border states stayed in the Union; President Lincoln suspended habeas corpus in many areas, for example, allowing the army to arrest suspected Confederate sympathizers without trial. The loyalty of the border to the Union, in other words, was not entirely a free choice. Still, it is notable that the Border South seems to have experienced less democratic erosion during the antebellum years and, ultimately, significantly less support for secession as compared to the rest of the South.

92 WHEN DEMOCRACY BREAKS

EVER BE, HENCEFORTH, AND FOREVER; AND WILL BE AN ABOLITIONIST OF THE
NORTH IN 1870![215]

Townsend's South Carolina was the first state to declare secession, on December 20, 1860. Preceding this outcome had been the October elections for the state legislature, which would call the secession convention. Secessionism seems to have been popular with South Carolina voters, and secessionists may well have won this election without manipulation. Yet they took no chances. One recent historian has aptly described the secessionists' election campaign as "paramilitary," largely run by vigilance committees and militia companies, who actively and sometimes violently suppressed dissent.[216] One South Carolinian later recalled that anyone "with a public reputation for unionism . . . would not have been allowed to live here."[217] In as many as half of all districts in the October elections, secessionists made sure that only one slate of candidates was running, pledged to vote for immediate secession if Lincoln won the presidency.[218] One well-known Unionist was threatened with hanging if he stood for election.[219] A Unionist farmer in Beaufort, where the declared candidates were all secessionists, later reported that "feeling ran so high" during the campaign that he did not even dare to "abstain from voting" and so cast a blank ballot.[220] Predictably, this election produced a legislature that one contemporary described as "tremendously out and out secession."[221] When it held an initial vote on whether to call a secession convention, only fourteen members were opposed, and they were quickly persuaded or pressured to change their position. The final vote was 117–0.[222] When the elections for convention delegates took place on December 6, secessionists controlled them even more tightly than they had the legislative contest; almost all of the candidates were publicly pledged to take South Carolina immediately out of the Union.[223] At the convention, delegates endorsed secession by a vote of 169–0.[224]

In no other Lower South state did secessionists achieve a unanimous convention vote, but in all of them advocates employed repressive tactics like those applied in South Carolina. In the various state elections for secession convention delegates, which for the Lower South (apart from South Carolina) all took place in January 1861, voter turnout was dramatically lower, by 20% or more, compared to

---

[215] [Townsend], *The Doom of Slavery*, 26–27, emphasis in original.
[216] McCurry, *Confederate Reckoning*, 47.
[217] McCurry, *Confederate Reckoning*, 49.
[218] McCurry, *Confederate Reckoning*, 50–51.
[219] Sinha, Counterrevolution of Slavery, 202, 235.
[220] McCurry, *Confederate Reckoning*, 49.
[221] McCurry, *Confederate Reckoning*, 51.
[222] McCurry, *Confederate Reckoning*, 52.
[223] McCurry, *Confederate Reckoning*, 51.
[224] Wooster, *Secession Conventions*, 22.

THE U.S. SECESSION CRISIS   93

the presidential election in November, and the low turnout seems to have helped secessionists. As one historian has noted, the "fewer people voting, the better secession did."[225] The low turnout may have partly resulted from the collapse of regular party competition during the secession crisis (a collapse with lasting effect: there would be no organized political parties in the Confederacy).[226] Yet the low turnout also apparently stemmed from intimidation of opponents of immediate secession, everywhere attacked as "submissionists" and "traitors," and from manipulation of the voting process. When a Unionist voter in Mississippi sought a Unionist ticket, for example, he was informed that "none had been printed, and that it would be advisable to vote a secession ticket."[227]

Another tactic used by secessionists was to seize federal property in the South, even before secession conventions had the chance to act, creating the perception that secession was a fait accompli. Several pro-secession governors, for example, ordered state militia to seize U.S. forts and arsenals (which was possible because most of them, at the time, were lightly defended).[228] In Louisiana, the secessionist governor issued such an order just days before the election of delegates to the secession convention.[229] In Alabama, Florida, and Georgia, secessionist governors each ordered the seizure of federal installations before (in the case of Alabama and Florida, just before) delegates at the respective state secession conventions were to decide whether to take their states out of the Union.[230]

The actions of secessionists in Georgia and Texas show the extent to which they were willing to manipulate the democratic process—and, arguably, violate the rule of law—to achieve their desired goal. In Georgia, there was considerable opposition to immediate secession. Most of the opponents were either "conditional Unionists," who thought secession might be justified under some circumstances but that Lincoln's election in and of itself was not one of them, or

---

[225] Merritt, *Masterless Men*, 301; David Williams, *Bitterly Divided: The South's Inner Civil War* (New York: New Press, 2008), 36.

[226] A classic study on this subject is Seymour Martin Lipset, *Political Man: The Social Bases of Politics*, expanded ed. (1960; Baltimore: Johns Hopkins University Press, 1981), chapter 11 ("The Emergence of the One-Party South—the Election of 1860").

[227] Merritt, *Masterless Men*, 301.

[228] U.S. House of Representatives, *Seizure of Forts, Arsenals, Revenue Cutters, and Other Property of the United States*, Report no. 91, Feb. 28, 1861, 3, reports that fourteen federal forts, as well as other federal property, such as mints and post offices, had been seized as of that time. See also Silvana R. Siddali, "'The Sport of Folly and the Prize of Treason': Confederate Property Seizures and the Northern Home Front in the Secession Crisis," *Civil War History* 47, no. 4 (2001): 310–33. Some of the seized federal installations were unoccupied (troops were stationed on island forts only in wartime, for example, and the country was at peace), or guarded by a token force (in at least one case, by just a single soldier); some forts were seized despite the presence of a federal garrison because the commanding officer lacked orders from the War Department to resist locals with force and wished to avoid needless bloodshed, and so withdrew; some commanding officers may have turned over their forts because they sympathized with the secessionists.

[229] McCurry, *Confederate Reckoning*, 55.

[230] Freehling, *Road to Disunion*, 2:484.

94 WHEN DEMOCRACY BREAKS

"cooperationists," who thought secession was feasible only if all Southern states agreed to leave the Union together. In the election for delegates to the Georgia state convention, on January 2, opponents of immediate secession apparently won a slim majority of the popular vote. The pro-secession governor, however, refused to release the result. Instead, the day after the election, he ordered the state militia to seize Fort Pulaski, the principal U.S. Army installation in the state. When the convention met in mid-January, secessionists turned out to have secured a narrow majority of the delegates.[231] In one key test vote, they prevailed 164–133, and in a second, 166–130. At this point, many anti-secessionists appear to have given up, and an ordinance of secession was passed 208–89. Secessionists then passed a resolution requiring all those who had voted against secession to sign "a pledge of the unanimous determination of this Convention to sustain and defend the State . . . without regard to individual approval or disapproval of its adoption." Six days later, the convention voted for an ordinance defining as a traitor to Georgia anyone who "shall adhere to her enemies," in particular, "the late United States of America." The punishment for treason was death. Finally, in late April, the governor released the delegate election results from January, which showed (falsely) that secessionists had won 57% of the popular vote.[232]

Texans, owing to the "troubles" of 1860, were already operating in a climate of fear when Lincoln was elected, which seems to have worked to the advantage of secessionists. Nonetheless, Texas secessionists faced a formidable obstacle: Governor Sam Houston, who was not only a firm Unionist but also personally popular. A hero to many Texans, he had won the governorship in August 1859 with almost 57% of the vote.[233] In the weeks after Lincoln's victory, the Texas legislature could not call a secession convention because it was out of regular session; Houston, as governor, could have called a special session, but he initially refused. A group of leading secessionists therefore resorted to an extra-constitutional process. They issued a "citizen's call" for a convention, "suggesting" that the people elect delegates on January 8 for a convention to meet

---

[231] The historian Anthony Gene Cary has concluded that because "delegates were elected by counties, even a closely divided statewide vote could, and did, translate into a controlling convention majority." Anthony Gene Carey, *Parties, Slavery, and the Union in Antebellum Georgia* (Athens: University of Georgia Press, 1997), 249. At the same time, the secessionist majority appears to have been augmented by several delegates, if not more, who campaigned as opponents of secession only to change position in the days after the election, perhaps partly in response to the seizure of Fort Pulaski. See Michael P. Johnson, "A New Look at the Popular Vote for Delegates to the Georgia Secession Convention," *Georgia Historical Quarterly* 56, no. 2 (1972): 266–267. Note that Johnson does not speculate as to why these delegates changed their position.

[232] McCurry, *Confederate Reckoning*, 55–59; Freehling, *Road to Disunion*, 2:484; Johnson, "A New Look at the Popular Vote for Delegates to the Georgia Secession Convention"; *Journal of the Public and Secret Proceedings of the Convention of the People of Georgia, Held in Milledgeville and Savannah in 1861: Together with the Ordinances Adopted* (Milledgeville: Boughton, Nisbet & Barnes, 1861), 26, 45, 382.

[233] *Guide to U.S. Elections*, 1650.

THE U.S. SECESSION CRISIS   95

in Austin on January 28.[234] Houston rejected these elections as illegal. He later noted that a "majority of the people stood aloof" from them; only a third of all voters participated, and 30 of the 122 organized Texas counties held no elections at all.[235] As in Georgia, secessionists refused to release the embarrassing official returns.[236] Nonetheless, Houston now felt compelled to call a special session of the legislature, which opened on January 21.[237] He evidently hoped the legislature would counter the convention, but it disappointed him. Lawmakers passed a resolution authorizing the Austin convention to "determine what shall be the future relations of this State to the Union."[238] Houston at this point recognized the authority of the Austin convention to consider secession. It voted to secede on February 1 and then submitted the question of secession to voters for ratification, in a referendum to be held on February 23.

Over the next few weeks, even though the people of Texas had not yet voted, secessionists acted as if their approval had already been granted. On February 4, the Austin convention chose delegates to represent Texas at the Confederate constitutional convention, then about to meet in Montgomery, Alabama. On February 18, the Committee on Public Safety that the Austin convention had appointed, backed by militia, negotiated the surrender of Major General David Twiggs, commander of U.S. forces in Texas.[239] Twiggs (a Georgian who would later take a Confederate command) gave the secessionists control of all federal forts and arsenals in Texas and promised that the more than two thousand U.S. soldiers there, comprising more than a tenth of the total U.S. Army at the time, would soon evacuate the state.[240] Just five days after this secessionist coup, Texas voters approved secession, 46,166 to 14,747.[241]

---

[234] For what is also known as the "Austin Call," see *Journal of the Secession Convention of Texas 1861* ([Austin]: Austin Printing Co., 1912), 9–13. The move for the Call was led by Texas Supreme Court justice Oran Milo Roberts (who referred to it as a "citizens' call" [9n]); he had helped inspire it with a speech delivered on December 1, 1860, which became a best-selling pamphlet, *Speech . . . upon the "Impending Crisis."* For the impact of the speech, see Freehling, *Road to Disunion*, 2:451.

[235] Houston, *Writings*, 8:280; Hart et al., "Address to the People of Texas!"; Walter L. Buenger, *Secession and the Union in Texas* (Austin: University of Texas Press, 1984), 143.

[236] Houston and other Texas Unionists complained of this. See Houston, *Writings*, 8:280; Hart et al., "Address to the People of Texas!"

[237] Houston, *Writings*, 8:220–221.

[238] Freehling, *Road to Disunion*, 2:452; *Journal of the Secession Convention of Texas 1861*, 13–14.

[239] *Journal of the Secession Convention of Texas 1861*, 8; Jeanne T. Heidler, "'Embarrassing Situation': David E. Twiggs and the Surrender of United States Forces in Texas, 1861," in *Lone Star Blue and Gray: Essays on Texas and the Civil War*, 2nd ed., ed. Ralph Wooster and Robert Wooster (1995; Denton: Texas State Historical Association, 2015), 65–80.

[240] On the size of federal forces in Texas, see J. J. Bowden, *The Exodus of Federal Forces from Texas, 1861* (Austin: Eakin Press, 1986), 3; on the size of the U.S. Army in March 1861, see Howard C. Westwood, "President Lincoln's Overture to Sam Houston," *Southwestern Historical Quarterly* 88, no. 2 (1984): 144.

[241] Joe T. Timmons, "The Referendum in Texas on the Ordinance of Secession, February 23, 1861: The Vote," *East Texas Historical Journal* 11, no. 2 (1973): 15–16.

96 WHEN DEMOCRACY BREAKS

A few weeks later, the Austin convention voted to require that all state officials take an oath to support the Confederate Constitution or be removed from office. On March 16, Governor Houston refused to take the oath, and the convention declared that he was no longer governor.[242] He issued a statement charging the convention with "usurpation": "I PROTEST IN THE NAME OF THE PEOPLE OF TEXAS AGAINST ALL THE ACTS AND DOINGS OF THIS CONVENTION, AND I DECLARE THEM NULL AND VOID!"[243] But he protested in vain, and was replaced as governor by the pro-secession lieutenant governor, Edward Clark.

Notably, Texas was the only state of the Lower South to have authorized a referendum on secession. Although in South Carolina and Georgia the question of calling a referendum was never officially raised, in Mississippi, Florida, Louisiana, and Alabama opponents of immediate secession did propose that the question of secession be submitted to the voters. These proposals were consistent with the constitutions of at least three and possibly all four of these states: the Mississippi, Florida, and Louisiana constitutions had each been ratified by referendum, and the constitutions of Mississippi, Alabama, and Louisiana specifically required that any constitutional amendment had to be ratified by referendum. Nonetheless, secessionists overrode these constitutional traditions and rules, refusing to submit the question of secession or any constitutional change resulting from it to a popular vote and successfully blocking all attempts to do so.[244]

In Virginia in May 1861, and Tennessee in June, referenda on secession were held, and in both cases voters approved secession by landslide margins—in Virginia, 125,950 to 20,373, and in Tennessee, 104,913 to 47,238.[245] Importantly, however, the Civil War was already underway by this point. South Carolina forces had fired on Fort Sumter on April 12, making war between North and South an established fact even before the plebiscites took place. Unionist voters in both Virginia and Tennessee, moreover, were subjected to violent intimidation and even arrest.[246] On election day in Virginia, J. W. Butler of Loudoun County voted no and was immediately seized by authorities; he would still be languishing in prison in February 1863. He was one of dozens of Unionist voters known to have been arrested.[247]

---

[242] *Journal of the Secession Convention of Texas 1861*, 183–184 (Mar. 16, 1861).

[243] Houston, *Writings*, 8:275, 278.

[244] Wooster, *Secession Conventions*, 37, 58–59, 73, 110–111; Poore, *Federal and State Constitutions*, 1:44, 330, 725n, 737–738; 2:1067n, 1077–1078.

[245] Wooster, *Secession Conventions*, 149, 188.

[246] On Tennessee, see Daniel Crofts, *Reluctant Confederates: Upper South Unionists in the Secession Crisis* (Chapel Hill: University of North Carolina Press, 1989), 345–347.

[247] Mark Neely Jr., *Southern Rights: Political Prisoners and the Myth of Confederate Constitutionalism* (Charlottesville: University Press of Virginia, 1999), 120–122.

THE U.S. SECESSION CRISIS   97

Officially, neither Virginia nor Tennessee seceded until its voters spoke. One Virginia secessionist announced as much, solemnly explaining in a public letter a week before the referendum that the people of Virginia could still reject secession, in which case, "in the war now carried on by the Government of the United States against the seceded States, Virginia must immediately change sides."[248] Yet in fact, secessionists in Virginia, as in Tennessee, fully anticipated the outcome and acted accordingly. On April 27, almost a month before the Virginia referendum, the Virginia secession convention invited the Confederate government to move from Montgomery to the Virginia capital, Richmond—an offer that was quickly accepted.[249]

Conclusion

Although the political breakdown associated with secession and the start of the Civil War was not the breakdown of a modern democracy, especially given the presence of slavery and severe restrictions on the franchise, it would be a mistake to ignore this example altogether. Indeed, as we have sought to show, there is much to learn from this troubling case. The decision of so many Southerners to reject the outcome of the 1860 presidential election—and to fracture their democratic institutions—did not emerge out of the blue. It followed decades of democratic erosion, in which Southern leaders had sacrificed core political freedoms of their white constituents in an effort to protect and affirm slavery at any cost. They had severely restricted rights to speech and association, and eventually demonized and effectively banned the Republican Party across most of the South, making meaningful cooperation with their political rivals all but impossible. Along the way, they had developed an exceptionally high tolerance for violating their own democratic norms (i.e., even those applicable only to white males) as well as basic rule of law in pursuit of their cause. In the end, they appear to have profoundly deceived themselves about the realities of slavery, and about the extent of their own power, after forcefully suppressing all opposition and dissent when it came to slavery over so many years. American democracy thus broke down not because of a sudden onslaught of self-consciously antidemocratic forces or thought, but because—at least in part—Americans who regularly celebrated their democratic values and institutions had gradually been willing to subordinate both to what they saw as a higher cause of sustaining a slaveholding society.

---

[248] Quoted in Edward McPherson, *The Political History of the United States of America, during the Great Rebellion*, 4th ed. (1864; Washington, DC: James Chapman, 1882), 7n.

[249] Virginius Dabney, *Richmond: The Story of a City*, revised ed. (Charlottesville: University Press of Virginia, 1990), 164.

Perhaps, as supporters and beneficiaries of this slaveholding society, Southern political leaders' democratic commitments were simply empty from the beginning, and there was nothing truly democratic for them to corrupt, erode, or break. But this perspective seems hard to reconcile with the democratic aspirations expressed by Southern slaveholders like Thomas Jefferson, who largely penned the Declaration of Independence, or James Madison, who was a principal author of both the Constitution and the Bill of Rights. Paradoxically, liberal democratic values did take root alongside slavery in the South, and the erosion of these values that an increasingly aggressive defense of slavery seemed to require proved both real and consequential.[250]

The critical question for us today (and for this volume) is whether the pattern of political breakdown that took hold in the antebellum South could have occurred *only* in a slaveholding society—and thus be of little relevance to us now—or whether the process of extended erosion and ultimate breakdown could also play out in a modern democracy, even in the absence of slavery. Particularly given the resonance with other accounts in this volume, it seems to us highly problematic, even reckless, to assume the former.

[250] A classic study of this paradox is Edmund S. Morgan, *American Slavery, American Freedom: The Ordeal of Colonial Virginia* (New York: W. W. Norton, 1975).

Appendix

Laws in Slaveholding States Restricting Speech Related to Slavery (Including Antislavery Speech and Other Speech Believed to Provoke or Inspire Resistance among Enslaved People), 1804–1861

Year law enacted	State or territory	Speech outlawed	Punishments mandated	Censorship of U.S. mail mandated
1804	Georgia	Speech "tending to incite" any slave or slaves "to sedition, tumult, or disorder"	*For speaking or causing to be spoken, or writing or publishing:* Banishment from the state "forever"; *for violation of banishment:* death	
1805	South Carolina	"[I]nflammatory discourse, tending to alienate the affection or seduce the fidelity of any slave or slaves"	*For writing or publishing, or delivering a public "discourse":* "punishment, not extending to life or limb, as shall be adjudged by the judge or judges presiding in the court"	
1820	South Carolina	Written or printed speech intended "to disturb the peace or security" of the state "in relation to the slaves of the people of this state"	*For circulating or bringing into the state:* *If white:* fine up to 1,000 dollars and prison up to one year *If "free person of color":* for first offense, fine up to 1,000 dollars; for second offense, up to 50 lashes and banishment from the state; *for violation of banishment:* death	

(*continued*)

Year law enacted	State or territory	Speech outlawed	Punishments mandated	Censorship of U.S. mail mandated
1824	Florida (territory)	Speech that excites or attempts to excite "an insurrection or revolt of slaves"	*For writing, speaking, or "otherwise"*: death *For "accessory threats"*: Fine up to 1,000 dollars, prison up to one year, and whipping up to 39 lashes	
1829	Georgia	Speech "exciting to insurrection, conspiracy, or resistance among the slaves, negroes, or free persons of color of this State"	*For circulating print or writing*: death	
1830	Louisiana	(1) Written or printed speech "having a tendency to produce discontent among the free colored population of the state, or insubordination among the slaves"; (2) Public or private speech, including "conversations . . . signs or actions," having the same tendency	*For writing, publishing, distributing (1)*: prison at hard labor for life, or death; *for (2), or for "knowingly" bringing (1) into Louisiana*: prison at hard labor for 3 to 21 years, or death	
1830	Mississippi	Written or printed speech "containing any sentiment, doctrine, advice or inuendoes [*sic*] calculated to produce a disorderly, dangerous or rebellious disaffection among the coloured population of this state, or in anywise to endanger the peace of society"	*For white people writing, publishing, circulating, or aiding and abetting doing so*: prison for 3 to 12 months and fine of 100 to 1,000 dollars; *for Black people circulating*: death	

1831	North Carolina	(1) Written or printed speech having the "evident tendency ... to excite insurrection, conspiracy or resistance in the slaves or free negroes and persons of colour within the State, or which shall advise or persuade slaves or free persons of colour to insurrection, conspiracy or resistance"; (2) speech that endeavors "to excite in any slave or slaves or free negro or person of colour a spirit of insurrection, conspiracy or rebellion"	*For publishing or circulating (1)*: for first offense, prison for one year or more and whipping at court's discretion; for second offense, death "without benefit of clergy"; *for (2)*: for first offense, prison for one year and whipping of 39 lashes; for second offense, death "without benefit of clergy"
1832	Alabama	Speech "tending to produce conspiracy, or insurrection, or rebellion, among the slaves or colored population"	*For publishing or circulating print or writing*: death
1832	Florida (territory)	Speech to "attempt ... to excite an insurrection or revolt of slaves"	*For writing, speaking, or "otherwise"*: death
1832	Virginia	Speech "advising persons of colour within this state to make insurrection, or to rebel"	*For writing, printing, publishing, circulating print or writing*: if Black: for first offense, whipping up to 39 lashes; for second offense, death; if white, fine of 100 to 1,000 dollars
1835	Maryland	Written or printed speech "having a tendency to create discontent among, and stir up to insurrection, the people of color of this State" or "of other States or Territories of the United States"	*For "knowingly" writing or printing, or for circulating within the state, or for carrying, sending or aiding in carrying or sending to another state or territory of the United States*: prison for 10 to 20 years

(*continued*)

Year law enacted	State or territory	Speech outlawed	Punishments mandated	Censorship of U.S. mail mandated
1836	Tennessee	Speech "calculated to excite discontent, insurrection or rebellion amongst the slaves or free persons of color"	*For writing, printing, drawing, etc.; or aiding and abetting doing so; or for possessing with intent to circulate, or circulating, or aiding and abetting circulation; or for communicating by words, gestures, or writing to "any slave or free person of color"*: for first offense, "confinement at hard labor" for 5 to 10 years; for second offense, the same for 10 to 20 years.	
1836	Virginia	(1) Speech of "any member of an abolition or anti-slavery society" coming to Virginia and advocating "the abolition of slavery"; (2) Written or printed speech "persuading persons of colour . . . to make insurrection, or to rebel, or denying the right of masters to property in their slaves, and inculcating the duty of resistance to such right"	*For (1)*: fine of 50 to 200 dollars and prison for 6 months to 3 years; *for (2)*: if Black, whipping up to 39 lashes and deportation; if white, prison for 2 to 5 years; *for U.S. postmasters in Virginia who refuse to censor the mail*: fine of 50 to 200 dollars	Yes
1837	Missouri	Speech intended "to excite any slave or slaves, or other persons of color, in this State, to rebellion, sedition, mutiny, insurrection, or murder"	*For writing, printing, or circulating writing or print*: for first offense, fine up to 1,000 dollars, prison up to 2 years; for second offense, prison up to 20 years; for third offense, prison for life	

1841	Alabama	Speech "calculated to excite discontent, insurrection or rebellion amongst the slaves or free persons of color"	*For printing, writing, drawing, etc., or aiding and abetting doing so:* prison for 10 or more years; *for circulating printing, writing, drawing, etc.:* prison for 10 or more years, or death	
1842	Maryland	Speech of "an inflammatory character, having a tendency to create discontent amongst or stir up to insurrection the people of color in this State"	*For free Black people "knowingly" calling for or receiving in the mail, or possessing, print, writing, drawing, etc.:* prison for 10 to 20 years	Yes (for free Black people)
1845	Missouri	Speech "tending directly to excite any slave or other colored person in this state to rebellion, insurrection, or murder"	*For speaking, "utter[ing]," writing, printing, or circulating:* for first offense, prison for 2 years; for second offense, prison for at least 5 years. Also, for white persons imprisoned under this law: permanent disqualification from voting, holding office, or serving on a jury in Missouri	
1848	Virginia	(1) Speech maintaining "that owners have not right of property in their slaves"; (2) Written or printed speech "with intent to advise or incite persons of colour . . . to rebel or make insurrection, or denying the rights of masters to property in their slaves, and inculcating the duty of resistance to such right"	*For free persons speaking or writing (1):* fine up to 500 dollars, and jail up to one year; *for free persons writing, printing, or circulating (2):* prison for 1 to 5 years; *for U.S. postmasters in Virginia who refuse to censor the mail:* fine up to 200 dollars	Yes

(*continued*)

Year law enacted	State or territory	Speech outlawed	Punishments mandated	Censorship of U.S. mail mandated
1850	Arkansas	(1) Speech maintaining "that owners have not right of property in their slaves"; (2) speech "with intent to advise or incite negroes in this State to rebel or make insurrection, or inculcating resistance to the right of property of masters in their slaves"	*For free persons:* *for speaking or writing (1):* fine up to 500 dollars and jail up to one year; *for writing, printing, or circulating (2):* prison for 1 to 5 years	
1854	North Carolina	Same as 1831 North Carolina law	Same as 1831 North Carolina law, except the penalty of death was no longer required to be "without benefit of clergy"	
1855	Missouri	(1) Speech having "the tendency . . . to excite any slave, or other colored person in this State, to insolence or insubordination towards his master or owner, or to rebellion, insurrection or murder, or to escape from his master or owner"; (2) speech "calculated to excite insurrection, revolt, conspiracy or resistance, on the part of slaves, negroes, or free persons of color in this State . . . or . . . to induce or encourage slaves to escape from their owners or masters"	*For writing, printing, speaking (1):* for first offense, prison for up to 5 years; for second offense, prison for at least 5 years; *for circulating writing or printing (2):* for first offense, prison for at least 2 years; for second offense, prison for at least 10 years; *for either:* permanent disqualification from voting, holding office, or serving on a jury in Missouri	

1859	South Carolina	Speech "calculated to disaffect any slave or slaves in this State, or tending to incite any insurrection or disturbance among the same"	*For, "with evil intent," writing, printing, drawing etc., circulating writing, etc., speaking, or subscribing to a publication:* if white, fine and prison; if free person of color, fine, prison, and "corporal punishment"; *for officials neglecting or refusing to enforce mail censorship:* fine up to 500 dollars	Yes
1860	Texas	(1) Speech uttered in the presence of any slave that would render the "slave discontented with his state of slavery"; (2) public speech maintaining that "masters have not right of property in their slaves"; (3) private speech that would "bring the institution of slavery (African) into dispute in the mind of any free inhabitant of this State, or of any resident for the time being therein"; (4) written or published speech "inculcating resistance to the right of property of masters in their slaves, or calculated to produce in slaves a spirit of insubordination with the intent to advise or incite negroes in this State, to rebel or to make insurrection"	*For free persons:* *for writing, speaking (1):* prison for 2 to 5 years; *for writing, printing, speaking (2):* prison for 2 to 4 years; *for (3):* prison for 2 to 5 years; *for writing, printing, or "knowingly" circulating (4):* prison for 2 to 7 years; *for subscribing to a (4) publication:* 500 dollar fine and/or jail for up to 6 months; *for officials neglecting or refusing to enforce mail censorship:* fine up to 200 dollars	Yes
1860	Kentucky	Speech "with intent to advise or incite negroes in the state to rebel . . . or inculcating resistance to the rights of property of masters in their slaves"	*For writing, printing, or "knowingly" circulating:* prison for 1 to 5 years	

(*continued*)

Year law enacted	State or territory	Speech outlawed	Punishments mandated	Censorship of U.S. mail mandated
1861	North Carolina	(1) Speech in print with the "evident tendency . . . to cause slaves to become discontented with the bondage in which they are held by their masters, and the laws regulating the same, and free negroes to be dissatisfied with their social condition"; (2) speech endeavoring "to excite in any slave or free negro or person of color, a spirit of insurrection, conspiracy or rebellion"; (3) "inflammatory language, the tendency of which would be to excite in any slave or free negro a spirit of insurrection, conspiracy or rebellion"	*For bringing (1) into North Carolina, publishing, circulating, or aiding and abetting doing so:* death; *for (2):* death; *for (3):* fine or prison	

Sources: **1804 Georgia**: *Acts of the General Assembly of the State of Georgia, Passed at the Sessions of May and November, 1804* (Louisville: Ambrose Day, 1805), 5–6; **1805 South Carolina**: *Acts and Resolutions of the General Assembly of the State of South-Carolina, Passed in December 1805* (Columbia: D. & J. J. Faust, 1806), 50–51; **1820 South Carolina**: *Acts and Resolutions of the General Assembly of the State of South-Carolina, Passed in December, 1820* (Columbia: D. Faust, 1821), 23–24; **1824 Florida**: *Acts of the Legislative Council of the Territory of Florida, Passed at Their Third Session, 1824* (Tallahassee: Florida Intelligencer, 1825), 208; **1829 Georgia**: *A Digest of the Laws of the State of Georgia,* 2nd ed. (Athens: Oliver Prince, 1837), 804; **1830 Louisiana**: *The Louisiana Digest* (New Orleans: Benjamin Levy, 1841), 1:521; **1830 Mississippi**: *Laws of the State of Mississippi, Embracing All Acts of a Public Nature, from January Session, 1824, to January Session 1838, inclusive* (Baltimore: John D. Toy, 1838), 328–329; **1831 North Carolina**: *Acts Passed by the General Assembly of the State of North Carolina, at the Session of 1830–31* (Raleigh: Lawrence & Lemay, 1831), 10–11; *Journals of the Senate & House of Commons of the General Assembly of the State of North Carolina, at the Session of 1830–31* (Raleigh: Lawrence & Lemay, 1831), 281; **1832 Alabama**: *A Digest of the Laws of the State of Alabama,* 2nd ed. (Tuscaloosa: D. Woodruff, 1836), 110; **1832 Florida**: *A Manual or Digest of the Statute Law of the State of Florida, of a General and Public*

Character (Boston: Charles C. Little and James Brown, 1847), 490; note: this became state law in 1845, when Florida became a state (490); **1832 Virginia**: *Acts Passed at a General Assembly of the Commonwealth of Virginia . . . 1831* (Richmond: Thomas Ritchie, 1832), 21–22; **1835 Maryland**: *Laws Made and Passed by the General Assembly of Maryland* (Annapolis: Jeremiah Hughes, 1836), [558–559]; **1836 Tennessee**: *Public Acts Passed at the First Session of the Twenty-first General Assembly of the State of Tennessee 1835-6* (Nashville: B. Nye, 1836), 145–146; **1836 Virginia**: *Acts of the General Assembly of Virginia, Passed at the Session of 1835-36* (Richmond: Thomas Ritchie, 1836), 44–45; **1837 Missouri**: *Laws of the State of Missouri Passed at the First Session of the Ninth General Assembly . . . [1836-1837]* (Jefferson: Calvin Gunn, 1837), 3; **1841 Alabama**: *Acts Passed at the Annual Session of the General Assembly of the State of Alabama . . . 1840* (Tuscaloosa: Hale & Phelan, 1841), 121; **1842 Maryland**: *Laws Made and Passed by the General Assembly of the State of Maryland [1841-1842]* (Annapolis: William McNeir, 1842), 232–233; **1845 Missouri**: *The Revised Statutes of the State of Missouri . . .* (St. Louis: J. W. Dougherty, 1845), 342–343; **1848 Virginia**: *Acts of the General Assembly of Virginia, Passed at the Session . . . 1847[-]48* (Richmond: Samuel Sheperd, 1848), 117, 125; **1850 Arkansas**: *Acts Passed at the Eighth Session of the General Assembly of the State of Arkansas* (Little Rock: Lambert A. Whiteley, 1851), 22–23; **1854 North Carolina**: *Revised Code of North Carolina, Enacted by the General Assembly at the Session of 1854 . . .* (Boston: Little, Brown, 1855), 63, 205–206; **1855 Missouri**: *The Revised Statutes of the State of Missouri, Revised and Digested by the Eighteenth General Assembly* (Jefferson: J. Lusk, 1856), 1:556–557; **1859 South Carolina**: *Acts of the General Assembly of the State of South Carolina, Passed in December 1859* (Columbia: R. W. Gibbes, 1859), 768–769; **1860 Texas**: *General Laws of the Eighth Legislature of the State of Texas* (Austin: John Marshall, 1860), 99–100; "An Act, Supplementary to [and] amendatory of an act, entitled an act to adopt and establish a Penal Code for the State of Texas," Title 19, Chapter 1, Article 653, Texas State Library and Archives; **1860 Kentucky**: Harvey Myers, comp., *A Digest of the General Laws of Kentucky . . .* (Cincinnati: Robert Clarke, 1866), 381; **1861 North Carolina**: *Public Laws of the State of North Carolina, Passed by the General Assembly, at Its Session of 1860-'61* (Raleigh: John Spelman, 1861), 39–40.

4

The Breakdown in Democracy in 1930s Japan

Louise Young

Consensus wisdom holds that Japanese democracy has been stable across the past seventy years, since the occupation reforms undertook to "democratize and demilitarize" political structures in the wake of Japan's defeat in World War II. Assessments of the political system prior to 1945 are more mixed. Early opinion was shaped by the Tokyo War Crimes Tribunal of 1946–1948, which passed judgment on the "deformed nature of prewar and wartime Japanese politics" that left the system susceptible to a "military seizure of power" in the 1930s, or as one influential study was titled, *Democracy and the Party Movement in Prewar Japan: The Failure of the First Attempt.*[1] Even as subsequent research took issue with the Tokyo Trial's "military takeover thesis" and began to look to the rational underpinnings of decision-making in the 1930s, the supports for military leadership among elite constituencies, and continuities in the political system going back to the late nineteenth century, no one has claimed that wartime Japan represented a moment of vibrant democracy.[2] Indeed, the parliamentary system created with the founding of constitutional monarchy in 1889 underwent an extended stress test during the 1930s, as economic collapse, a wave of political violence, and geopolitical crisis led to the hollowing out of democratic institutions built up over the preceding decades, culminating in a de facto military dictatorship by the end of the decade.

While few scholars dispute the claim that democracy broke down in some fundamental sense, beyond this very little is agreed upon. I would like to explore the causes of democratic breakdown along several avenues of inquiry. The first is

---

[1] Mark Peattie's characterization in his review of Gordon Berger, *Parties out of Power: Journal of Japanese Studies* 4, no. 1 (Winter 1978): 199; Robert Scalapino, *Democracy and the Party Movement in Prewar Japan* (Berkeley: University of California Press, 1953).

[2] James B. Crowley, *Japan's Quest for Autonomy: National Security and Foreign Policy* (Princeton: Princeton University Press, 1966) and Gordon Berger, *Parties Out of Power in Japan, 1931–1941* (Princeton: Princeton University Press, 1977); for a more recent historiographic assessment, see Stephen Large, "Oligarchy, Democracy, and Fascism," in *A Companion to Japanese History*, ed. William M. Tsutsui (West Sussex: Wiley-Blackwell, 2009), 156–171.

Louise Young, *The Breakdown in Democracy in 1930s Japan* In: *When Democracy Breaks*. Edited by: Archon Fung, David Moss, and Odd Arne Westad, Oxford University Press. © Oxford University Press 2024. DOI: 10.1093/oso/9780197760789.003.0004

THE BREAKDOWN IN DEMOCRACY IN 1930S JAPAN   109

the nature of the constitutional system established in 1889. The founders created a constitutional monarchy with a democratically elected national assembly. Yet the position of the emperor, the armed services, and the cabinet all anchored extraordinary powers in the executive branch. Did flaws in constitutional design create openings for the autocratic turn of the 1930s? Second, I will focus on the agents of democratic retreat—the antidemocratic actors who pushed to repurpose the state for authoritarian ends and the pro-democratic actors who sought to protect the status quo of party politics and freedom of expression. Who were the stakeholders in Japanese democracy? How committed were they to democratic rule? Why did key players turn against the system? Third, I will take up democracy as a process. We tend to think of democracy in linear terms, assuming that social and economic modernization bring about democratic progress. However, the devolution of Japanese democracy in the 1930s brings this formulation into doubt. What causes democratic institutions to evolve? What causes them to devolve? What are the ideas and norms, the social movements and organizations, and the political institutions that support democratic opening—and conversely promote democratic collapse?

This chapter answers these questions by tracing the longer arc of political history from the late nineteenth century through World War II. Examining the creation of a constitutional monarchy under the reign of the Meiji emperor (1868–1912), I argue that while by design the Meiji Constitution of 1889 created an asymmetry of power between the executive and legislative branches of government, it also provided the foundation for parliamentary democracy. Politics under the 1889 Constitution evolved to meet the pressures of an industrializing society, with the dramatic expansion of democratic institutions in the Taishō period (1912–1926). A concatenation of domestic and international crises in the late 1920s put Japanese democracy to a stress test. When parliamentary government proved incapable of responding effectively to the multifront crisis, the voting public lost faith in party politics during the early Shōwa period (1926–1989). Military leadership stepped into the political opening and carried out a slow-moving takeover of the state that culminated in de facto dictatorship by the end of the 1930s. However, the same susceptibility to legitimacy hazards that faced democracy also faced the wartime dictatorship. Having led the nation into a catastrophic war, military leadership, the armed services, and militarism in general were discredited, paving the way for their widespread rejection in the wake of World War II.[3]

---

[3] I adopt two Japanese conventions in this essay: a periodization that follows Japanese reign names (Meiji, Taishō and Shōwa eras) and proper names listing family name first, personal name second (Young Louise).

110 WHEN DEMOCRACY BREAKS

Founding the Modern Constitutional Order, 1868–1889

Since the promulgation of the Meiji Constitution in 1889, the Japanese political system operated as a constitutional monarchy, with strong executive power vested in the emperor, his advisory committees, and his cabinet. Political parties developed to represent male heads of propertied households who expressed the political will of the people via the lower house of a bicameral parliamentary system, in which an elected House of Representatives exercised limited powers and was held in check by an appointed House of Peers. This became known as the "transcendental cabinet system," to reflect governance by a bureaucratic elite that stood above and apart from the parliament of commoners.[4] Like founding moments in other democratic systems, the Meiji political and legal reforms created tensions in the meaning of democracy.

One aspect of this tension was the relationship between the legislative and executive branches of government. The Meiji constitutional system created a structure where political institutions and political power were defined by whether one was located inside or outside the formal vessel of government. Inside stood the cabinet, which constituted the critical decision-making body of government and controlled the levers of state power. Appointment to this body was determined by the small circle who advised the emperor—a group initially comprised of the founding generation of statesmen who built the modern state and was later made up of their designated protégés. Outside stood the people, who expressed their will through a national assembly, the Diet, meant to debate matters of political importance and serve in an advisory role to the cabinet and the government ministries. Significantly, there was no constitutional mechanism for the national assembly to nominate, elect, or approve members of the cabinet: the latter was explicitly sealed off from democratic control.

The Meiji Constitution embodied the vision of the activists who overthrew the feudal order in 1868—the event known as the Meiji Restoration. The reforms that followed established the modern Japanese nation-state. The restoration coalition represented specific interests from the previous Tokugawa governmental structure. Most were lower-ranking members of the former samurai, the bureaucratic-warrior elite that had occupied the top strata in a formal social hierarchy. Three centuries of peace under Tokugawa rule "tamed the samurai," transforming them from mobile fighting forces into an urbanized intellectual and administrative caste.[5] The twenty or so government leaders in the new Meiji

---

[4] Scalapino, *Democracy and the Party Movement in Prewar Japan*, 153–154. See also Itō Hirobumi, *Commentaries on the Constitution of the Empire of Japan* (Tokyo: Igirisu-hōritsu Gakkō, 1889), published simultaneously in English and Japanese to explain the principles of constitutionalism to a foreign and domestic audience.

[5] The phrase comes from the title of Eiko Ikegami's book *The Taming of the Samurai: Honorific Individualism and the Making of Modern Japan* (Cambridge, MA: Harvard University Press, 1997).

THE BREAKDOWN IN DEMOCRACY IN 1930S JAPAN   111

government hailed from only four of Japan's 280 domains and from the imperial court in Kyoto. They joined with the emperor and a few members of his court in rebellion against the Tokugawa house that had ruled a federation of semi-autonomous domains from a seat of government in Edo. A vestige of an earlier era of monarchic rule, the imperial court exercised a ceremonial role under the Tokugawa order but held no political or administrative function. Together reform-minded activists in the court and in the domains of Chōshū, Satsuma, Tosa, and Hizen overthrew the Tokugawa regime and restored power into the hands of the emperor, initially modeling the new structures of government along the lines of the seventh-century monarchy, itself based on the example of the Chinese bureaucratic state. This history, as well as their elitism and numerical limits, is captured in the term "the Meiji oligarchs," widely used to describe the founding generation of the modern state.[6]

Within a decade, the oligarchs abandoned East Asian statecraft for Western-style government, a course dictated in part by the threat of Western imperialism. Both the ongoing peril of gunboat diplomacy and the imperialism of free trade in East Asia triggered a program of self-strengthening and defensive modernization, carried out at breakneck pace in the 1870s and 1880s. High-speed state-building was necessitated as well by the economic and social instability of the 1870s, giving rise to a series of armed insurrections against the new government. The slogan "rich country strong military" captured the vision of economic and military modernization that inspired the oligarchs during the first two decades of the Meiji period. A core element of defensive modernization was the creation of a constitutional government and the rule of law recognizable to the great powers, in order to win entry of the Japanese state as an equal member of the Western-dominated interstate system.[7]

Political parties and the idea of a government opposition first emerged out of the factional struggles and breakup of the restoration coalition in the 1870s. Under the pressures of defensive modernization and the competing challenges of a comprehensive reform program, the oligarchs split into two irreconcilable groups. Unable to forge a compromise, the dissident faction resigned their positions to establish a base of political opposition outside the government and founded Japan's first political parties. Under the banner of the "people's rights

---

[6] Oligarchs/oligarchy is the English term for *hanbatsu* (literally: domain cliques), an antigovernment description of government leadership that circulated and became established during the popular rights and party movements of the 1870s and 1880s, though the English term lacks the opprobrium attached to *hanbatsu*. The number of members of the oligarchy varies: Stephen Large, "Oligarchy, Democracy, and Fascism," 156–171, identifies seven core members: Itō Hirobumi, Yamagata Aritomo, Inoue Kaoru, Matsukata Masayoshi, Kuroda Kiyotaka, Ōyama Iwao, and Saigō Tsugumichi.

[7] Louise Young, "Rethinking Empire: Lessons from Imperial and Post-imperial Japan," in *The Oxford Handbook on the Ends of Empire*, ed. Martin Thomas and Andrew Thompson, Oxford Handbooks Online, 2017, 2–6, https://doi.org/10.1093/oxfordhb/9780198713197.001.0001.

112   WHEN DEMOCRACY BREAKS

movement," they pressed for constitutional government and a national assembly to share power with the restoration state. With the breakup of the restoration coalition, oligarchic politics reorganized itself around those that remained inside and those leading the party movement on the outside. Insider government was dominated by old boy networks from Satsuma and Chōshū domains, derisively labeled "clique government," while the outsiders used connections from Tosa and Hizen domains to forge a common agenda for the new parties. Shared identity as former samurai, shared participation in the founding of the modern state, and shared commitment to the overarching goals of the Meiji reform program bound these men together and tempered the sharpness of the divide between government insiders and party outsiders. This sense of esprit de corps between the Satsuma-Chōshū clique government and their loyal opposition of former confederates endured over the subsequent decades, shored up by defections back and forth between government insiders and party outsiders.[8]

In mapping this division between insiders and outsiders onto the executive and legislative branches of government, the Meiji Constitution laid the foundations for parliamentary politics to evolve along several tracks: the factional politics of government ministry insiders, political party activism within the national assembly, and the combat and compromise between the two. Political battles and negotiations often went on behind closed doors, but also spilled out into an evolving public sphere. The latter was delineated through a spirited political press and an expanding reading public, as well as meetings, organizations, and speechmaking devoted to concerns of the common weal.[9] In this sense the determination of government policy involved not only cabinet officials and party men but also a vocal community of spectators who interpreted and commented on the political theater of the day.

The Meiji constitutional system represented the first political compromise between insiders and outsiders of modern politics. The insiders hewed to a vision of a bureaucratic authoritarian state that adapted Prussian-style government to indigenous traditions of rule; the outsiders sought to create a representative democracy that drew on French and British models, blending them with homegrown political philosophy. In spite of heated debates over the merits of these respective models, both "insiders" and "outsiders" agreed on the central tenets of defensive modernization: state-led industrialization, the creation of a competitive military force, and anchoring national loyalties to the emperor. These areas

---

[8] On the development of the constitutional system, see George Beckmann, *The Making of the Meiji Constitution: The Oligarchs and the Constitutional Development of Japan, 1868–1891* (Lawrence: University of Kansas Press, 1957); Banno Junji, *The Establishment of the Japanese Constitutional System*, trans. J. A. A. Stockwin (London: Routledge, 1992).

[9] Kyu Hyun Kim, *The Age of Visions and Arguments: Parliamentarianism and the National Public Sphere in Early Meiji Japan* (Cambridge, MA: Harvard Asia Center, 2008).

THE BREAKDOWN IN DEMOCRACY IN 1930S JAPAN   113

of overlap were expressed in the two most distinctive features of Japan's constitutional design: the identification of the state with the imperial institution and its putative sacrality as well as the special and direct relationship of the armed services to the imperial commander-in-chief, circumventing executive branch control via the cabinet. Both of these features would be weaponized in the 1930s to create a de facto military dictatorship.

Out of the debate over the shape of the modern constitutional order a lexicon of democracy emerged. These ideas circulated through the world of literate elites, a social group that grew exponentially with the establishment of a modern school system in the 1870s and the development of a modern publishing industry of book translations, newspapers, and magazines from the same time. Upper-class activists in town and country joined in debates over the shape of the new political order and even designed their own constitutions.[10] By the 1890s, the theater of politics had expanded beyond the world of male ex-samurai and rural landlords to include women and a wider stratum of commoners, where a robust public discussion trafficked terms such as "democracy," "parliament," "Dietman," "cabinet," "nation," "the public," "public speaking," "national assembly," "society," "commerce," and "constitution" that were composed both of neologisms and adaptations of indigenous concepts.[11] The Meiji political order thus signified the actions of government and party leaders, as well as the theater of cabinet pronouncements and Diet politics engaged by a wider reading public.

This became the foundation upon which Japan's political structure evolved. Over time the representation of "opposition" expanded out from an initial base of the men of samurai background from the restoration domains and traditional village leaders who were the prime beneficiaries of the privatization of land in the 1870s. By the turn of the twentieth century, opposition parties represented a more complex coalition of elite interests among industrialists, financiers, and the intelligentsia. Yet the restrictive vision of parliamentary politics that saturated the early debates on the movement for a national assembly in the 1870s carried through into the elitist character of mainstream parties.[12] In 1889 roughly 1% of the population held the right to vote, a figure that reflected the founders' vision of democracy for the upper classes. While the size of the electorate expanded in 1900 and 1919 with the lowering of the tax qualification, and universal manhood

[10] Daikichi Irokawa, *Culture of the Meiji Period*, trans. Marius B. Jansen (Princeton: Princeton University Press, 1988).

[11] For discussion of these terms, see Carol Gluck, *Japan's Modern Myths: Ideology in the Late Meiji Period* (Princeton: Princeton University Press, 1985) and Douglas R. Howland, *Translating the West: Language and Political Reason in Nineteenth-Century Japan* (Honolulu: University of Hawaii Press, 2002).

[12] For the debate on Itagaki Taisuke's 1874 Memorial calling for a National Assembly, see William R. Braisted, trans. and ed., *Meiroku Zasshi: Journal of the Japanese Enlightenment* (Cambridge, MA: Harvard University Press, 1976), xxxiii–xl.

114　WHEN DEMOCRACY BREAKS

suffrage was granted in 1925, the division between insiders and outsiders defined by proximity to political power continued to define parliamentary politics—as well as the larger fields of discourse and activism beyond the ballot box.

The Constitution of 1889 established a constitutional monarchy with some elements of democratic rule. Like constitutions more generally, this one represented a body of national law that set limits on the power of the state. Prior to 1889, there were no legal limits on state power in any area; now the government accepted certain limitations. In other words, the power of the state that was wielded in the name of the emperor was no longer absolute. Beyond this, the Meiji Constitution created deliberate ambiguities that permitted both the expansion of democratic institutions as well as the subsequent breakdown in democratic rule and the assertion of expansive state power in the name of the emperor. One source of ambiguity lay in the dueling constitutional principles of the transcendental cabinet system that constituted absolutist rule; another was the electoral democracy expressed through the Diet. The tensions between principles of absolutism and democracy in the Meiji Constitution gave rise to ongoing debate as different groups laid claim to the Constitution for their respective political purposes. Moreover, the Meiji Constitution left the question of sovereignty ambiguous, providing grounds for competing interpretations that were part of the constitutional debate. Was sovereignty vested in the emperor, who is identical with the state? Or was sovereignty vested more broadly in the nation and its people, with the emperor constituting an organ of the state?[13]

The ambiguities around the position of the emperor as well as the expansive powers of the executive branch of government in the Meiji Constitution handicapped Japan's democratic system from the outset. With so few avenues for public access, the bureaucratic state became the locus of politicking and gave rise to a pernicious factionalism. Moreover, the constitutional prerogatives of the armed services privileged military officials in the politics of the bureaucratic state. At the same time, the modern constitutional order replaced a feudal structure that contained no electoral mechanism for public input into state decision-making, with a democratic system whereby elected assemblies expressed the popular will. This represented an ideological and institutional paradigm shift and provided the foundation upon which democratic institutions and norms could expand. Constitutional design thus created the conditions of possibility for both bureaucratic/military authoritarianism and parliamentary democracy, and for each system to both flourish and falter.

---

[13] On the position of the emperor, see John W. Hall, "A Monarch for Modern Japan," in *Political Development in Modern Japan*, ed. Robert E. Ward (Princeton: Princeton University Press, 1968), 11–64; Marius B. Jansen, "Monarchy and Modernization in Japan," *Journal of Asian Studies* 36, no. 4 (1977): 611–622; David Anson Titus, *Palace and Politics in Prewar Japan* (New York: Columbia University Press, 1974).

THE BREAKDOWN IN DEMOCRACY IN 1930S JAPAN   115

Democracy from Above, 1890–1913

By the time of the Great War, twenty-five years of government under the Meiji Constitution had given rise to the expansion of the bureaucratic state and the political party system, as the oligarchs in the government and their loyal opposition in the Diet became fused into a new political inside. Over this period, some twenty ex-samurai insiders—the oligarchs—grew to number several hundred wealthy elites that included former samurai but also men of commoner background among business and landowning circles. This process opened the transcendent cabinet and its ministerial bureaucracies to new groups of elites; the state developed mechanisms to integrate this broader group of insiders as government institutions proliferated beyond the limits of oligarchic control. At the same time political parties established a base of support among elite interest groups and the rural upper class, and helped interpellate these groups as political subjects—the citizenry—through Diet representation. Finally, the interpenetration of government leaders and party politicians through deal-making created a new political establishment that included both Diet and cabinet. Because of these three developments, new tactics and norms of insider politics became the constituent elements of Japanese democracy. In what might be described as upper-class pluralism, parliamentary politics created procedures for political debate and vehicles for interest group representation that integrated an increasingly diverse elite and built democracy from above.[14]

Compromise between government leaders and party politicians was incentivized by the unworkability of a constitutional system expressly designed to seal off the executive branch from democratic control. In the first years of the Diet, the oligarchs quickly discovered the limitations of transcendental cabinets. The political parties in the lower house used their single lever of power by refusing to pass governmental budgets to great effect, frustrating the developmental initiatives of the oligarchs to build military and economic capacity. During the initial sessions of the Diet, the oligarchs traded off serving as prime minister, but none had much success in compelling the lower house to pass a budget or raise taxes on their landowning constituents—forcing a rapid sequence of Diet dissolutions and new elections as the oligarchs attempted to master the new political system. When their efforts to control the opposition parties through bribery and intimidation failed, government leaders responded by founding

---

[14] Standard accounts of political developments include the following: Peter Duus, *Party Rivalry and Political Change in Taishō Japan* (Cambridge, MA: Harvard University Press, 1968); Tetsuo Najita, *Hara Kei and the Politics of Compromise, 1905–1915* (Cambridge, MA: Harvard University Press, 1967); Mitani Taiichirō, "The Establishment of Party Cabinets, 1898–1932," trans. Peter Duus, in *Cambridge History of Japan*, vol. 6: *The Twentieth Century*, ed. Peter Duus (New York: Cambridge University Press, 1988), 55–96.

116 WHEN DEMOCRACY BREAKS

their own pro-government parties and directing their protégés to join existing parties.[15] In the process oligarchic rivalries and interministerial machinations spilled out into the Diet, adding to the political turbulence. For their part, party leaders sought to expand power and influence by insinuating themselves onto cabinet posts, which were used to direct government funds to pet projects of local elites and other constituents. Initially this included government funding for local schools and railways, and later expanded into road building, harbor works, and telephone and telegraph lines. This history of combat and compromise is recorded in the convoluted family tree of formations, dissolutions, and reformations, of splinters, offshoots, cross alliances, and mergers that constitutes the bloodline of Japanese political parties.

Civil and military services expanded in number and complexity to define the bureaucratic state. The cabinet system was created in 1885, with members overseeing nine government ministries of foreign affairs, home, finance, army, navy, justice, education, agriculture and commerce, and communication. New ministries were added to this core group, with a cabinet that ranged between ten and fifteen members for most of the prewar period. The ministries they oversaw grew rapidly: the upper ranks of the civil service (section and station chiefs, bureau chiefs, and cabinet ministers) numbered around four thousand in 1892, rising to thirteen thousand by 1928. The elite civil service and the officer corps became a prime channel for securing status through high salary, social connections, and other perks of office.[16]

During the Meiji period cabinet posts were monopolized by former samurai from the four domains of the restoration coalition; they were appointed by and among the oligarchs. As the bureaucracy of state expanded, the original oligarchs turned from direct operation of the machinery of government to wielding power via their protégés and patronage networks, and as "elder statesmen" they advised the throne. This structure lasted until the restoration generation of oligarchs died out around World War I. With the retreat of oligarchic control, an increasing fraction of cabinet ministers came from the imperial capital of Tokyo rather than the four domains of the restoration coalition. They were overwhelmingly Tokyo University Law School graduates, and included financiers and politicians in addition to the civil servants and military officers

---

[15] The first few elections were notorious for political violence, with government officials employing thugs to harass voters. Twenty-five people were killed and hundreds injured in violence at the polls in the election of 1892. Even though the cabinet scaled down their strong-arm tactics, ruffians and gangsters became a fixture in Japanese politics, from elections and campaigns to legislative debates; see Eiko Maruko Siniawer, *Ruffians, Yakuza, Nationalists: The Violent Politics of Modern Japan, 1860–1960* (Ithaca, NY: Cornell University Press, 2015).

[16] On the bureaucracy, see Robert Spaulding, *Imperial Japan's Higher Civil Service Examinations* (Princeton: Princeton University Press, 1967); Bernard Silberman, "The Bureaucratic Role in Japan," in *Japan in Crisis: Essays in Taishō Democracy*, ed. Bernard S. Silberman and H. D. Harootunian (Ann Arbor: University of Michigan Press, 1974).

that composed the first generation of cabinet members. Aside from cabinet ministers, who moved between ministries and other top-ranking posts, civil service and officer corps recruits stayed within their agencies and moved up the ranks under the patronage of their seniors. Over lifetime careers they developed intense sectional loyalties and a sense of rivalry with other ministries that competed for budgetary and other resources—the army ministry with the navy ministry, the home ministry with the justice ministry, and so forth. Moreover, different ministries developed networks of voluntary associations as an instrument of public policy: the army ministry with the reservist organizations, agriculture and commerce ministry with industrial cooperatives (*sangyō kumiai*), the ministry of finance with private banking associations. While voluntary organizations were conceived as a way to channel directives from the state to the people, to a modest extent they also operated as a mechanism for public opinion to reach government insiders.[17]

These patterns determined the trajectory of bureaucratic politics in the prewar and wartime period in several ways. First, while the oligarchs gradually lost the ability to manage the bureaucracy via personal networks, inter- and intraministerial patronage networks continued to define political fault lines within the bureaucratic state—and these multiplied over time. Second, as the social geography of power shifted from southwest Japan to the imperial capital, a new mechanism of integration replaced domain-based clique government with a Tokyo Imperial University old boys' network. The Tokyo-based power elite composed of professionals, academics, businessmen, and politicians were connected via common education at the faculty of law and the officers' school, connections cemented via recruitment channels to bureaucratic, company, newspaper, and university posts as well as family alliances sealed via arranged marriages. This social glue helped to patch over bureaucratic divisions, as common background and social connections provided both a reservoir of goodwill and a reserve of mediators to manage conflict.

Paralleling these developments within ministerial bureaucracies, Diet politics became more open to interest group organizing and coalition building among the expanding ranks of the upper class, which included owners of the publishing and entertainment industries, the big business groups known as *zaibatsu*, and wealthy landlords. Chambers of commerce organized in cities from the 1890s, representing commercial and manufacturing interests that were regional in character and that advocated for local development assistance to build railroads, ports, and schools. Later sectoral business organizations like the Japan Economic

---

[17] For an illuminating study of these kinds of connections in a Tokyo neighborhood, bureaucrats reach down into neighborhoods to foster engagement with groups they manage: Sally A. Hastings, *Neighborhood and Nation in Tokyo, 1905–1937* (Pittsburgh: University of Pittsburgh Press, 1995).

118   WHEN DEMOCRACY BREAKS

Federation emerged as powerful lobbying organizations to weigh in on issues such as labor legislation and tariff policy.[18]

The political press, which had emerged as an organ of the people's rights movement in the 1870s with a small readership among political activists, began in the 1890s to develop mass circulations among a newly literate public. Local and national papers affiliated with the major parties demonstrated the capacity to shape and mobilize public opinion on political issues. Editors of the Osaka- and Tokyo-based mass circulation dailies could wield power among various classes of newspaper readers with calls to action on questions of domestic and foreign policy.[19] Newspapers helped stir up periodic citizens' rallies in Tokyo and other urban centers that could turn violent, such as the "movement to protect the constitution" in 1912 and 1913 protesting the arrogance of the military high command in trying to dictate cabinet appointments. Newspaper editors and senior journalists on their staff were highly paid and occupied positions of public prominence; old-school ties and marriage alliances connected them to other segments of the upper class.

In the 1890s, political parties represented the interests of landlords almost exclusively, as they occupied the overwhelming share of the 1% entitled to vote because they paid the land tax. But even as landlord dominance of the parties thinned with the expansion of the franchise in 1900 and 1919, and with universal manhood suffrage in 1925, organizations like the Imperial Agricultural Association continued to represent the interests of large landlords with the Diet.[20] High-salaried public intellectuals were another constituency of political parties and shaped Diet politics from their perches at influential newspapers and magazines and in the universities.[21] Indeed, seven Tokyo University professors managed to stir up a hornet's nest in the Diet with a public campaign demanding the annexation of large portions of Manchuria after Japan's victory in the Russo-Japanese War—embarrassing the government and touching off nationwide protests against what were viewed as the humiliating terms of the peace treaty with Russia.[22] Political parties came to represent the complex interests of the power elite: large landlords, business leaders, public intellectuals, the higher civil service, and the senior officer corps. By the 1910s these interests shook out into two so-called establishment parties, whose interparty rivalries tended to pit an

[18] Miles Fletcher, *The Japanese Business Community and National Trade Policy, 1920–1942* (Chapel Hill: University of North Carolina Press, 1989).

[19] James L. Huffman, *Creating a Public: People and Press in Meiji Japan* (Honolulu: University of Hawaii Press, 1997).

[20] Teikoku nōkai was created in 1910 as an umbrella organization for local landlord associations established throughout the country from the 1880s.

[21] Byron Marshall, "Professors and Politics: The Meiji Academic Elite," *Journal of Japanese Studies* 3, no. 1 (1977): 71–97.

[22] Byron Marshall, *Academic Freedom and the Japanese Imperial University, 1868–1939* (Oxford: University of California Press, 1992), 8–15.

THE BREAKDOWN IN DEMOCRACY IN 1930S JAPAN   119

urban- and manufacturing-based party (the Kenseikai or Minseitō) against a rural-based party with ties to big landlords (the Seiyūkai). Thus, the establishment parties had expanded democratic representation, while keeping the reign of parliament tightly within the grasp of the upper class.

Over the first decades of the Meiji constitutional order, horse-trading and pork-barrel politics effectively dissolved the boundary between the parties and the cabinet. Parties were filled with bureaucrats, and party men were appointed to cabinet posts. They made deals in the smoke-filled rooms where policy was decided, and public opinion considered them all part of an establishment of insiders. This process culminated in the era of "party cabinets" begun in 1918, when Hara Takashi was appointed prime minister—the first time a party leader assembled a cabinet and led the government of Imperial Japan. Between 1918 and 1932, control of the cabinet changed hands back and forth between the two establishment political parties, the Seiyūkai and the Minseitō—a development championed by public intellectuals as the rise of a liberal political order.[23] Hara, the president of the Seiyūkai party, earned the signal honor of inaugurating party rule by an astute campaign to breach the walls of the bureaucracy during his appointment as home minister in multiple cabinets. From this base he appointed Seiyūkai-affiliated men to posts of prefectural governors and colonial governorships—extending party reach from local government into colonial administration. Hara's legacy was fusing the top-down vision of the transcendental cabinet system with the commitment to loyal opposition that carried over from the early party movement.[24] The Diet and the government ministries became effectively redefined as a single political inside—an upper-class pluralism that balanced interest group politics of the business community, wealthy landlords, public intellectuals, and the upper ranks of the civil service. Despite the rough and tumble of politics within the establishment, its stakeholders offered a united front against challenges from the outside. This represented a democracy built and expanded from above: the electoral system and party organization managed the complex interests of the power elite via representative government for wealthy men.

Democracy from Below, 1914–1928

The term "Taishō democracy" generally refers to the period between the Great War and the invasion of Manchuria in the early 1930s.[25] Though the reign of the Taishō emperor technically began in 1912 and ended in 1926, popular

---

[23] The Kenseikai was reorganized in 1927 as the Minseitō.

[24] On Hara Kei, see Najita, *Hara Kei and the Politics of Compromise*; Mitani, "The Establishment of Party Cabinets," 55–96.

[25] Some historians take the starting point for Taishō democracy back to the aftermath of the Russo-Japanese War of 1904–1905, with the first urban rioting against the terms of the Portsmouth

120   WHEN DEMOCRACY BREAKS

perception aligns the Taishō period with the global 1920s. For Japan this signified the flourishing of social movements to expand civil and political rights, the establishment of party governments, cultural experimentation and cosmopolitan modernism in the arts and literature, a boisterous political press with a nationwide readership, and the rise of left-wing radicalism. Taishō democracy is associated with the embrace of liberal internationalism embodied in the Washington Conference System in China (1922) and permanent membership on the Council of the League of Nations (1920), as well as a cooling toward military expansionism expressed in the fallout from the ill-fated Siberian Expedition (1918–1922), participation in the antiwar Kellogg-Briand Pact (1928) as one of the fifteen original signatories, and the negotiation of regional disarmament treaties with Britain and the United States at Washington (1922) and London (1930). Thus, the trends associated with Taishō democracy were liberal internationalism, leftist political opening, and cultural cosmopolitanism.

In theory, the Meiji oligarchs set up a system of limits on democracy, prescribing a servile citizenry, with political rights (for the 1%) expressed through the Diet, itself intended to act as a rubber stamp for the executive branch. In reality a very different form of democracy emerged by the 1920s. Despite obstacles to political activism, people organized themselves into interest groups, political parties, and social movements. They expressed their political will through the ballot box, and when that was unavailable, through protest and direct action. Even so, the imprint of the Meiji constitutional order left its mark on the democratic institutions that grew up upon its foundations, which were defined by the persistent logic of insider and outsider politics. As the composition of the "insiders" expanded, a new "outside" rose up in opposition to a government that appeared sealed off and unresponsive to public demands. In other words, the very success of democracy from above invited the movement for democracy from below.[26]

Focused on grooming their relations with the government, the establishment parties eschewed possibilities for expanding a base of power outside of their upper-class constituencies and focused their democracy project on increasing

---

Peace Treaty. Edward G. Griffin, "Taishō Democracy," in *Kodansha Encyclopedia of Japan* (Tokyo: Kodansha, 1983). Andrew Gordan, who coined the term "imperial democracy" to describe this phenomenon, also begins with the Hibiya Riots of 1905 and divides his study into the "movement for imperial democracy" from 1905 to 1918, "imperial democratic rule" from 1918 to 1932, and the "collapse of imperial democracy" from 1932 to 1940: *Labor and Imperial Democracy in Prewar Japan* (Berkeley: University of California Press, 1991).

[26] The idea of democracy from above and below riffs off Maruyama Masao's famous essay on Japanese fascism, which made the distinction between the movement for "fascism from below" by radical movements and "fascism from above" by agents of the government to convert the state to fascist form: "The Ideology and Dynamics of Japanese Fascism," trans. Andrew Fraser, in Maruyama Masao, *Thought and Behavior in Modern Japanese Politics*, ed. Ivan Morris (London: Oxford University Press, 1969), 25–83.

THE BREAKDOWN IN DEMOCRACY IN 1930S JAPAN   121

access to the state for themselves. Probably the most striking expression of their commitment to limiting representation was the specter of the largest party, the Seiyūkai, opposing the movement for universal suffrage in the early 1920s. Denying large segments of the population a voice in parliament left the field open for new forms of opposition to the political establishment to emerge, as many people took to the streets to assert claims to power and resources in a militant push for democracy from below. Although the passage of universal manhood suffrage in 1925 meant that the original electorate of 1% had grown to an estimated 20% of the population, this still left plenty of people without recourse to democratic representation. Twelve million male citizens over twenty-five qualified to vote in the first elections under the new law in 1928, out of a population of sixty-two million. In an interesting twist, this included Koreans living in the home islands but excluded all residents of the colonies, including ethnic Japanese.[27]

Left-wing radicalism exploded in the wake of World War I, and activists developed a toolkit of extraparliamentary and often extralegal tactics to express their political demands. Right-wing radicalism also gained steam, though on a smaller scale and with less overall impact. The movement for democracy from below was fueled by the energy of the left—a host of progressive political movements pushing for women's rights and universal suffrage, labor and farm tenant rights, civil rights for foreign workers (Koreans) and former outcast groups (*burakumin*), as well as Communist, Anarchist, and Socialist ideals. Right-wing organizations emerged to counter the left in universities, workers organizations, women's groups, and other sites of the social movement. The alternative to parliamentary activism was direct action, and this became the tool of choice for opposition groups across the 1910s and 1920s. Starting with the Hibiya Riots of 1905 against the Russo-Japanese War treaty, rallies, marches, strikes, and other forms of popular protest proved their efficacy in telegraphing opposition sentiments to a government unaccustomed to and uninterested in hearing from the lower orders. Popular protest proved able to force real changes in policy and on occasion brought down the cabinet. The Rice Riots of 1918 were a spectacular demonstration of the power of the crowd. As a form of social politics via direct action, they made both a symbolic and a material impact on politics going forward.[28]

---

[27] Neither Koreans, Taiwanese, nor Japanese residents in the empire were represented in the Diet. During the 1920s, limited forms of democratic local self-government were established in the colonies: Emer Sinead O'Dwyer, *Significant Soil: Settler Colonialism and Japan's Urban Empire in Manchuria* (Cambridge, MA: Harvard University Asia Center, 2015); Jun Uchida, *Brokers of Empire: Japanese Settler Colonialism in Korea, 1876–1945* (Cambridge, MA: Harvard University Asia Center, 2011).

[28] Michael Lewis, *Rioters and Citizens: Mass Protest in Imperial Japan* (Berkeley: University of California Press, 1990).

122 WHEN DEMOCRACY BREAKS

The rioting was touched off by price inflation and intermittent food shortages during the economic boom of World War I; unrest spread through the summer of 1918 to protest the price and availability of rice—targeting rice merchants and local elites who were perceived to have either caused the problem by manipulating supplies for profit or—just as bad—failed to use their wealth to help their fellow citizens. When police forces proved unable to prevent mobs breaking into rice warehouses and smashing the property of local elites, the government was forced to dispatch troops to 144 locations throughout the country. The mobilization of the army to put down the Rice Riots represented a signal failure of the state. The Terauchi Masatake cabinet fell in disgrace, demonstrating the ability of the un-enfranchised crowd to determine the fate of the prime minister. Moreover, through the Rice Riots crowd action forced a host of new policies concerning rice prices and rice supply, as well as new measures to address poverty and provide social services for the urban poor. Most of all, the riots burned into popular memory the image of a chain of cities engulfed in rioting—the specter of urban revolution. They heralded the beginning of new forms of social politics that, along with party cabinets, de-fined Taishō democracy. Excluded from the deliberations of parliament and lacking access to the bureaucratic patronage, these political outsiders developed their own toolkit to shape policy and influence the state.

Political organizations representing those excluded from the realm of estab-lishment politics proliferated rapidly and began to spread radical ideas through the mass media and culture industries. On the left, labor and tenant union mem-bership grew rapidly and unions established links to proletarian political parties. For the most part these were vanguard parties, led by intellectuals and other elites who cast themselves in the role of enlightening workers and directing their political action. The Japan Communist Party was founded in 1922 and quickly outlawed, but continued to organize from an underground base and through connections to student organizations in Tokyo's leading universities. Intellectuals created Socialist parties and press organs beginning in the turn of the century, and the burst of union activism from World War I energized the Socialist move-ment and gave it new direction. By the mid-1920s close to 10% of the workforce was unionized, including both factory workers and tenant farmers; they struck factories and fields in increasing numbers across the decade. They demanded wage hikes and rent reduction as well as improved working conditions, asking to be treated with dignity and respect; they also called for civil rights and a political structure that gave power "to the people." After the passage of universal man-hood suffrage in 1925, proletarian parties organized to run candidates for office, winning 3–4% of the Diet in the first elections after the new law was enacted and 10% by the mid-1930s.[29]

[29] Gordon, *Labor and Imperial Democracy in Prewar Japan.*

THE BREAKDOWN IN DEMOCRACY IN 1930S JAPAN   123

The dramatic rise of left-wing movements in the home islands was matched by the appearance of anticolonial nationalism in the overseas empire. In 1919, violent uprisings in the March 1 Movement in colonial Korea and the May 4 Movement in China deployed Wilsonian principles to call for national self-determination. Colonial elites in Taiwan, Korea, and Manchuria took up the language of "Taishō democracy" to push for local self-government, and Japanese colonists—who could not vote—also began to demand political representation. The movement for democracy from below was empire-wide.

While organized workers and their parliamentary representation constituted a small minority overall, they punched above their weight in terms of impact. The proletarian movement was strongest in the factories, in the universities, and in the farm suburbs of Tokyo and Osaka, where the upper class and establishment insiders were also concentrated. Japan's upper classes gazed with increasing alarm at the expanding organizational strength and rising militancy of the left; they viewed these developments against the backdrop of the spread of international socialism and the specter of worldwide revolution. They connected it with an alarming breakdown in social order and the spread of anticolonial nationalism in the empire.

In the meantime, the radical right organized into its own political parties and action groups, constituting hundreds of small organizations, sometimes loosely affiliated with each other, but more atomized than the left. With names like Blood Pledge League, Righteousness Corps of the Divine Land, and the Anti-Red League, radical right activists regarded themselves as heirs to so-called *shishi*, revolutionary men of spirit called to act in the political crisis of the 1850s. Now they called for a cleansing of the political system through Taishō and Shōwa restorations of a purified imperial rule. Like the left, they condemned the parliamentary establishment for corruption and self-dealing; they denounced the concentration of economic power in the hands of the big business combines known as *zaibatsu*; they blamed the upper classes for the suffering of the working poor. Unlike the left, the right-wing were animated by virulent anticommunism and embraced the ultranationalist ideas labeled "Japanism": the emperor cult, pan-Asianism, and hypermilitarism. To be sure, belief in the emperor-centered constitution, leadership in Asia, and the importance of a strong military were tenets of nationalist ideology shared across the political spectrum. Right-wing "Japanism" of the 1920s and 1930s simply pumped up and aggrandized these ideas, lending nationalism an extreme or "ultra" quality.[30]

---

[30] For a discussion of the "ultra" quality of "ultranationalism," see Maruyama, "The Ideology and Dynamics of Japanese Fascism"; Louise Young, "When Fascism Met Empire in Japanese-Occupied Manchuria," in "Axis Empires: Toward a Global History of Fascist Imperialism," special issue of *Journal of Global History* 12, no. 2 (June 2017): 274–296.

124   WHEN DEMOCRACY BREAKS

The radical right engaged in direct action of a different sort, as they mobilized militant gangs of followers to harass and beat up leftists; they drew up enemies' lists and sent members to China to operate in the shadowy underworld of continental adventurers. Like the specter of Socialist revolution evoked by the radical left, the right imposed its own psychic terror on the establishment through political violence. Most dramatically, rightists assassinated in 1921 both Hara Takashi, the architect of the transactional "politics of compromise" and head of the first party cabinet, and Yasuda Zenjirō, founder of one of the "big four" *zaibatsu*, who accrued his fortune through sweetheart deals with government insiders.[31] Symbols of unsavory deal-making and crony capitalism, Hara and Yasuda paid the ultimate price for the perceived injustice of upper-class pluralism.

By the late 1920s democratic political traditions had grown in significant and substantive ways out of the restrictive foundation in the Meiji constitutional order. These included a free and vigorous political press, a political party system, the public embrace of democratic norms, universal manhood suffrage, and support for further broadening civil rights. Labor and farm tenant unions pressed their claims on employers and in the public sphere. A system of higher education made space for marginalized people, including women, colonial peoples (Koreans, Chinese), and former outcasts (*burakumin*). Yet critical weaknesses constrained the system as well. The state held extensive censorship and police powers to regulate political activity. Passage of the Peace Preservation Law in 1925, and its amendment in 1928, greatly enhanced instruments of political repression available to the state. The establishment political parties answered to wealthy businessmen, big landlords, and bureaucrats; they saw little benefit in responding to demands for greater representation. All the limitations of the Meiji Constitution were still in place and, with the notable exception of universal manhood suffrage, much of the democratic opening was effected via changing norms and informal practices rather than legal reform.

Thus, at the end of the 1920s, the Japanese political system was poised to move either toward greater democratic opening or toward the consolidation of upper-class pluralism. Democracy from below could have forced the system to represent an increasingly broad group of constituents. Democracy from above could have battened down the hatches against the pressures from the outside. The politics of compromise could have continued to convert outsiders to insiders. However, democracy is not linear. What happened instead was a slow-moving takeover of the state by the armed services and the marginalization of political parties. As we shall see, a concatenation of external and internal shocks in the late 1920s disrupted democratic evolution, triggering an extended stress test of

---

[31] The phrase "politics of compromise" comes from Najita, *Hara Kei and the Politics of Compromise*.

THE BREAKDOWN IN DEMOCRACY IN 1930S JAPAN   125

Japan's political institutions. When the state seemed powerless to quickly resolve the multifront crisis, confidence in democratic governance disintegrated.

Shocks to the System, 1929–1932

The late 1920s and early 1930s proved challenging years for all industrialized societies, Japan not the least, as a decade of alternating inflation and deflation ended with a bank panic in 1927, and a tottering national economy slid ignominiously into the global crash of 1929.[32] At the same time, the diplomacy of liberal internationalism which had effectively managed the competing ambitions of Britain, the United States, and Japan in the Asia-Pacific was coming under increasing stress. Naval limitations to forestall a financially ruinous arms race in the Washington Conference in 1922 were broadly championed by the political elite, but the optics of the London Naval Conference of 1930 provoked a more critical and anxious response.[33] Japan signed onto both treaties, which dictated ratios for various classes of vessels, calculated to guarantee each power's security interests; the sticking point was whether Japan had enough firepower to prevail in a potential war with the United States. While naval leaders from all three powers grumbled at the restrictions, the issue proved particularly bitter for the Japanese Navy, which split into two antagonistic factions over how best to guarantee military security vis-à-vis the United States. After their narrow failure in 1930, the antitreaty "fleet faction" used every tool at their disposal to ensure the collapse of another round of treaty revision in 1936. In the meantime, the rising tide of Chinese nationalism and the push to recover economic and political rights signed away under gunpoint began to splinter the united front of great powers, as Chinese diplomats successfully pitted Britain, the United States, and Japan against each other. Pressures to restart the arms race and the breakdown of great power unity in the face of Chinese nationalism coincided with the contagion of trade protectionism and tariff wars. Amplifying hostility and fear between the United States, Britain, and Japan over their respective ambitions in Asia, the challenges of arms limitation, anticolonial nationalism, and trade wars undermined support for liberal internationalism among Japan's political elite.[34]

The sense of a gathering storm in the international arena coincided with heightened stress at home. The multifront socioeconomic crisis of the early

[32] Hugh Patrick, "The Economic Muddle of the 1920s," in *Dilemmas of Growth in Prewar Japan*, ed. James Morley (Princeton: Princeton University Press, 1971), 211–266.

[33] Roger Dingman, *Power in the Pacific: The Origins of Naval Arms Limitation* (Chicago: University of Chicago Press, 1976); J. Charles Schencking, *Making Waves: Politics, Propaganda, and the Emergence of the Imperial Japanese Navy, 1868–1922* (Stanford: Stanford University Press, 2005).

[34] The following discussion draws on Louise Young, *Japan's Total Empire: Manchuria and the Culture of Wartime Imperialism* (Berkeley: University of California Press, 1998), especially 21–182.

126 WHEN DEMOCRACY BREAKS

1930s—agrarian stagnation and mass starvation in Japan's Northeast, unprecedented urban unemployment in cities large and small, plummeting exports to all
of Japan's critical markets, the devastating decision to return to the gold standard
in 1930 only to abandon it a year later—fed an atmosphere of desperation and
panic.[35] In newspaper headlines and magazine articles, in passionate debate in
the halls of the Diet, and in speeches before citizens rallies, opinion leaders called
attention to a systemic economic crisis and demanded action. And yet, during
the crucial months of 1929 and 1930, the government was paralyzed by bureaucratic in-fighting and a reluctance to take action that might adversely impact
such core stakeholders as big landlords and business leaders. Looking out on the
sea of human misery that washed across the national landscape, Japan's political
establishment remained intent on self-dealing and incapable of mounting a competent and effective response.

The popular press was replete with examples of insider corruption and government impotence in those crucial years, but one will serve: the dollar-buying
incident involving Japan's big business firms, the *zaibatsu*. Big business suffered
from an image problem long before the dollar-buying scandal: the "big four"
firms Yasuda, Mitsubishi, Mitsui, and Sumitomo dominated the national
economy and were regularly criticized for the nefarious origins of their success,
their cozy relationship with the establishment political parties, their purchase
of aristocratic rank, and the numerous government corruption scandals with
which they were associated. Although business organizations hedged their political bets by spreading their money around, conventional wisdom maintained
that Mitsubishi *zaibatsu* had "bought" the Seiyūkai and that the Minseitō was
"in the pocket" of Mitsui *zaibatsu*. After insisting for years that Japan maintain
a convertible currency, the *zaibatsu* banks engaged in a fever of highly lucra-
tive speculation against the yen in September and October 1931, undermining
the frantic efforts of the government to shore up the value of the national currency in order to keep Japan on the gold standard. Moreover, the news that
Mitsui sold barbed wire to the Chinese 19th Route Army, against whom Japanese
troops were fighting in Shanghai in 1932, and salt to the enemy in Manchuria,
provoked outrage and condemnation of big business as traitors.[36] And yet the
government did nothing to bring Mitsui to account. To the public it appeared
that the *zaibatsu* and their political tools, the establishment parties, lined their
pockets while millions of ordinary Japanese were starving and out of work. For
the middle and working class, who felt disconnected and unrepresented by the
establishment political parties and who were bearing the brunt of the damage

---

[35] For a study of the rural dimension, see Kerry Smith, *A Time of Crisis: Japan, the Great Depression,
and Rural Revitalization* (Cambridge, MA: Harvard University Asia Center, 2001).

[36] Young, *Japan's Total Empire*, 189.

THE BREAKDOWN IN DEMOCRACY IN 1930S JAPAN   127

from the economic crisis, the ability of the wealthy to game the system and continue their privileged access to the government establishment was outrageous and intolerable. It showed that parliamentary democracy worked only for the rich and connected.

In the meantime, trouble was brewing in Japan's overseas empire, compounding the sense of a nation beset by crisis on all sides. Attention turned to China, where Japan's position appeared embattled by the rising nationalist movement. Focused increasingly on overturning the legal structure that underpinned Japan's railroad imperialism in Northeast China, Chinese nationalists boycotted Japanese goods and struck Japanese-owned factories to demand the recovery of rights signed away over decades of gunboat diplomacy. Against the backdrop of global trade friction and tariff wars, the China market became Japan's "imperial lifeline" and the justification for an army-led invasion of Manchuria in 1931.

This invasion began with a military conspiracy unsanctioned by insider decision-making within the cabinet in Tokyo. Yet the occupation of Northeast China and the creation of the puppet state of Manchukuo quickly became a fait accompli and ushered in a series of policy shifts of great consequence for Japan. It also established a pattern of actions by military actors in the empire that sequentially expanded the war front across the 1930s. The invasion of Manchuria, the escalation to all-out war with China in 1937, the attacks on Soviet Siberia in 1938 and 1939, and the destruction of the American and British fleets in the Asia-Pacific in 1941 were all teed up by military mission creep, where the creation of ever-changing facts on the ground generated forward momentum and closed off routes for retreat. What connected the serial openings of new war fronts were decisions by a small group of actors—military men on the spot, a faction within government—that did not represent a broader consensus of elite stakeholders within the prewar state. In each case, core groups fundamentally disagreed but were dragged along. They gave consent reluctantly or after the fact. In this sense the politics of military expansionism triggered a transformation of upper-class pluralism, shrinking the circle of insiders and making them less responsive to input from elite constituencies and interest groups.

The question remains: Why did the Japanese sphere of influence in Northeast China become the inflection point for democratic retreat? One answer is that Manchuria stood at the intersection of external and domestic crises, of diplomatic and economic dilemmas. For this reason, it served as the battleground between advocates of liberal internationalism and those of regional autarky. When elite consensus turned toward unilateralism in Manchuria, it signaled a broader pivot to go-it-alone Asianism and a rejection of the cooperative diplomacy of imperialism.

Japan acquired this sphere of influence after victory in the Russo-Japanese War in 1905, when Russia transferred to Japan leaseholds and development

128 WHEN DEMOCRACY BREAKS

rights in the Kwantung Territory, the ports of Port Arthur and Dairen, and the South Manchurian Railway Zone—all of which China had previously signed away to Russia under duress. On this foundation, Japan built the largest and most profitable company of the prewar period, the South Manchurian Railway, and dominated the world trade in soybeans. Manchuria also served as base for the crack troops of the imperial army, the garrison force known as the Kwantung Army. Japan's stake in Manchuria was substantial by any measure. South Manchurian Railway assets added up to a billion yen in 1930, boasting spectacular rates of return of 20%–30% over most years of operation, though in steep decline in the late 1920s. A quarter-million Japanese lived in railway towns along the South Manchurian Railway, a large fraction of whom were railway employees and their families.

Statesmen had long considered investments in Northeast China as a bridgehead for plans to expand Japanese interests into the more developed regions to the south. Manchuria was the centerpiece of a far-flung colonial empire, including Taiwan, Korea, and the Pacific Islands, and a foothold for expanding economic interests into the rest of China. For Japan's trade-dependent national economy, and amid the global economic crisis, the empire in Northeast Asia became a critical market for both exports and imports and the hub of global trade networks. When Matsuoka Yōsuke coined the term "lifeline" in 1930 to describe the significance of Manchuria for Japan, it took hold precisely because of this history of involvement. The Japanese economy was externally dependent: if markets controlled by Britain and the United States were at risk, Japan could double down on a safety net in Asia.

Manchuria also became a trouble spot in the politics of nationalism and imperialism in China. Boosted by the rising tide of Chinese nationalism, an anti-imperialist "rights recovery movement" sought to reverse decades of infringement on Chinese sovereignty through legal challenges to leaseholds, investments, and railroad-building permissions. Led by Chiang Kai-shek, the nationalist movement sought to reunify the country militarily under the Republican banner, reclaiming it from regional warlords and their foreign imperialist allies. Between 1926 and 1928, the Northern Expedition brought Chinese territory up to the Great Wall under Chiang's military control—coming dangerously close to the Japanese sphere of influence in South Manchuria. By the late 1920s panic had set in among South Manchurian Railway administrators and Kwantung Army officers, who feared the vast investments in Manchuria were put at risk by the Chinese nationalist movement and Chiang. And while Korea, Taiwan, and other parts of the empire appeared securely within Japan's grip, the Manchurian crown jewel was in peril. South Manchurian Railway employees and Kwantung Army officers pleaded with Tokyo to act to protect Japanese investments from the threat of Chinese nationalism. A radical clique within the

THE BREAKDOWN IN DEMOCRACY IN 1930S JAPAN   129

Kwantung Army chose to force the government's hand by triggering a military crisis in Manchuria.

On September 18, 1931, the conspirators within the Kwantung Army staged an explosion on the Japanese railway track in Mukden and left evidence incriminating Chinese troops. The alleged Chinese attack became the pretext for Japanese forces on the spot to launch an invasion of Manchuria, acting without authorization from the high command in Tokyo to mobilize their troops, bomb the city of Jinzhou in South Manchuria, and attack the troops of regional warlord Zhang Xueliang. The series of independent actions carried out by the Kwantung Army between 1931 and 1933 became known as the Manchurian Incident. In the wake of military action, diplomacy scrambled to calm the protests of Republican China, the United States, and Great Britain, but when these efforts failed, Japanese statesmen walked out of the League of Nations in 1933. The Manchurian Incident put the army firmly back in charge of colonial policy in Korea and Manchuria and laid the ground for the fait accompli as a method to overcome the impasse of bureaucratic conflict when the army didn't get its way.

The Manchurian Incident demonstrated to actors in the bureaucratic state, to party politicians, and to the public at large that the army possessed the capacity for decisive leadership. Force, momentum, and action served to "overcome the deadlock" of political paralysis and secure an economic lifeline in a dangerous world. While the invasion originated with a conspiracy by rogue army officers, eventually the high command and the rest of the political establishment went along, sanctioning military action after the fact and choosing to profit from new facts on the ground that brought all of Manchuria under Japanese control. In the process, they surrendered power to a shrinking pool of insiders, hollowing out the democratic advances of upper-class pluralism and halting the momentum for democracy from below in its tracks.

Agents of Military Takeover, 1932–1936

Japan's response to the gathering global crisis of the late 1920s proved fateful for democratic institutions. Yet the breakdown in democracy in wartime Japan did not occur suddenly or through institutional rupture. Rather, the Great Depression and the Manchurian Incident of late 1920s and early 1930s together touched off a slow-motion military takeover. A breakdown, not a break, the political shifts of the 1930s represented a series of actions and choices made by human agents. This included, notably, the people who inhabited the institutions of insider and outsider politics as well as the groups and organizations supporting a culture of pluralism and liberal democracy. Over the course of the early 1930s, the invasion of Manchuria, the creation of the puppet state of Manchukuo, the

130   WHEN DEMOCRACY BREAKS

intensification of conflict with regional powers, the withdrawal from the League of Nations, and the rejection of liberal world order all proved enormously popular with the public and were supported by government insiders and in the Diet. This support extended to the rising influence of the army in foreign policy decision-making and in the colonial empire at the expense of civilian ministries. Likewise, the public celebrated and the parliament supported "national unity" cabinets that augmented the power of the military, marking the effective end of party cabinets.[37] Army spokesmen commanded the airwaves, and their attacks on the incompetence and corruption of political parties resonated widely. Organized interest groups responded by putting their faith in army leadership in times of "national emergency." Thus, the military takeover of government and the accompanying retreat from democracy were broadly supported.

Why did supporters of parliamentary democracy decide to place their faith in army rule? Popular Japanese stereotypes of the "dark valley" of the 1930s conjure up images of a militaristic police state which exercised unlimited powers of political repression to coerce an unwilling but helpless populace into cooperating with the army's power play at home and abroad.[38] The reality was more complicated, with insiders and outsiders together steering the turn to an authoritarian, militaristic polity.

The military led the way in this effort by initiating the conspiracy in Manchuria, but equally important was a series of public relations campaigns carried out over the early 1930s that sold their Manchurian cover story (self-defense against Chinese necessitated the invasion) and promoted their worldview ("red peril" and "white peril" represented existential threats to the nation) through direct appeals to the public. Distributing a series of pamphlets making the army's case to libraries and neighborhood centers; organizing mass rallies with speeches, music, and popular entertainment; and sponsoring films, radio shows, and press releases, the army used new forms of propaganda with increasing sophistication to shape and define public opinion. Initially their efforts aimed to reverse antipathy toward the military, grown over the course of the 1920s and expressed in popular support for the reduction of military budgets and participation in arms limitation treaties, as well as an alarming rise in draft dodging. Later the goals of the campaign expanded to fomenting opposition to the Japan Communist Party and spreading "red peril" sentiments, to whipping up support for Japanese unilateralism in Manchuria, racism toward the Chinese, and hostility to the League

[37] The last time the armed services tried to bully executive branch insiders over the choice of prime minister triggered the Taishō Political Crisis of 1913. The military lost that power play: Andrew Gordon, *A Modern History of Japan: From Tokugawa Times to the Present* (London: Oxford University Press, 2014), 128–129.

[38] The dark valley mythology is mostly debunked in scholarly accounts of the 1930s but retains a strong hold in public memory, especially in museum representations of wartime Japan such as the Edo-Tokyo Museum and the National Shōwa Memorial Museum (Shōwa-kan), both in Tokyo.

THE BREAKDOWN IN DEMOCRACY IN 1930S JAPAN   131

of Nations, and to inciting panic about the putative "national emergency" (the military campaigns in China) and coming "crisis of 1936" (the Soviet military buildup). Though these campaigns began prior to the Manchurian Incident, the crisis on the continent made the public more receptive to the message. By the mid-1930s opinion effectively shifted on questions of empire and domestic politics—previous support for disarmament evaporated and even the proletarian parties moderated their anti-imperialist platforms to support the military occupation of Manchuria and take a harder line toward the Chinese Nationalists.

Critical to the success of army propaganda was the role of Japan's commercialized mass media in whipping up war fever and spreading the idea of a "national emergency." The jingoistic militarism of the mass media in the early 1930s represented a dramatic shift from the previous decade, when publishing and entertainment culture championed pacifism and international cooperation. Why did the media appear to switch sides, becoming unofficial propagandists for the army? One simple answer is that newspaper, magazine, and radio companies hyped the invasion because Manchuria sold so well in the highly competitive marketplace for news and infotainment.

Like "overcome the deadlock" and "Manchurian lifeline," the term "national emergency" saturated media coverage of the Manchurian Incident and became shorthand for promoting military action in China. After the story broke of the military clash on September 18, the news of the latest action on the continent commanded the headlines for months. War songs set the fashion in popular music and battlefield dramas filled the stage and screen. The big dailies spread the Kwantung Army's version of events in Manchuria and promoted their conspiracy as established fact. The opening of hostilities was reported on the front page of Japan's leading newspaper: "[I]n an act of outrageous violence, Chinese soldiers blew up a section of South Manchurian Railway track . . . and attacked our railway guards." From army press release to jingoistic headlines, Japanese audiences learned of the invasion of China from a credulous mass media.[39]

Against the backdrop of the gathering crisis in Manchuria and the outbreak of war fever, the radical right launched a sustained attack on democratic institutions. In the face of perceived government inaction and ineptitude, groups of junior military officers joined hands with civilian organizations to enact a rapid-fire series of violent conspiracies aimed at reclaiming command over the state. The plot to stage a pretext for the invasion of Manchuria was just one dramatic example, as a series of conspiracies back in Tokyo accompanied radical action in China. In March 1931 plans for a coup d'état by a group of officers in the ultranationalist organization called the Cherry Society fell apart at the last minute, though they regrouped for a second attempt in October, again halted

[39] Young, Japan's Total Empire, 57–58.

132   WHEN DEMOCRACY BREAKS

at the eleventh hour. In the spring of 1932, the Blood Pledge League drew up an assassination list that included business and political leaders; they executed the former finance minister Inoue Junnosuke and the head of the Mitsui business conglomerate, Dan Takuma, before the ringleaders were arrested. On May 15, remnants of the Blood Pledge League joined army cadets in another coup attempt, assassinating Prime Minister Inukai Tsuyoshi and launching abortive assaults on several government buildings before surrendering to the police. The wave of army terror culminated in the most spectacular and audacious coup attempt yet on February 26, 1936. Under the leadership of junior officers, fourteen hundred troops seized central Tokyo, killed several members of the government and their guards, and declared martial law with the support of sympathetic senior officers. But after several days of tense stand-offs between different factions of the military, the coup opponents prevailed and forced the rebels to stand down.

This wave of right-wing terror, memorably called "government by assassination" by an American journalist, heightened the intensity of war fever and created a climate of panic among the political establishment.[40] "Government by assassination" subjected the political system to a stress test that challenged the integrity of both the bureaucratic politics of the state as well as party politics in the Diet. The response revealed many points of weakness. Indeed, establishment political parties reacted to the war fever and the army's "national emergency" with opportunism and cowardice. In the 1920s, the Minseitō and Seiyūkai political parties were branded doves and hawks, respectively, based on their foreign policies (oppose or support military intervention in China; cooperate with great powers or act independently), and the approach to China tacked between these two poles depending on which party was in power. When the Kwantung Army launched their conspiracy in the fall of 1931, the Minseitō held the cabinet and initially tried to restrain military action. Amid war fever, attacks on their soft line proved effective, and elections swept the Seiyūkai into power. Both parties moved steadily to the right on foreign policy, outflanking each other to support army action and appease demands for "whole nation" (army-dominated) cabinets. In the wake of the assassination of Prime Minister Inukai in the May 15th Incident of 1932, army leaders insisted that the political parties step back from running the government to avoid further antagonizing restive elements in their ranks. Opportunists within both parties sought to direct this antiparty hostility toward their own internal rivals, marginalizing liberal internationalists within the parliament. These machinations effectively ended party rule in 1932.

Over the subsequent months and years, senior officers used the wave of violent conspiracies by junior officers to blackmail their bureaucratic opponents,

---

[40] Hugh Byas, *Government by Assassination* (New York: Knopf, 1942). The book was based on contemporaneous coverage in the *New York Times*.

THE BREAKDOWN IN DEMOCRACY IN 1930S JAPAN   133

demanding acquiescence to budget increases and the confrontational military policy on the continent. Together with the cowardice and opportunism of party politicians in the Diet, the dynamics of bureaucratic politics in the early 1930s ceded power to the military, which became the preeminent power broker within the political structure and whose authority only increased over the course of the decade. Military leaders worked hard to gather the levers of power in their hands. One important task was to get their own house in order, and after the coup attempt of 1936, the army cracked down on radical elements in its ranks. Conspirators were court-martialed and executed and sympathetic senior officers purged or demoted. Meanwhile, the military expanded its control over the bureaucratic state—with active-duty officers placed in charge of colonial governorships and with effective veto power over cabinet posts. Nothing about this slow-moving military takeover violated the Constitution. Indeed, the autonomy of the general staffs from cabinet control and the so-called right of supreme command that gave the military a direct line of authority to the emperor were key elements of constitutional design. The Meiji constitutional order provided army leaders the option to take over the state from within.

As the army moved to assume control over the levers of government, elite stakeholders in tandem relinquished control. Not only did the establishment parties shift dramatically to the right in support of army positions, but their core constituents also endorsed army moves toward unilateralism in Manchuria and militarization at home. Facing a rural crisis that both jeopardized their rents and heightened tensions with their tenants—who were demanding reduction in rents, access to low-interest loans, and better terms of trade for their farm produce—big landlords welcomed the distraction of colonial warfare. The rural elite also embraced plans to settle newly occupied rural Manchuria with Japanese tenant-farmers, allowing them to export the vexing problems of rural poverty and social strife. Finding themselves under attack from right and left radicalism, business interests sought to diffuse public antipathy through gestures of patriotism, making ostentatious contributions to home-front support campaigns during the "national emergency." Moreover, chambers of commerce and new business organizations like the Japan-Manchuria Business Council expressed great enthusiasm for the opportunities before them with the government pouring funds into efforts to "develop Manchuria." Intellectuals flocked to Manchuria, where demand for scientific know-how and research skills created a jobs bonanza during the economic downturn. Just as the state was limiting scope for free expression of ideas within the home islands, the army's puppet state in China offered intellectuals the opportunity to shape the future of the empire. In these ways, intellectual opinion leaders, landlord organizations, and the business community endorsed the occupation of Manchuria and retreated before the army's political rise at home.

134 WHEN DEMOCRACY BREAKS

Indeed, there were few reasons to argue with the retreat from liberal internationalism in the early 1930s. The Manchurian invasion was a spectacular success in military, economic, and diplomatic terms, and was broadly popular with both political insiders and outsiders. Militarily, Japan won! Zhang Xueliang's forces were driven out of Manchuria. Diplomatically, Japan paid little price for its violation of the "territorial integrity of China"—a fundamental tenet of great power engagement in the region since the turn of the century. Other regional stakeholders were consumed with domestic problems and chose not to block Japan: the Soviet Union with forced collectivization and a horrendous famine, Britain and the United States with the Great Depression, the Republic of China with its military campaigns against the Communists. The USSR sold its railway in North Manchuria to Japan and retreated to Siberia. Republican China laid down its arms and requested mediation from the League of Nations. America registered disapproval through a toothless "nonrecognition" doctrine. Britain initially worked to defend Japan in the League of Nations, and even though the British-run Lytton Commission Report of 1932 condemned the invasion, no action was taken when Japan decided to withdraw from the League in protest. Afterward, China acknowledged the loss of Manchuria with the Tangku Truce of 1933. In the meantime, rising military budgets and the investments pouring into Manchukuo reinflated the Japanese economy, pulling the country out of depression faster than any other industrial economy. The Manchurian war boom brought Japan back to full employment by 1934, and the deficit spending push by Finance Minister Takahashi Korekiyo anticipated the fiscal policy innovations of American John Maynard Keynes. Thus, in military, diplomatic, and economic terms, the turn to military imperialism represented a vindication of army leadership.

Just as the Manchurian Incident war boom was fading, and opposition to the inflated military budgets gathered among business organizations and local governments, the opening of new war fronts in North, Central, and South China in 1937 touched off yet another war fever, with greater reach and saturation. Like the national emergency that accompanied the Manchurian Incident, the crisis atmosphere of the China Incident provided cover to further shrink the influence of civilian bureaucrats and party men over government policy. But much like the crisis of the early 1930s, key constituencies—the big business community, landlord organizations, opinion leaders in the mass media—relinquished leadership to the military in exchange for something of value to them. By the time of the attack on Pearl Harbor and the launch of the Pacific War in 1941, Japan was a military dictatorship for all practical purposes. The military takeover and democratic retreat were mutually implicated processes, decided by a play for power on one side and a voluntary, if reluctant, relinquishing of influence on the other.

Repurposing the State, 1936–1940

Over the course of the 1930s, multiple developments served to augment military control and hollow out democratic institutions. With the dissolution of political parties into the mass party known as the Imperial Rule Assistance Association (IRAA) in 1940, the polity became a de facto military dictatorship. Many scholars have pointed out that the key difference between the rise of fascism in Germany, Italy, and Japan lay in the continuity of political institutions in Japan.[41] Government continued to operate under the Meiji Constitution, and the party system survived for a decade after the Manchurian crisis. Even with the creation of the IRAA in 1940, parties retained informal influence as factions within the single-party state. Bureaucratic government was not taken over by a fascist putsch from outside, but through the triumph of military factions from within. Interest groups like chambers of commerce and landlord associations continued to exercise influence on state policy, albeit with reduced access; wartime mobilization called on long-standing voluntary associations like youth groups and reservist associations. Thus, the expanding power of the state over the public, and the enhanced authority of the military within the state, relied on repurposing existing institutions rather than creating something new from whole cloth.

Even though institutions themselves endured, a hollowing out and redirection meant that their democratic function attenuated across the 1930s. This breakdown in democratic efficacy occurred across multiple sites, but three stand out as revelatory of this process. First, political parties were excluded from forming cabinets and were demoted to outsider status. As part of their power play, the army reasserted the principle of transcendental government, whereby the state stood above and apart from the people. Second, the tightening of censorship and unleashing of the "thought police" led to a dramatically expanded system of political repression and a de facto police state. Third, the requirements of mobilization for war in China and the drive toward economic autarky laid the ground for a national defense state. All three developments represented the repurposing of structures already in place that helped transform a democracy into a dictatorship.

---

[41] For overviews of the fascism debate, see Katō Yōkō, "The Debate on Fascism in Japanese Historiography," in *Routledge Handbook of Modern Japanese History*, ed. Sven Saaler and Christopher W. A. Szpilman (New York: Routledge, 2018), 225–236; Rikki Kersten, "Japan," in *The Oxford Handbook of Fascism*, ed. R. J. B. Bosworth (New York: Oxford University Press, 2004), 526–544; Louise Young, "Japan at War: History-Writing on the Crisis of the 1930s," in *The Origins of the Second World War Reconsidered*, 2nd ed., ed. Gordon Martel (New York: Routledge, 1999), 155–177. An influential essay rejecting the fascist concept for Japan is Peter Duus and Daniel Okimoto, "Fascism and the History of Pre-war Japan: The Failure of a Concept," *Journal of Asian Studies* 39, no. 1 (1979): 65–76. Key arguments supporting continuity in political structures are Kato Shūichi, "Taishō Democracy as Pre-stage for Shōwa Militarism," in *Japan in Crisis: Essays on Taishō Democracy*, ed. Bernard S. Silberman and H. D. Harootunian (Ann Arbor: University of Michigan Press, 1974), 217–236 and Berger, *Parties Out of Power in Japan*.

136   WHEN DEMOCRACY BREAKS

After 1932, political parties continued to function, elections were held, and establishment parties commanded most seats in the Diet, but they lost the informal right to appoint the prime minister and determine the composition of the cabinet. As before, the privy council formally nominated the prime minister, but with the advent of so-called national unity cabinets the army arrogated for itself an informal veto. Subsequent cabinets were headed by senior officers or peers approved by the military high command. Excluded from government decision-making by a shrinking number of insiders, parties returned to an outsider politics that focused on budgetary combat and responding to initiatives coming from the cabinet. Since many of these initiatives involved the extension of state power under the exigencies of total war, parties concentrated their firepower on defending their shrinking scope of authority. Much of the latter half of the 1930s was consumed with holding the line against radical proposals for a New Political Order that envisioned the "purification of politics" through the overturning of divisive, Western-style liberalism and the reform of a pluralist multiparty system in favor of a single mass organization. The parties ultimately lost this battle, conceding to their dissolution with the creation of the IRAA in 1940.[42]

Modeled on the Nazi Party, the IRAA, however, failed to live up to the hopes of the architects of the New Political Order. Rather than a mass organization that took shape organically, that could channel the popular will and would express fervent loyalty to the imperial state, the IRAA remained a prefabricated organization that forced into a single party the members of existing political organizations. Party men occupied a large fraction of the IRAA, where they maintained earlier ties with interest groups and with their regional base. Under the umbrella of the IRAA the Seiyūkai and the Minseitō continued to function as informal factions, and their social networks outside the party likewise persisted. Thus, the IRAA offers a prime example of the nature of the democratic break. This was a substantive change of institutional form from pluralism to a single-party state; as a political party the IRAA constituted a vehicle for channeling the will of the state to the people rather than the other way around. At the same time, it offered some limited scope for formal and informal mechanisms of party politics to endure as a "loyal opposition" under the dictatorship of the mass party, a faint echo of the chummy relationship between government insiders and party outsiders in the Meiji period.

Freedom of expression in the mass media and in political thought represented a second site where the breakdown in democracy was clearly felt. The legal and institutional infrastructure for surveillance and censorship of political thought was created in the Meiji period, with the Peace Police Law of 1900 and the

---

[42] Gordon, *Labor and Imperial Democracy in Prewar Japan*, 327–330; Gordon Berger, "Politics and Mobilization in Japan, 1931–1945," in Duus, *Cambridge History of Japan*, 6: 97–153.

THE BREAKDOWN IN DEMOCRACY IN 1930S JAPAN   137

Special Higher Police—also known as the "thought police"—established in 1911. Deployed initially against the fledgling Socialist movement, after the Great War the government used the Special Higher Police to control leftist and progressive activism. The Peace Preservation Act of 1925 greatly enhanced state powers and enabled the mass arrests of March 1928 for "thought crime" in an effort to crush the Communist movement. This inaugurated a dramatic expansion of the infrastructure of repression; after 1928 branches of the Special Higher Police were established in all prefectures and agents deployed overseas and to the empire.

In tandem with the expanded powers of the Special Higher Police, Home and Justice Ministries developed an extensive program of intellectual rehabilitation of thought criminals known as "conversion," or *tenkō*.[43] Between 1928 and 1941, the Home Ministry's Special Higher Police arrested sixty-six thousand thought criminals, mostly leftist intellectuals, labor leaders, and members of proletarian political parties. Once behind bars, prisoners were subjected to an elaborate program of psychological pressure meant to break their commitment to antigovernment ideals and convert them to imperial state ideology. Justice Ministry prosecutors spent hours and days with prisoners deploying a combination of carrot and stick to engineer *tenkō*. While threatening families with exposure (guilt by association) and reprisals (ostracism, loss of jobs), prosecutors also offered to waive charges and return prisoners to their former position if they publicly recanted their beliefs and declared their loyalty to the state. This was called "the special dispensation system," a kind of plea bargain whereby thought criminals could recant their beliefs in exchange for leniency. Initially developed after the first mass arrests of 1928, the system demonstrated its stunning success in 1933, when the two leaders of the Japan Communist Party, Nabeyama Sadachika and Manu Sanabu, recanted and triggered a cascade of conversions by other jailed members of the party. These jailhouse conversions of 1933 broke the back of the Communist movement in wartime Japan and eliminated a powerful voice for democracy from below.

Periodic mass arrests and the jailhouse pressures to convert were one element of the antidemocratic police state. While this targeted the radical left, the liberal intelligentsia became objects of state surveillance and repression via a different set of tactics that targeted freedom of expression in the elite universities. What was striking about the university environment of the 1920s was the coexistence of rightists, leftists, and liberals in the academy. Intellectual openness was tolerated even at Tokyo Imperial University, the flagship state academy and

---

[43] On *tenkō*, see Max Ward, *Thought Crime: Ideology and State Power in Interwar Japan* (Durham, NC: Duke University Press, 2019); Shunsuke Tsurumi, *An Intellectual History of Wartime Japan, 1931–45* (New York: Routledge, 1986); R. H. Mitchell, *Thought Control in Prewar Japan* (Ithaca, NY: Cornell University Press, 1966); P. G. Steinhoff, *Tenkō: Ideology and Social Integration in Prewar Japan* (New York: Garland, 1991).

138 WHEN DEMOCRACY BREAKS

training ground for upper civil servants. But this openness underwent a sharp transformation in the 1930s, as tolerance for any form of opposition shrank. Repression in the academy reflected a shift in the balance between fear of subversive ideas on the one hand and the value placed on the benefits of intellectual freedom on the other. On an unprecedented scale, conservative bureaucrats and right-wing scholars now purged from the academy intellectuals such as Takigawa Yukitoki and Minobe Tatsukichi, whose teachings had represented liberal orthodoxy and, in Minobe's case, had earned him a position in the House of Peers. In the series of university incidents that punctuated the decade, scientific analysis of Japan's history, polity, and society came increasingly under attack. Like mass arrests and jailhouse conversions, university purges were designed for both their specific targets as well as a broader form of police state terror. By making examples of celebrated intellectuals like Minobe, the state telegraphed the message that no one was safe to express opinions freely. Even so, liberal and even Marxist intellectuals continued some measure of public expression until a far-reaching purge of 1942–1943, when the thought police rounded up suspect intellectuals in universities, newspapers, publishing houses, and think tanks in major cities throughout the empire. This wiped out the last vestiges of press freedom and political expression for intellectuals.

Negative thought control through repression was supplemented by positive thought control via "spiritual mobilization," which also intensified across the course of the decade and corroded freedom of political expression and an independent press. Spiritual mobilization was part of a rapid growth of state power and activity over the course of the 1930s, an expansion that came at the expense of democratic control. This mobilization for total war represented the third site where democracy became transformed into military dictatorship. Underpinned by the shared belief among political actors in the efficacy of state action, successive cabinets expanded the purview of state control over labor, finance, politics, markets, ideas, trade, production, and other aspects of social, economic, and political life.

Much of this was directed by the cabinets of Konoe Fumimaro in the latter 1930s, under the rubric of the "new structure movement." Descendent of a powerful aristocratic family, Konoe's pedigree guaranteed him a position in the House of Peers and a glide path to the inner circles of executive power. After the failed military coup of 1936, he became a compromise figure among battling factions within the bureaucracy and led three cabinets during the crucial period between 1937 and 1941. One after another, Konoe rolled out a new order in Asia, a new economic order, a new order for labor, and a new political order. Promoted as replacing Western-style individualism and class conflict with Asian-style cooperation and mass unity, mechanisms to manage economy and society were created by technocratic officers and bureaucrats following some combination of

THE BREAKDOWN IN DEMOCRACY IN 1930S JAPAN   139

Nazi, Soviet, and Chinese blueprints. The national defense state of the late 1930s operated under the Meiji Constitution but supplanted the democratic norms and procedures that had emerged under Taishō democracy with technocratic-military rule. In this sense, the new structure movement replaced democracy from above with what Maruyama Masao called "fascism from above"—the fascization of the state from within.[44]

One example of this process was the reorganization of the relationship between capital and labor. During the Taishō era, business organizations occupied the political inside as constituents of the establishment parties and through their connections to government officials; workers organizations pushed for the expansion of rights and representation from outside the system. The national defense state replaced the democratic logic of combat and compromise between and among insiders and outsiders with top-down mechanisms for the state to dictate terms to interest groups and voluntary organizations. This meant that business leaders and workers organizations were no longer pitted against each other as proponents of democracy from above and below, but were jointly placed in subordination to a shrinking inner circle of decision-makers.

Launched in 1937, the New Order for Labor replaced unions with discussion councils of workers and managers that brought labor and capital together into a "single body." This project involved repurposing some existing company unions that already functioned as discussion councils, replacing more radical sectoral unions, and forcing the greater fraction of companies that were not unionized to organize workers councils in their factories. Factory councils were connected via regional branches to a central council, providing an organizational mechanism for the state to mobilize labor power in support of the war effort.

At the same time, the state wrangled control over business organizations through an expanding set of regulations limiting free markets. The New Economic Order adopted Soviet-style five-year planning to set targets for industrial development and government control. State planners established a list of types of industries that were subject to escalating levels of state management in what was called the controlled economy. Public utilities and industries related to national defense were reorganized into state-managed, privately owned companies; other industries were simply regulated. The series of laws that underpinned the various new orders concentrated decision-making in a new advisory body to the central government known as the cabinet planning council that relied on statistics and technocratic expertise to plan its way out of the national crisis.

Though both the New Order for Labor and the controlled economy fell short of their ambitious goals, they nonetheless expanded state power over society

---

[44] Maruyama, "The Ideology and Dynamics of Japanese Fascism," 25–83.

140 WHEN DEMOCRACY BREAKS

and reduced social influence over the state. Like the military takeover of government and the engorgement of the thought police, the apogee of the national defense state spelled the effective end of democratic politics in wartime Japan. In all three cases the transformation of democracy into dictatorship represented a gradual process rather than a sudden rupture and was accomplished through the repurposing of existing institutions rather than creating something new and revolutionary. In this sense the story of wartime Japan is one of continuity of both institutions and actors, suggesting that the seeds of dictatorship lay within the political system. In Japan's case political modernity established under the Meiji Constitution contained the possibility of both bureaucratic authoritarianism and parliamentarian democracy. With the paired passage of universal suffrage with the Peace Preservation Law during the high-water mark of Taishō democracy in 1925, the possibility of democracy opening wider emerged simultaneously with expanded tools for closing it down. A wildly popular imperialism spelled the end to democracy, as the popular embrace of the New Order in Asia swept an antidemocratic military regime into power.

Conclusion

What can we conclude about democratic breakdown in 1930s Japan? I would like to end with three observations. First, democracy is not linear. Despite the tenacity of a generalized modernization theory that envisions the evolution of democratic institutions and a trajectory of progress from less to more democracy, as well as the broadly held view that economic development brings political pluralism in its wake, Japan's case punctures both precepts of democratic ideology. In Japan, the arc of political history from the late nineteenth century tracked a zigzag course between democracy and authoritarianism, even amid steady movement through stages of industrial modernization. After Japan's defeat, democracy reemerged from the wartime state, with key institutions and actors once again shifting purpose, as political parties, bureaucratic ministries, and interest groups of political stakeholders, as well as higher education and mass media ecosystems, all survived the collapse of the war effort in 1945 and reemerged as the cornerstones of the new political order. From its foundations in the Meiji Restoration of 1868 the modern state became more democratic, then became more autocratic, then more democratic again. This suggests that we might think of dictatorship and democracy both as immanent to modern political systems, two sides of the same coin.

Second, both democracy and dictatorship are vulnerable to legitimacy hazards. The failure of democracy to deliver a solution to the geopolitical and economic crisis of the 1930s led to the rise of fascism. The even more catastrophic failure of military dictatorship to deliver victory in World War II led to the collapse of the institutional legitimacy of the military, the overturning of belief in military-led modernization as a nation-building project, and the rejection of militarism as an ideology. In this sense, what went wrong with democracy also went wrong with dictatorship—leading to the embrace of democratic institutions once again, and cementing support for the antiwar clause of the new "peace" Constitution promulgated in 1947.[45] Because expanding the empire was popular in the 1930s, military officials were able to take over and repurpose the state. Because losing the empire was unpopular after 1945, civilian officials were able to purge the military and repurpose the state once again.

Third, if the Japanese case offers any lessons for the defense of democracy against an authoritarian slide, it is the risk of making Faustian bargains with antidemocratic agents. The transactional opportunism of political parties to gain advantage over a rival faction or to ride the wave of jingoism secured only short-term gain and hastened the overall decline of party influence. Left-wing and liberal intellectuals who joined colonial state think tanks and worked with the military, hoping to have a voice at the table and temper the army's violent instincts, found themselves outmaneuvered and marginalized. They gave military imperialism legitimacy and expertise and got little in return. Cabinet officials gave way to military demands for troop surges and budget increases for fear of political retaliation or worse. Thousands of such bargains large and small enabled the slow-moving military takeover of the state. Core stakeholders in Japan's democratic system, like the establishment political parties, the metropolitan daily newspapers, and business organizations, engaged in short-term thinking and opportunism, abandoning their active support for democratic principles such as freedom of expression or party control over the cabinet in a classic case of the tragedy of the political commons.

---

[45] Article 9 of Japan's 1947 Constitution reads, "Aspiring sincerely to an international peace based on justice and order, the Japanese people forever renounce war as a sovereign right of the nation and the threat or use of force as a means of settling international disputes."

5

Weimar Germany and the Fragility of Democracy

Eric D. Weitz[*]

Over one hundred years after the German Revolution of 1918/19 and the founding of the Weimar Republic on August 11, 1919, "Weimar" continues to resonate all across the political and cultural spectrum. It stands as the premier example for the breakdown of democracy. Its brief, fourteen-year history is etched into the popular and academic imagination by hyperinflation, economic depression, endless street battles, louche sexuality, parliamentary paralysis, and the Nazi victory on January 30, 1933, which utterly vanquished German democracy. Germany and Germans, it seems, were not ready for democracy. Only utter defeat in World War II and American guardianship, so goes one line of thought, turned Germans into willing democrats.

Weimar is the celebrated symbol of alternative lifestyles as well as the dread warning signal of moral degeneration. A simple internet search for "Weimar" turns up thousands of links to articles, books, and websites. The conservative American pundit Patrick Buchanan, who is truly obsessed with Weimar, blames the collapse of the Republic on rampant homosexuality, and warns that America is on the same path unless there occurs a clear-cut reckoning with the forces of immorality.[1] Others offer accolades to the "degenerate chic" style of downtown New York City clubs precisely because they echo the nightlife of Berlin in the 1920s.[2] One website, depicting the 2017 racist demonstrations in Charlottesville, Virginia, links the slogan "Unite the right" with warning signals of "Weimar America."[3]

In Germany especially it has proven very difficult, nearly impossible, to offer a full-throttle recognition of Weimar's achievements. In one of History's grand tricks, comparable to Thomas Jefferson and John Adams both dying on

---

[*] Professor Weitz passed away July 1, 2022, after completing this chapter but before its publication, and was not able to personally review the proofs of his contribution.

[1] See, for example, the quotes in Ed Brayton, "Pat Buchanan's Bizarro History," Patheos, October 30, 2011, https://www.patheos.com/blogs/dispatches/2011/10/31/pat-buchanans-bizarro-history/.

[2] *New York Times*, arts section, July 17, 2007. See also Eric D. Weitz, "Not Just a Cabaret, Old Friend," *New York Times*, July 29, 2007.

[3] "Unite the Right Rally 2017: Weimar America," Know Your Meme, accessed October 10, 2019, https://knowyourmeme.com/videos/173466-2017-unite-the-right-rally.

Eric D. Weitz, *Weimar Germany and the Fragility of Democracy* In: *When Democracy Breaks.* Edited by: Archon Fung, David Moss, and Odd Arne Westad, Oxford University Press. © Oxford University Press 2024. DOI: 10.1093/oso/9780197760789.003.0005

the Fourth of July, November 9 occurs four times as a momentous occasion in Germany's twentieth century. Working backward, in 1989 it was the date that the Berlin Wall came down as thousands of East Berliners crossed over to the West, signaling the effective collapse of the German Democratic Republic and opening the path to German unification. In 1938, November 9 was the date of Reichskristallnacht, or the Night of Broken Glass, the vast, state-sponsored pogrom in which thousands of Jews were beaten and sent off to concentration camps, their homes, shops, and synagogues ransacked and destroyed. In 1923, it was the date of Hitler's first attempt to seize power, the so-called Beer Hall Putsch. And in 1918, it was the spark-date of the German Revolution. As thousands of soldiers, sailors, and workers demonstrated in cities and towns all across the country, Kaiser Wilhelm II abdicated the throne. From the balcony of the Reich Chancellery in Berlin the Social Democrat Philipp Scheidemann proclaimed the German Republic. A few hundred meters away, in front of the royal palace, the former Social Democrat now Communist Karl Liebknecht proclaimed a Socialist Republic.

Two grand democratic achievements (1918 and 1989) coupled with one farce (1923) and one very grim episode (1938), a prelude to the Holocaust. Nonetheless, it should be possible to memorialize the disaster of Nazi rule and the persecution of Jews at the same time one affirms the progressive and democratic traditions that have also been a part of German history since the late eighteenth century and came to fruition in the Revolution of 1918/19 and the Weimar Republic. Yet November 9 is always a muted affair in Germany. It is not even celebrated as the Day of German Unity. The government proclaimed October 3, the date when the formal unification of East and West Germany took place, as the national holiday. The requisite speeches are pronounced, appropriate lessons delivered in schools. But on neither October 3 nor November 9 is there anything quite like the popular celebrations of Bastille Day in France or the Fourth of July in the United States or many other such commemorations around the world.

Lost in all of this frantic mining of the past for today's cultural and political conflicts are the substantive achievements of the Weimar era, which were founded on Germany's 150-year-long humanistic and democratic tradition. It is worth providing some details here because so many people believe that Nazism was simply a fulfillment of German history in its entirety, as if the German tradition was only conservative and authoritarian.

We can start in Weimar, the city that gave its name to the Republic, because the constitution drafters retreated there while Berlin, in 1919, lay in virtual civil war. But the drafters' choice of the city was also symbolic. Weimar holds a revered place in German history because it was the site, in the late eighteenth and early nineteenth centuries, of the great flourishing of German culture. Goethe, Schiller, Herder, Fichte, and many others lived there for extended periods,

144 WHEN DEMOCRACY BREAKS

patronized by the Grand Duke, and produced their poems, plays, philosophical discourses, and scientific studies. However varied were the ideas expressed by these luminaries, along with Kant and many others, all were deeply impressed, at least for a time, by the French Revolution. For all their limitations—notably with Kant around the issue of race—all of them believed in the possibilities of a more expansive and freer human existence than had existed under the royal and princely regimes of the eighteenth century.

The humanist and democratic philosophical stream continued into the nineteenth century with early Socialists like Moses Hess and, of course, Marx and Engels, along with many others. In politics it was manifest in the Revolutions of 1848, both in Paris, where many German artisan émigrés lived, and in the many German states that experienced revolution. The failure of the German revolutions—an indelible theme in German history—did not, however, destroy liberal and Socialist ideas in Germany, while the many '48ers who went into exile strengthened those movements throughout the Americas, North and South.

These democratic and humanistic ideas influenced the creation of the German Reich in 1870/71.[4] Otto von Bismarck's famous "revolution from above" was both authoritarian and liberal with strong social components, the latter a response to the democratic and Socialist movements in the middle decades of the nineteenth century. The Reich as engineered by Bismarck had universal manhood suffrage and an electoral participation rate that puts the contemporary United States to shame.[5] The anti-Socialist laws from 1878 to 1890 could not prevent the continual rise of the Social Democratic Party (SPD), which by 1890 had become Germany's largest party by electoral count and in 1912 had the largest number of delegates in the Reichstag. (Gerrymandering had delayed that accomplishment.) A lively press and popular culture and the commitment to the rule of law (the famed German *Rechtstaat*) made the Kaiserreich anything but a straight-line dictatorship.[6] Bismarck's famed social welfare programs did nothing to dent the rise of the SPD and the trade unions, as he had hoped. In fact, one can argue that they only strengthened the movements, because the trade unions especially began to train functionaries who could advise workers and operate within the welfare state. The SPD in particular demanded a democratization that went far beyond the constitutional order of 1871. For so many of its partisans, democracy and Socialism were inextricably entwined. Germany was (and is today) a federal

---

[4] For the view that the empire embodied only authoritarian elements, see Hans-Ulrich Wehler, *The German Empire, 1871–1918*, trans. Kim Traynor (Leamington Spa: Berg, 1985).

[5] See Margaret Lavinia Anderson, *Practicing Democracy: Elections and Popular Culture in Imperial Germany* (Princeton: Princeton University Press, 2000).

[6] David Blackbourn and Geoff Eley, *The Peculiarities of German History: Bourgeois Society and Politics in Nineteenth-Century Germany* (Oxford: Oxford University Press, 1984).

system, and in some localities and states social reform and democratization went far beyond what existed at the national level.

In the years between the turn into the new century and the outbreak of World War I, the SPD, Progressive Party, and Catholic Center Party—the three parties that would form the Weimar Coalition—sought to strengthen parliamentary control of the state, though there were countermoves on the emergent extreme right and in the military, both of which fostered plans for something like a Bonapartist coup. That came to naught as World War I created, initially, a national consensus in favor of war. (Though there were always dissenters in local SPD organizations and on the streets who opposed the war.) The military dictatorship of the war years exercised severe repression. But by 1917, wildcat strikes in critical war industries and bread riots in many cities offered a prelude to the much more expansive popular activism that would emerge in the Revolution of 1918/19 and the Weimar Republic. As World War I dragged on, the three liberal and left-wing parties increasingly collaborated, leading to a peace resolution in 1917 and various other efforts, ultimately in vain, to bring the war to a negotiated close.

The democratic and humanistic tradition in Germany ran deep, even in the semi-authoritarian German Empire, its accomplishments substantial and hardwon. And that tradition served as the foundation for the vast expansion of democracy, social reform, and cultural efflorescence in the Weimar years.

* * *

The Revolution of 1918/19 began with a sailors' mutiny in Kiel in the last days of October 1918. The end to the war was in sight. Everyone knew that negotiations were underway between the United States and Germany. The sailors had no intention to join whatever last-minute heroics their officers were planning, especially not after suffering miserable rations for four years while their commanders enjoyed fine dining on linen tablecloths. So they refused orders to stoke the boilers so the ships could head out to sea. Instead, many sailors headed home from Kiel on the railroad, spreading the word of their mutiny and their demands for an end to the war and better conditions when back on board ship. Their mutiny sparked a popular revolution the likes of which Germans had not seen since 1848. Strikes and demonstrations spread like the proverbial wildfire.

The popular mobilizations forced the abdication of Kaiser Wilhelm II and all the other kings and princes who ruled the German states. The German Reich, forged by Bismarck in 1870/71 as a union of dynastic families and the territories they ruled, was gone, overthrown by the vast pressure exercised by soldiers, sailors, and workers (male and female) who took to the streets in great numbers to demand an end to World War I and an open and more democratic (and sometimes Socialist) system in Germany. The actions they took and the

146 WHEN DEMOCRACY BREAKS

institutions they forged, like the workers and soldiers councils, however fleeting, gave common people a sense of purpose and achievement, the power to mold the political order under which they lived.[7] Along with wage improvements, they forced the implementation of the eight-hour day, six and a half hours in the mines, a vast improvement over the twelve- and ten-hour days that prevailed before 1914. These councils were inspired, in part, by the Russian Revolution, but they were also an almost natural outgrowth of popular protest in the classic age of high industrialization. Similar institutions emerged in 1918–1919 in Italy, Hungary, Austria, and many other places. In Germany, the grandest hopes of some of the councils' supporters, for a Socialist democratic system, could not be sustained, but the councils did give people the experience of popular democracy.

Parallel with the popular insurgency, democratic reforms were underway at the top. Notably, in late September 1918, Field Marshal Paul von Hindenburg and General Erich Ludendorff, in a fit of panic, had gone to the Kaiser and told him that Germany no longer had the resources to prosecute the war and had to seek an armistice. A series of exchanges ensued with American president Woodrow Wilson and his advisors. The Americans made clear they would not negotiate with the Kaiser and his generals. Hindenburg and Ludendorff were only too happy to throw the responsibility of defeat onto a civilian government. So on October 3, 1918, the Kaiser called the liberal Prince Max von Baden to the chancellorship. Prince Max brought two Social Democrats into the cabinet, the first time the SPD was represented in the government. He freed political prisoners, including the inspiring radical Rosa Luxemburg, who began making their way to Berlin and other centers of the popular movement. Prince Max also eased censorship and instituted other democratic reforms. Notably, the new government established Germany as a constitutional monarchy and began to dismantle the inequitable suffrage systems that prevailed in Prussia and some other German states (though not at the national level).

Too little, too late. The popular movement surged forward. Germany would be a republic, that much was at least clear; what kind of republic was not. Germany entered the period of "dual power," as Leon Trotsky dubbed the months between the first Russian Revolution in March 1917 and the Bolshevik Revolution the following November. Would Germany be a liberal or a Socialist republic or something even more radical, perhaps akin to Soviet-style Communism? The issues were debated and fought out in the workers and soldiers councils, in the streets, in the various Socialist-led governments that took power at the national and individual state levels, and in the parliaments. The issues facing the country were enormous. Representatives of the SPD-led government had signed the

---

[7] The groundbreaking work is Peter von Oertzen, *Betriebsräte in der Novemberrevolution* (Düsseldorf: Droste, 1963).

armistice on November 11, 1918, but a final peace treaty lay months in the future. The army had to be demobilized and returned from its far-flung places of occupation, including France, Belgium, and Russia, along with the troops stationed in Germany's ally, the Ottoman Empire. The economy had to be demobilized and revved up for peacetime production. Hundreds of thousands of the war-wounded had to be treated. Would women continue to work in the factories in such large numbers? To Germany's east national wars, civil wars, and class and ethnic conflicts raged on until 1923, contributing to a great sense of insecurity.

On the same day the armistice was signed, the SPD leader Friedrich Ebert formed a coalition government with the more radical Independent Social Democratic Party. Ebert's slogan was "No Experiments!" The slogan was shouted and printed time and again. According to Ebert and his fellow SPD leaders, now was not the time to create Socialism. The tasks at hand were too great and Germany had to be placed on a steady course. People had to be fed and kept warm, and the winter of 1918–1919 was harsh. The country needed the expertise of the old regime. So Ebert moved quickly to sideline the workers and soldiers councils, his radical partners in the government, and the still more radical ex-SPD members like Luxemburg and Liebknecht who founded the Communist Party of Germany on January 1, 1919. Ebert's government called for elections in mid-January to establish a new government and a constitutional convention. The electorate gave the SPD a significant plurality, and it established a government, the Weimar Coalition, consisting of the SPD, Catholic Center Party, and liberal German Democratic Party (the former Progressive Party), reprising the wartime collaboration among the three. Both before and after the elections, Ebert also unleashed the regular army and paramilitaries on radical workers, resulting in a virtual white terror through the spring of 1919. Well-known radicals like Luxemburg, Liebknecht, and Kurt Eisner were assassinated, and many hundreds of lesser known workers and other radicals were killed.

The constitution drafters left Berlin for the more peaceful circumstances of small-town Weimar. They worked for over six months and produced a document that established the most democratic conditions under which Germans had ever lived. Globally, the Weimar Constitution was probably *the* most democratic constitution of its time. All the political rights enshrined in founding constitutions since the American, French, and Latin American revolutions of the late eighteenth and nineteenth centuries were written into the document, like freedom of speech, assembly, and press, and security of person and property. Men and women were declared equal under the law. The Constitution provided for universal suffrage and the recognition of trade unions. The population gained social rights as well, at least rhetorically. Notably, workers achieved the right to participate in the regulation of wages and conditions of labor.

148 WHEN DEMOCRACY BREAKS

The Weimar Constitution was a grand achievement. Its meaning lay not just in its specific words and strictures. Like the Revolution, its democratic spirit percolated through society. All during the 1920s people took to the streets in demonstrations, a lively if chaotic expression of democratic rights. Although the authorities sometimes shut down Communist newspapers, by and large Germany had an extremely active free press in the 1920s. Many localities, especially those led by the SPD or the Weimar Coalition parties, spearheaded social reforms. Local governments, trade unions, churches, and cooperatives, sometimes all together, built public housing with indoor plumbing and gas lines for cooking and heat. "Light, air, and sun" was the motto. Public housing, modern, sleek (for its day), and, most important, outfitted with running water, indoor toilets in each apartment, and gas for heating and cooking, greatly improved the living circumstances of those fortunate enough to gain entry to the new buildings. Public health clinics provided care and counseling of all sorts, not least about sex. A new openness prevailed regarding sex, including homosexuality. Jewish life flourished, despite the rise of anti-Semitic movements. Jews had far greater opportunities in business, culture, and society than at any previous time in German history, even if the state bureaucracy and army remained largely closed to them.

The democratic spirit of the Revolution and the foundation of the Republic also stimulated Weimar's lively and creative culture, which has endured down to the present day. The democracy existed not only in the formal political order but in culture and society as well. Writers, artists, and composers, along with activist workers, believed that they were creating a new world, a more open and progressive, modern world. New theatrical forms pioneered by Bertolt Brecht, among many others; the collages of John Heartfield and Hanna Höch; the extraordinary modernist buildings designed, not only by Walter Gropius but also lesser known (today) yet just as bracing and innovative architects like Erich Mendelsohn and Bruno Taut; the novels of Thomas Mann; the sculptures of Käthe Kollwitz; the philosophical reflections of Martin Heidegger; filmmakers like Walter Ruttmann and Billy Wilder, the latter among many who would go on to legendary Hollywood careers—these are just a few examples of the creative spirit that defined Weimar. Most of these individuals had begun their productive work prior to World War I. But it was the disaster of total war coupled with the Revolution and Weimar democracy that propelled them forward among the greatest of twentieth-century creative individuals. All of them, the luminaries and the lesser known, wrestled in their work with the meaning of modernity, its life-enhancing possibilities and its underside marked by alienation and the human wreckage of war. Despite popular understanding today, Weimar culture was never one-sided, never exclusively about fear, disaster, and bodily destruction. It was also about creating a better, sometimes utopian future.

These were some of the grand achievements of Weimar democracy. The supporters of the Republic were, by and large, Socialist workers, Catholic reformers and liberal professionals. But even the most fervent backers of the Republic would find their loyalties tested by the constant attacks from the right and the sheer volume and depth of the crises that consumed Weimar democracy.

* * *

The constraints on the Republic were great. Another inheritance, different from the democratic and humanistic one, rippled through the German landscape of the 1920s, and it was highly authoritarian. The Bismarckian unification of Germany had democratic elements, but it also remade for the modern era powerful conservative institutions and ideas. Power was embedded in the Kaiser, to whom both the military and the civilian cabinet answered. Neither institution was controlled by Parliament. Bismarck was largely able to manage his sovereign until Wilhelm II assumed the throne in 1888, leading ultimately to the chancellor's dismissal in 1890. Bismarck's less able successors and Wilhelm II's mercurial and not so bright personality lent something of an aura of instability or at least uncertainty to the system in the next two decades, which left more of an opening for the military cabinet to influence foreign policy. The three parties that would go on to form the Weimar Coalition—Progressive (later the German Democratic Party), Catholic Center, and SPD—struggled to assert parliamentary control and had some successes, but never could completely democratize the political system.

Within the state ministries strong conservative elements prevailed. The Foreign Office in particular was a bastion of the old nobility, and chancellors typically served as foreign secretaries as well. The economic ministries were tightly linked both to Junker (Prussian noble) agriculture—as unprofitable as most estates had become—and the coal and steel barons, along with the newer, somewhat more bourgeois sectors of chemicals and production and electric power generation. The infamous *Herr-im-Hause* (lord of the manor) ideology still dominated labor relations in industry, while the highly repressive, early nineteenth-century *Gesindeordnung* (rules of conduct governing servants) continued to determine life on the agricultural estates. (The latter would be one of the first laws abolished by the revolutionary government in 1918–19.) The Justice Ministry was also a reactionary bastion.

This old-style conservatism was both complemented and challenged by two developments from 1890 onward. The first was Kaiser Wilhelm II's self-proclaimed *Weltpolitik* (world policy), which threw off the restraints of the Bismarckian era. Germany, too, had a place in the sun, the Kaiser had determined. The result was the pursuit of imperial ambitions, especially in the Ottoman Empire, and a more forthright colonial policy. The series of reckless

150   WHEN DEMOCRACY BREAKS

comments and provocative actions that stemmed from the throne added layers of tension to the international order. More specifically, it destroyed the prospects of an Anglo-German alliance, something most observers had thought natural in the 1890s.[8]

At the same time, radical right-wing movements with a pronounced popular dimension emerged.[9] It goes too far to call them fascist. Most were steered by old-line officers or nobles, as was the case with the Naval League, the Agrarian League, and many others. But they certainly represented a politics that went beyond the limits of Bismarckian authoritarianism, including a potential hostility to the crown itself. A direct line runs from this kind of right-wing populism, significant though kept in check before 1914, to the more virulent and extensive right-wing radicalism of the Weimar years.

World War I brought all the authoritarian elements to the fore. Nationalist sentiment surged through Germany—though not completely so, as is often believed. In the last days of July and the first days of August 1914, numerous antiwar demonstrations occurred in cities throughout the country. The SPD's ultimate vote for war credits was determined by the party's long-standing fear of Russia, the continent's most autocratic power; a concomitant fear of repression and exclusion if the party placed itself outside the national chorus; and the nationalist sentiments that so much of the party leadership and rank and file felt deeply. No one anticipated the long, drawn-out, catastrophic war that ensued. Nor did anyone think (and why they did not is rather strange) that the *political* power of the military would only be enhanced as the country quickly came under martial law. In 1916, the third Supreme High Command under Field Marshal von Hindenburg and General Ludendorff constituted the virtual dictatorial power in Germany, surpassing even the Kaiser's authority.

Revolutions are never pretty. They are chaotic and bloody. But they also offer the possibility of profound and meaningful political and social transformation. As mentioned, the SPD-led governments continually pronounced the slogan "No Experiments!" Over the winter of 1918–1919 those governments limited the scope of revolution and in the process left in power the conservative elements that were hostile not only to Socialism but also to democracy.

In the winter of 1918–1919 all sides had their gaze firmly fixed eastward, on revolutionary Russia. No longer the feared giant, the autocratic power, Russia now signified Communism, terror, and chaos. All the conservative forces in Germany quaked at the thought that such conditions might spread to Germany. They were prepared to make compromises and accept the SPD-led governments

---

[8] See Paul Kennedy, *The Rise of the Anglo-German Antagonism, 1860–1914* (London: Allen and Unwin, 1980).

[9] Geoff Eley, *Reshaping the German Right: Radical Nationalism and Political Change after Bismarck* (New Haven: Yale University Press, 1980).

because they seemed the best bulwark against Bolshevism. The Social Democrats thought the same. For them, the gradual path to Socialism lay through representative democracy and the rule of law. They feared Bolshevism as much as the conservatives with whom they compromised. But the traditional conservatives would back the Republic only so long as they feared something more radical. Within months, for some even weeks, they would start to rescind their support.

The compromises with the old, conservative elites were embedded in a series of agreements over the winter of 1918–1919. In the most infamous, the Ebert-Groener Pact in November 1918 between the SPD chancellor and later first president of the Republic Friedrich Ebert and Quartermaster General Wilhelm Groener (Hindenburg and Ludendorff having more or less abdicated their power as well, if not their titles), entailed the army's recognition of the government in return for the SPD's promise not to challenge the order of command in the army. In other words, the old Prusso-German officer corps and its control of the armed forces would be left untouched by the revolutionary and Weimar governments, however restricted the army would be by the terms of the armistice and the Versailles Peace Treaty. The Stinnes-Legien Agreement between the head of the industrial association, Hugo Stinnes, and the trade union leader, Carl Legien, entailed business's recognition of the unions and, implicitly, the latter's support of private property rights. The government refused to conduct purges of the state bureaucracy in return for the civil service's tacit acceptance of the SPD-led governments. And no one was going to touch the influence of the churches, Catholic and Protestant. A more radical Socialist plan to ban religious education in the schools quickly ran aground in the spring of 1919.

The SPD's fear of "Bolshevik conditions" in Germany is understandable, although in retrospect a Russian-style revolution was hardly likely in Germany. Yet the SPD could have been far more adventurous in its political thinking. It had a brief window over the winter of 1918–1919 when it could have drawn on the popular uprising to institute more radical changes. It could have purged the officer corps and the state bureaucracy, assuring a more loyal army and state. It could have established a constitutional role for the workers and soldiers councils that would have granted them some power within the factories and mines, thereby limiting what would become, after 1923, a revival, at least to some extent, of the *Herr-im-Hause* method of domination. (The factory council law that was passed in March 1919 was essentially a sham.)

Revolutionary moments are rare and precious. In a society with strong authoritarian institutions, they can be used to radically reshape the political order, even though such reforms will always be less than what the most radical revolutionaries demand. But an overly cautious policy bears its own dangers. The limits of SPD thinking, the lack of political imagination in 1918–1919, kept in power those who were not just anti-Socialist but fundamentally antidemocratic

152   WHEN DEMOCRACY BREAKS

as well. They would go on the attack as soon as possible. The SPD's failures in 1918–1919 lay the seeds for the destruction of the Republic in 1933.

And then there were the Allies, who had their own limited political imagination. The problems with the Versailles Peace Treaty are well known and do not need here to be rehearsed in detail.[10] John Maynard Keynes laid them out already in 1919 in *The Economic Consequences of the Peace*, an immediate best-seller in Germany.[11] One can understand the French and Belgian desire for revenge and reparations. The British too needed reparations to fund the repayment of war debts to the United States. But the plain fact was that the Allies burdened the Republic, not the now-dead Kaiserreich, with the consequences of the war. The Allies should have nurtured the new German democracy, cultivated ties with similar-thinking republican elements in Germany. Instead, the stab-in-the-back legend became a leitmotif of German politics. It had its origins even before the end of the war, when Ludendorff and Hindenburg, in conversations with the Kaiser, threw the burden of defeat on traitors at home, notably Jews and Socialists. The Catholic Center politician Mathias Erzberger signed the armistice agreement on November 11, 1918. The representatives of the SPD-led government signed the Versailles Treaty on June 28, 1919. Every succeeding negotiation over reparations, even when they reduced the burden on Germany, was signed by representatives of the Republic. In negotiations the Allies gave the Weimar Republic almost nothing that it could take home and claim a victory (despite the efforts of the long-serving foreign secretary, Gustav Stresemann, whose public pronouncements always rang a bit hollow).

In that way, foreign affairs intersected with domestic German politics. Rather than supporting the Republic, the Allies gave its attackers ever more ammunition, even when they reduced the amount of reparations payments in the Dawes Plan (1924) and the Young Plan (1929). In the annals of international political failures, the Allied treatment of the Weimar Republic has to rank among the very top.

* * *

The right-wing attack on Weimar democracy began already in late winter and early spring 1919. It was unrelenting and took multiple forms. A series of radical worker and Communist uprisings in 1919, 1921, and 1923 were repressed by the army, militarized police, and paramilitary forces. A veritable white terror reigned at times in Saxony, Saxony-Anhalt, and the Ruhr, three of Germany's important industrial regions. SPD functionaries often commanded the militarized police forces or allowed

---

[10] Most recently, Jörn Leonhard, *Der überforderte Frieden: Versailles und die Welt 1918–1923* (Munich: Beck, 2018).

[11] John Maynard Keynes, *The Economic Consequences of the Peace* (London: Macmillan, 1919).

WEIMAR GERMANY AND THE FRAGILITY OF DEMOCRACY   153

them and the paramilitaries to operate with impunity. Political assassinations became rampant, those of Kurt Eisner, the head of the Bavarian revolutionary government in 1918–1919; the Catholic political figure Mathias Erzberger; and the Jewish
industrialist, public servant, and *litterateur* Walter Rathenau only the most renowned. The security forces—army, police, and paramilitaries—gained new leases
on life through their active suppression of working-class radicalism. As a result,
radical workers became increasingly alienated from the Republic. All around the
world the Bolshevik Revolution resulted in an angry division between Socialists and
Communists. In Germany, the divide ran deeper than anywhere else precisely because the Republic was associated with the SPD and because SPD-led police forces
often led the repression of radical workers. In the state of Prussia, for example, the
Social Democrat Carl Severing headed the Ministry of the Interior for virtually the
entire period of the Republic, while just below him the many conservative holdovers
from the Kaiserreich remained in place, only too happy to join in the brutal suppression of the radical left.

Weimar's many economic crises gave conservatives other openings to attack
the Republic. In the Revolution, as mentioned, workers had won trade union
recognition, the eight-hour day (six and a half in the mines), and higher pay.
The hyperinflation of 1923 undermined all those achievements. In that year of
extraordinary chaos, including the Nazis' first attempt to seize power, a botched
Communist revolution, and the utter devaluation of the German mark, any wage
gains won by workers quickly lost meaning, let alone the savings that a few skilled,
well-paid workers had been able to accumulate. To reduce a complicated set of
developments to their bare essentials, the government introduction of a new currency in November 1923 marked the effective expropriation of large segments of
the population. In negotiations among German industrialists and U.S. bankers
(both as proxies for their governments), along with representatives of France,
Belgium, and Great Britain, the French and Belgians agreed to withdraw from
their occupation of the Ruhr, Germany agreed to meet reduced reparations in a
timely manner, and American bankers opened their coffers to provide loans to
Germany. German business used the weakened position of workers to reinsti-
tute the prewar working day of twelve hours in the factories and eight and a half
hours in the mines, an enormous blow. One of the signal achievements of the
Republic was destroyed, leading to a crisis of legitimacy among even its most fervent supporters. True, over the next few years of economic growth, the Ministry
of Labor, led by reform-minded Catholics, gradually pushed back the working
day. Still, the Republic would never fully recover from the effects of both hyperinflation and stabilization.[12]

---

[12] For the most complete account, see Gerald D. Feldman, *The Great Disorder: Politics, Economics,
and Society in the German Inflation, 1914–1924* (New York: Oxford University Press, 1994).

154 WHEN DEMOCRACY BREAKS

Conservative sentiments were manifest not only on the estates of the nobility, the manors of industrial barons, and the offices of the state bureaucracy. They were present in popular culture as well, in the many *Kaisertreue* (loyal to the Kaiser) people from all classes and the indelible image of the male bicyclist, his head always bowed, a metaphor for the submissiveness of large segments of the population. Throughout the Weimar years, the annual conferences of the Catholic and Protestant churches provided major fora for the expression of hostility to the Republic, the fount, so the argument went, of moral dissolution, corruption, and political ineptitude. A cacophony of slogans and smears deprived the Republic and its leading exponents of legitimacy. *Schieberrepublik* (usurious or exploitative republic), *Schmährepublik* (republic of defamation), and *Judenrepublik* (Jew republic) were just a few of the insults hurled at Weimar in the popular press, presided over by the magnate Alfred Hugenberg, as well as in the publications of various radical right groups. The *Überfremdung* (foreign flooding) of Germany was another common expression. A photo of a paunchy Friedrich Ebert, president of the Republic, in a bathing suit, standing along with another SPD leader, Gustav Noske, in the waters of the Baltic, did not humanize him (Figure 5.1). Germans, accustomed to the pomp and circumstance of the House of Hohenzollern, the House of Wittelsbach, and so on, found only someone to ridicule. The photo "went viral" as much as the media landscape of the 1920s allowed. More seriously, libel and treason charges against Ebert, Erzberger, and other leaders of the Republic sapped their energies and demoralized them. The drive on the part of conservatives was not to capture or co-opt democratic institutions, but to destroy totally their legitimacy.

The emergence of the radical right was the new factor on the political scene. There were literally hundreds of such organizations in the 1920s. All espoused racial anti-Semitism, the abolition of the Socialist and Communist parties, the revival of Germany's great power status (meaning first of all the overthrow of the Versailles system), and the destruction of the Republic. Their popular activism and penchant for street violence marked them off from the traditional conservatives. Their supporters were a ragtag combination of displaced World War I veterans, disgruntled teachers and shopkeepers, some workers, and Protestants and Catholics appalled by the supposed immorality of the Weimar Republic.

Only gradually were the Nazis able to establish their hegemony over all these groups. Only gradually also did the traditional right and the radical right come to a rapprochement. Old-line conservatives considered the Nazis uncouth and unreliable, too low class. In the Golden Years of the Republic, 1924–1928, they could largely be ignored. But in the context of the ultimate crisis of Depression,

Figure 5.1 President Friedrich Ebert is on the right, his colleague Gustav Noske on the left.
Source: Bildagentur/Art Resource, NY.

156 WHEN DEMOCRACY BREAKS

when Chancellor Heinrich Brüning's policies only drove the economy deeper into the depths and political paralysis gripped the Parliament, the Nazis, as we shall see, increasingly became an attractive option for the old-line conservatives.

Still, when we look at Germany in 1928, we see glimmers of hope for the long-term stability of the democracy.[13] During the Golden Years, the living conditions for many people improved. The stabilization measures of 1924 had been harsh, but they did contribute to economic recovery. The diplomatic situation eased as the foreign minister, Gustav Stresemann, pursued the "policy of fulfillment," which meant that Germany would try to get the Versailles Treaty revised while adhering to its strictures and meeting the country's reparations obligations. The Nazis were a marginal political movement, a worry for the security forces but hardly a credible political threat. In the 1928 Reichstag elections, they won only 2.6% of the vote, while the SPD's share of the electorate increased significantly, to 29.8%, over its tallies in the early 1920s. (However, the SPD would never subsequently come close to the 37.9% of the electorate it won in 1919.)

* * *

And then came the world economic crisis, which hit Germany probably harder than any other country, including the United States. Right after Black Friday American banks quickly called in their loans to Germany. A financial crisis very soon became a demand and then a production crisis. Brüning, a highly conservative member of the Catholic Center Party, pursued a deflationary policy that only made matters worse. By 1932, one-third of the German labor force was unemployed.

The Great Depression finally destroyed the prospects for the stabilization of the democracy, prospects visible in 1928. A society already battered by the battlefield and home-front disasters of World War I, the difficulties of the transformation to a peacetime economy, the harsh strictures of the Versailles Treaty, and, especially, the results of hyperinflation and stabilization, now experienced another huge social and economic crisis.

Modern democracies have to deliver to their constituents. They have to provide order in society such that people feel a sense of personal security. They have to ensure that most people have opportunities to pursue gainful employment with the prospect of improving their personal and familial well-being. They have to guarantee that the institutions of state and economy are run with some quantum of fairness and thereby earn the respect or at least toleration of the population. On all these counts, Weimar, for all its great achievements, failed. Even

---

[13] For a cultural-historical perspective, see Rüdiger Graf, *Die Zukunft der Weimarer Republik: Krisen und Zukunftsaneignungen in Deutschland 1918 bis 1933* (Munich: Oldenbourg, 2008) and Moritz Föllmer und Rüdiger Graf, eds., *Die "Krise" der Weimarer Republik: Zur Kritik eines Deutungsmuster* (Frankfurt am Main: Campus, 2005).

during the Golden Years, constant street demonstrations from right and left created an aura of instability. The judiciary, a bastion of old-line conservatives, meted out stringent punishments to Socialists and Communists and let off rightwing activists with minimal or no sentences. And worst of all, the Republic could not master the economic crises it faced. Probably no democratic political order would long survive this litany of economic disasters, including reparations, hyperinflation and stabilization, and the Great Depression. Together, they blasted open a huge entryway for the traditional and radical right to launch their final assaults on the Republic.

In some ways, the Republic was already overthrown in 1930. A grand coalition government had been cobbled together after the 1928 election. It was never a model of cohesion, and it quickly fell apart after the Great Depression hit Germany. The central issue was unemployment insurance. A nationwide program had been passed by the Reichstag in 1927, a landmark piece of social legislation. It was envisaged as a way to ease the effects of temporary unemployment. No one imagined the massive employment crisis that ensued with the Great Depression. Quickly, the program's coffers emptied out. The Social Democrats demanded an increase in unemployment benefits and higher taxes on the wealthy. Chancellor Brüning, a member of the Catholic Center Party, called for a reduction in benefits in order to balance the budget. Brüning, in general, pursued the orthodox deflationary policies, akin to Herbert Hoover's in the United States, that only worsened the economic crisis. Moreover, like many conservatives, he wanted to use the economic crisis to accomplish two overarching goals: to overthrow both Weimar democracy and the Versailles Treaty.

So in one of the great political miscalculations of any democratic order, Brüning decided to call an election, confident that he would win enough popular support to carry out his program. Only hubris can explain why a sitting chancellor or prime minister could imagine that people would vote for him amid an economic disaster. In the Reichstag election of 1930, the Nazi vote suddenly soared to 18.3%. The shock cascaded through society and all the political parties. Even the Nazis were surprised. Nearly a dozen minor political parties together won 14%. The political order became even more fractured, helped along by a proportional voting system that set a very low bar for parties to win representation. The fracturing at the national level was replicated in most states; in some, the Nazis scored an even higher proportion of the votes.

Brüning remained chancellor, although it proved impossible to reach any political consensus. Between 1930 and 1932, Germany was governed by a presidential dictatorship. President Hindenburg, never a supporter of democracy, continually invoked emergency powers under Article 48 of the Weimar Constitution. The drafters had envisaged Article 48 as something to be used in rare and extreme circumstances; they were thinking of something like a

158 WHEN DEMOCRACY BREAKS

Bolshevik Revolution in Germany. Now it became a regular means of governance because a parliamentary majority could not be won for any piece of legislation, minor or major. By invoking Article 48, the president gave Brüning the power to legislate, which he did. His deflationary policies, even allowing the firing of individuals from the once-sacrosanct civil service, only worsened the economic crisis. Moreover, the two years of this presidential dictatorship further delegitimized the Republic all across the political spectrum. The SPD, fearing worse, adopted an official policy of toleration of the Brüning government, which alienated many of its own supporters. For the right, Brüning never went far enough in his attempts to destroy the democracy and the Versailles system.

Three major elections in 1932 only underscored the incapacity of the political system to deal with the immense crisis facing the nation. The first was a presidential contest. A host of parties, including the Nazis, fielded candidates. No one captured a majority, leading to a run-off between Hindenburg and Hitler. Hindenburg was by this point nearly eighty-five years old. He was a man of the nineteenth century, his mental capacity on the decline. Calculating that he was the lesser of two evils, the SPD threw its support behind him, a position that once again alienated radical and even moderate workers. Hindenburg prevailed in the election. For the Nazis, this second effort to seize power—the first being the 1923 putsch—led to internal dissension and, for Hitler, a personal crisis. He probably had a breakdown of some sort. He had not wanted to run, fearing a loss to the revered military leader Hindenburg, and did not know what to do once the loss had registered. But Hindenburg was convinced to dispose of Brüning and called to the chancellorship the still more conservative Franz von Papen. Two Reichstag elections and a succession of governments over the remaining nine months of 1932 only heightened the sense of governmental ineptitude and of the Weimar Republic in general. In the July 1932 election, the Nazis won 37.4% of the vote, the highest they would ever win in a free election. In November 1932, their tally declined to 33.1%, setting off another internal crisis within the party.

Indeed, it is possible to imagine the disintegration of the Nazi Party in these circumstances. Ultimately, Hitler and the Nazis were saved from oblivion by a small clique of powerful men around President Hindenburg. These noble estate owners, bankers, businessmen, and army officers, with Papen in the lead, prevailed upon the president to appoint Hitler chancellor of Germany on January 30, 1933. This deal marked the ultimate alliance of the traditional and radical right. The traditionalists shared with the Nazis a visceral hatred, not just of Socialism and Communism, but of democracy itself. They both wanted to destroy the left and rebuild Germany's great power status. The more traditional right was also anti-Semitic. If not murderously so like the Nazis, old-line conservatives also believed that Jews exercised overweening influence in Germany and that their power had to be curbed—despite the fact that Jews counted for all of 0.75%

of the German population. The traditional conservatives believed they could use the Nazis to overthrow the Republic and the Versailles system. The Nazis believed they could use the traditional conservatives to achieve the same goal and more. We know who won.

* * *

Weimar did not collapse like the proverbial house of cards. Nor was it a victim of too much "mass"—mass democracy, mass culture, mass society.[14] According to this viewpoint, too many people were constantly out on the streets demonstrating, too many political parties were active, too many demands were placed on the system. The underlying perspective in all of these works is that Germany (and, by implication, every society) needed a managed or administered democracy, not an overly popular democracy, to survive.[15]

The overwhelming issue, however, is that the Republic was systematically and relentlessly destroyed by the right, both the old-style conservatives and the dynamic Nazi Party, which represented something entirely new on the political scene.[16] The refusal of the SPD in 1918–1919 to purge the institutions of power—army, state, churches, business—of conservative elements hostile to the Republic proved a huge and tragic failure. From these bases, the old-line conservatives quickly withdrew their support for the Republic. Largely because of the Depression, the Nazis then proved capable of gathering in all those people and forces that despised democracy and Socialism, blamed Jews for Germany's defeat in World War I and everything else that had gone wrong in their lives, and thought that Germany needed to be, once again, a great power on the European stage. The attacks sapped the Republic of energy; even its supporters, by the end, were weary, beaten down by the intense, unstoppable hostility of Weimar's enemies and their own inability to master yet another set of economic and political crises.

---

[14] The sense of mass overload is present even in the classic, highly detailed account of Karl Dietrich Bracher, *Die Auflösung der Weimarer Republik: Eine Studies zum Problem des Machtverfalls in der Demokratie* (Stuttgart: Ring-Verlag, 1955). See also S. William Halperin, *Germany Tried Democracy: A Political History of the Reich from 1918 to 1933* (1946; New York: Norton, 1965). For more recent studies along these lines, see Heinrich-August Winkler, *Weimar, 1918–1933: Die Geschichte der ersten deutschen Demokratie* (Munich: Beck, 1993) and Ursula Büttner, *Weimar: Die Überforderte Republik, 1918–1933. Leistung und Versagen in Staat, Gesellschaft, Wirtschaft und Kultur* (Stuttgart: Klett-Cotta, 2008).

[15] This perspective is also evident, if *sotto voce*, in Peter Gay, *Weimar Culture: The Outsider as Insider* (New York: Harper & Row, 1968). Gay was close to and influenced by the older generation of German émigrés who were writing in the 1950s.

[16] See Hans Mommsen, *The Rise and Fall of Weimar Democracy*, trans. Elborg Forster and Larry Eugene Jones (Chapel Hill: University of North Carolina Press, 1996), as well as Eric D. Weitz, *Weimar Germany: Promise and Tragedy*, 3rd Weimar Centennial edition (Princeton: Princeton University Press, 2018).

Weimar is a warning sign for today, over one hundred years after the Revolution and the founding of the Republic, of what can happen when the institutions and personnel of a democracy are subject to unrelenting and often vicious attack; when politics becomes a war for total domination by one side; when certain groups are vociferously condemned and marginalized; when traditional conservatives traffic with the radical and racist right, granting it a legitimacy it would never be able to achieve on its own. And it is a warning signal that democracy is always a fragile thing. Democracies cannot prevail solely on commitment to the idea of popular participation. Democracies have to deliver, have to provide personal security, economic well-being, and political stability to their constituents. Otherwise it is all too easy for extreme nationalist and racist parties to gather support, blaming everything that has gone wrong on "outsiders," the minorities within and the migrants at the border gates.

6

The Failures of Czech Democracy, 1918–1948

John Connelly

Introduction

The collapse of Czech democracy in 1948 should command the attention of anyone interested in knowing how democracies survive. Before World War II, Czechoslovakia was a unique success story, the lone outpost of rule of, by, and for the people east of the Rhine, surrounded by the Nazi and Soviet dictatorships as well as authoritarian Hungary, Poland, and Austria. But Czechoslovakia had unusual advantages. Going back to the 1820s, the Czech national movement had portrayed the Czech nation as democratic: in order to exist and thrive, it needed self-rule. Moreover, the Czech lands possessed important prerequisites for democracy. The economy was balanced and prosperous and its population highly literate; Czechs benefited from liberalization in the Habsburg monarchy and had produced a full spectrum of political parties by the time war broke out in 1914. After World War I, thanks largely to Woodrow Wilson's patronage, the Czech political class came into possession of its own state, and a constituent assembly in Prague crafted a liberal constitution that functioned until Nazi troops occupied the country in March 1939.[1]

What happened to the Czech lands after the Nazi occupiers were expelled in 1945 is therefore mysterious.[2] Political life quickly revived, yet democracy was hobbled. Important right-leaning parties were now banished, and the once small Czechoslovak Communist Party, which had played no role in Czech governance

---

[1] This essay focuses on the Czechs. According to the Czech national mythology, Slovaks, whose language Czechs understand with little need for translation, were a fraternal people destined to share statehood for the sake of mutual assistance: they were two tribes and one people. The events of the early twentieth century, culminating in the political crisis of the 1990s, revealed that mythology to be a fiction. For background, see my *From Peoples into Nations: A History of Eastern Europe* (Princeton: Princeton University Press, 2020).

[2] Two exceptional studies have appeared in recent years, and I will make significant use of them in what follows: Igor Lukes, *On the Edge of the Cold War: American Diplomats and Spies in Postwar Prague* (New York: Oxford University Press, 2010); Bradley F. Abrams, *The Struggle for the Soul of the Nation: Czech Culture and the Rise of Communism* (Lanham, MD: Rowman & Littlefield, 2004).

John Connelly, *The Failures of Czech Democracy, 1918–1948* In: *When Democracy Breaks*. Edited by: Archon Fung, David Moss, and Odd Arne Westad, Oxford University Press. © Oxford University Press 2024. DOI: 10.1093/oso/9780197760789.003.0006

162   WHEN DEMOCRACY BREAKS

before 1939, now became the strongest party, claiming five important ministerial posts.[3] It did so not because of any electoral victory, but because the other legal parties—Czech National Socialists, Social Democrats, and Catholics (known as the People's Party)—had agreed to restrict the political spectrum and recognize the Communists as the leading force. Supposedly the future belonged to the left, whose dynamism and high morality were embodied by the Soviet Union, whose Red Army had freed Prague in May 1945.

But the Soviet Union did not impose its system on Czechoslovakia. Just six months later, that army, along with the U.S. armed forces that had liberated western Bohemia, evacuated the country, leaving the country's politicians to their own devices. In February 1948, after these politicians had ruled the country jointly in a government of four parties, the Communists exploited a mistake of their rivals to stage a full-scale takeover. On the surface, the mistake was procedural: the "democrats," as the non-Communists were known, complaining of Communist abuses of power, submitted their resignations on February 20. They expected that President Edvard Beneš would appoint a caretaker government and announce new elections. According to polling, the democrats were predicted to win in a landslide. They would then rule without the Communists.

However, they had miscalculated. The Communists and their allies among the Social Democrats (also a Marxist party) still held a majority of government posts and simply asked Beneš to appoint new ministers to replace those who had resigned.[4] This move was in keeping with provisions in the Constitution of 1920. They then called upon their hundreds of thousands of party members to form "action committees," which ousted their rivals from all positions of influence in state and civil society, and then began setting up a totalitarian order.

In what follows I trace how Czechoslovak democracy reached this conclusion after decades of formation and survival. The explanation is only partly about violence. As stated, there were no Soviet troops in the country, and if Czech Communists controlled the police in February 1948, they did not have complete mastery of the army. The explanation is more subtle, and extends into ideas about political legitimacy. Democracy did not simply collapse: it had been eroded in a process extending back to before the war.

In the eyes of many Czechs, the entry of Nazi troops into their capital in March 1939 had been enabled by Great Britain and France. The previous year, at the infamous Munich conference, the Western powers had presented Hitler with the fortified Czechoslovak borderlands (the Sudetenland) in exchange—they thought—for peace. Czech politicians had no say in these deliberations, but after

---

[3] There were sixteen ministerial posts in the first postwar Czechoslovak government: agriculture, social welfare, information, interior, and education went to the Communists. The prime minister and minister of defense were fellow travelers, and the deputy prime minister was a Communist.

[4] As explained below, these ministers were Communist fellow travelers in the democrats' parties.

THE FAILURES OF CZECH DEMOCRACY   163

German troops erased their sovereignty, they drew two lessons: Western powers thought that liberal democracy was good only for them, and if liberal democracy could not protect the Czechs' basic security, perhaps another form of government could. The Soviet Union also called itself democratic and seemed in 1945 to be a great success story, having carried the major burdens of defeating fascism. The world was tilting leftward, and Czechs had no choice but to adjust.

The Forming of Czech Democracy

Before 1918, the Czech lands seemed predestined for strong liberal democratic rule. The country's most evident advantage was social structure. Czech society was relatively egalitarian and featured relatively wealthy middle and working classes and peasantry, and a balanced economy with strengths across sectors, from farming and textiles to heavy industry and manufacturing. There was no native aristocracy or huge differences of wealth. Thanks in part to Austria, in part to the efforts of the national movement to foster Czech culture, the country boasted a complete education system and strong scientific establishment, with established professional classes, in the most developed of all Habsburg provinces. (It had provided the monarchy with its weapons.)[5] This self-confident and increasingly modern society articulated its interests through a variety of organizations that emerged after the 1870s: chambers of commerce, a lively press, sporting societies, institutionalized religious faiths, social clubs, and a full spectrum of political parties.

By the 1890s a transition had taken place, from a rather simplistic division between liberals and conservatives to parties stretching from Social Democratic and the more nationally minded National Socials (no relation to the German Nazi Party) on the left, then to political Catholicism and agrarianism. Further to the right, a National Democratic "camp" took shape, conservative in orientation, the right wing of which later flirted with fascism. The largest of all the parties were the Social Democrats, from which the far left splintered in 1921, making the Czech Communist Party, which, because of the land's relatively high level of socioeconomic development, was comparatively moderate.

The constitutional order of the Habsburg monarchy's western half (Cisleithania) became progressively more open and "liberal," and by 1907 it featured universal, equal, and direct male suffrage by secret ballot. Yet because of the difficulty in getting German and Czech politicians to work together, the

---

[5] Vaclav Benes, "Czechoslovak Democracy and Its Problems 1918–1920," in *A History of the Czechoslovak Republic, 1918–1948*, ed. Victor S. Mamatey and Radomír Luža (Princeton: Princeton University Press, 1973), 39–88.

164   WHEN DEMOCRACY BREAKS

Parliament in Vienna and the Diet in Prague could not produce governing majorities, causing the emperor to appoint prime ministers who ruled by decree, sometimes tolerated by Parliament, yet frequently blocked by obstruction. Czech elites failed to become reconciled to the Habsburg state because it never permitted them to control Bohemia in the way that the Hungarian elite controlled Hungary.[6] If Czech politicians became experts in obstruction, as a class they also came much more closely together, from left to right, than is normally the case. The point was to defend Czech interests against the other national clubs in Vienna, above all the German.

Still, Habsburg rule integrated the broad masses of the people, including peasants, into democratic practices, much in contrast to Romania, Bulgaria, Hungary, Russia, and to some extent Italy, where the majorities were disenfranchised and became fodder for radical movements. One unusual feature of the "plebian" nature of Czech society and absence of a native aristocracy, however, was widespread suspicion of social differentiation, which when combined with the demoralizing experience of Nazi occupation would produce enthusiasm for radical left parties after World War II that subsisted on ostracizing and demonizing others—first ethnic, then social.[7]

These institutional developments found support in Czech nationalist mythology. From the formation of the Czech movement in the 1820s to its consolidation later in the century under the philosophy professor T. G. Masaryk, democracy, freedom, and tolerance were portrayed as essential to the Czech character, going back to the proto-Protestant Hussite movement of the fifteenth century. Masaryk even had a grand idea whereby history moved forward, from monarchical and tyrannical rule (Austria) to scientific and democratic rule (the Czech people). The Czech question was therefore more than a concern of one tiny European people; it had supposed importance for the progress of humankind as a whole.[8] This notion worked well as long as conventional liberal democracy seemed to uphold the practical demands of the Czech movement for independence; when democracy in its liberal form ceased to guarantee the prospering of the Czech nation, however, its fate would become uncertain.

Such an explicit pro-democratic ideology was unique in Eastern Europe; indeed no other state on the continent (except France), produced a similarly strong

---

[6] Czechs wanted the monarchy divided into federal units, one of which would be under Czech control; that is, they wanted the deal that the monarch had struck with the Hungarian elite in 1867, permitting them to govern their own nation-state, while maintaining a union through the monarch with Cisleithania. (The ethnically diverse Hungarian lands were called Transleithania, lands across the Leitha River.) Vít Hloušek, "The Birth of Modern Czech Politics: 1848–1918," in *Czech Politics: From West to East and Back Again*, ed. Stanislav Balík, Vít Hloušek, Lubomír Kopeček, Jan Holzer, Pavel Pšeja, and Andrew Lawrence Roberts (Berlin: Verlag Barbara Budrich, 2017), 26.

[7] Hloušek, "The Birth of Modern Czech Politics," 18.

[8] Peter Bugge, "Czech Democracy 1918–1938: Paragon or Parody," *Bohemia* 47 (2006–2007): 22–23; Jan Holzer, "Politics in Interwar Czechoslovakia," in Balík et al., *Politics*, 35.

THE FAILURES OF CZECH DEMOCRACY   165

"nationalist republicanism." Masaryk preached that for Czechs "progress" was a moral but also a practical mission, of making minds and bodies strong and excluding no one, no matter how poor. Only a progressive program would permit Czechs to stand among Central European nations. The watchword was unity: according to Masaryk, "the modern national movement is politically and socially democratic."[9] The major threat was German nationalism, which was portrayed as undemocratic, authoritarian, and aggressive, whether in Prussian or Austrian guises.

The First Republic

This first Czechoslovak Republic of 1918 has been celebrated as the lone successful democracy in the East Central Europe of its time. In the 1990s Václav Havel called it "a modern, democratic, liberal State [that] was purposefully created on the basis of the values to which the entire democratic Europe of today is committed as well, and in which it sees its future."[10] The republic was indeed a formal democracy with freedoms to speak and organize, regular fair elections, representative bodies, and tolerance of minorities, political and otherwise.

Still, this democracy suffered from limitations because it was meant to serve the national movement. It was a creation and possession of Czechs and some Slovak allies, and Czech politicians, regardless of ideological orientation, cooperated to the exclusion of everyone else: the German and Hungarian parties and the Communists.[11] Slovakia was treated almost as a colony, with a marginal political presence in faraway Prague, and the real work of governing fell to the Czech parties, who governed as a bloc, of and for the Czech people, though constituting a bare majority of the state's population. (Germans were about one-fourth.)[12] What happened institutionally after 1918 was that the Czech parties learned to use "their" state for their own purposes.

The extraordinary cohesion of Czech parties meant stability. Where the Polish, German, or Yugoslav republics foundered on the inability of complex political spectrums to produce parliamentary majorities, the tight collaboration of Czech politicians guaranteed that democratic rule would survive. Throughout the

---

[9] T. G. Masaryk, paraphrased in Jaroslav Střítecký, "The Czech Question, a Century Later," *Czech Sociological Review* 3, no. 1 (1995): 67.

[10] Cited in Bugge, "Czech Democracy," 4.

[11] The actual doctrine of this Slavic state was "Czechoslovakism," the effective political myth propagated by Masaryk and other Czech and Slovak nationalists of the "brotherlike" relation between the two peoples, conferring upon them the destiny of unity in a common state of their own. But in fact it was the Czech elite that ran the state (Holzer, "Politics," 40).

[12] The exact proportion of Germans was 23.36% in 1921. Joseph Rothschild, *East Central Europe between the Two World Wars* (Seattle: University of Washington Press, 1974), 89.

166 WHEN DEMOCRACY BREAKS

interwar years, the five major parties (the *Pětka*) polled over half the votes and thus after each election formed coalitions that could govern. But their behavior also created a perception that no matter how the population's desires shifted, the same parties were always in power. Critics said the system caused people to believe that politics was the job of politicians, who, to make matters worse, failed to promote new leaders and lost all vital contacts with their base by the 1930s. They simply sorted out policy questions among themselves.[13]

Equally problematic was that the opposition in Parliament—Germans, Slovaks, Communists—was essentially ignored and took recourse to shouting and other forms of obstruction reminiscent of Czech behavior under the Austrian regime. Thus, while the Czech population became nationally integrated, with basic loyalty to the state, though not politically integrated, the German population was alienated in every sense and drifted rightward, producing by the late 1930s the largest support for a fascist movement achieved in any place at any time.[14]

The historian Jan Holzer has noted a problem in a democracy without real choices: namely, a conviction that political parties and contestation were a nuisance, harmful to the larger cause of national unity and national independence (something the *Pětka* system protected and ensured).[15] The system could prove intolerant when its survival seemed challenged. In 1933, Parliament passed a law permitting the shuttering of radical organizations, and throughout the 1930s a constitutional court, which might have challenged such extralegal acts, suffered from vacancies and never functioned properly. The absence of effective checks and balances would continue into the postwar years, when a strong and independent judiciary might have checked ministerial decrees and abuses of power leading to the February 1948 coup.

But with the background of the antidemocratic surge in Europe of this time, these appear quibbles. Despite administrative harassment, the Czechoslovak Republic featured a range of political options, and no serious infringements took place on civil liberties. Elements of the parliamentary system may have verged on the unconstitutional, for example the practice dating from 1919 that seats belonged to parties and not deputies, but what was the comparison? The French government banned a range of right-wing organizations in 1936 (which quickly reorganized), while Communists in every other state east of the Rhine could not

[13] "People spent political energies in the microcosms of the many party organizations, while general democratic integration, i.e. participation or interest in broader political issues, was low" (Bugge, "Czech Democracy," 16).

[14] Bugge, "Czech Democracy," 12, 28. In this they mirrored the attitude of their very popular president, T. G. Masaryk, of whom Roman Szporluk wrote, "The only institutional aspect of democracy which interested Masaryk was his rights as president of the new Czechoslovak republic" (cited in Bugge, "Czech Democracy," 20n64).

[15] Holzer, "Politics," 45.

THE FAILURES OF CZECH DEMOCRACY 167

operate legally. In Czechoslovakia the state tolerated Communists and fascists, though they aimed to destroy it.

Moreover, the disciplined and well-organized hierarchal parties of the permanent government coalition (the *Pětka*) formed an important counterbalance to the office of the president (called *Hrad*, or Castle), itself a power center, under the tolerant but elitist-minded Masaryk, the state's founder. Both he and his successor and collaborator, Beneš, believed that democracy was above all a defense against extremes of right and left and thus required a mediating institution above the parties, acting with little concern for formal aspects of democracy and constitutionalism.[16] The *Hrad* had allies and connections in civic associations and political parties; it intervened in public life when it (i.e., Masaryk) saw fit, considering itself a repository of wisdom that would ensure that democracy got proper ethical results.

Masaryk was likened to a monarch, a "democratic prince," and a "beloved potentate." George Bernard Shaw said he was the only man qualified as a potential president of a United States of Europe.[17] But how sound was a democratic regime that depended so heavily on the charisma and stabilizing force of one human being?

Masaryk had been dead for just over a year when the European powers— Germany, Italy, Great Britain, and France—decided to award Germany Czechoslovakia's border regions, with their overwhelmingly German population, on October 1, 1938. This was a disaster for Czechoslovak statehood because that area, commonly known as the Sudetenland, was a fortified border of hills, thick forests, and a band of modern defenses. Czechoslovak diplomats took no part in this conference at Munich and were given the choice of accepting or refusing its results. In the latter case, a British diplomat informed them, they would be on their own. Beneš decided to accept the diktat of the powers, arguing that he could not lead his nation to a slaughterhouse.[18] For his part, Hitler had cannily argued that including some 2.5 million Germans in Czechoslovakia against their wishes had violated the highest Wilsonian principle: national self-determination.

The effect of the capitulation on the mobilized Czechoslovak army of some one million men, and much of the citizenry, was demoralization. Neither

---

[16] "The *Hrad* [Castle] can be defined as a flexible, but at its core stable conglomerate of politicians, civil servants, businessmen, journalists, intellectuals and other people of influence, adhering to the President, his philosophy and worldview, and his political practice." The president intervened regularly in party politics, and also had control of some newspapers. He and his supporters also had an intelligence service (Bugge, "Czech Democracy," 18, 27).

[17] W. Preston Warren, *Masaryk's Democracy: A Philosophy of Scientific and Moral Culture* (Chapel Hill: University of North Carolina Press, 1941), 1.

[18] His words: "Should you reject this plan you'll be dealing with Germany completely on your own. The French will put it to you more elegantly, but believe me, they are in complete agreement with us. They will be disinterested." For a devastating critique of Benes for his "profound failure of psychological and political nerves," see Rothschild, *East Central Europe*, 132.

168   WHEN DEMOCRACY BREAKS

their leadership in Prague, nor the Western powers, felt democracy was worth fighting for. After the war, German generals said that their armies could not have broken through the Czechoslovak fortifications. Even now tourists can inspect the undisturbed concrete bunkers surrounding the Sudetenland. Yes, Prague would have been bombed, but perhaps the spectacle of a small nation fighting for its life would have shamed the Western powers—under pressure from their citizenries—and caused them to abrogate their deal with Hitler.[19] As it was, Germany made good use of Czech munitions when attacking France a little over a year later.

Beneš escaped to Britain, and the political system adjusted to what Czech politicians perceived as the will of the German hegemon. Soon they forbade the Communist Party and began working on racist legislation to ban Jews from professions. The press filled with chauvinist articles, and an intolerant nationalism crept into public discourse that had been unacceptable under Masaryk, with his ideology of "humanism."[20] How far Czech politicians would have gone in marginalizing racial and political enemies remains unknown, because Hitler's troops ended this experiment (known as the Second Czecho-Slovak Republic) with the invasion of the Czech lands on March 15, 1939. A German administration assumed control of what they called the Protectorate of Bohemia and Moravia, and Slovakia became nominally independent.

Czechoslovakia Becomes a People's Democracy

After the war, Beneš seemed vindicated. Czech towns were hardly touched by the fighting, and the population had grown. But his mood, and the mood of many Czechs, had shifted leftward because of the evident failure of Western-style democracy to protect their nationhood. Nowadays people say facts depend upon one's position in the political spectrum, but in 1945, whether one was Communist, Catholic, agrarian, or bourgeois, Czechs agreed that the "pre-Munich republic" had failed and there was no going back. Liberalism had delivered the Czechs' state to a genocidal regime. The anti-German uprising in Prague of May 1945 lasted only three days, but people claimed it was a sign of rupture, a "national revolution." The question was toward what.

---

[19] On the concerns of German generals, see William L. Shirer, *The Rise and Fall of the Third Reich* (New York: Simon and Schuster, 1960), 424–425. On recent work documenting the ability of Czechoslovakia to defend itself, and the likelihood of France and Great Britain coming to its aid, see Sven Felix Kellerhof, "Fast wäre es 1938 zum Krieg gekommen," *Die Welt*, September 18, 2018.

[20] Among these revisionists pointing to domestic roots of the problematic Second Republic are Peter Heumos and Jan Rataj (Bugge, "Czech Democracy," 6–7).

THE FAILURES OF CZECH DEMOCRACY   169

The first visible sign of change was the interim government, which had been assembled among Czech exile politicians in Moscow. It was called democratic but featured conditions not seen in liberal democracies. The major Czech political actors, Beneš's National Socialists, a Catholic party (the People's Party), Social Democrats, and the Communists, agreed to ban two right-wing parties, the Agrarians and National Democrats, for supposed collaboration. After that point, these four parties ruled in a National Front government and acted to hinder the emergence of other political parties. As a critic noted at the time, this was a regime without opposition.[21] But of course the idea that a handful of parties might control government was by no means new in Czechoslovakia, nor was the fact of no effective opposition.

Just before returning to Prague, the Czech politicians (with one Slovak party) worked out a governing program (the Košice program) that was left-wing and nationalistic at the same time, stipulating close alliance with the Soviet Union; nationalization of banks, industry, and insurance; land reform; but also punishment of traitors and the denial of citizenship to Germans and Magyars—some three million of the state's inhabitants. Until elections in May 1946, the parties governed through a provisional national assembly, by presidential decree, and by revolutionary "national councils."[22] Reminiscent of the grassroots "soviets" that emerged in the Russian Revolution, these councils were selected rather than elected and supposed to tap the people's will, bypassing bureaucratic details, vaulting ahead to purges of administration of those unfit for life in the new "people's" democracy. They featured a heavy Communist representation.

Though all four parties entered government, the Communists demanded key ministries from the start: agriculture, information, education, and interior. The last controlled the police, uniformed and secret. This was far more than their share, given that they had received only 10% of the vote in prewar elections, but no one objected. Thanks to their association with the Soviet Union, Communists claimed a paramount ability to protect the nation. They also asserted the left's supposedly crucial role in wartime resistance at home. And they were visibly growing. By 1948 the Communist Party of Czechoslovakia numbered 2.5 million members; among Czechs that was about a quarter of the population.[23] Unlike

[21] Paul Zinner, *Communist Strategy and Tactics in Czechoslovakia, 1918–1948* (New York: Pall Mall, 1963), 93. Beneš belonged to the National Socialists from 1919 to his election as president in 1935; see Otto Friedman, *The Break-up of Czech Democracy* (London: Victor Gollancz, 1950), 59.

[22] The provisional assembly had six parties, four Czech and two Slovak (and thus two Communist parties, one Czech and one Slovak), and operated according to a program worked out at Košice in April 1945. Each had forty representatives. The second Slovak party was the Democratic Party.

[23] Anna Grzymala-Busse, *Redeeming the Communist Past: The Regeneration of Communist Parties in East Central Europe* (Cambridge: Cambridge University Press, 2002), 32. The exact proportion was 25.3%.

170 WHEN DEMOCRACY BREAKS

members of the other parties, as we will see, Czech Communists were subject to party discipline and could be mobilized for party tasks.

Among the four parties, the Communists understood the tasks of building a left-leaning democracy most acutely and acted with brazen self-confidence, brooking no delay, gladly making use of the chaos of the early postwar months in order to cleanse public life of supposed wartime collaborators. They infiltrated organizations, including other political parties, but also workers' militias and factory councils.[24] The leading Social Democrat, Zdeněk Fierlinger, a personal friend of Beneš, accused by his critics of moral bankruptcy, was made interim prime minister, but in fact worked for the Communists, while commanding allegiance of the left wing of his party. Measures in the economy were part of this overall transformation: nationalization decrees, expulsions of Germans who legitimated property seizures. Beneš approved such measures through "decrees" which were rubber-stamped by the provisional parliament.

The leftward shift did not seem unusual and went beyond Czechoslovakia. In September 1945, Communist information minister Václav Kopecký told the National Front government, "The situation is no different in other European counties, namely in France, where one can count on a government with Thorez as premier, and the other ministers will be from the socialist and radical-socialist parties. The government in Italy will also be made up of leftist party groupings. This is leading to an unstoppable move to the left in all European countries, towards real and true democracies."[25] The new vocabulary was *lidovláda*, rule of the people, also described as "people's" or "real democracy"; even commentators right of center called the order *Socialist*.

Communists were of course the truest Socialists, but they insisted they were moderate; each country could go on a separate path. The Communist leader Klement Gottwald said that Czechoslovakia would go to Socialism without violence and disruption. Stalin agreed: it was possible in some cases to achieve Socialism without the dictatorship of the proletariat.[26] Beneš believed that given

---

[24] Maria Dowling, *Czechoslovakia* (London: Bloomsbury, 2002), 82. Because of criticism the trade unions dissolved militias in the fall of 1946, but not entirely, and they would be quickly reactivated in February 1948. Factory councils created in 1945 were very strong; they could form management boards and carry out purges. Martin Myant, *Socialism and Democracy in Czechoslovakia 1945–1948* (Cambridge: Cambridge University Press, 1981), 68.

[25] Cited in Karel Kaplan, *The Short March: The Communist Takeover in Czechoslovakia, 1945–1948* (London: Palgrave Macmillan, 1987), 1.

[26] For the views of Černý and Peroutka, as well as leading Catholics, see Igor Lukes, "The Czech Road to Communism," in *The Establishment of Communist Regimes in Eastern Europe 1944-1949*, ed. Norman Naimark and Leonid Gibianskii (Boulder, CO: Westview, 1997), 249–250; Radomír Luža, "Between Democracy and Communism," in *A History of the Czechoslovak Republic*, ed. Radomír Luža and Victor Mamatey (Princeton: Princeton University Press, 1973), 389.

THE FAILURES OF CZECH DEMOCRACY   171

the strong sympathies Czechs felt for the USSR, Stalin would have no reason to impose his system upon Czechoslovakia by force.[27]

The non-Communists were called "democrats" but shared basic understandings of history with the Communists. The USSR had miraculously advanced from agrarian empire to military-industrial superpower in a decade and was the war's major victor. By the time Western forces finally got around to launching their assault on Europe in June 1944, the Red Army was in Poland and Romania; less than a year later its soldiers stood at Europe's heart, in Prague, Vienna, and Berlin. As the most determined and bloodied antifascist force, Communists therefore displayed exuberant moral superiority.[28] They said that bourgeois democracy had proved unable to deal with challenges of economic development, and instead produced crisis and fascism and war. Similar to Polish intellectuals in Czesław Miłosz's *The Captive Mind*, Czech Catholics and liberals adopted the Hegelian view that history proceeds in stages; bourgeois democracy and the capitalism it undergirded belonged to the past, and the age of Socialist "people's democracy" was dawning. Communists would play the main role, but would be assisted by everyone else. Except of course traitors.

In our day no Czech intellectual better symbolizes the supposed liberal democratic option than Ferdinand Peroutka, a member of the Czech National Socialist Party who had known Masaryk (he belonged to "Castle" circles) and escaped to the West in 1948. But if we look at his argumentation, it was structurally identical to that of the Communists. He wrote in the fall of 1945 that "there is no turning back." Those who defend capitalism, he said, fail to ask tough questions about that old system's inability to solve the "social question." In any case, that old order belonged to the past. Though briefly stunned by the Nazi cudgel, Czech intellectuals had now awakened in a developing Socialist state. It was "pointless to prolong the feeling of inner turmoil, which plagues people who have refused to come to terms with the time in which they live [*se smířit s dobou*]. We have decided not to contribute to that feeling.... [P]eople have a chance of success only when they stand firmly on the basis of realities and not fantasies.... [T]he old world has died [and now]... only socialism is possible."[29]

A month later, President Beneš spoke on similar lines upon receiving an honorary degree from Charles University: "We accept the idea that liberal society

---

[27] Edward Táborský, "President Edvard Beneš and the Czechoslovak Crises of 1938 and 1948," in *Czechoslovakia: Crossroads and Crises*, ed. Norman Stone and Edward Strouhal (London and New York: St. Martin's Press, 1989), 132.

[28] For an evocation of this view, see the memoir of Heda Kovaly, a Czech Jew who survived Auschwitz: *Under a Cruel Star: A Life in Prague* (Cambridge, MA: Plunkett Lake Press, 1986), 52–66.

[29] Ferdinand Peroutka, "Není návratu," *Svobodné noviny*, November 25, 1945, emphasis added. A second leading liberal, Prokop Drtina, felt a new age was dawning: the whole world was moving leftward. Ondřej Koutek, *Prokop Drtina: Osud československého demokrata* (Prague: Institute for the Study of Totalitarian Regimes, Vyšehrad, 2011), 223–224.

172   WHEN DEMOCRACY BREAKS

theoretically and in practice belongs to the past." Commentators across the spectrum agreed that the interwar republic had been an instrument of class rule, which failed to solve the social question because only people of exalted social background had been permitted to occupy positions of authority. Real power had rested with finance capitalists, industrialists, and high-ranking civil servants, men with shady political pasts, who stood close to Czech fascists.[30] Even the liberals called Masaryk's democracy the *pre-Munich republic*, by implication a reactionary class state. Given that Beneš and Peroutka had themselves help run this state, such sentiments inspired guilt as well as an urgent determination to draw a line between themselves and that past.

And so now democracy had to be practiced more sincerely and successfully: all strata of the population would share in rule, and to those who felt shame about the past, that implied admitting Communists, mainly of working-class background, into positions of authority. There was of course truth to the allegation that the old top-heavy system had discouraged participation of average citizens; this was a mistake the revolutionary new regime would not repeat.[31]

No one specified what in the institutional makeup of liberal democracy had to be abandoned. One evident casualty in retrospect was tolerance of a range of opinions. Given the supposedly unquestionable failings of "bourgeois democracy," not to support the fledgling leftist people's democracy—whatever its real institutional substance—was concomitant to being a fascist and, worse than that, a traitor. Communists insisted that the nation would "tolerate no return to the political conditions [of the first republic], even in disguised form."[32] "Disguised" meant that the new order could tolerate only open, ostentatious loyalty and support; any opposition to the most antifascist force—the Communists—was by definition treasonous.

The most evident enemies, for whom it became treasonous to imagine equal rights, were aliens to the "people." The Košice program spoke of the "Slavic orientation of our cultural politics . . . in accord with the new meaning of Slavdom in international but also our Czechoslovak politics."[33] Though otherwise an optimist, Beneš believed that the Sudeten Germans had supported the destruction of Czechoslovakia in league with Nazi Germany. Even after that state was vanquished, Germany would remain a mortal threat for at least a century. Therefore the fifth column of Germans, one-third of Bohemia's population, including children and the aged, as well as antifascists and a handful of culturally

---

[30] Abrams, *Struggle*, 332n3; Christiane Brenner, *"Zwischen Ost und West": Tschechische politische Diskurse 1945–1948* (Munich: Collegium Carolinium, 2009), 91.

[31] Aside from some isolated Catholics, the view pervaded the political spectrum that party pluralism and "liberalism" had gone too far. Otherwise people's tendency was to say that the interwar state was a complete failure (Brenner, *"Zwischen Ost und West,"* 84–86).

[32] Brenner, *"Zwischen Ost und West,"* 90.

[33] Brenner, *"Zwischen Ost und West,"* 368.

THE FAILURES OF CZECH DEMOCRACY   173

German Jewish survivors, had to leave. Beneš believed the Western powers would oppose such a massive transfer and therefore leaned on the Soviet Union even more heavily.

Once Allied permission was secured, the expulsions proceeded rapidly: some 2,256,000 Germans were sent over the border in 1946 alone, causing Bohemia's population to drop by 20%.[34] Though mostly done by plan and supposedly "orderly and humane," the expelling involved seizing of property and routine violence, including rapes, to which the postwar ("Slavic") judicial system was insensitive. If democracy was not to be simply "on paper," as in the pre-Munich republic, then the "people" really had to decide by way of organs that had real authority.[35] The task of identifying and expelling Germans and Hungarians thus fell to revolutionary national councils through which the left invited mass participation.[36] There was no quibbling over fine points; the councils made use of hearsay and innuendo coming from people who felt aggrieved (or sought to cover the tracks of their own collaboration) or wanted to settle prewar political scores, and employed people with no qualifications as judges.

And law was really secondary. The measures' severity—the allowance of only forty kilograms of possessions and three days' worth of food, often preceded by humiliating detention—derived from views of collective guilt; at one point Beneš said that all Germans were responsible for the massacre at Lidice that had followed upon the assassination of Reinhard Heydrich by Czech paratroopers in 1942. A later dissident critic said that the vengeance of the early postwar months had paved the way for February 1948: security forces had "learned" to practice blatant illegality in these early postwar days, placing one group of citizens beyond the protection of the state. Now the traitor was of a different ethnicity; later he would be of a different class.[37]

President Beneš issued decrees legitimating the transfer of property, but the Communists got the credit because they were the force most clearly identified with revolutionary justice. They were heavily represented in the national councils and controlled the Ministry of Agriculture, which distributed millions of acres of land as well as a wealth of houses and livestock to often landless Czech peasants from central Bohemia. In May 1946 Czechs rewarded them with some 40% of the votes in their half of the country, the strongest support of a Leninist organization in free elections at any time. Among the strongest supporters were young people (the voting age was dropped from twenty-one to eighteen) and peasants

[34] Myant, *Socialism,* 64.
[35] Brenner, *"Zwischen Ost und West,"* 98–101. The Communists were the people's true "advocates."
[36] For an excellent account, see Benjamin Frommer, *National Cleansing: Retribution against Nazi Collaborators in Postwar Czechoslovakia* (Cambridge: Cambridge University Press, 2005).
[37] Danubius (Jan Mlynařík), "Tézi o vysídleni československých němcův," *Svědectví* 15, no. 57 (1978): 371–376.

174 WHEN DEMOCRACY BREAKS

anticipating even more largesse, as well as factory workers. Though Soviet troops had just left the country, the elections took place under vague threats: hints were dropped that Red Army troops in neighboring countries might cross into Czechoslovak territory.[38] Communist leader Gottwald now became prime minister.

The democrats felt they had no choice but to continue in government. Prokop Drtina, the National Socialist minister of justice, wrote that no single party could govern; even two parties could not rule with a solid majority. Therefore Czechs—following their basic democratic sentiments—had voted that all parties govern through a continuation of the National Front. All four parties had agreed to deep structural reforms, going beyond a cosmetic makeover, in order to make sure Munich did not recur, and the rhetoric of the National Front made unclear whether there even should be rivalry among them. Characteristically it was a centrist Social Democrat, the later dissenter Bohumil Laušman, who called for the most radical program of nationalization.[39] The term "nationalization" was particularly fitting in the Czech context because it meant putting property in the hands of Slavs, in a sense concluding a battle with Bohemia's Germans for what was called *nationaler Besitzstand* that went back to the 1840s.[40]

Democracy Recovers

Despite its limitations, the National Front government still guaranteed free expression, and among quiet dissenters, questions began to arise about this strange new form of governance: Why the pleonasm "people's democracy"? Was it not enough to say "democracy" if what was meant was rule of the people? Or was the point that the "people" meant something else: those who did not contradict the Communist Party?[41]

By early 1947, tales of violence and brutality toward the expelled Germans began seeping through the Czech press, fueling a sense of unease among much of the public. But non-Communist politicians found it difficult to switch from their rhetoric of accommodation, in which criticism of Soviet-style practice was taboo, to honest political contestation. President Beneš, for instance, never publicly uttered a harsh word about Communist methods or practice, though he

[38] The threats were made in May 1946. See Dowling, *Czechoslovakia*, 82–83; Václav Veber, *Osudové únorové dny* (Prague: NLN—Lidové Noviny, 2008), 46–47.

[39] Kaplan, *Short March*, 9.

[40] The idea was that Czechs were merely getting back what rightfully was theirs. Pavel Sajal, *Za 300 miliard hodnot vrací se do rukou českého národa* (Prague: Čs. sociální demokracie, propagační oddělení, 1946).

[41] This was a question posed by Helena Koželuhová of the People's Party in a book of 1946 (Brenner, *"Zwischen Ost und West,"* 111–112).

THE FAILURES OF CZECH DEMOCRACY   175

had plenty to say privately. (The same was true of Masaryk's son Jan Masaryk, the foreign minister, who belonged to no party.) Debates occasionally flared in Parliament about whether to return to rule of law after the "wild" retributions were finished, yet those who favored equal protection of all citizens were accused of betraying promises made during the war to hunt down every last collaborator.[42]

Therefore the contest pitting the values of Western versus Eastern democracy fell to a younger generation, perhaps because the trauma of Munich had not affected them personally. In 1946, non-Communist students had won majorities in student council elections in the Brno and Olomouc universities. The campaign rhetoric was a fierce blend of national and class-based innuendo, hurled from both sides. In the spring of that year, Vladimir Šoffr, a Czech army major who had spent the war years in Nazi camps like Auschwitz and Nordhausen, told students in a class on military studies at Brno that they were not "simple-minded workers, who saved up Reichsmark after Reichsmark, and voluntarily worked overtime, for whom life's essential purpose seemed to consist in black market trading.... [T]he intelligentsia is the center of the atom, everyone else must keep an honest distance."[43]

He was questioning the left-wing narrative according to which wartime resistance had been entirely an affair of the left; in fact it was mostly class based: the intelligentsia had been overrepresented, most dramatically in the demonstrations of November 1939, after which some twelve hundred students were sent to concentration camps, and nine "ringleaders" executed. (In the course of the war a further thousand students were arrested for resistance activities.)[44] The result was a storm of outrage in the left-wing press, and the major's immediate dismissal from teaching. Communists asked not how Czech munitions workers had indeed behaved during occupation, nor how many students and members of the intelligentsia had lost their lives, and instead vilified Major Šoffr as a fascist because he criticized *them*.[45] In response to a student protest before the headquarters of the Brno Communist newspaper, the local Communist cell called in workers from the Zbrojovka armaments plant, a factory praised by Hitler, where workers voluntarily worked overtime during the war.[46]

[42] Koutek, *Prokop Drtina*, 268.
[43] *Čin* (Brno), May 23, 1946.
[44] Jan Havránek, "Czech Universities Communism," in *Universities under Dictatorship*, ed. John Connelly and Michael Grüttner (University Park: Pennsylvania State University Press, 2005), 167–168. On the relatively privileged position of industrial workers in Nazi-occupied Czech lands, see Chad Bryant, *Prague in Black: Nazi Rule and Czech Nationalism* (Cambridge, MA: Harvard University Press, 2007), 85.
[45] The mostly middle-class Sokol gymnastics club was the strongest organization in support of the small resistance movement, and lost over a thousand members executed. Detlev Brandes, *Die Tschechen unter deutschem Protektorat* (Munich: R. Oldenbourg Verlag, 1975), 2:60–62.
[46] See the recollections of Daruše Burdová of Brno at U.S. Holocaust Memorial Museum oral history project, https://collections.ushmm.org/search/catalog/irn87814.

176   WHEN DEMOCRACY BREAKS

In late March 1947 the critical focus upon the Communists intensified as more became known about police excesses during the expulsion of Germans from northern Bohemia.[47] Communist disregard for "bourgeois" rule of law began alienating otherwise loyal Social Democrats, who joined the "democrats" (National Socialists and Catholics) in condemning the violence as well as "limitations on free speech represented by police assistance [i.e., presence] at public meetings. Czech students, who were the first to taste fascist methods and for whom Masaryk's humanistic ideals are sacred, cannot bear joint responsibility for the elements of fascism which we see in contemporary Czech life, only in another color and another form." Of the forty-one students who cast votes, twenty-nine supported the resolution, three opposed it, and nine abstained.[48] The Communists could not openly defend police violence, but they refused to support the resolution since it seemed an outright affront to "our state," meaning the "people's democratic" regime.

Communist students suffered more defeats in student council elections. In late November 1947, they were voted down in Prague's faculty of commercial studies by 1,500 to 250, surprising the *New York Times* correspondent on the scene. "Careless of considerations that make older politicians hesitate," the democrats took down portraits of Stalin and Tito in student faculty offices when the Communists removed portraits of Roosevelt and Churchill, and set up a board to investigate a Communist functionary who had referred to professors at his faculty as "fascists." Anyone using that word had to present evidence that it really applied; it could not be a class-based tool of abuse.[49]

Though there was no open disagreement between the National Socialists and Communists in the central government, a coarse rhetoric was beginning to set into national politics as well, reflecting suspicions of enemy forces bent on subversion and total power. In January 1947, Communist leader Gottwald said that to defeat the (still hidden) reactionary forces in the National Front, his party would need an absolute majority. Its policy must be "active struggle, gaining new position after new position, pushing the enemy into the defensive."[50] Yet Communists stood little chance of achieving even a plurality. In early 1948, the opinion research institute in Communist Václav Kopecký's Ministry of

---

[47] *Svobodné Slovo*, March 27, 1947. On this case and others of mistreatment of Germans by supposed partisans protected by their membership in the Communist Party, see Tomáš Staněk, *Verfolgung 1945: Die Stellung der Deutschen in Böhmen, Mähren, und Schlesien* (Vienna: Böhlau, 2002), 83–84, 129.

[48] Charles University Archive (Prague), SVS 140.

[49] The exact tally is 1,382 for National Socialists and People's Party, 259 for the Social Democrats, and 253 for the Communists. Albion Ross, "Prague Students Fight Reds Openly: Faculty Elections Continue to Pile Humiliating Defeats on Totalitarian Elements," *New York Times*, November 29, 1947.

[50] Josef Korbel, *The Communist Subversion of Czechoslovakia* (Princeton: Princeton University Press, 1959), 183.

Information determined that his party would get 28% of the vote in the elections scheduled for May.[51] Communists could not come to power by the ballot box.

As relations worsened between West and East, the tension between the pro-West internal stance of Czech democratic politicians and their external subservience to the Soviet Union was approaching a breaking point. At the Paris Peace Conference in the summer of 1947, U.S. secretary of state James Byrnes cabled instructions to Washington to stop the extension of a credit of fifty million dollars to Prague when the Czechoslovak delegation applauded Soviet foreign minister Vyshinsky's charge that the "United States was trying to dominate the world with hand-outs."[52] Yet to the Czechs that seemed unfair: what Byrnes had failed to note was that only the Communists (two of ten) had clapped.[53] Yet if the United States seemed unsympathetic to their dilemma of bridging East and West, the Soviets were making loyalty an absolute condition. In July the Czechoslovak government agreed to accept the U.S. invitation to participate in Marshall Plan aid. Yet Stalin forbade it from collecting, saying the Plan was a hostile act. President Beneš might have objected, still traumatized by Munich, but chose not to. At this time he also suffered his first stroke.[54] Foreign Minister Jan Masaryk famously lamented that he was no longer the foreign minister of an independent country, but at the time this was no more than a private gripe.

In September 1947, Stalin summoned Europe's Communist leaders to Szklarska Poręba, a mountain resort in Polish Silesia, to found the Communist Information Bureau—Cominform—that would coordinate the work of "progressive" forces. The Soviets urged the radical Yugoslav delegation to humiliate French and Italian comrades for sharing government with bourgeois forces and imagining they could seize power via the ballot box. The charges also implicated Czechoslovak Communists who likewise shared power with non-Communists and were gearing up for elections. Upon returning to Prague, Party General Secretary Rudolf Slánský informed the Politburo that Czechoslovak Communists must place their country squarely on the track to Socialism. They would have to shift the party's line: the previous year, party chief Gottwald had been speaking of a "Czechoslovak road to socialism" without the violence of the Soviet model.[55] Slánský also said the reactionaries were increasingly aggressive; what he really meant was that Czech Communists' popularity was declining.

---

[51] That was a drop of 10% from 1946. Tad Szulc, *Czechoslovakia since World War II* (New York: Viking Press, 1971), 37.

[52] Vít Smetana, "Pod křídla Sovětů: Mohlo se Československo vyhnout 'sklouznutí' za železnou oponu?," *Soudobé dějiny* 15, no. 2 (2008): 275–277.

[53] The United States also opposed Czechoslovak plans to deport 100,000 Hungarians (Korbel, *The Communist Subversion of Czechoslovakia*, 179).

[54] This is the analysis of Táborský, "President Edvard Beneš," 139. That stroke was suffered on the night of July 9 to 10, 1948.

[55] Vojtech Mastny, *The Cold War and Soviet Insecurity* (Oxford: Oxford University Press, 1996), 33; Jiří Pernes, "Specifická cesta KSČ k socialismu," *Soudobé dějiny*, nos. 1–2 (2016): 11–53.

178   WHEN DEMOCRACY BREAKS

The most specular danger sign was the Social Democrats' party congress at Brno in mid-November 1947, where by 283 to 182 the delegates replaced party chief and fellow traveler Zdeněk Fierlinger with centrist Bohumil Laušman. The vote sent Communists into alarm mode because it showed that the moderate Marxists could not be counted on to partner with them in the coming elections. Communist chances of getting a majority would be nonexistent. A Soviet official told the National Socialist Hubert Ripka that the defeat of "comrade" Fierlinger reflected anti-Soviet tendencies among Czech and Slovak "reactionaries."[56] But here too was a chance for Beneš and other non-Communists—including Masaryk—to rally forces in the name of democracy. They failed to use it, however. The *New York Times* reflected gloomily that the Soviets held all the trump cards and unless a miracle occurred, "we must stand by and watch the dark curtain descend upon Prague."[57]

The reporter was observing what seemed an unstoppable momentum: the "totalitarian" left had already devastated the opposition in Romania, Poland, Hungary, and, most shocking, in Bulgaria. In June 1947, police had arrested the Bulgarian Agrarian leader Nikola Petkov in the chambers of Parliament and put him on trial for attempting to restore "fascism." (In fact he had been in the resistance.) Refused counsel and unable to summon witnesses, Petkov was sentenced to death, hanged, and denied Christian burial. The Central Committee of Bulgaria's trade unions issued a statement read over Radio Sofia: "To a dog, a dog's death!" Before Petkov's arrest numerous politicians and army officers were tortured to produce evidence against him. In the weeks that followed the Communists disbanded all remaining parties except for a branch of the Agrarians loyal to them.[58]

In late 1947, Czechoslovak Communist officials openly threatened violence. Gottwald said his party would "settle accounts" with Laušman for betraying them, and he told Minister of Justice Drtina, "[Y]ou will meet a bad end."[59] Communist information minister Václav Kopecký spoke with undisguised disdain of opposition students. "You cannot work with people like [democratic student leader Emil] Ransdorf," he said, "only fight them. Agitation against the Communist Party of Czechoslovakia can be taken as an act of a fascist character." When Ransdorf questioned the legality of expropriating capitalists, Kopecký

---

[56] Ripka was minister of foreign trade (Korbel, *The Communist Subversion of Czechoslovakia*, 189).

[57] "Crisis in Czechoslovakia," *New York Times*, November 18, 1947. On Beneš's silence, see Albion Ross, "Beneš Rules Out Isolation of Reds," *New York Times*, November 22, 1947.

[58] Michael Padev, *Dimitrov Wastes No Bullets. Nikola Petkov: The Test Case* (London: Eyre and Spottiswoode, 1948); Frederick B. Chary, *A History of Bulgaria* (Santa Barbara, CA: Greenwood, 2011), 127; *Sydney Morning Herald*, September 25, 1947; R. J. Crampton, *Concise History of Bulgaria* (Cambridge: Cambridge University Press, 1997), 186.

[59] Korbel, *The Communist Subversion of Czechoslovakia*, 193, 201.

THE FAILURES OF CZECH DEMOCRACY   179

called for his arrest.[60] He had good reason to believe the democratic leaders in government would not object. To this point they had acceded to all measures of expropriation, as well as the far-reaching nationalizations. They even objected to allegations that they were not Socialist.[61]

The Communist Coup

Plans for seizing power had emerged during the war years, but only in February 1948 did the Communists follow through. The final confrontation might have been ignited by numerous disagreements, for example on agricultural policy or taxation, but it exploded suddenly over flagrant Communist infiltration of the police. Interior Minister Václav Nosek, a Communist politician judged reasonable during London emigration, had recently fired eight non-Communist commanders in the Prague force and put men in their places loyal to him. On February 13, the democratic deputies voted to censure Nosek and demanded the dismissed commanders be reinstated. Nosek and Gottwald ignored the vote, and twelve non-Communist ministers resigned on February 20, believing President Beneš would call for early elections after appointing a caretaker government. Instead, Beneš refused to diverge from the National Front model and required that all parties continue to be represented in government. He was acting from the ingrained conviction that he must mediate among the parties in the tradition of the interwar *Hrad*.

On February 19, the Soviet deputy foreign minister Valerian A. Zorin flew into Prague and told the wavering Czech Communists that this was their moment. He visited Foreign Minister Masaryk, in bed with laryngitis at his apartment in the Czernin palace, and informed him of Soviet displeasure at the activities of Czechoslovak "reactionaries." He also called on the Social Democrat Laušman and threatened Soviet intervention if his party maintained contact with the ministers who had resigned, alleging they were in contact with "reactionary governments."[62] A huge team of KGB functionaries arrived in Prague, and news filtered in of Soviet forces in Hungary gathering on the Slovak border.[63]

---

[60] Compiled from reports by *Národní osvobození*, December 5, 1947; *Svobodné Slovo*, December 4, 1947.

[61] See the self-defense of Ferdinand Peroutka from February 1948, who argued that he and his political allies were indeed Socialists, but that did not conflict with demands for humanity and legality. He recognized that the Communist notion of Socialism demanded silence in the place of criticism. Vítězslav Houska, ed., *Polemiky Ferdinanda Peroutky* (Prague: Český spisovatel, 1995), 218–221.

[62] Kaplan, *Short March*, 175; Szulc, *Czechoslovakia*, 38; Veber, *Osudové únorové dny*, 275. Zorin had been ambassador from 1945 to 1947.

[63] Karel Kaplan, *Poslední rok prezidenta* (Brno: Institute of Contemporary History of the ASCR, 1994), 36.

180 WHEN DEMOCRACY BREAKS

The Communists reactivated the revolutionary people's militias that had been disbanded in 1946, and on February 20, Deputy Commander Josef Smrkovský (later a hero of the Prague Spring) told militiamen to be ready for a "state of battle" the following day. Seven thousand of them received ammunition from the armament works in Brno. President Beneš failed to summon the army as a countermeasure, perhaps unsure of its loyalty because Communists and Soviet agents infiltrated the higher ranks. Fellow traveler and Defense Minister General Ludvík Svoboda (also later a hero of the Prague Spring) said that Czechoslovakia could maintain its freedom only under Soviet protection, a view that Beneš did not and could not oppose. For him, freedom for Czechs was national independence and not personal "liberal" freedom, and he made frequent references to the Munich debacle. Though Germany was divided into four zones, he would not renounce Soviet protection against Germany; thus, rather than a threat, he saw the Red Army as an ultimate guarantee of sovereignty.[64]

The democratic ministers had counted on three Social Democratic ministers who failed them. Gottwald thus still had a majority in the cabinet and drew up a list of fellow-traveler politicians from the National Social and Catholic parties who would replace those who had resigned. Technically, he was acting within the bounds of the 1920 Constitution, but while he negotiated with Beneš, below the Castle Communist-controlled police were arresting lower-ranking democratic politicians, supposedly for attempting a seizure of power. Beneš had pledged to his secretary in June 1947, "[T]he Communists could seize power in this country only over my dead body," yet on February 25 he signed Gottwald's new cabinet list, arguing, as in 1938, that he could not bear responsibility for a mass slaughter of innocent people.[65] Gottwald had allegedly threatening violence in the streets if the president refused to comply.[66]

Yet Gottwald's threats were verbal, and nothing hindered Beneš from calling his bluff. Would the Red Army have staged an armed intervention if he and Masaryk had rallied the public to their side? We know from internal correspondence that the Soviet leadership was not willing to send troops into Czechoslovakia; moreover, Stalin tended to be cautious in foreign policy.[67] By

---

[64] Kaplan, *Poslední rok*, 36. On February 23, he addressed a meeting of the Renewed National Front, declaring that the "army goes with the nation. . . . [W]ho disturbs the unity of the nation is a menace and must be removed." Szulc, *Czechoslovakia*, 39.

[65] Táborský, "President Edvard Beneš," 136.

[66] The report of threats is from Beneš's physician. See Szulc, *Czechoslovakia*, 40; Jon Bloomfield, *Passive Revolution: Politics and the Czechoslovak Working Class, 1945–1948* (London: Allison and Busby, 1979), 231.

[67] Táborský thinks they would have used less direct means, like economic pressure. Foreign Minister Molotov refused the request of Czech Communists to move troops in Austria or Germany closer to the Czech borders, let alone to transport them into Czechoslovakia. The

THE FAILURES OF CZECH DEMOCRACY   181

his mere name Masaryk commanded the loyalties of a majority of Czechs. In any case, these men's wavering postures were more than counterbalanced by the Communist drive for quick resolution of a festering problem, most memorably embodied in the "people's" militiamen who stormed into and occupied the headquarters of non-Communist parties (seeking "traitors").[68]

Later, Beneš cursed the "treasonous" Social Democrats, including his onetime confidant Fierlinger, whom he said should be destroyed like a "snake," or better yet, hanged from the nearest tree.[69] He complained that the democratic ministers had surprised him; Masaryk called them idiots and buffoons and showed them no solidarity. For their part the democrats were upset that Benes summoned the Communists and Social Democrats for consultations, but not them.[70] But Beneš also wondered why the non-Communists failed to organize resistance. When Central Prague was flooded with workers supporting Gottwald's coup, one could not find even two members of the Sokol (the bourgeois national gymnastics association) or Legionaries on Wenceslaus Square. The lone group to mobilize for democracy were some ten thousand students who twice marched up to the Prague Castle, but Beneš did nothing to encourage them.[71]

In the months that followed, the student dissidents were purged, depleting the country of a young liberal leadership stratum and consigning liberal ideas about politics to decades of oblivion. Some were sent to camps, others to uranium mines, still others to the military. Beginning on February 21, the party had summoned loyal cadres to form "action committees," which swept public life with the harsh broom of revolution, scouring all organizations of "traitors," including political parties, schools, factories, newspapers, and of course

methods used were more subtle; for example, Moscow supported the trip of Polish socialists whose task was to warn Czech Social Democrats not to align themselves with the "right," that is, the democrats. The tone of the Soviet press was of course hostile to the Czech democrats (Veber, *Osudové únorové dny*, 275–278).

[68] Jonathan Haslam, *Russia's Cold War: From the October Revolution to the Fall of the Wall* (New Haven: Yale University Press, 2011), 100. For an argument that Beneš had lost his ability to reach and command the use of the army, see the recollections of his chancellor Jaromír Smutny, in Korbel, *The Communist Subversion of Czechoslovakia*, 225. On the use of the people's militia to seize the Social Democratic headquarters on February 24, see Jan Stransky, *East Wind over Prague* (New York: Random, 1950), 201.

[69] He said this in March. Václav Černý, *Paměti 1945–1972* (Prague: Atlantis, 1992), 182.

[70] He said they had failed to coordinate their action with the president; whether the president would have supported them was a question Masaryk did not entertain. His allegiance to Moscow, which some date to 1935, did not brook doubt. Karel Kaplan, *Pět kapitol o únoru* (Brno: Doplněk, 1997), 445. For their part, the democrats believed they had acted with Beneš's approval (Lukes, *On the Edge*, 193). On their disappointment with Beneš, see Veber, *Osudové únorové dny*, 279.

[71] Organizers said about twenty thousand to thirty thousand students took part; the leading student of the events, Zdeněk Pousta, places the figure around nine thousand (Veber, *Osudové únorové dny*, 300).

182   WHEN DEMOCRACY BREAKS

state administration. These acts were illegal, but when the action committees encountered resistance they threatened use of the police to enforce their will. (The police now took personal oaths of loyalty to Communist chief Gottwald.)[72]

But resistance was rare. On February 24, action committees at the seat of government told the non-Communist ministers they were no longer welcome in their offices, and they departed without complaint. The head of the Catholic People's Party, Father Jan Šrámek, once president of the government in exile, declared his party dissolved in order to protect its good name. (In March he would be apprehended trying to flee abroad.)[73] After Beneš confirmed Gottwald's cabinet, the new political leadership, citing supposed dangers of subversion and treason, justified the work of the action committees retroactively. Charges emerged, *almost three years after the war*, that non-Communist student leaders were Nazi collaborators. Sometimes the action committees went further than the party leadership had thought prudent, for example by firing the rector of Charles University just before the institution was to celebrate its six hundredth anniversary. Foreign dignitaries canceled their attendance at the festivities.

The coup was not a seizure of power by a small clique, but rather an activation of the instruments that Communists—with much support among the democrats—had created in 1945–1946 to cleanse society. Then and now revolutionary committees targeted traitors to the people, in the first case understood in ethnic terms, now in class terms. The enduring principle was collective guilt, the idea that a certain group of citizens stood beyond all legal protection. Still, victors as well as victims recognized a common logic: only the Soviet Union could guarantee that Munich would not be repeated. At the height of the February crisis, two determined opponents of Communism, Vladimir Krajina and Prokop Drtina, repeated the mantra that Czechoslovakia's alliance with the Soviet Union was beyond questioning.[74]

---

[72] Communists and fellow travelers, supporters of Zdeněk Fierlinger's wing of Social Democracy would seize offices, have locks changed, exclude and then fire those considered unreliable. See Josef Korbel's recollection of E. Loebl, a mild-mannered, jovial Communist official in the Ministry of Foreign Trade, who in February 1948 headed an action committee in the ministry and denied his superiors the right to enter their own offices, then purged the ministry of all non-Communists. The head of the Ministry of Posts, Monsignor Hala, was told not to appear at his ministry, otherwise the action committee would "summon all the means the working class has at its disposal" (Korbel, *The Communist Subversion of Czechoslovakia*, 148–149, 227). Loebl was tortured and tried with Rudolf Slánský, rehabilitated in the 1960s, and later became a professor at Vassar College. On the oaths, see Philip Selznick, *The Organizational Weapon: A Study of Bolshevik Strategy and Tactics* (New York: McGraw-Hill, 1952), 267.

[73] Pavel Horák and Vilém Prečan, eds., *Únor 1948 očima poražených* (Prague: Masaryk Institute—NLN, 2018), 317–318.

[74] It did not occur to them that the Soviet Union was the force insisting that they, the democrats, must be ousted from power (Kaplan, *Pět kapitol*, 349). Krajina was among the few who tried to stop the action committee from seizing power of the National Socialist Party headquarters (Veber, *Osudové únorové dny*, 297). For a discussion of the precedent set by the postwar expulsions, and the larger motivating force of "Munich," see Karel Kaplan, *Pravda o Československu 1945–1948* (Brno: Panorama, 1990), 20–21.

In the 1946 elections, Czech Communists had achieved the greatest electoral victory ever for a Leninist party, and the 1948 coup, propelled by the action committees, tapped the greatest popular energy ever applied to the construction of a monolithic Communist regime. The phrase that comes to mind, with the Chinese and Russian cases in mind, is "cultural revolution." The most enthusiastic purgers were young Communists who two decades later regretted their actions and formed a core of leadership for the Prague Spring, with its calls for legal projections of dissenting minorities and a return to the democratic and humanitarian ideals of T. G. Masaryk. They understood that "people's democracy" had been a shortcut to Stalinism; within two years the Party was subjecting its own top cadre to show trials, and Rudolf Slánský, so useful in organizing the 1948 coup, was himself hanged as a traitor to the people.

Conclusions

Among the factors conditioning the collapse of Czechoslovakia's formidable democracy, most striking was the country's precarious international position. In both 1938 and 1948, Czechoslovakia possessed a powerful economy, high standard of living, and robust civil society, yet in both years a consensus emerged in the hegemonic neighboring state that Western-style Czechoslovak democracy, indeed Czechoslovak independence, was incompatible with its interests. And in both cases Czech democratic elites adjusted their rhetoric and practice to suit the new circumstances.

In the short-lived Czecho-Slovak Second Republic (October 1938–March 1939) they transformed the political system, still mostly within First Republic legality, to an authoritarian racial state, seeking to secure the economic and cultural well-being of the ethnically Czech people under Nazi tutelage. Beneš and other liberals who had escaped to London then adjusted their understanding of politics to anticipate the requirements of the new regional hegemon after 1945, the Soviet Union.

They unwittingly prepared the ground intellectually and institutionally for the 1948 coup, by stating that Czechoslovakia was unshakably bound to the USSR, and then in concocting various pseudo-profound theories about the need for new kinds of democracy. Beneš had written as early as 1934 about the need to synthesize individualism with collectivism in "societism," a principle supposedly exemplified both in the USSR and in fascism. Liberalism, he claimed, was "dead." After the war, he said that democracy had to be a "corrected democracy, newly formulated," and he anticipated a synthesis of "democratic liberty and the necessary degree of governmental authority."[75]

---

[75] Antoine Mares, *Edvard Beneš: Un drame entre Hitler et Staline* (Paris: Perrin, 2015), 377. The word "pseudo-profound" is Joseph Rothschild's. See his *East Central Europe*.

184   WHEN DEMOCRACY BREAKS

The "people's democracy" that he and his colleagues consolidated in Prague in May 1945 tolerated limits on the right of association (for example, of new parties), on freedom of speech (an implicit ban on criticism of the USSR), on the right to own property, and on the security of the person, at first, for Germans and Magyars. Yet soon the regime was seizing possessions from Czechs as well in the name of "nationalization," while permitting no right of appeal.[76] Beneš and other "democrats" agreed that not democracy but "Socialism" had a high public value, and thus found themselves within the Communist mindset, according to which humanity had moved beyond capitalism along with the institutions that supported it, like "bourgeois" rule of law. Socialism took on a higher value because it served the ultimate source of meaning: the Czech nation.

What happened in 1948 was thus not so much a coup as a clear statement: that people's democracy really was different from all that preceded it, and there was no point in countering demands coming from the heart of the people's democratic order in Moscow. If in 1948 the democrats hardly conceived of, let along organized, resistance, that was because *they had nothing to fight and die for that they had not already surrendered.*[77] The rhetorical power of Socialism in its Leninist form was such that one Communist intellectual, Arnošt Kolman, later recalled feeling like a "matador" after battles of words with his most determined liberal and Catholic opponents.[78] What he and his comrades were propounding was more than a worldview; it was a "secular faith" that accounted for everything that had happened or would happen: the failure of the West in 1938, the temporary victory of fascism, the guaranteed future in which war and suffering became things of the past.

More than simply illiberal, this was an alternative to liberalism, far more compelling than anything authoritarians like Putin, Orban, Salazar, Franco, or Pinochet might dream up. The Socialist order did not call itself a belief: it claimed to be modern, fostering enlightenment and the good of humankind, putting all racism, profiteering, and corruption in the past. Most confounding for its Czech opponents, this "new faith" even managed to cloak itself in the colors of democracy, as a continuation of the nation's long heritage of promoting national liberation (without which liberation of the individual was meaningless), supposedly extending back to Jan Hus. In 1950 the Socialist state would rebuild the church he preached from, and for several years it even celebrated T. G. Masaryk's birthday

---

[76] Kamil Nedvědický, "Únor 1948 jako počátek nelegitimního režimu," *Securitas imperii* 17 (2010): 65.
[77] Brenner, "*Zwischen Ost und West,*" 113.
[78] Kolman was later a victim of Stalinism. John Connelly, *Captive University: The Sovietization of East German, Czech, and Polish Higher Education, 1945–1956* (Chapel Hill: University of North Carolina Press, 2000), 75.

THE FAILURES OF CZECH DEMOCRACY   185

(March 7) as a national holiday. Party propaganda claimed the old philosopher-king would have supported the coup.[79]

In 1947 the conviction took hold in much of the younger generation that people's democracy was in fact a cover for totalitarian rule, and real political contestation shifted to student councils, where the democrats stoked outrage over injustices done to Germans in which their elders, like National Social justice minister Drtina, had been complicit. (Few of those democratic leaders would later ponder in their bile-laden memoirs whether it had been possible to limit democracy to a single class or ethnic group.) The democratic students demonstrated that faith in Western democracy had not eroded beyond repair, yet in two marches to the Castle in February 1948 they were the only group in Czech society that came out vocally against the Communist coup.

But these young democrats carried no weapons, had no police behind them and no hope. The left-wing intelligentsia would portray the seizure of power ("victorious February") as the fulfillment of progressive dreams, yet ultimately it was the new secular faith combined with threats of police and militia violence that guaranteed that the "action committees" could work without hindrance, purging Czechoslovak political life of dissent. Soon came show trials, first hitting "bourgeois" politicians (and costing Czech women's advocate Milada Horáková her life in 1949), before turning upon the Communist Party itself.

As during the Munich crisis of 1938, much hinged on Beneš. He might have said no to Stalin in July 1947 and at least made use of the limited capital he possessed to appeal to Czechoslovak citizens. After all, even Gottwald and his comrades supported the acceptance of Marshall Plan aid, and the idea of U.S.-sponsored assistance was popular. In February 1948, Beneš might have moved more rapidly and skillfully, appointing an interim cabinet of experts, ordering the army to stand by to maintain order, and appealing directly to the nation over the radio. He could have exploited levers he undoubtedly possessed.[80]

But why did the health of the postwar order in Czechoslovakia depend so much on the acts of a single man? A democracy should be bolstered by the actions of free citizens operating in civil society organizations; its institutions ought to check one another. Robust courts should have declared action committees unconstitutional. Yet here one can trace problems that became fully evident in 1948 to the original construct, the short-lived democracy of T. G. Masaryk (1918–1938). Precisely because it emerged in a country where ethnic Czechs were a bare majority, this democracy had been led by a strong hand, first of President Masaryk himself, but then through an informal device that coordinated policy outside of Parliament, the *Pětka*, or committee of five, consisting of the leaders

---

[79] Robert Bruce Lockhart, "Report on Czechoslovakia," *Foreign Affairs*, April 1955.
[80] Táborský, "President Edvard Beneš," 139.

186   WHEN DEMOCRACY BREAKS

of ethnically Czech parties (Social Democrats, National Socialists, Catholics, Agrarians, National Democrats). Though the National Front of the postwar period was a Communist idea, it continued this tradition of politics managed by experts and unchecked by courts; in a sense the National Front was the *Pětka* with two parties removed and one added: the Communists.

Like the *Pětka*, the National Front carried on deliberations with little outside scrutiny. Thus, if public opinion failed to mobilize against Communist infiltration of the police in February 1948, that is because it was poorly informed.[81] Beneath the surface, the police had been transformed from an instrument serving liberal democracy—within well-known constitutional constraints—to the phalanx of an "organizational weapon," prepared to function as the tool of a totalitarian elite. But the weapon embodied in Communism went beyond party operatives who had been smuggled into the ranks of the police. Communist Party members were not just rank-and-file associates who paid dues and attended meetings; they were cadres imbued with faith and constrained by discipline, ready to be rapidly deployed in the extralegal councils and committees.[82]

Where the Czech case goes beyond classic totalitarian theory is that these cadres believed they embodied the people's will, transcending what the party leadership had explicitly told them to do, and in the process overcoming the apathy of the old managed democracy. Their frenetic activity *from below* (in the action committees) supposedly raised the Czech nation to a higher level of self-governance, achieving results that had eluded liberals constrained by rule of law. The origins of their self-righteous fury had little to do with class: the Communists and their opponents belonged to a wealthy modern society, without the gaping inequalities of other places. From the beginning of the Czech national movement, small differences in material comforts or status could generate huge dissatisfaction in Czech national politics; after the war, Marxism in its Leninist guise provided a platform for one group of bourgeois intellectuals to strike out at another.

The self-righteousness of the Communist side also drew from the humiliation of the war years. At Munich, a liberal political elite had surrendered a successful economy, a relatively equitable social system, and a superficially perfect

---

[81] See, for example, the reminiscence of Hubert Ripka, minister of trade from the National Socialist Party: "On the following day, *Svobodne Slovo*, the official organ of the National Socialist party, published a documented article entitled: 'We Will Not Permit a Police Regime.' It caused tremendous excitement, for it was the first time the public had been informed of the abuses committed by the Communist officials of the interior." That was February 20, when the coup was already under way. Hubert Ripka, *Czechoslovakia Enslaved: The Story of the Communist Coup d'etat* (London: Victor Gollancz, 1950), 223. Similarly, Benes was plagued by the idea that the public did not really know what he had done and thought in early 1948 (Černý, *Paměti*, 185).

[82] Selznick, *Organizational Weapon*, 20, 268.

THE FAILURES OF CZECH DEMOCRACY   187

democracy without a shot. Thus, the tasks of expelling Germans and taking their property compensated for six years of impotency.

Precisely because the Czech resistance had been meager, the controversies over its legacy were bitter. Against the Communist narrative of having single-handedly defeated fascism, Major Šoffr said that the anti-Nazi movement was drawn largely from the intelligentsia: right, center, and left. Insinuations and counterinsinuations carried into the student council battles of 1947, when liberal students questioning revolutionary justice were made out to be traitors and fascists. February 1948 saw an intensification of the fury against enemies who had supposedly survived the first rounds of purging. Major Šoffr was now put behind bars, along with thousands of other members of the "bourgeois" elite. The coup was like a reenactment of the 1938 crisis, with the same cast of characters in the Castle—Benes and his staff—but below, it was Czech against Czech. Perhaps if Benes had acted to protect democracy—of the sort he helped establish in 1918—free elections would have taken place in May 1948 and the Soviet Union would have had a difficult choice to make: to show that people's democracy did not require tanks to survive. (That evidence would be provided in 1953 in East Berlin, 1956 in Budapest, and 1968 in Prague.)[83]

By 1948, Czech Communists had succeeded in deepening a deeply moralistic "us-them" division among Czechs, on which the other side was made to stand for fascism. They asked not are you for or against democracy, but rather are you for or against the enslavement of the Czechoslovak people to foreign powers. Truman and Churchill were made to stand as one with Hitler. Zdeněk Mlynář, a young Stalinist student in 1948, said his generation was brought up believing in a world where they, the righteous, stood on one side, and the enemy on the other: "We were children of the war who, having not actually fought against anyone, brought our wartime mentality with us into those first postwar years, when the opportunity to fight for something presented itself *at last*."[84]

There were also banal forces behind the Communists' victory. They did well among people opting for radical social change, similar to supporters of Labour in the United Kingdom, and when 40% of Czechs cast ballots for them in 1946 the Communists could claim major levers of power, like the Interior Ministry.[85] Czechs were not voting for Stalinism, however, but for a supposedly different Czechoslovak road to Socialism.

---

[83] Other indices: the student council elections of the fall, the fall of Fierlinger as well as the crushing victory of Ladislav Feierabend in elections to Kooperativa, the purchasing agency of the agricultural cooperatives in May 1947 (Lukes, *On the Edge*, 170).

[84] Zdenek Mlynář, *Nightfrost in Prague: The End of Humane Socialism* (New York: C. Hurst, 1980), 1–2, emphasis added: the point was, after six years of humiliating passivity.

[85] Gottwald and his comrades based their claim on Taborsky, "President Edvard Benes," 135.

188   WHEN DEMOCRACY BREAKS

Still, there was an edge to the polemics, most strongly present in student politics, which grew razor sharp just before the coup, suggesting that Communist victory would indeed by accompanied by the uncompromising cleansing of "cultural revolution." Supporters of the Communist Party of Czechoslovakia cast their votes not just for the utopian equality of "Socialism" but because ethnic revolution led by the early national committees had permitted widespread distribution of other people's property. Much of the clientele of the 1946 elections had been "bought." Critics said the striking continuity through the zero hour of 1945 was such people's self-seeking, subordinate approach to politics, a "protectorate mentality," permitting self-enrichment at the expense of one enemy or another.[86] What the critics did not say was that this posture, of being the beneficiary of rather than contributing to liberal institutions, went back even further, to the impressive social welfare regimes rewarded to the Czechs, beginning with Austria. Perhaps Emperor Franz Joseph and then the wise "founder president" T. G. Masaryk were the ultimate guarantors of the once formidable Czech liberal democracy.

The adjective "liberal" suggests that democracy is never pure but always of a certain type. A conviction had taken hold among close to a majority of Czechs after World War II that democracy of the liberal type had outlived its usefulness for the nation—the only relevant demos—and did not require defending. In this postwar "discourse" all defense was class-based, and democracy itself became a weapon for a just cause. Millions of Czechs acting to destroy democracy claimed they were acting in its service. Subsequent experience suggests that they were operating under a convenient illusion: democracy always requires basic protections of civil rights. No class of human beings should be expropriated, expelled, or imagined as outside the demos. What is unclear is which failure was most important: the failure of the institutions, or the failure of the convictions in which such institutions must rest, or the failure of leaders, at home and in the West, who convinced themselves that institutions could be sacrificed to a higher principle, whether for the sake of "peace" or "history" or, most destructive, "the nation."

---

[86] The Czech writer and psychoanalyst Bohuslav Brouk—one of the few Czech intellectuals to oppose Communism publicly after the war—wrote that "a great many people join the Communist Party and remain in it because of their defeatist, Protectorate mentality. They came to know in the occupation the sad fate of politically unorganized people in a state with only one party. . . . [S]adly the German tyranny cultivated chicken-heartedness in the souls of many of our people." Critics pointed to a behavioral syndrome from the occupation days, when people came passively to adapt to demands of overwhelming force. Father František Hála of the People's Party likewise said the Nazis had corroded the national spirit, especially of people willing to sell their convictions for selfish reasons. Across the political spectrum—from President Beneš and the Catholic Pavel Tigrid, to the Communist intellectual Zdeněk Nejedlý—critics agreed that Czechs had absorbed elements of fascism ("fascism in ourselves") (Abrams, *Struggle*, 115).

7

September 11, 1973

Breakdown of Democracy in Chile

Marian Schlotterbeck

On September 4, 1970, Chile captured the world's attention when it elected Socialist senator Salvador Allende Gossens as president. With his leftist Popular Unity coalition, Allende promised a peaceful transition to Democratic Socialism could be won at the ballot box instead of on the battlefield. At the height of the Cold War, Chile appeared to offer an alternative path to both U.S. capitalist liberal democracy and Soviet-style Communism. At a time when enthusiasm for the 1959 Cuban Revolution had declined as Fidel Castro moved into the Soviet orbit, Allende offered a top-down economic development model that would redistribute wealth by occupying the state rather than destroying it. Chile's competitive multiparty, political system shared much in common with Western European countries like Italy, Portugal, and France. Allende's election would test the viability of having a Marxist government democratically elected as opposed to taking power via armed revolution.

There was plenty of reason for optimism in 1970 for the prospects of Allende's government and the so-called Chilean path to Socialism. Chile had enjoyed uninterrupted democratic rule since 1932. Unlike most other Latin American countries, the Chilean military did not intervene in politics, elections happened on schedule, freedom of the press was guaranteed, and openly Marxist parties not only legally participated in politics but also formed part of coalitional governments. Despite his election at the height of the Cold War, Allende believed his model of ideological pluralism could flourish in the context of superpower rapprochement.

His victory represented the culmination of a decades-long strategy by the Chilean left to take state power through peaceful means. Starting in the late nineteenth century, a strong labor movement emerged in the northern nitrate mines and the southern textile and coal-mining communities. This leftist, often Marxist-oriented labor movement allied itself to the emergent political parties that represented the working class: the Communist Party and the Socialist Party. Across the twentieth century, the goal of the two largest parties on the

---

Marian Schlotterbeck, *September 11, 1973* In: *When Democracy Breaks.* Edited by: Archon Fung, David Moss, and Odd Arne Westad, Oxford University Press. © Oxford University Press 2024. DOI: 10.1093/oso/9780197760789.003.0007

190   WHEN DEMOCRACY BREAKS

left was to channel social struggle through electoral participation. As a result, Chilean democracy became synonymous with competitive elections, coalition governments, and representation of nonelite sectors (*sectores populares*) within the political process.

On election night, voters gave Allende a slim 39,000-vote margin (36.2%) over the right's candidate, Jorge Alessandri (34.9%). The centrist Christian Democrats, the party of sitting president Eduardo Frei, finished last (27.8%). When there was such a three-way split in Chilean politics, presidents were typically elected with a plurality, not a majority, of the vote. Under Chilean law, when no candidate won an outright majority, Congress determined the outcome of the election between the two top candidates in the popular vote. Previous congresses had always respected the popular vote. Yet in 1970, despite precedent, there were some indications that Congress might not choose Allende.

Thus, before he could even assume office, Allende faced an organized and well-funded opposition. Although presidential elections occurred on September 4, it would be nearly two months before Congress met to certify the popular vote and name the next president. From the outset, the U.S. government and the Chilean political right, representing elite landowners, mass-media moguls, and industrialists allied with foreign capital, operated as antidemocratic forces in Chile. Openly fascist and anti-Communist Chilean groups joined their ranks, including Patria y Libertad (Fatherland and Liberty), which was partially funded by the CIA. Patria y Libertad carried out violent acts of sabotage during the years ahead and engaged in street skirmishes with Allende supporters.

These sectors used the two-month delay between September and November 1970 to devise a number of political and military schemes to prevent Allende from assuming the presidency. Lobbying for Washington to intervene began almost immediately from both Chilean and U.S. business sectors, most notably with Augustin Edwards, owner of Chile's largest newspaper, *El Mercurio*, who conveyed a warning to U.S. president Richard Nixon and his secretary of state Henry Kissinger that Chile was about to go Communist, while International Telephone and Telegraph, a U.S. corporation with large holdings in Chile, offered the CIA one million dollars to stop Allende. On September 15, 1970, Nixon met with top advisors and issued a directive to the CIA to initiate covert operations to prevent Allende from taking office and to promote a coup in Chile.[1]

U.S. covert operations consisted of two tracks: a constitutional path that lobbied legislators to declare the second-place candidate Jorge Alessandri of the National Party the winner. Alessandri would then call new elections

---

[1] Richard Helms, "Meeting with the President on Chile at 1525," CIA, September 15, 1970. For more on U.S. covert operations in Chile, see Peter Kombluh, *The Pinochet File: A Declassified Dossier on Atrocity and Accountability* (New York: The New Press, 2003).

BREAKDOWN OF DEMOCRACY IN CHILE   191

which would pave the way for outgoing president Frei to be reelected.[2] Despite the influx of covert funding and U.S. pressure, Christian Democrats refused to break with tradition, but not before, "Frei and some of his ministers seriously considered the possibility of a coup in September–October 1970," reflecting "a mindset dominated by a deep fear and an intransigent rejection of the Marxist Left."[3]

The second track of U.S. covert policy was a military solution. The CIA channeled arms and funds to right-wing military officials and civilian conspirators, including Patria y Libertad members, who devised a plot to kidnap the head of the armed forces, General René Schneider, a strict constitutionalist who opposed military intervention. The kidnapping would be blamed on leftist extremists, which would provoke sufficient panic to justify a military coup or to convince Christian Democrats to vote for Alessandri over Allende. Instead of kidnapping, the CIA-supported conspirators assassinated General Schneider. This egregious act of political terrorism shocked the nation. When the identities of those responsible came to light, instead of the desired military coup, the Chilean armed forces, Congress, and the country rallied behind Allende's congressional confirmation on October 24, 1970.

Allende's inauguration on November 4, 1970, marked the beginning of a period of three years in which the Popular Unity government attempted to put in place its policies and in which the opposition inside and outside of Chile became increasingly convinced the only way to prevent Allende from succeeding was by creating sufficient conditions of chaos to provoke a military coup. As long as Allende moved toward Socialism *within* a constitutional framework, those opposed to him would have to destroy the legitimacy of Chile's political institutions, the very same institutions that Allende now occupied. During Allende's government, one of the principal challenges presented by the Liberal democratic system—by the organization of the Chilean state—was that the main players did not trust each other, and different agendas controlled different branches of government. Eventually, this produced a crisis of legitimacy for the entire political system that ultimately spelled the end of Allende's presidency and Chilean democracy.

On September 11, 1973, the military seized power, following the aerial bombardment of the presidential palace, La Moneda. While those on the right who opposed Allende from the outset had both financial resources and political influence on their side, they did not have a sufficient base of support to overthrow his government, despite encouragement and aid from the United States.

---

[2] Chile's Constitution stipulated that sitting presidents could not be reelected for a second term. But new elections would allow Frei to return to office.

[3] Sebastian Hurtado, *The Gathering Storm: Eduardo Frei's Revolution in Liberty and Chile's Cold War* (Ithaca, NY: Cornell University Press, 2020), 201–202.

192 WHEN DEMOCRACY BREAKS

Rather the Christian Democrats, who held the presidency from 1964 to 1970 and represented the political center, eventually concluded that the best prospects for getting back into power were not a political solution—waiting until the 1976 presidential elections—but a military one: throwing their support behind the antidemocratic right to destabilize the Allende government and calling for military intervention. The Chilean middle class, politically aligned with the Christian Democrats, provided a nonelite base of public support for a military intervention. The coup led by General Augusto Pinochet and the brutal seventeen-year dictatorship that followed sought not only to overthrow a Marxist president and a democratic transition to a Socialist economy but also to turn back the decades-long struggle of working people for full inclusion as citizens in Chile's democracy.

Explanations for Democratic Breakdown

Explanations for the overthrow of democracy in Chile emerged in the immediate aftermath of the 1973 military coup, with seminal studies, such as Arturo Valenzuela's *The Breakdown of Democratic Regimes: Chile* (1978), appearing by the end of the decade. This first wave of scholarship, much of it produced by political scientists, sociologists, foreign journalists, and Chilean politicians, emphasized to varying degrees four different factors: class conflict, U.S. imperialism, errors by the left in power, and polarization of political elites and the electoral system, particularly the centrist Christian Democrats.[4] In the nearly fifty years since the coup, historical research has provided a more complete and nuanced understanding of the motivations that guided different actors during the tumultuous thousand days of Allende's presidency. In many respects similar to Weimar Germany, Chile in 1970 had both "a strong authoritarian tradition and a strong democratic tradition."[5]

Within Latin America, Chile is often cast as a democratic exception. In the early national period of the nineteenth century, Chile stood out among the new Latin American republics for its political stability. Chile did not experience ongoing interelite conflict between liberals and conservatives nor disruptive cycles of military strongmen and military coups. Living under authoritarian rule in the 1980s, Chilean social scientists based at NGOs and think tanks began to question this "myth of Chilean exceptionalism." Chilean historian María Angélica Illanes

---

[4] For an excellent summary of the English-language literature, see Alfredo Joignant and Patricia Navia, "El golpe a la cátedra: Los intelectuales del primer mundo y la vía chilena al socialismo," in *Ecos mundiales del golpe de Estado: Escritos sobre el 11 de septiembre de 1973*, ed. Alfredo Joignant and Patricia Navia (Santiago: Ediciones Universidad Diego Portales, 2013), 11–52. For a survey of the Chilean scholarship, see Mario Garcés and Sebastian Leiva, *Perspectivas de análisis de la Unidad Popular: Opciones y omisiones* (Santiago: Universidad Arcis, 2004).
[5] See Eric Weitz's chapter in this volume.

BREAKDOWN OF DEMOCRACY IN CHILE   193

dates the myth's origins to the 1920s, when, during a period of political and economic crisis, a group of conservative historians consciously sought to resurrect Bernardo O'Higgins and Diego Portales as founding fathers. By casting Portales as a heroic figure who saved Chile from the "anarchy" of the 1820s Liberal governments and consolidated a strong central state in the 1830s dominated by Chile's small oligarchy, these historians celebrated the institutional stability of the "Portalian state" as responsible for Chile's unique path.[6] Throughout the twentieth century, the narrative of Chilean exceptionalism gained currency across the political spectrum, as competing groups refashioned it to support divergent political projects. The staying power of these beliefs—that the military respected the constitutional order and lacked vocation for political office, led many politicians on the left, including Allende, to erroneously believe the military would not intervene in Chile's political crisis, and those in the center, such as Frei, to assume that if it did, it would not stay in power.[7]

When the military junta seized power in September 1973, they justified their actions as necessary to save Chilean democracy from the threat of Marxism and international Communist conspiracy, citing "resolutions by Congress, the Supreme Court, and the Contraloría General denouncing the constitutional and legal violations by the Allende government."[8] Moreover, as political scientist Brian Loveman points out, the military consolidated its rule by drawing on "key authoritarian features of Chile's constitutional tradition, political institutions and political practices."[9] As Diego Portales famously observed in 1832, "[T]he social order is maintained in Chile by *the weight of the night* . . . [and] the masses' general passivity is the guarantee of public tranquility."[10] Should the "weight of the night" be lifted, "Portales and his successors never hesitated to use 'the stick' to secure that tranquility."[11] Thus, in a reappraisal of the Chilean state's seemingly remarkable stability, scholars have increasingly acknowledged the exclusionary elements at its core: elite rule, traditional social hierarchies, and repression of popular movements.[12]

---

[6] María Angélica Illanes Oliva, *La batalla de la memoria: Ensayos históricos de nuestro siglo, Chile 1900–2000* (Santiago de Chile: Planeta, 2002), 165–166.

[7] James Petras, "Chile after Allende," in *Revolution and Counterrevolution in Chile,* ed. Paul M. Sweezy and Harry Magdoff (New York: Monthly Review Press, 174), 163.

[8] Brian Loveman, "The Political Architecture of Dictatorship: Chile before September 11, 1973," *Radical History Review* 124 (January 2016): 12.

[9] Loveman, "The Political Architecture of Dictatorship," 15.

[10] Diego Portales, "The Authoritarian Republic," in *The Chile Reader: History, Culture, Politics,* ed. Elizabeth Quay Hutchinson, Elizabeth Quay Hutchison, Thomas Miller Klubock, Nara B. Milanich, and Peter Winn (Durham, NC: Duke University Press, 2014), 141.

[11] Brian Loveman, *Chile: The Legacy of Hispanic Capitalism,* 3rd ed. (New York: Oxford University Press, 2001), 4–5.

[12] Alfredo Jocelyn-Holt Letelier, *El Peso de la Noche: Nuestra Frágil Fortaleza Histórica* (Santiago de Chile: Ariel, 2000).

194 WHEN DEMOCRACY BREAKS

By documenting how political norms were traditionally upheld at the expense of addressing social inequality, scholars have highlighted the repeated use of states of exception, amnesties, and political violence directed at the lower classes.[13] Chile's democracy endured as long as social relations in the countryside, particularly on the large, landed estates (*haciendas*), remained unchanged. If this tenuous political compromise "was threatened, political toleration ended."[14] For Chile's traditional landed elites, represented politically in the twentieth century by the National Party, the beginning of the end came not with Allende's election in 1970 but with his predecessor Christian Democrat Frei's passage of the 1967 Agrarian Reform Law.[15] By examining how political violence was a constitutive element of state formation across the nineteenth and twentieth centuries, scholars suggest that the sudden shock of the September 11, 1973, military coup was less of an aberration in Chile's democratic tradition than previously thought. By contrast, the exception appears to be the short decade from 1964 to 1973, corresponding to the "Revolution in Liberty" led by Christian Democrat Frei (1964–1970) and the "Democratic Path to Socialism" under Allende (1970–1973), a period marked by remarkable advances in democratization and nonelite political participation.

Chilean Popular Front: Democratic Expansion and Contraction in the 1930s and 1940s

In contrast to the authoritarian traditions within the Chilean political system, the advent of mass politics in the 1920s enabled the development of a strong democratic culture, particularly among the lower classes. In the 1930s and 1940s, Popular Front governments were a prototype for the kind of multiparty, multiclass coalition that brought Unidad Popular (Popular Unity) candidate Allende to office in 1970. This experiment made manifest, historian Jody Pavilack contends, "deep divisions over the definition and practical content of democracy."[16] At the same time, the pattern of democratic expansion followed by

---

[13] Elizabeth Lira and Brian Loveman, *Las Ardientes Cenizas Del Olvido: Via Chilena de Reconciliacion Politica, 1932–1994* (Santiago: LOM, 2000). See also Gabriel Salazar, *La Violencia Política y Popular en las "Grandes Alamedas". La Violencia en Chile 1947–1987 (una perspectiva histórico popular)* (Santiago: LOM, 2006). Florencia Mallon, *Courage Tastes of Blood: The Mapuche Community of Nicolás Ailío and the Chilean State, 1906–2001* (Durham, NC: Duke University Press, 2005), 21; Lessie Jo Frazier, *Salt in the Sand: Memory, Violence, and the Nation-State in Chile, 1890 to the Present* (Durham, NC: Duke University Press, 2007).

[14] Loveman, *Chile*, 3rd ed., 202.

[15] Fernando Mires, *La rebelión permanente: Las revoluciones sociales en América Latina* (Mexico City: Siglo XXI, 1988), 337.

[16] Jody Pavilack, *Mining for the Nation: The Politics of Chile's Coal Communities from the Popular Front to the Cold War* (University Park: Pennsylvania State University Press, 2011), 31.

BREAKDOWN OF DEMOCRACY IN CHILE   195

contraction and repression in important respects foreshadowed the tragic end to Allende's Popular Unity government.

Chile, like many other industrializing countries in South America, went through a period of populist governments, particularly in the 1930s and 1940s, when Popular Front governments, which included Socialists and Communists, came to power. The Popular Front governments were led by middle-class parties, especially the Radical Party, but as members of the governing coalition, the Socialists and Communists held important ministry positions. Under each of these governments, urban workers gained rights and saw a rapid expansion of their political participation.[17] In her study of southern Chile, Pavilack documented how Chilean coal miners aligned with the Communist Party mobilized "to make representational politics effectively serve the interests of popular sectors, not just those of the oligarchic and bourgeois elites or foreign investors."[18] She adds, "[D]emocracy, as it was embraced by Marxist parties and their working-class followers in mid-twentieth century Chile, was an intrinsically contentious project. Organization and mobilization from below came to be seen by workers not as a way to overthrow Chilean democracy or halt its capitalist advance, but rather as a way to participate fully. Workers were prepared to fight within existing systems rather than against them, but this did not mean an end to class conflict."[19]

Between 1946 and 1947, Chilean copper and coal miners, allied with the Communist Party, launched a series of strikes that threatened to bring Chile's export-oriented economy to a standstill. Pressured by the U.S. government and the U.S. owned-mining companies, President Gabriel González Videla ended the strikes in October 1947 by declaring a state of siege and sending the military to occupy the southern coal zone. Over the next four months, between six thousand and seven thousand Communist workers and their families were forcibly deported to internment camps. Afterward, President González Videla passed the Law for the Permanent Defense of Democracy (1948), which banned his former allies the Chilean Communist Party and disenfranchised some forty thousand voters. As a young army captain in 1947–1948, Augusto Pinochet Ugarte spent time in northern Chile at the Pisagua internment camp before assuming command of the military occupation in the southern coal-mining zone. He would later attribute the origin of his anti-Communism to these experiences.[20]

---

[17] Mario Garcés Durán, *La Unidad Popular y la revolución en Chile* (Santiago: LOM, 2020).
[18] Pavilack, *Mining for the Nation*, 6.
[19] Pavilack, *Mining for the Nation,* 34.
[20] John R. Bawden, *The Pinochet Generation: The Chilean Military in the Twentieth Century* (Tuscaloosa: University of Alabama Press, 2016), 56. See also Augusto Pinochet, *The Crucial Day: September 11, 1973* (Santiago: Editorial Renacimiento, 1982).

196 WHEN DEMOCRACY BREAKS

Despite urban workers' efforts to deepen and expand democracy, the Popular Front revealed the limits of Chile's political system to tolerate not only political pluralism but also nonelite empowerment. While urban workers gained important rights, including the right to unionize, engage in collective bargaining, and strike, rural workers continued to be deprived of these same rights, and other important social sectors, including women, indigenous people, peasants, and illiterates, remained disenfranchised.[21] The 1948 Cold War proscription of the Chilean Communist Party, which would not be legalized again until 1958, and the subsequent internment of many working-class Communist militants mirrors a pattern in Latin America in which populist governments in the 1930s and 1940s ended with persecution of workers, unions, and leftist political leaders. As historian Marcelo Casals contends, anti-Communism as an ideology was not merely reactive; it was dynamic and adaptable in providing a powerful social script.[22] By midcentury anti-Communism was already deeply embedded in Chilean political culture and informed how opposition inside and outside of Chile viewed Allende's presidential campaigns in 1958 and 1964. From this perspective, his subsequent electoral victory in 1970 symbolized "the materialization of all anticommunist fears."[23]

Cold War Politics in Chile and U.S. Intervention in the 1950s and 1960s

If the 1948 Law for the Permanent Defense of Democracy marked Chile's alignment with the United States in Cold War era politics, U.S. government interest in Chile would grow in the decades ahead. The U.S. government found a new ally in the Chilean Christian Democratic Party (PDC), founded in 1957, and celebrated leader Eduardo Frei as the "last best hope" for countering Communism in Latin America.[24] In less than a decade, the Christian Democrats became Chile's largest political party and captured the presidency in 1964.

---

[21] For more on the exclusion of rural Chile from the benefits of the Popular Front governments, see María Angélica Illanes, *Movimiento en la tierra: Luchas campesinas, Resistencia patronal y política social agraria, Chile, 1927–1947* (Santiago: LOM, 2019).

[22] Marcelo Casals, "The Chilean Counter-revolution: Roots, Dynamics and Legacies of Mass Mobilisation against the Unidad Popular," *Radical Americas* 6, no. 1 (June 2021): 1–17. See also Marcelo Casals, *La creación de la amenaza roja: Del surgimiento del anticomunismo en Chile a la "campaña del terror" de 1964* (Santiago: LOM, 2016).

[23] Marcelo Casals, "Anticommunism in 20th-Century Chile: From the 'Social Question' to the Military Dictatorship," *Oxford Research Encyclopedia of Latin American History*, online, March 2019. https://doi.org/10.1093/acrefore/9780199366439.013.666.

[24] Leonard Gross, *The Last, Best Hope: Eduardo Frei and Chilean Democracy* (New York: Random House, 1967).

By the middle of the twentieth century, the preferences of the Chilean electorate broke down into three thirds: right, center, and left. Each of these political blocs occupied the presidency: first, Conservative Jorge Alessandri in 1958, then the center represented by Frei and the Christian Democrats in 1964, and finally the Socialist Allende leading the leftist Popular Unity coalition in 1970. In 1958, the right's candidate, Alessandri, won with 31.2% of the popular vote, narrowly beating a leftist coalition headed by Allende, who earned 28.5% ahead of Frei, who earned 22%. Had there not been a fourth spoiler candidate, a renegade leftist priest, who received 3.3% of the vote, Allende might plausibly have been elected one year before the 1959 Cuban Revolution.

The Cuban Revolution unquestionably altered the political landscape in Latin America and in U.S.-Latin American relations. Unlike in Central America and the Caribbean, the U.S. influence in South America was fairly limited prior to World War II. In 1947, the U.S. government created the Central Intelligence Agency and also signed the Río Treaty (1947) with most Latin American countries, including Chile. In line with the Truman Doctrine, this Cold War mutual security agreement treaty gave the U.S. government influence that it never had before in South America, particularly in the training of military forces. Under the broad doctrine of national security, Latin America in the mid-twentieth century experienced multiple forms of U.S. intervention, resulting in the removal of governments that were perceived as threats to U.S. political and economic interests: Guatemala in 1954, Guyana in 1961, Brazil in 1964, and the Dominican Republic in 1965.

After the April 1961 Bay of Pigs military invasion failed to oust Cuban revolutionary Fidel Castro, President John F. Kennedy sought to open a new chapter in U.S.–Latin American relations with the Alliance for Progress. Driven by the desire to avoid another Cuba, U.S. policymakers laid out an ambitious ten-year, $20 billion economic and military aid program. U.S. policymakers acknowledged the need for social reforms in a region where the high levels of poverty and disenfranchisement made Socialist revolution appealing. Kennedy's vision sought to stave off the threat of revolution by improving standards of living across the hemisphere.

Founded in 1957, the PDC sought to provide a "third way" by pursuing a social reform agenda that was capitalist and anti-Marxist.[25] Its social base was primarily the urban-professional middle class and managerial class.[26] In 1964, Eduardo Frei Montalva campaigned for the presidency promising a "Revolution in Liberty," a middle-class revolution that was in large part bankrolled by the

---

[25] In addition to Sebastian Hurtado's *Gathering Storm*, see Mario Amorós, *Entre la araña y la flecha: La trama civil contra la Unidad Popular* (Madrid: Ediciones B, 2020).

[26] Alan Angell, *Politics and the Labour Movement in Chile* (London: Oxford University Press, 1972), 182.

198 WHEN DEMOCRACY BREAKS

U.S. government's Alliance for Progress. The right opted not to run its own candidate and threw its support behind Frei, who received a stunning 56% of the popular vote in 1964, handily defeating Allende. While the previous political center had been occupied by the pragmatic Radical Party, the Christian Democrats represented "the rise of an ideological Center," which, as Arturo Valenzuela, notes "aggravated" political polarization.[27]

Over half of Frei's 1964 presidential campaign was funded directly by the CIA, which spent an additional $3 million on an anti-Communist propaganda campaign against Allende. Known as the "campaign of terror," its purpose was to convince voters that the election of a Marxist president would undermine respect for the family and traditional gender roles. Thus, by 1964, Chilean political actors on the right, the CIA, and conservative Brazilian women had already established a transnational anti-Communist network that tapped into anxiety over changing gender roles as a key narrative for its anti-Allende messaging.[28]

Lifting "the Weight of the Night": Mobilization of Chilean Society in the 1960s

Polarization of society figured prominently in early scholarship on democratic breakdown in Chile. Explanations ranged from highlighting the "hypermobilization" of society to the detriment of governability, concluding that "the real problem is whether the masses can be controlled,"[29] and the assessment that national political parties' ideological positions overtook civil society, preventing autonomous social organizations from flourishing.[30] These perspectives diminish the significant agency exercised by nonelite actors and incorrectly suggest that social organizations functioned as mere mouthpieces for political parties. The reality on the ground was far more complex.[31]

---

[27] Arturo Valenzuela, *Chile: The Breakdown of Democratic Regimes* (Baltimore: Johns Hopkins University Press, 1978), xiii.

[28] Marcelo Casals, " 'Chilean! Is This How You Want to See Your Daughter?' The Cuban Revolution and Representations of Gender and Family during Chile's 1964 Anticommunist Campaign of Terror," *Radical History Review* 136 (January 2020): 122; Margaret Power, "Who but a Woman? The Transnational Diffusion of Anti-Communism among Conservative Women in Brazil, Chile and the United States during the Cold War," *Journal of Latin American Studies* 47, no. 1 (2015): 93–119. For more on Brazil's role in undermining democracy in Chile, see Roberto Simon, *El Brasil de Pinochet. La dictadura brasileña, el golpe en Chile y la guerra fría en América del Sur.* Trad. Pablo Diener. (Santiago: LOM, 2022).

[29] Henry A. Landsberger and Tim McDaniel, "Hypermobilization in Chile, 1970–1973," *World Politics* 28, no. 4 (July 1976): 540.

[30] Manuel Antonio Garretón, *The Chilean Political Process*, trans. Sharon Kellum (Boston: Unwin Hyman, 1989).

[31] Marian Schlotterbeck, *Beyond the Vanguard: Everyday Revolutionaries in Allende's Chile* (Oakland: University of California Press, 2018).

BREAKDOWN OF DEMOCRACY IN CHILE   199

Motivated by the desire to win in highly competitive elections, political parties across the spectrum, but particularly on the center and left, as historians Gabriel Salazar and Julio Pinto have argued, encouraged social mobilization and popular empowerment, "only to subsequently repress" these lower-class movements or "to actively contain this impulse from below."[32] Politicization of social organizations was a key feature of Chilean politics in the 1960s and 1970s. It was accelerated by three of the Christian Democrats' key reforms: (1) the expansion of the electorate, (2) agrarian reform with land redistribution in the countryside, and (3) the creation of Promoción Popular (Popular Promotion) programs that incentivized organizing by the urban and rural poor.[33] While moderate in many respects, these reforms rattled traditional social hierarchies and the political status quo, which rested on the exclusion of peasants and other marginal sectors from political life.

As more and more Chileans had a stake in the system, they began to demand something of it. When given the opportunity to organize, people did. Peasants formed unions and cooperatives, went on strike, and occupied land. Landless urban poor (*pobladores*) organized neighborhood councils and homeless committees and carried out land occupations. Labor militancy and strikes multiplied.[34] As one observer noted, "[W]hat is certain is that with its reforms, the PDC unleashed social forces that from the beginning escaped their control, creating a climate of social agitation that the parties of the Left had not been able to create."[35]

The Christian Democrat's relationship to the landless urban poor exemplifies this dynamic of mobilization and subsequent repression when popular sector actions and demands exceed institutional control. Despite encouraging community-organized neighborhood councils as a key step to resolve Chile's housing crisis, the Frei administration began to crack down on illegal land occupations (*tomas*), most notoriously in the March 1969 "Massacre of Puerto Montt," in which Chilean national police violently dispersed an illegal land occupation, killing ten people.[36] As Sebastián Hurtado concludes, President Frei

---

[32] Gabriel Salazar and Julio Pinto, *Historia contemporánea de Chile V: Niñez y juventud* (Santiago: LOM, 2002), 214.

[33] Eduardo Frei carried out an ambitious agrarian reform program (1967) endorsed by the U.S. Alliance for Progress. The extension of the right to unionize and strike to rural workers aimed to counter the appeal of more revolutionary options and to expand the Christian Democrats' electoral base. Similarly, under Frei's government, electoral changes lowered the voting age from twenty-one to eighteen and extended the right to vote to illiterate Chileans, who accounted for approximately 10% of the population. The 1970 presidential election was the first with the newly expanded electorate (Loveman, *Chile*, 3rd ed.).

[34] Peter Winn, "Loosing the Chains: Labor and the Chilean Revolutionary Process, 1970–1973," *Latin American Perspectives* 3, no. 1 (1976): 73.

[35] Mires, *La rebelión permanente*, 338.

[36] Angela Vergara, "Revisiting Pampa Irigoin: Social Movements, Repression, and Political Culture in 1960s Chile," *Radical History Review* 124 (January 2016): 43–54. For more on Chile's housing rights movement in the twentieth century, see Mario Garcés, *Tomando su sitio: El movimiento de pobladores*

200   WHEN DEMOCRACY BREAKS

"chose to enforce the rule of law with great determination, following the historic pattern of the Chilean state's violent repression of modes of mobilization perceived as unacceptable challenges to the social order."[37] Just three years earlier, the Chilean military left eight people dead in the northern mining town of El Salvador after President Frei called them in to break a copper miners' strike in 1966. By end of Frei's term, the Christian Democrats faced not only a crisis of political representation but also one of power when, on October 21, 1969, the military went on strike over poor wages in the so-called Tacnazo.[38]

By the late 1960s, many Chileans who had first mobilized under the auspices of Frei's Revolution in Liberty had become disenchanted with the centrist, middle-class Christian Democrat's unfulfilled promises. The contradiction of encouraging the mobilization of workers, peasants, and urban poor, only to revert to the historical practice of the state using violence against the activism that these mobilizations gave rise to, produced serious rifts within the party. While President Frei led the largest and most conservative wing, a sizable faction led by former Christian Democratic student leaders and key figures from the agrarian reform program, like Jacques Chonchol, argued for accelerating and deepening social reforms begun under Frei. This more progressive, leftist faction broke from the party in May 1969 to form the Popular Unitary Action Movement (MAPU), which soon joined Allende's Popular Unity coalition.

In 1970, the Christian Democrats ran candidate Radomiro Tomic, from the center-left wing of their party, with a platform that in many ways resembled the one supported by the Popular Unity coalition. Tomic called for nationalization of the U.S.-owned copper mines, which expanded the Frei government's "Chileanization of copper" with the purchase of the majority share of Chile's largest copper mines. Whereas in 1964, the Christian Democrats formed an electoral alliance with the right, as historian Sebastian Hurtado notes, "so powerful and appealing was the message of the Left for a considerable part of the Chilean polity that even within the PDC a good number of members, [including Tomic,] promoted an alliance with the coalition of Communists and Socialists."[39] Tomic contended that an alliance of "the truly progressive forces" would ultimately have the best chance of carrying out much needed structural reforms and held that Frei's "ideological refusal to reach an understanding with the Marxist parties was an intellectual and strategic mistake."[40] After Tomic finished a distant third in the

---

de Santiago, 1957–1970 (Santiago: LOM, 2002) and Edward Murphy, For a Proper Home: Housing Rights in the Margins of Urban Chile, 19560–2010 (Pittsburgh: University of Pittsburgh Press, 2015).

[37] Hurtado, Gathering Storm, 202.
[38] Mires, La rebelión permanente, 341–342.
[39] Hurtado, Gathering Storm, 199.
[40] Hurtado, Gathering Storm, 121, 200.

BREAKDOWN OF DEMOCRACY IN CHILE   201

1970 presidential elections, Frei and the more conservative Christian Democrats took back control of the party.

Just as the labor movement predated the emergence of Chile's Communist and Socialist parties in the early twentieth century, popular movements composed of workers, students, peasants, and *pobladores* drove the democratization of Chilean society across the 1960s, carrying the five-party Popular Unity coalition to power in 1970 and forming the milieu out of which Chile's New Left parties emerged. In this sense, Allende's election reprised a familiar dynamic in which lower-class organization and mobilization preceded and subsequently facilitated electoral victories for leftist parties. Allende campaigned on promises to radically redistribute power "from the established dominant groups to the workers, peasants and progressive middle-class sectors in the city and the countryside."[41] In his inaugural speech on November 4, 1970, Allende declared, "[T]he *pueblo*, at long last having reached the Government, takes leadership over the nation's destiny."[42]

Allende's election in 1970 reflected the heightened expectations raised by Frei's Revolution in Liberty and the extent to which the Chilean electorate had both expanded and moved to the left in the 1960s. The 56% of the popular vote Frei received in 1964 (from right and center) had become 64% of Chileans who voted for platforms by Allende and Tomic that promised substantive social and economic change.[43] Thus, while Allende won with a plurality and occupied a minority position within the government, many supporters optimistically interpreted the leftward shift in the electorate as a popular mandate.

Allende's commitment not to use violence against his working-class supporters signaled an important break from the historical pattern of elites' use of the state to exercise violence in support of their interests. As the Popular Unity's 1969 campaign platform contended, "the development of monopoly capitalism prevents the spread of democracy and encourages the use of violence against the people."[44] The election of a *compañero* president thus expanded the possibilities for social mobilization on an even greater scale than under Frei. The perception of expanding horizons inspired some Chileans to carry out actions that went beyond the promises of the Popular Unity platform. Historian Peter Winn characterized this grassroots activism as "the revolution from below" to

---

[41] Unidad Popular, *Programa básico de gobierno de la Unidad Popular* (Santiago: Comando de la Unidad Popular, 1969), 12.

[42] Salvador Allende Gossens, "Primer discurso político del Presidente Dr. Salvador Allende: Pronunciado el día 5 de noviembre de 1970, en el Estadio Nacional" (Santiago: Ministerio de Relaciones Exteriores, n.d.), 5.

[43] Lois Hech Oppenheim, *Politics in Chile: Democracy, Authoritarianism and the Search for Development,* 2nd ed. (Boulder, CO: Westview Press, 1999), 40.

[44] Unidad Popular, *Programa de gobierno de la Unidad Popular* (Santiago: Comando de la Unidad Popular, 1969) 5.

differentiate it from Allende and the Popular Unity government's top-down revolution from above. While Allende remained steadfast in his commitment to
democratic procedure, not all of his supporters did. Motivated by a desire for
social justice and immediate redistribution, the direct-action tactics associated
with the revolution from below, particularly carrying out illegal land takeovers
(*tomas*) in the city and countryside, challenged the rule of law and questioned
the slow pace of institutional reform carried out within existing democratic
processes.

Founded in 1965, the Revolutionary Left Movement (MIR) was another important actor in the Allende years. As a Marxist-Leninist party, participants
drew inspiration from the model of the Cuban Revolution, but they also drew
on Chile's much longer tradition of anarchism and labor activism. At the time,
the MIR's endorsement of armed struggle and its admiration for the Cuban
Revolution were not unique in Chile or Latin America. Much like the left wing
of Allende's own Socialist Party, the MIR had been skeptical of Allende and the
moderate left's strategy to take power through electoral means. Yet unlike in
Argentina and Uruguay, Chile's Marxist-Leninist left did not become an urban
guerrilla organization. Instead, following Allende's election, the MIR engaged
in grassroots organizing among the rural and urban poor. Their more militant wing worked with young Socialists to form Allende's personal bodyguard.
Despite several overtures from President Allende, the MIR never joined his
Popular Unity coalition. Relations between the moderate Communists and the
radical MIR remained strained. While the MIR's inflated revolutionary rhetoric antagonized the Christian Democrats, the Communists blamed the MIR
for undermining the government's goal for a controlled top-down transition
to Socialism.[45] Yet the extent to which the MIR controlled the revolution from
below is debatable. A defining feature of the era was the Chilean lower classes'
significant autonomy and sense of historical agency, encapsulated in the phrase
"When we made history."[46]

Early Signs of Democratic Erosion

In addition to the right's plot to deny Allende the presidency with the assassination of General Schneider in October 1970, other earlier indicators of democratic erosion existed. The Christian Democrats in Congress agreed to vote for
Allende only after he signed a Statute of Constitutional Guarantees, in which

---

[45] Valenzuela, *Chile*, 108–109.

[46] Julio Pinto Vallejos, *Cuando hicimos la historia: La experiencia de la Unidad Popular*
(Santiago: LOM Ediciones, 2005), 5.

he pledged to protect and obey the Constitution. No other president in Chilean history had to sign such a document, essentially stating the well-understood principle that constitutionally elected presidents will respect and uphold the Constitution. Political scientist Arturo Valenzuela observed that the Christian Democrats' extraction of this concession from Allende in exchange for their confirmation votes in November 1970 indicates that from the outset, his government confronted "a breakdown in mutual understanding" that signaled "the fragility of Chilean institutions."[47]

At the same time, under the terms of Chile's existing Constitution and political system, Allende had little reason not to anticipate exercising his constitutional powers. His predecessors had similarly faced opposition-controlled congresses. Perhaps underestimating the powerful forces lining up against him, Allende expected that working within the existing political norms of negotiation, compromise, and coalitions would enable him to resolve political conflict. He knew that Chile's democratic institutions were not built to enact rapid, sweeping changes. Along with the moderate Communist Party and the moderate wing of the Socialist Party, Allende remained committed to a phased implementation of Popular Unity's program, working with Christian Democrats to pass specific legislation. For these sectors, the goal was to consolidate an electoral majority in the 1976 elections, which meant not alienating the middle class. The left wing of the Popular Unity coalition, principally represented by the Socialist Party, Christian left, and MAPU, advocated for moving faster and relying principally on working-class support. In this regard, the left wing of Popular Unity and the more radical MIR aligned ideologically.

The lack of internal cohesion within Allende's Popular Unity coalition resulted from the fact that it was a coalition, not a single party. The process for decision-making often resembled a parliamentary system within the governing coalition. His political program's stated goals contained several contradictions that became increasingly difficult to reconcile or balance, including how to stabilize the political system and economy while promising revolutionary change, how to support grassroots activism, and how to channel activism through existing institutions. Politically, disagreements within the Popular Unity coalition hampered Allende's ability to govern effectively and efficiently and slowed the government's response time at critical junctures.

The next section traces the unfolding chronology of Allende's presidency with attention to the internal and external factors that contributed to democratic erosion across important groups, including the Christian Democrats, the middle class, and the military.

---

[47] Valenzuela, *Chile*, 49.

204 WHEN DEMOCRACY BREAKS

Salvador Allende and the Popular Unity Project

With more than twenty years as a senator, Allende was deeply invested in the political institutions and norms that he had helped build. He believed in the possibilities of both popular democracy and the capacity of the state to improve the lives of Chile's poor majority (*el pueblo*).[48] Like many other Latin American leaders and Marxist intellectuals, Allende looked to dependency theory to diagnose the region's historic challenge of underdevelopment. First advanced by Latin American economists working for the United Nations Economic Commission for Latin America, dependency theory contended that the development of the First World had been achieved through colonialism and the capitalist exploitation of the developing world. Third World poverty was thus seen as the product of this unequal relationship. Allende and the other Popular Unity leaders believed that a majority of Chileans would never support a revolution characterized by collective violence or state terror. Instead, the Popular Unity government hoped that by implementing structural reforms—land redistribution and nationalization of key industries—economic strength would translate into political support as it sought to persuade the majority of Chileans to vote for Socialism by the end of Allende's term in 1976.

With the goal of creating a state-run economy, Allende expanded many reforms begun during Frei's Revolution in Liberty (1964–1970). Allende had campaigned on a platform to end foreign and monopoly control of the economy, grow the public sector, and deepen democracy through the creation of worker control in state-run factories. Within a year of taking office, Allende's government had nationalized the American-owned copper mines with unanimous approval in Congress. In just eighteen months, his government implemented one of the most extensive land redistributions in world history without widespread violence. By the one-year anniversary in November 1971, Chile's GNP had increased, as had social spending and workers' share of the national income. These gains translated to an increase in support for Popular Unity at the polls. In the April 1971 municipal elections, the first elections since Allende took office and widely seen as a referendum on the democratic road to Socialism, Popular Unity candidates received just under 50% of the popular vote—a remarkable increase from Allende's plurality victory in September 1970. The Popular Unity government interpreted these elections as signaling widespread approval for its policies as well as raising the possibility that the electoral majority necessary to legislate a democratic transition to Socialism could be obtained ahead of the 1976

---

[48] Steven S. Volk, "Salvador Allende," Oxford Research Encyclopedia of Latin American History, November 2015, doi:10.1093/acrefore/9780199366439.013.106.

elections.[49] Typically, the left could count on 30% of the votes and the right could get 25%–30%. Within Chile's tripartite political blocs, the center functioned as a swing vote. In this scenario, Popular Unity would need to maintain their existing base of support and expand it to include more middle-class sectors from the political center.

Along with land reform, Allende's signature economic proposal was the creation of a socialized area of the economy, the Área de Propiedad Social (APS). The Popular Unity platform identified changes in property relations as an essential step toward breaking both Chile's historically dependent role within the world capitalist system and the power of domestic economic elites. In the case of agrarian reform, Allende's government applied the 1967 Agrarian Reform Law passed by the Christian Democrats, which contained specifications for the size of rural estates and the circumstances under which they could be expropriated. The Popular Unity government had no such legal precedent for how to create a socialized sector, nor was there agreement within the leftist coalition over the size of enterprises that should be included or the mechanisms by which they should transition to state ownership. It took the government nearly a year to introduce legislation, which further contributed to uncertainty among business sectors fearing possible expropriation.

Political Opposition: Christian Democrats in Congress

In addition to the hostility of the U.S. government and the Chilean political right, Allende faced a number of institutional constraints once in office. While he had won the powerful executive branch within a presidential system, this was the only branch of government he controlled. The Popular Unity parties accounted for just over one-third of the seats in Congress, making them a minority. Since congressional elections in Chile would not be held until March 1973, Popular Unity had no chance to alter this balance of power in the majority Christian Democrat Congress during Allende's first years in office. The judiciary, including the Supreme Court and Constitutional Court, was also controlled by the right. Political scientist Lois Oppenheim observed the "built-in contradiction" of Allende's position was his commitment to "carry out revolutionary change . . . within the legal confines of a political system in which [his government] had very limited political power."[50] The rhetoric of Allende's government,

---

[49] Peter Winn, "The Furies of the Andes," in *A Century of Revolution: Insurgent and Counterinsurgent Violence during Latin America's Long Cold War,* ed. Greg Grandin and Gilbert M. Joseph (Durham, NC: Duke University Press, 2010), 241.

[50] Oppenheim, *Politics in Chile,* 65; Mires, *La rebelión permanente,* 374–375.

206   WHEN DEMOCRACY BREAKS

with its focus on the working-class as its primary constituency, also differentiated it from previous administrations.

Without a majority in Congress, the Popular Unity government needed to reach agreements with opposition parties, essentially the Christian Democrats, to pass legislation critical to advance its program. Allende repeatedly tried to negotiate deals around specific legislation with the Christian Democrats in December 1971, March 1972, and June–July 1972. These negotiations were hampered by ideological disagreements within the Popular Unity government over the necessity and possibility of reaching an agreement with the Christian Democrats. The moderate wing of Popular Unity, led by the Communists, saw an agreement with the Christian Democrats as critical to success. Despite Allende's dogged persistence trying to reach political compromises to pass key legislation, he became increasingly isolated politically.

There was little strategic incentive for the Christian Democrats to compromise with the Popular Unity government. The Popular Unity parties represented the primary competition at the polls and in social bases, including among sectors like the urban poor and peasants, who had first been organized by the Christian Democrats. After Allende's election, all political parties maintained their electoral mobilization, which contributed to increased polarization. Second, as U.S. allies in the Cold War, the Christian Democrats were anti-Marxist, pro-capitalist, and anti-Communist. A sizable segment of the more conservative wing of the Christian Democrats was deeply resistant to forming any kind of legislative alliance with the Communist Party. Third, the Christian Democrats were a large, heterogeneous party that was internally divided. Following the departure of the MAPU in 1969, another splinter group from the Christian Democrats formed the Christian Left in 1971 and joined the governing Popular Unity coalition. President Allende had desperately tried to convince the Christian Left to remain within the Christian Democrats. Despite additional congressional seats for the government's coalition, ironically, the Christian Left's departure decreased Allende's chances of reaching a compromise with the Christian Democrats since the progressive Congress members, who had been most inclined to work with Allende, had abandoned the Christian Democratic Party to its more conservative leaders.

From the start, the creation of the socialized area of the economy (APS) proved contentious and put Allende on a collision course with the political right and center. Between 1971 and 1972, Congress blocked government-backed legislation, so Allende circumvented Congress with executive decree-laws. Congress passed a Christian Democrat–sponsored constitutional amendment to undo the APS, which Allende vetoed, then Congress voted to overrule his veto. This political stalemate produced a constitutional crisis that was not easily or quickly resolved. Allende resisted congressional attempts to overrule his veto, which would have effectively created a parliamentary system in place of the existing presidential one. The failure of the mid-July 1972 Popular Unity–PDC talks in some respects signaled the defeat of the Popular Unity moderates' strategy. In the face of political roadblocks, Allende's social base mobilized to show their support for the president and their rejection of politicians' attempts to halt the expansion of the socialized public sector.

Allende and the more moderate wing of the Popular Unity government remained committed to moving toward Socialism within a constitutional order. They stretched the institutional bounds in creative ways. For example, without a majority in Congress, Allende's government utilized several decree-laws from the 1930s to intervene and requisition industries for the socialized state sector. By the end of his first year in office, Allende had nationalized ninety-one of the largest monopoly firms, including banks, insurance companies, and foreign companies, and had expropriated key industries like textiles, steel, and coal. The government had searched for any legal means possible and had used the constitutional powers of a strong executive branch in order to implement structural changes and redistribute wealth. These actions infuriated the opposition.

One classic explanation for the breakdown of democracy in Chile centers on the political system and its democratic institutions. Politically, Allende had difficulty governing because he controlled only the presidency but not the other three branches of government. The opposition, which controlled 59% of Congress, wanted to block Allende's agenda. They were short of the 66% needed to impeach Allende, but impeachment of ministers required only a simple majority. So by 1973, Congress had impeached Allende's entire cabinet. This level of turnover made it impossible for Allende to govern effectively. The case of Chile in the early 1970s illustrates the risk that occurs in a democracy when political opposition to the sitting president is so intense that an opposition-controlled Congress is willing to undermine the basic functioning of government just to block the president's agenda. In questioning Allende and his government's legitimacy, the political right and center ultimately weakened the entire democratic system.

With a stalemate between Allende in the executive and an opposition-controlled Congress, political conflict became increasingly displaced to society. The failure of Allende's moderate strategy to reach an agreement with the Christian Democrats signaled the erosion of the political center. As Arturo Valenzuela notes, the Christian Democrats "should have realized more fully the necessity of coming to an agreement when the [Popular Unity] government coalition was willing, in the crucial negotiations of June and July 1972."[51] Traditionally, the political center played a moderating role in Chile's political system. Instead, in the year ahead, Chile's institutions and society would polarize.

---

[51] Valenzuela, *Chile*, 107.

208   WHEN DEMOCRACY BREAKS

The center would swing to the right, leaving the Allende and the moderate left increasingly isolated.

Conflict Moves to the Streets: The Opposition's Mass Strategy to Defeat Allende, December 1971

In the second year of Allende's government, the opposition strategy moved from Congress into the streets. This was a play not just for the political center but also for the middle class. In doing so, it mobilized a sizable segment of Chile's population against the constitutionally elected government. Between November and December 1971, Cuba's revolutionary leader Castro visited Chile. There is no doubt that his extended presence and the publicity surrounding his stay served to galvanize the opposition around a common cause. On December 1, 1971, near the end of Castro's trip, the forces opposed to the Popular Unity government took their protest to the streets in the first "March of the Pots and Pans," in which elite right-wing women guarded by the fascist Patria y Libertad's shock troops marched down Santiago's streets, symbolically banging pots and pans to suggest the hardships imposed by Allende's government.

The March of the Pots and Pans unveiled the opposition's new "mass strategy" that would seek to challenge Allende's economic policies directly in the streets—adopting the organizing tactics traditionally used by the Chilean left. These marches were geared toward frightening the middle class since the right wanted the middle third of voters to suffer under Allende. Broadly, the opposition sought to create conditions of sufficient political and economic chaos that the middle class would join the anti-Allende movement and the Chilean military would be persuaded to remove Allende from power. The post-Watergate 1973 Church Report by the U.S. Senate Intelligence Committee observed that "throughout the Allende years, the CIA worked to forge a united opposition"; to that end, between 1971 and 1973, the U.S. government channeled direct payments to the Christian Democrats and the National Party.[52]

The opposition's mass strategy, which debuted with the March of Pots and Pans, intensified in the years ahead. It accused Allende not only of breaking the Constitution but also of undermining traditional gender roles and, by extension, the foundations of society and civilization. Elite right-wing groups like Feminine Power successfully mobilized a cross-class alliance of "apolitical" women by organizing around their shared identity as mothers and housewives and galvanizing a sense of uncertainty in the face of social and economic

---

[52] U.S. Senate, Select Committee on Intelligence Activities, Staff Report. *Covert Action in Chile, 1963–1974* (Washington, DC: U.S. Government Printing Office, 1975).

BREAKDOWN OF DEMOCRACY IN CHILE   209

dislocations. The Popular Unity government underestimated the uneasiness of the Chilean middle class when confronted with dramatic social change, which partly explains why ideas about the family, gender roles, and school choice became rallying cries for the opposition. Historians, including Heidi Tinsman, Margaret Power, and Gwynn Thomas, have demonstrated how the Chilean left's inability to see women as political actors and to address women's needs as women was a strategic and ideological shortcoming.[53]

The Allende government had staked much on the success of its economic transformations, which left it vulnerable to criticism and attacks from their domestic political opposition and from the Nixon-Kissinger machinations. Even with the creation of a socialized area of the economy, the Popular Unity government still controlled only part of the economy and did not control distribution chains. By 1972, the second year of Allende's government, serious shortages of foodstuffs and other basic goods emerged. The shortages were caused, in part, by the initial success of Allende's redistributive policies, which meant more people had more money. The assumption of Keynesian stimulus spending was that production would increase to meet the new demand. This did not happen in Chile, in part because production could not be expanded to keep pace with rising demand, but also because some producers who were opposed to Allende opted to forgo profits by producing less. Similarly inclined shopkeepers hoarded goods in warehouses, which could then be sold for greater profit on the black market.

The decisive factor in the Chilean economic crisis and consequent unrest was a calculated U.S. policy, known as the "invisible blockade." Long before Castro's visit, Nixon in September 1970 issued a directive to "make the economy scream."[54] The 1975 Church Report found that soon after Allende's election, "the United States cut off economic aid, denied credits, and made efforts—partially successful—to enlist the cooperation of international financial institutions and private firms in tightening the economic 'squeeze' on Chile."[55] Ultimately, Nixon's directive in September 1970 had long-term destabilizing effects. While the Allende government's unwieldy coalition and inexperience contributed to its economic woes, it is difficult to imagine any government adept enough to withstand the Nixon administration's clandestine international offensive.

Unlike the political right, economic elites, and the U.S. government, Chile's middle class was neutral toward Allende at the start of his presidency. In the

---

[53] Heidi Tinsman, *Partners in Conflict: The Politics of Gender, Sexuality, and Labor in the Chilean Agrarian Reform, 1950–1973* (Durham, NC: Duke University Press, 2002); Margaret Power, *Right-Wing Women in Chile: Feminine Power and the Struggle against Allende, 1964–1973* (State College: Pennsylvania State University Press, 2002); Gwynn Thomas, *Contesting Legitimacy in Chile: Familial Ideals, Citizenship and Political Struggle, 1970–1990* (State College: Pennsylvania State University Press, 2011).

[54] Helms, "Meeting with the President on Chile at 1525.".

[55] U.S. Senate, *Covert Action in Chile.*

210 WHEN DEMOCRACY BREAKS

struggle for the middle third, the economy took center stage. The objective was to polarize Chilean society, particularly by making life difficult for the middle class, which would eventually push them toward the conservative opposition. For much of the twentieth -century, the fate of the Chilean state had been intertwined with the Chilean middle class, which held a privileged place as both a beneficiary of state policies and a participant in creating them. The Popular Unity government discursively put the working class at the heart of its political project. In doing so, it neglected the "long-standing norms that had governed" the special relationship between the Chilean state and the middle class.[56] Social mobilization, often associated with the revolution from below, sought to accelerate the pace of Allende's reforms and often challenged private property rights. For example, in southern Chile, the MIR and its peasant wing, the Revolutionary Peasants Movement (Movimiento de Campesinos Revolucionarios, MCR), collaborated with indigenous Mapuche peasants to reclaim ancestral lands and accelerate the pace of Popular Unity's agrarian reform. Their actions prompted a violent response from landowners and extensive media coverage, which tended to inflate the scope of the threat of "violent *tomas*" and the MIR/MCR as "guerrilla groups." The Christian Democrats, through the opposition-controlled media, promoted "distorted depictions of the local situation [which] served as ammunition in the national political conflict."[57] Historian Marcelo Casals concludes that both "real and imagined threats to middle-class social status, such as the expansion of state property, inflation, massive shortages of basic goods, and street violence," eroded middle-class neutrality toward Allende.[58]

In response to the opposition's mobilization, Allende called a high-level meeting of Popular Unity at Lo Curro in June 1972. On the one hand, the moderate Communists advocated for consolidating the social gains already achieved and continuing negotiations with the Christian Democrats. On the other side, the more leftist Socialists called for accelerating the pace of reforms and backing the workers. The moderate side advocating class reconciliation, which reflected Allende's own position, carried the day. Allende informed his supporters the following month, "[T]o continue governing in the service of the workers, it is my obligation to defend tirelessly the democratic institutional regime."[59]

[56] Marcelo Casals, "The Insurrection of the Middle Class: Social Mobilization and Counterrevolution during the Popular Unity Government, Chile, 1970–1973," *Journal of Social History* 54:3 (Spring 2021): 944–969.

[57] Claudio Robles-Ortiz, "Revolution From Below in Panguipulli: Agrarian Reform and Political Conflict under the Popular Unity in Chile," *Journal of Agrarian Change* 18 (2018): 622. See also Casals, "The Chilean Counter-revolution," 3.

[58] Casals, "Insurrection of the Middle Class," 3.

[59] "Enérgico rechazo de Allende a la 'Asamblea del Pueblo,'" *El Mercurio*, August 1, 1972, 8.

The Bosses Lockout: October 1972

In October 1972, the counterrevolutionary opposition launched a nationwide action aimed at creating the conditions for a coup. Politicians declared the Popular Unity government to be operating outside the law, going so far as to declare, "[T]he moment to act has arrived."[60] Christian Democrats, the National Party, and the openly fascist paramilitary group Patria y Libertad marched together in the streets of downtown Santiago. A strike by truck owners in the remote southern province of Aysén in October 1972 soon spread across the country, threatening to bring the Chilean economy to a standstill. This was not a coincidence; it was "the culmination of more than a year of planning, and organization by Chile's economic elites" to bring middle-class sectors over to their side.[61] In the late 1960s, as the Frei administration's reforms threatened their class interests, Chilean economic elites began to open their business associations, like the chamber of commerce and the National Agriculture Society, to smaller merchants, shopkeepers, farmers, and manufacturers. While this business movement remained controlled by elites, its visible face during the October Strike was the middle-class leaders "who could more effectively portray the action as a broad-based, popular rejection of Marxism."[62] According to the U.S. government's Church Report, "anti-government strikers were actively supported by several of the private sector groups which received CIA funds," which financially subsidized the lengthy strike that effectively prevented the movement of goods to markets and to consumers.[63]

What the organizers of the Bosses Lockout had perhaps underestimated was the degree of popular support that Allende still held, despite the economic turmoil of the previous year. One sign at a pro-Allende rally read, "With this government, you have to wait in line, but this government is mine."[64] Allende's supporters, particularly workers, mobilized to defend the government, occupying factories and opening shops to keep the economy running. The Bosses Lockout, moreover, had strong class connotations. Unlike the illegal land occupations (*tomas*) in the city and countryside, the workers' mobilization did not challenge the legal order: the lockout was illegal; to work was legal.[65] October 1972 also marked an important advance in grassroots democratic participation and popular-sector organizing through the creation of supply and price boards,

---

[60] Senator Alberto Baltra (PIR), quoted in Mires, *La rebelión permanente*, 358.
[61] Peter Winn, *Weavers of Revolution: The Yarur Workers and Chile's Road to Socialism* (New York: Oxford University Press, 1986), 235.
[62] Thomas C. Wright, *Latin America in the Era of the Cuban Revolution,* 3rd ed. (Santa Barbara, CA: Praeger, 2018),157.
[63] U.S. Senate, *Covert Action in Chile.*
[64] Illanes, *La batalla de la memoria*, 158.
[65] Mires, *La rebelión permanente*, 359.

212   WHEN DEMOCRACY BREAKS

industrial belts (*cordones industriales*), and myriad other territorial organizations. These were not "soviets" or alternative institutions to the Chilean state—despite being decried as such by the opposition and celebrated as "embryos of power" by the far-left MIR and Socialist Party. Instead, they were grassroots social organizations that sought to deepen and expand democratic participation in the context of defending the democratically elected government. It was this mobilization from below that ultimately saved the Allende government in late 1972.

The left-wing Popular Unity pointed to this mass mobilization as evidence that revolutionary advance was possible and Allende should throw his support behind the workers. Yet by October 1972, Allende's government was largely in a defensive position. Time and again, Allende reiterated that "he would not endorse an armed road to revolution nor suspend the Constitution. He would find a solution by continuing to navigate and stretch the inherited institutional framework."[66] At the insistence of the opposition to guarantee congressional elections would be held in March 1973, Allende ultimately ended the Bosses Lockout by incorporating military officers into his cabinet.

Failure of a Political Resolution via the March 1973 Congressional Elections

After the October 1972 Bosses Lockout, the new battleground in the campaign to unseat Allende became the March 1973 congressional elections. The National Party and the Christian Democrats joined forces to form the Democratic Confederation. This center-right alliance vowed to attain the two-thirds majority in the Senate necessary to impeach Allende. The Nationalist Party (right) openly called not just for a new balance of power in Congress but also for a new government, accusing Allende of imposing Marxist totalitarianism. For its part, the Popular Unity government sought to rally its bases and secure a majority mandate for continued reforms. Consistent with Chile's pluralist democratic traditions, it made sense to all sides of the political spectrum that the March 1973 congressional elections would be a referendum on the revolutionary process.

If Chileans looked to the polls for a resolution to the political crisis, the election results only reinforced the existing stalemate. Both sides could claim victory in the March elections. In absolute numbers the center-right coalition received 54.6% but failed to secure the two-thirds majority in Congress needed to impeach Allende. The left picked up seats in Congress, garnering 43.5% of the vote. Despite economic turmoil and growing unrest in the streets, support

---

[66] Steve J. Stern, *Battling for Hearts and Minds: Memory Struggles in Pinochet's Chile, 1973–1988* (Durham, NC: Duke University Press, 2006), 19.

for Allende's government went from 36% when he was elected in September 1970 to nearly 44% in March 1973. Although lower than the 50% in the March 1971 municipal elections, the results still indicated a remarkable level of support from Chile's poor majority for the changes carried out in the previous two years. The left-wing Popular Unity and MIR called for a revolutionary option to push forward support for worker mobilization. Allende steadfastly eschewed the idea that violence was necessary for revolution, refused to consider arming the workers, and relied, perhaps too heavily, on his skills at political negotiation to carry him through crisis points.

To the very end, Allende and the moderates continued to seek a negotiated political solution, only to face a Christian Democratic Party no longer interested in compromise. By 1973, the Frei-led conservative wing of the Christian Democrats not only dominated the party but also "sabotaged all attempts to reach an agreement with the government," including those sponsored by the Catholic Church.[67] Former president Frei concluded that "Marxism was the gravest threat to the institutions of liberal democracy and, to confront that challenge, unconstitutional and undemocratic measures could be temporarily warranted."[68] Without the numbers to impeach the president, the center and right in Congress could not remove Allende constitutionally. The National Party and the Christian Democrats arrived at the same conclusion: a military solution to the country's political impasse. The pivot of the Christian Democrats, who held the presidency from 1964 to 1970, to throwing their support behind the most authoritarian elements within the right indicates the extent to which politics can become so polarized that they become antidemocratic.

In the months ahead, the opposition movement gained greater traction and visibility. There were several aspects of the Popular Unity program that left it vulnerable to being exploited by the opposition. As manifested by the March of the Pots and Plans, the opposition successfully tapped into widely held beliefs about the obligation of the state to protect and provide for Chileans families as a rallying cry to delegitimize the government.[69] In March 1973, Catholic schoolchildren marched in the streets to protest the Allende government's educational reform plan. Despite being aligned with UNESCO's recommendations for modernization, the opposition painted it as an effort to circumvent parental authority and warned of children being shipped off to Cuba and the Soviet Union for political indoctrination. Second, the APS socialized sector of the economy benefited only some workers, not all, which opened the door for challenges from the revolution from below and their far-left political allies in the form of factory seizures

---

[67] Casals, "Insurrection of the Middle Class," 15.
[68] Hurtado, Gathering Storm, 201.
[69] Gwynn Thomas, "The Legacies of Patrimonial Patriarchalism: Contesting Political Legitimacy in Allende's Chile," Annals of the American Academy 636 (July 2011): 69–87.

214   WHEN DEMOCRACY BREAKS

and demands for inclusion in the APS. Meanwhile, the Christian Democrats successfully exploited preexisting labor petitions for salary adjustments to back a segment of copper miners as they launched a months-long strike.[70] The image of Catholic university and high school students marching alongside the copper miners underscored the sense that Allende had lost even the workers' support.

The Creeping Coup: June–September 1973

In late June 1973, the Allende government staved off a coup attempt, known as the Tanquetazo. As tanks rolled down Santiago's streets, leftist activists mobilized across Chile to defend workplaces and neighborhoods as they had during the Bosses Lockout in October 1972. Within hours, General Carlos Prats and forces loyal to the Constitution successfully put down the anti-Allende rebellion in Santiago. Congress refused to grant Allende's request for extraordinary powers to respond to the seditious uprising. Not only did the conspiratorial elements within the military escape punishment, but Allende once again brought the military back into his government, appointing General Prats as minister of defense. Despite vociferous demands from the left wing of his coalition, Allende never gave serious consideration to arming workers.[71]

Allende's decision to incorporate the military into his cabinet was likely the only way to end the October 1972 Bosses Lockout, but it had the effect of further politicizing the armed forces, which remained in the government until the March 1973 elections and again, following the failed military uprising in June 1973. Allende can be criticized for tolerating seditious right-wing elements within the military, for misjudging the extent of U.S. national security indoctrination, and for underestimating the anti-Communism among his officers corps. He trusted that the military would remain loyal to the Constitution, or at the very least, that his repeated efforts to demonstrate his respect for the Constitution would dissuade or sufficiently isolate any pro-coup tendencies, which had periodically surfaced with the 1969 failed military uprising under Frei, the 1970 Schneider assassination, and the failed coup attempt in June 1973.[72] Internally, this final failed coup attempt served as an opportunity for the military to purge its ranks of those loyal to Allende. By June 1973, an important part of the high

---

[70] Thomas Miller Klubock, *Contested Communities: Class, Gender, and Politics in Chile's El Teniente Copper Mine, 1904–1951* (Durham, NC: Duke University Press, 1998), 282–295; Angela Vergara, *Copper Workers, International Business and Domestic Politics in Cold War Chile* (State College: Pennsylvania State University Press, 2008).

[71] Tanya Harmer, *Allende's Chile and the Inter-American Cold War* (Chapel Hill: University of North Carolina Press,) 232–234.

[72] Tanya Harmer, "Towards a Global History of the Unidad Popular," *Radical Americas* 6, no. 1 (June 2021): 6–7.

BREAKDOWN OF DEMOCRACY IN CHILE   215

command of the armed forces of Chile had lost respect for the democratically elected government.

The political right did not share Allende's belief that the military should respect constitutional order. An openly seditious right engaged in "a propaganda campaign of terror, a legislative campaign of total obstructionism, and a secret conspiracy of treason against the democratic institutions that it publicly professed to defend."[73] Unable to instigate a coup in 1970, the Chilean political right and the U.S. government actively courted the Chilean armed forces. Coup plotting began to take shape in earnest in November 1972, shortly after the resolution of the Bosses Lockout. Based on firsthand accounts, mid-rank military officers met with middle-class activists, Christian Democrat–affiliated labor leaders, and business leaders, intentionally excluding segments of the top brass considered to be loyal to the Constitution.[74] After March 1973, the conspiracy widened to include the right wing of the Christian Democrats.

Writing in 1978, political scientist Arturo Valenzuela concluded that the Christian Democrats failed to appreciate how the "political game shifted" after the March elections and June 1973 Tanquetazo: "[I]n combating the dubious prospect of 'Marxist totalitarianism,' to the bitter end, they failed to realize how much of a stake they had in the democratic political order they thought they were defending. By not moving forcefully to structure a political solution, they seriously undermined the position of the president and his advisers who were clearly ready to reach a mutual accommodation."[75] This failure of moderate political elites on the left and center to reach an agreement in mid-1973 weakened not only the authority of Allende's government but also the legitimacy of the political class altogether. The front lines would increasingly be in the streets and in the barracks.

In 1970, the Chilean armed forces were essentially divided between those who opposed Allende's election on ideological grounds and those who remained sympathetic, or at least neutral, to Popular Unity's vision for national development.[76] At that time, Chilean military training incorporated elements from homegrown anti-Communism alongside counterinsurgency tactics promoted by the United States in the National Security Doctrine.[77] Yet they were by no

[73] Oppenheim, *Politics in Chile,* 91.

[74] Johnathan Kandell, "Chilean Officers Tell How They Began to Plan the Take-over Last November," *New York Times,* September 27, 1973, 3.

[75] Valenzuela, *Chile,* 107.

[76] Verónica Valdivia Ortiz de Zárate, "'¡Estamos en Guerra, Señores!' El régimen militar de Pinochet y el 'Pueblo,' 1973–1980," *Historia* 43, no. 1 (January–June 2010): 170. See also Verónica Valdivia Ortiz de Zárate, *El golpe después del golpe: Leigh vs. Pinochet, Chile, 1960–1980* (Santiago: LOM, 2003).

[77] For more on National Security Doctrine in Cold War South America, see Francisco Leal Buitrago, "La doctrina de seguridad nacional: materialización de la guerra fría en América del Sur," *Revista de Estudios Sociales* 15 (2003): 74–87.

216   WHEN DEMOCRACY BREAKS

means the dominant ideologies. By 1973, however, the military had started to interpret events within Chile through the National Security Doctrine framework, which opened the door to define segments of the civilian population as an internal enemy. After the failed June 1973 Tanquetazo, the military's internal analyses became dotted with references to the enemy within and internal warfare. Unlike Argentina and Uruguay in the 1970s, Chile had no armed revolutionary groups to challenge the military or the state's monopoly on violence. Instead, it was the armed forces that launched preemptive assaults on Allende's working-class supporters in July 1973.

Acting on the advice of General Prats and as a gesture of compromise, President Allende ratified the October 1972 opposition-sponsored Arms Control Law, which gave the Chilean armed forces the discretionary authority to search and seize weapons from the general population. Historian Peter Winn has argued that the application of the law served the dual purpose of intimidating Allende supporters and acclimating conscript soldiers—often drawn from poor sectors—to the abuse of fellow citizens.[78] Following the failed coup attempt in June 1973, the armed forces began to apply the law, carrying out raids in factories and working-class neighborhoods across Chile. Despite the fascist paramilitary Patria y Libertad's ongoing acts of sabotage, the military almost exclusively targeted pro-Allende working-class supporters, particularly the *cordones industriales* (industrial belts) that had organized to resist the Bosses Lockout. This "creeping coup" gutted the left and in many respects explained the weakened position of Allende's social base prior to the coup.

During this same period, the military carried out an internal house cleaning, detaining and torturing soldiers and marines suspected being loyal to Allende or the Constitution.[79] In August 1973, several sailors and civilian naval base workers were arrested on charges of sedition, and the national leadership of the Socialist Party, the MAPU, and the MIR were accused of attempting to infiltrate the Chilean armed forces. Secret meetings between the groups had taken place, but the initiative came not from above, but from below. Low-ranking sailors and civilian workers had overheard their superiors discussing coup plans, and they took action to warn the Popular Unity government. The opposition-controlled press amplified the charges as a left-wing conspiracy to infiltrate the armed forces.

On August 22, 1973, the Chilean Congress passed a partisan but nonbinding resolution declaring that Allende's government had violated the Constitution through its use of decree orders to carry out appropriations. Many scholars point

[78] Winn, "The Furies of the Andes," 260–226.

[79] Jorge Magasich, *Los que dijeron No: Historia del movimiento de los marinos antigolpistas de 1973* (Santiago: LOM Ediciones, 2008); Danny Monsálvez, "Agosto 1973: Proa al golpe en la armada: Los marineros antigolpe," *Revista Tiempo y Espacio* 14 (2004): 203–233.

BREAKDOWN OF DEMOCRACY IN CHILE   217

to this event as sealing Allende's fate, as it "provided a fig leaf of legitimacy for a military coup."[80] The following day, General Prats resigned as commander-in-chief of the Chilean Army. He had served as minister of the interior, a role equivalent to vice president in Chile, following the October 1972 Bosses Lockout. After his appointment as minister of defense in June 1973, right-wing women staged regular demonstrations to sprinkle chicken feed on the lawns of military officers, especially targeting General Prats. The failed June 29 coup attempt and the gendered protests convinced Prats that he had lost his officers' support and he resigned along with two other pro-Allende generals. The path had widened for the coup conspiracy to move forward. To replace Prats, President Allende respected the chain of command and appointed the next general in line: Augusto Pinochet Ugarte.

By September 1, 1973, the coup plan was already in place, with the Chilean navy taking the lead. It is unlikely the military would have been deterred by last-minute political negotiations between the Christian Democrats and Allende's government, nor by Allende's plans to hold a plebiscite. On September 10, fifty officers suspected of loyalty to Allende, including three generals and one admiral, were arrested. Those elements within the armed forces who might have defended democracy were preemptively neutralized.

September 11, 1973, Military Coup and the Legacies of Authoritarian Rule

One of the earliest, if now largely discredited, explanations for the breakdown of democracy in Chile framed it as an act of U.S. imperialism directed by President Nixon and his top advisor, Secretary of State Henry Kissinger. Unlike coups in Iran (1953) and Guatemala (1954), the Chilean coup was not CIA orchestrated or executed. Nor did it directly involve the U.S. military, as had occurred as recently as 1965 with the marine invasion to depose the democratically elected government of Juan Bosch in the Dominican Republic. Washington's actions did contribute to the destabilization of Allende's government, particularly as Nixon's September 1970 directive to "make the economy scream" materialized in mid-1972 along with U.S. material aid to key opposition groups like the striking truck drivers and copper miners. As has so often been the case in Latin America, the U.S. government was no friend to democracy. Pro-coup Christian Democrats, including Eduardo Frei, erroneously believed that after the coup, the United States would exert sufficient pressure for new elections and a return to civilian

---

[80] Elizabeth Quay Hutchinson, Thomas Miller Klubock, Nara B. Milanich, and Peter Winn, eds., *The Chile Reader* (Durham, NC: Duke University Press), 351.

government. Instead, the Nixon administration immediately granted diplomatic recognition to the military junta, and despite mounting evidence of the systematic violation of human rights, U.S. military and economic aid readily flowed to the Pinochet regime over the next seventeen years.

Rather than understand the Latin American Cold War as derivative of superpower conflict, recent historical studies have suggested it was largely fought over different types of democracy.[81] As elsewhere during Latin America's "democratic spring" in the 1930s and 1940s, Chile under the Popular Front governments witnessed tremendous gains by urban labor and the expansion of mass politics. For both the Communist and non-Communist left, democracy entailed striving for economic equality and guaranteeing the rights of social citizenship. Initially the United States backed these reforms and promoted the consolidation of Latin American welfare states, particularly with the Alliance for Progress aid program. Yet by the late 1960s, Washington increasingly jettisoned any notion of social citizenship in favor of a more limited definition of democracy centered on political and individual rights. Strong authoritarian tendencies in Latin American political thought, emboldened by Cold War anti-Communism with varying degrees of support from Washington, coalesced with violent fury to crush the left in Latin America and reverse decades of democratic gains.

The tragic end to Allende's government and Chile's democratic tradition was by no means inevitable. It was the result of contingent political decision-making by several actors: the Chilean armed forces with the active endorsement of the political right and center and the United States. It counted on the support of business sectors inside and outside of Chile and a sizable portion of the Chilean middle class mobilized through associations of professionals, small shop owners, truck drivers, students, and women.

The rhetoric and actions of the political right consistently undermined institutional stability. Historically, whenever the status quo had been challenged, Chile's upper classes had repeatedly turned to violent repression to retain power. Still smarting from the 1967 Agrarian Reform Law passed during Christian Democrat Frei's administration, they were vehemently opposed to Allende's election and the Popular Unity platform.[82] Unlike the political left and center, the right did not share the belief that the military should respect constitutional order, underscoring the absence of "moral limits when it comes to defeating those it identifies as its mortal enemy."[83]

---

[81] Greg Grandin, *The Last Colonial Massacre: Latin America in the Cold War* (Chicago: University of Chicago Press, 2004), introduction; Greg Grandin, "Living in Revolutionary Time: Coming to Terms with the Violence of Latin America's Long Cold War," in Grandin and Joseph, *Insurgent and Counterinsurgent Violence during Latin America's Long Cold War*, 1–42.

[82] Casals, "The Chilean Counter-revolution," 7.

[83] Casals, "The Chilean Counter-revolution," 3.

While this antidemocratic camp was a small minority in 1970, by mid-1972 it had become a powerful mass movement "that would end up paving the way for the military coup."[84] The Chilean middle class, politically aligned with the Christian Democrats, represented the linchpin as a nonelite base of public support for a military intervention. They had been economically squeezed by inflation and shortages; politically, their leaders in the Christian Democratic Party had already moved to the right; and anti-Communist and seditious messages were widely disseminated in the media. Anti-Communism, already deeply embedded in Chilean political culture, offered a coherent script to mobilize and expand the opposition's ranks.

Despite the Chilean armed forces' application of the National Security Doctrine as a framework, Chile was not experiencing a military crisis in 1973. Rather, military intervention responded to the country's political, social, and economic crisis. Among the factors that stoked the military's anti-Communist mindset and facilitated their move into politics, historian Veronica Valdivia points to the "capacity of the opposition to intensify the confrontational climate" gripping the country and conflict over private property.[85] On September 11, 1973, the military's declaration of internal warfare against an enemy within did not correspond to reality: Chile had no leftist guerrilla movement. Rather, this National Security Doctrine framework served as justification for systematic violence against the Chilean lower classes and their political allies on the left. State terror aimed at eradicating the political, social, and cultural spaces built by the lower classes in the preceding century, particularly as social mobilization multiplied, and democratic participation flourished in the decade from 1964 to 1973.[86]

The commitment of citizens, particularly those without significant economic or political power, to work within existing channels contrasted with the willingness of political elites to abandon democracy. Those who came to defend the Allende government and Chilean democracy were nonelites—the ordinary men and women who mobilized to keep the economy running during the Bosses Lockout in October 1972 and the low-level soldiers who tried to warn party leaders on the left of their superior officers' conspiratorial plans, only to be detained and tortured. The same sectors experienced a creeping coup in the months running up to September 11, 1973, and disproportionately figure among those targeted for human rights abuses under military rule. In the seventeen years of military rule, state agents assassinated more than 3,000 citizens. More

---

[84] Casals, "The Chilean Counter-revolution," 1.

[85] Valdivia, " '¡Estamos en Guerra, Señores,' " 170.

[86] Francisco Domínguez, "Violence, the Left, and the Creation of *Un Nuevo Chile*," in *Political Violence and the Construction of National Identity in Latin America*, ed. Will Fowler and Peter Lambert (New York: Palgrave Macmillan, 2006), 150.

220 WHEN DEMOCRACY BREAKS

than 38,000 Chileans survived imprisonment and torture in clandestine detention centers, and an additional 100,000 were subjected to torture during raids on working-class neighborhoods and mass round-ups following public protests.[87]

Chile in 1973 offers a cautionary example of how class tensions reached a level where politicians and a significant amount of the electorate came to reject the basic principles and shared understandings that underpin democracy. By 1973, these sectors came to see "the price of inclusion of the masses—for example, wages, inflation, and property transfer, not to mention the ultimate possibility of radical social displacement"—as greater than the risks of direct conflict and military rule.[88] Unlike the ideologically divided left, antidemocratic actors successfully developed a more unified and better organized counterrevolutionary movement. Yet even those politicians and civilians, especially in the center, who actively courted military intervention and initially celebrated September 11, 1973, as Chile's liberation, paid a much higher cost in the long run for losing democracy.

[87] Stern, *Battling for Hearts and Minds*, 392–395.

[88] Paul W. Drake, *Socialism and Populism in Chile, 1932–1952* (Urbana: University of Illinois, 1978), 340.

8

The Indian Emergency (1975–1977) in Historical Perspective

Sugata Bose and Ayesha Jalal

Democracy and authoritarianism have been historically bound in a complex and sometimes intimate relationship. The global emergence of quite a few democratically elected authoritarian leaders today has made explicit what had always been an underlying feature of the history of democratic practice. The authoritarian strain was perhaps more marked in countries aspiring to democracy by shedding an inheritance of colonial despotism.[1] India's experiment with democracy after winning independence from British rule offers a fascinating case study of the struggle to establish democratic norms amid the lure of falling back on the structures of an authoritarian legacy.

Foundations and Frailties of India's Democracy

Constitutional reforms in British India during the early twentieth century, in 1909, 1919, and 1935, introduced elements of limited representative government while denying substantive democracy. These were measures to protect and perpetuate colonial rule under the changed political circumstances of an intensifying nationalist challenge. The British had alternated between attempts at communalizing and provincializing Indian representative politics in order to keep power at the all-India center firmly in their own hands. Since 1909 separate electorates were introduced for religious minorities. The 1919 and 1935 legislations sought to direct Indian political attention toward local and provincial arenas. The Indian National Congress, led by Mohandas Karamchand Gandhi from 1920 onward, orchestrated mass movements across the country to circumvent the constraints of the representative institutions with very restricted electorates set up by the British raj. Indians learned the value of democracy less from its example in the metropolis and more from the practice

---

[1] Ayesha Jalal, *Democracy and Authoritarianism in South Asia: A Comparative and Historical Perspective* (Cambridge: Cambridge University Press, 1995).

Sugata Bose and Ayesha Jalal, *The Indian Emergency (1975–1977) in Historical Perspective* In: *When Democracy Breaks*. Edited by: Archon Fung, David Moss, and Odd Arne Westad, Oxford University Press. © Oxford University Press 2024. DOI: 10.1093/oso/9780197760789.003.0008

222 WHEN DEMOCRACY BREAKS

of authoritarianism in the colony. The rule of colonial difference had ensured that what was good for the metropolis was not considered good for the colony. "Democracy," as Subhas Chandra Bose put it in 1928, "is by no means a Western institution; it is a human institution." India, he believed, should become "an independent Federal Republic." He warned Indian nationalists not to become "a queer mixture of political democrats and social conservatives." He explained, "If we want to make India really great, we must build up a political democracy on the pedestal of a democratic society. Privileges based on birth, caste or creed should go, and equal opportunities should be thrown open to all irrespective of caste, creed or religion. The status of women should also be raised, and women should be trained to take larger and a more intelligent interest in public affairs."[2] With independence on the horizon nearly two decades later, a Constituent Assembly was convened on December 9, 1946, to begin the task of laying the constitutional foundation of India's democracy.

On November 26, 1949, the Constituent Assembly adopted a set of principles enshrined in a lengthy written document that have guided India's political destiny for over seven decades. The Republic envisioned in the Constitution was formally inaugurated on January 26, 1950. Its most far-reaching provision was for a universal adult franchise in a country with a literacy rate hovering near 12%. India was to have a parliamentary democratic system with a directly elected House of the People (Lok Sabha) and a Council of States (Rajya Sabha) indirectly elected by state legislatures.

India was extremely fortunate that as stringent a critic of mainstream nationalism as the "depressed classes" leader Dr. B. R. Ambedkar placed his intellectual prowess at the service of the nation for five crucial years, from December 9, 1946, to October 12, 1951, when he resigned as law minister from Jawaharlal Nehru's cabinet in protest against conservative opposition to the reformist Hindu Code Bill. As the minorities face the cold winds of exclusion from the powers that be in today's India, it is pertinent to recall what Ambedkar said on the question of minority protection while introducing the draft constitution on November 4, 1948. "To diehards who have developed a kind of fanaticism against minority protection," he declared, "I would like to say two things. One is that minorities are an explosive force which, if it erupts, can blow up the whole fabric of the State. . . . The other is that the minorities in India have agreed to place their existence in the hands of the majority. . . . They have loyally accepted the rule of the majority which is basically a communal majority and not a political majority. It is for the majority to realize its duty not to discriminate against minorities."[3]

---

[2] Quoted in Sugata Bose, *His Majesty's Opponent: Subhas Chandra Bose and India's Struggle against Empire* (Cambridge, MA: Belknap Press of Harvard University Press, 2011), 73.

[3] *Constituent Assembly Debates* (New Delhi: Government of India, 1950), vol. 7, November 4, 1948, 39.

THE INDIAN EMERGENCY   223

In the same speech Ambedkar responded to critics who asserted that there was "nothing new in the Draft Constitution, that about half of it has been copied from the Government of India Act of 1935 and that the rest of it has been borrowed from the Constitutions of other countries." Ambedkar explained that he had borrowed and not plagiarized. He was only sorry that the provisions taken from the Government of India Act of 1935 related mostly to the details of administration. He agreed that ideally administrative details should have no place in the Constitution but argued that it was necessary in the Indian situation. It was in this context that Ambedkar invoked the concept of constitutional morality described by Grote, the historian of Greece, as "a paramount reverence for the forms of the Constitution, enforcing obedience to authority acting under and within these forms yet combined with the habit of open speech, of actions subject only to definite legal control, and unrestrained censure of those very authorities as to all their public acts combined too with a perfect confidence in the bosom of every citizen amidst the bitterness of party contest that the forms of the Constitution will not be less sacred in the eyes of his opponents than in his own."[4]

However, Grote had written of a situation wherein people were saturated with constitutional morality and could, therefore, take the risk of omitting details of the administration from the Constitution. In India of the late 1940s Ambedkar believed such a diffusion of constitutional morality could not be presumed. "Constitutional morality," he contended, "is not a natural sentiment. It has to be cultivated. We must realize that our people have yet to learn it."[5]

Ambedkar followed up this contention with a debatable proposition: "Democracy in India is only a top-dressing on an Indian soil, which is essentially undemocratic."[6] In today's climate some would probably label him unpatriotic or antinational for having said so. But a mature democracy ought to ponder his remark and embrace the value of constitutional morality as respect for forms and processes that enable the negotiation, adjudication, and resolution of differences by transcending what Grote described as "the bitterness of party contest." In the course of the Constituent Assembly debates another eloquent member, Zairul-Hasan Lari, pointed out that constitutional morality was a value that not just citizens but also the government must learn.[7] Just because the government has the power to act does not mean it should. The spirit underlying the Constitution and not just the words must guide and restrain the government.

If Ambedkar had profound insights into freedom of conscience, minority protection, and constitutional morality, he and the Constituent Assembly

[4] *Constituent Assembly Debates,* 37–38.
[5] *Constituent Assembly Debates,* 37–38.
[6] *Constituent Assembly Debates,* 38.
[7] *Constituent Assembly Debates,* vol. 7, November 8, 1948, 298.

224 WHEN DEMOCRACY BREAKS

collectively fell short on the question of emergency provisions and federalism. The Constitution was framed under the dark shadow of the dislocations wrought by partition. The loss and division of the Muslim-majority provinces reduced the voices that would have argued against an overcentralizing impulse. Ambedkar was originally elected to the Constituent Assembly from Bengal thanks to the magnanimity of Scheduled Caste leaders led by Jogendra Nath Mondal. The list of members who registered and presented their credentials on December 9, 1946, from Bengal had been a veritable roll of honor: Mr. Sarat Chandra Bose, Dr. B. R. Ambedkar, Mr. Kiran Shankar Roy, Mr. Frank Reginald Anthony, Mr. Satya Ranjan Baksi, Dr. Prafulla Chandra Ghosh. The list included twenty-five members from Bengal, among them the distinguished Communist leader Somnath Lahiri.[8] Once the partitioner's axe fell on Bengal, the Jessore and Khulna constituency that Ambedkar represented through an indirect election was given away to the new Constituent Assembly of Pakistan. At that moment in July 1947 Ambedkar had to be hastily reelected from Bombay province to a seat vacated by M. R. Jayakar.

Ambedkar candidly acknowledged that the Indian Constitution, unlike the American one, was not cast in the pure federal mold. The Constitution of India, he claimed, "can be both unitary as well as federal according to the requirements of time and circumstances. In normal times, it is framed to work as a federal system. But in times of war it is so designed as to make it work as though it was a unitary system." "Once the President issues a Proclamation which he is authorized to do under the Provisions of Article 275," he went on to say, "the whole scene can become transformed and the State becomes a unitary state."[9] We now know from what transpired between 1975 and 1977 how this lacuna in the form of emergency provisions can allow authoritarianism to get the better of both federalism and democracy. Even fundamental rights are not as inviolable in the Indian Constitution as the Bill of Rights in the United States. "Though imbibing the principles of democratic Constitutions," Asok Chanda wrote in his 1965 book, *Federalism in India*, "the Indian Constitution is not altogether free from authoritarian trends which it inherited in accepting the basis of the 1935 Act."[10]

Did no one in the Constituent Assembly foresee the dangers posed to federalism and democracy by the states of exception written into the Constitution?

---

[8] *Constituent Assembly Debates*, vol. 1, December 9, 1946, 10.

[9] *Constituent Assembly Debates*, vol. 7, November 4, 1948, 34–35.

[10] Asok Chanda, *Federalism in India: A Study of Union State Relations* (London: George Allen and Unwin, 1965), 67. Until 1965 there was a lively intellectual tradition of critical scholarship on the Indian Constitution. The following year Granville Austin's *The Indian Constitution: Cornerstone of a Nation* (Oxford: Clarendon Press, 1966) was published. Austin was a U.S. State Department employee in the 1950s and 1960s. This foreigner's praise of the liberal features of the Constitution was lapped up in Indian ruling circles. Austin did not take seriously the objections raised in the Constituent Assembly to the inclusion of the emergency provisions, which were to be invoked within a decade of the publication of his book.

THE INDIAN EMERGENCY   225

A few did. But their far-sighted amendments were typically voted down or "negatived," to use the parliamentary jargon. Hari Vishnu Kamath, a close associate of Subhas Chandra Bose during the freedom struggle, rang the alarm bells during the debate on draft Article 275 on August 2, 1949:

> I have ransacked most of the constitutions of democratic countries of the world—monarchic or republican—and I find no parallel to this Chapter on emergency provisions in any of the other constitutions of democratic countries in the world. The closest approximation, to my mind, is reached in the Weimar Constitution of the Third Reich which was destroyed by Hitler taking advantage of the very same provisions contained in that constitution. That Weimar Constitution of the Third Republic exists no longer and has been replaced by the Bonn Constitution. But those emergency provisions pale into insignificance when compared with the emergency provisions in this chapter of our Constitution.[11]

Ambedkar's colleague T. T. Krishnamachari made light of "the constitutional dictatorship envisaged in Article 48 of the Weimar Constitution." Kamath intervened once more to say to Krishnamachari, "[T]he point I made out with reference to article 48 of the Weimar Constitution is that Hitler used those very provisions to establish his dictatorship." Ambedkar reckoned "much time" had been taken up in the debate and "thought that no reply was necessary because Mr. T. T. Krishnamachari had replied to the points already." The president of the Constituent Assembly, Rajendra Prasad, terminated the debate with a show of some impatience. The Constituent Assembly passed the motion empowering the president to proclaim an emergency if the security of India was threatened "whether by war or external aggression or internal disturbance" or if he was satisfied there was "imminent danger thereof."[12]

The next day Kamath rose to the defense of federalism during the debate on draft Article 277-A that would let the Union government intervene in the internal affairs of states in case of "internal disturbance." He brought an amendment to replace that phrase with "internal insurrection or chaos." The article proposed intervention by the president on receipt of a report from the state governor "or otherwise." Kamath considered "otherwise" to be a "mischievous word." He refused to be party to such "a foul transaction, setting at naught the scheme of even the limited provincial autonomy which we have provided for in this Constitution, and I shall pray to God that he may grant sufficient wisdom to

[11] *Constituent Assembly Debates*, vol. 9, August 2, 1949, 105.
[12] *Constituent Assembly Debates*, vol. 9, August 2, 1949, 123, 125–127.

226   WHEN DEMOCRACY BREAKS

this House to see the folly, the stupidity, the criminal nature of this transaction."[13] Kamath received some support from K. T. Shah, Shibbun Lal Saxena, Hirday Nath Kunzru, Renuka Ray, and Biswanath Das in taking a stand against the emergency provisions and overcentralizing tendencies. They were outvoted, and Kamath's plea to lay "the foundation of a real democracy" sounded like a voice in the wilderness.[14] "I do not altogether deny," Ambedkar conceded, "that there is a possibility of these articles being abused or employed for political purposes. . . . [T]he proper thing we ought to expect is that such articles will never be called into operation and that they would remain a dead letter."[15] That was a pious hope waiting to be belied.

"The proceedings of this Constituent Assembly would have been very dull," Ambedkar said in his final speech in the Constituent Assembly, "if all members had yielded to the rule of party discipline. Party discipline, in all its rigidity, would have converted this Assembly into a gathering of 'yes' men. Fortunately, there were rebels." He went on to list by name Hari Vishnu Kamath, Dr. P. S. Deshmukh, R. K. Sidhva, Professor Shibban Lal Saksena, Pandit Thakur Das Bhargava, Professor K. T. Shah, and Pandit Hirday Nath Kunzru. "That I was not prepared to accept their suggestions," Ambedkar generously stated, "does not diminish the value of their suggestions nor lessen the service they have rendered to the Assembly in enlivening its proceedings."[16]

Reduced to enlivening the proceedings rather than contributing to the substance of the final product, the rebels did not disguise their feelings of regret that their amendments were rejected. Rising to extend "limited and qualified support" to the motion moved by Ambedkar to pass the Constitution, Kamath suggested that "[w]e, the people of India" had come to the end of a long journey which was, however, "the beginning of a longer, a more arduous and a more hazardous one." "True to the Indian genius," he noted, "our struggle, our awakening, began with a spiritual renaissance which was pioneered by Ramakrishna Paramahansa, Swami Vivekananda and Swami Dayananda. In the wake of those spiritual leaders came the political renaissance and the cultural renaissance of which the torchbearers, the leaders, the guides were Lokamanya Tilak, Aurobindo and Mahatma Gandhi and, last but not the least, Netaji Subhas Chandra Bose." He recalled the part

[13] *Constituent Assembly Debates*, vol. 9, August 3, 1949, 138, 140. K. T. Shah had already on November 15, 1948, brought an amendment to Article 1 of the Constitution: "India shall be a Secular, Federal, Socialist Union of States." It was voted down. *Constituent Assembly Debates*, vol. 7, November 15, 1948, 399–401.

[14] *Constituent Assembly Debates*, vol. 9, August 3, 1949, 142.

[15] *Constituent Assembly Debates*, vol. 9, August 4, 1949, 177.

[16] *Constituent Assembly Debates*, vol. 11, November 25, 1949, 974. For an analysis of the intellectual lineage of the dissenters, especially Hari Vishnu Kamath, see Aniket De, "A Rebel's Constitution: States of Exception and Anticolonial Alternatives in the Making of the Indian Republic," in *Nation, Partition, Federation: South Asia's Freedom in Global Perspective*, ed. Sugata Bose and Ayesha Jalal (forthcoming).

played in the freedom struggle by Sheikh Abdullah in Kashmir and Khan Abdul Ghaffar Khan and his brother Dr. Khan Sahib in the North West Frontier Province. "That part of India is no longer with us," Kamath said, "but our hope and our faith is that whatever the differences between the part that has gone from us and the part that still remains to us, those differences will be removed, will be smoothened and our relations will become happier day by day, and Pakistan and India will live on the most cordial terms as years roll by." The Constitution that had been settled by the Assembly he described as "a centralized federation with a facade of parliamentary democracy." He and his friends Shibban Lal Saksena, P. S. Deshmukh, R. K. Sidhva, Mahavir Tyagi, Thakur Das Bhargava, Naziruddin Ahmad, K. T. Shah, Hirday Nath Kunzru, and Brajeshwar Prasad had all tried "to make the Constitution conform to the Preamble" but "found that the horoscope of the Drafting Committee was strong."[17]

Between 1951 and 1971 India held five general elections to the Lok Sabha, the directly elected House of the People, based on universal adult franchise and supervised by a neutral Election Commission. Its credentials as a formal electoral democracy were established beyond question. It had a vibrant and free print media, even though radio and television (available only since the early 1970s) were under state control. The Indian National Congress was the dominant political party, which in partnership with the bureaucracy sought to control the commanding heights of the political economy of development. A wide array of somewhat fragmented opposition parties failed to dislodge the Congress party in a first-past-the-post parliamentary democratic system. The central government resorted to repression in Kashmir and India's northeast, especially Nagaland, in the 1950s. In 1959 a duly elected Communist government in the state of Kerala was dismissed by the center. The war with China in 1962 occasioned an external emergency and the curtailment of fundamental rights.

Jawaharlal Nehru, India's first prime minister (1947–1964), had relied on provincial party bosses and dominant social groups to bring in the vote for the Congress party. The limitations of this oligarchical form of democracy were revealed in the 1967 elections in which the Congress party barely scraped through to power at the national level while losing to opposition parties in as many as eight states. This set the stage for further interventions by the center in the affairs of the states. Democratic political processes had empowered various subordinate social groups, which were now poised to break free of erstwhile patron-client linkages. Nehru's daughter, Indira Gandhi, rose to the challenge of widening and deepening the social bases of support of her party. She split the party in 1969, throwing out the organizational deadwood, and launched a left-leaning populist social and economic program encapsulated in the slogan "Garibi Hatao"

---

[17] *Constituent Assembly Debates*, vol. 11, November 19, 1949, 689–692.

228 WHEN DEMOCRACY BREAKS

(Remove Poverty). She nationalized fourteen private banks and abolished the privy purses of India's erstwhile princes. She called early general elections in March 1971, winning close to a two-thirds majority in Parliament with a significantly higher vote share than the undivided Congress party in 1967. Indira Gandhi's decisive leadership during the Bangladesh crisis of 1971 enhanced her prestige, and even the opposition leader in Parliament, Atal Behari Vajpayee, was effusive in her praise. The Congress Party handily won a series of state elections in 1972, reversing the downward trajectory of 1967.[18]

The Breakdown of India's Democracy

And yet, just three years later, democracy broke down in India, giving way to a nineteen-month spell of overt rather than just covert authoritarianism. At the midnight hour of June 25–26, 1975, a pliant president invoked the constitutional provision to declare a state of internal emergency at the instance of the prime minister. The cabinet, which had been kept in the dark, fell in line at dawn. Power had been shut off to the printing presses, so there were no newspapers that morning. A predawn swoop had been conducted on opposition leaders, including the venerable Jaya Prakash Narayan. One of the many political opponents to be arrested was none other than Hari Vishnu Kamath, who had warned about the dangers posed by the emergency provisions in the Constituent Assembly decades earlier. Altogether nearly 110,000 opposition political leaders and activists, independent editors and reporters, as well as dissenting students and youth were imprisoned during the Emergency. Fundamental rights, including the right to life and liberty enshrined in Article 21 of the Constitution, were suspended, and courts could not entertain writs of habeas corpus. A series of constitutional amendments were bulldozed through Parliament, further restricting, among other things, judicial review of executive decisions. The Supreme Court in a 4–1 decision with Justice H. R. Khanna dissenting upheld the government's position on the inadmissibility of habeas corpus petitions. The republic adorned itself with two additional adjectives—secular and socialist—in the preamble to the Constitution by means of the Forty-Second Amendment.

In addition to the deployment of a constitutional provision allowing for a state of exception to the rule of law, an extraconstitutional center of power emerged around Sanjay Gandhi, the younger son of the prime minister. It was Sanjay Gandhi and the coterie around him who were behind what came to be called the "excesses" of the Emergency. These included coercive methods of population

---

[18] Sumantra Bose, *Transforming India: Challenges to the World's Largest Democracy* (Cambridge, MA: Harvard University Press, 2013), 22–31.

THE INDIAN EMERGENCY   229

control, including drives toward compulsory sterilization in northern India, and forcible demolition of urban slums, notably in the Turkman gate area of Delhi. These assaults on the most vulnerable sections of society, including Dalits and Muslims, led "the wits to comment that having failed to get rid of poverty the Congress had taken to getting rid of the poor."[19]

Resistance to the Emergency was fitful. The opposition and labor leader George Fernandes went underground and engaged in the polemics of defiance through his political pamphlets, until he was tracked down in June 1976. The judiciary, with the honorable exception of Justice Khanna, caved to the executive's will, arguing that the constitutional provisions permitting the lawful suspension of rights limited their freedom of maneuver. Papers like the *Indian Express* and *The Statesman* stood up to the Emergency; courageous and principled journalists like Gourkishore Ghosh and Kuldip Nayyar went to jail. Yet there was something to the Jana Sangh leader L. K. Advani's complaint about the mainstream media: "They asked you to bend, and you crawled." The Indira Gandhi regime deployed Article 19(2) of the Constitution, citing "security of the state" and "promotion of disaffection," to effectively muzzle the media.

In January 1977 Indira Gandhi announced her decision to relax the Emergency (it was not repealed until two months later) and called for general elections in March. It is not entirely clear why she did so. The most plausible explanation is that she received intelligence that she would win the election. Macroeconomic management by her government had been reasonably effective; inflation had been tamed. It is also possible that Nehru's daughter was uncomfortable with the label of autocrat being attached to her even by erstwhile friends in foreign lands. A proven vote-getter and charismatic campaigner, she may have craved democratic legitimacy for her authoritarian leadership. As soon as opposition leaders were released from detention, they combined five different political entities to form the Janata (People's) Party. In a sign of impending trouble, two key Congress leaders from Uttar Pradesh and Bihar—Hemvati Nandan Bahuguna and Jagjivan Ram—defected to form the Congress for Democracy and joined forces with the Janata Party. The people's verdict was loud and clear: the Congress party suffered a humiliating rout in northern India, with Indira Gandhi and Sanjay Gandhi losing their own seats in Uttar Pradesh. The Congress Party's strong performance in the south suggests that people voted against the "excesses" of the Emergency rather than in defense of democracy in the abstract. Overall, the Janata party won a majority and formed the first non-Congress government at the center. The resort to overt authoritarianism had been emphatically repudiated by India's electorate.

---

[19] Jalal, *Democracy and Authoritarianism*, 76.

Causes of the Breakdown

Explanations for the breakdown in India's democracy range from personal and proximate triggers to the structural and deep historical factors at work. At one end of the spectrum is the claim that Nehru's "halting yet honest attempts to promote a democratic ethos" were "undone by his own daughter, and in decisive and dramatic ways."[20] At the other end is the view that "Indira did not concoct the Emergency regime out of ether" and that "historical forces with roots in the past and implications for the future were at work in the extraordinary turn of events of 1975–77."[21] In between, there is the view that acknowledges the Emergency represented a style of rule but neglects to delve into its roots in the Nehruvian era.[22] The contrast between Nehru and his daughter is surely overdrawn. The architect of India's parliamentary democracy equated communists and federalists with terrorists in the late 1940s; let the Gandhian Potti Sriramalu die of starvation in 1952 when he called for the linguistic reorganization of states; threw his friend Sheikh Abdullah into prison in 1953, compounding the Kashmir problem; turned a blind eye to human rights violations in Nagaland in 1956; and acquiesced in the dismissal of a duly elected state government of Kerala in 1959.[23] It is clear that "events which have been explained mainly in terms of Indira Gandhi's flawed leadership qualities, and more specifically her personal paranoia, are more meaningfully analyzed in the context of the structural contradictions within the Indian state structure and economy."[24]

Among the more proximate causes of the erosion of public support for Indira Gandhi's government between 1973 and 1975 was the first international oil shock that adversely affected India's balance of payments and fueled inflation. The difficult international economic environment hampered the democratically elected government's efforts to deliver on its socioeconomic promises regarding poverty and unemployment. The electoral victories of 1971 and 1972 drawing on the mobilization of subordinate social groups, including Dalits and minorities, had not dented rural power structures at the regional level or the clout of trading classes in urban areas. In Gujarat and Bihar, for example, the opposition made the ostensibly undemocratic demand for the dissolution of duly elected state

[20] Ramachandra Guha, *India after Gandhi: The History of the World's Largest Democracy* (New York: Harper Collins, 2007), 515.

[21] Gyan Prakash, *Emergency Chronicles: Indira Gandhi and Democracy's Turning Point* (Delhi: Penguin, 2018), 38–39.

[22] Christophe Jaffrelot and Anil Pratinav, *India's First Dictatorship: The Emergency, 1975–77* (New York: Oxford University Press, 2021). See Aniket De's review in *Global Intellectual History*, November 21, 2021, ahead of print, https://www.tandfonline.com/doi/full/10.1080/23801883.2021.1994742.

[23] Sugata Bose, *The Nation as Mother and Other Visions of Nationhood* (Delhi: Penguin Viking, 2017), 153–157.

[24] Jalal, *Democracy and Authoritarianism*, 75.

assemblies. But there were credible allegations of corruption against the Gujarat government, and after talks with the opposition leader Morarji Desai, Gandhi yielded to the coercive demand for fresh elections. The role of university and college students in the anticorruption movements of Gujarat and Bihar gave them a measure of moral legitimacy even before Jaya Prakash Narayan offered them his stamp of approval. Narayan was not averse to taking the help of the Hindu majoritarian Jana Sangh and the Rashtriya Swayamsevak Sangh in support of his movement for "Total Revolution." In such a scenario Gandhi needed to bolster the Congress party organization and delegate authority to capable regional readers in her party. Instead, she dispensed with any semblance of inner-party democracy from 1973, fearing potential challengers within her own party as much as the opposition. Determined to make the center the fount of all political authority and socioeconomic reforms, she buttressed an already overcentralized state and crafted a top-heavy party structure.

The personal and political became conjoined on June 12, 1975. That day the Allahabad High Court held Indira Gandhi guilty of electoral malpractice in 1971 on a technicality and barred her from being a member of Parliament for six years. On the same day came news of the Congress Party's defeat at the hands of an opposition alliance in the Gujarat state elections. On June 24, 1975, the Supreme Court conditionally stayed the Allahabad judgment, permitting Indira Gandhi to attend Parliament but not take part in any vote. A breakdown might have been averted if Indira Gandhi had stepped down as prime minister until she was fully cleared by the Supreme Court. She opted instead for the sovereign's right to declare an exception from the norm that had been left as a legacy from colonial times.

The breakdown of India's democracy in 1975 cannot be understood without reference to this state of exception and its inheritance at the moment of decolonization in 1947 and the constitution-making process between 1946 and 1950. Beginning with Regulation III of Bengal in 1818, the jurisprudence of emergency had a checkered history during colonial rule. John Stuart Mill in his tract on representative government had spelled out the nature of this exception: "[A] rude people, though in some degree alive to the benefit of civilized society, may be unable to practice the forbearances which it demands. . . . [I]n such a case, a civilized government, to be really advantageous to them, will require to be in a considerable degree despotic."[25] Emergency powers were embedded in the rule of law propagated by the colonial state. They found pride of place in the Defence of India Act and the Defence of India rules in the first half of the twentieth century and provided the context, for example, not to mention an otiose

---

[25] John Stuart Mill, *Considerations on Representative Government* (New York: Prometheus, 1991), 16.

232   WHEN DEMOCRACY BREAKS

justification, for the Amritsar Massacre of April 13, 1919. A major study of colonialism and the rule of law concludes by emphasizing "the continuity between the ideas and practices of law and emergency of the colonial state and the nationalist state."[26]

The Congress party leadership, notably Jawaharlal Nehru and Vallabhbhai Patel, had insisted on partition in order to inherit the unitary center of the British raj. The specter of partition violence was invoked to further bolster centralized state authority and entrench emergency powers in the Constitution. Partition had depleted the ranks of federalists in the Indian Constituent Assembly. Only a few ethical and eloquent voices arguing for greater democracy and federalism remained. Hari Vishnu Kamath had argued strenuously against the emergency provisions (draft article 275, later renumbered Article 352 and Article 359) during the Constituent Assembly debates in August 1949. His warning included a reference to Article 48 of the Weimar Constitution, used cunningly to subvert democracy in Germany.[27] "Part XVIII of the Constitution conferring emergency powers upon the President," Sarat Chandra Bose wrote in a critique in January 1950 in the *Indian Law Review*, "has a remarkable family-likeness to Section 42, 43 and 45 of the Government of India Act, 1935, the quintessence of which is re-incarnated in our Constitution with a minimum of verbal changes." He described the emergency provisions as "time-bombs." He further pointed out that Article 21 of the Constitution "does not secure due process of law; it secures procedural process only."[28] This lacuna enabled the suspension of the fundamental right to life and liberty in 1975 and played a key role in the Supreme Court's ruling on habeas corpus. The breakdown of India's democracy had deep historical roots in colonial jurisprudence that formed the basis of the postcolonial republic. Either sheer lack of knowledge or deliberate obfuscation of this history has resulted in some shallow, uncritical scholarship on the republic's founding moment.

Aftermath

The Janata experiment in democracy lasted about as long as the Emergency. Before the Janata government collapsed under the weight of its own contradictions, some of the more egregious legal amendments of the Emergency era were reversed by the Forty-Third Amendment of the Constitution. Most of

[26] Nasser Hussain, *The Jurisprudence of Emergency: Colonialism and the Rule of Law* (Ann Arbor: University of Michigan Press, 2003), 119, 135–139.

[27] *Constituent Assembly Debates*, vol. 9, August 2, 1949.

[28] Sarat Chandra Bose, *I Warned My Countrymen* (Calcutta: Netaji Research Bureau, 1968), 333–344.

THE INDIAN EMERGENCY   233

the colonial inheritance of the states of exception remained on the statute books, including the law on sedition enshrined as Section 124A of the nineteenth-century Indian Penal Code. It is deployed today to brand as "antinational" those expressing disaffection toward a government that has done incalculable harm to the very idea of India. In May 2022 the Supreme Court at long last began hearing challenges to this colonial-era law. Faced with this judicial review, the government of Narendra Modi and his home minister Amit Shah has brought an amended law before Parliament, removing the term "sedition" while making its terms more stringent under the guise of Sanskritic Hindi terminology.

As secularism and socialism lost legitimacy as justificatory ideologies of a centralized postcolonial state since the 1980s, an implicit and then explicit resort was made to Hindu religious majoritarianism to shore up central state authority against myriad regional and subaltern challenges. That trend reached its apogee in the victory of the Bharatiya Janata Party and the installation of Narendra Modi as prime minister in 2014 and his reelection in 2019. The relentless onslaught on democratic institutions, including the media and the judiciary, in recent years has led opposition leaders and political commentators to talk darkly about an undeclared emergency in today's India.[29] The dominance of a democratically elected authoritarian leader along with the organizational muscle provided by the Rashtriya Swayamsevak Sangh arguably poses a graver challenge to the world's largest democracy than the one that was overcome in 1977.

It is majoritarianism masquerading as democracy that undergirds the authoritarian turn in contemporary global politics. In that sense, Modi is not unique and is of a piece with Erdogan, Trump, and Bolsonaro in the manipulation of religious or race-based majorities. He certainly precedes and rivals Donald Trump in the use of the language of citizenship and illegal immigration to mask virulent antiminority prejudice. During the election campaign in 2014 he proclaimed that on the day the results were to be announced he would drive all "illegal immigrants" across the border of Bangladesh. The citizenship crisis that erupted in December 2019 can be traced back to the tenor of the election campaign in 2014.

During Modi's first term there were concerns expressed about his regime's fomenting of "intolerance," a euphemism for a wave of unreason, injustice, and inhumanity that swept across India. Students raising the cry for freedom were charged with sedition and assaulted by stormtroopers of the ruling party inside court premises. Scholars and writers faced systematic intimidation, and a few were killed. To disagree with the government was to be antinational. So-called

---

[29] Dexter Filkins, "Blood and Soil in Narendra Modi's India," *New Yorker*, December 9, 2019; "Modi Makes His Bigotry Even Clearer," *New York Times*, December 18, 2019; "India Is at Risk of Sliding into a Second Emergency," *Financial Times*, December 22, 2019.

intolerance took the most grotesque form of lynching Muslims and Dalits suspected of eating beef or taking part in the beef trade. There have been scores of such horrible incidents since 2014. In 2015 Muhammad Akhlaque, the father of an Indian Air Force officer, was killed by a mob not far from Delhi on the suspicion of storing beef in his refrigerator. The attack symbolized the death of "akhlaque" or the ethics of good governance in India. In most cases, it was the victims and not the perpetrators of these hate crimes who were subjected to the strong arm of the law. From the topmost echelons of the government there were the feeblest of disapprovals or disavowals of the taking of precious human life in the name of protecting the cow.[30]

Speaking in the 16th Lok Sabha on August 9, 2017, Prime Minister Modi proclaimed that the five years from 2017 to 2022 would replicate the extraordinary journey of 1942 to 1947 from *sankalp* to *siddhi*, from resolution to realization. Outside Parliament, Modi had remarked that the next five years would be transformative because the holders of the top constitutional posts all subscribed to the same ideology. It was not difficult to infer that he had resolved to realize the ideological project of political *Hindutva* by building the edifice of a Hindu *rashtra*. Once he was reelected prime minister for a second term in 2019, Modi and his home minister, Amit Shah, began spearheading the attempt to redefine the idea of India in the religious majoritarian mold by the time of the seventy-fifth anniversary of India's independence.

In July 2019 the government railroaded through Parliament an amendment to the Unlawful Activities Prevention Act that empowered the regime to proclaim an individual a terrorist and hold such a person in detention without trial for a period up to two years. This law bore a striking resemblance to the Rowlatt Act of a hundred years ago against which Gandhi had launched his first all-India *satyagraha* in 1919. The Mahatma had dubbed it a "lawless law" enacted by a "satanic government." The Modi regime's stance on preventive detention was a clear indication of its intent to behave more and more like its authoritarian colonial predecessor.

On August 5, 2019, the government extinguished the vestiges of democracy in Jammu and Kashmir. The autonomy for Jammu and Kashmir enshrined in Article 370 had already been whittled down by successive Congress regimes since 1954. A dead letter for decades, an audacious BJP government chose to give it an unceremonious burial. But it did much more. Through an accompanying legislation that downgraded and bifurcated the state to the status of two union territories, it heaped humiliation on a regional people and declared its determination to achieve integration through the force of arms. What followed was an

---

[30] For Sugata Bose's speeches in the 16th Lok Sabha (2014–2019) against majoritarianism masquerading as democracy, see Bose, *The Nation as Mother*, 175–215.

indefinite and unprecedented communication lockdown hand in hand with a military clampdown on the Kashmir valley.[31] A brazen and reckless assault on federalism and democracy, the government's move is certain to provoke further alienation instead of nurturing a sense of belonging to the Indian Union. A supine Supreme Court failed to entertain writs of habeas corpus filed on behalf of leaders and activists imprisoned without trial. Instead, a five-member bench, including the chief justice Ranjan Gogoi, delivered a verdict on the long-standing land dispute in Ayodhya, rewarding in their astonishing judgment the vandals who had torn down a historic mosque in 1992.

Emboldened by their seemingly unimpeded march toward establishing a Hindu majoritarian state, the government used its parliamentary majority to pass the Citizenship Amendment Act (CAA) in December 2019. Ostensibly designed to provide a fast track to citizenship to non-Muslim immigrants from the Muslim-majority countries of Afghanistan, Bangladesh, and Pakistan, this move introducing for the first time a religious test for citizenship struck a raw nerve and provoked large-scale protests led by students and youth against the discriminatory law. The law came to be viewed in conjunction with repeated threats issued by the home minister, Amit Shah, to compile for the whole country a National Register of Citizens (NRC), which would form the basis for weeding out "illegal immigrants" and "infiltrators" Shah described as "termites." An exercise to draw up an NRC in the northeastern state of Assam had already left nearly two million excluded people facing the specter of statelessness and confinement in detention camps. A cynical move by the regime to target minorities came to be seen as a declaration of war on the undocumented poor. As the resistance against the CAA and NRC (and also the National Population Register, which would facilitate an exclusionary NRC) gathered momentum, a flustered government responded with police brutality, especially in BJP-ruled states such as Uttar Pradesh. The anti-CAA movement waned with the onset of the pandemic in 2020.

The de facto suspension of the fundamental rights to life and liberty, including habeas corpus, lends credence to the view that India faces an undeclared emergency. Protesters all across India, especially brave young men and women, recited the uplifting Preamble to the Constitution, wherein "the People" grant themselves liberty, equality, fraternity, and justice. There is a need for idealistic youth to recognize the importance of resorting to both reason and emotion in upholding the spirit of the Constitution against the cunning use of certain constitutional provisions by a majoritarianism determined to transform a democracy

---

[31] See Sumantra Bose, *Kashmir at the Crossroads: Inside a 21st-Century Conflict* (New Haven: Yale University Press, 2021).

into a dictatorship and a federation into a unitary state.[32] India must brace for a prolonged *satyagraha* in defense of the values enshrined in the anticolonial movement. A postcolonial constitution retaining the myriad states of exception of the colonial era does not afford sufficient protection against democratically elected authoritarian rulers. There will be no safe anchor until "We, the People" are able to decisively overturn the current parliamentary majority. It will then remain to be seen if the constitutional legacy of Parliament as a living organism can be deployed with wisdom to strengthen the features of federalism and democracy and make fundamental rights and habeas corpus as inviolable as possible, so that India may be free from the scourge of majoritarian tyranny.

---

[32] This was the message for India's protesting youth in Sugata Bose, "Assault on the Edifice," *Indian Express*, February 6, 2020.

9
Democratic Breakdown in Argentina, 1976

Scott Mainwaring

This chapter analyzes the democratic breakdown in Argentina in 1976, the final breakdown in Latin America before the first democratic transition of the third wave in the region (the Dominican Republic in 1978).[1] Although Argentina was, after Brazil, the second most populous Latin American country to experience a breakdown between 1964 and 1976, this breakdown has received little scholarly attention in the United States and United Kingdom. Likewise, although Adam Przeworski and his coauthors[2] famously observed that Argentina in 1976 had a higher per capita GDP than any other country in the world that experienced a democratic breakdown between 1945 and 1990, the English-language scholarly literature that has explored this puzzle is thin. Why did a fairly wealthy country with moderate income inequalities experience a breakdown?

My argument about the Argentine breakdown focuses on three factors. First, extreme radicalization[3] on the left and right greatly increased the stakes of democracy and quickly led powerful actors to shift away from supporting or accepting the regime. Argentina had long had right-wing sectors that were hostile toward democracy.[4] One thing that changed before the 1973–1976 period is

---

[1] I developed some of the core ideas in this chapter in collaboration with Aníbal Pérez-Liñán. A few paragraphs come from our book, *Democracies and Dictatorships in Latin America: Emergence, Survival, and Fall* (New York: Cambridge University Press, 2013). I am grateful to María Victoria De Negri for excellent research assistance and comments, and to Carlos Gervasoni, Frances Hagopian, María Matilde Ollier, Aníbal Pérez-Liñán, Luis Schiumerini, Emilia Simison, Natán Skigin, Eduardo Viola, participants at the conference on When Democracy Breaks, and the staff of the Tobin Project for comments. I dedicate this chapter to the memory of María Matilde Ollier, one of Argentina's great champions of democracy.

[2] Adam Pzeworski, Michael E. Alvarez, José Antonio Cheibub, and Fernando Limongi, *Democracy and Development: Political Institutions and Well-Being in the World, 1950–1990* (New York: Cambridge University Press, 2000).

[3] Radical actors are situated "*toward* one pole of the ideological spectrum . . . in conjunction with an urgency to achieve those preferences in the short to medium term where they do not represent the status quo, or with an intransigent defense of the status quo where these positions represent the status quo" (Mainwaring and Pérez-Liñán, *Democracies and Dictatorships in Latin America*, 14). An extensive contemporary literature highlights the impact of polarization on dampening democratic commitments.

[4] Edward L. Gibson, *Class and Conservative Parties: Argentina in Comparative Perspective* (Baltimore: Johns Hopkins University Press, 1996); Alberto Spektorowski, *The Origins of Argentina's Revolution of the Right* (Notre Dame, IN: University of Notre Dame Press, 2003);

Scott Mainwaring, *Democratic Breakdown in Argentina, 1976* In: *When Democracy Breaks*. Edited by: Archon Fung, David Moss, and Odd Arne Westad, Oxford University Press. © Oxford University Press 2024. DOI: 10.1093/oso/9780197760789.003.0009

238   WHEN DEMOCRACY BREAKS

that a revolutionary left and powerful radicalized labor and student movements emerged. The radical labor movement challenged the mainstream "verticalist"[5] unions that had loyally obeyed Juan Perón since the 1940s. The revolutionary left never had any chance of capturing power, but it galvanized an extremist response with the emergence of right-wing death squads, which were created and funded by the state. The revolutionary left and the radical labor and student movements generated fear in the conservative and centrist establishment, including most of the Peronist Party, the military, business, most of the Catholic Church leadership and clergy, and the centrist and conservative unions. The country was besieged by right-wing and left-wing bombings, kidnappings, politically motivated assassinations, factory seizures, and violent attacks on companies, newspapers, and cultural organizations. Violent antisystem actors from the right hoped to annihilate the radical violent left, and vice versa, with complete disdain for democracy.

Second, the democratic government proved woefully incapable of handling Argentina's problems on the economic and public security fronts. Mismanagement created a profound economic crisis. Ill-designed policies produced hyperinflation (around 3,500% annualized) in July 1975 and again early in 1976; first-quarter 1976 inflation annualized reached 3,000%.[6] Incoherent policies created a gaping fiscal deficit of 17% of GDP in 1975.[7] In tandem with hyperinflation, economic crisis, frequent strikes, and many factory and university takeovers, escalating terrorism from the far left and far right generated a widespread sense of chaos. The state, through state-created and - funded death squads and later by inviting military involvement in combating the left and sanctioning gross human rights violations, was largely responsible for right-wing terrorism. Thus, the state not only failed to solve the public security threat; it was directly responsible for much of the violence. In response to the sense of chaos and, after July 1975, the growing sense of a power vacuum, actors that had welcomed democracy in 1973 clamored for a coup in 1976.

Third, even in the context of some extremely radical actors, democracy might have survived if nonextremist actors, especially the government, had embraced democracy. Attitudes about democracy affected the outcome because they shaped actors' behavior. President Perón could have dampened radical extremism and bolstered the democratic camp if he had been committed to

---

Eduardo Viola, "Democracia e Autoritarismo na Argentina Contemporânea" (PhD diss., University of São Paulo, 1982).

[5] The "verticalist" unions faithfully obeyed Perón and viscerally opposed dissident unions and dissident movements within unions.

[6] William C. Smith, *Authoritarianism and the Crisis of the Argentine Political Economy* (Stanford: Stanford University Press, 1989), 230.

[7] Smith, *Authoritarianism and the Crisis of the Argentine Political Economy.*

DEMOCRATIC BREAKDOWN IN ARGENTINA   239

democracy. Instead, he initially opportunistically encouraged the revolutionary left and then, from the outset of the new democracy, turned to right-wing death squads to contain the revolutionary left. His support for extremist antidemocratic actors helped forge the cauldron in which democracy died. His decision to have his wife, Isabel Perón, be his vice president quelled potential tussles within the Peronist camp in 1973, but it proved to be disastrous for democracy after he died. Isabel Perón (1974–1976) was an extremely weak leader, and her closest advisor conspired against democracy by forming right-wing death squads. By 1975, only one major actor, the main opposition party, the centrist Radicals (Unión Cívica Radical, UCR), firmly supported democracy. But the UCR was in a weak initial position that grew weaker over time. The other main actors were either indifferent to democracy (the powerful labor confederation, most of the Peronist Party, and initially some business groups and leaders) or hostile to it (the right-wing death squads, right-wing sectors of the military, other business groups, and the revolutionary guerrillas). It is very difficult for democracy to survive if the main actors are hostile or indifferent to its survival.

The Argentine breakdown of 1976 is emblematic of the dynamics that led to many democratic failures between 1964 and 1976 in the shadow of the Cuban Revolution. Radical antisystem actors were committed to their own political goals even if their methods and objectives imperiled democracy. Extremism on one side of the political spectrum begat extremism on the other, making democracy untenable. The breakdowns that were most similar to Argentina 1976 in this respect were Chile and Uruguay in 1973. Conservative fears about leftist extremism were an important ingredient in most breakdowns in Latin America between 1964 and 1976;[8] the Argentine breakdown of 1976 was part of this larger dynamic. In this way, international influences contributed to the Argentine breakdown. And for this reason, the Argentine breakdown opens a window into the dynamics of some breakdowns in Latin America from the time of the Cuban Revolution until the end of the Cold War—especially those with powerful extremist authoritarian leftist forces.

Contributions

The Argentine literature on specific actors in the 1973–1976 period is rich, as is the literature on the political history of the period. Many works have analyzed the revolutionary left, organized labor, the Peronist governments, and the military, among others. Several books have focused on the 1976 breakdown; among

[8] Kurt Weyland, *Revolution and Reaction: The Diffusion of Authoritarianism in Latin America* (New York: Cambridge University Press, 2019).

240   WHEN DEMOCRACY BREAKS

the best are those by Liliana De Riz[9] and Eduardo Viola.[10] However, to my knowledge, there are no major works in English on the democratic breakdown— although some excellent English-language books on a few specific actors during the 1973–1976 period supplement the extensive Spanish-language literature.[11]

This chapter draws extensively on these literatures. I hope to add in two ways to this existing work. First, I hope to enhance the limited English-language work on the 1976 breakdown. Second, this is one of the first works to use the Argentine case to contribute to broader theoretical and comparative debates about why democracies break down. Although there is an extensive Argentine literature on the 1973–1976 period, little of it has deeply engaged broader theoretical and comparative debates about breakdowns. One of my aspirations is bringing this case into these broader theoretical and comparative discussions. I analyze the Argentine case in light of these broader literatures, believing that it sheds light on them; conversely, it is illuminating to consider the Argentine case from the perspective of the broader comparative and theoretical work on democratic breakdowns. Historical cases can teach a great deal theoretically about democratization and democratic breakdown—especially if the case directly engages the theoretical and comparative literatures. Case studies are crucial for understanding the dynamics of breakdowns, and these dynamics often enhance theoretical understanding.

Theoretical Notes about Democratic Breakdowns

In this section, following Mainwaring and Pérez-Liñán,[12] I articulate four general points about studying democratic transitions, survival, and breakdowns. First, democracies emerge and survive or break down because of the purposeful action of concrete historical actors: presidents, militaries, foreign powers, political parties, labor unions, business associations and lobbies, paramilitaries, and others. Democracies break down if the actors that want to subvert them have the power to do so. They survive if the actors that are invested in its continuity are more powerful than the actors that try to subvert it.[13] I therefore focus on specific historical actors.

---

[9] Liliana De Riz, *Retorno y derrumbe: El último gobierno peronista* (Mexico City: Folios, 1981).

[10] Viola, "Democracia e Autoritarismo na Argentina Contemporânea."

[11] On the Montoneros, see Richard Gillespie, *Soldiers of Perón: Argentina's Montoneros* (Oxford: Clarendon Press, 1982). On the guerrillas, see María José Moyano, *Argentina's Lost Patrol: Armed Struggle, 1969–1979* (New Haven: Yale University Press, 1995).

[12] Mainwaring and Pérez-Liñán, *Democracies and Dictatorships in Latin America.*

[13] Michael McFaul, "The Fourth Wave of Democracy and Dictatorship: Noncooperative Transitions in the Postcommunist World," *World Politics* 54, no. 2 (2002): 212–244.

DEMOCRATIC BREAKDOWN IN ARGENTINA 241

This perspective is a contrast to analyses that see the likelihood of democratic survival or breakdown as being heavily conditioned by structural, cultural, or other contextual factors. Structural and cultural factors condition who the actors are and what their preferences are—but within very broad boundaries. Democracy can survive in difficult structural and cultural conditions, as countless cases show,[14] and it can break down despite favorable structural contexts, as the Argentine case of 1976 demonstrates.

In structural approaches, the nature of the actors and their preferences are more or less dictated by structural conditions. Yet who the key actors are and what their preferences are have great autonomy in relation to structural conditions. Broad structural and cultural forces exert only indirect influences on the formation, worldview, and behavior of actors. To understand democratic transitions, breakdowns, and survival, we need to analyze the actors themselves rather than assume that structures or cultures strongly condition outcomes.

The second point involves who the actors are in democratic transitions, politics, and breakdowns. In the analysis of the Argentine breakdown, I focus on the four presidents from 1973 to 1976 and on organizational actors—the two main parties, the guerrillas, the military, organized labor, the paramilitary extreme right, and business associations. By focusing on presidents and organizational actors, I locate my approach between structural or long-term cultural approaches, on the one hand, and agency and contingent action approaches, on the other.[15] Having said that, because Juan Perón, who was the president from October 12, 1973, until his death on July 1, 1974, is easily the most prominent political figure in Argentina since 1946 and influenced many other actors, his decision-making figured prominently in the fate of democracy.

Some class approaches to political regimes see the poor, middle classes, and rich as the fundamental actors.[16] I do not see this as a useful way to study democratic transitions and breakdowns in most contexts. The poor, middle classes, and rich are rarely cohesive political actors. Rather, they are usually politically divided along many lines, including race, religion, geography, ethnicity, nationality, and economic sector. In the United States, for example, poor African

[14] Scott Mainwaring and Tarek Masoud, eds., *Democracy in Hard Places* (New York: Oxford University Press, 2022).

[15] For converging perspectives, see Nancy Bermeo and Deborah J. Yashar, "Parties, Movements, and the Making of Democracy," in *Parties, Movements, and Democracy in the Developing World*, ed. Nancy Bermeo and Deborah J. Yashar (New York: Cambridge University Press, 2016), 1–27; Giovanni Capoccia and Daniel Ziblatt, "The Historical Turn in Democratization Studies: A New Research Agenda for Europe and Beyond," *Comparative Political Studies* 43, nos. 8–9 (2010): 931–968; Daniel Ziblatt, *Conservative Parties and the Birth of Democracy* (Cambridge: Cambridge University Press, 2017).

[16] Daron Acemoglu and James A. Robinson, *Economic Origins of Dictatorship and Democracy* (New York: Cambridge University Press, 2006); Carles Boix, *Democracy and Redistribution* (Cambridge: Cambridge University Press, 2003).

242   WHEN DEMOCRACY BREAKS

Americans have different voting patterns and political beliefs than poor white people; religious individuals have different voting patterns and political beliefs than secular voters; and residents of large cities have different voting patterns than rural voters. These well-established facts suggest problems for thinking about the rich, middle sectors, and poor as cohesive political actors.

In many cases where there is conflict over the political regime, class does not predict organizational actors' position about the regime in any clear way. In democratic politics, organizational actors and presidents (or prime ministers) usually hold the most power. Many important political actors are not clear expressions of social classes (or of the poor, the middle class, or the rich).

The third question is what the important issues are in democratic politics and breakdowns. Class approaches to democracy see conflicts over distribution as the only important issue.[17] However, in most historical cases, including Argentina 1973–1976, other issues have been equally or more important. In Argentina, governmental incompetence, rampant political violence, and a widespread establishment fear of a leftist threat and a breakdown of social order were more important than battles over income redistribution. Except in cases of retrograde business sectors, there is little reason why moderate redistribution should motivate profound animus toward a democratic regime.

Whereas Daron Acemoglu and James Robinson and Carles Boix implicitly see routine income distribution and Socialist revolution as part of a continuum, they are often sharply conflicting goals. In Argentina, labor unions and wide swaths of the popular sectors vigorously favored income redistribution, but most union and popular leaders completely rejected revolution. Whereas routine redistribution was not a central contributing factor to the Argentine breakdown, conservative and centrist fears about revolutionary and radical struggles that would have led to wholesale property expropriations and a complete reordering of Argentine society were.

The final general theoretical point is a cautionary note about essentialist assumptions that some classes consistently support democracy or authoritarianism. Acemoglu and Robinson and Boix posited that when revolution is not possible, the poor will support democracy because it redistributes income to them, and the rich will oppose democracy for the same reason. However, organized labor and most other actors are best seen as conditional democrats or conditional authoritarians.[18] In Argentina, organized labor mobilized vigorously

[17] Acemoglu and Robinson, *Economic Origins of Dictatorship and Democracy*; Boix, *Democracy and Redistribution*.

[18] Michael Albertus, "Landowners and Democracy: The Social Origins of Democracy Reconsidered," *World Politics* 69, no. 2 (2017): 473–501; Eva Bellin, "Contingent Democrats: Industrialists, Labor, and Democratization in Late-Developing Countries," *World Politics* 52, no. 2 (2000): 175–205; Steven Levitsky and Scott Mainwaring, "Organized Labor and Democracy in Latin America," *Comparative Politics* 39, no. 1 (2006): 21–42.

against a series of dictatorships from 1955 to 1973, but when democracy was restored in 1973, on the whole it manifested indifference toward the regime's survival.

Most of the work on Argentina and most case studies on democratic breakdowns are consistent with these four points. However, they form a contrast to some prominent theoretical work on political regimes published in the past two decades.

Prelude to Democracy

Along with Chile and Uruguay, Argentina had one of the earliest democracies in Latin America, from 1916 to 1930. Until the 1976 coup, it was usually the wealthiest or second wealthiest (after Venezuela) country in Latin America. Argentina experienced previous democratic breakdowns in 1930, 1951,[19] 1962, and 1966; the country was one of the world champions of democratic breakdowns in the twentieth century.

The military dictatorship that took power in 1966 aspired to govern for a long time, but in 1969 it fractured and began to collapse. The two main political parties, the powerful labor movement, and youthful leftists mobilized against the regime, and its support crumbled. Violent protests in 1969 helped bring down the dictatorship of General Juan Carlos Onganía (1966–1970) in a military coup in June 1970. His successor, General Roberto Levingston, lasted only nine months (June 1970 to March 1971) before he was ousted by another coup. Finally, General Alejandro Lanusse (1971–1973) from the outset planned to restore power to civilians, and did so by allowing elections in 1973.

Democratic Advantages and Challenges at the Dawn of Democracy in 1973

Although it unraveled quickly, democracy in Argentina (1973–1976) was not doomed to failure from the outset. Conventional structural factors such as the level of development and the level of inequality were favorable to democracy. Przeworski et al. famously observed that no democracy had ever broken down with a per capita GDP higher than Argentina's in 1975.[20] In 1973, Argentina had

---

[19] A military coup overthrew Juan Perón (1946–1955) in 1955. However, by 1951 Perón had installed a competitive authoritarian regime; democracy had already broken down. The government committed large-scale violations of political, civil, and human rights, and elections were no longer free and fair. Thus, I date the breakdown of democracy to 1951.

[20] Pzeworski et al., *Democracy and Development*, 98.

244   WHEN DEMOCRACY BREAKS

the second highest per capita GNI ($9780 in constant 2015 U.S. dollars) in Latin America, behind only Venezuela; Argentina's per capita GNI was nearly four times higher than that of South Korea ($2,548).[21] At least from the 1950s (and probably earlier, but there are no good data) until the 1976 coup, Argentina had moderate income inequalities by world capitalist standards. Against this backdrop of moderately high income and moderate inequalities, Argentina has long been seen as an anomalous case of repeated democratic breakdowns despite favorable structural conditions.

Some other factors were auspicious. One of the biggest obstacles to democracy from 1946 through 1970, the profound enmity between the country's two largest parties, the Peronists and Radicals, dissipated. In November 1970, the two parties signed an agreement to work together for democracy and to eliminate the proscription of Peronists. The Radicals' acceptance of the Peronists as a legitimate electoral contender boded well for democracy. The inclusion of the Peronists in the democratic game and their landslide wins in 1973 gave them a large stake in the regime. This rapprochement had the potential to build a core of democratic actors that dominated electoral politics and to end a major source of democratic destabilization.

In 1973, when the new democratic regime began, the military was discredited. The military dictatorship of 1966–1973 had fractured badly,[22] and the ascendant sectors of the armed forces led the transition to democracy. Most business groups defected from supporting the dictatorship and seemed willing to accept democracy.

I do not want to overstate the democratic potential that existed in 1973; I claim merely that democracy had a chance. If Perón and the first president of the democratic period, Héctor Cámpora (May 25 to July 13, 1973), had not stoked the revolutionary left in ways that alarmed conservative and centrist actors; if Perón had chosen a capable vice president; and if economic policies had been sound, democracy could have survived. Democracy would have had an even better chance if Perón and an able successor had been able to push organized labor toward more restraint. There were some adverse circumstances from the outset—especially the authoritarian predilections of some actors—but these actors were reinforced by grave missteps by the sequence of presidents. These missteps pushed critical actors such as the military, most business groups, most

---

[21] World Bank Development Indicators, online, accessed Nov. 17, 2023, https://databank.worldb ank.org/source/world-development-indicators#.

[22] On the dictatorship of 1966–1973, see Guillermo O'Donnell, *El estado burocrático autoritario* (Buenos Aires: Editorial de Belgrano, 1982); María Matilde Ollier, *El fenómeno insurreccional y la cultura política (1969-1973)* (Buenos Aires: Centro Editor de América Latina, 1986); María Matilde Ollier, *Orden, poder y violencia (1968-73)*, 2 vols. (Buenos Aires: Centro Editor de América Latina, 1989); María Matilde Ollier, *Golpe o revolución: La violencia legitimada, Argentina 1966-1973* (Buenos Aires: EDUNTREF, 2005).

DEMOCRATIC BREAKDOWN IN ARGENTINA   245

of the establishment, most church leaders, and most of Argentine society from a willingness to try democracy in 1973 to supporting a coup in 1976.

From Birth to Breakdown: A Tragedy in Four Presidents

Act 1: The Government of Héctor Cámpora (May 25 to July 13, 1973)

Argentina's fifth democratic or semi-democratic regime of the twentieth century began in 1973 as its most democratic ever. For the first time since 1951, the Peronists were allowed to field a presidential candidate. Running as Juan Perón's officially designated candidate, Héctor Cámpora (1909–1980) won a landslide in a free and fair presidential election on March 11, 1973,[23] and he assumed office on May 25. Cámpora ran because Perón had been banned, and his authority stemmed from having been designated by Perón.

Cámpora was a traditional left-of-center Peronist, and his seven-week term marked the apogee of power for the left. It was a period of massive popular mobilizations, including scores of factory takeovers[24] and increasing left-wing violence. The last five years (1968–1973) of the military dictatorship had witnessed the emergence of the revolutionary left. It was much weaker than the authoritarian right, but it had a profoundly polarizing impact. One of the most powerful leftist guerrilla movements in the history of Latin America, it embraced violence as a way of life and of effecting political change.[25] The left expanded rapidly among student groups after 1969. By 1970, the Peronist groups Montoneros (originally of Catholic nationalist origins) and Revolutionary Armed Forces (Fuerzas Armadas Revolucionarias), as well as the Trotskyite ERP (Ejército Revolucionario del Pueblo, People's Revolutionary Army) were in full operation.

The Montoneros were close to the Peronist Youth (Juventud Peronista), a separate organization that first established an important political presence in the 1960s in the resistance against successive governments. The Peronist Youth

---

[23] Cámpora won 49.5% of the vote. Second-place finisher Ricardo Balbín of the UCR captured 21.3%.

[24] Elizabeth Jelin reports an average of 30.5 strikes per month from June to September 1973; 43% of these strikes included workers taking over factories, so there were about 13 seizures of factories every month—almost one every other day. Elizabeth Jelin, "Conflictos laborales en la Argentina," *Revista Mexicana de Sociología* 40, no. 2 (1978): 457, Table 1.

[25] Gillespie, *Soldiers of Perón*; Ollier, *El fenómeno insurreccional y la cultura política*; Ollier, *Orden, poder y violencia*; María Matilde Ollier, *De la revolución a la democracia: Cambios privados, públicos y políticos de la izquierda argentina* (Buenos Aires: Siglo XXI/Universidad Nacional de San Martín, 2009); Viola, "Democracia e Autoritarismo na Argentina Contemporânea"; Peter Waldmann, "Anomia social y violencia," in *Argentina, hoy*, ed. Alain Rouquié (Buenos Aires: Siglo XXI, 1982), 206–248.

246 WHEN DEMOCRACY BREAKS

radicalized over time, and in 1967 some members created the Fuerzas Armadas Peronistas (Peronist Armed Forces). The revolutionary left deeply penetrated Argentina's public universities. From then until its defeat around 1977, it waged constant violence against the armed forces, the police, leaders of the political right, and bureaucratic (conservative) labor leaders.

In his first day in office, Cámpora issued a pardon, signed into law the next day by the Congress, that granted amnesty to 371 jailed members of left-wing revolutionary organizations.[26] Many of these individuals had committed serious crimes, including homicide, kidnapping, theft, and assault. Cámpora's pardon had negative repercussions. It reinforced the hostility of the security forces, the Argentine right, and much of the center toward Cámpora; it convinced the security apparatus and the right that it might be impossible to combat the revolutionary left through legal means; and it gave a boost to the revolutionary left.

From the outset, the revolutionary left was a powerful pernicious influence in the new democracy. It contributed to a spiral of violence that weakened democracy and fostered the breakdown. It generated fear among other political actors. María José Moyano estimates that by 1974, the revolutionary guerrilla movement had five thousand members.[27] She constructed a data set based on Buenos Aires newspaper accounts of violent actions committed by the revolutionary left, the paramilitary right, and collective actors for the four years before the democratic transition (1969–1973) and during the democratic period of 1973–1976. Even though these newspapers did not register all violent acts,[28] Moyano reported that the guerrilla forces undertook 1,935 operations during the democratic period: 812 bombings, 481 killings, 251 attacks on property, 143 seizures of buildings or groups of buildings including 15 attempted seizures of military installations, 140 kidnappings, 107 thefts of arms, and one hijacking of an airplane. The actions of the revolutionary left and the radical left encouraged the formation of right-wing death squads, most of which functioned within the Peronist movement.[29] Left-wing and right-wing violent extremes flourished.

On June 20, 1973, Perón returned to Argentina after almost eighteen years in exile. Perhaps two million people, including hundreds of thousands of leftist supporters, flocked to the Ezeiza International Airport near Buenos Aires to greet him. In an early adumbration of what was to come, the terrorist right wing organized a sniper attack known as "the Ezeiza massacre" against the left at the

---

[26] Moyano, *Argentina's Lost Patrol*, 103.

[27] Moyano, *Argentina's Lost Patrol*, 2.

[28] Moyano included only incidents that were reported in a few major newspapers published in Buenos Aires. These newspapers could not have reported all violent actions, especially those outside of Buenos Aires and probably particularly those by the right-wing death squad, AAA. Crimes committed by the AAA with the collaboration of the police were less likely to be officially reported than other crimes, and they were probably therefore less likely to appear in newspaper accounts.

[29] Moyano, *Argentina's Lost Patrol*, 56.

airport, resulting in at least sixteen deaths and several hundred wounded.[30] The minister of social welfare José López Rega, who had been Perón's personal secretary while he was in exile in Spain, masterminded the attack. This event marked the first major public appearance of the paramilitary right-wing Peronists and the definitive break between the Peronist extreme left and extreme right.

Although Argentina had a long history of right-wing extremism before 1973, the far right had new elements during the 1973–1976 period. Right-wing death squads kidnapped, tortured, and killed guerrillas, left-wing activists, and sympathizers in vastly greater numbers than ever before. The far right developed a more Manichaean and apocalyptic worldview that legitimated, in its eyes, the sadistic extermination campaign that it unleashed against the revolutionary left and leftist labor leaders, lawyers, public officials, and intellectuals.

The most important right-wing paramilitary organization was the Argentine Anti-Communist Alliance (AAA), secretly created in 1973 by López Rega. Because of its access to vast state funds (López Rega funded it from the Ministry of Social Welfare), the AAA was by far the best-resourced and largest of the right-wing death squads, and the one that assassinated most people and caused most damage to Argentine democracy. The AAA assassinated an estimated two thousand leftist and center-left politicians, labor leaders, leaders of leftist parties and popular organizations, judges, and others from 1973 to 1976.[31] Although it was an underground organization, the AAA collaborated closely with the Federal Police.

On June 8, a government initiative led to the signing of an agreement between the main labor confederation, the General Labor Confederation (CGT, Confederación General del Trabajo), and the General Economic Confederation (Confederación General Económica), which primarily represented Argentine business sectors close to the Peronist orbit. The agreement, known as the Social Pact, was the centerpiece of Perón's economic policy. It attempted to contain the inflation rate, increase real wages, generate labor peace in a country that had been rocked by violent massive working-class protests in the previous four years, and boost economic growth. The plan proposed freezing prices and granting significant wage increases, but then freezing wages for two years. It greatly accentuated state intervention in the economy, with considerable state control over prices and increased subsidies and regulations.[32] Until the first quarter of 1974, the Social Pact lowered inflation and boosted real wages and growth, but these positive effects were short-lived. The General Economic Confederation supported the government until the unraveling of the Social Pact in the second quarter of 1974.

---

[30] Moyano, *Argentina's Lost Patrol*, 36. Solid estimates have never been established.

[31] Marina Franco, "La 'seguridad nacional' como política estatal en la Argentina de los años setenta," *Antítesis* 2, no. 4 (2009): 865.

[32] De Riz, *Retorno y derrumbe*.

248   WHEN DEMOCRACY BREAKS

After 1945, Argentina had the most powerful labor movement in Latin America. From 1945 until 1983, most of the labor movement was intensely loyal to Perón but indifferent to democracy.[33] Organized labor prioritized political power and material gains over democracy and unquestioningly accepted Peronism's authoritarian proclivities. Parts of the movement radicalized in the struggle against the military dictatorship of 1966–1973, and labor insurgency helped bring down that dictatorship. This was the first time since 1946 that the left had made substantial inroads in Argentina's labor movement.

In office for only seven tumultuous weeks, Cámpora and the leftist members of his cabinet resigned on July 13 and called for new presidential elections to allow Perón to run. Perón and the Peronist center and right wanted to get rid of Cámpora because radical labor mobilizations and the revolutionary left's violence threatened to displace him and had already generated a sensation of social chaos and political threat. In a few months, the perception of the right and the center had shifted from considering Perón a threat to considering him a way to contain the growing leftist mobilization.

Act 2: Raúl Lastiri (July 13 to October 12, 1973)

Raúl Lastiri, the president of the Chamber of Deputies and a leader of the right wing of Peronism, assumed the presidency on an interim basis when Cámpora resigned. Lastiri's short tenure marked a turn toward the right wing of Peronism. His father-in-law, José López Rega, was Argentina's most notorious far-right Peronist.

Act 3: Juan Perón (October 12, 1973, to July 1, 1974)

Perón won the September 23 election even more decisively than Cámpora had, capturing almost 62% of the vote. He took office on October 12, 1973. Although Perón was more willing to accept democracy in 1973 than he had been from 1946 to 1955, his democratic transformation proved to be shallow, as evinced by his opportunistic support for the revolutionary left until May 1973 and his support for right-wing death squads after that.

His eight and a half months as president were marked by escalating economic problems, a growing militarization of politics, his repudiation of the Peronist

---

[33] James McGuire, *Peronism without Perón: Unions, Parties, and Democracy in Argentina* (Stanford: Stanford University Press, 1997); Juan Carlos Torre, *Los sindicatos en el gobierno, 1973–1976* (Buenos Aires: Centro Editor de América Latina, 1983); Viola, "Democracia e Autoritarismo na Argentina Contemporânea," 510–511, 516–518.

left, and the shattering of the coalition that brought him to power. During the 1973–1976 period, the Peronist Party was probably more ideologically heterogeneous than any other major party in the history of modern democracy. Until the falling out between Perón and the Montoneros in 1974, the ideological span ranged from revolutionary Socialists, including sectors with ruthless totalitarian mentalities, to extremist reactionaries who formed death squads aimed at killing the revolutionary left and leftist students, labor leaders, lawyers, intellectuals, judges, and others. This extraordinary ideological heterogeneity was an asset when Peronism opposed the military dictatorships of 1966–1973, but inevitably it led to severe conflicts within Peronism after the transition. The Peronist Party itself was highly subordinate to Perón for most of the period from its creation in 1946 until his death in 1974; it was never an important independent actor until his death. It was always more of a movement than a professionalized party.[34]

In November 1973, a revision to the Law of Professional Associations led to the displacement of many radical left labor leaders, giving the upper hand to the conservative Peronist loyalists. The law imposed greater centralization and discipline in the labor movement at a time of massive factory-level mobilization and unrest.

Perón had expected that the revolutionary left would bend to his will, but this proved not to be the case. It viewed mainstream labor leaders as sellouts and believed that replacing them with leftists was essential to the revolutionary cause. Less than three weeks before Perón assumed the presidency, on September 25, 1973, the Montoneros assassinated the secretary general of the CGT, José Rucci, who had been close to Perón.

Perón intensified the offensive against the Peronist Youth and the leftist revolutionaries. In late 1973, he signed the Act of Commitment for National Security, which created a National Security Council and expanded the legal authority to prosecute the left. In January 1974, after seventy members of the ERP audaciously attacked a two-thousand-person army garrison in Azul, Buenos Aires, the government passed a new penal code to make it easier to prosecute the left. Perón denounced the ERP and called for "annihilating these criminal terrorists."[35] The new legislation banned factory occupations and made it easier to repress illegal strikes. In response to the ERP attack, Perón pressured a democratically elected leftist Peronist, Oscar Bidegain, to resign as governor of the Province of Buenos Aires.

---

[34] Steven Levitsky, *Transforming Labor-Based Parties in Latin America: Argentine Peronism in Comparative Perspective* (New York: Cambridge University Press, 2003).

[35] Cited in Liliana De Riz, "De la movilización popular al aniquilamiento (1973–1976)," in *Argentina: 1976: Estudios en torno al golpe de estado*, ed. Clara E Lida, Horacio Crespo, and Pablo Yankelevich (Mexico City: El Colegio de México, 2007), 41.

250 WHEN DEMOCRACY BREAKS

On February 28, 1974, a police coup overthrew the democratically elected center-left Peronist governor of the province of Córdoba, Ricardo Obregón Cano, and his vice governor. Perón subsequently announced his support for the coup. Córdoba had been the site of the country's most disruptive labor and student mobilizations against the previous military dictatorship, and it was home to some of the most combative left-wing labor unions.

In March 1974, the Montoneros assassinated Rogelio Coria, secretary general of the Construction Workers of the Argentine Republic (Unión de Obreros de la Construcción de la República Argentina). On May 1, 1974, Labor Day in Argentina, in a major speech in one of the country's most important public spaces, the Plaza de Mayo, an enraged Perón denounced the Montoneros, saying that they were "mercenaries representing foreign interests."[36] Perón was angry about the Montoneros' assassination of Peronist labor leaders; their disdain for his wife, Isabel Perón; and their repeated clashes with his allies and government. This moment marked the definitive break between Perón and the Montoneros. Another leftist Peronist governor, Alberto Martínez Baca of Mendoza, was removed from office on June 6, 1974, weeks after the May 1 rupture and weeks before Perón's death.[37] With Perón's support, the AAA stepped up its assassinations of leftist labor leaders. In response to its dislocation from institutional spaces of power in the labor movement and in Peronist circles, the revolutionary left increasingly resorted to violence.[38]

In the 1973–1976 period, the labor movement was sharply divided, in part along ideological lines, and also in conflicts between union leaders and radical factory-level leaders.[39] The peak leadership and dominant orientation of the main labor confederation, the CGT, was staunchly Peronist and anti-leftist. After the Montoneros assassinated José Ignacio Rucci in September 1973, the most prominent labor leader was Lorenzo Miguel, head of the Metalworkers' Union (Unión Obrera Metalúrgica, UOM) and of the "62 Organizations," a large group of unions that were unflinchingly committed to Perón. Some of these traditional labor leaders advocated strict adherence and subordination to Perón, while others, such as Miguel, demanded that labor function as a somewhat independent pressure group. Until July 1975, this faction had privileged access to power,[40] but after Perón's death, even it faced increasing repression. The unions that followed the CGT line confronted the left, often violently.

[36] Cited in De Riz, *Retorno y derrumbe*, 136.
[37] Unlike the coup against the governor of Córdoba, the subsequent Peronist removals of leftist Peronist governors were effected legally through the constitutional mechanisms of an impeachment or a federal intervention.
[38] De Riz, *Retorno y derrumbe*, 104–112.
[39] Because of space constraints, I do not discuss the conflict between radical bases and conservative union leaders. See Jelin, "Conflictos laborales en la Argentina," and Torre, *Los sindicatos en el gobierno*.
[40] Torre, *Los sindicatos en el gobierno*.

DEMOCRATIC BREAKDOWN IN ARGENTINA   251

The radical factions combated the bureaucratic traditional union leadership, and vice versa. The radical factions ranged from some Peronist center-left unions, known as "the combatives" (*combativos*), to revolutionary Peronism and unions with a Marxist leadership, known as "classist" (*clasista*) unions.[41] To simplify, I combine these factions and refer to them as the radical or leftist unions. These center-left (the *combativos*) and leftist factions had spearheaded the radical opposition to the military dictatorship of 1966–1973.[42] The radical labor movement included the electric and auto workers in Córdoba, the printers' union in Buenos Aires, telephone workers, civil servants, railway workers, sugar workers, the Naval Construction Union, and typographers.[43]

Act 4: Isabel Perón (July 1, 1974, to March 24, 1976)

After less than nine months in office, Perón died on July 1, 1974, at the age of seventy-eight. His widow and vice president, María Estela (Isabel) Martínez de Perón, took office. Isabel Perón's government was incompetent. It inherited a difficult situation because of the far-left and far-right violence, the extraordinary heterogeneity of the Peronist coalition, and the unraveling of the Social Pact. The government was completely unequipped to deal with the situation. Its manifest ineptitude, combined with its involvement in the extreme right, including death squads, deepened apathy and hostility toward the democratic regime.

Isabel was ill-prepared to become president, and she leaned heavily on her closest advisor, López Rega. Her term marked a sharp but erratic turn toward the authoritarian far right, with occasional shifts back to Peronism's labor base. The regime degenerated quickly. Armed confrontations between leftist guerrillas and rightist paramilitary groups escalated. López Rega quickly became the central figure in Isabel's government, leading to the ascension of the far-right sectors of Peronism and to increasing violence and legal measures against the left. The main political dynamics during Isabel's presidency revolved around conflicts

---

[41] Mónica Gordillo, "Sindicalismo y radicalización en los setenta: Las experiencias clasistas," in Lida, Crespo, and Yankelevich, *Argentina, 1976*, 59–84; Daniel James, *Resistance and Integration: Peronism and the Argentine Working Class, 1946–1976* (Cambridge: Cambridge University Press, 1988), 215–242; McGuire, *Peronism without Perón*, 156–157.

[42] James, *Resistance and Integration*, 215–242; McGuire, *Peronism without Perón*, 265–270; O'Donnell, *El estado burocrático autoritario*.

[43] On the labor movement during the 1973–1976 period, see Julio Godio, *El movimiento obrero argentino [1955–1990]: Venturas y desventuras de la columna vertebral desde la resistencia hasta el menemismo* (Buenos Aires: Editorial Legasa, 1991); Daniel James, "The Peronist Left, 1955–1975," *Journal of Latin American Studies* 8, no. 2 (1976): 273–296; Daniel James, "Power and Politics in Peronist Trade Unions," *Journal of Interamerican Studies and World Affairs* 20, no. 1 (1978): 3–36; Jelin, "Conflictos laborales en la Argentina"; McGuire, *Peronism without Perón*; Juan Carlos Torre, "El movimiento obrero y el último gobierno peronista (1973–1976)," *Crítica & Utopía* 6 (1982): 1–16; Torre, *Los sindicatos en el gobierno*.

among forces that had initially supported Juan Perón in 1973, and in particular conflicts between (and within) the revolutionary left, the labor movement, and the extreme right. The offensive against the left involved both institutional/legal and increasing state repression and paramilitary extrajudicial killings. In turn, the revolutionary left stepped up its campaign of assassinations, kidnappings, bombings, and other violent tactics to gain power.

The radical labor movement became marginalized and faced increasing repression while Juan Perón was president and even more so after his death. Some prominent radical labor leaders were legally removed from their positions in July 1974 just after Perón's death, and the "classist" and "combative" leaders became increasingly isolated. The loyalist bureaucratic leadership supported the removal, repression, and killing of leftists. The radical leaders were increasingly displaced because of the repression and new regulations that made it easier to remove them.

In September 1974, the Congress approved a new national security law (Law 20840), making it easy to arbitrarily detain individuals, declare strikes illegal, intervene in unions, and ban media. The law fostered a reduction in the number of strikes and gave the union leadership more control over the rank and file.[44] Between August and October 1974, government interventions dismantled some of the most aggressive independent unions and removed opposition union leaders.[45] On September 6, 1974, in response to the growing repression and legal measures against the left, the leader of the Montoneros declared that it was time to go clandestine.

Isabel's government removed leftist Peronist governors in the provinces of Santa Cruz (Jorge Cepernic, October 7, 1974) and Salta (Miguel Ragone, November 23, 1974). On November 6, 1974, in response to the Montoneros' assassination of Alberto Villar, head of the Federal Police and a leader and a founder of the AAA, the government decreed a state of siege, which effectively ended most constitutional guarantees. The 62 Organizations, the unions that adopted a conservative pro-Perón line, publicly supported the state of siege.

The government's offensive against the left extended to higher education. Richard Gillespie writes that after August 1974, the government intervened fifteen of sixteen federal universities and replaced the rectors (university presidents). "By July 1975 . . . 4000 faculty members had been sacked, and 1600 students had been imprisoned."[46]

The militarization of politics worsened as the AAA stepped up its campaign to murder leftists. As Isabel Perón's government became more isolated,

---

[44] Jelin, "Conflictos laborales en la Argentina."
[45] Jelin, "Conflictos laborales en la Argentina," 441.
[46] Gillespie, *Soldiers of Perón*, 157.

DEMOCRATIC BREAKDOWN IN ARGENTINA 253

it increasingly turned to the military in the hopes of garnering its support. The military governments' failures from 1966 to 1973 and the deep internal schisms these failures had resulted in a temporary military retreat from overt political involvement during the presidencies of Cámpora, Lastiri, and Juan Perón. However, under Isabel's government, the military became deeply involved in politics, as in the past, as a profoundly antidemocratic actor.[47]

The federal government formally decreed military interventions in the provinces of Tucumán in May 1974 (while Juan Perón was alive), in Catamarca in August 1974, and again on February 5, 1975, in Tucumán, where the ERP had a strong presence. These military interventions reengaged the armed forces as a political actor actively involved in repression and combating the revolutionary left. Juan Perón had wanted to keep the armed forces out of politics, but Isabel and López Rega demanded that the military combat the revolutionary left and leftist labor leaders. These military interventions granted the armed forces sweeping powers in the efforts to defeat the revolutionary left. The 1975 military intervention in Tucumán, known as "Operation Independence" (Operativo Independencia), marked the establishment of the first clandestine detention center and the de facto escalation of the "dirty war," with the regular use of torture and "disappearances."

By 1975, the democratic regime had degraded deeply. Democracy is a political regime characterized by (1) free and fair elections for the head of government and the legislature; (2) wide adult suffrage rights (nearly universal in today's world); (3) respect for political rights and civil liberties and the institutions designed to protect them; and (4) civilian control over the military and paramilitary forces; the officials who are elected in free and fair elections must be able to carry out their policies without vetoes from armed actors.

Although democracy in Argentina began with free and fair elections in 1973, as the above discussion makes clear, it was vitiated from an early time by glaring democratic deficits. The regime squarely met the second condition of democracy (full suffrage for adults), and in 1973 it met the first (free and fair elections). However, starting in 1974, the police coup against the democratically elected leftist Peronist governor of Córdoba and constitutional but democratically dubious removals of freely and fairly elected leftist Peronist governors in four other provinces (Mendoza, Buenos Aires, Santa Cruz, and Salta) violated the principle that free and fair elections determine who governs. From the outset, with an escalation after Perón's death, there were massive human rights violations (the third principle of democracy). Moreover, in violation of the fourth principle of democracy, Isabel Perón's government invited growing military involvement in

---

[47] Liliana De Riz, *Retorno y derrumbe: el último gobierno peronista*, 2nd ed. (Buenos Aires: Hyspamérica, 1987), 190, 201.

254   WHEN DEMOCRACY BREAKS

politics in an effort to combat the left-wing terrorist threat.[48] Also in violation of the fourth principle of democracy, paramilitary death squads and the military increasingly dictated major public policies (e.g., how the government dealt with the revolutionary left, other sectors of the left, and the radical working-class movement).

The best democracy indicator, V-Dem, gives Argentina a very low (for a democracy) liberal democracy score of 0.33 in 1974 and 0.31 in 1975.[49] In light of the massive violations of human rights, the coup against and removals of democratically elected governors, and by 1975 the lack of military subordination to civilian authorities, these low scores are appropriate. By the second half of 1975, the regime had degenerated so profoundly that I view it as a competitive authoritarian regime. Córdoba after the democratically elected governor was removed by a coup in 1974 had an unequivocally subnational authoritarian regime, as did Tucumán by early 1975, given the extensive powers of the military, the existence of a clandestine detention center, and massive human rights abuses. De facto, then, Argentina was a case of erosion to competitive authoritarianism before it became a case of breakdown via military coup—but a strange one because the widespread sense of a power vacuum in Argentina in 1975–1976 stands in contrast to the purposeful machinations of leaders such as Hugo Chávez and Nicolás Maduro in Venezuela, Viktor Orbán in Hungary, Recep Erdoğan in Turkey, Narendra Modi in India, and Daniel Ortega in Nicaragua.

The revolutionary left continued to assassinate mainstream labor leaders. In 1975, the Montoneros killed Hipólito Acuña, vice secretary (*secretario adjunto*) of the 62 Organizations, which represented the country's unions that were faithful to Perón and rejected leftist positions, and Teodoro Ponce, vice secretary of the UOM. The Peronist Armed Forces murdered Marcelino Mansilla, the secretary general of the Union of Construction Workers of Mar del Plata (Unión Obrera de la Construcción) on August 27, 1975, and the ERP assassinated Atilio Santillán, secretary general of the Federación Obrera Tucumana de la Industria Azucarera on March 22, 1976, two days before the military coup, claiming that he had betrayed the working-class struggles.

On October 5, 1975, in an audacious operation, sixty Montoneros attacked an army garrison in the northern province of Formosa. As part of the operation, they hijacked an airplane and seized control of the local airport. That month, while Ítalo Luder, the president of the Senate, was acting president, the government announced a military intervention throughout the whole of Argentina, extending the role of the armed forces in combating the revolutionary left and the combative and classist union movement.

---

[48] Franco, "La 'seguridad nacional' como política estatal en la Argentina de los años setenta."
[49] These scores range from 0 (extraordinarily authoritarian) to 1 (extraordinarily democratic).

Whereas public opinion had accepted and even supported the revolutionary left's use of violence to defeat the dictatorship of 1966–1973, under democracy society became tolerant of right-wing extremism as a way of restoring order.[50] Left-wing violence led the public to shift away from supporting the democratic regime. By 1976, actors that had supported the return of democracy in 1973 embraced the toppling of democracy. After the economic collapse and hyper-inflation of mid-1975, the government and the democratic regime lost support, and the opposition became more fervent. Nobody believed that Isabel Perón's government was capable of addressing the panoply of serious problems.

The Peronist Party was occasionally an important actor after Perón's death—especially in the decision about whether to democratically remove Isabel Perón from the presidency in 1975.[51] With the defection of one faction of the Peronist Party to the opposition, Isabel lost majority control in the Chamber of Deputies. Because of deteriorating health, she took a leave from September 13 to October 17, 1975. During this period, as the acting president, Ítalo Luder on October 6 created the Consejo de Seguridad Interior (Council of Domestic Security), which formally deepened the military's role in "the struggle against subversion" and subordinated the Federal Police and the National Penitentiary System to the military. Isabel resumed the presidency on October 17. The Peronist leadership in Congress could plausibly have worked with the UCR to explore ways of removing her, but instead, it endorsed the traditional Peronist orthodoxy of "verticalism." By late 1975, it resigned itself to the impending coup.

Right-wing business groups began to mobilize against the democratic regime after Juan Perón's death. The most visible pro-coup business organization was a new association, formed in August 1975, the Permanent Assembly of Business Associations (Asamblea Permanente de Entidades Gremiales Empresarias, APEGE). It went on the offensive against the government after the hyperinflation and economic collapse of July 1975. APEGE represented Argentina's main business associations, including the Argentine Rural Society, the Argentine Rural Confederations (Confederaciones Rurales Argentinas), the Argentine Business Chamber (Cámara Argentina de Comercio), the Argentine Construction Chamber (Cámara Argentina de la Construcción), the Argentine Commercial Union (Unión Comercial Argentina), and many others. From its creation, the APEGE worked to undermine Isabel Perón's government, denounced the economic and social chaos, demanded drastic policy changes, and in *sotto voce* encouraged a coup. Big agricultural producers launched some de facto strikes

---

[50] Ollier, *Orden, poder y violencia*, 101.
[51] Mario D. Serrafero, "Juicio político y derrumbe institucional en la Argentina (1976)," *Estudios Interdisciplinares de América Latina y el Caribe* 8, no. 2 (1997): 41–66.

256 WHEN DEMOCRACY BREAKS

against the government in September and November 1975, provoking food shortages.

By late 1975, the military was contemplating overthrowing the government. On December 18, 1975, a coup attempt launched by air force officials failed. As Liliana De Riz notes, by then a widespread expectation that a coup was imminent prevailed.[52] Five days later, the ERP attacked Argentina's largest army base in a poor suburb of Buenos Aires, Monte Chingolo, to disastrous effect; it was their last major military operation. Early in 1976, some Peronist leaders continued to look for a way to replace Isabel, but to no avail. In January, she again changed her cabinet in a futile attempt to regain political support and initiative. By then, almost everyone expected a breakdown.

On March 24, 1976, the coup finally came. It ended Argentina's shortest-lived competitive regime and intensified a reign of terror that had begun when Juan Perón was in office and became dramatically worse after his death. The coup enjoyed widespread popular support;[53] the failures of the democratic regime were many and profound. In response to the leftist threat and the chaos that followed Perón's death, some factions of the military, including those that led the 1976 coup and governed from 1976 until 1981, were far more virulent than previous military dictators.

The coup was the final blow to democracy in Latin America before the onset of the third wave of democratization only two years later. When Isabel Perón was swept out of office, seventeen of the twenty countries in Latin America had authoritarian regimes. Only Costa Rica and Venezuela had democracies, and Colombia had a semi-democratic regime. The period from 1964 to 1976 was one of the worst for democracy in Latin America in the twentieth century.

Explaining the Democratic Breakdown

Three main factors contributed to the breakdown. First, powerful antisystem actors on the far left and the far right made it very difficult for democracy to survive—much as occurred in the German and Czech cases studied in this volume and in Spain between 1931 and 1936. Kurt Weyland argued that during the 1960s and 1970s, the establishment greatly overestimated the radical leftist threat in most Latin American countries, and that based on the fear created by this exaggerated threat, it undertook a series of military coups that ousted democratic governments.[54] This argument about the overestimated leftist threat

---

[52] De Riz, *Retorno y derrumbe*, 141.

[53] Marcos Novaro and Vicente Palermo, *La dictadura militar, 1976–1983: Del golpe de estado a la restauración democrática* (Buenos Aires: Paidós, 2003).

[54] Weyland, *Revolution and Reaction*.

DEMOCRATIC BREAKDOWN IN ARGENTINA   257

is correct for some cases, but in Argentina the radical left threat was real. The radical left had absolutely no chance of capturing state power, but it had enormous disruptive capacity, as evidenced by the huge number of kidnappings, political assassinations, factory takeovers, bombings, violent student and popular protests, and massive riots. When rampant violent collective protest continued under the new democracy, it began to generate a sense of uncontrollable violence and chaos. Moyano reported that from May 25, 1973, to March 24, 1976, there were 28 collective violent attacks on property, 265 seizures of property, 129 bombings, 49 kidnappings, and 42 assassinations, not including the guerrilla attacks and attacks by right-wing groups.[55] Citing an Argentine newspaper, *La Opinión* of March 19, 1976 (just five days before the coup), Gillespie affirmed that there was a politically motivated assassination every five hours and a bomb explosion every three.[56]

Some guerrilla attacks displayed remarkable operational capacity and audacity—although terrible judgment about the political effects of the violence they spewed.[57] Before they went clandestine, the Montoneros and the Peronist Youth frequently mobilized scores of thousands of people in the streets, and sometimes hundreds of thousands.[58] Gillespie observes that the Montoneros were "the mightiest urban guerrilla force ever seen in . . . Latin America."[59] In 1975, the ERP controlled a significant percentage (perhaps 33%) of the territory of the province of Tucumán. Moyano summarized, "[T]he seizure (of property) frenzy conveyed the sense of a generalized crisis of authority, that the established hierarchical order in the public and private spheres was under siege."[60] Even though guerrilla attacks on police and military units had limited success, they demonstrated a military capacity and audacity that galvanized the armed forces, Perón and the Peronist right wing, and most of the centrist and conservative establishments. The belief that there was a real subversive threat was central to the motivations of the Argentine military when it toppled Isabel Perón's government.

The combative and classist labor unions were also radical actors. In addition, many unions controlled by the conservative labor leadership faced radical grassroots opposition. Hundreds of thousands of university and high school students, even those who never joined the Peronist Youth or one of the guerrilla organizations, mobilized for radical change. Students and workers occupied factories and universities on a seemingly constant basis. These other radical

---

[55] Moyano, *Argentina's Lost Patrol*, 70.
[56] Gillespie, *Soldiers of Perón*, 223.
[57] Gillespie, *Soldiers of Perón*, 193–205.
[58] Gillespie, *Soldiers of Perón*, 134–135, 148–149.
[59] Gillespie, *Soldiers of Perón*, 163.
[60] Moyano, *Argentina's Lost Patrol*, 72.

258   WHEN DEMOCRACY BREAKS

leftist actors did not take up arms, but they often supported the revolutionary left and embraced violent tactics, and they were indifferent to liberal democracy.

Even under otherwise favorable circumstances, it is difficult for democracy to survive massive leftist collective violence that generates wide fear and anxiety. Under democracy, left-wing widescale kidnappings, property seizures and factory occupations (with some frequency accompanied by taking hostages), wildcat strikes, bombings, violent attacks on property, and politically motivated assassinations usually engender a right-wing response that can undermine democracy. Few democracies have survived a radical leftist threat as deep as that posed by the Argentine left from 1973 to 1976. Again, this is not because the revolutionary left had any chance of taking power, but it did pose a real threat to life and property. The extreme right-wing and left-wing mobilization in Argentina during those years, and the ruthless and sanguinary war each side waged against the other, have similarities to what occurred during Weimar Germany and the Spanish Republic of 1931–1936—and, with far fewer assassinations, in Chile from the late 1960s until the 1973 coup.

Assassinations and kidnappings carried out by the extreme right outpaced the number carried out by the left. Based on the newspaper accounts that generated her database, Moyano reported 1,165 assassinations, 458 kidnappings, and 264 bombings carried out by the right between Cámpora's inauguration and the March 24, 1976, coup.[61] Table 9.1 shows comparative data on violent acts

Table 9.1 Violent Acts by Kind of Actor, May 25, 1973, to March 24, 1976

	Guerrilla operations	Collective violent protest	Right-wing violence	Total
Theft of arms	107	-	-	107
Attacks on property	251	75	64	390
Seizures of buildings	143	265	37	445
Bombings	812	129	264	1,205
Kidnappings	140	49	458	647
Hijackings (airplanes)	1	-	-	1
Deaths	481	42	1,165	1,688
Total	1,935	560	1,988	4,483

Source: María José Moyano, *Argentina's Lost Patrol: Armed Struggle, 1969–1979* (New Haven: Yale University Press, 1995), pp. 56, 70, 81–82.

[61] Moyano, *Argentina's Lost Patrol*, 82.

DEMOCRATIC BREAKDOWN IN ARGENTINA 259

committed by the guerrillas, collective actors, and right-wing actors.[62] Even though Buenos Aires newspapers could not have counted all violent politically motivated actions, Table 9.1 provides a glimpse of the extraordinary turmoil that afflicted Argentina: in just thirty-four months, 107 episodes in which the guerrillas stole arms, 390 attacks on property, 445 buildings seized (often factories or university buildings), 1,205 bombings, 647 kidnappings, and 1,688 politically motivated assassinations.

Violence by the left and the right generated deep public insecurity and a sense of Hobbesian chaos. By the end of 1975, two hundred security companies had sprouted to offer business executives and others private protection services just in the federal capital.[63] After Cámpora's inauguration, right-wing violence did not seize the Argentine imaginary as much as the leftist violence; most of the establishment supported the right-wing assassination campaign. Nevertheless, through its campaign of terror against the left, the extremist right undermined democracy well before the March 1976 coup. Until the revolutionary left was defeated, right-wing terrorism fueled left-wing terrorism; the revolutionary left hardened its positions in response to right-wing terrorism.

In the media, the discourse about a subversive threat became ubiquitous.[64] Although data on homicides capture only a small part of the perceived subversive threat, there was a sharp increase in violent crime in the final year of the 1966–1973 military dictatorship and the democratic period. In the province of Buenos Aires, the only for which data are available in this source, the homicide rate increased from 7.6 per 100,000 inhabitants in 1969 to 14.2 in 1974, the last year for which Waldmann presents data—an increase of 87%.[65] During those years, for purposes of comparison, Germany and France had homicide rates of 1.2 and 0.8 per 100,000, respectively.[66] The incidence of serious injuries caused by attacks also increased, from 19.6 to 26.1 per 100,000 inhabitants, an increase of 33%.[67]

Labor unrest, kidnappings of business executives, strikes, factory takeovers, and high labor absentee rates were chronic, adding to the widespread chaos. Labor conflict was so intense that Fiat closed its plant that produced railroad equipment because of the "lack of order, authority, and security."[68] The guerrillas were militarily severely weakened before the March 1976 coup, but in the

---

[62] As noted earlier, Franco provides a significantly higher estimate of assassinations carried out by the AAA: two thousand ("La 'seguridad nacional' como política estatal en la Argentina de los años setenta," 865).

[63] Gillespie, *Soldiers of Perón*, 213–214.

[64] Franco, "La 'seguridad nacional' como política estatal en la Argentina de los años setenta."

[65] Waldmann, "Anomia social y violencia," 216.

[66] Waldmann, "Anomia social y violencia," 216.

[67] Waldmann, "Anomia social y violencia," 216.

[68] Jelin, "Conflictos laborales en la Argentina," 449.

260 WHEN DEMOCRACY BREAKS

right-wing and centrist imaginary, the leftist threat remained real,[69] and the government seemed incapable of establishing order and of governing.

If the government had been competent in other spheres, such as economic policy, and if some core actors (especially the presidents and government) had been committed to democracy, the regime probably could have defeated the leftist threat without succumbing to a coup and without resorting to massive human rights violations. But powerful extremist antidemocratic actors posed a stiff challenge.

Government Ineptitude and the Economic Crisis

A substantial literature indicates that poor economic performance can sink new democracies.[70] In Argentina, it was not an economic crisis per se as much as the widespread belief that government ineptitude had caused it and, after July 1975, that the government was completely incapable of resolving it that contributed to the breakdown.

From the outset in 1973, economic policies were highly statist, nationalist, ill-conceived, and incoherent.[71] The Cámpora government took office at a favorable expansionary moment for the Argentine economy, albeit with inflation running slightly above 100%. The Social Pact, the economic plan established during the early days of Cámpora's government, was designed to achieve economic and labor stability and increase real wages and growth. Labor agreed to not negotiate new contracts for two years in exchange for significant wage increases (20%) and an agreement that business would freeze prices. The Social Pact produced a drop in inflation and other short-term successes.[72] However, across-the-board 20% wage increases without allowing for compensatory price increases are usually not viable in modern economies under democratic regimes. The success of the plan rested on effective state monitoring of prices and wages and on stability in import and export prices so as not to upset the internal balance of prices and to maintain an equilibrium in the balance of payments. This is an extraordinarily unlikely proposition in a complex modern economy. Constant labor pressures

---

[69] In *Argentina's Lost Patrol*, Moyano argues—against conventional wisdom—that the revolutionary left was not militarily defeated until after the coup.

[70] Mark J. Gasiorowski, "Economic Crisis and Political Regime Change: An Event History Analysis," *American Political Science Review* 89, no. 4 (1995): 882–897.

[71] Roberto L. Ayres, "The 'Social Pact' as Anti-Inflationary Policy: The Argentine Experience since 1973," *World Politics* 28, no. 4 (1976): 473–501.

[72] Adolfo Canitrot, "La viabilidad económica de la democracia: Un análisis de la experiencia peronista, 1973–1976," Estudios Sociales #11, May 1978, Centro de Estudios de Estado y Sociedad, Buenos Aires; Pablo Gerchunoff and Lucas Llach, *El ciclo de la ilusión y el desencanto: Un siglo de políticas económicas argentinas* (Buenos Aires: Emecé, 2010), 344–345.

DEMOCRATIC BREAKDOWN IN ARGENTINA   261

for wage increases and other concessions, business maneuvering for higher prices, and a major disruption in import prices with the oil crisis of 1973–1974 made the plan unviable.

Oil prices quadrupled between October 1973 and February 1974, creating a massive external imbalance. Argentina's terms of trade deteriorated sharply; using 1970 as an index = 100, the index fell from 120.2 in the second quarter of 1973 to 65.0 in the second quarter of 1974.[73] Juan Perón tried to compensate for the increase in import prices by subsidizing some imports, but this measure added to the escalating fiscal deficit.[74] Because of the price controls, firms began withholding some products from the market.[75] Exacerbating the effects of the oil crisis, in July 1974 European markets suspended the import of Argentine beef. By March 1974, for all practical purposes, the Social Pact collapsed when Perón decreed a new wage increase of 13%, with a 30% increase in the minimum wage.[76] With these wage increases, the government hoped to regain labor peace at a time of radical labor demands. But predictably, these increases were soon eroded by inflation. Perón seemed to expect that massive state intervention in setting wages and prices would lead to labor peace, but it had the opposite effect: it made government decisions about prices and wages highly politicized and conflictual. In November 1974, labor won another 15% wage increase. With the Social Pact imploded and inflation on the rise, José Gelbard resigned as the minister of the economy in November 1974.

An overvalued and fixed exchange rate, with multiple exchange rates led to trade imbalances, frequent runs against the Argentine currency, and a raging black market for the dollar. In 1974 and 1975, on average, the black market rate for the dollar was more than three times the official commercial exchange rate, and at times it was as much as 4.7 times higher.[77] In U.S. dollars, exports increased by 20.4% in 1974, but imports increased by 62.6%. In 1975, exports plummeted by 24.7% while imports increased by another 8.6%.[78] The overvalued exchange rate generated disincentives for exports, protected inefficient sectors of national industry, and led to high internal prices for many products, thereby weakening the competitive capacity of domestic producers. After growing rapidly from 1968 to 1974, GNP fell by 1.3% in 1975 and 2.9% in 1976 (and per

[73] Canitrot, "La viabilidad económica de la democracia," 28, Figure 8.
[74] Canitrot, "La viabilidad económica de la democracia"; Torre, *Los sindicatos en el gobierno.*
[75] De Riz, *Retorno y derrumbe* (2nd ed.), 140–141; Torre, *Los sindicatos en el gobierno.*
[76] Jelin, "Conflictos laborales en la Argentina," 434; Torre, *Los sindicatos en el gobierno.*
[77] Guido Di Tella, *Argentina under Perón, 1973–76: The Nation's Experience with a Labour-Based Government* (London: Palgrave Macmillan, 1983), Table 8.2, 222–223.
[78] Di Tella, *Argentina under Perón*, Table A.4.1, 216–217; Gary W. Wynia, *Argentina in the Postwar Era: Politics and Economic Policy Making in a Divided Society* (Albuquerque: University of New Mexico Press, 1978), 227.

262 WHEN DEMOCRACY BREAKS

capita GNP fell more).[79] The fiscal deficit exploded in 1975 when public sector expenditures reached 41.7% of GNP compared to 25.7% of GNP for revenue.[80]

A new restrictive and nationalist Law of Foreign Investments crushed international enthusiasm for investing in Argentina. State regulations, increasing taxes, at times increasing real wages, escalating inflation, and a highly uncertain investment climate because of terrorism, frequent kidnappings of business executives, labor militancy, and erratic policymaking depressed investment.[81] Occasional devaluations to address the external imbalances generated inflation and eroded real wages. Union power was at its height, and the unions often successfully pushed the government into granting wage increases even when inflationary pressures were severe. Extensive price controls led to shortages of some goods and dampened investment. To address imbalances, the government relaxed price controls, but unions then insisted on wage increases to compensate for the higher prices.

To protect real wages, public sector prices were kept at low levels, generating huge public sector deficits and adding to the inflationary pressures. On top of these ill-conceived economic policies, frequent kidnappings and assassinations of business executives by the guerrillas, constant labor conflicts including factory takeovers, and chronic high levels of social conflict and mobilization made for an abysmal business climate. The government frequently undermined its own economic policymakers by granting new wage concessions or through other policies.

The economic crisis spiraled out of control in June 1975 as Economic Minister Alfredo Gómez Morales (October 21, 1974, to June 2, 1975) resigned in response to being undermined by a new wage increase of 38%.[82] His successor, Celestino Rodrigo, tried to implement an orthodox stabilization plan. He devalued the currency by 100%, increased prices for most public sector goods, including gas, by 181%,[83] and attempted to jettison the failed price controls. Grassroots labor protests broke out across Argentina's main cities. The CGT organized a massive general strike on July 7–8, 1975—the first ever against a Peronist government. The general strike paralyzed the country, led to López Rega's and Celestino Rodrigo's downfalls, and won huge (from 60 to 200%) but completely unsustainable wage increases. On average, real wages increased by almost 60% in June 1975.[84] The CGT had inflicted a temporary defeat on the right-wing sectors of Peronism. López Rega was expelled from Argentina on July 19, 1975. However,

[79] Di Tella, *Argentina under Perón*, Table A.1.1, 210–211.
[80] Di Tella, *Argentina under Perón*, Table A.1.7, 235.
[81] Ayres, "The 'Social Pact' as Anti-Inflationary Policy"; Di Tella, *Argentina under Perón*, Table A.1.2, 212–213.
[82] De Riz, "De la movilización popular al aniquilamiento," 50.
[83] Mario Rapoport, *Historia económica, política y social de la Argentina (1880–2000)* (Buenos Aires: Ediciones Macchi, 2000), 700–701.
[84] Di Tella, *Argentina under Perón*, Table A.16, 234.

DEMOCRATIC BREAKDOWN IN ARGENTINA   263

labor's victory was Pyrrhic; the wage increases unleashed hyperinflation. The increase in the consumer price index in July 1975 was 34.7%[85]—an annualized inflation rate of 3,468%, anticipating the Latin American hyperinflations of the 1980s. The economic crisis and the government's incoherent response fueled the rising tide against the democratic regime.[86] Pedro Bonnani replaced Celestino Rodrigo on July 22, but he fell three weeks later because of labor pressures, resigning on August 11, 1975. Antonio Cafiero, the fifth minister of the economy since the democratic transition, replaced Bonnani, but he, too, was unable to secure labor peace. After the massive increases of June 1975, real wages fell sharply, declining about 60% from June 1975 to March 1976.[87]

Faced with an economy in shambles, Cafiero resigned on February 3, 1976, replaced by Emilio Mondelli. On February 16, APEGE led a highly publicized and effective business lockout that was widely interpreted as coup-mongering. According to Ricardo Sidicaro,[88] twelve hundred business associations joined the lockout. Inflation again raged out of control; the increase in consumer prices averaged 38.0% in March 1976,[89] which would be 4,670% on an annualized basis. For the year that ended March 31, 1976, inflation was 566%.[90]

Democracies can survive deep economic crises. But in a context of extremist actors and weak commitments to democracy, the Argentine economic crisis contributed to defections from the democratic coalition and accretions to the coup coalition. Government ineptitude in economic policy helped convince the expanding coup coalition that, in addition to the leftist threat, there was a power vacuum that could not be solved within the confines of democracy.

Lack of Commitment to Democracy

In his classic 1971 book, *Polyarchy: Participation and Opposition*, Robert Dahl argued that elites' commitment to democracy was an important variable in sustaining democracy, or in failing to sustain it. Dahl cited Argentina as a leading example of a country with many favorable conditions that had nevertheless gone through repeated democratic failures. He argued that elites' lack of commitment to democracy was an important reason for the failure of democracy in Argentina. Dahl's argument helps shed light on the 1976 breakdown.

---

[85] De Riz, *Retorno y derrumbe*, first edition, 128.
[86] De Riz, *Retorno y derrumbe*, first edition, 124–129.
[87] Di Tella, *Argentina under Perón*, Table A.16, 234.
[88] Ricardo Sidicaro, *Los tres peronismos: Estado y poder económico 1946–1955, 1973–1976, 1989–1999* (Buenos Aires: Siglo Veintiuno Editores Argentina, 2002), 137–138.
[89] Di Tella, *Argentina under Perón*, Table A.2, 214.
[90] Novaro and Palermo, *La dictadura militar*, 17.

264   WHEN DEMOCRACY BREAKS

From 1973 to 1976, several powerful actors worked for or supported the destruction of democracy, and most others were indifferent. The fact that no major actors except the UCR were normatively committed to democracy helped sink the regime.[91] Even programmatically nonradical actors did little or nothing to defend democracy.

The hostility of some powerful actors toward liberal democracy and the indifference of most of the rest from 1973 to 1976 continued the sad legacy that Dahl mentioned in his analysis of Argentina. The revolutionary left's activities destabilized democracy. After an initial period of restraint, the revolutionary left treated the semi-democratic regime as if it were the same as the antecedent dictatorship. The revolutionary and combative sectors of the labor movement employed violence against physical property and seized factories on a regular basis. The extremist right undermined democracy through massive human rights abuses, and then it sabotaged democracy through a military coup.

Even most actors that did not have extremist policy agendas did little or nothing to protect democracy. Juan Perón, the moderate sectors of the labor movement, and the Peronist Party could have done much more to safeguard democracy. Unlike the extremist actors, Perón, the labor moderates, and the Peronist Party moderates were not normatively opposed to democracy. However, neither their discourse nor their behavior expressed a commitment to preserving democracy. If they had been committed to democracy, different behavior might have led to a more favorable outcome.

In 1973–1974, Perón was less authoritarian than he had been in 1946–1955, but he was still no steadfast democrat. He made four decisions that were highly damaging to democracy. In 1972, he pointedly refused to repudiate the armed revolutionary left even after the country was moving toward democratic elections: "People have been pressuring me to make statements against violence, but . . . the full blame for this violence falls on the dictatorship. . . . For every person that the Montoneros have killed, the military dictatorship has killed 100." As María Ollier summarized, "Perón legitimated, clearly and plainly, armed violence."[92]

Until 1974, Perón had great credibility among most of the Argentine left, so his decision to legitimize revolutionary violence had an impact. Legitimizing the left's violence against the dictatorship in 1972–1973 when a transition to democracy was under way made it difficult for Perón to tame its violence after the

---

[91] A normative commitment to democracy means that actors value democracy because of its intrinsic procedural properties and protections—the guarantee of free and fair elections, full suffrage rights, and civil liberties and political rights—rather than for strictly instrumental purposes or because of the substantive outcomes it produces.

[92] María Ollier, *El fenómeno insurreccional y la cultura política (1969–1973)* (Buenos Aires: Centro Editor de América Latina, 1986), 146.

transition. By the time Perón definitively broke with the Montoneros on May 1, 1974, he had lost his ability to rein in the revolutionary left. Given his influence among most of the Argentine left in the 1960s and 1970s, it is likely that if he had not explicitly supported violent actions and the Peronist revolutionary left during the transition to democracy (1972–1973), there would have been less revolutionary fervor and therefore a less destructive impact on democracy.

Second, after he took office, Perón supported López Rega even as the latter created the AAA to combat the left.[93] Thus, Perón was responsible for allowing the creation and expansion of right-wing death squads. The right-wing death squads directly undermined democracy and contributed to the spiral of violence and extreme polarization that plagued Argentina during the 1973–1976 period. In this and other ways, Perón was complicit as right-wing actors undermined democracy. If he had not supported the expansion and violence of the extremist left and the extremist right, democracy might have stood a chance.

Third, Peron's decision to allow his wife to be the vice-presidential candidate proved destructive. Perón was seventy-seven years old and not in good health when he assumed the presidency. Choosing a vice president who had the potential to be a good successor was a paramount democratic responsibility. He enjoyed unassailable prestige within Peronist ranks, so he could have chosen a capable running mate without incurring a cost. Isabel Perón had a fifth-grade education and was wholly unqualified to become president. In 1973, she was a convenient way for Perón to maintain his unwieldy coalition intact; nobody dared challenge his choice. His decision was also a product of his preference for a loyalist inner circle. As president, Isabel was grossly incompetent. She consistently supported López Rega until his ouster in July 1975. Without gaining support on the right, she alienated the Peronist left and center and virtually the entire non-Peronist establishment. She wavered incoherently between supporting finance ministers who attempted to stabilize the economy and giving in to labor demands for huge wage increases. Democracy would have stood a better chance with a competent president.

Finally, from the outset, Juan Perón opted for ill-advised, incoherent economic policies. Many business sectors and most of Argentine society were willing to give democracy a chance. When the government wavered incoherently between stabilization policies and massive wage increases, when businesses and citizens experienced the uncertainty generated by erratic and incoherent policies, when they faced deep economic losses and a downward economic spiral, and when they saw constant turmoil and fear produced (in their view) by the revolutionary and radical left, they defected.

[93] Liliana De Riz, *La política en suspenso, 1966/1976* (Buenos Aires: Paidós, 2000), 148–153.

266 WHEN DEMOCRACY BREAKS

If labor unions had been committed to democracy, they would have made different choices that would have had less destructive economic consequences and less pernicious political ones. Most labor leaders displayed complete indifference to democracy. Even at the expense of contributing to an inflationary spiral that eroded real wages, they fought relentlessly for higher wages, more political power, and more control over government policy.[94] Even though their actions added to the sense of chaos and disorder, the radical leaders and bases pressed for factory takeovers and strikes. Their goal was labor power and radical social change or revolution. Even if it meant degrading the regime, conservative union leaders supported the assassinations and removals of their radical competitors.

Admittedly, many union leaders were under pressure from radicalized bases during the 1973–1976 period. This situation reduced their ability to prioritize democracy over short-term economic interests (demanding constant wage increases). A few union leaders resisted these short-term and narrow temptations and attempted to work for a democratic solution. In October 1975, UOM leader Victorio Calabró, who became the governor of Buenos Aires (he replaced Oscar Bidegaín in January 1974 when Perón pushed the latter to resign), joined a coalition that hoped to convince Isabel to resign. However, orthodox Peronists and Isabel herself defeated this attempt. Calabró was expelled from the party in November 1975 and removed as governor the following month. The Argentine experience of 1983–1989, when workers suffered great material setbacks but fought valiantly to defend democracy, showed that labor is sometimes willing to prioritize democracy. Organized labor bears some responsibility for the 1976 breakdown—although certainly far less than the revolutionary left and the reactionary right.

Likewise, Peronist politicians thwarted plausible steps to salvage democracy. Some Peronist leaders in Congress defected to the opposition after the hyperinflation and growing power vacuum in July 1975. Led by Ítalo Luder, this group hoped to convince Isabel Perón to resign when she took her leave in September 1975. She agreed to move the elections up from 1977 to October 17, 1976, but with the support of the "verticalist" labor leaders (led by Lorenzo Miguel) and eleven Peronist governors (led by Carlos Menem of La Rioja, later president of Argentina from 1989 to 1999), she blocked the effort to remove her. The verticalist labor leaders and governors were more interested in preserving their positions than in saving democracy.[95] The small core of actors that were committed to democracy—the UCR and a small part of the Peronist Party—were not able to find a democratic way of replacing Isabel.

[94] Torre, *Los sindicatos en el gobierno.*
[95] Torre, *Los sindicatos en el gobierno,* 144.

By October 1975 it would have been difficult to rescue democracy even with a competent president, but the Peronist factions headed by Luder might have had a chance in tandem with the UCR and moderate labor leaders. They might have been able to overcome the vacuum of power and massive cynicism and lack of confidence that beset a feeble, incompetent, and increasingly authoritarian president. With Isabel restored in the presidency, the fate of democracy was more or less sealed.

Only one main actor, the centrist UCR, embraced liberal democracy. The Radicals remained mostly true to democratic practices and attitudes until the final agony of the regime in March 1976.[96] The UCR denounced growing human rights abuses, but it had limited popular support. Its presidential candidate won only 21% of the vote in the March 1973 presidential election and 24% in the September 1973 election, and the party captured only 51 of 245 seats in the Chamber of Deputies in 1973. As violence overwhelmed politics, it became a less central player, and its voice was drowned out in the cacophony of violence.

Although it is analytically useful to conceptualize extremist actors, the weakness of actors committed to democracy, and governmental incompetence and bad policy results as separate factors that contributed to the breakdown, these three factors interacted. For example, because he was not a true democrat, Perón nurtured the extremist antisystem left and then supported the creation of the right-wing death squads that helped undermine democracy. Likewise, government ineptitude and the power vacuum and chaos reinforced antidemocratic actors.

The 1976 breakdown differed significantly from the breakdowns of 1951/55, 1962, and 1966. In the earlier breakdowns, the deep antipathy between Peronists and Radicals, the electoral hegemony of the Peronists coupled with the steadfast refusal of the military and conservative establishment to allow the Peronists to run after 1955, the Peronists' mobilization against successive regimes including the semi-democratic regimes of 1958–1962 and 1963–1966, frequent divisions within the armed forces, and widespread societal opposition to the authoritarian regimes were central.[97] The 1970 rapprochement between Peronists and Radicals and the end of the proscription of the Peronists ended this earlier source of democratic instability. The emergence of a powerful revolutionary left and the radicalization of parts of the labor movement and student movement, coupled with the strengthening of a more virulently authoritarian and violent right wing, also made the 1976 breakdown very different from the previous ones. Governmental

---

[96] Acuña, *De Frondizi a Alfonsín*, 208; De Riz, *Retorno y derrumbe* (2nd ed.), 154; De Riz, *La política en suspenso*, 179.

[97] Guillermo O'Donnell, *Modernization and Bureaucratic-Authoritarianism: Studies in South American Politics* (Berkeley: Institute for International Studies, University of California, 1973); O'Donnell, *El estado burocrático autoritario*.

268   WHEN DEMOCRACY BREAKS

incompetence and a widespread sense of social and political chaos and a power vacuum were crucial elements in the 1976 breakdown, more so than in the earlier breakdowns.

One common element to all four breakdowns between 1951 and 1976 is that, for an extended time in Argentine history, almost no actors valued democracy more than instrumental substantive outcomes. When substantive outcomes are bad, as almost inevitably happens from time to time, democracy easily becomes vulnerable if no actors defend it on normative grounds.

Evaluating Explanations for the Breakdown

How can we be confident that these three explanations are valid—indeed, that they might constitute the best explanations for the breakdown? One reason is that some social scientists and historians implicitly agree the first two explanations are valid and important.[98] Although social scientists' and historians' implicit agreement does not prove that an explanation is correct, it increases the confidence that it is.

Another is what leading actors themselves said at the time and after the coup. The actors that supported the 1976 coup consistently explained their support based on the threats, the sense of chaos, fear, and uncertainty generated by radical actors; and on governmental incompetence, the vacuum of power, and the economic and public security crises. Actors are not always aware of the motivations for their behavior, and they sometimes use discourse strategically or instrumentally to disguise their true motivations. However, in this case, the actors that supported the coup had no obvious reason to dissemble. Moreover, the sequence of events supports the argument that leftist radicalism and the deep economic and public security crisis fueled growing support for an authoritarian right-wing reaction. As noted, the authoritarian right-wing reaction began in 1973, and it intensified over time as the guerrilla movement grew and as radical labor protest continued. The severe economic crisis from July 1975 on also generated growing opposition to the democratic regime.

Hence, it is useful to document how actors explained their positions and their support for the coup. In December 1975, the APEGE (which represented business associations) issued a statement decrying the "lack of authority, and absence of security and order in which Argentines live."[99] On January 21, 1976, APEGE stated, "The systematic persecution (of business interests), whether

---

[98] De Riz, *Retorno y derrumbe*; De Riz, *La política en suspenso*; Viola, "Democracia e Autoritarismo na Argentina Contemporânea."

[99] Quoted in Gonzalo Sanz Cerbino, "El huevo de la serpiente: La Asamblea Permanente de Entidades Gremiales Empresarias y el golpe de estado de 1976," *Realidad Económica* 251 (2010): 14.

DEMOCRATIC BREAKDOWN IN ARGENTINA   269

through the system of price controls, through labor conflicts and threats that stem from the constant increase of unions' power, through the excessive tax burden . . . are parts of a perfectly structured plan to reach our gradual and inexorable annihilation."[100]

APEGE and other business associations began issuing thinly veiled calls for coups on the grounds that the government of Isabel Perón was incapable of resolving the economic crisis and the subversive threat. On March 10, 1976, APEGE denounced the "corruption, lack of security for people and goods, and the generalized social chaos. . . . The efforts and sacrifice of life of our army forces and security forces are worth little if they must fight against the counterweight of policies that foster the causes of subversive delinquency. . . . Some Argentines are not willing to remain passive in the face of the destruction of their country. The path must be corrected in a clear and definitive way."[101]

On March 20, 1976, the Federation of Entrepreneurs of Buenos Aires (Federación de Empresarios de Buenos Aires) warned, "The crisis that affects our country has reached its limits. . . . Nobody expects anything from a regime [*sistema de poder*] that has not and does not have any answer that would enable us to resolve the dramatic situation that overwhelms us. . . . The blindness, lack of capacity, and immorality of our leaders . . . have unleashed this chaos."[102] That same day, Confederation of Rural Associations of Buenos Aires and La Pampa (CARBAP) warned that "nobody will be surprised if the government or the legislative, political, entrepreneurial, or union institutions disappear, crushed by the weight of their own incapacity or failure to operate."[103] A right-wing party, Nueva Fuerza (New Force), echoed these themes, declaring just before the coup that it was imminent because of the economic chaos, corruption, and "total decadence."[104]

In an analysis of the attitudes of a major Argentine newspaper, *Clarín*, about the coup, Micaela Iturralde wrote, "In the months leading up to the coup, *Clarín*'s characterization of the national situation in terms of 'chaos' and 'national crisis,' went along with its equally positive assessment of the armed forces as the

---

[100] Cited in Horacio Raúl Bustingorry, "Historia de APEGE: La huelga patronal del 16 de febrero de 1976," paper presented at the Eleventh Symposium of History Departments, University of Tucumán, Argentina, quoting *La Nación*, January 22, 1976, 9.

[101] Quoted in Verónica Baudino and Gonzalo Sanz Cerbino, "Las corporaciones agrarias e industriales frente al golpe del '76: Apuntes para la reconstrucción de la fuerza social contrarrevolucionaria," Young Researchers' Working Paper No. 30 (2011), Gino Germani Institute, University of Buenos Aires, 131–132, http://biblioteca.clacso.edu.ar/Argentina/iigg-uba/2012030 2023339/dji30.pdf.

[102] Sanz Cerbino, "El huevo de la serpiente," 27–28.

[103] Cited in Baudino and Sanz Cerbino, "Las corporaciones agrarias e industrials frente al golpe del '76," 132.

[104] Cited in Rapoport, *Historia económica, politica y social de la Argentina*, 679.

270 WHEN DEMOCRACY BREAKS

necessary guarantors of 'order' and 'national security,' in the light of the violence unleashed by the armed organizations."[105]

In their March 24, 1976, proclamation after seizing power, the generals explained their motivation: "Faced with a tremendous power vacuum that could have plunged us into dissolution and anarchy . . . the lack of a global strategy . . . to confront subversion; the lack of solutions for the country . . . the manifest irresponsibility of the management of the economy . . . the Armed Forces . . . have assumed leadership of the state. . . . This decision has an objective of ending the power vacuum [*el desgobierno*], corruption, and the subversive scourge."[106] Six days later, in a speech on March 30, 1976, President Jorge Videla repeated these themes: "The intervention of the armed forces was the only possible alternative given the deterioration provoked by the power vacuum [*el desgobierno*], corruption, and complacency. . . . We have never experienced such disorder."[107]

Even some Peronist leaders expressed support for the coup for similar reasons. Jorge Paladino, who served as secretary general of the National Justicialist Movement from 1968 to 1972, later stated, "With the coup, the Armed Forces did nothing more than accept a request that they confront a survival crisis of the nation that the formal institutions and civic organizations had proven incapable of and impotent to resolve. You can't even claim that the military overthrew a government. The state had been acephalous since July 1, 1974."[108] As Marcos Novaro and Vicente Palermo wrote, "[S]ociety was bankrupt and desperate to end the situation of chaos."[109]

Many powerful actors expressed their support for the military takeover because of their perception of a radical left threat and a profound economic and security crisis. In April 1976, the head of Confederation of Rural Associations of Buenos Aires and La Pampa, Jorge Aguado, declared that the military had taken power "to impede the continuation of a government that, because of its own incapacity and immorality, had plunged the country in a profound social, economic, and political crisis."[110] In a September 1976 publication, the country's most traditional and powerful association of landowners, the Argentine Rural Society (Sociedad Rural Argentina), stated, "During the 1975–76 period, the

---

[105] Micaela Iturralde, "El diario *Clarín* y la construcción discursiva del golpe de Estado de marzo de 1976 en Argentina," *Quórum Académico* 10, no. 2 (2013): 199–223.

[106] Jorge R. Videla, Emilio Massera, and Orlando Agosti, "Proclama del 24 de marzo de 1976," http://servicios.abc.gov.ar/docentes/efemerides/24marzo/htmls/decadas/descarga/proclama.pdf.

[107] Jorge Videla, "Discurso pronunciado el día 30 de marzo de 1976 por el Excelentísimo Señor Presidente de la Nación, teniente general Jorge Rafael Videla al asumir la Primera Magistratura de la República Argentina," In *Mensajes presidenciales: Proceso de Reorganización Nacional, 24 de marzo de 1976* (Buenos Aires: Imprenta del Congreso de la Nación Argentina, 1977), 1:7–8.

[108] Cited in Novaro and Palermo, *La dictadura militar*, 24.

[109] Novaro and Palermo, *La dictadura militar*, 28.

[110] Cited in Baudino and Sanz Cerbino, "Las corporaciones agrarias e industriales frente al golpe del '76," 146.

DEMOCRATIC BREAKDOWN IN ARGENTINA   271

country experienced perhaps its greatest social, political, and economic convulsion since the period of national organization. This turmoil, the product of a demagogic and populist regime, nearly brought the country to its dissolution. This disgraceful outcome was avoided thanks to the military intervention of March 24."[111]

A year after the coup, the Confederation of Rural Associations of the Rosafé Zone[112] (Confederación de Asociaciones Rurales de la Zona Rosafé) also invoked the chaos and subversive threat for their supporting the military intervention: "When the armed forces took over the government on March 24, 1976, a sensation of hopeful faith was manifest in the Argentine citizenry. One year later, it is apparent how much has been achieved for the country's good." Along similar lines, the Argentine Rural Society exalted, "The struggle against subversion has been carried out with high valor and growing success. . . . The actions that will lead Argentina to a destiny of order, progress, and happiness have been carried out."[113]

The discourse from establishment actors ignores the right's deep complicity in the breakdown. The steep degeneration of democracy as manifested in massive human rights abuses, the coup against a democratically elected governor and the democratically dubious removals of several other governors, the growing power of paramilitary death squads, and the increasing political involvement of the military were the result of authoritarian right-wing actors.

The argument about actors' normative commitments has a different status in the logic of explanation. It is based on a counterfactual, namely, that if some programmatically moderate powerful actors had been normatively committed to democracy, they would have taken different steps that could have averted the democratic breakdown. I focused on the nonradical actors because the antisystem actors were committed to the destruction of democracy, whereas the programmatically moderate actors were not. Of course, it is difficult to definitively adjudicate explanations based on counterfactuals.

The Argentine Breakdown and Theories of Democratization

The Argentine experience of 1973–1976 helps illuminate the four theoretical points about democratization that I elaborated earlier in this chapter. First, to understand breakdowns, we need to examine specific actors rather than primarily

---

[111] Cited in Sidicaro, *Los tres peronismos*, 141–142.

[112] The Rosafé Zone is a highly productive agricultural area that includes the farmland outside of two major cities in the province of Santa Fe: Rosario and Santa Fe.

[113] Both quotes in this paragraph come from Carlos del Frade, *Matar para robar, luchar para vivir: historia política de la impunidad, Santa Fe, 1976–2004* (Rosario: Ciudad Gótica, 2004), 216.

272   WHEN DEMOCRACY BREAKS

invoking structural or cultural conditions. Although in most historical periods, the chances of democratic survival have been better in wealthier countries, the Argentine breakdowns of 1951, 1962, 1966, and especially 1976 show that democracies sometimes fail despite auspicious structural conditions. A fairly high standard of living and moderate inequality did not inoculate democracy.

Argentina had perhaps the most powerful labor movement in Latin America. According to Dietrich Rueschemeyer, Evelyne Huber Stephens, and John D. Stephens, a powerful organized working class should be good for democracy.[114] Yet organized labor had an instrumental attitude toward democracy and supported Perón, who used democratic elections to come to power but then ran roughshod over it. Democracy was a means toward institutional power for labor leaders, and for wage growth and social benefits for workers if Perón was in office. Under these circumstances, a powerful organized labor movement was a hindrance to democracy.

Second, the Argentine breakdown of 1976 underscores that it is useful to focus the analysis on concrete historical actors—presidents and organizations—rather than conceptualizing the actors as social classes or the "rich," "middle classes," and "poor." In Argentina, the key actors, except for organized labor and business associations—the leftist revolutionaries, the presidents, the military, the right-wing death squads, and the two largest parties—cannot readily be analyzed in class terms. Moreover, organized labor was deeply divided from 1973 to 1976 along ideological lines, in ways that could not be predicted on the basis of the economic activities of the different sectors of the working class. Organized business was also divided until around the time of Perón's death.

We cannot understand regime dynamics in Argentina from 1973 to 1976 along such simple lines. In May 1973, when democracy began, most poor and middle-class people supported the new regime. By March 1976, most poor, middle-class, and rich people opposed it. To understand regime dynamics, we need to study organizational actors and presidents, not the rich and poor. The cleavage lines regarding policy positions and the political regime were complex.

In Argentina from 1968 to 1977, some of the most important actors were leftist revolutionaries. Revolutionary groups claimed to act on behalf of the people, workers, or the poor, but there was a chasm between the revolutionary left and the people on whose behalf they purported to act.[115] After the transition to democracy in 1973, most labor leaders repudiated the revolutionary left, and there is a widespread perception that common citizens did as well. Likewise, although the Argentine military implemented a far-right agenda after it seized

[114] Dietrich Rueschemeyer, Evelyne Huber Stephens, and John D. Stephens, *Capitalist Development and Democracy* (Chicago: University of Chicago Press, 1992).

[115] Gillespie, *Soldiers of Perón*; Moyano, *Argentina's Lost Patrol*.

power in March 1976, it would be facile to generally reduce the military to an instrument of class interests.[116] Some military regimes (for example, Peru from 1968 to 1975 and Portugal from 1974 to 1975) have implemented a leftist policy agenda. Rather than treating militaries as expressions of class interests, social scientists and historians need to examine the identities and institutional interests of the armed forces.[117] Likewise, it is usually excessively simplistic to treat political parties and churches as expressions of class interests. In sum, to comprehend regime dynamics, we need to study organizational actors and presidents, not the rich and poor (or the middle classes) as more or less unitary actors.

Third, the Argentine case shows that battles over income distribution are not always the defining issue of democratic politics.[118] In Argentina during this time, battles over income distribution *were* important, but extremism on the right and left and governmental incompetence were more important. When the new government implemented the Social Pact in 1973, many business leaders grumbled, but they were willing to absorb higher labor costs if it won them labor peace and social peace. When the economy grew in 1973 and early 1974, businesses could fare well enough with some redistribution. Redistribution became a major conflict only when the economy started to experience deep problems and the security situation unraveled. Actors increasingly opposed the political regime on the grounds of governmental incompetence, a power void, widespread political violence, and massive social and political convulsions. These issues had far more weight for most actors than conflicts over routine redistribution.

In one superficial respect, the Argentine breakdown of 1976 conforms to Acemoglu and Robinson's and Boix's expectations: until late 1975, most labor leaders continued to support Isabel Perón's government and for this reason largely abided by the democratic regime, and most business interests and the wealthy applauded the March 24, 1976, coup. However, the logic of the actors in Argentina largely contradicts the expectations of these two works. Business and the wealthy applauded the coup despite the fact that economic policy and results veered sharply against labor after July 1975; the process of turning Argentina from Latin America's most equal society into a much more unequal society started during Isabel Perón's government. Income distribution, which is central to Acemoglu and Robinson's and Boix's accounts of why different classes support democracy or dictatorship, mispredicts actors' positions in Argentina at the time of the breakdown in 1976.

---

[116] Dan Slater, Benjamin Smith, and Gautam Nair, "Economic Origins of Democratic Breakdown? The Redistributive Model and the Postcolonial State," *Perspectives on Politics* 12, no. 2 (2014): 353–374.

[117] Alfred Stepan, *The Military in Politics: Changing Patterns in Brazil* (Princeton: Princeton University Press, 1971).

[118] Stephan Haggard and Robert R. Kaufman, *Dictators and Democrats: Masses, Elites, and Regime Change* (Princeton: Princeton University Press, 2016), 219–300; Slater, Smith, and Nair, "Economic Origins of Democratic Breakdown?"

274 WHEN DEMOCRACY BREAKS

For most actors, a more important issue in Argentina in 1973–1976 revolved around a basic Hobbesian or Huntingtonian[119] question: how to secure peace and order. The period witnessed tremendous social convulsions and constant political violence. The left-wing extremist actors posed an existential threat to establishment actors, especially the military, the police, business leaders, "verticalist" union leaders, and the church. Right-wing extremists killed leftists and leftist sympathizers in large numbers, and the government removed leftists and sympathizers from their positions in government, labor unions, and universities—and often imprisoned them. This, and the ubiquitous sense that there was a power vacuum and that Isabel Perón's government was grossly ill-equipped to resolve any of the country's problems, were far more important in the breakdown of democracy than battles over income distribution.

Finally, the Argentine experience of 1973–1976 underscores the problematic nature of the essentialist position that the working class is consistently pro-democratic[120] and that the poor are consistently democratic only if revolution is not viable.[121] In Argentina, no major faction of the labor movement was committed to liberal democracy between the late 1940s and 1976. Organized labor supported the democratic transition in 1973, but its support for democracy as a regime type was instrumental. The bureaucratic "verticalist" labor leaders supported the democratic transition as a way of gaining political power and winning economic concessions for workers; they were indifferent to democracy. Radical labor leaders wanted radical change, not democracy.

Whereas for Acemoglu and Robinson and Boix, the potential champions of revolution are the poor, in Argentina (as in Chile and Uruguay in the 1970s), the revolutionaries were mostly well-educated middle-class young people.[122] In Argentina, most of the top labor leadership repudiated the leftist guerrillas. And by 1975, the poor overwhelmingly repudiated them.

International Actors and Influences

International actors were not directly terribly important in the demise of democracy in Argentina in 1976, but international influences cast a dark shadow over this ill-fated regime. In the southern half of South America, the period from 1964 to 1976 represented the height of the Cold War, and democracy was one of its

[119] Samuel P. Huntington, *Political Order in Changing Societies* (New Haven: Yale University Press, 1968).

[120] Rueschemeyer, Stephens, and Stephens, *Capitalist Development and Democracy*.

[121] Acemoglu and Robinson, *Economic Origins of Dictatorship and Democracy*; Boix, *Democracy and Redistribution*. Levitsky and Mainwaring make this point broadly for Latin America in "Organized Labor and Democracy in Latin America."

[122] Moyano, *Argentina's Lost Patrol*.

victims. Under Presidents Richard Nixon (1969–1974) and Gerald Ford (1974–1977), the United States was largely indifferent toward the fate of democracy in Latin America. In the notorious case of the Chilean coup of September 11, 1973, the United States actively supported democracy's demise. The Argentine military and other pro-coup actors were aware that they would not face sanctions if they struck against democracy. This awareness certainly affected their willingness to undertake a coup.

Throughout the southern half of South America, the left radicalized in the 1960s and early 1970s, drawing inspiration from the Cuban Revolution and radical movements elsewhere, including Vietnam. In response to the leftist threat, military dictatorships sprouted even in the two southern cone countries with long histories of democracy, Chile and Uruguay. Right-wing forces galvanized against guerrillas and revolutionary and radical movements, parties, and intellectuals.[123] After the Chilean coup in September 1973, Argentina was surrounded by dictatorships on all sides: in Brazil, Uruguay, Chile, Paraguay, and Bolivia. At the time, democracy had limited publicly expressed normative appeal in Brazil and the southern cone. The extraordinary economic growth in Brazil from 1968 to 1974 helped create legitimacy for military dictatorships. In Argentina, Bolivia, Brazil, Paraguay, and Uruguay, militaries and conservative actors believed that dictatorship was an essential bulwark against revolutionary and radical forces. The climate in the southern half of South America was deeply inhospitable to democracy. The fact that dictatorship was normalized throughout the region undoubtedly affected actors' perceptions in Argentina.

Conclusions

I close with three general conclusions that flow directly from the Argentine case. It is difficult to sustain democracy when powerful extremist actors are committed to its destruction. All too often, including in Argentina from 1973 to 1976, extremism begets extremism.[124] If antisystem extremist actors take power, other actors will face huge, potentially catastrophic losses. If they fear cataclysmic losses, almost all actors will prefer an authoritarian regime that is likely to protect their core interests. Democracy can survive extremist actors committed to its destruction if those actors are isolated, but the challenge is much more daunting with powerful extremist actors. It is difficult to name a democracy that survived such powerful violent extremist actors as Argentina had from 1973 to 1976.

---

[123] Wynia, *Argentina in the Postwar Era*.
[124] Mainwaring and Pérez-Liñan, *Democracies and Dictatorships in Latin America*; Weyland, *Revolution and Reaction*.

276   WHEN DEMOCRACY BREAKS

These extremist actors were not an ex-ante condition that doomed democracy from the outset. As noted, Perón first encouraged the revolutionary left and then tolerated the creation of the right-wing death squads to combat it. Moreover, many actors that defected to the pro-coup camp had been willing to give democracy a chance.

Second, in the context of violent extremist actors and weak normative commitments to democracy, bad government performance makes it more difficult to sustain democracy. All political regimes are susceptible to periods of bad government performance, and countless democracies have survived poor government performance, including Argentina from 1983 to 1990, from 1998 to 2002, and since 2012. However, when poor government performance is combined with powerful violent extremist actors and with weak normative commitments to democracy, the prospects are dim.

Third, democracy is more likely to survive if some powerful actors, especially the government and the largest opposition party or parties, are normatively committed to it. Normative commitments to democracy provide an inoculation. They help enable democracies to weather difficult times. If most actors perceive democracy merely instrumentally, for the substantive outcomes it produces, they are likely to engage in practices that eventually hollow democracy and make it vulnerable to incremental erosion or sudden breakdown. In Argentina, even most nonextremist actors were normatively indifferent to democracy. Democracy was a means to achieve other goals. When they found they could not achieve those goals, they turned against democracy, and democracy broke down with little support.

10

Why Russia's Democracy Broke

Chris Miller

Why did Russia's democracy break in the early 2000s? In the 1990s, after independent Russia emerged from the Soviet Union, the country had competitive elections to Parliament and the presidency that had substantial impact on public policy. Today the results of the country's most important elections are known in advance, and genuine opposition politicians are jailed or prevented from running for office. The political system changed in the early 2000s, as the Russian government eliminated the independent political power of the country's oligarchic business elite. In the 1990s oligarchs funded Russia's political parties, providing a genuine if deeply flawed type of political competition. Russia's politics in the 1990s failed to provide for stable living standards or responsive government, however, which many people blamed on the oligarchs. Putin came to power in 2000 promising to limit oligarchs' political power. The tools he used—abusing his legal authority, centralizing control over the media, and drastically expanding the power of the security services—succeeded in limiting the oligarchs' power, but also eliminated any space for political competition.

Russian democracy collapsed not under pressure from the political extremes but rather from the elite's and the security services' frustration with political competition. Many people, in the elite and the populace more broadly, believed that centralized authority would provide for more effective governance. There was hardly any ideological support for democracy per se, and the only groups that provided real political competition—the oligarchs—were self-interested and deeply unpopular. Putin's campaign against the structures that provided for political competition was therefore broadly popular, even if the stagnation and corruption that Russia's new political system have bred are not. The contrast between post-Soviet Russia and Ukraine is instructive: Russia used its security services to crack down on its oligarchs, eliminating most political competition in the process. In Ukraine, where the security services were always weaker, oligarchs have played a major role in politics, guaranteeing that they have shaped public policy—but also guaranteeing that no single force has monopolized control over the country's politics.

Chris Miller, *Why Russia's Democracy Broke* In: *When Democracy Breaks*. Edited by: Archon Fung, David Moss, and Odd Arne Westad, Oxford University Press. © Oxford University Press 2024. DOI: 10.1093/oso/9780197760789.003.0010

278 WHEN DEMOCRACY BREAKS

Weimar Syndrome, Russian-Style?

When Yegor Gaidar, the first prime minister of independent Russia, looked back on his country's politics in the fifteen years after it emerged from the wreckage of the Soviet system, he saw little cause for optimism. Gaidar had designed President Boris Yeltsin's program to cast off Soviet-style state Socialism. While in office, he believed that Russia was building a European-style liberal democracy. A decade and a half later, long after he had been ejected from power, Russian politics was on a different trajectory. By 2006, when Gaidar published his book *Collapse of an Empire,* Russia was clearly no longer Soviet. But nor was it democratic, by any definition of the word. Russia had built a functioning, independent state, which looked very different from its Soviet predecessor. But though the country had cast off state Socialism, Russia's political elite no longer aspired to a competitive political system. Nor, it seemed, did many Russian citizens. Coming to power in 2000, President Vladimir Putin ended open political competition, consolidated control over the media, and harassed opposition voices.

Gaidar sensed this shift in Russian politics and believed he knew the malaise from which Russia suffered: Weimar syndrome. Like Weimar Germany, Gaidar argued, post-Soviet Russia suffered from postimperial nostalgia. Most Russians looked back fondly on the days of Leonid Brezhnev, a growing number showing sympathy even for Stalin. "There was a fifteen-year gap between the collapse of the German Empire and Hitler's rise to power and fifteen years between the collapse of the USSR and Russia in 2006–07," Gaidar wrote that year, sensing that this was not a coincidence.[1] "Few remember," he continued, "that the imperial state regalia and symbols were restored in Germany eight years after the empire's collapse, in 1926, and in Russia, after nine years, in 2000. Not many more know that an important Nazi economic promise was to restore the bank deposits lost by the German middle class during the hyperinflation of 1922–1923," mirroring the false promises made by many Russian politicians.[2]

Gaidar was far from alone in sensing an impending Weimar-style authoritarian shift. Many Russian intellectuals, from journalist Yevgenia Albats to academics Irina Starodubrovskaya and Vladimir Mau, drew similar comparisons.[3] Foreign observers also asked whether Russia was headed along a similar path. Academic journals in the 1990s were full of debate about similarities between pre-Nazi Germany and post-Communist Russia.[4]

---

[1] Yegor Gaidar, *Collapse of an Empire* (Washington, DC: Brookings Institution Press, 2007), xiii.

[2] Gaidar, *Collapse of an Empire,* xv.

[3] Yevgenia Albats, "Bureaucrats and the Russian Transition: The Politics of Accommodation, 1991–2003" (PhD diss., Harvard University, 2004), 41, 68; Vladimir Mau and Irina Starodubrovskaya, *Challenge of Revolution* (New York: Oxford University Press, 2001), 306–322.

[4] Stephen Shenfield, "The Weimar/Russia Comparison," *Post Soviet Affairs* 14, no. 4 (1998): 355–368; Stephen E. Hanson and Jeffrey S. Kopstein, "The Weimar/Russia Comparison," *Post-Soviet*

Economists noted that both 1990s Russia and 1920s Germany experienced devastating hyperinflation that not only destroyed household savings but also undermined the popularity of democratic politics.[5] Political scientists pointed out that both Weimar Germany and 1990s Russia had fragmented political parties, weak institutions, and large numbers of people who lamented the collapse of their countries' empires.

What is "Weimar syndrome"? In the 1990s, analysts who feared that Russia faced a Weimar-style slide into authoritarianism pointed toward the large chunk of votes received by overtly nationalist politicians. In 1993, the lead vote-winner in parliamentary elections was a party led by Vladimir Zhirinovsky, a flamboyant, anti-Semitic populist who advocated extending Russian rule to the boundaries of the old Soviet state—and even beyond. Zhirinovsky lamented the "zionization" of Europe and foresaw that "Islam—whether yellow or black—is rolling over Christian Europe."[6] He saw only one solution: "Russia can be saved only with an authoritarian regime."[7] "What is needed is a strict, centralized authority."[8] Zhirinovsky's party won the largest share of votes in the 1993 Duma elections, sparking fears that he would bring to power the authoritarian methods he thought necessary to govern Russia.

Zhirinovsky remains a fixture on the Russian political scene today, but he was outmaneuvered in the mid-1990s by Communist Party leader Gennady Zyuganov, who rebranded Communism by melding it with Russian nationalism, religious conservatism, and reinvigorated sympathy for Stalin. "Two basic values lie at the foundation of the Russian idea," Communist leader Zyuganov explained in the early 1990s: "Russian spirituality, which is inconceivable without an Orthodox Christian outlook and a realization of one's true purpose on Earth, and Russian statehood and great-power status."[9] "West European–style social democracy stands no chance in Russia," Zyuganov declared on a different occasion.[10]

Affairs 13, no. 3 (1997): 252–283; Andrei Melville, "Weimar and Russia: Is There an Analogy?," in *Currents* (Berkeley: Institute of International Studies, University of California at Berkeley, 1994); Leonid Luks, " 'Weimar Russia?' Notes on a Controversial Concept," *Russian Politics & Law* 46, no. 4 (2008): 47–65; Marcel H. Van Herpen, *Putinism: The Slow Rise of a Radical Right Regime in Russia* (London: Palgrave Macmillan, 2013); Alexander Yanov, *Weimar Russia and What We Can Do about It* (New York: Slovo-Word, 1995).

[5] Neil Ferguson and Brigitte Granville, "Weimar on the Volga," *Journal of Economic History* 60, no. 4 (2000): 1061–1087.

[6] Andreas Umland, "The Fascist Threat in Post-Soviet Russia," NATO, 57–59, accessed October 13, 2023, https://www.nato.int/acad/fellow/96-98/umland.pdf.

[7] Umland, "The Fascist Threat in Post-Soviet Russia," 60.

[8] Jacob W. Kipp, "The Zhirinovsky Threat," *Foreign Affairs* 73, no. 3 (1994): 77.

[9] Stuart J. Kaufman, "The Russian Problem," *Journal of Conflict Studies* 16, no. 2 (1996): 8.

[10] James P. Gallagher, "Communist Gennady Zyuganov Makes U.S. Nervous," *Chicago Tribune*, April 18, 1996, https://www.chicagotribune.com/news/ct-xpm-1996-04-18-9604180081-story.html.

280 WHEN DEMOCRACY BREAKS

He was not wrong. Against Russia's right-wing Communists and the openly fascist Liberal Democratic Party of Zhirinovsky stood Boris Yeltsin, Russia's president throughout the 1990s. Unlike his two main opponents, Yeltsin vocally supported democracy in Russia. In practice, though, he was far from a flawless democrat. He inherited a deep recession, a collapse in the government's administrative capacity, and a separatist dispute in Chechnya. Yet when a clash with Parliament over the scope of presidential authority reached a stalemate in 1993, he ordered the military to shell Parliament and force fresh legislative elections.

At no point in post-Soviet Russia has civil society or the population at large played a major role in politics beyond participation in elections. There was a moment in the final years of the Soviet Union when civil society groups called *neformaly* organized in Moscow and other large cities and tried to implement politics.[11] But the shock of the Soviet collapse—and the social and economic upheaval that accompanied it—removed much of the impulse behind them. The post-Soviet Russian government and Parliament were barely influenced by such groups. More influential were regional elites and business managers, who had been in power during the late Soviet period and who largely remained in power in post-Soviet Russia.[12] These elites had ascended to power via a nondemocratic system and had no reason to support political competition unless they had a specific personal interest to do so. The "democratic" political coalitions that had mobilized in Moscow and St. Petersburg in the late Soviet period are better described as anti-Soviet rather than pro-democracy. When the Soviet Union collapsed, so too did these coalitions. A small share of the population—part of the intelligentsia in Moscow and other large cities, for example—remained ideologically committed to democracy as a form of politics. But most of society, and even much of the intelligentsia, had no particular attachment to democratic institutions such as free elections, independent courts, or competitive politics. A belief in the need for a strong hand, by contrast, had been promoted by the Soviet government and had deep roots in Russian political culture. The last Soviet leader, Mikhail Gorbachev, and the first Russian leader, Boris Yeltsin, were more commonly criticized for being too weak than for being too authoritarian.

When Yeltsin talked about democracy, moreover, it was never clear what he meant. Certainly Yeltsin-style democracy meant something different from the Soviet system. Returning to the Soviet era was never popular, even though Russians missed the social benefits the Soviet state provided. To Yeltsin, building democracy appeared to mean something like building a European-style society, wealthier and more "modern" than Russia's. His goal, he said, was to "jump from

---

[11] V. A. Pecheneva, ed., *Neformaly—Kto oni, kuda zovut* (Moscow: Politizdat, 1990); Carole Sigman, *Clubs Politiques et Perestroika en Russie: Subversion sans Dissidence* (Paris: Karthala, 2009).
[12] Grigorii Golosov, "Russian Political Parties and the 'Bosses,'" *Party Politics* 3, no. 1 (1997): 5–21.

WHY RUSSIA'S DEMOCRACY BROKE   281

the gray, stagnant, totalitarian past into a cloudless, prosperous, and civilized future."[13] Because the prosperous West had elections and other democratic institutions, Russia needed them, too. Many Russians at the time believed there was a link between democracy, modernity, and prosperity. But the social instability of the 1990s in Russia discredited the idea that political competition would necessarily produce prosperity. Absent that, support for democracy per se was weak. The Soviet media and educational system had spent decades insisting that democracy was a fraud and that citizens' preferences did not matter. Russia's deeply flawed political system of the 1990s, in which average citizens were very weakly represented, appeared to many Russians to prove the Soviet critique correct.

Postimperial nostalgia, a weak party system, hyperinflation, unemployment, anti-Semitism, nationalism, and a violent struggle for executive power: the first decade of independent Russia replicated the ills of Weimar politics. It is easy to understand, therefore, why many analysts lived through the 1990s in constant anticipation of a coup, a revolution, a Reichstag fire, or a fascist electoral victory.

Yet Russian democracy did not end in a flash or a fire. It limped on for nearly a decade after Yeltsin's storming of Parliament, only to be snuffed out by the next generation of political elites. And rather than being overturned in a coup or a rebellion, Russian democracy was degraded steadily over time, via bogus court proceedings and a takeover of the media. Russian democracy did not end with the victory of nationalist parties. In elections today, Putin continues to face the nationalists of the 1990s, and he is far more popular than they, even though he presents himself as a moderate alternative. The Kremlin has used victorious wars—most notably, the annexation of Crimea in 2014—to bolster its popularity. But this nationalist shift in Kremlin politics followed rather than preceded the collapse of Russia's democracy, coming a decade after Putin consolidated power. The Russian government's use of alleged "fifth-columnists" to justify repression, a trend that intensified around the annexation of Crimea, also came well after Russia's democratic breakdown.

To understand why Russia's democracy broke, therefore, Weimar Germany provides a useful foil. Russians and foreigners in the 1990s feared that the country's democracy would be imperiled by a fascist putsch, facilitated by a far-right electoral victory, inspired by economic discontent, and justified by citing enemies at home and abroad. In fact, Russia's democracy was broken by a coalition of the center that was less ethnically nationalist than the country at large. Russian democracy broke at a time when Russia's economy was booming and when the country enjoyed relatively amiable relations with neighbors and other

[13] Timothy Colton, *Yeltsin: A Life* (New York: Basic Books, 2008), 2.

282   WHEN DEMOCRACY BREAKS

great powers. Russia's democracy survived the "Weimar moment" of the 1990s, in other words, and broke at exactly the point that it should have consolidated.

Why did this happen? This chapter will first examine different metrics and definitions of Russian democracy, noting that even in the 1990s, Russia's political system was deeply flawed and can be considered democratic only under the loosest definition. Yet it was at least competitive, in a way it has not been since. There was a notable slump in political competition and media diversity in the early 2000s, following Putin's consolidation of power. Second, the chapter will examine three explanations of why political competition in Russia disappeared: structural hangovers from the Soviet period, the centralization of power in the 1990s under President Yeltsin, and the policies implemented by Russia's president after 2000, Putin. Third, the chapter examines the crucial years between 1999 and 2003, when Russian political competition ended and when control over the media was centralized.

Finally, the chapter will contrast Russia's experience with its neighbor Ukraine. Like Russia, Ukraine had a tumultuous and semi-democratic 1990s; like Russia, Ukrainian democracy was dominated by oligarchs and only occasionally responsive to popular demands. But in the mid-2000s, the two countries' paths diverged. Democratic competition in Russia ended during its 2003 parliamentary and 2004 presidential elections, neither of which was genuinely competitive. Ukraine's 2004 presidential election was also deeply flawed, because the first iteration of the election was rigged in favor of the incumbent's preferred successor. Yet because, unlike in Russia, the Ukrainian state had not crushed all competition, the rigged election sparked mass protests that succeeded in demanding a new, clean vote that brought the rival candidate to power. Russia's 2004 presidential election was rather different: Putin was reelected to a second term with 71% of the vote, in an election devoid of debate, substantive media coverage, or genuine competition. The end of political competition in Russia, in turn, left no check on the government's power when the Kremlin decided to begin restricting rights more broadly.

When Did Russian Democracy Break?

The structure of Russian politics is different today than it was in 2000, when Putin was first elected president. Russia's Constitution today has no provisions that are incompatible with democratic governance. The country has political parties, a variety of candidates, and elections in which the votes are usually (though not always) tallied broadly accurately.[14] If you don't look closely—and

---

[14] Notable exceptions include the 2018 Primoriye gubernatorial contest; the 2011 parliamentary election; and nearly every vote in Chechnya. See Andrew Konitzer, *Voting for Russia's Governors: Regional*

WHY RUSSIA'S DEMOCRACY BROKE   283

Russia's government does not encourage anyone to do so—you could mistake the formal institutions of Russian politics for those of a democracy.

If you do look closely, however, you see that political institutions don't work in the same way as do similar institutions in democratic systems. The winner of Russian presidential elections, for example, is known in advance. The country's four major political parties compete for parliamentary seats, but they almost never criticize Putin.[15] The parties run candidates for president, but only with the aim of winning second place. The state-controlled media covers presidential and parliamentary elections diligently but ensures that candidates with critical ideas get no airtime. Any politician who opposes Putin and has a chance of winning a medium-size following is harassed by the legal system and prevented from competing.

In the 1990s, before the Putin era, politics worked differently. To be sure, Russia's government in the 1990s was far from a model of democracy. It was unrepresentative, unresponsive, and at times authoritarian. It had deep and enduring flaws. Its only real political party was the Communist Party, which retained Soviet-era authoritarian instincts. Legislators sold their votes to the highest bidder, while judges sold court decisions and journalists sold favorable news coverage. A small class of oligarchs played an outsized role. There were few independent organizations, whether NGOs or labor unions, to mediate between the population and the government. By many tests of democratic governance, Russia in the 1990s would have failed. Yet there is one test that it would have passed: Russian electoral politics were competitive and unpredictable—a sharp

---

Elections and Accountability under Yeltsin and Putin (Baltimore: Johns Hopkins University Press, 2005); "Russian Communist Hunger Strike over 'Rigged' Far East vote," BBC, September 17, 2018, https://www.bbc.com/news/world-europe-45546006; "'Miraculous' Election Win for Kremlin-Backed Candidate Causes Protests in Russia's Far-East," *Independent*, September 17, 2018, https://www.independent.co.uk/news/world/europe/russia-election-primorsky-krai-kremlin-communist-voters-fraud-a8541006.html; "Ищенко сообщил о подаче исков по возможным нарушениям на выборах в Приморье," *RIA*, September 17, 2018, https://ria.ru/20180917/1528709563.html; "'Голос' сообщил о массовой фальсификации на повторных выборах главы Приморья," *Novaya Gazeta*, December 25, 2018, https://novayagazeta.ru/articles/2018/12/25/147911-golos-soobschil-o-massovoy-falsifikatsii-na-povtornyh-vyborah-glavy-primorya; "Сказка об украденных выборах в Приморье," *Golos*, December 25, 2018, https://www.golosinfo.org/ru/articles/143130.

[15] Hans Oversloot and Ruben Verheul, "Managing Democracy: Political Parties and the State in Russia," *Journal of Communist Studies and Transition Politics* 22, no. 3 (2006): 383–405; Neil Robinson, "Classifying Russia's Party System: The Problem of 'Relevance' in a Time of Uncertainty," *Journal of Communist Studies and Transition Politics* 14, nos. 1–2 (1998): 159–177; Jonathan Riggs and Peter J. Schraeder, "Russia's Political Party System as an Impediment to Democratization," *Demokratizatsiya* 12, no. 2 (2004): 265–293; Kenneth Wilson, "Political Parties under Putin: Party-System Development and Democracy," in *Institutions, Ideas and Leadership in Russian Politics,* ed. Julie Newton and William Tompson (London: Palgrave Macmillan), 137–158; Henry E. Hale, *Why Not Parties in Russia? Democracy, Federalism, and the State* (Cambridge: Cambridge University Press, 2005).

284   WHEN DEMOCRACY BREAKS

contrast from today's Russia, in which all important political questions are decided before elections occur. In the 1990s, the winner of elections was not known in advance, and the government often lost. I will define democracy as a form of government that includes three aspects:

- Regular, free, fair, and competitive elections.
- Broad-based participation in political processes.
- Protection of individual and minority group political rights.

By each of these metrics, Russia was at best a partial democracy in the 1990s. It is substantially less of a democracy today.

Modern Russia has had only a handful of competitive elections for Parliament or the presidency. There have been none since current President Putin and his team consolidated control. Over the past two decades, not a single Russian election could have realistically caused a turnover in power. In today's Russia, elections serve multiple political purposes. They are most important as a tool for Moscow to test the competence of local elites, who are judged in part based on voter turnout.[16] What elections have not done is offer voters a real choice. Instead, voters are given a fake choice, between President Putin (or, briefly, Dmitry Medvedev) and candidates from large parties that do not seek to oust Putin (e.g., the Communists, the far-right Liberal Democrats) or from small parties that will win at most several percentage points of the vote. Genuine opposition candidates who threaten to win a sizable vote share, such as Alexei Navalny, are not allowed to run. In addition to not offering voters a real choice, Kremlin-backed candidates have access to state resources to support their campaigns, while opposition candidates are all but barred from TV.

Russian elections were not always so stale. The vote that brought Yeltsin to power in 1991 was a surprise victory against the establishment candidate, Nikolai Ryzhkov.[17] The 1996 presidential election, in which Yeltsin faced Communist candidate Gennady Zyuganov, surprised everyone—Yeltsin included—when Yeltsin won reelection. True, these elections were marred by widespread allegations of illegal campaign tactics, notably of businesses and oligarchs violating campaign finance laws and buying votes. Yet the votes were probably counted roughly accurately, and in providing voters a clear, policy-relevant choice between Yeltsin and Zyuganov, the election passed a low bar of basic

---

[16] Stephen Holmes and Ivan Krastev, "An Autopsy of Managed Democracy," *Journal of Democracy* 23, no. 3 (July 2012): 33–45.
[17] Stephen White, Ian McAllister, and Olga Kryshtanovskaya, "El'tsin and His Voters: Popular Support in the 1991 Russian Presidential Elections and After," *Europe-Asia Studies* 46, no. 2 (1994): 285–303.; Viktor Sheinis, "August 1991: A Pyrrhic Victory," *Russian Politics & Law* 45, no. 5 (2007): 6–25.

democratic practice.[18] In Russia's 1996 presidential election, for example, voters were given a choice, crude though it was, between retaining Yeltsin and his advocacy of private property or opting for the Communist Zyuganov, who promised to roll back capitalism.[19] The result was unpredictable and had meaningful ramifications for government policy.[20] By contrast, Russia's most recent presidential vote, in 2018, had no policy ramifications, and candidates made no effort to stake out positions different from Putin's, especially on issues that mattered. In the 1990s, in other words, Russia had a deeply flawed political system, with limited popular participation in governance, few independent institutions, yet nevertheless competitive and unpredictable elections. Today's Russia has all the flaws of the 1990s, but it has dispensed with the competition.

Three Explanations of Why Russia's Democracy Failed

Why did Russia abandon electoral competition? Scholars have put forth three major explanations. The first focuses on structural forces that delegitimized democracy, reducing Russians' willingness to defend it and increasing the number of people who saw no value in democracy. As Russia first abandoned Soviet authoritarianism in the early 1990s and forged new political institutions, multiple factors delegitimized competitive politics. First, the period of democratization was also a period of deep economic crisis, marked by social dislocation and falling living standards.[21] Though this crisis was mostly a holdover from the final years of the Soviet Union, the population blamed economic pain on the new political system. In addition, the emergence of competitive politics coincided with a collapse in central state capacity and a rise in the influence of mafias and oligarchs. The Russian public blamed this shift, too, on the country's new democratic institutions. Finally, democratization in the late 1980s and early 1990s

---

[18] David S. Mason and Svetlana Sidorenko-Stephenson, "Public Opinion and the 1996 Elections in Russia: Nostalgic and Statist, Yet Pro-Market and Pro-Yeltsin," *Slavic Review* 56, no. 4 (1997): 698–717; Mikhail Myagkov, Peter Ordeshook, and Alexander Sobyanin, "The Russian Electorate, 1991–1996," *Post-Soviet Affairs* 13, no. 2 (1997): 134–166; Erik Depoy, "Boris Yeltsin and the 1996 Russian Presidential Election," *Presidential Studies Quarterly* 26, no. 4 (1996): 1140–1164; Michael McFaul, *Russia's 1996 Presidential Election: The End of Polarized Politics* (Stanford: Hoover Press, 1997); Daniel Treisman, "Why Yeltsin Won," *Foreign Affairs* 75, no. 5 (September 1996): 64–77; Yitzhak Brudny, "In Pursuit of the Russian Presidency: Why and How Yeltsin Won the 1996 Presidential Election," *Communist and Post-Communist Studies* 30, no. 3 (1997): 255–275.

[19] Andrew Wilson's discussion of "virtual politics"—a common post-Soviet situation where voters are given fake choices—does not wholly apply to Russian politics in the 1990s, where at key moments such as the 1993 and 1996 elections voters were given real choices between far-right nationalists, Communists, and capitalist candidates; see Andrew Wilson, *Virtual Politics: Faking Democracy in the Post-Soviet World* (New Haven: Yale University Press, 2005).

[20] Michael McFaul, "Russia's 1996 Presidential Election," *Post-Soviet Affairs* 12, no. 4 (1996): 344.

[21] Peter Reddaway and Dmitri Glinksi, *The Tragedy of Russia's Reforms: Market Bolshevism against Democracy* (Washington, DC: U.S. Institute of Peace, 2001).

286   WHEN DEMOCRACY BREAKS

coincided with the collapse of the Soviet/Russian Empire, causing nationalistically inclined Russians to associate democracy with geopolitical weakness. All these factors reduced the popularity of democracy.

A second explanation for the failure of Russia's democracy focuses on the decisions of Russia's first president, Yeltsin. Some scholars argue that Russia's competitive politics would have been preserved if only Yeltsin's instincts were more democratic. For example, at a moment of constitutional crisis in 1993, Yeltsin ordered the military to storm Parliament and pushed through a new constitution by force, which set a precedent for resolving constitutional disputes violently and which substantially expanded presidential power. Second, during the 1996 presidential election, Yeltsin relied on illegal donations from oligarchs to fund his reelection campaign. Had Yeltsin not centralized power in 1993, and had he run a cleaner campaign in 1996 (a campaign that might have resulted in his defeat), many scholars argue, Russia would have entered the 2000s with a tradition of rotating presidential power via elections and with a stronger Parliament that would have been able to check executive branch excesses.[22]

A third explanation focuses on the decision and policies of Yeltsin's successor, Putin. Even if the circumstances of Russia's democratization in the early 1990s were not favorable for developing deep democratic roots, and even if Yeltsin was a mediocre steward of the country's democratic institutions, Russia could have retained competitive electoral politics were it not for a slow-motion coup under President Putin. Upon becoming president, Putin centralized authority by extralegal means, accumulating far more power than Yeltsin ever had. He began by taking down news outlets owned by oligarchs who criticized him, such as Boris Berezovsky and Vladimir Gusinsky, exiling both oligarchs on trumped-up charges.[23] Then Putin jailed oligarch Mikhail Khodorkovsky, again on bogus charges, sending a message that unauthorized political action would be punished.[24] Yeltsin's main rivals were elected to Parliament; Putin's, by contrast, were jailed.

Putin had the power to take these steps because he mobilized security service networks in government and in the business world, drawing on his background in the KGB.[25] The number of current and former security services personnel in top Russian government positions increased markedly in Putin's early years.[26]

---

[22] For an argument that a strong presidency and weak Parliament facilitated the decline of democracy, see, e.g., Steven Fish, *Democracy Derailed in Russia: The Failure of Open Politics* (Cambridge: Cambridge University Press 2005).

[23] See, e.g., Peter Baker and Susan Glasser, *Kremlin Rising: Vladimir Putin's Russia and the End of Revolution* (New York: Scribner, 2005).

[24] For an overview, see Chris Miller, *Putinomics: Power and Money in Resurgent Russia* (Chapel Hill: University of North Carolina Press, 2018), chs. 2–3.

[25] Nikolai Petrov, "The Security Dimension of the Federal Reforms," in *The Dynamics of Russian Politics*, ed. Peter Reddaway and Robert Orttung (Lanham, MD: Rowman & Littlefield, 2003), 2:7–32.

[26] Olga Khryshtanovskaya and Stephen White, "Putin's Militocracy," *Post-Soviet Affairs* 19, no. 4 (2003): 289–306.

WHY RUSSIA'S DEMOCRACY BROKE   287

With the support of the security services, Putin defanged the media and ended electoral competition. Yeltsin's allies lost every parliamentary election they contested during his presidential term. Putin's party, by contrast, won majorities in every parliamentary vote.

Contrasting Russia's 1999 and 2003 Parliamentary Elections

How do we know that the Soviet legacy, the economic collapse, and Yeltsin's centralization of power were not the key factors in undermining Russian democracy? One reason is that the last parliamentary election of Yeltsin's time in office was the cleanest and most competitive that independent Russia ever had. The Organization for Security and Cooperation in Europe (OSCE) has monitored each of independent Russia's presidential and parliamentary elections, studying whether the media environment was fair, incumbents and challengers had a level playing field, and votes were counted accurately. The OSCE monitors described the 1999 parliamentary elections—the last elections before Putin took power—as "a benchmark in the [Russian] Federation's advancement toward representative democracy."[27] The subsequent parliamentary vote, in 2003, was assessed rather differently by OSCE monitors: votes were counted accurately, but "the election failed to meet a number of OSCE commitments for democratic elections, most notably those pertaining to: unimpeded access to the media on a non-discriminatory basis, a clear separation between the State and political parties, and guarantees to enable political parties to compete on the basis of equal treatment."[28]

This difference in electoral quality was visible in election results. Voters responded to a lack of competition in 2003 by voting "against all"—or by not voting at all. Turnout was lower in 2003, at 55%, compared to 61% in 1999.[29] In 2003, 4.7% of voters chose "against all," compared to 3.3% in 1999.[30] The biggest change, however, was the distribution of parliamentary seats. In 1999, given real competition, the opposition Communist Party won the largest vote share, with 24% of the vote by party list.[31] The Fatherland–All Russia Party, led by Yeltsin's rival Yevgeny Primakov, won 13%. Parties that were sympathetic to Yeltsin,

---

[27] Organization for Security and Cooperation in Europe, "Russian Federation: Elections to the State Duma 19 December 1999 Final Report," Warsaw, OSCE, 2000, 3.

[28] Organization for Security and Cooperation in Europe, "Russian Federation: Elections to the State Duma 7 December 2003," Warsaw, OSCE, 2004, 3.

[29] OSCE, "Elections to the State Duma 19 December 1999," 26; OSCE, "Elections to the State Duma 7 December 2003," 23.

[30] OSCE, "Elections to the State Duma 19 December 1999," 26; OSCE, "Elections to the State Duma 7 December 2003," 24.

[31] OSCE, "Elections to the State Duma 19 December 1999," 26.

288   WHEN DEMOCRACY BREAKS

including Unity and the Union of Rightist Forces, won 23% and 8%, respectively. Per Russian electoral law, half of parliamentary seats were distributed by party-list and half by single-mandate districts. In the districts, many candidates ran as independents, so neither the opposition nor the pro-presidential parties had a majority in Parliament. Yet the opposition held the largest bloc, and with 40% of seats had a strong voice in parliamentary affairs.[32]

The results of the 2003 vote were quite different. A new party—United Russia—was created with the aim of backing President Putin. It won 37% of the party-list vote, and thanks to strong performance in single-mandate districts won a total of 223 seats in the Duma—nearly a majority. Opposition parties were crushed. The Communists lost over half their seats, declining from 113 to 52. Liberal parties were all but ejected from Parliament, with the right-liberal Union of Right Forces winning only 3 seats, down from 29, and the left-liberal Yabloko winning 4, down from 20. A new political party, Rodina, was created by Putin allies to attract voters who previously supported the Communists.[33] It won 36 seats, enough to give pro-Kremlin parties a decisive majority.[34]

What explains the difference between the 1999 and 2003 parliamentary vote in Russia? One explanation might be the country's strong economic performance in the early 2000s or approval of Putin's policies in Chechnya and his efforts to centralize power. Putin was genuinely popular in the early 2000s, but the electoral success of his allies relied on more than presidential charisma. Some of the irregularities noted by OSCE observers in 2003 were visible in previous parliamentary votes. For example, both the 1999 and 2003 elections were criticized by OSCE monitors for failing to meet international best standards in polling and counting, but this does not appear to have significantly affected either set of results.[35]

Yet the 2003 parliamentary election was far more biased in favor of pro-presidential parties than previous votes had been, a bias which made real competition impossible. The media was significantly more centralized in 2003. To be sure, the 1999 parliamentary election included biased and tendentious media coverage, which was shaped by the oligarchs who owned the country's national TV channels. The OSCE described the 1999 TV environment as a "media war," noting that TV station ORT, influenced by oligarch Boris Berezovsky, had coverage highly favorable to the pro-government party Unity, while "TVcentre showed obvious support for [Yeltsin's rival] Yuri Luzhkov."[36]

---

[32] This 40% figure counts the Communists and Fatherland–Our Russia as opposition.

[33] Tom Parfitt, "'Racist' Russian TV Advert Investigated," *Guardian*, November 10, 2005, https://www.theguardian.com/world/2005/nov/10/russia.tomparfitt.

[34] OSCE, "Elections to the State Duma 7 December 2003," 24.

[35] OSCE, "Elections to the State Duma 7 December 2003," 20–23; OSCE, "Elections to the State Duma 19 December 1999," 20–25.

[36] OSCE, "Elections to the State Duma 19 December 1999," 16.

WHY RUSSIA'S DEMOCRACY BROKE   289

The 2003 parliamentary election was also structured by undemocratic media practice—but unlike in 1999, which saw oligarchs competing via their control of TV stations, in 2003 all the TV stations parroted the government line, a line that was established in a centralized fashion, via meetings in the Kremlin.[37] There were no competing points of view. "Throughout the campaign," OSCE monitors reported, "the majority of media coverage was devoted to reports on the activities of President Putin. . . . Most media coverage was characterized by an overwhelming tendency of the State media to exhibit a clear bias in favour of [pro-government] United Russia and against the [opposition] CPRF [Communist Party of the Russian Federation]."[38] Private broadcasters were more balanced, but this could not balance out the pro-government bias on state channels. The OSCE reported:

> *First Channel* provided 19 per cent of its political and election news coverage to United Russia, all positive or neutral; the CPRF received 13 per cent of mostly negative coverage. *TV Russia* devoted 16 per cent of its prime time news to United Russia, with an overwhelmingly positive tone; in contrast, while the CPRF received a comparable amount of time, the tone of its coverage was mainly negative. *TV Centre*, a television controlled by the Moscow City administration, allocated 22 per cent of its prime time news coverage to United Russia, with an overwhelmingly positive slant, while the CPRF received 14 per cent of mainly negative coverage. State-funded broadcasters also produced a number of prime time news items discrediting the CPRF.[39]

The government's control of media coverage in the 2003 parliamentary vote encouraged even more aggressive media control during the 2004 presidential election, during which the OSCE observed that "state-controlled media comprehensively failed to meet its legal obligation to provide equal treatment to all candidates, displaying clear favouritism toward Mr. Putin."[40] Russian government control of the media has only tightened since.

---

[37] Vasily Gatov, "How the Kremlin and the Media Ended Up in Bed Together," *Moscow Times*, March 11, 2015, https://themoscowtimes.com/articles/how-the-kremlin-and-the-media-ended-up-in-bed-together-44663; Maria Lipman, "Media Manipulation and Political Control in Russia," Chatham House, January 2009 https://www.chathamhouse.org/sites/default/files/public/Research/Russia%20and%20Eurasia/300109lipman.pdf.

[38] OSCE, "Elections to the State Duma 7 December 2003," 15–16.

[39] OSCE, "Elections to the State Duma 7 December 2003," 16.

[40] Organization for Security and Cooperation in Europe, "Russian Federation: Presidential Election 14 March 2004," Warsaw, OSCE, 2004, 15.

290 WHEN DEMOCRACY BREAKS

The End of Political Competition

How was Putin's government able to consolidate control over the media and the electoral process and thereby end political competition? There was no coup, no crisis, no substantial change in legislation. The key change in Russian politics between 1999 and 2003 was Putin's assault on the oligarchs who had played a dominant and disruptive role in Russia. To do so, Putin turned to the security services to pressure the oligarchs, sending several into exile and jailing Russia's richest man. Those who remained got the message: they were not to participate in politics, nor to disagree with anything Putin did. Without the oligarchs, there were no remaining political forces who could contest elections, fund political parties, support media outlets—or compete with Putin.

On July 28, 2000, Putin held a meeting with twenty-one oligarchs in the Kremlin's Ekaterinsky Hall. "No clan, no oligarch, should come close to regional or federal authorities," he declared. "They should be kept equally far from politics."[41] "I don't really like the world 'oligarch,'" he explained. "An oligarch is a person with stolen money, who continues to plunder the national wealth using his special access to bodies of power and administration. I am doing everything to make sure this situation never repeats in Russia."[42] Yet not all the oligarchs listened. Putin decided to send a message.

The first oligarch to fall was Vladimir Gusinsky. Just months after Putin took power, Gusinsky, a banker turned media magnate, was arrested. Gusinsky was later released on the condition that he sell NTV, his television station that had been critical of Putin, and leave Russia. He promptly complied. Four months later, a second oligarch was attacked. Boris Berezovsky, whose businesses spanned automobiles to airlines, announced while traveling abroad that he would not return to Russia, fearing that the government would press charges against him, too. The exile of Gusinsky and Berezovsky was a devastating blow for Russian media, as these two oligarchs had each invested heavily in newspapers and TV stations. True, these media outlets usually parroted their owners' opinions, but they at least provided a point of view different from the government's.[43]

Not all oligarchs got the message from the exile of Gusinsky and Berezovsky. "These people who fuse power and capital: there will be no oligarchs of this kind as a class," Putin threatened, alluding to Stalin's campaign of eliminating kulaks—rich peasants—as a class. Many thousands were killed in Stalin's

---

[41] Thane Gustafson, *Wheel of Fortune* (Cambridge, MA: Belknap Press, 2017), 292, translation adjusted; cf. Maura Reynolds, "Putin Reaches Out to Oligarchs," *Los Angeles Times*, July 29, 2000, http://articles.latimes.com/2000/jul/29/news/mn-61087.

[42] Richard Sakwa, *Putin: Russia's Choice* (London: Routledge, 2007), 149.

[43] "Under Yeltsin, we 'oligarchs' helped stop Russia from reverting to its old, repressive ways," Berezovsky bragged; see Boris Berezovsky, "Our Reverse Revolution," *Washington Post*, October 16, 2000.

anti-kulak campaign. Putin wanted the oligarchs to understand: he was tough too. "The state has a club, the kind that you only need to use once: over the head," Putin explained. "We haven't used the club yet. But when we get seriously angry, we will use this club without hesitation."[44] Russia's richest man, banking and oil magnate Mikhail Khodorkovsky, was uniquely unwilling to play by the new rules. Khodorkovsky remained involved in politics, buying the support of Duma members and even getting his firm's executives elected to the Duma.[45] One legislator in Khodorkovsky's pay once made a speech on the floor of the Duma with a cell phone pressed to his ear, reciting words fed to him by Khodorkovsky's staff.[46] On top of this, Khodorkovsky meddled in Russian foreign policy, opening talks to build an oil pipeline to China, in direct contradiction of the government's wishes.[47] And he accused Putin's ally Sergei Bogdanchikov, the chair of the state-owned oil firm Rosneft, of corruption.[48]

In 2000, Putin allowed Gusinsky and Berezovsky to leave Russia and live in exile (though Berezovsky died under suspicious circumstances in 2013). Yet Khodorkovsky refused to submit, aiming to play a major role in the 2003 parliamentary vote, and—many suspected—planning to run for president himself in 2004.[49] The threat of exile was not enough, so Putin opted for tougher measures. When Khodorkovsky's private jet landed to refuel in the Siberian city of Novosibirsk on October 25, 2003, it was surrounded by troops from the FSB's Alfa Brigade, the country's most elite security force. Khodorkovsky was thrown in jail. His business was seized and resold to one of Putin's allies at a knockdown price. Khodorkovsky himself spent a decade behind bars.

How was Putin able to take down the oligarchs? Above all, by drawing on security services networks and strengthening their role in Russian politics. The means Putin used to trap opposing oligarchs, including trumped-up legal cases and arrests by elite special forces personnel, were facilitated by his KGB background. It let him mobilize the security services in a way that Yeltsin, for example, could not.

Putin appointed a slew of current and former security services personnel to top positions.[50] Of the seven officials initially appointed to head federal districts, for

---

[44] Miller, *Putinomics*, 1.
[45] Gustafson, *Wheel of Fortune*, 295.
[46] Gustafson, *Wheel of Fortune*, 295.
[47] Gustafson, *Wheel of Fortune*, 290–291.
[48] Gustafson, *Wheel of Fortune*, 286, 290–292.
[49] Seth Midans and Erin A. Arvedlund, "Police in Russia Seize Oil Tycoon," *New York Times*, October 26, 2003, https://www.nytimes.com/2003/10/26/world/police-in-russia-seize-oil-tyc oon.html; Alex Rodriguez, "Push into Politics Cited for Russian Tycoon's Fall," *Chicago Tribune*, November 16, 2003, https://www.chicagotribune.com/news/ct-xpm-2003-11-16-0311160141-story.html; Richard Sakwa, *Putin and the Oligarch: The Khodorkovsky-Yukos Affair* (London: I. B. Tauris, 2014).
[50] The subsequent paragraphs draw on Miller, *Putinomics*, ch. 2.

292 WHEN DEMOCRACY BREAKS

example, two were KGB officers, two were army generals, and one was a police general. Only two of the seven were said to be civilians, and even one of these was alleged to have KGB ties.[51] Chief federal inspectors in each region were drawn from the ranks of the security services.[52] Putin solidified his personal control over the security services, naming Sergey Ivanov as defense minister and Boris Gryzlov as interior minister. Meanwhile, Mikhail Fradkov was put in charge of the tax police. Both Ivanov and Fradkov are believed to have a background in the KGB, while Gryzlov was a St. Petersburg politician and a former classmate of FSB director Nikolai Patrushev.[53] The security forces increasingly answered to Putin personally.[54]

The expansion of Russia's security services in politics that occurred during the early 2000s was not inevitable. Putin's predecessor as Yeltsin's prime minister, Sergey Kiriyenko, had no deep security services ties.[55] When Kiriyenko tried to confront gas company Gazprom over its nonpayment of taxes in 1998, the firm's leader asked, "Who do you think you are? . . . You're just a little boy."[56] The Gazprom boss faced no punishment. By contrast, the only three oligarchs who dared to treat Putin in such a way met very different fates: Gusinksy was exiled, Khodorkovsky was jailed, and Berezovsky was exiled and possibly murdered. To pressure the oligarchs, Putin used a full range of tools—legal pressure, media criticism, police raids, and the threat of assassination—to ensure that they stayed out of politics. By the 2003 parliamentary elections, all those who remained in Russia understood the message. As the oligarchs withdrew from politics, however, they were not replaced by civil society, independent media, or real political parties. They were replaced by centrally controlled media and fabricated political parties, all puppets of the Kremlin.

Why Ukraine and Russia Diverged

The end of political competition between 1999 and 2003 was the goal of the anti-oligarch campaign. Many Russians celebrated the demise of the independent

---

[51] Masha Gessen, *The Man Without a Face: The Unlikely Rise of Vladimir Putin* (London: Penguin Random House), 181.

[52] Petrov, "The Security Dimension of the Federal Reforms," 7–8.

[53] Petrov, "The Security Dimension of the Federal Reforms," 7–8; Miriam Elder, "Fradkov Named Foreign Spymaster," *Moscow Times*, October 8, 2007, https://www.themoscowtimes.com/archive/fradkov-named-foreign-spymaster; see also Andrei Soldatov and Irina Borogan, *The New Nobility: The Restoration of Russia's Security State and the Enduring Legacy of the KGB* (New York: Public Affairs, 2011).

[54] This paragraph draws on Miller, *Putinomics*, ch. 2.

[55] Kiriyenko's grandfather, however, had been an agent. Victor Yasmann, "Russia: Sergei Kiriyenko—Russia's 'Kinder Surprise,'" RFE/RL, February 15, 2006, https://www.rferl.org/a/1065790.html.

[56] Andrei Shleifer and Daniel Treisman, *Without a Map* (Cambridge, MA: MIT Press, 2001), 153.

political influence of the country's corrupt and self-interested oligarchs. Though some of the oligarchs had real business acumen, many had bribed and stolen their way to wealth and influence. But in their pursuit of self-interest, they provided electoral competition which Russia's political system has since lacked. In the 1990s, anti-Yeltsin political parties relied on oligarchs and businesses for financing and logistical support. After the defeat of the oligarchs, Russia's government did not become more responsive to popular demands. Civil society and labor groups, which never played a major role in post-Soviet politics, did not fill the gap. The media did not become more objective or more constructive. The defeat of the oligarchs did not make space for democracy; it ended political competition. Indeed, this was the goal: Russian elites—and not only those in the security services—believed that politics in the 1990s had been too tumultuous. The solution, they believed, was more centralization and less competition, which they thought would provide better governance.

The quality of Russian governance did improve during the 2000s, and the economy grew rapidly. Economic growth was caused in part by rising oil prices, in part by the recovery after the country's 1998 financial crisis, and in part by better administration. Governance improvements were the result largely of projects begun in the late 1990s, as technocrats reshaped the post-Soviet administrative structure, adapting it to a new society and new economy. One positive effect of the defeat of the oligarchs was an increase in tax revenue, as the government managed to extract more tax from energy companies in the 2000s.[57] Yet in the medium term, Russia's government tax take is probably lower today than it would be if Russia were a democracy. Russians have no means of demanding higher-quality public services, which polls suggest they would like and which competitive elections might have made possible. And to speak of the "defeat" of the oligarchs is only partially correct: they were tamed politically, but in economic terms they are as dominant as ever. They can still break laws, and often do—but only when the president backs them, which he often does. The defeat of the oligarchs did not, in other words, cause an evident improvement in the quality of governance.

A second argument made in favor of Putin's crackdown on the oligarchs is that oligarch-driven political competition offered no benefits over the uncompetitive system that Russia has today. There is little doubt that a political system based on oligarchic competition is far from optimal. It is perhaps the worst type of competition. But the divergent experiences of Ukraine and Russia after 2000 suggest that the worst type of competition is better than no competition at all.

The structural argument for Russia's democratic failure—the economic collapse, the weak institutions, the postimperial syndrome—at first glance appears to be a powerful explanation of why Russian democracy broke. It is difficult to

---

[57] See Miller, *Putinomics*, chs. 2–3.

294 WHEN DEMOCRACY BREAKS

imagine a less auspicious environment for solidifying a nascent democratic system. Yet many of Russia's neighbors faced a similar array of challenges, and not all ended up with a political system as autocratic as Russia's. The post-Soviet country that began its independence in a position most like Russia's is Ukraine. True, thanks in part to energy riches, Russia always was and remains significantly wealthier than Ukraine.[58] By most other metrics, however, the two countries looked similar in 1991. In both countries, roughly 70% of the population lived in cities. The two countries had similar tertiary-school enrollment rates (45% in Ukraine versus 49% in Russia) and similar life expectancies (sixty-nine and sixty-seven, respectively).[59] Both are multiethnic countries, and Ukraine is to a large extent bilingual. Both countries saw political mobilization and fracturing along ethnic, linguistic, and regional lines. Both faced recurring disputes over borders and competing demands for centralization and autonomy. Neither country had a clearly defined and universally accepted sense of political community.[60]

Both Russia and Ukraine had contested, unpredictable, and substantive elections during the 1990s. Control of the presidency and Parliament was decided by elections. Parties represented different political ideologies, interest groups, and regions. Opposition parties often defeated incumbents, as in 1994 in Ukraine, when President Leonid Kravchuk was unseated by Leonid Kuchma, and in Russia, where opponents of President Yeltsin repeatedly won majorities in Parliament. Results were often unpredictable, as in Russia's 1996 presidential election, when Yeltsin surprised most analysts by defeating Zyuganov. In both Russia and Ukraine during the 1990s, opposing political forces sought power via the electoral system, and voters could express preferences about policy regarding economics and identity by voting for rival parties.

Russia and Ukraine also shared many similar problems in their democracies in the 1990s. In both countries, media outlets such as TV stations and newspapers were controlled by competing oligarchs, with few quality or objective sources of information.[61] In both countries, a small group of oligarchs played an outsized role in the political process. They stole funds, they bought members

---

[58] International Monetary Fund, "IMF DataMapper," accessed January 23, 2019, https://www.imf.org/external/datamapper/NGDPDPC@WEO/UKR/RUS.

[59] World Bank Group, "Data Bank World Development Indicators," accessed January 23, 2019, https://databank.worldbank.org/data/reports.aspx?source=2&country=RUS.

[60] The only post-Soviet country that comes as close to Ukraine in its similarity to Russia is Belarus—a country which today is governed as autocratically as Russia. Yet to understand why Russia's democracy broke, comparison with Belarus is less insightful than comparison with Ukraine, for a simple reason: Belarus never had democracy. Only two and a half years separated the collapse of the Soviet Union from the establishment of an autocratic government under Aleksandr Lukashenko, the dictator who rules Belarus to this day. In 1992 and 1993, before Lukashenko consolidated power, the country's government was de facto controlled by the old Soviet-era regime, which had no interest in democracy and did everything possible to prevent it from emerging.

[61] Laura Belin, "The Russian Media in the 1990s," *Journal of Communist Studies and Transition Politics* 18, no. 1 (2002): 139–160; Olena Nikolayenko, "Press Freedom during the 1994 and 1999

WHY RUSSIA'S DEMOCRACY BROKE   295

of Parliament, and they corrupted the media. Yet Russia's crackdown on the oligarchs—and Ukraine's lack of a crackdown—demonstrates that oligarchs were the main force for political competition in both countries.

Russia was not the only post-Soviet country in the early 2000s in which the ruling elite tried to squash electoral competition. In Ukraine's 2004 presidential election, outgoing president Leonid Kuchma backed candidate Viktor Yanukovych, who was supported by the oligarchs Rinat Akhmetov and Viktor Medvedchuk.[62] Behind in the polls, Yanukovych and his backers tried to rig the electoral process, blatantly changing the vote count in certain regions. Yet unlike in Russia, where the population accepted the end of electoral competition in the 2000s, the Ukrainian population did not. The middle classes of Kyiv and other cities took to the streets demanding a new vote, free of manipulation. The protests could not have succeeded without the anger of the Ukrainian population, their persistence in mobilizing, or their bravery in confronting the government despite the risk that it would crack down violently. Yet the protests for a clean election in 2004—which came to be known as the Orange Revolution— succeeded only because Ukraine's oligarchs and regional elites were also divided.

Consider, first, the political coalition that backed the orange candidate, Viktor Yushchenko. Yushchenko himself was a technocratic former head of the country's central bank. He made a name for himself by pushing economic and governance reforms and was supported by many small and medium-size businesses.[63] Yet key to Yushchenko's coalition was a political party leader named Yuliya Tymoshenko, who had come to prominence in a partnership with politician and oligarch Pavel Lazarenko, who played a major role in Ukraine's gas sector, from which he is reported to have stolen huge sums.[64] Tymoshenko would play a major role in Ukraine's deeply corrupt energy sector over the subsequent decade.[65] Yushchenko's political coalition, in other words, depended on oligarchic support. Had Ukraine's government pushed the oligarchs out of politics, as had Russia's, Yushchenko could not have succeeded in challenging a candidate backed by an incumbent president.

Ukraine's media landscape was also different in 2004 than Russia's. As in precrackdown Russia, Ukraine's TV channels were largely owned by oligarchs, who

---

Presidential Elections in Ukraine: A Reverse Wave?," *Europe-Asia Studies* 56, no. 5 (2004): 661–686; Natalya Ryabinska, "The Media Market and Media Ownership in Post-Communist Ukraine," *Problems of Post-Communism* 58, no. 6 (2011): 3–20.

[62] Anders Aslund, *How Ukraine Became a Market Economy and Democracy* (Washington, DC: Peterson Institute for International Economics, 2009), 181.

[63] Anders Aslund, "The Economic Policy of Ukraine after the Orange Revolution," *Eurasian Geography and Economics* 46, no. 5 (2005): 327–353.

[64] Aslund, *How Ukraine Became a Market Economy and Democracy*, 94–97.

[65] M. E. Sharpe, *The Challenge of Integration* (New York: East West Institute, 1998).

296 WHEN DEMOCRACY BREAKS

shaped news coverage in their personal interest. In Ukraine's 2004 vote, most of the oligarchs who owned TV stations supported Yanukovych, creating a relatively uniform media landscape. Yet unlike in Russia, where the media was purged following the exile of the media barons, Ukraine's TV stations still included journalists with a diverse array of political views. As it became clear that Yanukovych had stolen the election, journalists on Ukrainian TV stations openly revolted. On one prominent station, 1 + 1, "the entire news team of producers, reporters, and editors walked out, forcing the station's news director and government loyalist Vyacheslav Pikhovshek to hold multi-hour talk marathons by himself."[66] Such moves kept the opposition from the airwaves—but made it impossible for pro-Yanukovych forces to pretend that the country was unified behind him.

The competing forces in Ukrainian politics made it easier for Yushchenko to negotiate with his opponents for a new election to replace the one that Yanukovych had rigged. One of Yushchenko's strategies was to peel off parts of Yanukovych's oligarchic coalition by promising oligarchs that their interests would be respected under a Yushchenko presidency.[67] Yushchenko was able to make commitments that interlocutors found credible because the competitive nature of Ukraine's political system meant that no election was winner-take-all. Yushchenko would be constrained by a disparate coalition, by regional governments that he would not control, security services that were themselves politically divided, and by a fractious Parliament.[68] There were many different parties and factions in Parliament, with membership amorphous and parliamentarians often selling votes to the oligarch willing to pay the most that day.[69] An optimal democracy this was not—but nor was it a system conducive to consolidating authoritarian power. When, a decade and several election cycles later, Yanukovych won the presidency and tried to create a more authoritarian system, he was ousted after the Maidan protests in 2014—again by a coalition of Kyiv's middle classes and self-interested oligarchs. Yanukovych cycled in and out of power, despite his best efforts at establishing an authoritarian regime. Putin, by contrast, has proven impossible to dislodge.

Had Ukraine's government pushed its oligarchs out of politics in the early 2000s, stealing the 2004 election would have been far easier. In Russia, potentially popular opposition candidates such as Yushchenko are often barred from

[66] Adrian Karatnycky, "Ukraine's Orange Revolution," in *Crisis in Ukraine*, ed. Gideon Rose (New York: Foreign Affairs, 2014).

[67] Taras Kuzio, "Ukrainian Economic Policy after the Orange Revolution," *Eurasian Geography and Economics* 46, no. 5 (2005): 359.

[68] On political divisions in the security services and among regional governments, see Andrew Wilson, *Ukraine's Orange Revolution* (New Haven: Yale University Press, 2006), 135.

[69] Aslund, "The Economic Policy of Ukraine after the Orange Revolution," 340.

WHY RUSSIA'S DEMOCRACY BROKE   297

running for office on trumped-up charges. Had Russia not cracked down on the political role of its oligarchs, the 2003 parliamentary election and the 2004 presidential vote would almost certainly have been more competitive. One of the reasons Putin is said to have decided to arrest Khodorkovsky in 2003 is that the oligarch planned to play a role in the parliamentary vote and was considering running against Putin in the 2004 presidential race.[70]

"Consolidating Society" versus Consolidating Democracy

The argument that Russia lost electoral competition because the country's oligarchs were pushed out of politics is not a comfortable conclusion for those who believe that oligarchy is an antidemocratic form of governance. Putin himself claimed that his crackdown on the oligarchs was a move to bolster Russian democracy, and in the early 2000s many genuine democrats agreed with him. They feared a Weimar-style putsch, a victory of the far right, or a return of the Communists, this time in authoritarian-nationalist garb. Many observers, Russian and foreign, saw a "red-brown" coalition between fascists and Communists as the key threat to Russian democracy in the 1990s and early 2000s. Did Weimar Germany not face similar divisions, both the Nazis and the Communists attacking the center-left and center-right, degrading not only the popularity of those parties but popular faith in democracy itself? Surely the lesson of Weimar was that the centrist parties needed more backbone and more authority in the face of antidemocratic opponents? When oligarchs attacked the political center—often using illegal means to do so—surely a forceful response to their meddling was needed to uphold democracy against its opponents? Surely the center needed to be bolstered against the fascist and Communist-authoritarian parties that threatened the political center in the 1990s? What better way of limiting their influence than by cutting off their ability to raise funds from oligarchs?

The oligarchs were certainly an easy target. In the 1990s, Russian politics had been dominated by oligarchs and failed to provide for popular well-being. Many people's living standards fell. The quality of public services declined. The collapse of the Soviet system upended society, but the new system of the 1990s, in which oligarchs and mafias played a large role, hardly seemed more just. Russia needed a strong hand to discipline the oligarchs, reestablish state authority, and reorient government toward the public interest, many Russians believed. In his final years in office, Yeltsin had spoken of the need for leaders who were "democratic

---

[70] Sergei Guriev and Andrei Rachinsky, "The Role of Oligarchs in Russian Capitalism," *Journal of Economic Perspectives* 19, no. 1 (2005): 131–150.

298 WHEN DEMOCRACY BREAKS

and innovative yet steadfast in the military manner."[71] When he selected Putin as his successor, Yeltsin predicted that Putin would have the skills needed for "consolidating society"—which meant something different from consolidating democracy.[72]

Coming to power in the early 2000s, Putin promised stronger central authority that would better provide for the public interest. The promise of consolidating society underpinned the crackdown on the oligarchs, which everyone knew was made possible not by the rule of law but by force mobilized by Putin and his security services allies. For a moment in the early 2000s, it seemed plausible that the newly empowered government might prove more responsive to public interests. But its method of centralizing power, destroying the media, bending the courts to its will, and ending political competition eliminated the institutions by which the public can force governments to address their concerns.

It is possible to imagine a different method of limiting the oligarchs' power that could have bolstered rather than degraded democracy in Russia. Such a campaign would have used genuine legal cases and higher taxes rather than police raids and show trials. Yet this option was not on offer. There were no popular political parties that could have promoted or executed such a policy. Parties such as Yabloko advocated popular measures such as legal restrictions on oligarchic influence, but they never had the resources to win a large following, regularly taking less than 10% of the vote. The most powerful forces in Russian politics were not parties but oligarchs and the security services. In the 1990s, Yeltsin and the Duma had balanced these forces off each other, and they in turn provided competition between Yeltsin and his opponents. In the 2000s, Putin leaned heavily on the security services, using them to marginalize the oligarchs, and in exchange giving the security services the dominant role in politics.

In contrast to Russia, Ukraine's oligarchs remained politically influential. In the process, they have provided funding and administrative support to different political parties, guaranteeing electoral competition of a sort. At key moments when Ukraine was on the verge of sliding into single-party authoritarianism, as in 2004 and 2013, competing oligarchs provided support for street protests and opposition parties, without which these popular movements would likely have failed. Ukraine's political system, despite flaws, is far more competitive than Russia's. Russia, by contrast, has marginalized its oligarchs but sunk into authoritarian rule that might continue for the remainder of Putin's life. In the early 2000s, Russia and Ukraine faced a similar, unappealing choice: unchecked oligarchs or unchecked central authority. It is better to have no oligarchs in politics. But it is worse to have only one.

---

[71] Colton, *Yeltsin*, 431.
[72] Colton, *Yeltsin*, 432.

11

A Different "Turkish Model"

Exemplifying De-democratization in the AKP Era

Lisel Hintz

Introduction

The 2002 coming to power of the newly formed Justice and Development Party (Adalet ve Kalkınma Partisi, AKP) invoked optimism among many domestic and foreign observers hoping that Turkey smooth out its somewhat jittery path toward democracy. Although Turkey transitioned to a multiparty system in 1950, a combination of military interventions, restrictions on civil liberties such as freedoms of speech and religion, and a brutal campaign against Kurds and Kurdish identity prevented Turkey from being considered a fully consolidated democracy. Moves to address each of these issues, particularly in the AKP's first term, led observers to herald the sum of the party's accomplishments as a "Turkish model" that could be exported to other parts of the Muslim world.[1] Although the term lacked specificity—did they mean a model of economic development, a mix of Islam and democracy, civilianization of the military, something else entirely?—the new party's professed commitment to conservative democratic values, European Union membership, and neoliberal growth strategies promising enough to replicate. In particular, AKP members' explicit eschewing of the label "Muslim democrats,"[2] despite their own experiences coming up through the ranks of Turkey's most prominent Islamist movement, along with their championing of clean government—the *ak* in the party's preferred moniker *Ak Parti* means "pure/white," a term carrying a moral connotation of "uncontaminated"—provided a reassuring alternative for many who were concerned about threats to secularism and frustrated with rampant corruption. Finally, the AKP's parliamentary majority, achieved through a combination of a 10% electoral threshold and disillusionment with previous parties' inability to avoid economic

---

[1] On the debate surrounding Turkey as a "model," see Meliha Benli Altunışık, "The Turkish Model and Democratization in the Middle East," *Arab Studies Quarterly* 27, nos. 1–2 (2005): 45–63.
[2] See Vali Nasr, "The Rise of Muslim Democracy," *Journal of Democracy* 16, no. 2 (2005): 13–27.

Lisel Hintz, *A Different "Turkish Model"* In: *When Democracy Breaks*. Edited by: Archon Fung, David Moss, and Odd Arne Westad, Oxford University Press. © Oxford University Press 2024. DOI: 10.1093/oso/9780197760789.003.0011

300   WHEN DEMOCRACY BREAKS

crisis, provided much needed political stability as well as an opportunity to push through the democratizing reforms the party advocated.

Those initially optimistic observers have now had to admit that, despite initial signs of what seemed to be democratic progress, under later terms of AKP rule Turkey regressed significantly. In Charles Tilly's formulation, identified as nonlinear pathways of democratization and de-democratization, Turkey is now firmly on a de-democratizing trajectory.[3] At the time of writing, the AKP has been in power for over twenty years, Turkey is governed through a highly centralized presidential system ruled by a hypermasculine nationalist populist, and the 2023 elections were neither free nor fair.[4] Although Turkey's traditionally fragmented opposition showed signs of being able to forge ties around local elections, as they did to win the Istanbul and Ankara mayoral election in 2019, they are struggling to do so ahead of the next round of local elections scheduled for 2024. Opposition officials are also hampered in their ability to govern at the local level by interference from Ankara. Thus, while prominent former AKP members, including Ali Babacan and Ahmet Davutoğlu, formed their own parties to offer new challenges to President Recep Tayyip Erdoğan and his AKP, the question of whether elections truly matter anymore is unresolved.

Far from being a "model" for political tolerance, Turkey after two decades of AKP rule exemplifies in microcosmic form many of the processes of de-democratization seen across the globe. Common authoritarian consolidation practices in AKP-era Turkey included institutional takeover in the judiciary and the security forces, processes that accelerated and expanded following the 2016 coup attempt via purges and strategic placements. The post-putsch state of emergency also augmented the executive presidency's heavy-handed use of decrees, amounting to "rule by law." A significant degree of media capture further allowed the AKP to control narratives, silence criticism, and vilifying opposition[5] and created a regime-stabilizing culture of self-censorship in the process. As an obvious example, Turkey held the infamous title of being the world's largest jailer of journalists for several years. From a political economy perspective, a complex network of holding groups with interests in construction, mining, real estate, and other industries gives the AKP powerful influence over 90%–95% of Turkey's media outlets. Also seen in other cases of de-democratization, freedom of assembly was drastically curtailed. In the Turkish case, peaceful protests against issues such as environmental destruction, unsafe labor conditions, civilian casualties in the Kurdish southeast, and violence against women, faced

---

[3] Charles Tilly, *Democracy* (New York: Cambridge University Press, 2007).

[4] Berk Esen and Şebnem Gümüşçü, "How Erdoğan's Populism Won Again," *Journal of Democracy* 34, no. 3 (2023): 21–32.

[5] Bilge Yeşil, "Authoritarian Turn or Comtinuity? Governance of Media through Capture and Discipline," *South European Society and Politics* 23, no. 2 (2018): 239–257.

A DIFFERENT "TURKISH MODEL" 301

harsh crackdown by security forces. In view of these and many other, similarly antidemocratic factors, Turkey has often been classified as competitive authoritarian,[6] but the illusion of competitiveness may in fact be a constitutive component of the AKP's regime durability.[7] Given the immense role Erdoğan's own background and persona play in inspiring support among those who see him as their unimpeachable "Captain" (Reis), the equally immense decision-making power he commands in both domestic and foreign policy realms, and the pervasive belief among many observers that no AKP successor could match his level of charismatic legitimacy, the dynamics of the Turkish case under Erdoğan might also be classified as a personalistic authoritarian regime.[8]

Whichever term we settle on, what explains this case of rapid regime change? Turkey's story of democratic breakdown is as puzzling as it was quick. As will be obvious throughout the chapter, Erdoğan's role looms large in accounting for the shift from democratization to de-democratization, but focusing on the motivations, actions, and influence of one individual gives us only part of the story. A frequent debate within Turkey's highly fragmented opposition, for example, revolves around who saw through AKP leader Erdoğan's authoritarian ambitions first, who objected to them most vocally, and thus who could have saved Turkey from democratic demise if only the world had heeded their warnings. The purpose of this chapter is not to engage this debate, nor to answer the age-old question of whether Erdoğan planned his rise to supreme authority early in his political career or whether absolute power corrupts absolutely. What this chapter focuses its efforts on instead is the interrelated processes by which Turkey's system of governance slides so quickly and drastically from democratization to de-democratization, resulting in what in practice is equivalent to one-man rule at the national level.

Because these processes are intricately linked, the analysis of how they led to democratic breakdown could be framed in a host of different ways. A focus on the use of economic tools to ensure loyalty to the party even in the face of antidemocratic practices, for example, links directly to co-optation and control of the media via the political economy of Turkey's mega-holding groups, as mentioned above, but also links to the role the construction industry played in the AKP's consolidation, and abuse, of power. An illustrative example serves to demonstrate the point.

---

[6] Berk Esen and Şebnem Gümüşçü, "Rising Competitive Authoritarianism in Turkey," *Third World Quarterly* 37, no. 9 (2016): 1581–1606.

[7] Meral Uğur-Cınar, "Elections and Democracy in Turkey: Reconsidering Comeptitive Authoritarianism in the Age of Democratic Backsliding," *The Political Quarterly* 94, no. 3 (2023): 445–451.

[8] See Mark Gasiorowski, "The Political Regimes Project," in *On Measuring Democracy: Its Consequences and Concomitants*, 3rd ed., ed. Alex Inkeles (New Brunswick, NJ: Transaction, 2006).

302   WHEN DEMOCRACY BREAKS

The economic reforms undertaken in the early years of AKP rule contributed to Turkey's growth as a whole, garnering the party widespread support, while particularly supporting the rise of a conservative middle class of small and medium enterprise owners, nicknamed "Anatolian Tigers." The growth these reforms fueled in turn enabled Erdoğan to preside over massive building projects, such as a third bridge over the Bosphorus, a metro-accessible tunnel under it, a new airport, and thousands of mosques, including the Çamlıca Mosque, which stood as Turkey's largest upon its completion in 2016. These construction projects served to impress many Turks excited to see tangible markers of the development Erdoğan promised to continue from his days as Istanbul's mayor from the Islamist Welfare Party (*Refah Partisi*) in the 1990s. When I asked why they voted for the AKP, numerous blue-collar workers cited these projects, along with other, less showy but more functional forms of infrastructure. Their common response was "Look what Tayyip [Erdoğan] did! What did the others do?"

Each of these projects was controversial, however, and can be seen as intricately linked with Turkey's de-democratization. For AKP opponents the mushrooming of construction sites was evidence not of modernization and development but rather of corruption, environmental degradation, and human rights abuses. The unprecedented Gezi Park protests of 2013, which grew into nationwide mobilization against the AKP's increasingly authoritarian rule, began as a small demonstration to protect one of Istanbul's remaining green spaces from being paved over to build a shopping mall and Ottoman-style barracks. Protests over the construction of what is now the Istanbul New Airport centered around massive deforestation and evidence that the consortium that won the construction tender was bullied into buying a failing pro-AKP media outlet,[9] as well as intolerable labor conditions.[10]

To tie together economic development, the construction industry, and factors indicating de-democratization, including violations of human rights and freedom of speech, these megaprojects that garner electoral support from impressed and employed voters are acquired and financed through sweetheart deals that favor party loyalists willing to overlook violations of democratic norms. Specifically, those invested in the construction of the new airport had little incentive to object to the arrest of protesting workers, nor to improve their unsafe working conditions; official statistics cite the number of construction

---

[9] Andrew Finkel, "Corruption Scandal Taints Turkish Construction," *Financial Times*, May 6, 2014, https://www.ft.com/content/68196132-cc98-11e3-ab99-00144feabdc0. For an overview, see Fikret Adaman, Bengi Akbulut, and Murat Arsel, eds., *Neoliberal Turkey and Its Discontents: Economic Policy and the Environment under Erdoğan* (London: I. B. Tauris, 2017).

[10] Emma Sinclair-Webb, "Construction Workers at Istanbul's New Airport Jailed for Protesting Work Conditions," *Human Rights Watch Dispatch*, September 21, 2018, https://www.hrw.org/news/2018/09/21/construction-workers-turkeys-new-airport-jailed-protesting-work-conditions.

deaths during airport construction as fifty-five,[11] but an opposition lawmaker filed a formal inquiry over reports claiming it is as high as four hundred.[12] While impossible to judge the real number from afar, workers' dubbing of the construction site as the "the cemetery" is worth noting.[13] The link between AKP-led development and infringements on labor rights and free speech is also seen in the 2014 Soma mining disaster in which three hundred workers died due to lack of safety oversight; an iconic photo shows a man protesting the government's handling of the disaster being kicked by Erdoğan's aide.[14] The role of crony capitalism in exacerbating death and destruction in the February 2023 earthquakes—via amnesty permits that enabled buildings out of line with code to remain, transportation hubs built in "no-go" zones on top of fault lines, and the lack of experience and preparedness among many of those working in the Disaster and Emergency Management Presidency—is a particularly devastating recent example.[15]

Clearly, the AKP's use of economic tools played a role in the power consolidation that produced democratic breakdown. As Esen and Gümüşçü argue from a different political economy angle, the politicization of state financial and judicial organs that could target and punish those in the opposition was also a key element of the AKP's ability to erode democratic practices.[16] One could also focus on the consequences of promoting a narrative that replaced gender equality with gender justice[17] and sought to protect "family values" at the expense of women's and LGBTQ+ rights,[18] on the rise of violent pro-government groups self-tasked with vigilante justice,[19] or on the decreasing prospects that

---

[11] Umut Erdem, "55 Workers Died during Istanbul Airport's Construction: Minister," *Hürriyet Daily News*, January 18, 2019, http://www.hurriyetdailynews.com/55-workers-died-during-istan bul-airports-construction-minister-140600.

[12] "'3. Havalimanında 400 İşçi Hayatını Kaybetti' İddiası Meclis Gündeminde," *HaberSol.org*, February 13, 2018, http://haber.sol.org.tr/toplum/3-havalimaninda-400-isci-hayatini-kaybetti-iddi asi-meclis-gundeminde-228335ç.

[13] Tim Nelson, "Why Workers Are Calling Istanbul's New Airport 'The Cemetery,'" *Architectural Digest*, October 15, 2019, https://www.architecturaldigest.com/story/why-workers-are-calling-istanbuls-new-airport-the-cemetery.

[14] Alexander Christie-Miller, "Miners Say Safety Declined after Turkey Privatized Mine," *Christian Science Monitor*, May 15, 2014, https://www.csmonitor.com/World/Middle-East/2014/0515/Min ers-say-safety-declined-after-Turkey-privatized-Soma-mine.

[15] "Çiğdem Mater 'Depremi' Sordu, Mücella Yapıcı Yanıtladı," interview published on Kısa Dalga site, February 16, 2023, https://kisadalga.net/haber/detay/cigdem-mater-depremi-sordu-mucella-yapici-yanitladi_57137.

[16] Berk Esen and Şebnem Gümüşçü, "Building a Competitive Authoritarian Regime: State-Business Relations in the AKP's Turkey," *Journal of Balkan and Near Eastern Studies* 20, no. 4 (2017): 349–372.

[17] Çağla Diner, "Gender Politics and GONGOs in Turkey," *Turkish Policy Quarterly* 16, no. 4 (2018): 101–108.

[18] Evren Savcı, *Queer in Translation: Sexual Politics under Neoliberal Islam* (Durham, NC: Duke University Press, 2020).

[19] Howard Eissenstat, "Uneasy Rests the Crown: Erdogan and 'Revolutionary Security' in Turkey," *Project on Middle East Democracy Snapshot*, December 20, 2017, https://pomed.org/pomed-snaps hot-uneasy-rests-the-crown-erdogan-and-revolutionary-security-in-turkey/.

304   WHEN DEMOCRACY BREAKS

EU membership incentives or other forms of external pressure could prompt democratization.[20]

In this chapter I examine three processes in which the AKP engaged that are inextricably linked to these other dynamics: (1) the reshaping of the institutional playing field to remove what I define as identity obstacles to the party's rise, (2) the rhetorical vilification of opposition actors to justify their marginalization, and (3) the unprecedented manipulation of the electoral system. These processes are sequentially and constitutively linked, in that the first allows the second and the second allows the third. The AKP would not have had the power necessary to declare the (first) 2019 Istanbul municipal election null, for example, without first co-opting the Supreme Electoral Board and declaring through pro-government media that opposition "terrorists" rigged their win via an "electoral coup."[21] Before examining these three processes, the chapter proceeds by briefly sketching Turkey's experiences with democratization and de-democratization prior to the AKP. The next two sections examine the processes of institutional consolidation and vilification of the opposition in depth. The conclusion takes on the electoral manipulation that has been made possible by these processes while considering prospects for the future of Turkey's opposition.

Democratization Interrupted

What makes Turkey's democratic breakdown such a puzzling case is not just the rapidity with which it took place but also the progress along Tilly's democratization trajectory the country had taken in recent years—even including the first term of AKP rule. Turkey also took some significant democratizing steps early on, especially compared to other Western countries. In 1930, just seven years after the founding of the republic, women gained the right to vote; this move toward gender equality, along with many Westernizing and secularizing reforms, including switching from the Arabic to the Latin script and banning the fez, was part of founding father Mustafa Kemal Atatürk's nation-making project. After crushing rebellions such as the Kurdish-Islamist Sheikh Said Rebellion in 1925 in the name of establishing security within the boundaries of the new republic, Atatürk viewed the role of his Republican People's Party (*Cumhuriyet Halk*

---

[20] Tanja Börzel and Bidzina Lebanidze, "'The Transformative Power of Europe' beyond Enlargement: The EU's Performance in Promoting Democracy in Its Neighborhood," *East European Politics* 33, no. 1 (2017): 17–35.

[21] See the pro-government claim in Ibrahim Karagül, "A Coup Was Conducted through Elections on March 31," *Yeni Şafak Gazetesi*, April 3, 2019, https://www.yenisafak.com/en/columns/ibrahim karagul/a-coup-was-conducted-in-turkey-through-elections-on-march-31-feto-terrorists-were-used-for-a-project-targeting-istanbul-the-first-moves-for-post-july-15-plans-have-been-made-so-elections-in-istanbul-should-be-re-held-2046998.

A DIFFERENT "TURKISH MODEL"   305

Partisi, CHP) as presiding over cultural, political, and economic modernization during a period of single-party rule. Institutionalizing a "responsible, though not responsive" political system thus took precedence over democratization.[22]

Following one brief attempt at political pluralism in 1930 with the creation of the Liberal Republican Party (Serbest Cumhuriyet Fırkası) as a check on the CHP, which scholars point to as a signal of Atatürk's intentions to democratize Turkey before his untimely death in 1938,[23] and another with a two-party election tilted heavily against the challenging Democrat Party (*Demokrat Parti*, DP) in 1946, 1950 marked the beginning of generally free and fair multiparty elections. The 1950 contest was remarkable in the sense that the incumbent CHP unexpectedly lost to the DP but quickly handed over power. This partial democratic transition is due largely to party leader, "national chief" (*milli şef*), and president İsmet İnönü's commitment to democracy, the influence of the Turkish Armed Forces (*Türk Silahlı Kuvvetleri*), and relatedly, the post–World War II environment. Dictatorial regimes had been disgraced, and the prospect of NATO membership to secure Turkish interests against Soviet aggression incentivized domestic change.[24]

Following the transition, however, Turkey experienced moves along Tilly's continuum in fits and starts. In 1960, for example, the DP-led government that so unexpectedly unseated the CHP was overthrown by a military coup, and three of its leaders were hanged. Holding various forms of control following various degrees of intervention, the military also removed democratically elected governments in 1971, 1980, and 1997. Although threats to the principle of secularism enshrined in all of modern Turkey's constitutions (1924, 1961, 1982) are often cited as the main reason for the military's interventions, other destabilizing and antidemocratic factors also played powerful roles. These include rampant mismanagement leading to economic crisis and seizure of state resources (1960, 1971) and street clashes between radical leftists and (state-aided) right-wing ultranationalists that devolved into terrorist attacks and civil war–like conditions (1971, 1980). The 1997 intervention, however, dubbed a "postmodern coup" because no physical act of force was used, centered directly on the military's belief that Turkey's secularist state was under siege. In the beginning of what would become known as the "February 28 process," the National Security Council delivered an ultimatum to Turkey's first Islamist prime minister, Necmettin

---

[22] See Kemal H. Karpat, "The Republican People's Party, 1923–1945," in *Political Parties and Democracy in Turkey*, ed. Metin Heper and Jacob M. Landau (London: I. B Tauris, 1991): 42–64.

[23] See, for example, Walter F. Weiker, "The Free Party, 1960," in Heper and Landau, *Political Parties and Democracy in Turkey*, 85.

[24] See Hakan Yılmaz, "Democratization from Above in Response to the International Context: Turkey, 1945–1950," *New Perspectives on Turkey* 17 (1997): 1–37; Feroz Ahmad, *The Making of Modern Turkey* (London: Routledge, 1993), 102–120. On İnönü, see Metin Heper, *İsmet İnönü: The Making of a Turkish Statesman* (Boston: Brill, 1998).

306 WHEN DEMOCRACY BREAKS

Erbakan. The demands ultimately forced Erbakan's Welfare Party to resign from the coalition government it led; the party was dissolved by the Constitutional Court in 1998. As part of the February 28 Process, religious schools were closed, headscarves were banned on university campuses, and hundreds of individuals in the military and civil service suspected of Islamist leanings were fired. These events are detailed here as they powerfully shape the AKP's approach to institutional reconfiguration discussed in the next section.

Of these military interventions, each justified by "the need to reestablish or safeguard democracy and/or the state,"[25] the military actually took the reins of governance only in 1980. The military's intended goal may have been to reshape the country's political system such that "a viable democracy could take root,"[26] but the means used to do so not only were brutal but also in some ways impeded democratization in the long term. Political violence, including disappearances, torture, and extrajudicial killings, targeting leftists and Kurds, combined with bans on union activity and other associational restrictions decimated the country's social democratic basis for mobilization. As a scholar of Turkey's center-left notes, "[F]rom the left's point of view . . . the coup was specifically targeted to crush the CHP and the leftist movement."[27] From a civil society perspective, much of the explanation for why Turkey's opposition has been unable to mobilize sufficiently to topple Erdoğan's AKP can be traced to the legacies of the 1980–1983 military-led regime. Intra-opposition feuds over the meaning of social democracy, the limits of secularism, and the Kurdish question continued to divide those otherwise united in their desire to oust the increasingly authoritarian AKP throughout the 2010s.

Further, the draconian Constitution promulgated by the military in 1982 remains in place. A 2017 report submitted by a Turkish NGO to the High Commissioner for Human Rights noted that the Constitution reflected an antidemocratic perception in which individual freedoms were viewed as a threat to the continuity of the state.[28] Although the Constitution was amended several times through referenda (2007, 2010, 2017), reforms focused more on consolidating power in ways that advantaged the AKP and Erdoğan's personal control as president than on addressing key grievances citizens raised. Multiple attempts at a new constitution, including convening demographically

---

[25] Frank Tachau and Metin Heper, "The State, Politics, and the Military in Turkey," *Comparative Politics* 16, no. 1 (1983): 17–33.

[26] Üstün Eder, "The Motherland Party, 1983–1989," in Heper and Landau, *Political Parties and Democracy in Turkey*, 152.

[27] Sinan Ciddi, *Kemalism in Turkish Politics: The Republican People's Party, Secularism, and Nationalism* (Abingdon: Routledge, 2009), 69.

[28] Journalists and Writers Foundation, "Shrinking Civil Society Space," submission to the OHCHR, 2017, http://jwf.org/jwf/wp-content/uploads/2018/06/Shrinking-Civil-Society-Space-.pdf.

A DIFFERENT "TURKISH MODEL"   307

representative "wise men" committees, came to naught.[29] In 2011, for example, then–Prime Minister Erdoğan made the drafting of a civilian constitution a campaign promise to Kurdish voters hoping to see exclusionary references to the "Turkish nation" removed; comparative constitutional law experts suggested the more inclusive term *Türkiyeli*, meaning "of Turkey," as it carried no ethnic criterion for membership.[30] However, this and other democratizing efforts aimed at Kurds collapsed along with the government's negotiations with the Kurdistan Workers' Party (Partiya Karkeren Kurdistan, PKK) in 2015. After unexpected votes for the pro-Kurdish Peoples' Democratic Party (*Halkların Demokratik Partisi*, HDP) in June 2015 elections threatened the AKP's parliamentary majority for the first time since 2002, and conflict with the PKK resumed, the AKP turned to court Turkey's ultranationalists to replace the electoral support it could no longer count on from Kurds.

Turkey's Kurdish question is largely regarded as the country's "most important problem."[31] Kurdish issues are deeply intertwined with democratization and human rights concerns, and not just the security concerns that the AKP and other previous governing actors have emphasized. At various periods in Turkey's history Kurds have faced repressive measures such as forced migration,[32] bans on the Kurdish language and alphabet[33] and Kurdish media,[34] and the state's co-optation of Kurds' Spring Newroz celebrations as the refashioned Turkish Nevruz (without the banned letter "w").[35] Kurds also disproportionately experienced the effects of various periods of emergency rule,[36] and tens of thousands of Kurdish civilians were killed, disappeared, imprisoned, tortured, and displaced since the initiation of conflict between the PKK and the Turkish state, particularly in the "lost years" of the 1990s. Although the AKP took steps toward extending cultural rights to Kurds—coinciding with the ramp-up of Turkey's European Union

---

[29] See Onur Bakıner, "How Did We Get Here? Turkey's Slow Shift to Authoritarianism," in *Authoritarian Politics in Turkey: Elections, Resistance, and the AKP*, ed. Bahar Başer and Ahmet Erdi Öztürk (London: I. B. Tauris, 2017): 21–46.

[30] Hakan Kolcak, "A New Constitution for a Stable Nation: A Constitutional Study on the Long-Running Kurdish Question in Turkey," *Journal of Ethnic and Cultural Studies* 2, no. 1 (2015): 29–48.

[31] Henri Barkey and Direnç Kadıoğlu, "The Turkish Constitution and the Kurdish Question," Carnegie Endowment for International Peace, report, August 1, 2011, https://carnegieendowment.org/2011/08/01/turkish-constitution-and-kurdish-question-pub-45218.

[32] Ayşe Betül Çelik, "'I Miss My Village!' Forced Kurdish Migrants in Istanbul and Their Representation in Associations," *New Perspectives on Turkey* 32 (2005): 137–163.

[33] Welat Zeydanlıoğlu, "Turkey's Kurdish Language Policy," *International Journal of the Sociology of Language* 217 (September 2012): 99–125

[34] Ece Algan, "Local Broadcasting as Tactical Media: Exploring Practices of Kurdish Activism and Journalism in Turkey". *Middle East Journal of Culture and Communication* 12 (September 2019): 220–235.

[35] Lerna Yanık, "'Nevruz' or 'Newroz?' Deconstructing the 'Invention' of Contested Tradition in Contemporary Turkey," *Middle Eastern Studies* 42 (August 2006): 285–302; Lisel Hintz and Allison Quatrini, "Subversive Celebrations: Holidays as Sites of Minority Identity Contestation in Repressive Regimes," *Nationalities Papers* 49 (March 2021): 289–307.

[36] Zafer Üskül, *Olağanüstü Hal Üzerine Yazılar* (Istanbul: Büke Yayınları, 2003).

308   WHEN DEMOCRACY BREAKS

accession bid in the early years of AKP rule—and initiated a peace process (çözüm süreci) with the PKK in 2012, the breakdown of the ceasefire in 2015 and the AKP's subsequent nationalist turn marked another case of democratization interrupted. The AKP's rhetorical vilification of Kurdish political actors as terrorists, discussed below produced numerous undemocratic outcomes. To list a few, the overwhelming majority of the pro-Kurdish HDP mayors democratically elected in 2019 were removed and replaced by AKP trustees,[37] former HDP co-chair Selahattin Demirtaş and other leading party members were jailed,[38] and the party faced dissolution by the Constitutional Court.[39]

Other key issues related to civil liberties and political freedoms that had held Turkey back from higher democracy scores historically included restrictions on freedoms of speech and assembly. The infamous Article 301 of the Turkish Penal Code prohibiting speech and acts denigrating Turkishness, the Republic, or institutions of the state, for example, was cited in criminal investigations opened against author Elif Şafak and assassinated Armenian journalist Hrant Dink for referring to the massacres of Armenians in 1915 as a genocide.[40] Although the wording was revised several times during the AKP's early years of democratizing reforms, the law is still objectionable to the European Court of Human Rights and still being cited; in May 2018 a case was opened against Armenian HDP member Garo Paylan for comparing the killings of Kurdish civilians and imprisonment of HDP MPs to the 1915 genocide.[41] Although these charges are being brought under the rule of a party that has deep roots in political Islam rather than that of a military regime, the use of legislation to silence opposition looks remarkably the same.[42]

Indeed, it is precisely the AKP's resort to a familiar politics of oppression to maintain power that most frustrates those initially optimistic about the party's proclaimed big-tent democratic aspirations. To understand how Turkey's regime went from fast progress on Tilly's democratization path to even faster movement toward de-democratization, what remains of this chapter applies an identity politics lens to democratic breakdown. To add new insight to the many

---

[37] Zeynep Kaya and Matthew Whiting, "The HDP, the AKP, and the Battle for Democracy," Ethnopolitics 18, no. 1 (2019): 92–106.

[38] Ödül Celep, "The Moderation of Turkey's Kurdish Left: The Peoples' Democratic Party (HDP)," Turkish Studies 19, no. 5 (2018): 723–747.

[39] "Top Prosecutor Repeats Call for Closure of HDP," Hürriyet Daily News, November 30, 2021, https://www.hurriyetdailynews.com/top-prosecutor-repeats-call-for-closure-of-hdp-169755.

[40] Bülent Algan, "The Brand New Version of Article 301 of Turkish Penal Code and the Future of Freedom of Expression Cases in Turkey," German Law Journal 9, no. 12 (2008): 2237–2252.

[41] "Garo Paylan Being Investigated for 'Insulting Turkishness,' under Turkey's Notorious Article 301," Armenian Weekly, May 17, 2018, https://armenianweekly.com/2018/05/17/garo-paylan-being-investigated-for-insulting-turkishness-under-turkeys-notorious-article-301/.

[42] Hakan Övünç Ongur, "Plus Ça Change . . . Rearticulating Authoritarianism in the New Turkey," Critical Sociology 44, no. 1 (2018): 45–59.

excellent studies of power consolidation and opposition marginalization cited above, the following two sections examine the role competing understandings of Turkishness played in these two processes. Briefly, I argue that Erdoğan was able to secure his place as the most powerful individual in Turkey since Atatürk—indeed, openly challenging the founder's legacy by putting in place a "New Turkey" undergirded by a fundamentally different understanding of what it means to be Turkish. Specifically, I examine how (1) the weakening and reconstituting of *Republican Nationalist* institutions that served as obstacles to the AKP's *Ottoman Islamist* understanding of national identity and (2) the rhetorical vilification of those in the opposition facilitated the AKP's rise to and hold on power.

Institutional Transformation: Removal of Identity Obstacles

This section seeks to identify, trace, and interrogate the channels through which the AKP consolidated institutional power. Specifically, I focus on the weakening and transformation of institutions that previously defined parties in the AKP's tradition of political Islam—the National Outlook Movement, *Milli Görüş Hareketi*—as threats. As this section highlights, many of the civil-military, judicial, and other reforms that were implemented under the AKP served to neutralize secularist threats to its own tenure rather than more broadly institutionalizing democratic norms and processes. Judicial reforms, for example, while in line with EU accession criteria, also helped reconfigure the personnel makeup of institutions responsible for blocking the rise of *Milli Görüş* actors in the past.

In contrast to the previously dominant understanding of national identity rooted in founding father Atatürk's principles of secularism, modernization, and Western orientation—what I refer to as "Republican Nationalism"[43]—the AKP's Ottoman Islamism as a competing proposal for Turkishness is based on Sunni conservatism, patriarchal state-society organization, and a regional leadership role for Turkey legitimized by its imperial legacies. Laying the content of these identities side by side, it is clear that there are points of contestation between them, and that supporters of one proposal would logically seek to defend its principles against the threat of incursion by the other. Republican Nationalists' attempts to do so included explicitly inserting conservative clauses into the current constitution, as discussed above. Article 4 states, for example, that Articles 1 through 3, which deal with characteristics of the republic such as its language

---

[43] Lisel Hintz, "'Take It Outside!' National Identity Contestation in the Foreign Policy Arena," *European Journal of International Relations* 22, no. 2 (2016): 335–361.

310   WHEN DEMOCRACY BREAKS

and its citizens' loyalty to Atatürk, "cannot be amended and no amendments can be proposed." Article 68 states that political parties and their platforms "may not be contrary to the democratic and secular principles of the Republic"; Article 69 states that parties violating this clause will be subject to dissolution.[44]

The AKP was established as successor to a string of parties that shared an Ottoman Islamist identity and that had been removed from power and/or shut down by institutions established to safeguard Republican Nationalist principles, only to reopen under a new name each time. Party founders Erdoğan, Abdullah Gül, and others learned from this history, acting pragmatically and cautiously upon coming to power in 2002. Its leadership worked under the knowledge that policies seen to threaten secularism domestically or to alter Turkey's historically Western foreign policy orientation could be seen as provocation by the military and thus cause for intervention and possible overthrow of the government. The fate of Necmettin Erbakan, the founder of the *Milli Görüş* movement in which Erdoğan cut his political teeth, served as a cautionary tale of the potential outcome of such provocation.

Erbakan had seen his National Order Party (*Milli Nizam Partisi*) and National Salvation Party (*Milli Selâmet Partisi*) dissolved by the Constitutional Court following Turkey's 1971 and 1980 coups, respectively, and had been banned from politics himself. By reorganizing and mobilizing the extensive and extremely efficient networks of *Milli Görüş* around his newly founded Welfare Party, however, Erbakan achieved what was unthinkable and intolerable for Republican Nationalists in becoming Turkey's first Islamist prime minister in 1996. His success was quite short-lived, as the Ottoman Islamist direction in which he took Turkey—including an increased presence of Islam in the educational system, civil society, and the business community; personal appeals by Erbakan for the instatement of sharia law; a state visit to Libya; Arab sheiks visiting the Prime Ministry; and the explicit rejection of a Western orientation for Turkey in favor of membership in an international Islamic Union—prompted a predictable Republican Nationalist reaction. On February 28, 1997, the very powerful National Security Council delivered a set of eighteen directives to Erbakan's cabinet designed to roll back what the Turkish Armed Forces perceived as encroachments on Turkey's inviolably secular nature. Erbakan's Welfare Party–led coalition government collapsed on June 18, 1997, and the Constitutional Court dissolved his party in 1998.

The purges of those with suspected ties to political Islam that followed as part of the February 28 Process exemplify the immediate factors underlying much of the AKP's cautiousness. The constitutive effect the process had on former

---

[44] Turkish Grand National Assembly, Constitution of the Republic of Turkey, accessed October 16, 2023, http://www.tbmm.gov.tr/anayasa/anayasa82.htm.

A DIFFERENT "TURKISH MODEL"   311

Welfare Party members held particular resonance for Erdoğan, who as a party-affiliated mayor of Istanbul was arrested for reciting a poem that, it was claimed, incited religious hatred. He spent four months in prison and was temporarily barred from politics, delaying his assumption of Turkey's premiership until 2003, despite his party's coming to power in 2002. As a cumulative lesson learned from personal and party organization-level experiences, in their first years in power Erdoğan and other AKP leaders emphasized that the term "conservative democrat" best encapsulated the identity that shaped their political platform, explicitly eschewing terms such as "moderate Islamist" and even "Muslim democrat" to insist "[W]e are against politics based on religion."[45]

Also helping to defuse fears based on the AKP's Milli Görüş heritage, and in a 180-degree departure from the "Islamic Union" foreign policy orientation pursued by Erbakan, the AKP immediately declared Turkey's membership in the EU to be a primary pillar of foreign policy. With its parliamentary majority the party started working diligently to implement political and economic reforms that were in line with the accession criteria of the EU's Copenhagen Agreement, as if trying to prove to skeptics that the AKP was completely different and that its intentions were genuine. Republican Nationalists doubted the AKP's commitment to EU accession, just as they doubted its professed commitment to democratization, pointing to numerous public speeches made by Erdoğan during his time as Welfare Party mayor of Istanbul just five years earlier. His statement that "for us, democracy can never be a goal" but merely a "vehicle" is exemplary of the sources of these doubts.[46]

Reasons to doubt the AKP's commitment to both democratization and EU membership have come to light in its subsequent terms (2011–present), although divining initial intent is methodologically challenging, as is attributing intention to an entire party. Nevertheless, the so-called liberals who initially viewed the AKP as a positive corrective to Turkey's history of military tutelage and human rights "taboos" later came to criticize the party, if not to directly admit that they were wrong in trusting the party in the first place. Among these liberals were well-known journalists, public intellectuals, and others who came to be known as *Yetmez Ama Evet'çiler*, "Those who say 'It's not enough but yes,'" because of their willingness to vote yes on the AKP's constitutional amendments in the 2010 referendum that many now cite as a turning point in the party's consolidation of power. That temporary support from this group of intelligentsia helped facilitate this consolidation is a particularly bitter sticking point for ardent Republican Nationalists who believed they knew best all along. An EU ministerial official

---

[45] "Erdoğan: Din Üzerinden Siyasete Karşıyız," *Hürriyet Gazetesi*, January 10, 2004, http://www.hurriyet.com.tr/gundem/erdogan-din-uzerinden-siyasete-karsiyiz-38556005.

[46] "Erdoğan: Demokrasi Amaç Değil, Araçtır," *Hürriyet Gazetesi*, March 6, 2011, http://www.hurriyet.com.tr/gundem/erdogan-demokrasi-amac-degil-aractir-17197745.

312 WHEN DEMOCRACY BREAKS

I interviewed made clear the lack of connection between the reforms the AKP had been pushing through and the EU accession process, stating that a particular constitutional amendments package had nothing to do with the EU; it was already on the ministry's desk and needed to be justified as part of the EU process.[47]

In the same way, the AKP was able to target obstacles to its pursuit of Ottoman Islamist hegemony by shifting the arena of contestation to the EU process. By engaging ardently in EU negotiations and citing the need to prove Turkey's commitment to accession, the AKP was able to justify the need for civil-military and judicial reforms, thus taking on the most powerful obstacles to Ottoman Islamism in an arena in which the military and the courts could not compete. By adhering to the civil-military reforms necessitated by the EU's Copenhagen Agreement during its first few years in power, for example, the AKP was able to institutionalize civil authority over the military and remove its "special status," legislating a total of nine harmonization packages between 2002 and 2004. In its 2004 Regular Report, the European Commission noted that "over the past year the Turkish government has shown great determination in accelerating the pace of reforms," enthusiastically approving of reforms targeted toward "civilian control of the military."

Arguably the most effective step toward reducing threats from an autonomous, staunchly Republican Nationalist institution was taking control of the National Security Council. This was the body that issued an ultimatum forcing the Welfare Party to step down from its governing coalition in 1997, and the "main tool for shaping politics" in the pre-AKP era. The influence of this previously powerful body was greatly constricted through these reforms, to making recommendations to the Council of Ministers in a "purely consultative function." Before these reforms, Article 118 of the 1982 Constitution had stipulated that the government would give priority to decisions made by the National Security Council. Further, the body was removed as a member of the Council of Higher Education and the Supreme Board of Radio and Television, shrinking the power it wielded over university life and curricula and the content broadcast by the media, respectively. In critically evaluating the impact these EU-mandated changes would have on the military's influence over the people of Turkey, a Republican Nationalist blogger warned that the army was being "liquidated" along the path to EU democracy.[48]

The reforms also included making a civilian the head of the National Security Council for the first time and increasing the number of civilians within the

---

[47] Parts of this section draw on Lisel Hintz, *Identity Politics Inside Out: National Identity Contestation and Foreign Policy in Turkey* (New York: Oxford University Press, 2018), 104–110.

[48] The blogger headlined a section "AB demokrasisi yoluyla ordu tasfiye ediliyor." Filiz Doğan, "Böl-parçala, AB'ye uy," Turksolu, May 26, 2003, http://www.turksolu.com.tr/31/dogan31.htm.

institution, changing its makeup as well as its influence. The 2007 EU Progress Report—published at the beginning of the AKP's second term in power—praised the Council's "new role," the drastic reduction in its overall size, and the halving of the number of military personnel in the institution. Tellingly, those areas in which successive reports have criticized a lack of progress, including civilian control over the gendarmerie and civilian oversight over defense expenditures, involved issues that did not constitute direct threats to AKP rule. The report also criticized the Turkish military's statement against AKP Islamist presidential candidate Abdullah Gül in 2007, a move that could have posed a threat to the AKP in the past, when the military had stronger influence over politics. Gül's conservative upbringing, career in the Milli Görüş tradition of political Islam, and, particularly, his wife's wearing of the headscarf represented red lines for Republican Nationalists' social purpose of protecting Atatürk's principle of secularism. That nothing came of the military's famous "e-memorandum" warning of a possible intervention if the candidacy of Gül was not rescinded, that soldiers stayed in their barracks instead, testifies to the AKP's success in reducing the role of a Republican Nationalist institution through foreign policy channels.

Emboldened by these institutional reforms mandated by the AKP's EU-oriented foreign policy, which made possible the election of Gül despite the open objection of the military, supporters of an Ottoman Islamist proposal went further in applying EU democratization criteria to the military obstacle. One of the most sweeping instances of this is the investigations and prosecutions over the course of 2008–2012 that comprised the *Ergenekon* and *Balyoz* trials, labeled by media outlet *Al Jazeera* as "Islamists' revenge against the army." The hundreds of individuals charged in these cases—including serving and former military personnel, journalists, and politicians—were accused of forming a clandestine secularist organization that sought the overthrow of the AKP government by inciting terror throughout society. Including indictment titles such as "Plan to Intervene in Democracy" (Demokrasiye Müdahale Planı), the two cases centered around the claims that those accused were part of a "deep state" organization plotting to create chaos through bombings and assassinations. These attacks, the indictments argued, would show the public that the AKP was unable or unwilling to provide for the security of its opposition and thus would justify a military coup against the democratically elected government. Prosecutors attempted to draw links among attacks, such as the 2006 assassination of a Council of State judge and the bombing of the *Cumhuriyet* (Republic) newspaper, and evidence of planned assassinations of navy admirals, the Greek patriarch, and non-Muslim minorities.

Initially heralded as a step forward in the democratization of civil-military relations by applying the rule of law even to former chief of general staff and president of Turkey Kenan Evren, the trials came to be seen as a way of obviating

314   WHEN DEMOCRACY BREAKS

the threat of powerful individuals, as well as tarnishing the institutional credibility of the armed forces, secular newspapers, and other disparate institutions and individuals united only in their opposition to the AKP. Signs that evidence used in the trials was illegally gathered and even manufactured—supposedly damning CDs containing plans written during the Balyoz coup plot in 2003 were written in Calibri, a font Microsoft released only as part of Windows 2007—also pointed to the cases serving more as a platform for political targeting than for the objective application of due process. The strong presence of members of the Gülen movement (a brotherhood, or *cemaat*, led by exiled cleric Fethullah Gülen, who has recently become one of Erdoğan's arch rivals) in the police and the judicial institutions responsible for gathering evidence and prosecuting the cases also raised suspicions about the motivations behind the trials.

Also as part of its EU foreign policy, the AKP pushed through judicial reform that ended the jurisdiction of military courts over civilians and abolished the State Security Court used to try crimes against the state, including violations of the principle of secularism. It was the State Security Court that had sentenced Erdoğan to prison for reading an allegedly Islamist reactionary (*irticai*) poem and had him temporarily banned from politics. The Constitutional Court, another looming obstacle to the AKP's pursuit of hegemony for Ottoman Islamism, also became a target of the judicial reforms carried out in line with EU accession criteria. The AKP began to move forward in these reforms after its amendment meant to override the decisions of university rectors, discussed below, and guarantee the right of university students to wear the headscarf was overturned by the court in 2008. Further, the party barely survived a closure case—a move likened to a military coup—in the same year thanks to the last-minute vote of the court's new president and then AKP sympathizer Haşim Kılıç.[49] While the AKP gained an automatic advantage when Gül became president, as the president selects all the members of the Constitutional Court, the AKP strove to quickly change the makeup of the court by proposing seventeen regular justices rather than the existing eleven regular and four substitute justices. While the reform was in "harmony" with the EU standard of delimiting justices' term limits to twelve years, this set up the AKP to rotate out justices nominated by previous Republican Nationalist president Ahmet Necdet Sezer and replace them with AKP-friendly justices.[50] Further, all justices continue to be selected by the president or by the heavily AKP-majority Parliament. These institutional reforms, ostensibly taken

[49] See "Ak Parti'yi Kapatma Kararı Askeri Darbeden Farksız Olur," *Yeni Şafak Gazetesi*, May 10, 2008, https://www.yenisafak.com/yerel/ak-partiyi-kapatma-karari-askeri-darbeden-farksiz-olur-116288.
[50] See Serap Yazıcı, "Turkey in the Last Two Decades: From Democratization to Authoritarianism," *European Public Law* 21, no. 4 (2015): 635–656.

A DIFFERENT "TURKISH MODEL"   315

in pursuit of EU membership, also greatly advanced the AKP's prospects for transforming institutional identity obstacles.

As an illustration of how civil-military and judicial reforms subsequently facilitated the AKP's transformation of other institutions, I also briefly examine the understudied role of universities and their leadership. The sequence is important here, as the AKP became better equipped to tackle the obstacle of university rectors because it first tackled the obstacle of the military. By swiftly reducing the role of the military in politics through EU-mandated reforms, the AKP facilitated the confirmation of Gül as president, despite the now weakened military's objections. The formerly Republican Nationalist institution of the presidency, another key identity obstacle, has the authority to appoint the head of the Council of Higher Education, the council responsible for both state and private universities, as well as to appoint heads of the former. By clearing the way for an Ottoman Islamist president through EU reforms, the AKP thus ensured that, at least for the time being, a supporter of its identity proposal would wield a significant amount of power over Turkey's university rectors. Gül's tenure as president, while largely symbolic in terms of actual decision-making authority, broke the taboo of having an Islamist politician with a headscarfed wife in the role, paving the way for Erdoğan himself to move into the position, one in which power would be much more heavily concentrated.

Upon becoming the first popularly elected president in 2014, Erdoğan actively used his authority in choosing rectors to weaken the Republican Nationalist domination of the influential institution of the university rector. As one columnist put it, university rectors became the "next domino in Erdoğan's path" toward eliminating dissension and filling these powerful positions with supporters willing to implement his wishes.[51] Although this institutional restacking of the deck has been particularly prominent since the July 2016 coup attempt, multiple instances of Erdoğan hand-selecting university rectors occurred prior to the state of emergency. Overriding majorities cast by "social democrats," Erdoğan instead appointed individuals supported by the "conservative" (*muhafazakar*) segment of votes at prominent universities across Turkey.[52] The AKP further facilitated the spread of Ottoman Islamism in universities by restricting the autonomy of "board selection in private universities, tenure and promotion reviews, and granting of equivalency to degrees obtained abroad."[53] Notably, with Executive

[51] Mustafa Akyol, "Turkish Universities Latest Domino in Erdoğan's Path," *Al Monitor*, November 7, 2016, https://www.al-monitor.com/pulse/iw/originals/2016/11/turkey-erdogan-took-full-cont rol-of-universities.amp.html.

[52] Sinan Tartanoğlu, "Cumhurbaşkanı Kendi Rektörünü Seçiyor," *Cumhuriyet Gazetesi* 20 (March 2015), http://www.cumhuriyet.com.tr/haber/turkiye/232935/Cumhurbaskani_kendi_rektor unu_seciyor.html.

[53] A. Kadir Yıldırım "The Slow Death of Turkish Higher Education," *Al Jazeera*, July 10, 2014, http://www.cumhuriyet.com.tr/haber/turkiye/232935/Cumhurbaskani_kendi_rektorunu_seci yor.html.

316 WHEN DEMOCRACY BREAKS

Order 676 as one of many preventative/punitive measures taken following the coup attempt, Erdoğan institutionalized complete control over the administration of higher education in Turkey in the executive by granting the president the power to appoint private as well as state university rectors. Further, the intra-university vote was eliminated in public universities; the president now chooses whomever he wishes without input from the faculty.

Thus the AKP transformed the previously Republican Nationalist institutions of the military, the judiciary, university rectors, the presidency, and more by weakening and or reconstituting them in the name of democratization and EU accession. Having neutralized these identity obstacles, the party creates space for marginalizing opposition actors with a reduced fear of recrimination through institutional checks. The following section details the strategies of rhetorical vilification used to delegitimize those opposed to the AKP's consolidation of power and justify crackdowns against them.

Rhetorical Vilification of Opposition

In February 2019, renowned criminal turned Erdoğan supporter Sedat Peker gave a speech in which he advised "good" people to arm themselves with guns as "insurance" against opposition members in the run-up to the local elections to be held in March.[54] With deep mafia links, Peker is no stranger to violence, but he recently brought his solution to problems from the private to the public sphere. In pro-AKP rallies (before launching a YouTube campaign to expose governmental corruption), he called for the beheading of academics that signed a peace petition and once declared, "[W]e will spill barrels of blood and shower in the blood" of those who protest killings of Kurdish civilians in the military's campaign against the PKK in Turkey's southeast.[55] Peker was by no means alone in advocating or threatening violence against those who express criticism. Pro-AKP writer Cem Küçük seems to have made a career out of menacing public appearances in which he singles out individuals he states must pay a price for betraying their nation.[56] Explicit death threats, like the ones sent to primetime TV anchor Fatih Portakal after he speculated on air that Turkey might experience protests similar to France's "Yellow Vest" demonstrations,[57] are a common

[54] "Sedat Peker'den 'Silahlanın' Çağrısı," Bianet, February 4, 2019, https://bianet.org/bianet/diger/205171-sedat-peker-den-silahlanin-cagrisi.
[55] "Notorious Criminal Threatens Academics Calling for Peace in Turkey's Southeast," *Hürriyet Daily News*, January 13, 2016, http://www.hurriyetdailynews.com/notorious-criminal-threatens-academics-calling-for-peace-in-turkeys-southeast-93834.
[56] See, for example, Post Medya, "Cem Küçük'ten Can Dündar, Arzu Yıldız, ve Fatih Yağmur'a Ölüm Tehdidi," YouTube, September 15, 2015, https://www.youtube.com/watch?v=WHv2k9s2Oow.
[57] "Turkey's Fox TV Anchorman Portakal Says He Has Received a Death Threat," *Hürriyet Daily News*, December 20, 2017.

A DIFFERENT "TURKISH MODEL"   317

phenomenon for journalists, academics, lawyers, and others who do not toe the government's line.

Importantly for this chapter's analysis, death threats and ominous messages often follow public statements from Erdoğan that draw attention to those deemed in need of being reminded where "their place" is. The threats received by TV newsman Portakal—a popular theme included Turks stabbing oranges, as *portakal* means "orange" in Turkish—followed a typical rebuke from Erdoğan: "Know your place, and if you don't know, the people of this country will smack you [*enseni patlatır*]."[58] The Turkish president used similar language about main opposition CHP leader Kemal Kılıçdaroğlu after the latter encouraged workers and union members to protest Yellow Vest–style. Again equating being in the opposition with something akin to treason, Erdoğan stated, "There are Yellow Vests in France, and the CHP is also there. There were Gezi Park protests and Mr. Kılıçdaroğlu was also there. There preparations once again, but you are waiting in vain. We will make you pay a heavy price."[59] With the passing of a 2018 government decree interpreted by many to encourage vigilante justice, a "skyrocketing" rise in both gun sales and gun deaths over the past three years,[60] and the post-coup establishment of pro-government militias that train members in weapons use,[61] the threat of deadly violence toward those who feel deputized into action by their leaders' words leaves today's Turkey closely resembling the widespread street wars of the 1970s.

Aside from the very real security concerns, do menacing words by a leader matter when assessing the level of democracy in a country? Can violence-themed rhetoric, whether acted upon vigilante-style or not, contribute to suppression of freedom of the press, and perhaps even the erosion of the rule of law? Turkey's journalist advocacy groups such as Reporters Without Borders and the Journalists' Union of Turkey certainly think so.[62] In grappling with these questions in the context of democratic breakdown in Turkey, this section of the chapter explores the various rhetorical devices the AKP government and its

[58] "Cumhurbaşkanı Erdoğan'dan FOX TV Fatih Portakal'a Sert Sözler!," *Haber7*, December 18, 2018, http://www.haber7.com/medya/haber/2785607-cumhurbaskani-erdogandan-fox-tv-fatih-portakala-sert-sozler.

[59] "Opposition MP Blasts Erdoğan for Threatening CHP Leader Kılıçdaroğlu," *Ahval News*, December 17, 2018, https://ahvalnews.com/chp/opposition-mp-blasts-erdogan-threatening-chp-leader-kilicdaroglu.

[60] "Turkey's Umut Foundation Calls for Gun Ownership Reform as Violence Toll Soars," *Hürriyet Daily News*, May 9, 2018, http://www.hurriyetdailynews.com/turkeys-umut-foundation-calls-for-gun-ownership-reform-as-violence-toll-soars-131554.

[61] See Howard Eissenstat, "Uneasy Rests the Crown: Erdoğan and 'Revolutionary Security' in Turkey," Project on Middle East Democracy, Washington DC, 2017, https://pomed.org/pomed-snapshot-uneasy-rests-the-crown-erdogan-and-revolutionary-security-in-turkey/.

[62] "Turkish Media Groups Reps. Express Concern over Erdoğan's Targeting of News Anchor," *Ahval News*, December 18, 2018, https://ahvalnews.com/turkish-media/turkish-media-group-reps-express-concern-over-erdogans-targeting-news-anchor.

318   WHEN DEMOCRACY BREAKS

supporters use to marginalize and delegitimize those who express opposition to its rule. Verbal and written rants do not inherently constitute a violation of democratic norms—indeed some could argue wars of words should be embraced in democratic regimes as part of freedom of expression and a marketplace of ideas. As I discuss here, however, AKP leaders' targeting of opposition members with vilifying terms promotes alienation that is contrary to the spirit of democracy, exacerbates us-versus-them tensions that lead supporters to seek vigilante justice, and justifies the use of state violence and punishment. The most significant inflection point in this use of vilification, in terms of the scope of those being targeted and the international attention brought to it, occurred during the 2013 Gezi Park protests but would be honed and wielded later. Initially begun as a small environmental demonstration to protect a park off Istanbul's central Taksim Square from being converted into a shopping mall and Ottoman-style barracks, the Gezi protests exploded into nationwide mobilization against the AKP government following viral images of police beating protesters and torching their tents with people still in them. Media silence by Turkish news outlets following multiple incidents of police violence against peaceful demonstrators added to protesters' grievances and fueled their momentum to continue turning out into the streets despite the injuries and deaths. While police beatings continued to produce casualties, most were due to the disproportionate and reckless use of tear gas canisters that were fired at head-level.

In what follows in this section, I analyze how the AKP literally added insult to injury to demobilize and discredit its opposition using Gezi as a mini case study. To do so, and to contribute to wider discussions of us-versus-them dynamics used by government in painting opposition actors as threats that need quashing, I identify three mechanisms of rhetorical vilification: naming, blaming, and framing. By "naming," I mean the use of derogatory and belittling terms used repeatedly by AKP members and spread through government-influenced media outlets to identify Gezi protesters as a hostile "other" to be feared and condemned. This mechanism serves to criminalize the actions of protesters and thus justify harsh measures used against them, while fueling a societal polarization of "us" (good government supporters) versus "them" (bad opposition agitators) that would have lasting consequences. Blaming consists of focusing on rare occurrences of violence and, much more often, fabricating antisocial and even immoral behavior for which Gezi protesters must be held accountable. Finally, the mechanism of framing enabled the AKP rhetorically to situate the behavior of the protesters into preexisting frames with negative connotations. This further solidified beliefs in its supporters' minds that Gezi protesters were miscreants with ulterior, and often externally supported, antigovernment motives.

The AKP's use of naming as a mechanism to delegitimize and "other"-ize those supporting the Gezi protests was quite explicit in its marginalization of the

A DIFFERENT "TURKISH MODEL"   319

extent of antigovernment opposition. Indeed, although the millions of peaceful protesters represented diverse backgrounds ranging from nationalist soccer fans and LGBTQ+ activists to Anti-Capitalist Muslims,[63] the government's use of rhetorical vilification attempted to paint them all as disruptive ne'er-do-wells. The AKP Istanbul governor initially reacted to the uprisings on his watch as the work of a few 'marginal groups' (*marjinal gruplar*),[64] a theme Erdoğan repeated many times. By declaring the protesters to be marginal, the AKP was able to both reduce public perceptions of the number of people protesting and relegate their grievances to the category of minor or even illegitimate. The AKP's practice of naming protesters with derogatory language took many other forms, some of which directly engage Turkey's tumultuous history with terrorism. By calling anyone who went to the streets to express their discontent with the government a terrorist (*terörist*), a term most vocally applied by then–EU Minister Egemen Bağış, the AKP identified Gezi protesters as inherently dangerous to Turkey.

The word "terrorism" in Turkey immediately evokes images of the PKK, the Kurdish nationalist militant group that has waged a violent struggle against the Turkish state for over thirty years and against which many Turkish families fear their sons will be conscripted to fight. "Terrorist" also has leftist connotations dating from Turkey's deadly political struggles in the 1960s and 1970s and often associated with Turkey's (non-Sunni) Alevis, who were targeted with violence by ultranationalists. Berkin Elvan, a fourteen-year-old Alevi child who was shot in the head with a tear gas canister while out to buy bread in his neighborhood, was called a terrorist by Erdoğan in several public speeches.[65] In another vilifying act of naming, EU Minister Bağış tweeted that those who attended Berkin's funeral were "necrophiliacs" (*nekrofiller*); perhaps sensing he had gone too far even for his party's supporters, he later softened his epithet to "provocateurs."[66]

In perhaps the most widely reported form of naming as a mechanism of vilification, Erdoğan frequently termed Gezi participants *çapulcu*, a word meaning "looter" or "hooligan." Similar to how U.S. president Donald Trump used the racially charged word "thug" to vilify Black Lives Matter protesters mobilizing in the wake of the police killings of Ahmaud Arbery, George Floyd, Breonna Taylor, and others,[67] Erdoğan's use of the term *çapulcu* immediately evokes images of

---

[63] See Isabel David and Kumru Toktamış, eds., *"Everywhere Taksim": Sowing the Seeds for a New Turkey at Gezi* (Amsterdam: Amsterdam University Press, 2015).

[64] "Vali Mutlu: Müdahale Fevkalade Düzgün," *Cumhuriyet Gazetesi*, 15 June 2013: https://www.cumhuriyet.com.tr/haber/vali-mutlu-mudahale-fevkalade-duzgun-428036.

[65] "Erdoğan Berkin Elvan'ı Terörist İlan Etti," *Cumhuriyet Gazetesi*, March 14, 2014, http://www.cumhuriyet.com.tr/video/video_haber/50741/Erdogan_Berkin_Elvan_i_terorist_ilan_etti.html#.

[66] "Nekrofil'i Sildi 'Provakatör' Dedi," *Hürriyet Gazetesi*, March 13, 2014.

[67] Nicole Chavez and Ray Sanchez, "Trump Calls Protesters 'Thugs' Despite Peaceful Demonstrations in Tulsa and Much of the US," CNN, June 20, 2020, https://www.cnn.com/2020/06/20/us/nationwide-protests-saturday/index.html.

320 WHEN DEMOCRACY BREAKS

wanton, unruly destruction that requires a law-and-order response. In a speech marking the opening of an Ottoman archives building, Erdoğan declared, "[W]e won't be frightened off by the provocations . . . of a couple of *çapulcu*."[68] Such statements, however, were far from the largely peaceful, environmentally friendly political culture that demonstrators created (and even self-policed when necessary, as I observed in rare instances of deviation from the predominant norms of behavior). In a creative and spirited effort to counteract such disparaging acts of naming, protesters began defiantly calling themselves *çapulcu*, using the term in witty riffs on AKP policies to which they objected.[69] In a critique of Erdoğan's call for all women to have at least three children, one woman held a sign reading, "I'll have three kids, I promise," which included stick-figure drawings of children named ÇapulCan, ÇapulNaz, and ÇapulNur—adding common Turkish names to the *çapulcu* insult.[70] A photo reprinted in a volume titled *A Çapulcu's Guide to Gezi* shows the phrase "you banned alcohol, we sobered up" spray-painted on a wall in response to newly imposed restrictions on alcohol sales.[71] While the humorous co-optation of the insult temporarily bolstered morale and helped to foster bonds of solidarity among disparate groups of protesters all facing the same insults and injuries,[72] the AKP's rhetorical vilification—particularly when distributed through media sources with complex government links[73] while other outlets were being censored—instilled fear of and animosity toward protesters among AKP supporters.

A related government strategy of highlighting those rare occasions in which Gezi protesters deviated from the peaceful norms of protest the great majority attempted to enforce, as well as falsely blaming protesters for incidents of violence and destruction, also served effectively to paint all those engaging in antigovernment opposition demonstrations with the vilification brush. Blaming Gezi protesters not only for damage done to storefront windows but also for the decline in these stores' business, Erdoğan declared that shopkeepers were legally justified in using violence against demonstrators.[74] In one instance of false blaming much publicized by the AKP, protesters were accused of drinking

---

[68] "Başbakan Erdoğan, Üç Beş Çapulcu'nun, Tahriklerine Pabuç Bırakmayız," speech, YouTube, June 2, 2013, https://www.youtube.com/watch?v=vrli7hJ3iW0.

[69] See *Çapulcu'nun Gezi Rehberi* (Istanbul: Hemen Kitap, 2013).

[70] Ibid., p. 169.

[71] *Çapulcu'nun Gezi Rehberi*, 13.

[72] Lisel Hintz, "The Might of the Pen(guin)," *Foreign Policy*, June 10, 2013, http://foreignpolicy.com/2013/06/10/the-might-of-the-penguin-in-turkeys-protests/.

[73] "The Turkish Media Muzzle," *Al Jazeera*, April 2, 2013, http://www.aljazeera.com/programmes/listeningpost/2013/04/201342104340948788.html.

[74] "Erdoğan: Esnafın Palalı Eylemi Hukuk Çerçevesinde," *Yurt Gazetesi*, July 8, 2013, http://www.yurtgazetesi.com.tr/politika/akp-esnafin-palali-eylemi-hukuk-cercevesinde-h38095.html.

alcohol in a mosque—behavior considered inexcusable and immoral for pious AKP supporters. *Yeni Şafak* correspondent Süleyman Gündüz, who was present at the mosque when the supposedly alcohol-consuming protesters sought shelter from the tear gas being used by police, countered this claim by stressing that not only was alcohol not consumed but that those entering "took off their shoes" as a sign of respect.[75] Although the mosque's imam corroborated the journalist's story, the rhetorical damage was done for many who repeated the story long after the supposed incident.

Finally, the government's strategic use of framing placed those who supported the Gezi movement in subversive company with foreign agents recognizable in Turkey as plotting the country's downfall. A common narrative stressed by AKP leaders was that foreign "lobbies"—from an interest rate lobby (*faiz lobisi*)[76] to an Israel/Jewish lobby (*İsrail/Yahudi lobisi*)[77]—were conspiring to prevent Turkey from becoming the powerful regional leader it deserved to be. In a country in which conspiracy theories are immensely popular (and often at least half-true), the idea that Gezi protesters—already named hooligans and blamed for immoral behavior—could be organized and/or funded by scheming external forces proved too tantalizing to resist. Interviewees cited foreigners' presence during the protests—some of whom were deported—as evidence that Western agents were infiltrating Turkey in the hopes of creating enough instability to provoke a coup and thus unseat the AKP.[78] Given the U.S. involvement in previous cases of regime change in Turkey, the frame of Western-sponsored military coups proved effective in bringing the true motives of the protesters into question. Devastating economic crises exacerbated by currency speculators and the AKP's stoking of anti-Semitic flames during its rule in Turkey created plausible and logically coherent frames into which the opposition manifested during the Gezi protests could be placed.

Adopting a broader perspective, we see the social polarization that has ossified in the wake of the Gezi protests. The AKP's vilifying rhetoric has gained tremendous momentum, targeting many different forms of opposition and cementing antagonistic us-versus-them relations along multiple identity lines. A terrifying sentiment following the Ankara terrorist bombings in October 2015 in which more than one hundred Kurds, leftists, and others who had gathered for a peace march were killed was that they had in coming; if they were Kurds or leftists, so

---

[75] "Erdoğan 'Camiye İçkiyle Girdiler' İddiasını Tekrarladı," *Hürriyet Gazetesi*, June 10, 2013, http://www.hurriyet.com.tr/gundem/23468860.asp.

[76] Barış Balcı, "'Gezi' mi Faiz Lobisinden, Faiz mi Gezi'den?," *Hürriyet Gazetesi*, June 11, 2013, http://www.hurriyet.com.tr/gezi-mi-faiz-lobisinden-faiz-mi-gezi-den-23476867.

[77] "GEZİ Senaryosunu Yahudi Lobisi Yazdı, Yahudi Sermayesi Finans Etti," *Yeni Akit*, June 13, 2013, http://www.yeniakit.com.tr/yazarlar/mehtap-yilmaz/gezi-senaryosunu-yahudi-lobisi-yazdi-yahudi-sermayesi-finanse-etti-bes-1803.html.

[78] Author's interview with AKP official, Eskişehir, August 2013.

322 WHEN DEMOCRACY BREAKS

this thinking goes, they were probably terrorists anyway. Despite such worrisome outcomes, naming, blaming, and framing—related but distinct mechanisms in how they function—seem to have gained currency among supporters as legitimate practices. When the power struggle between the AKP and its former close allies in the Gülen movement erupted into an all-out war, for example, Erdoğan coined the nickname of the movement's leader Fethullah Gülen as *Pensilvanya*.[79] This evocation of Gülen's exile in the United States, which rapidly spread among AKP supporters, cast him and his "parallel structure" (*paralel yapı*) as foreign and thus inherently suspect. Following the July 15, 2016, coup attempt, the blame for which Erdoğan places squarely on Gülen and his supporters, the shadowy parallel structure reference was dropped and replaced with FETÖ—Fethullahcı Terrorist Organization. The term FETÖcu, or member of the organization, is now used widely to characterize anyone with remote, and often fabricated, links to Gülen. The application of this label has been wielded in justifying the purges and arrests of hundreds of thousands of Turkey's citizens, an aspect considered in this chapter's concluding discussion of challenges facing the country's opposition.

From a broader perspective, the term "terrorist" has been wielded to marginalize and justify the arrest of opposition actors from university students[80] to vegetable vendors.[81] What cohered as a countermobilization strategy against Gezi protesters has evolved into everyday politics in Turkey. Although rhetorical vilification should not be seen as a sole causal factor in the dissipation of demonstrations, its uses in justifying harsh measures against protesters carry over into methods of delegitimizing anyone who voices criticism. Today those using xenophobic insults against AKP opponents are lauded;[82] those using injury are rewarded with political promotion.[83] When examining the mechanisms by which democratic and hybrid regimes can slide along the path of dedemocratization, the long-term, society-wide consequences of naming, blaming, and framing play a key role.

[79] "Erdoğan'dan Paralel Yapı Açıklaması," *Takvim*, October 11, 2014, http://www.takvim.com.tr/guncel/2014/10/11/erdogandan-paralel-yapi-aciklamasi.

[80] Lisel Hintz, "Why Recep Erdogan Is Calling Turkish Students Terrorists," *Washington Post*, April 12, 2018, https://www.washingtonpost.com/news/monkey-cage/wp/2018/04/12/what-turkeys-president-wanted-to-achieve-when-he-called-students-terrorists/.

[81] "Turkish President Erdoğan Launches War on Food Price Terror," *Hürriyet Daily News*, February 11, 2019, http://www.hurriyetdailynews.com/turkish-president-erdogan-launches-war-on-food-price-terror-141168.

[82] "Erdoğan Attends 'Ak Troll' Wedding, Chats with Suspect," *Hürriyet Daily News*, June 15, 2015, http://www.hurriyetdailynews.com/erdogan-attends-ak-troll-wedding-chats-with-well-known-suspect.aspx?pageID=238&nID=84013&NewsCatID=338.

[83] "Controversial Former AKP MP in Anti-*Hürriyet* Protests Promoted to Deputy Minister," *Hürriyet Daily News*, December 18, 2015, http://www.hurriyetdailynews.com/controversial-former-akp-mp-in-anti-hurriyet-protests-promoted-to-deputy-minister.aspx?pageID=238&nID=92693&NewsCatID=338.

Conclusion: Electoral Manipulation and the Challenges of Turkey's Opposition

The transformation of institutions that could formerly serve as a check on the power of Erdoğan and his AKP opened the space for vilification that served to marginalize Turkey's opposition actors as well as justify the purges, arrests, and other antidemocratic actions against them. In both processes, identity contestation lies at the heart of Turkey's de-democratization. Of course, these processes of institutional transformation and opposition vilification are aided by other variables that more traditionally receive focus in studies of democratic breakdown. Turkey's complex networks of media influence, the preexisting fractures among its opposition, the political economy of patronage, and many more factors mentioned above and elsewhere combine to ease power consolidation and limit rebellion against it.

A main challenge that Turkey's opposition now faces both defines Turkey's de-democratization and facilitates it. The increasing presence of electoral manipulation from the most local to the most national level constrains the ability of parties challenging AKP rule through established channels. While the AKP had consistently won elections since coming to power in 2002, the March 2014 elections that followed the nationwide Gezi protests were the first clear indication that electoral manipulation had entered the party's playbook. Legislative changes instituted prior to the election shifted the boundaries and makeup of metropolitan municipalities to distort voting in a manner that significantly advantaged the AKP and disadvantaged the CHP.[84] On polling day itself, from power outages during vote-counting blamed on a cat to districts with over 100% turnout to reports that Ankara mayoral candidate Mansur Yavaş received no votes in his own district,[85] the elections set a precedent for victories plagued by irregularities. The March 2014 local elections are thus an important turning point in considering the constriction of space for political contestation through party challengers.

In addition to legislative changes such as redistricting and day-of manipulation of voting conditions on the ground, the AKP's increasing influence over institutions as discussed above made its presence clear in the electoral sphere in 2017. The stakes of Turkey's April 2017 referendum were particularly high, as the outcome would decide whether to institute the presidential system Erdoğan so stridently advocated, a shift that would greatly consolidate power in, presumably, his own hands. While forensic analysis shows evidence of on-the-ground

---

[84] Cenk Aygül, "Electoral Manipulation in March 30, 2014 Turkish Local Elections," *Turkish Studies* 17, no. 1 (2016): 181–201.
[85] "Ankara'da Oy Sayımı İçin Büyük Mücadele!," Haber, April 1, 2014, https://haber.sol.org.tr/dev let-ve-siyaset/ankarada-oy-sayimi-icin-buyuk-mucadele-haberi-90295.

324   WHEN DEMOCRACY BREAKS

interference such as ballot-stuffing and voter intimidation,[86] the referendum's "yes" vote's very narrow win (51.4%) came after the Supreme Electoral Board (Yüksek Seçim Kurulu, YSK) declared late in the day that ballots missing the official stamp would be counted.[87] Opposition MP Bülent Tezcan summed up the frustrations of those in the "no" camp: "The YSK is paving the way for us to enter an unfortunate period that accepts the principle of elections under judicial manipulation rather than under judicial supervision. . . . [E]lections will face a serious legitimacy problem."[88] Although Tezcan was referring to the controversy surrounding the referendum, his words presage the politicization of the electoral and judicial systems that was to come.

In the race for the position of the presidency itself in 2018, opposition actors overcame their discombobulation at the move of the presidential election along with parliamentary elections from November to June and, at least temporarily, their skepticism about the unevenness of the playing field to rally behind CHP candidate Muharrem İnce. However, despite the unexpected boost they gained when Erdoğan told his supporters he would step down from leadership if the nation said "Enough" (*Tamam*), spurring a humorous *Tamam*-themed campaign that brought hope and enthusiasm to opposition voters,[89] Erdoğan's early declaration of victory based on "unofficial results" on election night seemed to function as a fait accompli. The YSK made this result official soon after, despite ongoing ballot counting. Erdoğan supporters had already streamed into the streets, while İnce disappeared from media view for hours. Documented cases of electoral violence, discarded ballots, voter list irregularities, and polling stations moved just before polls opened also cast doubt on the integrity of the elections.[90] Despite such doubts, Erdoğan's influence over the media, the YSK, and the judiciary allowed his declaration of victory to go relatively unchallenged. Any major challenge the opposition might have raised was effectively nullified by İnce's (possibly inadvertent and still puzzling) midnight concession on live television as a news anchor read a personal text message from the candidate stating,

---

[86] Peter Klimek, Raul Jimenez, Manuel Hidalgo, Abraham Hinteregger, and Stefan Thurner, "Election Forensic Analysis of the Turkish Constitutional Referendum 2017," arXiv preprint, arXiv:1706.09839, June 29, 2017.

[87] "Turkey's Supreme Election Board Says Unsealed Ballot Papers Accepted in Vote," *Hürriyet Daily News*, April 16, 2017, https://www.hurriyetdailynews.com/turkeys-supreme-election-board-says-unsealed-ballot-papers-accepted-in-vote--112087.

[88] CHP MP Bülent Tezcan, quoted in Barın Kayaoğlu, "Erdogan's Referendum Win No Clean Sweep," *Al Monitor*, April 17, 2017, https://www.al-monitor.com/pulse/originals/2017/04/turkey-ref erendum-passes.html.

[89] Pınar Tremblay, "Turkish Opposition Motto Comes from Unexpected Contributor: Erdogan," *Al-Monitor*, May 11, 2018, https://www.al-monitor.com/originals/2018/05/turkey-best-opposition-motto-provided-by-erdogan.html.

[90] See the Election Observation Mission Final Report of the OSCE Office for Democratic Institutions and Human Rights, "Republic of Turkey: Early Presidential and Parliamentary Elections 24 June 2018," Warsaw, September 21, 2018.

A DIFFERENT "TURKISH MODEL" 325

"[T]he guy won."[91] Opposition election observers abandoned their posts, sealing Erdoğan's victory.

When even the AKP's multiple institutional levers of influence are insufficient in producing the desired results, as was the case in İmamoğlu's victory over AKP candidate and former prime minister Binali Yıldırım in a rerun of the 2019 Istanbul mayoral election, the ruling party uses other measures to limit the power of opposition actors. Examples include the sentencing of CHP Istanbul chair Canan Kaftancıoğlu, a key player in organizing Kurdish votes for İmamoğlu, to nearly ten years in prison for her tweets,[92] and the appropriation of political and financial decision-making and even land from the CHP-led metropolitan municipality to the AKP-dominated city council and to national ministries.[93] Attempts to curtail the opposition's ability to govern and mobilize following election victories are even starker in Kurdish-majority municipalities, where the arrests and replacements of HDP majors with AKP trustees left the HDP in 2020 in control of just one-fifth of the cities it won in 2019.[94] Kurdish areas are targeted with the highest levels of interference in both election processes and outcomes—a case of disproportionately regional de-democratization supported by the AKP's institutional takeover of the judiciary and the rhetorical vilification of HDP members as engaging in "terrorist" activities.

It is worth noting that both the 2018 presidential and parliamentary elections and the April 2017 referendum were held under a state of emergency that had been in place since the July 15, 2016, coup attempt. Despite the official lifting of emergency measures shortly after Erdoğan's victory, some of which were institutionalized into law by presidential decree,[95] the AKP's power over elections and their outcomes remains formidable. This power is not, however, unshakeable.

İmamoğlu's victory in the election rerun may have signaled much of what can challenge the AKP in the future: the unification of generally contentious opposition groups behind one candidate, the eschewing of identity politics in favor of condemnation of antidemocratic and corrupt practices, and more.[96] Whether the political space for such a challenge from the opposition remains

---

[91] "İnce 'Adam Kazandı' Dediğinde Halk TV," YouTube, March 18, 2019, https://www.youtube.com/watch?v=jLFo9Khy14U&t=0s.

[92] "CHP Istanbul Chair Sentenced to Nearly 10 Years in Prison," *Hürriyet Daily News*, September 6, 2019, https://www.hurriyetdailynews.com/chp-istanbul-chair-sentenced-to-nearly-10-years-in-prison-146355.

[93] "İBB'nin Varlıkları AKP'li Belediyelere Bedelsiz Olarak Verildi," *Finans Gündem*, November 27, 2019, https://www.finansgundem.com/haber/ibbnin-varliklari-akpli-belediyelere-bedelsiz-olarak-verildi/1453385.

[94] Ayla Jean Yackley, "Turkey's Crackdown on Mayors Amounts to Coup, Says Opposition Party," *Al Monitor*, May 19, 2020, https://www.al-monitor.com/pulse/originals/2020/05/turkey-crackdown-opposition-mayors-coup.html.

[95] Kaya and Whiting, "The HDP, the AKP, and the Battle for Democracy."

[96] F. Michael Wuthrich and Melvyn Ingleby, "The Pushback against Populism: Running on 'Radical Love' in Turkey," *Journal of Democracy* 31, no. 2 (2020): 24–40.

open following the AKP's 2023 win depends greatly on Erdoğan himself, given his personalization of politics and consolidation of power in the executive over which he presides. It also depends heavily on the opposition's ability to unite despite the intra-coalition and intra-party tensions that plagued them in the 2023 presidential and parliamentary elections, and continue to create divides in the run-up to local elections scheduled for March 2024. Similarly, whether Turkey democratizes or de-democratizes under any potential constellation of new leadership in the future will rest heavily on the choices made by those entering into such a highly consolidated system. The influence of the conservative right that supported the AKP's heavy-handed governance in the past would likely remain strong in any coalition. Although objection to the presidential system that the AKP's power consolidation became a rallying point for six traditionally contentious opposition parties in the run-up to the 2023 elections, whether this would have become a policy priority had the opposition won was not guaranteed.

The fact that some opposition leaders at least initially moved away from the polarizing identity politics that facilitated prolonged AKP rule may serve to strengthen Turkey's chances for democratization in the long run. The softening of red lines against engaging with pro-Kurdish political actors was instrumental in wresting Istanbul from AKP control—but also alienated nationalists who might otherwise have voted for the opposition coalition in 2023. If continued with strong political will in the face of such inevitable nationalist backlash, this outreach could open the space for future coalitions that are better poised to erode divisiveness and resolve conflict. If combined with engagement with other groups marginalized in the AKP and previous eras, including women's and LGBTQ+ platforms, non-Muslim minorities, and Alevis, Turkey can more firmly shift its de-democratizing trajectory in the other direction.

12

Venezuela's Autocratization, 1999–2021

Variations in Temporalities, Party Systems, and Institutional Controls

Javier Corrales

Venezuela experienced multiple forms of regime change starting in the late 1990s, all in the direction of deeper forms of authoritarianism, all under the same ruling party. The country transitioned from unstable democracy in the 1990s to semi-authoritarianism in the 2000s and then full-fledged authoritarianism starting in 2015. Venezuela thus raises questions about the "how and why" of autocratization.

My first goal in this chapter is to provide a description of Venezuela's democratic backsliding since the 1990s, showing the aspects that were typical (i.e., frequently replicated by other cases), less typical, and even sui generis. My second goal is to advance the causal claim that backsliding was mostly related to two permissive factors: (1) changes in party system features, specifically, variations in party system fragmentation, along with (2) ruling party capture of key state institutions, namely the judiciary and the electoral authorities. This is the argument I make in my 2023 book, *Autocracy Rising*.

An illiberal president is more likely to make inroads in democratic backsliding under conditions of asymmetrical party system fragmentation, meaning the ruling party becomes strong and unified while the opposition fragments. This happened in Venezuela between 1998 and 2005.[1] This party system feature facilitated the transition from democracy to semi-authoritarianism.

The transition from semi-authoritarianism to full-fledged authoritarianism, in contrast, is more likely when the ruling party loses electoral competitiveness. This is what happened in Venezuela starting in the early 2010s. Under declining competitiveness, the ruling party faces the choice of losing power if it leaves the regime unchanged. It can remain in office only if it restricts liberties further, including eroding electoral freedoms further. An illiberal president will choose the

---

[1] Scott Mainwaring, "From Representative Democracy to Participatory Competitive Authoritarianism: Hugo Chávez and Venezuelan Politics," *Perspectives on Politics* 10, no. 4 (2012): 955–967.

Javier Corrales, *Venezuela's Autocratization, 1999–2021* In: *When Democracy Breaks*. Edited by: Archon Fung, David Moss, and Odd Arne Westad, Oxford University Press. © Oxford University Press 2024.
DOI: 10.1093/oso/9780197760789.003.0012

328 WHEN DEMOCRACY BREAKS

latter if the ruling party has a reservoir of coercive institutions and practices to draw from (see Bueno de Mesquita). The second vital condition for transition from semi- to full authoritarianism is thus the president's capturing of the bureaucracy, especially the judicial system and the electoral system, which permits him or her to engage in deeper forms of autocratic legalism (Corrales 2016, 2022; Scheppele; Gibler et al 2011). Capturing the judicial and electoral systems is the essential institutional reservoir that allows the regime to deepen its restrictions of the political system and punish opponents. Autocratic intensification was also helped by the fact that the ruling party captured two additional parts of the bureaucracy: agencies controlling the main economic driver (the oil sector) and of course, the coercive apparatus.

I begin by reviewing the characteristics of the regime prior to democratic backsliding (the 1980s and 1990s), arguing that there were signs of both democratic stress and democratic renewal. I then look at the factors that allowed Hugo Chávez to undermine liberal democracy (the early 2000s). I identify the typical and nontypical aspects of this process. I then discuss the last stage, transition to full-fledged autocracy (2013 to the present), with a focus on the factors that prompted this transition and made it possible for the regime to prevail in its efforts.

The Preamble: Democratic Degradation and/or Renovation in the 1990s

Scholars agree that Venezuela in the 1960s had a strong, early rising democracy. It was strong in that Venezuela managed to establish most institutions typically associated with liberal democracy. It was early rising in that democracy emerged in the early 1960s, much sooner than in the rest of the Global South, long before the start of the Third Democratic Wave in the 1980s. According to some indices, Venezuela's democracy in the 1960s came close to matching U.S. scores, at least in terms of liberal democratic criteria.

Scholars disagree, however, regarding the course of democracy in Venezuela in the 1980s and 1990s, when the country was hit by two severe external economic shocks: the onset of the Latin American debt crisis in 1982 and the drastic drop in oil prices between 1981 and 1983 (see Hausmann and Rodríguez 2014). (Ever since the 1920s, when Venezuela became one of the world's leading oil exporters, Venezuela's economy has been highly dependent on oil exports.)

While scholars agree that these external shocks took a disproportionately large toll on the economy,[2] there is a debate on their impact on democratic

---

[2] See Ricardo Hausmann and Francisco Rodriguez, "Introduction," in *Venezuela before Chávez: Anatomy of an Economic Collapse*, ed. Ricardo Hausmann and Francisco Rodriguez (University Park: Pennsylvania State University Press, 2014), 1–14.

VENEZUELA'S AUTOCRATIZATION   329

institutions.[3] For some scholars, democratic institutions decayed irremediably in the 1990s. Institutions of representation stopped delivering and became corrupt to the core. For others, democracy came under stress, no doubt, but there were also signs of rebirth.

For the former school of thought, irremediable democratic decline in the 1990s explains the political instability of the period (interrupted market reforms in the early 1990s, two coup attempts in 1992, a devastating banking crisis in 1994–1996, and the electoral collapse of traditional parties by 1998). It also explains the rise of political maverick Hugo Chávez in the 1998 presidential election. This school of thought would contend that Chávez, a lieutenant colonel with no political experience until his 1992-coup attempt, prevailed in the 1998 elections because he promised a complete overhaul of Venezuela's democratic institutions, which resonated with the large majority of Venezuelans precisely because democratic atrophy was profound. For this school, the decline in the quality, functioning, and delivery of democratic institutions explains the huge electoral demand for an antisystem leader like Chávez.

For the latter school of thought, the explanation for the rise of Chávez is different. Chávez rose not exclusively because democratic institutions were moribund but because of democratic openings in the 1990s, despite the chaos of the period. In response to much of the economic instability of the time, leaders introduced political reforms such as decentralization and more electoral opportunities at the regional level. Civil society also became more mobilized and independent of parties. The press acquired greater freedoms, and journalistic quality expanded. Without these democratic openings in the 1990s, a political maverick would not have been able to rise. The old political parties and elites would have blocked him.

Either way, there is no disagreement that Venezuela's democracy was under serious stress in the 1990s, besieged by economic crisis, policy paralysis, instability, and party system volatility. Perhaps the best summary is this: in some areas, democracy was faltering, but in other areas, it was regenerating itself. At the very least, there was an opening of the party system with changes in electoral rules facilitating new parties and leaders to compete in a larger number of arenas than ever before. The party system, because of both economic crisis and political reforms, experienced a sort of opening. And this opening in turn created conditions that could be exploited by nontraditional individuals, rising outside of traditional parties, to compete electorally and win. The Venezuelan case suggests that preexisting instability of the party system can create conditions for

---

[3] See Javier Corrales, "Explaining Chavismo: The Unexpected Alliance of Radical Leftists and the Military in Venezuela under Hugo Chávez," in Hausmann and Rodriguez, *Venezuela before Chavez*, 371–406.

330   WHEN DEMOCRACY BREAKS

nontraditional, antisystem candidates to rise, who may either choose to reform the system or overhaul it entirely, and this instability was the result of both economic stresses as well as political openings.

Venezuela's Democratic Backsliding, 1999–2010: Common Elements

Chávez chose to overhaul the system in the direction of autocratization (see Lührmann and Lindberg). The process began soon after his election in 1998. By 2006, Chávez had transformed Venezuela into a semi-autocracy. The president came close to enjoying full dictatorial powers, even if some civil liberties remained in place.

The entire process of autocratization in Venezuela was representative in some respects as well as unusual in other respects. It was representative because the first phase of the process, democratic backsliding, displayed many characteristics that are typical of democratic backsliding elsewhere. It was unusual in that some aspects of this backsliding do not occur in most cases of backsliding. This section discusses the common elements.

Liberal Democracy as the First Target

The first feature of Venezuela's democratic backsliding, as in most other cases, was a rapid assault on the institutions of liberal democracy (Carothers 2002; Diamond 2002, 2014; Levitsky and Way 2010; Lust and Waldner 2015; Schedler 2006). Other institutions of democracy stayed unchanged or declined less rapidly. But institutions of liberal democracy were immediately targeted by the president. This is typical of most cases of backsliding.

Institutions of liberal democracy consist of those rules and norms that regulate the system of checks and balances on the executive branch and government-opposition relations (see Coppedge et al. 2011). In almost all forms of executive-driven backsliding, these institutions are the first to be targeted by the president, leading to enormous concentration of power in the executive branch, along with the rise of rules and norms aimed at hindering the ability of the opposition to compete electorally (Corrales 2015; Huq and Ginsburg 2018). This is what Nancy Bermeo describes as executive aggrandizement.[4]

Figure 12.1 shows how rapidly the descent of liberal democracy occurred. The figure traces the steep decline in V-Dem's liberal democracy index, which

---

[4] Nancy Bermeo, "On Democratic Backsliding," *Journal of Democracy* 27, no. 1 (2016): 5–19.

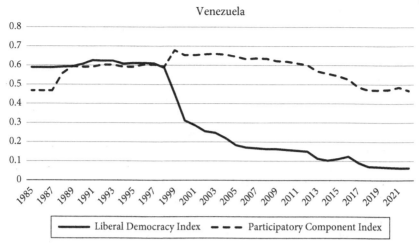

Figure 12.1 Venezuela: Different rates of democratic backsliding according to institution type. Source: Corrales (2022) based on V-Dem. The liberal democracy index measures a regime's commitment to protecting liberal democracy principles, such as individual and minority rights and limits placed on government through the enforcement of constitutionally protected civil liberties, rule of law, an independent judiciary, and effective checks and balances. The participatory component index measures a regime's commitment to active participation by citizens in all political processes, electoral and nonelectoral, including mechanisms for direct rule wherever practicable.

is meant to capture checks and balances on the executive branch, among other features.

This undermining of liberal democratic institutions was facilitated, in fact was possible only because of asymmetrical party fragmentation (a ruling party that was unified and strong with an opposition that was fragmented). Initially, the steps were mixed. The 1999 Constitution gave the impression that newer checks on the power of the president were created through the establishment of new participatory mechanisms, including the option of a recall referendum. However, signs of executive aggrandizement proliferated even under the new, presumably more inclusive constitution: the constitution extended the president's term in office from five to six years, eliminated the Senate (and thus a potential veto actor), restricted public financing for parties, and gave more powers to the president to manage military affairs without legislative oversight.

Executive aggrandizement continued even after the adoption of the new constitution, with the announcement of numerous executive decrees in 2001 that bypassed the legislature, renamed the National Assembly. Dismayed by these

332 WHEN DEMOCRACY BREAKS

power grabs, opponents of the ruling party began to stage street protests—including massive marches—that culminated in a strange coup. The government called on the military to repress the protests, but the military refused, asking the president himself to resign instead. A new president was sworn in, but the optics were counterproductive: despite having the support of unions, the new president was the leader of Venezuela's leading business federation, producing the image of corporate power deposing a popularly elected president. In a sign of rising polarization, Chávez's supporters took to the streets to demand his return, and the military, in an unexpected about-face, decided to restore Chávez to the presidency less than forty-eight hours after his ouster. No other ousted president in Latin America since the 1980s has been reinstalled.

Once returned to power, Chávez showed few signs of changing his ways. Consequently, more street protests followed in 2003–2004. Chávez responded by further concentrating power rather than softening his rule: he fired oil workers who went on strike and expanded presidential control over the affairs of the oil company in 2003. More broadly, he staffed the bureaucracy with loyalists, firing the professional staff. By 2004, Chávez had essentially eliminated or reformed most economic laws to give himself more discretionary power in the use of oil money and he eroded the autonomy of the Central Bank.

In 2003, Chávez used every possible tactic to delay a recall referendum sponsored by civic groups, and when he finally agreed to allow it, he engaged in massive social spending, aimed at expanding clientelism and diverting enough funds to co-opt business elites. Chávez used the influx of petrodollars that began flowing into the country in large volumes in late 2003, heavy dominance of the airwaves, and other electoral irregularities to prevail electorally. This tactic of giving the ruling party unrestricted access to petrodollars while denying funding to the opposition has been the hallmark of Chavismo to this day.

Perhaps the most decisive turn in the assault on the institutions of liberal democracy was the overhaul of the courts. Chávez began his administration by threatening members of the Supreme Court. The Constituent Assembly sacked and replaced most members of the Supreme Court. Then, in 2004, Chávez's party in the legislature expanded the Supreme Court from twenty to thirty-two seats, appointing seventeen new justices to fill the new seats and existing vacancies. A new law defied the 1999 Constitution by granting Chávez's party the power to remove judges from the court with a simple majority in the legislature. The judicial administration had already failed to protect judicial independence, firing three judges who had decided controversial cases against the Chávez regime.

Chávez also eroded the autonomy of the electoral body in charge of monitoring elections, the National Electoral Council (CNE). He allowed the now partisan Supreme Court to appoint its members in 2005, contravening the constitutional stipulation that nominations would come from civil society and

VENEZUELA'S AUTOCRATIZATION   333

the legislature. The CNE became another partisan body. Almost every scholar studying Venezuela's elections from the 2004 recall referendum and through the rest of the Chávez period raised alarms about the lack of impartiality of the CNE, its favoritism toward the ruling party, its whimsical enforcement and manipulation of electoral rules and norms, its decision starting in 2006 to stop international observations, and its unwillingness to investigate fraud allegations.

With control of the courts, the electoral authorities, the oil sector, the bureaucracy, the military, and the legislature, Chávez obtained what Michael Penfold and I called an "institutional resource curse" (Corrales and Penfold 2015).[5] This institutional control allowed the government to introduce laws, regulations, and practices that restricted the operation of independent state and societal actors. An important early victim of this autocratic legalism was the independent media. By 2005, Chávez was already restricting content, imposing fines, denying resources, refusing to allow import of paper, and banning journalists from covering certain stories.

In 2005, the opposition made a costly mistake. It decided to respond to democratic backsliding by boycotting the elections for the 2005 National Assembly. This decision to boycott, always tempting to many opposition parties in backsliding cases, did nothing to stop backsliding. It actually empowered the ruling party more. The ruling party ended up with 100% control of the National Assembly. From then on, the legislature became a mere rubber stamp of the presidency. By 2006, other important institutions of government that were supposed to remain fairly independent—the attorney general, the Ombudsman Office, the Central Bank, the state-owned oil company—also became subservient to the executive branch.

In short, by 2006, merely seven years after Chávez's coming to power, the mixed signals of democratic backsliding were less mixed. The president had moved decisively forward with executive aggrandizement—using autocratic legalism to favor the president (Corrales 2015), electoral irregularities to disfavor the opposition (Corrales 2020), and heavy spending to co-opt both the poor and the very wealthy (Corrales and Penfold 2015). Institution after institution—the Constituent Assembly of 1999, the courts, the CNE, the bureaucracy, the military, the oil company, and the legislature—fell into the hands of the ruling party. This institutional control allowed the government to create laws, decrees, regulations, rulings, and norms that increasingly granted the president more power to act and greater restriction of dissidents hoping to block the government's agenda. Courts and law enforcement officials would look the other way each time the president did something illegal. This use, abuse, or lack of use of the law to help

---

[5] Javier Corrales and Michael Penfold, "Venezuela: Crowding Out the Opposition," *Journal of Democracy* 18, no. 2 (2015): 99–113.

334   WHEN DEMOCRACY BREAKS

the president and hurt the opposition is the essence of autocratic legalism. It is perhaps that most inevitable effect stemming from presidential attacks on institutions of liberal democracy. If there was something less typical about this relentless attack on institutions of liberal democracy it was how far Chávez was able to reach. Few backsliding presidents achieve so much control of so many institutions in such a short period of time as Chávez did in his first seven years in office.

Unevenness

The second commonality of Venezuela's backsliding was initial ambiguity. At the beginning of the process, it is not easy for all societal actors to notice with clarity that backsliding is taking place. The ambiguity stems from the fact that even as one key aspect of democracy—liberal democracy—declines rapidly, other aspects of democracy may not decline as much, as fast, or at all. Consequently, not all actors are able to see the signs of backsliding right away.

Although the literature on democratic backsliding tends to distinguish between two temporalities of democratic regression—gradual and rapid forms of regression[6]—most often, democratic backsliding shows both temporalities occurring *simultaneously*, with some institutions declining fast and others more slowly, if at all.

In the specific case of Venezuela, the aspect of democracy that did not decline rapidly at first had to do with participatory features.[7] This is clear from V-Dem's participatory index. The index actually improves (briefly) and stays relatively strong before it begins to decline by the end of the 2000s. In other words, while the president was concentrating powers in the early part of the regime, he was also bolstering institutions designed to give Venezuelans new opportunities to participate in politics.

Chávez's defenders and several scholars contend that the regime actually expanded participatory democracy.[8] There is little question that the 1999 Constitution expanded some institutional avenues of inclusion: it recognized

---

[6] See Johannes Gerschewski, "Erosion or Decay? Conceptualizing Causes and Mechanisms of Democratic Regression," *Democratization* 28, no. 1 (2020): 43–62.

[7] V-Dem defines the participatory principle of democracy as a measure of "active participation by citizens in all political processes, electoral and non-electoral. It is motivated by uneasiness about a bedrock practice of electoral democracy: delegating authority to representatives. Thus, direct rule by citizens is preferred, wherever practicable. This model of democracy thus takes suffrage for granted, emphasizing engagement in civil society organizations, direct democracy, and subnational elected bodies" (https://v-dem.net/graphing/).

[8] See, for example, Gregory Wilpert, *Changing Venezuela: The History and Policies of the Chavez Government* (New York: Verso, 2007); Steve Ellner, *Rethinking Venezuelan Politics: Class, Conflict, and the Chávez Phenomenon* (Boulder, CO: Lynne Rienner, 2009).

VENEZUELA'S AUTOCRATIZATION   335

indigenous rights, called for greater racial integration, introduced the possibility of recall referenda for presidents, and created mechanisms for citizens to participate in nominations for certain public offices. In addition, Many of Chávez's policies were also predicated on mobilizing the poor and the nonwhite, such as creating new communal councils to promote local participation, dramatically expanding funding for social services, and establishing free health clinics in poor neighborhoods.[9] These reforms persuaded many voters, especially the president's supporters, that democracy was actually expanding rather than contracting.

Over time, however, the evidence of participation expansion became more dubious (see Figure 12.1). Chávez soon began to distort participatory democracy by making it sectarian and conditional.[10] New groups were incorporated and given new powers, provided they were demonstrably loyal to the ruling party; others were explicitly excluded or even ostracized. For instance, members of the ruling party were given priority in hiring decisions in state-owned corporations. These were the most appealing jobs because they offered incomparable job security. In contrast, nonloyalists were systematically excluded from any state-provided public services. Thus, new labor unions, civic organizations, neighborhood committees, and schools and universities were created—all of which incorporated people and sectors that were traditionally underprivileged and underrepresented, but with the condition that they needed to show support for the president. Participation became sectarian, and *chavista* groups became increasingly nonpluralistic. Being identified as a member of the opposition, or even a *chavista* with contrarian views, carried huge risks: unemployment, disqualification from access to state services, public ostracism.

Polarization, with a Large "Neither/Nor" Group.

A third commonality is the rise of polarization, with a sizable, disaffected middle. The regime's initially mixed track record (different rates of decline of different institutions of democracy) causes a major split across the political system. On the one hand, the leaders of the opposition will of course notice the decline in liberal democracy—those leading to executive aggrandizement, degradation of

---

[9] Ryan Brading, *Populism in Venezuela* (London: Routledge, 2013); Margarita López-Maya, "Hugo Chávez Frías: His Movement and His Presidency," in *Venezuela Politics in the Chávez Era*, ed. Stele Ellner and Daniel Hellinger (Boulder, CO: Lynne Rienner, 2003), 73–92; Jesús María Herrera Salas, "Ethnicity and Revolution: The Political Economy of Racism in Venezuela," in *Venezuela: Hugo Chávez and the Decline of an "Exceptional Democracy,"* ed. Steve Ellner and Miguel Tinker Salas (Lanham, MD: Rowan and Littlefield, 2007); Wilper, *Changing Venezuela*; Ellner, *Rethinking Venezuelan Politics*; Roger Burbach and Camila Piñeiro, "Venezuela's Participatory Socialism," *Socialism and Democracy* 21, no. 3 (2007): 181–200.

[10] Kirk A. Hawkins, "Who Mobilizes? Participatory Democracy in Chávez's Bolivarian Revolution," *Latin American Politics and Society* 52, no. 3 (2010): 31–66.

336   WHEN DEMOCRACY BREAKS

rights, and an uneven playing field—more than any other actors in part because they are the most direct cost-bearers of this type of decline. These groups will actually panic. But for the rest of the electorate, the outlook is not that clear-cut. In Venezuela, the ruling party offered followers not only opportunities to participate in politics but also copious amounts of social spending. The part of the electorate that cares more about the aspects of democracy that are not declining that much (in the case of Venezuela, participation, access to social services) may end up ignoring or forgiving the decline of institutions of liberal democracy—they see plenty of hope with the other indicators that they value more.

In other words, the initially mixed process of democratic decay, at least in the beginning, leads to an electorate that is very divided about the actual democratic trajectory of the regime. For some, democracy is crashing; for others, democracy is resurfacing. The result is rising polarization.

The president sometimes intentionally exacerbates this polarization by adopting increasingly extremist public policies, in addition to the extreme power grabs that always occur with backsliding. In Venezuela, these extremist public policies focused mostly on expanding the role of the state in economic matters, which culminated in a massive nationalization drive between 2008 and 2010 that was so large it was reminiscent of Communist regimes during the Cold War. These nationalizations were mostly done by executive decrees and often at the whim of the president. Policy extremism of any kind angers and even threatens the opposition even further. In the case of Venezuela, where public extremism focused so much on nationalization, even labor groups mobilized against the president since many were opposed to expanding state control of the economy.

This polarization, which results from the combination of the president's power grabs, intentional policy extremism, and unevenness in attacks on democratic institutions, can paradoxically help the incumbent politically. Under heightened polarization, government sympathizers become very forgiving of the president's excesses and mistakes because they become very hateful of opponents. Supporters morph easily into rabid fans; opponents, into threatened actors ready to embrace extremist positions, which in turn helps the president's supporters turn more hard-line.

That said, even with this polarization, the process of backsliding also produces a group in the electorate that is turned off by the acrimony between both camps. These voters see little difference between—or little to admire about—the extremist positions adopted by either side. In Venezuela, this group was called the *ni/nis* (the neither/nors), meaning that they sided with neither group. Their tendency was to abstain politically. An important part of the political battle centers on capturing this group, or preventing it from voting with the other side. The dilemma facing the opposition leadership is that if it becomes extreme, it risks alienating this middle group. But if it becomes too moderate, it risks losing the

VENEZUELA'S AUTOCRATIZATION   337

support of hard-line opponents, who begin to see the opposition leadership as sellouts. Polarization is thus not easy for the opposition leadership to manage.

Less Typical or Sui Generis Characteristics

Other aspects of backsliding in Venezuela were more atypical, meaning that they were not necessarily inevitable elements of backsliding even if they were signature elements in the Venezuelan case. First, Chávez's assault on liberal institutions of democracy was justified using a left-wing (populist) discourse, which is common in some but not all forms of backsliding. The "antagonistic binarism" that is typical of populism, that is, dividing the electorate between "we the *people* versus the *elite*," (see Müller 2016; Mudde and Rovira Kaltwasser 2017; Collier 2001; Pappas 2019) was heavily deployed by Chávez, but using a heavy dose of Marxist discourse. "We the people" was defined in terms of workers, low-income people, and underrepresented ordinary folks; elites were described as oligarchs, capitalists, multinationals, pro-American agents (*pitiyankis*). In typical populist fashion, all forms of dissent were subsumed under this category of class-based elites and, thus, not worth having a place at the table.

Second, the process also involved a heavy dose of militarism from the start. This was especially odd considering that the influence of the military in Venezuela and in Latin America was perhaps at an all-time low when backsliding began in 1999 (Martínez and Mares 2014; Mainwaring and Pérez-Liñán 2014). Since the very beginning of his administration, Chávez was intent on creating a "civil-military alliance."[11] He promoted this alliance in a country that had essentially achieved military subordination to civilian control in the early 1960s, a feat that most analysts of democracy in the Global South consider fairly admirable and rare.[12] Chávez came to power openly praising the military. He appointed military and former military officers to his cabinet, encouraged them to run for office, reduced the ability of the legislature to monitor military affairs, expanded the military budget for personnel, facilities, and equipment, and consulted with them more frequently than with members of Parliament. He also purged the military of officers who did not display loyalty to the ruling party. This allowed him to co-opt, restaff, and thus, de-professionalize the military to a degree that few other democratic presidents ever achieve. While many backsliding presidents ultimately end up siding closely with the military and, in fact, must find a way to coup-proof their regimes by courting the military heavily, it is less common

---

[11] Hugo Chávez et al., *Understanding the Venezuelan Revolution: Hugo Chávez Talks to Marta Harnecker* (New York: Monthly Review Press, 2005).
[12] Deborah L. Norden, *Venezuela: Coup-Proofing from Pérez Jiménez to Maduro* (London: Oxford University Press, 2021).

338 WHEN DEMOCRACY BREAKS

to see a president promote so much militarism from the very beginning of the backsliding process.[13]

Third, the process involved a heavy dose of social spending, possibly more on a per capita basis than even other petrostates at the time. Chávez took advantage of the spectacular boom in oil prices from 2004 to 2008 to expand social spending. Social spending was channeled to society via the creation of special social programs called "missions," each charged with different social services (literacy campaigns, health clinics, food distribution). These missions gave the government an image at home and abroad of being incredibly generous toward the poor. That said, it is important not to exaggerate the pro-poor aspect of the regime's social spending. By 2008 social spending had declined significantly. Many social missions were underfunded.[14] Most social programs generated unimpressive or declining returns as well as a high degree of corruption.[15] Incomes did not rise as much. While poverty declined, returns were incommensurate with the size of fiscal outlays. Returns were also not any better than most other comparable countries.[16] Despite these huge inconsistencies, Chávez gained a reputation early on of being a progressive distributionist. This reputation earned him allies at home and plenty of praise from abroad.

The Evolution of Opposition Tactics and the End of Asymmetrical Party System Fragmentation

The opposition changed tactics halfway during the backsliding process, for the better. In the initial stages, the opposition, in its desperation, supported extreme measures: massive protests in 2001, followed by open support for the early removal of Chávez (with the slogan, *Chávez vete ya*; "Chávez leave now"). which resulted in the 2002 coup, encouraging oil company workers to go on strike to strangle the country economically (2002–2003), and calling for election boycotts and abstentionism (in 2005).

After 2005, opposition tactics became far less extreme. Most of the opposition adhered to democratic norms and constitutional avenues to challenge Chávez. Starting in 2006, the opposition focused mostly on mobilizing the vote, seeking unity in decisions on candidates for elections, and protesting peacefully.

---

[13] Jun Koga Sudduth, "Coup Risk, Coup-Proofing and Leader Survival," *Journal of Peace Research* 54, no. 1 (2017): 3–15.

[14] Brading, *Populism in Venezuela*.

[15] Francisco Rodríguez, "An Empty Revolution: The Unfulfilled Promises of Hugo Chávez," *Foreign Affairs* 87, no. 2 (2008): 49–62; Thais Mangón, "Política social y régimen de bienestar, Venezuela 1999–2014," *Estudios Latinoamericanos Nueva Época* 38 (July–December 2016): 115–143.

[16] Kevin Grier and Norman Maynard, "The Economic Consequences of Hugo Chávez: A Synthetic Control Analysis," *Journal of Economic Behavior and Organization* 125 (2010): 1–21.

VENEZUELA'S AUTOCRATIZATION   339

Extremists remained active but were sidelined by the majority of opposition parties. This change in tactics from disruptive extremism to more institutional avenues paid off for the opposition (see Bunce 2010). From its low point in 2005, the opposition achieved increasingly strong results at almost every election between 2006 and 2015, this despite the increasing electoral obstacles posed by the government. In 2013, the opposition came very close to defeating the ruling party in presidential elections. In 2015, the opposition defeated Chavismo in the elections for the National Assembly.

In short, by the early 2010s, the opposition was able to shift the party system away from asymmetrical fragmentation. Opposition parties campaigned jointly for most elections, thus lessening party fragmentation. Starting in 2008, the opposition's catch-all electoral coalition became known as the Democratic Unity Roundtable (Mesa de la Unidad Democrática). It also opted to encourage electoral participation rather than boycotts. The opposition realized that rather than seeking unity at the level of ideology (which was nearly impossible due to the diversity of parties and viewpoints), it was better to focus mainly on fielding unified candidacies (rather than multiple candidacies) per post. This led to a rise in the opposition's electoral competitiveness, and thus in the party system's asymmetry, with the advantage gradually shifting toward the Democratic Unity Roundtable.

This shift in power balances had repercussions for regime dynamics from 2013 to 2019. For the first time since 1998, the ruling party felt electorally threatened. The regime faced a stark choice: to keep the regime and electoral rules unchanged, which, however biased toward the ruling party, would have still led to defeats, or to restrict the electoral opportunities for the opposition more severely and even repress protests. The regime chose the latter. This choice resulted in the autocratic intensification phase of Venezuela's democratic backsliding.

The Autocratic Intensification Phase: The Maduro Regime, 2013–Present

Venezuela's transition from semi-authoritarianism to full-fledged authoritarianism began in 2013. During this period, Venezuela achieved levels of autocracy similar to those of Cuba, one of the most autocratic states in the world. No other cases in Latin America except Nicaragua,[17] and few cases of democratic backsliding worldwide, end up undergoing this degree of autocratic

---

[17] Freedom House, *Freedom in the World*, https://freedomhouse.org/report/freedom-world; Javier Corrales, "Radical Claims to Accountability," in *Democracy and Its Discontents in Latin America*, ed. Joe Foweraker and Dolores Trevizo (Boulder, CO: Lynne Rienner, 2016), 115–131; Peter H. Smith and Melissa R. Ziegler, "Liberal and Illiberal Democracy in Latin America," *Latin American Politics and Society* 40, no. 1 (2008): 31–57.

340 WHEN DEMOCRACY BREAKS

intensification. Few cases of democratic backsliding worldwide started from such a high level of democracy and ended so low as Venezuela.[18]

The Why: Triggers and Capabilities

In my book *Autocracy Rising*, I deploy a functional and an institutional argument to explain Venezuela's autocratic intensification in the 2010s. The functional argument is that the regime needed to respond to deep political and economic crises that were threatening regime survival. Chávez's successor, Nicolás Maduro, needed to come up with desperate survival tactics with the rise of the opposition's strength. If he had allowed electoral politics to run its course, the ruling party would not have survived in office. The regime needed to be altered. The institutional argument is that Maduro's alteration focused on reinforcing and repurposing autocratic institutions already in place. To put down each and every crisis he confronted, Maduro drew from the toolkit left in place by Chávez. Maduro's contribution was to reinforce, update, or deepen these inherited tools. Autocratization emerged therefore as a response to both functional needs (economic crises, declining electoral competitiveness) as well as an institutional endowment (inherited autocratic practices, laws, and institutions), along with some clever adaptations.

The main crises afflicting Venezuela's ruling party in the early 2010s were twofold. First, the economy deteriorated sharply, mostly as a result of underperformance of the oil sector and in fact all state-owned enterprises established during Chávez's massive nationalization drive of 2008–2010. Second, the opposition continued to make electoral inroads, taking advantage of new opportunities (widespread grievances stemming from the economic crisis) and persevering on its strategy since 2006 of mobilizing the vote and maintaining unity during electoral races.

As the competitive authoritarian regime became *less* competitive electorally, it opted to become *more* authoritarian.[19] Signs of declining competitiveness were clear in the 2013 presidential election, the first after Chávez's death. Running as Chávez's chosen heir, Maduro won by a shockingly small margin and under suspicious circumstances. Clearer signs of declining competitiveness emerged in the 2015 legislative elections. The government lost the election, and thus control of the legislature, despite an electoral system rigged to its advantage.[20]

---

[18] Stephan Haggard and Robert R. Kaufman, *Dictators and Democrats: Masses, Elites, and Regime Change* (Princeton: Princeton University Press, 2016).

[19] Corrales and Penfold, "Venezuela."

[20] See Brading, *Populism in Venezuela*; Javier Corrales, "Democratic Backsliding through Electoral Irregularities: Venezuela 1999–2019," *European Review of Latin American and Caribbean Studies* 109

VENEZUELA'S AUTOCRATIZATION   341

The response of the regime to this declining competitiveness was to turn more authoritarian. This response required making use of, fortifying, and repurposing some of the authoritarian features adopted by the regime in previous years.

The How: The End of Unevenness

Whereas under Chávez democratic institutions were attacked unevenly, under Maduro the three fundamental aspects of democracy—minimal, liberal, and participatory institutions—were attacked fully and simultaneously. Mixed temporality disappeared in favor of across-the-board attack on all aspects of democracy. This change in temporality is the reason, I argue, the regime under Maduro qualifies as fully authoritarian rather than semi-authoritarian.

First, Maduro essentially eliminated minimal democracy between 2017 and 2021. He either stopped electoral processes altogether or made them so irregular that they ceased to have any semblance of fairness and freedom. For instance, Maduro blocked a petition to carry out a recall referendum. Using questionable rulings from his co-opted court and unfair statements from his co-opted Electoral Council, the government argued groundlessly that the opposition did not comply with technical requirements to request a recall referendum. This marked the first time that electoral irregularities in Venezuela caused the outright cancellation of an election rather than just tilting the playing field.

All the elections that did take place between 2017 and 2021 were unprecedentedly irregular and adverse to the four main parties of the opposition: Primero Justicia, Voluntad Popular, Acción Democrática, and Un Nuevo Tiempo. Maduro organized an impromptu election for a new Constituent Assembly, charged officially with the task of drafting a new constitution but, in reality, designed to supersede the legislature. For this election, the regime used some of the most irregular electoral practices in the history of elections in Latin America. For instance, some Venezuelans (mostly pro-government) were allowed to vote twice— once to select a member at large, which was a right granted to all Venezuelans, and then for special "section representatives," which was a right granted mostly to loyalists. Opposition figures were not given enough time to get organized. Many were banned from running campaigns. Then came the 2018 presidential election. This election featured bans on major opposition candidates, excessive use of public funds and public media to benefit the ruling party, manipulation of the timing of the election to leave little time for the opposition to campaign and organize observation teams across polling stations, and significant repression of

(2020): 41–65; Raúl Jiménez and Manuel Hidalgo, "Forensic Analysis of Venezuelan Elections during the Chávez Presidency," *PLOS One* 9, no. 6 (2014): 1–18.

342 WHEN DEMOCRACY BREAKS

protests (in 2017). A portion of the opposition decided to boycott the election. The portion of the opposition that did participate and came in second did not recognize the results. The government refused to audit the results.

In 2021, the government organized elections for a new National Assembly. For this election, most opposition parties were officially "taken over" by the government. Again, using rulings from the court, the government forced the replacement of the existing leaders of parties with leaders who were more conciliatory toward the regime. In many ways, the government created fake opposition parties and further divided the opposition.

Second, Maduro attacked not just minimal democracy but also the little that was left of liberal democracy. In 2015, for instance, right before the new legislature was about to be installed, Maduro reaffirmed the regime's penchant for court-packing: the government rushed the appointment of thirteen new justices before the start of the new congress in 2015. He devoted most of 2016 trying to bypass Congress, again using court rulings to declare invalid and illegal any law or resolution coming from the National Assembly. In fact, going forward with an impromptu election for a Constituent Assembly could be construed as a form of self-coup against the legislature, because the Constituent Assembly was granted enormous legislative powers after it came into being.

Finally, Maduro redoubled the attacks on institutions of participatory democracy. Local governments and communal councils, which became ubiquitous under Chávez, morphed essentially into cells of the ruling party, inaccessible to anyone who was not a party loyalist. Communal councils were granted enormous powers to distribute economic assistance during the economic crisis. They also engaged in communal watching, keeping tabs on the activities of neighbors, especially whether they participated in protests. And within the ruling party, pluralism diminished even more. Dissident voices were suppressed and many people were arrested.

In short, the regime drew from preexisting institutional resources control of electoral authorities, autocratic legalism, and disdain for pluralism in participatory institutions[21] to respond to new threats and target the opposition. Existing tools of repression were updated, fortified, and deployed.

A good example of this updating was military policy under Maduro. No doubt, Maduro inherited from Chávez a regime in which the military had been deeply incorporated into governance structures. It was thus relatively easy for Maduro

---

[21] Miriam Kornblith, "Venezuela: Calidad de las elecciones y calidad de la democracia," *América Latina Hoy* 45 (2007): 109–124; Allan R. Brewer-Carías, Dismantling Democracy in Venezuela: The Chávez Authoritarian Experiment (Cambridge: Cambridge University Press, 2010); Daniel Levine and J. E. Molina, *The Quality of Democracy in Latin America* (Boulder, CO: Lynne Rienner, 2011); Mainwaring, "From Representative Democracy to Participatory Competitive Authoritarianism"; Corrales and Penfold, "Venezuela."

to resort to the military to entrench his power deeper during the opposition-rising phase—the military was an available institutional asset at his disposal. But Maduro adapted this inheritance by giving the military far more economic power and autonomy than Chávez ever did. This included granting the military full control of the oil company, privileged access to imports and exports, greater presence in state-owned corporations, control over the distribution of consumer goods and public assistance. Maduro even went as far as to allow the military to engage in illicit activities with almost complete impunity (black market operations, smuggling goods across the Colombian border, exporting gold illegally, and abetting with drug trafficking). As extreme as Chávez's civil-military alliance was, it paled in comparison to Maduro's overutilization of the military institution and diversification of military roles.

Maduro's military policy can be classified as an example of what I call function fusion:[22] giving an existing institution functions that are normally assigned to other institutions. In the case of the military, the institution was given mostly economic functions (licit and illicit). Function fusion was also applied to civilians (who were given military functions as paramilitaries, or *colectivos*, as they are called in Venezuela), judges (who were given the function of business leaders, regulators, and legislators), and ruling party governors (who were allowed to become semi-dictators within their jurisdiction). By giving different institutional actors so many overlapping functions and prerogatives, Maduro was able to maintain a coalition of support from these institutional actors, without needing to offer as many economic handouts as one would have expected. Function fusion is how Maduro was able to offer payoffs to institutional groups in the context of declining economic resources.

Polarization during Autocratic Intensification

The Venezuelan case suggests that even within periods of autocratic intensification, polarization across the electorate does not necessarily dissipate. Rather, polarization will center on different issues.

For supporters of the regime, the issue is no longer agreement with policies, but rather, fear that the opposition, if allowed to return to power, will turn punitive: take away any institutional gains, remove regime supporters from any job or position held, or ostracize them for having supported the regime.

The issue for the opposition is no longer confusion about how to interpret signs of democratic decline, as is the case in the early stages of backsliding, but

---

[22] Javier Corrales, "Authoritarian Survival: Why Maduro Hasn't Fallen," *Journal of Democracy* 31, no. 3 (2020): 39–53.

344   WHEN DEMOCRACY BREAKS

rather, how best to confront the growing closure of institutional avenues to compete. Disagreements within the opposition will emerge, focusing less on interpretations than on the best strategy to fight back. Fighting back through institutional means becomes hard, not just because the opposition is prone to disagreements about strategy (how confrontational to be) but also because the institutional channels shrink continuously.

Thus, for the 2018 presidential election, as the regime turned more hard-line, the opposition split, one group deciding to compete and vote, and a significant group calling for abstention. The combination of repression in 2017, enormous electoral irregularities heading into the elections of 2018, and divisions within the opposition allowed the government to prevail electorally. None of the leaders of the opposition recognized the results.

The opposition had a brief revival in 2019–2021. On the day that Maduro was supposed to be sworn in for his second term in early 2019, the leadership of the National Assembly, still controlled by the opposition, refused to recognize his new term. At that point, the newly designated president of the National Assembly, Juan Guaidó, made the clever legal argument that Maduro's swearing-in ceremony constituted an "act of usurpation of power:" because Maduro never really won a free and fair election, he was illegally arrogating to himself the presidency by starting his second term. The National Assembly invoked the constitutional clause stating that in the absence of a legitimate president, the presidency is transferred to the president of the National Assembly, in this case, Guaidó. Guaidó received the support of most leaders of the opposition, as well as a broad international coalition that included the United States, the European Union, the Organization of American States, and the majority of the countries in the Western Hemisphere.

With encouragement from the Trump administration, Guaidó became increasingly hard-line. He brushed aside most forms of negotiations with Maduro, calling for Maduro's departure as a precondition for any new election. In fairness to Guaidó, Maduro hardly approached the negotiations with any intention of making major concessions (i.e., Guaidó's hard-line policy was surpassed by Maduro's extremism). Guaidó also encouraged military uprisings. And he welcomed economic sanctions from the United States, Canada, and the European Union. In short, there was a return to the strategies deployed by the opposition in the early years of Chavismo: electoral boycotts, a *vete ya* posture, economic crippling, and calls for military uprising.

The regime responded by actually upping the pressure on the opposition and within its ranks. The courts issued increasingly adverse rulings against opposition parties and its leaders. The pandemic (2020–2021) was used as an excuse to curtail the incidence of protest and freedom of the press. The ruling party turned further to illicit economic activities—and condoned loyalists engaged in illicit activities—as ways to retain power. The military, and especially *colectivos*, were given full discretion to repress protests. Espionage was reinforced and deployed specifically to the military, leading to a large number of dismissals and arrests within the military. The government responded to Western sanctions by strengthening its ties with autocratic regimes in Russia, Turkey, and Iran and relying increasingly on smuggling of mineral exports and even drugs. Ties with autocratic regimes and illicit transnational economic actors allowed the regime to find international loopholes to the sanctions regime imposed by the West.

In short, the transition from semi-authoritarianism in the 2010s was prompted first by a dramatic change in the party system (declining ruling party competitiveness), which encouraged the president to turn more autocratic to survive. The regime managed to turn more autocratic because it had a reservoir of autocratic institutions and tools at its disposal that could be redeployed and adapted to deal with the new political challenge posed by Venezuela's new party system (a co-opted court and electoral council, a coercive apparatus designed to engage in corruption, a mobilized group of paramilitaries, and illicit economic ties with business groups across society). The regime responded to political threats by updating existing autocratic practices and bringing them to new levels. Had there not been an arsenal of autocratic tools to draw from, the regime would not have been able to deploy autocratic tools as swiftly and effectively as it did in the 2016–2021 period. It either would have been overthrown or would have had to negotiate some form of regime liberalization, which most likely would have resulted in Chavismo losing control of the executive branch. And that is the one political loss that autocratic presidents never tolerate and will prevent if they have the right tools for the job. The economic sanctions imposed from abroad were insufficient to disarm the autocratic tools at the regime's disposal. After the initial shock experienced by the arrival of the sanctions, the regime deployed its autocratic tools, allowing the regime to weather the storm and transfer the costs of sanctions to opponents. Venezuela 1999–2023 thus confirms the long-standing hypothesis that autocratic regimes that trade strongly with non-Western nations can show far more resilience than democracies in the face of external economic shocks.

Conclusion

This chapter made a conceptual and a theoretical contribution to the study of democratic backsliding. The conceptual contribution is the idea that democratic backsliding can occur with different temporalities simultaneously: the presidency targets some dimensions of democracy but not others, leading to some institutions declining quickly while others decline slowly, if at all. This has at least two implications. First, this unevenness is one reason that backsliding leads to polarized electorates, some groups noticing the democratic decline quite clearly, and others hardly noticing it or perceiving improvements instead. Second, this polarization can be exploited by backsliding presidents to their advantage, because it turns supporters into a more forgiving constituency. Thus, backsliding presidents will act as both inadvertent as well as intentional polarizers.

The theoretical contribution is the idea that backsliding is related to party system features and institutional capturing. Initial backsliding is more likely under conditions of pro-incumbent asymmetrical party fragmentation: the ruling party becomes strong and cohesive, while opposition parties become fragmented. This is the condition that allows illiberal presidents in democracies to go far in concentrating power and attacking institutions of liberal democracy. This claim is not meant to deny that preexisting socioeconomic conditions (e.g., rising societal discontent with the status quo) are unimportant contributors to backsliding. In fact, democratic backsliding in Venezuela started with an external economic shock that no doubt contributed directly (by producing anti–status quo sentiment) and indirectly (by facilitating the change in the party system). But without the change in the party system toward asymmetrical fragmentation (1999–2006), backsliding would have been harder for the anti–status quo leader to achieve.

Asymmetrical party fragmentation, together with the recovery of oil prices (starting in 2004), allowed Chávez to overhaul or colonize a good number of democratic institutions in the country. At first, Chávez's backsliding record was mixed: even while attacking institutions of liberal democracy, he did introduce or promote some democratic innovations. But by mid-2000s, the democratic innovations had disappeared and the democratic reversals had acquired speed and scope.

During this period of steady democratic backsliding (2006–2012), the opposition and many civic organizations managed to remain independent and very active, but they were unable to stop the process of democratic backsliding: the state, the ruling party, the economy, and the restrictions imposed on independent organizations were too strong.

The process of autocratic intensification (2013 to the present) was the result of changes in the party system again as well as institutional capacity. Unlike backsliding, the autocratic intensification phase is more likely when the competitive-authoritarian regime loses competitiveness. At that point, the ruling party's only chance of hanging on to the presidency is to impose greater restrictions on party competition and turn more repressive toward opponents. Maduro was able to impose those restrictions because he had inherited a reservoir of autocratic practices and institutions that could be updated and repurposed to confront the challenges posed by Venezuela's new party system.

These autocratic responses succeeded politically, but only to a point. The responses managed to contain the political reverberations from the crises Maduro inherited (economic collapse, leadership vacuum, and declining competitiveness). Dissent was repressed, opposition parties were denied freedoms and opportunities to compete, and loyalists in the military and the ruling party were showered with favors, often including autonomy to engage in illicit economic activities. However, autocratization did not fundamentally solve, and in fact actually exacerbated, the country's governance crisis and, by extension, the ruling party's weak electoral competitiveness. By 2022, the regime's top leaders, including Maduro, had some of the lowest approval ratings of any government in Latin America.

Because of these policy failures, Venezuela's autocratic regime entered the 2020s with vulnerabilities. The regime has the capacity to survive in office, but it is far from consolidated. The president intensified autocracy, but the regime is not entirely free from the risk of internal implosion or being toppled even by actors within or connected to the ruling party.

References

Bermeo, Nancy. "On Democratic Backsliding." *Journal of Democracy* 27, no. 1 (2016): 5–19.

Brading, Ryan. *Populism in Venezuela*. London: Routledge, 2013.

Brewer-Carías, Allan R. *Dismantling Democracy in Venezuela: The Chavez Authoritarian Experiment*. Cambridge: Cambridge University Press, 2010.

Bueno de Mesquita, B., and A. Smith. *The Dictator's Handbook: Why Bad Behavior Is Almost Always Good Politics*. New York: Public Affairs, 2012.

Bunce, V. J., and S. L. Wolchik.. "Defeating Dictators: Electoral Change and Stability in Competitive Authoritarian Regimes." *World Politics* 62, no. 1 (2010): 43–86.

Burbach, Roger, and Camila Piñeiro.. "Venezuela's Participatory Socialism." *Socialism and Democracy* 21, no. 3 (2007): 181–200.

Carothers, T. "The End of the Transition Paradigm." *Journal of Democracy* 13, no. 1 (2002): 5–21.

Chávez, Hugo, Marta Harnecker, and Chesa Boudin. *Understanding the Venezuelan Revolution: Hugo Chavez Talks to Marta Harnecker*. New York: Monthly Review Press, 2005.

Collier, Ruth Berins. "Populism." In *International Encyclopedia of Social and Behavioral Sciences*, edited by Neil J. Smelser and Paul B. Baltes, 11813–11816. Elsevier, 2001.

Coppedge, M., J. Gerring, et al. "Conceptualizing and Measuring Democracy: A New Approach." *Perspectives on Politics* 9, no. 2 (2011): 247–267.

Corrales, Javier. *Autocracy Rising: How Venezuela Transitioned to Authoritarianism*. Washington, DC: Brookings Institution Press, 2022

Corrales, Javier. "The Authoritarian Resurgence: Autocratic Legalism in Venezuela." *Journal of Democracy* 26 (2015): 37–51.

348 WHEN DEMOCRACY BREAKS

Corrales, Javier. "Authoritarian Survival: Why Maduro Hasn't Fallen." *Journal of Democracy* 31, no. 3 (2020): 39–53.

Corrales, Javier. "Democratic Backsliding through Electoral Irregularities: Venezuela, 1999–2019." *European Review of Latin American and Caribbean Studies* 109 (2020): 41–65.

Corrales, Javier. "Explaining Chavismo: The Unexpected Alliance of Radical Leftists and the Military in Venezuela under Hugo Chávez." In *Venezuela: Anatomy of a Collapse*, edited by Ricardo Hausmann and Francisco Rodríguez, 371–406. University Park: Pennsylvania State University Press, 2014.

Corrales, Javier. "Radical Claims to Accountability." In *Democracy and Its Discontents in Latin America*, edited by Joe Foweraker and Dolores Trevizo, 115–131. Boulder, CO: Lynne Rienner, 2016.

Corrales, Javier, and Michael Penfold. *Dragon in the Tropics: Venezuela and the Legacy of Hugo Chávez*. 2nd edition. Washington, DC: Brookings Institution Press, 2015.

Corrales, Javier, and Michael Penfold. "Venezuela: Crowding Out the Opposition." *Journal of Democracy* 18, no. 2 (2015): 99–113.

Diamond, Larry. "Thinking about Hybrid Regimes." *Journal of Democracy* 13, no. 2 (2002): 21–35.

Ellner, Steve. *Rethinking Venezuelan Politics: Class, Conflict, and the Chávez Phenomenon*. Boulder, CO: Lynne Rienner, 2009.

Freedom House. *Freedom in the World*. https://freedomhouse.org/report/freedom-world.

Gerschewski, Johannes. "Erosion or Decay? Conceptualizing Causes and Mechanisms of Democratic Regression." *Democratization* 28, no. 1 (2020): 1–20.

Gibler, Douglas M., and Kirk A. Randazzo. "Testing the Effects of Independent Judiciaries on the Likelihood of Democratic Backsliding." *American Journal of Political Science* 55, no. 3 (July 2011): 696–709.

Grier, Kevin, and Norman Maynard.. "The Economic Consequences of Hugo Chavez: A Synthetic Control Analysis." *Journal of Economic Behavior & Organization* 125 (2016): 1–21.

Haggard, S., and Robert R. Kaufman. *Dictators and Democrats: Masses, Elites, and Regime Change*. Princeton: Princeton University Press, 2016.

Hausmann, Ricardo, and Francisco Rodríguez. "Introduction." In *Venezuela before Chávez: Anatomy of an Economic Collapse*, edited by Ricardo Hausmann and Francisco Rodríguez, 1–14. University Park: Pennsylvania State University Press, 2014.

Hawkins, Kirk A. "Who Mobilizes? Participatory Democracy in Chávez's Bolivarian Revolution." *Latin American Politics and Society* 52, no. 3 (2010): 31–66.

Huq, Aziz, and Tom Ginsburg. "How to Lose a Constitutional Democracy." *UCLA Law Review* 78 (2018): 80–168.

Jiménez, Raúl, and Manuel Hidalgo. "Forensic Analysis of Venezuelan Elections during the Chávez Presidency." *PLOS One* 9, no. 6 (2014): 1–18.

Kornblith, Miriam. "Venezuela: Calidad de las elecciones y calidad de la democracia." *América Latina Hoy* 45 (2007): 109–124.

Levine, Daniel, and J. E. Molina. *The Quality of Democracy in Latin America*. Boulder, CO: Lynne Rienner, 2011.

Levitsky, Steven. and Lucan Way. *Competitive Authoritarianism: Hybrid Regimes after the Cold War*. Cambridge: Cambridge University Press, 2010.

Llanos, Mariana, and Leiv Marsteintredet, eds. *Presidential Breakdowns in Latin America: Causes and Outcomes of Executive Instability in Developing Democracies.* London: Palgrave Macmillan, 2010.

López-Maya, Margarita. "Hugo Chávez Frías: His Movement and His Presidency." In *Venezuelan Politics in the Chavez Era*, edited by Steve Ellner and Daniel Hellinger, 73–92. Boulder, CO: Lynne Rienner, 2003.

Lührmann, Anna, and Staffan I. Lindberg. "A Third Wave of Autocratization Is Here: What Is New about It?: *Democratization* 26, no. 7 (2019): 1095–1113.

Lust, Ellen, and David Waldner. *Unwelcome Change: Understanding, Evaluating, and Extending Theories of Democratic Backsliding.* Research Report. Washington, DC, USAID, 2015.

Maingón, Thais. "Política social y régimen de bienestar, Venezuela 1999–2014." *Estudios Latinoamericanos Nueva Época* 38 (July–December 2016): 115–143.

Mainwaring, Scott. "From Representative Democracy to Participatory Competitive Authoritarianism: Hugo Chávez and Venezuelan Politics." *Perspective on Politics* 10, no. 4 (2012): 955–967.

Mainwaring, Scott, and Aníbal Pérez-Liñán. *Democracies and Dictatorships in Latin America: Emergence, Survival.* Cambridge: Cambridge University Press. 2014.

Martínez, R., and D. R. Mares. "Introduction." In *Debating Civil-Military Relations in Latin America*, edited by D. R. Mares and R. Martínez, 1–17. Chicago: Sussex Academic Press, 2014.

Mudde, Cas, and Cristóbal Rovira Kaltwasser. *Populism: A Very Short Introduction.* Oxford University Press, 2017.

Müller, Jan-Werner. *What Is Populism?* Philadelphia: University of Pennsylvania Press, 2016.

Naim, Moisés, and Ramón Piñango, eds. *El Caso Venezuela: Una Ilusión de Armonía.* Caracas: IESA, 1984.

Norden, Deborah L. *Venezuela: Coup-Proofing from Pérez Jiménez to Maduro.* London: Oxford University Press, 2021.

Pappas, Takis S. *Populism and Liberal Democracy: A Comparative and Theoretical Analysis.* Oxford University Press, 2019.

Rodríguez, Francisco. "An Empty Revolution: The Unfulfilled Promises of Hugo Chávez." *Foreign Affairs* 87, no. 2 (2008): 49–62.

Schedler, A., ed. *Electoral Authoritarianism: The Dynamics of Unfree Competition.* Boulder, CO: Lynne Rienner, 2006.

Scheppele, Kim Lane. "Autocratic Legalism." *University of Chicago Law Review* 85 (2018): 545–583.

Smith, Peter H., and Melissa Ziegler. "Liberal and Illiberal Democracy in Latin America." *Latin American Politics and Society* 40, no. 1 (2008): 31–57.

Sudduth, Jun Koga. "Coup Risk, Coup-Proofing and Leader Survival." *Journal of Peace Research* 54, no. 1 (2017): 3–15.

Wilpert, Gregory.. *Changing Venezuela: The History and Policies of the Chavez Government.* New York: Verso, 2007.

Index

For the benefit of digital users, indexed terms that span two pages (e.g., 52–53) may, on occasion, appear on only one of those pages.

Tables and figures are indicated by *t* and *f* following the page number

62 Organizations (Argentina), 250, 252, 254

Abdullah, Sheikh, 226–27, 230
abolitionist movement (antebellum United
    States)
    Black Americans' participation in, 55
    democracy-oriented arguments advanced
        by, 48–49
    international slave trade opposed by, 53
    mass mailing campaign (1835) by, 57–58
    Missouri Compromise (1820) opposed by, 53
    Northern opponents of, 54, 59
    Quakers and, 53
    Southern states' suppression of, 54–55, 57–58
    violence against members of, 61
Acción Democrática, 341–42
Acemoglu, Daron, 242–43, 273, 274
Acuña, Hipólito, 254
Advani, L. K., 229
Agrarian League, 150
Aguado, Jorge, 270–71
Ahmad, Naziruddin, 226–27
Ahmed, Fakhruddin Ali, 10–11
Akhlaque, Muhammad, 233–34
Akhmetov, Rinat, 295
AKP. *See* Justice and Development Party (AKP)
Alabama
    antislavery speech suppressed in, 55–56,
        59–60, 99–107
    federal lands seized during secession
        crisis by, 93
    pro-slavery vigilante groups in, 70
    secession from United States of, 84, 96
Albats, Yevgenia, 278–79
Alcibiades, 33
Alessandri, Jorge, 190–91, 197
Alevis, 319, 326
Alexander the Great, 31
Allende, Salvador
    Bosses Lockout (1972) and, 211–12

Christian Democratic opponents of, 202–3,
    205–8, 209–10, 213, 217
commitment to nonviolence of, 212–13
coup (1973) against, 193, 217–20
democratic socialism and, 189, 191, 194, 207
dependency theory and, 204
education reforms under, 213–14
election of 1958 and, 196–97
election of 1964 and, 196, 198
election of 1970 and, 8–9, 189–90, 196–97, 201
election of 1973 and, 212–13
faith in Chilean democratic institutions
    of, 204
Lo Curro summit (1972) and, 210
military officers in the cabinet of, 214–15
military suppression of supporters of, 216
nationalization of sectors of Chilean
    economy under, 204–5, 206–7,
    209, 213–14
Popular Unity coalition and, 189, 191, 197,
    200–3, 206, 208–9, 210, 212–13, 215–16
Revolutionary Left Movement and, 202
right-wing street demonstrations against,
    208–10, 215
Alliance for Progress, 197–98, 218
Ambedkar, B. R., 10–11, 222–27
American Anti-Slavery Society (AASS), 53
Amritsar Massacre (India, 1919), 231–32
"Anatolian Tigers," 302
Ankara terrorist bombings (2015), 321–22
Anthony, Frank Reginald, 223–24
Anti-Red League, 123
Appeal to the Colored Citizens of the World
    (Walker), 55, 56–57, 67
Archidamian War (431–421 BCE), 31–32
Área de Propiedad Social (APS, Chile), 205,
    206–7, 213–14
Argentina
    Act of Commitment for National Security
        (1973), 249

352 INDEX

Argentina (*cont.*)
  Catholic Church in, 237–38
  Council of Domestic Security in, 255
  coup attempt (1975) in, 256
  coup (1976) in, 9–10, 256, 270–71
  coups against provincial governments (1974–1975) in, 250, 253–54
  democratic collapses (1930–1966) in, 9–10
  democratic erosion prior to 1976 coup in, 9–10, 252, 253
  democratic government success (1916–1930) in, 243
  economic crisis prior to coup (1976) in, 260–63
  elections of 1973 in, 245, 248, 253–54
  Federal Police in, 247, 252, 255
  human rights violations in, 253–54
  hyperinflation in, 238, 255–56, 262–63, 266
  income equality levels in, 243–44, 273
  labor unions in, 242–43, 248, 250–51, 252, 257–58, 259–61, 262, 264, 266, 272, 273–74, 276
  lack of commitment to democracy before 1985 in, 263–68, 274
  Law of Foreign Investments in, 262
  Law of Professional Associations in, 249
  left-wing extremism and violence in, 237–38, 246, 249–52, 254–55, 256–59, 258*t*, 262, 264–65, 272–73, 274, 275–76
  military dictatorship government (1966–1973) in, 243, 244, 245, 248, 255
  military intervention in provinces (1974–1975) in, 253
  National Penitentiary System in, 255
  national security law (1974) in, 252
  per capita income in, 15–16, 243–44
  right-wing business groups in, 255–56, 263, 268–69, 273
  right-wing extremism and violence in, 237–38, 246–47, 250, 251–53, 255, 258–59, 258*t*, 265, 268, 274, 275–76
  semi-democratic regimes (1958–1966) in, 267–68
  Social Pact (1973–1974) in, 247, 251, 260–61, 273
  universities in, 252
Argentine Anti-Communist Alliance (AAA), 246n.28, 247, 250, 252–53, 265
Arginusae case (Athens), 38–39
Aristotle, 33, 41
Arkansas, 70, 84, 99–107
Armenian genocide (1915), 308
Atatürk, Mustafa Kemal, 12–13, 304–5, 308–10, 312–13

Athens
  Arginusae case in, 38–39
  The Assembly in, 29, 31–33, 37–39, 40
  Chaeronea, battle (338 BCE) of, 41
  The Council (Boule) in, 29, 32–33, 37–38
  courts in, 29
  democratic collapse (411 BCE) in, 6–7, 26, 28, 35–39
  democratic era (508–322 BCE) in, 25, 31
  democratic political culture in, 6–7, 30, 36–37
  democratic restoration (403 BCE) in, 27, 35, 39–41
  Eleusis mass killings (404/403 BCE) and, 35
  empire of, 31–32
  graphe paranomon procedure in, 33, 38–39
  income equality levels in, 30
  Mytilene revolt (427 BCE) and, 38–39
  nomothesia (lawmaking institution) in, 40
  oligarchic rule (411–403 BCE) in, 6–7, 27, 32–35, 36–37, 39, 41–42
  Peloponnesian War (431–404 BCE) and, 6–7, 26, 27, 31–32, 33–34, 35–36
  Persian Wars (490 and 480–479 BCE) and, 31
  probouloi (ten elders) in, 32–33
  Sicily military campaign (413 BCE) and, 6–7, 31–32, 35–36, 37–38, 39
  slavery in, 26–27, 30
  Social War of 357–355 BCE and, 41
  taxes in, 30
  The Ten (oligarchs) in, 35
  The Thirty (oligarchs) in, 32, 34–35
  voting rights restricted in, 4
Aurobindo, 226–27
Austria, 145–46, 161, 163, 164
Aysén strike (Chile, 1972), 211

Babacan, Ali, 300, 325–26
Bağış, Egemen, 318–19
Bahuguna, Hemvati Nandan, 229
Baksi, Satya Ranjan, 223–24
Balyoz trial (Turkey), 313–14
Bangladesh, 227–28, 233
Bay of Pigs invasion (Cuba, 1961), 197
Beer Hall Putsch (Germany, 1923), 142–43, 153
Belgium, 146–47, 153
Beneš, Edvard
  coup (1948) against, 180–82, 185, 187
  democracy as mediating institution for, 167
  elections scheduled for 1948 and, 178, 179
  on end of liberal democracy in Czechoslovakia, 171–72, 183
  exile during World War II of, 168, 183

INDEX 353

expulsion of German population from
Czechoslovakia and, 173–75
German population in Czechoslovakia
viewed as threat by, 172–73
Marshall Plan and, 177
Munich Conference (1938) and, 167, 187
National Front government crisis (1948),
162, 170
"people's democracy" program and, 184
Soviet Union and, 170–71
Berezovsky, Boris, 286, 288, 290–92
Berlin Wall, 142–43
Bewley, Anthony, 76, 78–80
Bharatiya Janata Party (BJP), 233, 234–35
Bidegain, Oscar, 249
Bihar state (India), 230–31
Bismarck, Otto von, 144–46, 149–50
Black Americans
as abolitionists, 55
Black Lives Matter movement and, 319–20
Black Methodists and, 75–76
political violence against, 20
proposed deportation of, 52–53
slavery and, 44, 45, 47, 51, 52, 97
Black Lives Matter movement, 319–20
Blood Pledge League, 123
Bogdanchikov, Sergei, 290–91
Boix, Carles, 242–43, 273, 274
Bolshevik Revolution (1917), 145–47, 152–
53, 169
Bolsonaro, Jair, 233
Bonnani, Pedro, 262–63
Bose, Netaji Subhas Chandra, 221–22, 226–27
Bose, Sarat Chandra, 223–24, 232
Bosses Lockout (Chile, 1972), 211–12, 214–15,
216–17, 219–20
Brazil, 197, 275
The Breakdown of Democratic Regimes (Linz
and Stepan), 23
Brecht, Bertolt, 148
Brezhnev, Leonid, 278
Brouk, Bohuslav, 188n.86
Brüning, Heinrich, 154–58
Buchanan, James, 68, 84–85
Buchanan, Patrick, 142
Bulgaria, 164
Butler, J. W., 96
Byrnes, James, 177

Cafiero, Antonio, 262–63
Calabró, Victorio, 266
Calhoun, John C., 60–61
Çamlıca Mosque, 302

Cámpora, Héctor
amnesty to left-wing revolutionaries granted
by, 246
Argentine economy under, 260–61
extremism and violence under, 259
manipulation of left-wing forces by, 244–45
mass popular mobilization under, 245
military retreat from politics during
government of, 252–53
resignation from presidency after seven
weeks of, 248
Casals, Marcelo, 196, 209–10
Castro, Fidel, 189, 197, 208
Catholic Center Party (Germany), 145, 147,
149, 156, 157
Central Intelligence Agency (CIA), 190–91, 197,
208, 211, 217–18
Chaeronea, battle (338 BCE) of, 41
Chanda, Asok, 224
Chávez, Hugo
clientelism and, 332
consolidation of power under, 332
coup attempts (2001 and 2002) against,
331–32, 338
democratic erosion under, 5, 328
economic nationalization programs under,
336, 340
economic performance under, 15–16
election of 1998 and, 5, 329
militarism under, 337–38
opposition electoral mobilization
against, 338–39
participatory democracy features
under, 334–35
partisan control over courts under, 13–14
partisan control over elections under, 13–14
populist discourse under, 337
press restrictions under, 13–14
semi-authoritarian nature of regime
of, 13–14
social service programs under, 334–36, 338
street protests (2003–2004) against, 332
Chechnya War (Russia), 280, 288
Cherry Society, 131–32
Chiang Kai-shek, 128–29
Chile
Agrarian Reform Law (1967) in, 8–9, 194,
205, 218
Arms Control Law (1972) in, 216
authoritarian tradition in, 192–93
Bosses Lockout (1972) in, 211–12, 214–15,
216–17, 219–20
cabinet impeachments (1970–1973) in, 207

354 INDEX

Chile (*cont.*)
campaign of terror (1964) in, 198
Castro's visit (1971) to, 208
Cold War and, 189, 196
Congress in, 190, 202–3, 205–8, 214, 216–17
Constitutional Court in, 205–6
coup (1973) in, 8–9, 191–93, 217–20
democratic erosion prior to 1973 coup in, 8–9, 202–3
democratic socialism and, 189, 191, 194, 207
democratic tradition in, 192–93, 194–95
election of 1964 and, 196–98
election of 1970 in, 8–9, 189–91, 196–97, 200–1
election of 1973 in, 212–13
land occupations in, 199–200
Law for the Permanent Defense of Democracy (1948) in, 195
March of the Pots and Pans (1971) in, 208
middle class in, 191–92, 209–10, 219
military government (1973–1990) in, 8–9, 219–20
nationalization of sectors of the economy in, 204–5, 206–7, 209, 213–14
National Security Doctrine in, 215–16, 219
political polarization in, 198, 206, 213
Popular Front governments in, 8–9, 194–96, 218
Popular Unity coalition in, 189, 191, 197, 200–3, 206, 208–9, 210, 212, 215–16
populist governments during 1930s and 1940s in, 195
Promoción Popular programs in, 199
"Revolution in Liberty" (1964–1970) in, 194, 197–98, 200, 201, 204–5
shortages (1972) in, 209
socialized area of the economy (APS) in, 205, 206–7, 213–14
Statute of Constitutional Guarantees (1970) and, 202–3
supply and price boards in, 211–12
Supreme Court in, 193, 205–6
Tanquetazo coup attempt (1973) in, 214, 215
United States and, 8–9, 190–92, 196, 197–98, 208–9, 211, 217–18
Chonchol, Jacques, 200
Christian Democratic Party (PDC, Chile)
agrarian reform and, 199
Allende presidency opposed by, 202–3, 205–8, 209–10, 213, 217
Christian Left's split (1971) from, 206
coup (1973) and, 8–9, 191–92, 218
election of 1964 and, 197–98

election of 1970 and, 191, 200–1
elections of 1973 and, 212–13
founding (1957) of, 196, 197
land occupations and, 199–200
middle class and, 219
Popular Unitary Action Movement's break (1969) from, 200
United States and, 196, 197–98, 208
Christian Left (Chilean political party), 206
Church Report (United States, 1975), 208, 209, 211
Clark, Edward, 96
Cleisthenes, 2–3, 18
Cobb, Howell, 85–86
Cold War
Chile and, 189, 196
Latin American domestic politics during, 218
Río Treaty (1947) and, 197
Truman Doctrine and, 197
Colombia, 256
Communist Information Bureau (Cominform), 177
Communist Party (Chile), 189–90, 195–96, 203
Communist Party (Czechoslovakia)
coup (1948) by, 179–83, 187
establishment (1921) of, 163
expulsion of German population from Czechoslovakia and, 173–75, 184
interwar era and, 165–66, 172
National Front government (1945–1948) and, 8, 161–62, 169–71, 176, 177, 186
"people's democracy" program and, 174
people's militias and, 180
resistance movement in World War II and, 175, 187
universities and, 176
Communist Party (Germany), 147, 152–53, 156–57
Communist Party (Japan), 122, 130–31, 136–37
Communist Party of the Russian Federation (CPRF), 283–84, 287–88, 289
Confederate States of America (CSA), 43, 83–84, 95. *See also* Southern United States (antebellum era)
Confederation of Rural Associations of the Rosafé Zone, 271
Congress for Democracy (Indian political party), 229
Congress Party (India), 227–28, 229, 230–32, 234–35
Constitutional Union Party, 48–49
Costa Rica, 256
Crimea War (2014), 281

Critias, 34–35
Cuba
  authoritarian regime in, 13–14, 339–40
  Bay of Pigs invasion (1961) and, 197
  revolution (1959) in, 189, 197, 202, 239, 275
Curtis, Michael Kent, 63n.90
Czechoslovakia
  Bohemia region in, 162, 163–64, 168, 172–73, 174, 176
  Constitution of 1920 in, 162
  coup (1948) in, 8, 161, 179–83, 185, 187
  Czech national movement and, 161, 164–65, 186
  democratic erosion prior to 1948 coup in, 8, 162, 183
  egalitarian society in, 164
  elections scheduled for 1948 in, 178
  expulsion of German and Hungarian population (1946–1947) from, 8, 173–75, 184, 186–87, 188
  German population in, 8, 165–66, 169, 172–73
  Habsburg era in, 163–64
  Hungarian population in, 8, 165, 169
  intellectuals in, 171
  Interior Ministry in, 8, 169–70, 187
  Jews in, 168
  judiciary in, 166
  Košice program in, 169, 172–73
  Marshall Plan (1947) and, 177
  Munich Conference (1938) and, 8, 162–63, 167, 174, 175, 177, 180, 182, 185, 186–87
  National Front government (1945–1948) in, 8, 161–62, 169–71, 174, 176–77
  Nazi occupation (1939–1945) of, 161, 162–63, 168
  Paris Peace Conference (1947) and, 177
  The *Pětka* (interwar coalition of five major parties) in, 165–67, 185–86
  Prague Spring (1968) and, 183, 187
  radical organizations outlawed in interwar era in, 166
  resistance movement in World War II and, 175, 187
  Slovak population in, 8, 165–66, 168
  socialism and national identity in, 184–85
  Soviet Union and, 161–62, 169, 171, 173–74, 177, 179–80, 182, 183, 187
  student dissidents in, 181–82, 185
  Sudetenland region and, 162–63, 167–68, 172–73
  United States and, 177, 185
  university elections (1946–1947) in, 175, 176, 185, 187

voting rights in, 163–64

Dahl, Robert, 263–64
Dairen (Manchuria), 127–28
Dalits, 228–29, 230–31, 233–34
Das, Biswanath, 225–26
Davutoğlu, Ahmet, 300, 325–26
Dawes Plan (1924), 152
Dayanand, Swami, 226–27
Declaration of Independence, 51–52, 98
Delaware, 68, 71
Demirtaş, Selahattin, 307–8
democracy. *See also* democratic collapse; democratic erosion
  in Athens, 30, 31, 36–37, 39, 41–42
  in Chile, 194–95
  constitutional morality and, 3, 10–11, 18, 223
  culture of, 2–3, 19
  definition of, 3–4, 283–84
  democratic commitment levels and, 24, 263, 276
  descriptive legitimacy and, 28, 36–37
  free speech and free association rights in, 49
  in Germany, 143–45, 148
  illiberal democracy and, 23–24
  in Japan, 129–30
  liberalism and, 26–27, 30
  majoritarianism and, 3–4
  modernization theory and, 140
  right to dissent and, 3–4
  role of sentiment in, 2–3, 10–11, 21–22, 174, 223
  structural *versus* cultural approaches to analyzing, 241
  voting rights and, 4, 49–50
democratic collapse
  agency-oriented explanations of, 271–72
  age of country's democracy and, 14, 21, 22, 25
  British colonial heritage and, 16
  crises of legitimacy and, 28, 37, 41–42, 140–41
  democratic erosion prior to, 17–18, 20, 23
  income inequality levels and, 14, 17, 25–26
  macroeconomic performance and, 14–16
  military defeats and, 37, 41
  per capita income levels and, 15–16, 17
  political polarization and, 14–16
  in presidential *versus* parliamentary systems, 14, 16, 17, 25–26
  refusal to accept election losses and, 7–8, 18–19
democratic erosion
  jailing of political opponents and, 17–18

356 INDEX

democratic erosion (cont.)
political polarization and, 5–6, 19–20
political violence and, 5–6, 17–18
quantitative measures of, 20–21
suppression of political speech and, 17–18
Democratic Party (United States), 46, 48–49, 69–70
Democratic Unity Roundtable (Venezuela), 339
democratization, third wave of, 1, 237, 256, 328
Democrat Party (Turkey), 305
dependency theory, 204
De Riz, Liliana, 239–40, 256
Desai, Morarji, 230–31
Deshmukh, P. S., 226–27
Dessalines, Jean-Jacques, 54
Dink, Hrant, 308
Dominican Republic, 197, 217–18, 237
Dred Scott ruling (1857), 85–86
Dresser, Amos, 58
Drtina, Prokop, 174, 178–79, 182, 185

Ebert, Friedrich, 147, 154, 155f
Ebert-Groener Pact (1918), 151
Edwards, Augustin, 190
Eisner, Kurt, 147, 152–53
Ejército Revolucionario del Pueblo (ERP, Argentina), 245, 249, 253, 254, 256, 257
Eleusis mass killings (404/403 BCE), 35
Elvan, Berkin, 319
Emancipation Proclamation (United States, 1863), 83–84
Engels, Friedrich, 144
Erbakan, Necmettin, 305–6, 310–11
Erdoğan, Recep Tayyip
authoritarian regime of, 300–1
consolidation of power under, 300, 308–9, 325–26
constitution of Turkey and, 306–7
construction projects under, 302
coup attempt (2016) against, 315–16, 321–22
democratic erosion under, 12–13, 301
election of 2018 and, 324–25
Gülen movement and, 313–14
imprisonment of, 12–13, 310–11, 314–15
Islamism and, 12–13
as Istanbul mayor, 302
judiciary power reduced under, 12–13
military power reduced under, 12–13
presidential system referendum (2017) and, 323
republican nationalism challenged by, 310
state control of media under, 324–25
universities and, 315–16

vilifying rhetoric utilized by, 12–13, 316–22
Welfare Party and, 310
Ergenekon trial (Turkey), 313
Erzberger, Mathias, 152–54
Euboea, 33, 36n.37
European Union (EU)
Copenhagen Agreement, 311–12
European Court of Human Rights and, 308
Turkey and, 12–13, 299–300, 303–4, 307–8, 311–13
Venezuela and, 344
Evet'çiler, Yetmez Ama, 311–12
Evren, Kenan, 313–14
Ezeiza massacre (Argentina, 1973), 246–47

Fatherland–All Russia Party, 287–88
Federation of Entrepreneurs of Buenos Aires, 269
Fernandes, George, 229
Fierlinger, Zdeněk, 170
The Five Thousand (oligarchs in Athens), 32, 33–34
Florida
antislavery speech suppressed in, 55–56, 66, 99–107
federal lands seized during secession crisis by, 93
pro-slavery vigilante groups in, 70
secession from the United States of, 84, 89–90, 96
Floyd, John, 56–57
Ford, Gerald, 274–75
Fort Pulaski (Georgia), 93–94
Fort Sumter, battle (1861) of, 89–90, 96
The Four Hundred (oligarchs of Athens), 32, 33–34
Fradkov, Mikhail, 291–92
France
commitment to democracy in, 164–65
left-wing postwar government in, 170
Munich Conference (1938) and, 162–63, 167
reparations from Weimar Germany to, 153
revolution (1789) in, 69–70, 143–44
right-wing organizations banned (1936) in, 166–67
voting rights in, 48–49
World War II and, 167–68
Yellow Vest movement in, 316–17
Franz Joseph (Austrian emperor), 188
Frei, Eduardo
Agrarian Reform Law (1967) and, 194, 218
Allende presidency and, 213
coup (1973) and, 217–18

INDEX   357

election of 1964 and, 196, 197–98
election of 1970 and, 190–91
land occupations and, 199–200
Revolution in Liberty programs and, 194,
  197–98, 201, 204–5
suppression of political opponents under,
  199–200
United States and, 196, 198
Frémont, John C., 68, 70–75
Fuerzas Armadas Peronistas (Peronist Armed
  Forces), 245–46

Gaidar, Yegor, 278–79
Gandhi, Indira, 10–11, 227–28, 229–31
Gandhi, Mohandas Karamchand ("Mahatma"),
  221–22, 226–27, 234
Gandhi, Sanjay, 228–29
Gazprom, 292
Gelbard, José, 261
General Economic Confederation (Argentina), 247
General Labor Confederation (CGT,
  Argentina), 247, 249, 250, 262–63
Georgia
  antislavery speech suppressed in, 54, 55–57,
    59–60, 99–107
  federal lands seized during secessionist
    crisis by, 93
  free blacks as subject of restrictions in, 56
  opposition to secession in, 93–94
  secession from United States of, 84, 94–96
German Democratic Party, 147, 149
German Democratic Republic (East Germany),
  142–43, 187
Germany. See German Democratic Republic;
  Weimar Germany
Gezi Park protests (Turkey, 2013), 302, 317–23
Ghosh, Gourkishore, 229
Ghosh, Prafulla Chandra, 223–24
Gillespie, Richard, 252, 256–57
Gogoi, Ranjan, 234–35
Gómez Morales, Alfredo, 262–63
González Videla, Gabriel, 8–9, 195
Gorbachev, Mikhail, 280
Gottwald, Klement
  ascent as prime minister (1946) of, 173–74
  coup (1948) and, 180–82
  Marshall Plan and, 185
  National Front government and, 176–77
  political violence threatened by, 178–79
  "socialism without violence" promise of,
    170–71, 177
Great Britain
  abolitionist movement in, 82

Great Depression in, 134
India and the empire of, 221–22, 231–32
Japan and, 119–20
Munich Conference (1938) and, 162–63, 167
reparations from Weimar Germany to, 152
US Civil War (1861–1865) and, 83–84
US secession crisis (1860–1861) and,
  81, 82–83
voting rights in, 48–49
Gropius, Walter, 148
Grote, George, 2, 3, 6–7, 10–11, 18, 223
Gryzlov, Boris, 291–92
Guaidó, Juan, 344
Guatemala, 197, 217–18
Gujarat state (India), 230–31
Gül, Abdullah, 310, 312–15
Gülen, Fethullah, 313–14, 321–22
Gündüz, Süleyman, 320–21
Gusinsky, Vladimir, 286, 290–91
Guyana, 197

Habsburg monarchy, 161, 163–64
Haiti, 54
Hála, František, 188n.86
Hammond, James Henry, 81
Hara Takashi, 119
Havel, Václav, 165
Heartfield, John, 148
Hedrick, Benjamin Sherwood, 72–74
Heidegger, Martin, 148
Helper, Hinton
  economic criticisms of slavery by, 64–66, 81
  election of 1860 and, 66
  Southern states' suppression of the writings
    of, 67, 77–78
Hemings, Sally, 51–52
Hess, Moses, 144
Heydrich, Reinhard, 173
Hibiya Riots (Japan, 1905), 121
Hindenburg, Paul von, 6, 146, 150, 151,
  152, 157–58
Hindutva movement, 234
Hitler, Adolf
  appointment as chancellor (1933) of,
    6, 158–59
  election of 1932 and, 5
  emergency powers of Weimar constitution
    utilized by, 10–11, 225
  Munich Conference (1948) and, 162–
    63, 167–68
Höch, Hanna, 148
Holzer, Jan, 166
Hoover, David, 74–76, 77–79

358 INDEX

Hoover, Herbert, 157
Horákova, Milada, 185
Houston, Sam, 82–84, 85–86, 94–96
How Democracies Die (Levitsky and Ziblatt), 23
Hugenberg, Alfred, 154
Hungary, 145–46, 161, 163–64, 178, 187, 254
Hurtado, Sebastián, 199–201
Hus, Jan, 164, 184–85

Illanes, María Angélica, 192–93
illiberal democracy, 23–24
The Impending Crisis (Helper), 64, 66–68, 77–78
Imperial Agricultural Association, 118–19
Imperial Rule Assistance Association
(IRAA), 135–36
İnce, Muharrem, 324–25
India
Amritsar Masacre (1919) in, 231–32
Bangladesh emergency (1971) and, 227–28
British colonial era in, 221–22, 231–32
China's war (1962) with, 227
Citizenship Amendment Act (2019) in, 235
constitution (1949) of, 10–11, 221–27, 228–
29, 232–33, 234–35
Defence of India Act (1915) and, 231–32
elections of 1951–1971 in, 227
elections of 1977 in, 10–11, 229
emergency government (1975–1977) in, 10–
11, 224, 228–29
Government of India Act (1935) in, 221–22,
223, 224, 232
Hindu Code Bill (1951) in, 222
Hindu religious majoritarianism in, 233–34
House of the People (Lok Sabha) in, 222, 227
immigration law in, 233, 235
international oil shock (1973–1975)
and, 230–31
judiciary in, 228–29, 231
Kashmir region and, 226–27, 230, 234–35
Muslims in, 233–34
National Population Register in, 235
Regulation III of Bengal (1818) in, 231–32
Rowlatt Act (1919) in, 234
Supreme Court in, 228, 231–33
Unlawful Activities Prevention Act (2019)
in, 234
Indian National Congress, 221–22, 227. *See also*
Congress Party (India)
İnönü, İsmet, 305
International Telephone and Telegraph, 190
Inukai Tsuyoshi, 131–32
Isocrates, 41
Italy, 11–12, 135, 145–46, 164, 167, 170

Ivanov, Sergey, 291–92

Jammu region (India), 234–35
Jana Sangh, 230–31
Janata Party (India), 229, 232–33
Japan
bank panic of 1927 in, 125
cabinets during Meiji period in, 116–17
China invaded (1937) by, 127
coup attempts (1931 and 1936) in, 131–33
democratic erosion during interwar period
in, 135–40
democratic erosion (1910–1930) in, 11–12
dollar-buying scandal (1931) in, 126–27
Great Britain and, 119–20
Great Depression and, 11–12, 125–
26, 129–30
Hibiya Riots (1905) in, 121
House of Peers and House of Representatives
in, 110
jailing of political opponents during interwar
period in, 137–38
labor unions in, 122, 124, 139
landlord dominance of parties in early
twentieth century in, 118–19
left-wing radicalism during interwar period
in, 121
Manchuria invaded (1931) by, 11–12,
127, 134
Meiji constitutional system (1889) in, 108–
10, 112–13, 114–15, 124
Meiji Restoration (1868) in, 110–11, 140
military dictatorship during World War II
in, 11–12
naval forces in, 125
New Order policies in, 136, 138–39
oligarchs in, 115–17, 120
party cabinets era (1918–1932) in, 119
"peace" Constitution (1947) in, 140–41
Peace Police Law of 1900 in, 136–37
Peace Preservation Law (1925) in, 124
political party ban (1940) in, 11–12
political violence during interwar period in,
11–12, 124, 131–32
press and press control in, 118, 124,
135, 136–37
Rice Riots of 1918 in, 121–22
right-wing radicalism during interwar period
in, 123–24
Russo-Japanese War (1905) and, 118–19,
121, 127–28
Satsuma-Chōshu clique government in, 112
Siberian Expedition (1918–22) and, 119–20

Special Higher Police in, 136–37
"spiritual mobilization" during interwar period in, 138–39
Taishō period of democracy (1912–1926) in, 11–12, 109, 119–20, 122, 123, 138–40
Tokugawa regime in, 110–11
Tokyo War Crimes Tribunal (1946–1948) and, 108
United States and, 119–20
voting rights in, 113–14, 120–21, 124, 139–40
war propaganda during 1930s in, 131
World War II and, 108, 109, 127, 134
zaibatsu business conglomerates in, 117–18, 123–24, 126–27
Japan Communist Party, 122, 130–31, 136–37
Japan Economic Federation, 117–18
Japanism, 123
Japan-Manchuria Business Council, 133
Jefferson, Thomas, 2–3, 51–53, 55, 73, 98, 142–43
Jelin, Elizabeth, 259–60
Jews
in Czechoslovakia, 168
in Weimar Germany, 142–43, 148, 152, 154, 158–59
Justice and Development Party (AKP)
civilian control of the military and, 312
constitution of Turkey and, 306–7
construction industry and, 301–2
democratic erosion under, 300–1, 302–3
economic reforms under, 302
election of 2002 and, 299–300
European Union and, 311–12, 313–15
Gezi Park protests (2013) and, 317–18
headscarf politics and, 314–15
human rights violations under, 302–3
Islamism and, 299–300, 310, 312, 315–16
Kurdish population of Turkey and, 306–8
Milli Görüş Hareketi and, 311
partisan control over elections of, 304, 323–25
partisan control over judiciary of, 303–4, 309
republican nationalism challenged by, 308–10, 312–13
state control of media by, 300–1
universities in Turkey and, 315
vilifying rhetoric used by, 12–13, 307–8, 316–22

Kaftancıoğlu, Canan, 325
Kamath, Hari Vishnu, 10–11, 224–27, 228, 232
Kant, Immanuel, 143–44
Kashmir region (India), 226–27, 230, 234–35

Kellogg-Briand Pact (1928), 119–20
Kennedy, John F., 197
Kentucky
antislavery speech suppressed in, 60–61, 66, 99–107
election of 1856 in, 71, 72–73
election of 1860 in, 68
pro-slavery vigilante groups in, 70
Kerala state (India), 227, 230
Keynes, John Maynard, 134, 152, 209
KGB (Soviet secret police), 179, 286–87, 291–92
Khan, Khan Abdul Ghaffar, 226–27
Khanna, H. R., 228–29
Khodorkovsky, Mikhail, 286, 290–92, 296–97
Kiel Mutiny (Germany, 1918), 145
Kılıç, Haşim, 314–15
Kılıçdaroğlu, Kemal, 317
Kiriyenko, Sergey, 292
Kissinger, Henry, 190, 209, 217–18
Know-Nothing Party, 48–49, 70
Kollwitz, Käthe, 148
Kolman, Arnošt, 184
Konoe Fumimaro, 138–39
Kopecký, Václav, 170, 176–77, 178–79
Korea, 123, 128–29
Krajina, Vladimir, 182
Kravchuk, Leonid, 294
Krishnamachari, T. T., 225
Kuchma, Leonid, 294–95
Küçük, Cem, 316–17
Kunzru, Hirday Nath, 225–27
Kurdistan Workers' Party (PKK), 306–8, 316–17, 319
Kwantung Army, 127–28

Lahiri, Somnath, 223–24
Lanusse, Alejandro, 243
Lari, Zairul-Hasan, 223
Lastiri, Raúl, 248, 252–53
Latin America. *See also specific countries*
Alliance for Progress and, 197–98, 218
authoritarian turn (1964–1976) in, 256, 275
conservative fears of leftist extremism in, 239
debt crisis (1982) in, 328
dependency theory and, 204
domestic politics during Cold War in, 218
third wave of democratization and, 1
Laušman, Bohumil, 174
Lazarenko, Pavel, 295
League of Nations, 119–20, 129–30, 134
Levingston, Roberto, 243
Levitsky, Steven, 23
Liberal Democratic Party (Russia), 280, 284

360 INDEX

Liberal Republican Party (Turkey), 305
Lidice massacre (Czechoslovakia, 1942), 173
Liebknecht, Karl, 142–43, 147
Lincoln, Abraham
 antislavery positions supported by, 43–44, 86–87
 election of 1860 and, 7–8, 43, 51, 68, 79–80, 84–86
 Emancipation Proclamation (1863) and, 83–84
 First Inaugural Address (1861) by, 86–87
Linz, Juan, 4 n.9, 23–24, 49–50
López Rega, José, 246–47, 248, 251–52, 253, 262–63, 265
Louisiana
 antislavery speech suppressed in, 55, 99–107
 federal lands seized during secession crisis by, 93
 pro-slavery vigilante groups in, 70
 secession from the United States of, 84, 96
Loveman, Brian, 193
Ludendorff, Erich, 146, 150, 151, 152
Luder, Ítalo, 254–55, 266–67
Luxemburg, Rosa, 146, 147
Lysander, 34–35
Lytton Commission Report (1932), 134

Macedon, 25, 31, 41
Madison, James, 2–3, 21–22, 98
Maduro, Nicolás
 authoritarian intensification under, 13–14, 340, 341, 347
 economic power granted to military by, 342–43
 election of 2018 and, 344
 opposition's electoral mobilization against, 341–42, 344
 participatory democratic institutions attacked by, 342
 partisan control of elections and, 341–42
 partisan control of judiciary under, 342
Maidan protests (Ukraine, 2014), 296
Mainwaring, Scott, 16
Manchuria
 Chinese nationalism in, 128–29
 Japan's invasion (1931) of, 11–12, 127, 134
 Japan's plans to settle rural areas in, 133
 as "lifeline to Japanese empire," 128
 Manchukuo puppet state (1932–1945) in, 127, 129–30, 134
 Manchuria Incident (1931–1933) and, 11–12, 129–31, 134
 South Manchurian Railway and, 127–29, 131

Mann, Thomas, 148
Mansilla, Marcelino, 254
Manu Sanabu, 137
March 1 Movement (Korea), 123
March of the Pots and Pans (Chile, 1971), 208
Marcy, William, 60
Marshall Plan (1947), 177
Martínez Baca, Alberto, 250
Maruyama Masao, 138–39
Marx, Karl, 144
Maryland
 antislavery speech suppressed in, 59–60, 99–107
 election of 1856 in, 71, 72–73
 election of 1860 in, 68
 pro-slavery vigilante groups in, 70
Masaryk, Jan, 174–75, 177–78, 179, 180–81
Masaryk, T. G.
 Communist Party's treatment of the legacy of, 184–85
 Czech national movement and, 164–65
 as Czech president, 167
 death of, 167
 humanistic and democratic values of, 168, 176, 183, 188
Matsuoka Yōsuke, 128
Mau, Vladimir, 278–79
Medvedchuk, Viktor, 295
Medvedev, Dmitry, 284
Melian dialogue, 37–38
Mendelsohn, Erich, 148
Menem, Carlos, 266
Metalworkers' Union (UOM), 250
Methodist Episcopal Church (MEC), 75–76
Miguel, Lorenzo, 250, 266
Mill, John Stuart, 231–32
Milli Görüş Hareketi (National Outlook Movement, Turkey), 309–10, 312–13
Miłosz, Czesław, 171
Minobe Tatsukichi, 137–38
Minseitō (Japanese political party), 118–19, 126–27, 132, 136
Mississippi
 antislavery speech suppressed in, 55, 99–107
 pro-slavery vigilante groups in, 70
 secession from the United States of, 84, 89–90, 96
 slave population in, 47, 51
Missouri
 admission to United States (1820) of, 53
 antislavery speech suppressed in, 54–55, 61, 99–107
 election of 1856 in, 72

INDEX 361

election of 1860 in, 68
pro-slavery vigilante groups in, 70
Mitsubishi, 126–27
Mitsui, 126–27, 131–32
Mlynář, Zdeněk, 187
Modi, Narendra, 233–34, 254
Mondal, Jogendra Nath, 223–24
Mondelli, Emilio, 263
Monte Chingolo attack (Argentina, 1975), 256
Montoneros
  emergence during late 1960s of, 245
  move to underground by, 252
  Peronist Youth and, 245–46
  Perón's falling out (1974) with, 248–49,
    250, 264–65
  political violence by, 249, 250, 254, 264
  street mobilization by, 257
Moyano, María José, 246, 256–57, 258–59
Munich Conference (1938)
  Czechoslovakia excluded from deliberations
    at, 167
  Czechoslovakian postwar politics and, 174,
    175, 177, 180, 182, 185, 186–87
  Czechoslovakian territory surrendered to
    Nazi Germany following, 8, 162–63, 167
Mutlu, Hüseyin Avni, 318–19
Mytilene revolt (427 BCE), 38–39

Nabeyama Sadachika, 137
Nagaland region (India), 227, 230
Narayan, Jaya Prakash, 228, 230–31
National Agriculture Society (Chile), 211
National Democrats (Czechoslovakia), 169
National Order Party (Turkey), 310
National Party (Chile), 194, 208, 211, 212–13
National Salvation Party (Turkey), 310
National Socialists (Czechoslovakia), 161–62,
    163, 169, 171, 176–77, 180, 185–86
Naval League, 150
Navalny, Alexei, 284
Nayyar, Kuldip, 229
Nazi Party (Germany)
  anti-democratic ideology of, 158–59
  anti-Semitism and, 158–59
  Beer Hall Putsch (1923) and, 142–43, 153
  election of 1930 and, 157
  election of 1932 and, 5, 158
  Great Depression and, 154–56
  Hitler's appointment as chancellor (1933)
    in, 158–59
  Weimar Germany dissolved by, 142
Nehru, Jawaharlal, 227–28, 230, 232
New York State, 60

Nicaragua, 13–14, 254, 339–40
Nixon, Richard, 8–9, 190, 209, 217–18, 274–75
North Carolina
  antislavery speech suppressed in, 55–56, 59–
    60, 61–62, 99–107
  election of 1856 in, 72–74
  free blacks as subject of restrictions in, 56
  political violence in, 7–8
  Republican Party suppressed in, 72–74
  secession from the United States of, 84
  voting rights in, 48–49
Northern Methodists, 75–76, 79
Northern United States (antebellum era)
  abolitionist movement's opponents in, 54, 59
  Civil War (1861–1865) and, 84
  electoral power of, 84–85
  free labor system in, 45
  free press protections in, 60
Nosek, Václav, 179
Noske, Gustav, 154, 155f
Novaro, Marcos, 270
November 9 events (German history), 142–43
NTV (Russian television station), 290
Nueva Fuerza (right-wing party in
    Argentina), 269

Obregón Cano, Ricardo, 250
O'Higgins, Bernardo, 192–93
Onganía, Juan Carlos, 243
Oppenheim, Lois, 205–6
Orbán, Viktor, 254
Organization of American States, 344
Ortega, Daniel, 254
Otis, Harrison Gray, 56–57, 59

Pakistan, 223–24, 226–27
Paladino, Jorge, 270
Palermo, Vicente, 270
Paramahansa, Ramakrishna, 226–27
Paris Peace Conference (1947), 177
Patel, Vallabhbhai, 232
Patria y Libertad (Chilean anti-Communist
    group), 190, 191, 208, 211, 216
Paylan, Garo, 308
Pearl Harbor, battle (1941) of, 11–12, 134
Peker, Sedat, 316–17
Peloponnesian War (431–404 BCE), 6–7, 26, 27,
    31–32, 33–34, 35–36
People's Democratic Party (HDP, Turkey),
    306–8, 325
People's Party (Czechoslovakia), 161–62, 169,
    180, 182, 185–86
Pericles, 26, 27

362 INDEX

Permanent Assembly of Business Associations
 (APEGE, Argentina), 255–56, 263, 268–69
Perón, Isabel Martínez de
 ascent to presidency (1974) of, 9–10, 238–
  39, 251
 cabinet of, 256
 coup (1976) against, 256, 270
 labor unions and, 273
 leave from presidency (1975) of, 255, 266
 military involvement in the government
  of, 252–54
 Montoneros and, 250
 political violence supported by, 9–10
 right-wing business groups and, 255–56,
  269, 273
 right-wing turn under, 251–52, 265
Perón, Juan
 Córdoba province coup (1974) and, 250
 death of, 9–10, 251
 election of 1973 and, 248
 labor unions and, 248, 250, 272
 lack of commitment to democracy of, 264,
  265, 267
 manipulation of left-wing forces by, 238–39,
  244–45, 248, 264–65, 267, 276
 manipulation of right-wing forces by, 238–
  39, 248, 265, 267, 276
 military retreat from politics during
  government of, 252–53
 Montoneros' falling out (1974) with, 248–49,
  250, 264–65
 return from exile (1973) of, 246–47
 statist economic policy under, 261, 265
Peronists
 fear of left-wing radicalism among, 237–38
 ideological heterogeneity among, 248–
  49, 251
 lack of commitment to democracy among,
  238–39, 264, 266–67
 Radicals' agreement (1970) with, 244, 267–68
Peronist Youth, 245–46
Peroutka, Ferdinand, 171–72
Persian Empire, 31, 33
Persky, Joseph, 63n.90
Petkov, Nikola, 178
Philip of Macedon, 41
Pierce, Franklin, 84–85
Pikhovshek, Vyacheslav, 295–96
Pinochet, Augusto, 8–9, 184–85, 191–92,
 195, 216–17
Piraeus (port of Athens), 35
"Plan to Intervene in Democracy"
 (Demokrasiye Müdahale Planı), 313

Plato, 41
Poland, 161, 171, 178
Ponce, Teodoro, 254
Popular Unitary Action Movement (MAPU),
 200, 203, 206, 216
Popular Unity coalition. *See under* Chile
Poręba, Szklarska, 177
Portakal, Fatih, 316–17
Portales, Diego, 192–93
Port Arthur port (Kwantung Territory), 118–19
Power, Margaret, 208–9
Prague Spring (Czechoslovakia, 1968), 183, 187
Prasad, Brajeshwar, 226–27
Prasad, Rajendra, 225
Prats, Carlos, 214, 216–17
Primakov, Yevgeny, 287–88
Primero Justicia (political party in
 Venezuela), 341–42
Progressive Party (Germany), 145, 149
Przeworski, Adam, 15–16, 17, 26–27,
 237, 243–44
Putin, Vladimir
 ascent to presidency (2000) of, 277
 Chechnya War and, 288
 Crimea War (2014) and, 281
 decline of political competition under, 284,
  286, 288
 election of 2004 and, 296–97
 oligarchs and, 290–92, 296–97, 298
 Russia's economic performance under, 288
 security services and, 12, 286–87, 291–92
 state control of media under, 12, 286, 289–90
 Yeltsin and, 297–98

Quakers, 53

Radical Party (Chile), 8–9, 195, 197–98
Radical Party (UCR, Argentina), 238–39, 244,
 264, 267–68
Ram, Jagjivan, 229
Randolph, Thomas Jefferson, 52–53
Ransdorf, Emil, 178–79
Rashtriya Swayamsevak Sangh, 230–31
Rathenau, Walter, 152–53
Ray, Renuka, 225–26
Reichskristallnacht pogrom (Germany,
 1938), 142–43
republican nationalism (Turkey)
 Atatürk and, 12–13, 309–10
 European Union and, 311
 judiciary in Turkey and, 314–15, 316
 Justice and Development Party's challenges
  to, 308–10, 312–13

Ottoman Islamism as challenge to, 309–10
secularism and, 312–13
Turkey's constitution and, 309–10
Turkish military and, 12–13, 316
universities and, 315–16
Republican Party (United States)
antislavery positions supported by, 7–8, 43–
44, 45, 45–46n.9, 66, 84–85, 86–87
"Black Republicans" as political epithet
against, 69–70, 79–80, 86–87, 91
election of 1856 and, 68–69, 70, 71–72
election of 1860 and, 66, 68–69
founding (1854) of, 68
Southern states' suppression during 1850s of,
7–8, 43–44, 68–80, 97
Republican People's Party (CHP, Turkey), 300,
305–6, 317, 325
Revolutionary Armed Forces (Argentina), 245
Revolutionary Left Movement (MIR), 202–3,
209–10, 211–13, 216
Revolutionary Peasants Movement
(MCR), 209–10
Righteousness Corps of the Divine Land, 123
Río Treaty (1947), 197
Ripka, Hubert, 178, 186n.81
Robinson, James, 242–43, 273, 274
Rodina (political party in Russia), 288
Rodrigo, Celestino, 262–63
Romania, 164, 171, 178
Rousseau, Jean-Jacques, 18
Rowlatt Act (India, 1919), 234
Roy, Kiran Shankar, 223–24
Rucci, José Ignacio, 249, 250
Russia
anti-Semitism in, 281
Bolshevik Revolution (1917) in, 145–47,
152–53, 169
Chechnya separatist dispute and, 280, 288
constitution of, 282–83
Crimea War (2014) and, 281
decline of political competition in, 277, 282–
84, 286, 288, 292–93, 296–97
democratic erosion during twenty-first
century in, 12, 281–82, 286
Duma elections of 2003 and, 288
economic crisis during 1990s in, 285–86,
287, 297–98
election of 1991 in, 284–85
election of 1993 in, 279
election of 1996 in, 284–85, 294
election of 1999 in, 287–88, 289
election of 2003, 287–89
election of 2004 in, 282, 296–97

hyperinflation in, 278–79, 281
jailing of political opponents in, 277
lack of commitment to democracy in, 280–81
late Soviet era elites' power in, 280
oil and gas sector in, 293–94
oligarchs' political role in, 12, 277, 283–84,
286, 289, 290–93, 294–95, 296–98
Organization for Security and Cooperation
in Europe monitoring of elections
in, 287–89
post-imperial nostalgia in, 278
Russo-Japanese War (1905) and, 118–19,
121, 127–28
security services in, 12, 277, 286–87, 291–
92, 298
state control of media in, 12, 286, 288–90,
292–93, 295–96
"Weimar syndrome" and, 278–79, 281–82
World War I and, 150
xenophobia in, 279
Ruttmann, Walter, 148
Ryzhkov, Nikolai, 284–85

Şafak, Elif, 308
Sahib, Khan, 226–27
Saint-Domingue. See Haiti
Saksena, Shibban Lal, 226–27
Samos, 33
Santillán, Atilio, 254
Saxena, Shibbun Lal, 225–26
Scheidemann, Philipp, 142–43
Schneider, René, 191, 202–3, 214–15
Seiyūkai (Japanese political party), 118–19,
120–21, 126–27, 132, 136
Severing, Carl, 152–53
Sezer, Ahmet Necdet, 314–15
Shah, Amit, 234, 235
Shah, K. T., 225–26
Shaw, George Bernard, 167
Sheikh Said Rebellion (Turkey, 1925), 304–5
Sicily military campaign (Athens, 413 BCE),
6–7, 31–32, 35–36, 37–38, 39
Sidhva, R. K., 226
Singer, Matthew, 15–16
Slánský, Rudolf, 177, 183
Smrkovský, Josef, 180
Social Democratic Party (SPD, Germany)
Brüning government (1930–1932)
and, 157–58
conservative antidemocratic forces tolerated
during Weimar era by, 6, 159
election of 1919 and, 147
election of 1928 and, 156

364 INDEX

Social Democratic Party (SPD, Germany) (*cont.*)
  growth during late nineteenth century
    of, 144–45
  police forces in Weimar Germany and, 152–53
  Russian Revolution and, 150–51
  unemployment insurance in Great
    Depression and, 157
  Versailles Treaty and, 152
  Weimar Coalition and, 145, 147, 149, 157
  World War I and, 145, 146–47, 150
Social Democrats (Czechoslovakia), 162, 163,
    169, 176, 178, 181, 185–86
Socialist Party (Chile), 189–90, 195, 202, 203,
    211–12, 216–17
Social War (357–355 BCE), 41
Šoffr, Vladimir, 175, 187
Soma mining disaster (Turkey, 2014), 302–3
South Carolina
  antislavery speech suppressed in, 54–55, 56,
    57–58, 59–60, 66–67, 99–107
  Fort Sumter, battle (1861) of, 96
  free blacks as subject of restrictions in, 56
  Lynch Men vigilantes (1835) in, 57–58
  peculiar constitutional and representation
    system in, 50–51
  secession from United States by, 50, 84, 89–
    90, 92–93, 96
  slave population in, 47
  voting rights in, 50
Southern Methodists, 75–76
Southern United States (antebellum era). *See
  also specific states*
  abolitionist movement and antislavery
    speech suppressed in, 54–63, 66–68, 80
  Civil War (1861–1865) and, 83–84
  criticisms of slavery prior to 1830 in, 51–52
  economic arguments against slavery in,
    62–66, 73
  exaggerated sense of Southern economic
    power in, 80
  free blacks in, 47, 56
  opponents of secession in, 82–84, 85–86,
    91, 92–96
  refusal to accept results of 1860 presidential
    election in, 43, 51, 87, 97
  Republican Party suppressed in, 7–8, 43–44,
    68–80, 97
  slavery in, 44, 45, 47, 51, 97
  voting rights in, 47, 48–49, 50, 97
Soviet Union
  collapse (1991) of, 277, 280, 285–86
  collectivization campaigns during 1930s
    in, 134

Czechoslovakia and, 161–62, 169, 171, 173–
    74, 177, 179–80, 182, 183, 187
  neformaly civil society in, 280
  Red Army of, 161–62, 171, 173–74, 180–81
Spain, 246–47, 256–57
Sparta, 6–7, 31–36. *See also* Peloponnesian War
    (431–404 BCE)
Šrámek, Jan, 182
Sriramalu, Potti, 230
Stalin, Josef
  anti-kulak campaign and, 290–91
  Cominform and, 177
  Czechoslovakia and, 170–71, 180–81, 185
  Marshall Plan and, 177
  Russian public opinion regarding, 278,
    279, 290–91
Starodubrovskaya, Irina, 278–79
Stepan, Alfred, 23
Stephens, Alexander, 85–86
Stevenson, William, 67
Stinnes-Legien Agreement, 151
Stresemann, Gustav, 152, 156
Sumitomo, 126–27
Svoboda, Ludvík, 180
Syracuse, 32–34

Taiwan, 123, 128–29
Takahashi Korekiyo, 134
Takigawa Yukitoki, 137–38
Takuma, Dan, 131–32
Tanquetazo coup attempt (Chile, 1973), 214, 215
Taut, Bruno, 148
The Ten (oligarchs of Athens), 35
Tennessee
  antislavery speech suppressed in, 58, 99–107
  pro-slavery vigilante groups in, 70
  secession from the United States of, 84, 87–
    88, 96–97
Terauchi Masatake, 122
Texas
  antislavery speech suppressed in, 66,
    76, 99–107
  Dallas fire (1860) in, 78
  election of 1856 in, 72–73, 75
  election of 1860 in, 79–80
  Northern Methodists in, 75–76, 79
  opponents of secession in, 82–84, 85–
    86, 94–96
  political violence in, 7–8, 75
  pro-slavery vigilante groups in, 70
  Republican Party suppressed in, 74–80
  secession from United States by, 51, 84,
    87–88, 96

state constitutional convention in, 88–89
Texas Troubles (1860) and, 78–80
Tezcan, Bülent, 323–24
Thakur Das Bhargava, Pandit, 226
The Thirty (oligarchs in Athens), 32, 34–35
Thomas, Gwynn, 208–9
Thucydides, 26, 31–34, 38
Tilak, Lokamanya, 226–27
Tilly, Charles, 300, 304–6, 308–9
Timber Creek Conference (1859), 76–77
Tinsman, Heidi, 208–9
Tocqueville, Alexis de, 47–49
Tokyo Imperial University, 137–38
Tokyo War Crimes Tribunal (1946–1948), 108
Tomic, Radomiro, 200–1
Townsend, John, 69–70, 81–82, 89–90n.212, 91–92
Trotsky, Leon, 146–47
Truman Doctrine, 197
Trump, Donald, 233, 319–20, 344
Tucumán (Argentina) military interventions
    (1974–1975), 253, 254
Turkey
    anti-Semitism in, 321
    Armenian genocide (1915) and, 308
    civil liberties restrictions in, 299–300, 308
    Constitutional Court in, 305–6, 307–8,
        310, 314–15
    constitution of, 306–7, 309–10, 312
    coup attempt (2016) in, 315–16, 321–22
    coups (1960–1997) in, 305–6
    democratic erosion in, 12–13, 300–1, 302–
        3, 308–9
    election of 1946 in, 305
    election of 1950 in, 305
    election of 2002 in, 299–300
    election of 2018 in, 324–25
    election of 2019 in, 300
    elections of 2023 in, 325–26
    European Union and, 12–13, 299–300, 303–
        4, 307–8, 311–13
    Gezi protests (2013) in, 302, 317–23
    headscarf politics in, 314–15
    human rights violations in, 302–3
    Islamic Union foreign policy in, 310–11
    jailing of journalists in, 300–1
    Kurdish population in, 12–13, 299–301, 304–
        5, 306–8, 316–17, 319, 321–22, 325, 326
    LGBTQ activism in, 303–4, 318–19, 326
    military government (1980–1983) in, 306
    military role in society of, 305–6, 312
    National Security Council in, 305–6, 310, 312–13
    North Atlantic Treaty Organization (NATO)
        and, 305

partisan control of elections in, 304, 323–25
partisan control of judiciary in, 303–4, 309
political violence in, 306
presidential system referendum (2017)
    in, 323
secularism initiatives in, 304–6
Sheikh Said Rebellion (1925) in, 304–5
state control of media in, 300–1, 324–25
state of emergency (2016–2017) in, 325
State Security Court in, 314–15
Supreme Electoral Board (YSK) in,
    304, 323–24
universities in, 315
voting rights in, 304–5
Turner, Nat, 7–8, 52–53, 55
Twiggs, David, 95
Tyagi, Mahavir, 226–27
Tymoshenko, Yuliya, 295

Ukraine
    election of 1994 and, 294
    election of 2004 in, 282, 295–97
    election of 2014 in, 296
    Maidan protests (2014) in, 296
    oligarchs' role in politics in, 277, 282, 294–
        97, 298
    Orange Revolution (2004) in, 295
Underwood, John C., 71–72
Union of Rightist Forces (Russian political
    party), 287–88
United Kingdom. See Great Britain
United States. See also United States secession
    crisis (1860–1861)
    Chile and, 8–9, 190–92, 196, 197–98, 208–9,
        211, 217–18
    constitution of, 88–89, 224
    Czechoslovakia and, 177, 185
    Great Depression and, 16, 20, 134, 156
    House of Representatives in, 84–85
    political violence in, 20
    proposed deportation of free black people
        from, 52–53
    Second Party System in, 46
    slavery in, 44, 45, 47, 51, 52, 97
    Supreme Court in, 85–86
    Venezuela and, 344
    voting rights in, 4, 50
    white supremacy doctrine in, 48–49
    World War I and, 145
United States secession crisis (1860–1861). See
    also Confederate States of America (CSA)
    Civil War (1861–1865) following,
        44, 83–84

366 INDEX

United States secession crisis (1860–1861) (*cont.*)
  democratic erosion in Southern States prior
    to, 7–8, 19, 44–45, 46, 51, 97
  Fort Sumter, battle (1861) of, 89–90, 96
  Great Britain and, 81, 82–83
  presidential election of 1860 in, 7–8, 43, 51,
    66, 68, 79–80, 84–86, 87, 97
  Southern opponents of secession and, 82–84,
    85–86, 91, 92–96
  Southern states' seizure of federal property
    during, 93
  state referendums and, 51, 87–88, 95–97
  supralegislative conventions and, 87–90
Unity (Russian political party), 287–88
University of North Carolina-Chapel Hill, 74
Uruguay, 202, 215–16, 239, 243, 274–75
Uttar Pradesh state (India), 229, 235

Vajpayee, Atal Behari, 227–28
Valdivia, Veronica, 219
Valenzuela, Arturo, 192, 197–98, 202–3, 207–
  8, 215
Venezuela
  asymmetric party system fragmentation in,
    327, 331, 346
  autocratic intensification after 2013 in, 339–
    45, 346–47
  banking crisis (1994–1996) in, 329
  Constituent Assembly in, 332, 333–34, 341–42
  constitution in, 331–32, 334–35
  coup attempt (1992) in, 329
  coup attempt (2001) in, 331–32
  Covid-19 pandemic and, 344–45
  democratic erosion in, 5, 13–14, 327, 328–30,
    331f, 334–35, 346
  democratic openings of 1990s in, 329–30
  democratic regime strength (1960–1999)
    in, 328
  economic nationalization programs in,
    336, 340
  election of 1998 in, 5, 329
  election of 2005 in, 333, 338
  election of 2013 in, 338–39
  election of 2015 in, 338–39
  election of 2018 in, 344
  election of 2021 in, 342
  European Union and, 344
  militarism in, 337–38
  National Assembly in, 331–32, 333, 338–39,
    342, 344
  oil sector in, 328, 338, 340
  partisan control over elections in, 13–14,
    327–28, 332–34, 341–42

  partisan control over judiciary in, 13–14,
    327–28, 332, 333–34, 342
  political polarization in, 336–37, 343–45
  social service programs in, 334–36, 338
  street protests (2003–2004) in, 332
  United States and, 344
Versailles Peace Treaty (1919), 151, 152, 154,
  156, 157–59
Videla, Jorge, 8–9, 195, 270
Villar, Alberto, 252
Viola, Eduardo, 239–40
Virginia
  antislavery speech suppressed in, 55, 56–57,
    58–60, 66, 99–107
  election of 1856 in, 71–73
  election of 1860 in, 68
  emancipation debate at state legislature
    (1831–1832) in, 52–53
  pro-slavery vigilante groups in, 70
  Republican Party suppressed in, 71–72
  secession from the United States of, 84, 87–
    88, 96–97
  state constitutional convention in, 88–89
  Turner's slave rebellion (1831) in, 52–53
  voting rights in, 48–49
Vivekananda, Swami, 226–27
Voluntad Popular (Venezuelan political
  party), 341–42
Von Baden, Max, 146
Von Papen, Franz, 158–59

Walker, David, 7–8, 55, 56–57, 67, 75–76
Washington Conference (1922), 119–20, 125
Weber, Max, 28, 36–37
Weimar Germany
  authoritarian tradition in German history
    and, 22, 143, 149–50, 151–52
  business-labor relations in, 151
  constitution and Article 48 emergency
    powers in, 6, 10–11, 20–22, 147, 157–58,
    225, 232
  creative culture in, 148
  democratic and humanistic tradition in
    Germany history and, 22, 143–45
  democratic erosion in, 5, 6, 20–21, 159
  election of 1919 and, 147
  election of 1928 and, 156
  election of 1930 and, 157
  election of 1932 and, 5, 158
  founding (1919) of, 142
  German Revolution of 1918–1919 and, 142,
    145, 152–53, 159
  "Golden Years" (1924–1928) in, 154–57

Great Depression and, 6, 16–17, 20, 142, 154–57
hyperinflation in, 142, 153, 156, 278–79
Interior Ministry in, 152–53
Jews in, 142–43, 148, 152, 154, 158–59
labor unions in, 147–48
left-wing uprisings in, 152–53
military's role in society of, 151
Nazi Party's vanquishing (1933) of, 142
political polarization in, 17, 20
political violence in, 6, 20, 258
press freedoms in, 148
Reichstag elections in, 156, 158
Reichstag fire (1933) in, 5, 6, 281
Überfremdung ("foreign flooding") concerns in, 154
Versailles Treaty and reparations for, 152–53
voting rights in, 147
Weimar Coalition and, 145, 147, 149, 157
xenophobia in, 154
Young Plan (1929) and, 152
Welfare Party (Turkey), 302, 305–6, 310–11, 312
Weyland, Kurt, 256–57
Whig Party, 46, 48–49
Wilder, Billy, 148
Wilhelm II (kaiser of Germany), 142–43, 145–46, 149–50
Wilson, Woodrow, 146, 161

Winn, Peter, 201–2, 216
Worth, Daniel, 67–68, 73, 75–76
Wyllys, Harold, 67

Yabloko Party (Russia), 288, 298
Yanukovych, Viktor, 295–96
Yasuda Zenjirō, 124
Yavaş, Mansur, 323
Yellow Vest demonstrations (France), 316–17
Yeltsin, Boris
    democratic values espoused by, 280–81
    economic programs under, 284–85
    election of 1996 and, 284–85
    election of 1999 and, 287–88
    Putin and, 297–98
    shelling of parliament (1993) by, 280, 281, 286
Yıldırım, Binali, 325
Young Plan (1929), 152
Yushchenko, Viktor, 295–97

zaibatsu (big business conglomerates in Japan), 117–18, 123–24, 126–27
Zhang Xueliang, 129, 134
Zhirinovsky, Vladimir, 279–80
Ziblatt, Daniel, 23
Zorin, Valerian A., 179
Zyuganov, Gennady, 279, 284–85, 294